# MARKETING RESEARCH

# MARKETING RESEARCH

*Second Edition*

## Ronald M. Weiers
*Indiana University of Pennsylvania*

Prentice Hall
*Englewood Cliffs, New Jersey 07632*

*Library of Congress Cataloging-in-Publication Data*

WEIERS, RONALD M.
  Marketing research.

  Includes bibliographical references and index.
  1. Marketing research.   I. Title.
HF5415.2.W43    1988      658.8'3      88-2541
ISBN 0-13-558479-5

Cover design: *Ben Santora*
Manufacturing buyer: *Barbara Kittle*

Photo credit: The Stock Market © Ann Heimann

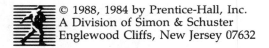 © 1988, 1984 by Prentice-Hall, Inc.
A Division of Simon & Schuster
Englewood Cliffs, New Jersey 07632

Printed in the United States of America

10  9  8  7  6  5  4  3  2  1

ISBN   0-13-558479-5   025

Prentice-Hall International (UK) Limited, *London*
Prentice-Hall of Australia Pty. Limited, *Sydney*
Prentice-Hall Canada Inc., *Toronto*
Prentice-Hall Hispanoamericana, S.A., *Mexico*
Prentice-Hall of India Private Limited, *New Delhi*
Prentice-Hall of Japan, Inc., *Tokyo*
Simon & Schuster Asia Pte. Ltd., *Singapore*
Editora Prentice-Hall do Brasil, Ltda., *Rio de Janeiro*

To Mom and Dad

# CONTENTS

# PREFACE

The image of the typical research book is similar to that of the typical lending institution—cold, impersonal, and intimidating. The first edition penetrated this unfriendly barrier to provide useful marketing research knowledge in a more readable and informal fashion than previous books.

The basic intent remains to familiarize you with a variety of popular techniques used in the collection and analysis of marketing information, and to develop your proficiency in their use and interpretation. Because it may have been some time since you were exposed to business statistics, necessary statistical concepts continue to be reviewed and explained as they become relevant to the textbook material involved. In addition, the second edition allows for better understanding and a more flexible course by presenting the more quantitative topics in separate chapters or sections, better allowing your instructor to tailor the course according to your background and needs.

The second edition continues to make liberal use of flow diagrams, charts, figures, and tables to reinforce key topics described in the text. It also includes numerous "real-world" photographs and illustrations to better communicate the involvement of companies, interest groups, governments, and a wide variety of other organizations in practical, everyday applications of marketing research to which we can all relate. Because so much marketing information is obtained from outside sources, especially research suppliers, government publications, and syndicated services, the discussion of such secondary data sources has been greatly expanded. The practical orientation of the text has been further enhanced through coverage of the important role of the microcomputer in marketing research, and the inclusion of realistic case studies—one set for each of the five sections of the book.

As with the first edition, the text tries to develop a sense of purpose and caution in planning and carrying out studies and experiments designed to generate marketing information. This objective, in addition to assisting you in your own research, is intended to help you become a more informed "consumer" of claims and findings offered by others, especially those inevitable sources who are either (a) downright unethical or (b) well meaning, but unscientific in their approach. This is vital, since most marketing students will become customers, rather than generators, of marketing research information.

Where other texts devote but a single (often token) chapter to ethics and misapplications in research, the second edition features self-defense techniques for the research consumer throughout the chapters. This approach includes frequent real-life exhibits where researchers: (a) came up with results conveniently highly supportive of the organization's product or goals; (b) relied on techniques or research approaches that were inappropriate or questionable; or (c) arrived at findings completely opposite to those uncovered by other researchers whose organizations happened to have exactly opposite products or interests. These examples, representing a variety of organizations and applications, are designed to further strengthen the uniqueness of this book as "the marketing research text with a conscience."

As with the first edition, the alert reader will notice a bit of demented humor here and there from the convoluted mind of some person whose name sounds like "wires." Throughout the book, remember that it was written with *you* in mind, with the goal of helping you learn about marketing research and its role in business and in society. Best wishes for a positive and enjoyable learning experience.

*Ronald M. Weiers, Ph.D.*
*Professor of Marketing*
*Indiana University of Pennsylvania*

# ACKNOWLEDGMENTS

The author wishes to thank his students and colleagues, both past and present, for their support, ideas, and valuable feedback regarding materials in the text. Special thanks are due to those who provided reviews and suggestions that contributed to the first and/or second editions of the text: Professor Boris W. Becker, Oregon State University; Professor Phillip E. Downs, Florida State University; Professor Michael Ursic, University of Florida; Professor Jerry C. Olson, Pennsylvania State University; Professor Amiya Basu, University of Illinois; Professor Theodore A. Clark, SUNY New Paltz; and Professor Linda Jamieson, Northeastern University. An expression of gratitude is also in order for Professor Thomas Bertsch, James Madison University; Professor Wayne Hemberger, Edinboro University of Pennsylvania; Professor Alan Ammann, Converse College; Professors Starr F. Schlobohm and Duncan G. LaBay, University of New Hampshire; and Professors Vincent P. Taiani and William T. Sheehe, Indiana University of Pennsylvania.

The author is especially indebted to two of the most proficient, conscientious and professional individuals with whom he has ever been associated. Student assistant Lisa Ofman, whose natural aptitude for marketing is matched only by her capacity for hard work, calmly and quickly attended to the many, varied, and often frustrating tasks which inevitably accompany a project of this magnitude. In addition, graduate assistant Nils Pallmann was both invaluable and relentless as he applied his unique blend of intellect, perseverance, and uncanny precision to helping the second edition become a reality. Thanks, everyone.

# 1

# A PREVIEW OF MARKETING RESEARCH

## Marketing Research Keeps American Flying High

American Airlines, an extensive user of marketing research, has been surveying its passengers for over 40 years and has had a consumer research staff for more than 30. The company's research activities are especially vital since government deregulation of the airline industry. According to director of consumer research Gerald Thiel, "It has become even more important for us to know our customers, their travel habits, and what they need from us."

One means toward this end is American's practice of surveying passengers on 1% of the airline's 1300 daily flights, making each flight a survey topic about once each 100 days. These In-Flight Tracking Surveys provide American with customer ratings of services along with a wide range of passenger characteristics, such as age, occupation, educational background, income, and travel plans. More than 320,000 customer responses were obtained in 1984 alone.

In addition, American employs daily telephone interviews with the public, conducts surveys of other airlines' passengers, and relies on opinions provided by an advisory panel of over 200 frequent fliers. The company also conducts up to 40 surveys per year on topics of special interest.

*Source:* Based on Brad Edmondson, "Airline Research the American Way," *American Demographics*, November 1985, p. 18.

**Figure 1-1.** American Airlines relies heavily on marketing research to gain information about customers, including their flying habits and their satisfaction with American and competing airlines. (Photo courtesy of American Airlines.)

One of many decisions based on such research was American's introduction of Ultimate Super Saver fares in 1985, an industry first. Research continues to be important in determining when discount fares will fill otherwise-unoccupied seats as opposed simply to decreasing revenues on flights that would have been full anyway. Mr. Thiel observes, "On a flight where there is low demand, every seat may be eligible for the Ultimate Super Saver fare. On high demand flights, such as the business runs from New York to Chicago, we may allow only a few seats for the deep discount. This is called yield management strategy, and it relies heavily on research."

## *INTRODUCTION*

1. "I think that marketing research will be too _____."
2. "It seems that most of my textbooks were written by _____."
3. "Marketing researchers spend most of their time doing _____."

As you read each of the preceding statements, you probably finished each one with one or more words describing your feelings about marketing research at this point in your course. If you're like many of the young men and women I've encountered as a university professor, chances are that your responses were something like:

1. "... mathematical."
2. "... eggheads."
3. "... surveys."

If you didn't provide the above answers, don't worry. After all, this isn't a *Reader's Digest* "Test your ..." quiz. Anyway, congratulations—you've just learned about a research technique called *sentence completion*, and I think you'll agree that it's a lot more common sense than it is mathematical. It's just one of many approaches we'll discuss for measuring consumer attitudes.

Regarding typical responses to statements 1 and 2, it's true that many research texts are overly mathematical, and look as though they were written by an esoteric cousin of the Wizard of Oz. While marketing research does depend partly on mathematics and statistics, our discussions will involve these on a "friendly" level—no deeper than necessary to convey the basis of a research technique.

As suggested by the typical response to statement 3, many people seem to equate marketing research with "survey taking." This is unfortunate, since the survey is just one of a storehouse of techniques available to the marketing researcher. Surveys are important, but the researcher who knows nothing else will be as well prepared as the NFL quarterback who is unacquainted with the forward pass.

In the sections that follow, we'll begin by defining marketing research and describing some of the typical applications for which it has been used. After exploring its relatively recent origins and its impressive growth in popularity, we'll go on to consider the roles it plays and the "customers" it serves.

We'll then talk about a theme that prevails throughout the book—how specific research techniques can be misused, often to the benefit of those who are unethical. Depending on what you'd like to see as a research "finding," there's almost always a way to bias a study so that you get the results desired. Finally, we'll preview the overall organization of the book and look at how the various research pieces fit together. Along the way, our discussion will be presented under these topics:

  I. Definition and typical applications
 II. Origins and growth of marketing research
III. Marketing research today
 IV. Research techniques: Tool kit or bag of tricks?
  V. Organization of the text

## DEFINITION AND TYPICAL APPLICATIONS

### Definition

Among the attempts made to describe marketing research briefly and accurately, the following adaptation from Philip Kotler sums it up quite well:

> Marketing research is the systematic design, collection, analysis, and reporting of data and findings relevant to a specific marketing situation.[1]

The "specific marketing situation" often involves a marketing decision, such as whether to introduce a new product, drop a distribution channel, or change a promotional appeal. However, marketing research is also used as a monitoring device to keep management aware of marketplace conditions and competitive pressures, thus serving as an "early warning" mechanism for anticipating problems and opportunities before they actually arise.

According to Eugene J. Kelley, former president of the American Marketing Association, marketing researchers are "investigators, the eyes and ears of our profession." Kelley's prediction for the remainder of the twentieth century is that marketing research "can and will become the strategic lifeline on which businesses will come to rely."[2]

The information supplied by marketing research is indispensable to a wide variety of marketing organizations, with consumer product firms especially dependent on research guidance. General Foods, which conducted extensive research before introducing its Crystal Light powdered soft drink, is typical, and its research director observes: "We collect a lot of material. . . . From a consumer point of view, almost every product you buy has gone through some sort of research."[3]

### Typical Applications

Before examining more closely the spectrum of marketing research activities, let's take a brief look at some typical applications that demonstrate its value and versatility.

---

[1] Philip Kotler, *Principles of Marketing*, 3rd ed. (Englewood Cliffs, N.J.: Prentice-Hall, Inc., 1986), p. 93. The definition here is slightly shortened from that presented by Kotler. Adapted by permission.

[2] "AMA President Kelley: Marketing Researchers Will Become 'Strategic Lifelines' of Corporations," *Marketing News*, January 21, 1983, sec. 1, p. 1, published by the American Marketing Association.

[3] Robert Garfield, "Researchers Put Us under Microscope," *USA TODAY*, January 8, 1985, p. 1B. Copyright 1985 by *USA TODAY*. Excerpted with permission.

## Sweetening Sales for Fanny Farmer

Faced with sagging sales, Fanny Farmer Candy Shops, Inc., conducted consumer preference research to identify product and store changes that could improve the chain's performance in the marketplace. The survey found that 75% of Fanny Farmer's customers were women, 50% were ages 22 to 40, and that most customers had annual earnings above $30,000.

Based on these and other findings, the company moved toward a more contemporary, upscale image. Besides upgrading their packaging and gift containers, as shown in Figure 1-2, they embarked on a complete renovation of the 300 existing stores located in 23 states. According to company president William Jorgenson, "We wanted to create a shopping environment that is warm and feminine, with a sense of style and flair." Following the changes suggested by marketing research, the firm made plans to add 60 to 80 new stores over a three-year period.[4]

## Launching a New Sunday Newspaper Supplement

On the heels of two years and $400,000 worth of marketing research, 1985 saw *The Los Angeles Times* introduce its new Sunday supplement, *The Los Angeles Times Magazine.* According to Donald F. Wright, president of the *Times,* the

**Figure 1-2.**  Marketing research results inspired Fanny Farmer's change from a Victorian silhouette to the more contemporary "Gibson Girl" design shown at the right,. (*Source:* "Consumers Give Fanny Farmer the Recipe for Sweet Comeback," *Marketing News,* January 31, 1986, p. 12, published by the American Marketing Association. Photo courtesy of Fanny Farmer Candy Shops, Inc.)

---

[4] "Consumers Give Fanny Farmer the Recipe for Sweet Comeback," *Marketing News,* January 31, 1986, p. 12, published by the American Marketing Association.

paper's marketing department implemented "the biggest research project ever undertaken by this newspaper," the purpose being to find a replacement for *Home*, the previous Sunday supplement the paper had carried since 1945. Research included the use of surveys and focus group interviews to identify strengths and weaknesses of two magazine prototypes that had been formulated for testing. The result is a general-interest magazine retaining the best features of *Home*, covering serious topics from a human relations perspective, and using its "strong local flavor" to serve as a showcase of the southern California lifestyle.[5]

### Monitoring the TV Family

Based on their study of prime-time TV programming, the National Commission on Working Women has accused the networks of presenting a distorted view of family life. In particular, the commission claims that family life on TV does not represent the difficult task that working mothers must perform in balancing job and child-rearing duties. This observational study analyzed five weeks of prime-time network programs featuring children under 18 and reached the following among its conclusions: (1) two-thirds of the TV children live with one parent, stepparents, or guardians, whereas 80% of real-world children live with both natural parents; (2) nearly half of all TV families are upper middle class or wealthy, while the actual median income for families with two working parents is around $30,000; (3) whereas all of TV's single parents are middle class or above, 69% of actual households headed by women are in poverty; and (4) while more than half of all TV children live with single fathers, over 90% of children in single-parent homes live with their mothers. The commission also found that child-care centers, so valuable in the real world, do not exist on TV. According to report author Sally Steemand, "Television is a powerful teacher, sending messages to viewers regarding the significant issues of society and the important concerns of life. Given that enormous power, the commission calls on TV writers and producers to integrate real-world concerns into the comedic and dramatic programs they develop for entertainment television." Alexis Herman, chairwoman of NCWW, puts it a little more strongly, observing that "American viewers deserve more from this medium than repetitive portrayals of affluent families where the mothers work as spies, corporate presidents and oil tycoons."[6]

### Throwing a Strike for Bowling

The National Bowling Council, representing 8500 retail outlets across the country (see Figure 1-3), conducted a descriptive research study of bowlers and came up with some surprising facts. Unlike the middle-aged, beer-drinking,

---

[5] "Huge Research Effort Guided Newspaper Magazine Launch," *Marketing News*, January 3, 1986, p. 50, published by the American Marketing Association.

[6] Ron Weiskind, "TV Distorts Family Life, Women's Group Says," *Pittsburgh Post-Gazette*, August 26, 1985, p. 21.

**Figure 1-3.** A study by the National Bowling Council claimed there were 64,000,000 bowlers in the United States. The ensuing "Bowling Facts Book" helped increase the visibility of bowling in a variety of media, including advertising for other products. (*Source:* Morton B. Elliot, "Bowling Pins Success to Unique Promo Tie-Ins," *Advertising Age*, March 9, 1981, p. 52. Copyright © 1981 by Crain Communications, Inc. Photo courtesy of AMF Bowling Companies, Inc.)

factory-worker stereotype that had long prevailed, the median bowler was found to be young (age 31) and relatively affluent ($2000 over median national income). In addition, over 40% had attended or graduated from college, and one-half held white-collar jobs. Before their report (the "Bowling Facts Book") had been out for very long, they had more than 10,000 requests for the book and its data describing America's 64 million bowlers. The bowling industry soon attracted the attention of many major corporations, with (1) more companies depicting bowling and bowling scenes in their advertising, and (2) increased promotional tie-ins between advertising and the bowling industry.[7]

---

[7] Morton B. Elliot, "Bowling Pins Success to Unique Promo Tie-Ins," *Advertising Age*, March 9, 1981, p. 52. Copyright © 1981 by Crain Communications, Inc.

### Who's Watching the Fish?

The New England Aquarium (see Figure 1-4), with a wide variety of penguins, seals, and assorted finny friends, receives about a million visitors a year and is one of the region's most-visited attractions. Serving both tourists and the local community, the aquarium uses marketing research in devising advertising strategies and special programs to best suit these diverse groups. In conjunction with a Boston consulting firm, the aquarium uses visitor interviews and micro-computers to analyze visitor demographics and service-usage patterns because, in the words of marketing director Cynthia Mackey, "We want to get a feel for what our audience is at different times of the year. This will help us to schedule special events, programs, and exhibit openings. . . . It helps us get away from guesswork." According to consultant Glenn Wasek, "The aquarium wants to pinpoint the most effective ways of deploying its resources. For example, if there is a large difference between the audiences which attend on weekends vs. week-days, and the goal is to increase weekend attendance, then advertising can be targeted at the characteristics of weekend audiences."[8]

### Finding Out Which Color Makes the Best Deodorant

A major toiletries manufacturer had finalized the package design for a new roll-on deodorant, but was still unsure as to which of three possible color schemes to use. This key decision was facilitated by the results of an experiment in which all three colors were submitted to in-home trial use. Participants were

**Figure 1-4.** This rockhopper penguin doesn't know it, but the New England Aquarium is using marketing research to ensure that as many visitors as possible come to see his antics. (*Source:* "Aquarium Fishes for Marketing Research Answers with Micros," *Marketing News,* November 9, 1984, p. 14, published by the American Marketing Association. Photo courtesy of the New England Aquarium.)

---

[8] "Aquarium Fishes for Marketing Research Answers with Micros," *Marketing News,* November 9, 1984, p. 14, published by the American Marketing Association.

told that they were to evaluate the effectiveness, fragrance, and ease of use of three slightly different formulations of a new deodorant. Since the three differed *only in the color schemes on their packages*, the results are especially interesting:[9]

**Color scheme A.**    This color arrangement nearly got the company into legal difficulties, as several users developed underarm rash and three actually visited a dermatologist.

**Color scheme B.**    The winner by an overwhelming margin, the deodorant in *this* package was praised as being fast-drying, having a pleasant fragrance, and protecting against wetness for as long as 12 hours.

**Color scheme C.**    Though the same physical product as the other two, this "formulation" was heavily criticized for its strong aroma and its short-lived (only a few hours) wetness protection.

## ORIGINS AND GROWTH OF MARKETING RESEARCH

It's nothing new for sellers to be interested in their customers, and some very early marketers even made use of some of the techniques discussed in this text. For example, it's been said that jade dealers used to shield their eyes when examining stones for possible purchase. The reason? They were afraid the seller might notice the pupils of their eyes dilating in reaction to an especially attractive stone, and raise the price.[10] In a later chapter, we'll discuss further this physiological indicator of interest or excitement, and how it can be measured by a device called the *pupilometer*.

There were scattered applications of marketing research techniques early in U.S. history—for example, an 1824 preelection poll published by a Pennsylvania newspaper.[11] However, it was not until the early 1900s that more formal approaches came into being. In 1911, the Curtis Publishing Company established the first formal marketing research department.[12] The department manager, Charles Parlin, was apparently a very innovative research pioneer.

Mr. Parlin, faced with the problem of convincing Campbell Soup (a large potential advertiser) that blue-collar families bought soup in cans, came up with an interesting research solution. Campbell had insisted that blue-collar wives made their soup the homemade way, peeling, scraping, and mixing the ingredients from

---

[9] Walter Stern, "Design Research: Beauty or Beast," *Advertising Age*, March 9, 1981, p. 43. Copyright © 1981 by Crain Communications, Inc.

[10] "What's Physiological Testing?" *Advertising Age*, January 19, 1981, p. 62. Copyright © 1981 by Crain Communications, Inc.

[11] From "History and Develoment of Marketing Research," by Lawrence C. Lockley in Robert Ferber (ed.), *Handbook of Marketing Research*, pp. 1–3 to 1–15. Copyright © 1974, McGraw-Hill. Used with the permission of McGraw-Hill Book Company.

[12] Kotler, *Principles of Marketing* (Englewood Cliffs, N.J.: Prentice-Hall, Inc., 1980), p. 141.

scratch. To disprove Campbell's contention, Parlin had garbage from blue-collar and white-collar routes systematically collected and dumped on the floor of an armory. When the counting was done, it turned out that *wealthy* consumers were the ones eating homemade soup—apparently prepared by their servants. However, the blue-collar refuse contained an abundance of empty soup cans. Thus convinced, Campbell became a regular advertiser in a prime Curtis publication, *The Saturday Evening Post.*[13]

Although Mr. Parlin didn't have access to any marketing research texts in his time, he did an excellent job of using an observational technique we'll be discussing later. Overall, the history of marketing research in the United States can be described as passing through the following phases:[14]

*1880–1920: the industrial statistics phase.*    Census work became increasingly important, and survey research was developed.

*1920–1940: the random sampling, questionnaire, and behavioral measurement development phase.*    This phase featured better questionnaires and more efficient sampling of populations.

*1940–1950: the management awareness phase.*    Managements began to take increased interest in marketing research for its value in decision making instead of being just a device for gathering information. "Market research" became "marketing research."

*1950–1960: the experimentation phase.*    Researchers began applying experimental techniques and more-scientific methodology to answering marketing questions.

*1960–1970: the computer analysis and quantitative methods phase.*    This phase emphasized the building of mathematical models to facilitate marketing decision making, and included application of the computer to marketing information and decision analysis.

*1970–1980: the consumer theory development phase.*    This phase featured the improvement of qualitative research concepts and methods for explaining and predicting the behavior of consumers.

*1980–present: the "high-tech" phase.*    Characterized by advancing electronic technologies: for example, microcomputers in on-line interviewing, computer databases for rapid information search and retrieval, and the

---

[13] Kenneth A. Hollander, "Audacious Audi Ad Echoes Parlin's Iconoclasm," *Marketing News,* January 27, 1978, p. 17, published by the American Marketing Association.

[14] Periods from 1880 through 1980 based on Gerald Zaltman and Philip C. Burger, *Marketing Research: Fundamentals and Dynamics* (Hinsdale, Ill.: Dryden Press, 1975), pp. 4–6; Robert Bartels, *The History of Marketing Thought,* 2nd ed. (Columbus, Ohio: Grid Publishing, Inc., 1976), chap. 9; and Jack J. Honomichl, "Since First Straw Vote in 1824, Research Grows," *Advertising Age,* April 19, 1975, pp. 106–9; in Kotler, *Principles of Marketing,* p. 142. Period 1980–present as observed by the author.

combined application of electronic monitoring devices for identifying TV viewing habits and scanner techniques for measuring shopping behavior.

As indicated by the diversity and richness of the innovations during these phases, marketing research has enjoyed the benefits of knowledge and experience from a wide range of other disciplines. Key contributors have been statistics, psychology, and a wide variety of other natural and social sciences.[15] As one observer puts it, "The marketing researcher usually is a very special kind of professional—a social scientist whose population is probably larger and more constantly researched than any other in the social sciences."[16]

Ever since Curtis Publishing set up that first marketing research department, an increasing number of firms have seen the value of research activities and added departments of their own. Figure 1–5, based on responses from 426 companies with research departments, shows the steady and rapid pace at which departments have been formed over the years.

## MARKETING RESEARCH TODAY

### Who Uses Marketing Research, and Why?

Earlier, we discussed a few typical applications of marketing research that proved to be quite informative for the companies or organizations involved. While users of marketing research are many and varied, key users tend to be in the following categories: (1) manufacturers of consumer products, (2) manufacturers of industrial products, (3) publishers and broadcasters, (4) advertising and public relations agencies, (5) financial institutions and services, (6) independent marketing research and consulting firms, (7) retailers and wholesalers, (8) government agencies, and, more recently, (9) not-for-profit organizations such as museums, zoos, theaters, symphony orchestras, and special-interest groups.

Of these groups, the biggest users of marketing research are manufacturers of consumer and industrial products, while retailers and wholesalers are not so heavily reliant on research activities. Government agencies generate vast quantities of published data, much of which are collected and analyzed through the use of marketing research techniques. Table 1-1 shows the average amount that various users spent on marketing research activities in 1983.[17]

---

[15] For an excellent discussion of these disciplines, and their respective contributions to marketing research, see Timothy Joyce, "The Role of the Expert in Marketing Research," *Commentary: The Journal of the Marketing Research Society*, Winter 1963, pp. 19–24.

[16] Emanuel H. Demby, "The Marketing Researcher: A Professional Statistician, Social Scientist—Not Just Another Business Practitioner," *Marketing News*, January 6, 1984, sec. 1, p. 20, published by the American Marketing Association.

[17] Dik Warren Twedt, *1983 Survey of Marketing Research* (Chicago: American Marketing Association, 1983), p. 28.

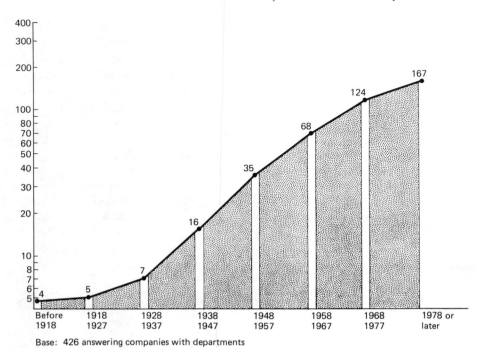

Base: 426 answering companies with departments

**Figure 1-5.** Since 1918, marketing research departments have been forming at a rapid rate. Of 426 responding companies in this study, over one-third of their marketing research departments had been formed during the five years preceding the survey. (*Source:* Adapted by permission from Dik Warren Twedt, *1983 Survey of Marketing Research*, p. 21, published by the American Marketing Association.)

As Table 1-1 indicates, companies participating in the 1983 American Marketing Association survey report substantial increases in research expenditures. These data are consistent with those reported by other studies of marketing research budgets. For example, in a study by Data Development Corporation, nearly 7 of 10 companies with a marketing research department revealed that their research budgets increased in 1985, with two-thirds anticipating an increase in research spending for 1986.[18]

To answer the "why" portion of this discussion, consider the wide range of applications reported by the five key user categories of Table 1-2. Of 33 kinds of applications shown, different kinds of organizations tend to concentrate on those most suitable for their own purposes. However, a number of similarities

---

[18] "Research Budgets Climbing," *Advertising Age*, January 13, 1986, p. 48. Copyright © 1986 by Crain Communications, Inc.

*TABLE 1-1. Expenditures on marketing research in 1983 versus 1978. While expenditures increased significantly for most reporting firms, financial services and consumer goods manufacturers showed especially large increases.*

| Type of firm | Average amount spent on marketing research | | Increase, 1978 to 1983 (%) |
|---|---|---|---|
| | *1978* | *1983* | |
| 139 manufacturers of consumer goods | $1,072,000 | $1,899,000 | 77 |
| 116 manufacturers of industrial goods | 257,000 | 379,000 | 47 |
| 51 advertising agencies | 500,000 | 741,000 | 48 |
| 62 publishers and broadcasters | 358,000 | 379,000 | 6 |
| 100 financial services | 153,000 | 287,000 | 88 |
| 91 others | 242,000 | 376,000 | 55 |

*Source:* Dik Warren Twedt, *1983 Survey of Marketing Research,* American Marketing Association, Chicago, 1983, p. 28.

do exist. For example, in 28 of the 33 categories, industrial and consumer product manufacturers are fairly similar in their research interests. As might be expected, the major emphasis of advertising agencies is on activities such as advertising instead of product research, and market analysis.[19]

## The Roles of Marketing Research

### Research and the Marketing Concept

The marketing concept stresses that the successful firm must (1) identify and (2) satisfy consumer needs. In the United States we spend about $2 billion a year to find out what the consuming public wants, thinks, or believes, and it has been estimated that this activity has been growing by about 15% each year since 1982.[20]

> The marketing concept holds that the key to achieving organizational goals consists in determining the needs and wants of target markets and delivering the desired satisfactions more effectively and efficiently than competitors.[21]

To the extent that a firm practices the marketing concept, marketing research serves the role of finding out what the consumer wants and evaluating

---

[19] Twedt, *1983 Survey,* pp. 40–44.

[20] Pamela G. Hollie, "What's New in Market Research," *The New York Times,* June 15, 1986, p. F19.

[21] Kotler, *Principles of Marketing,* p. 15.

**TABLE 1-2.** *Key users of marketing research, and their areas of research application. In 28 of the 33 categories, consumer and industrial companies are fairly similar.*

| | Percent of the companies engaging in this research activity | | | | |
|---|---|---|---|---|---|
| Type of research activity | *Consumer companies* | *Industrial companies* | *Advertising agencies* | *Publishers and broadcasters* | *Financial services* |
| Advertising research | | | | | |
| A.  Motivation research | 61% | 29% | 92% | 28% | 41% |
| B.  Copy research | 78 | 55 | 99 | 35 | 53 |
| C.  Media research | 72 | 57 | 93 | 78 | 65 |
| D.  Studies of ad effectiveness | 86 | 67 | 96 | 71 | 82 |
| E.  Studies of competitive advertising | 73 | 54 | 95 | 65 | 71 |
| Business economics and corporate research | | | | | |
| A.  Short-range forecasting (up to 1 year) | 97 | 98 | 52 | 76 | 94 |
| B.  Long-range forecasting (over 1 year) | 96 | 94 | 49 | 76 | 91 |
| C.  Studies of business trends | 90 | 99 | 77 | 76 | 92 |
| D.  Pricing studies | 91 | 90 | 50 | 60 | 94 |
| E.  Plant and warehouse location studies | 71 | 78 | 19 | 46 | 84 |
| F.  Acquisition studies | 81 | 89 | 29 | 53 | 79 |
| G.  Export and international studies | 69 | 82 | 32 | 19 | 29 |
| H.  MIS (management information system) | 89 | 90 | 38 | 56 | 89 |
| I.  Operations research | 71 | 68 | 38 | 46 | 78 |
| J.  Internal company employees | 73 | 80 | 55 | 63 | 87 |
| Corporate responsibility research | | | | | |
| A.  Consumers' "right to know" studies | 21 | 12 | 19 | 12 | 25 |
| B.  Ecological impact studies | 37 | 35 | 4 | 7 | 9 |
| C.  Studies of legal constraints on advertising and promotion | 58 | 46 | 40 | 25 | 55 |
| D.  Social values and policies studies | 47 | 29 | 49 | 32 | 37 |
| Product research | | | | | |
| A.  New product acceptance and potential | 89 | 73 | 76 | 68 | 89 |

**TABLE 1-2. (continued)**

| Type of research activity | Percent of the companies engaging in this research activity | | | | |
| --- | --- | --- | --- | --- | --- |
| | Consumer companies | Industrial companies | Advertising agencies | Publishers and broadcasters | Financial services |
| B. Competitive product studies | 97 | 92 | 83 | 76 | 96 |
| C. Testing of existing products | 98 | 86 | 81 | 71 | 76 |
| D. Packaging research: Design or physical characteristics | 91 | 61 | 80 | 54 | 54 |
| Sales and market research | | | | | |
| A. Measurement of market potentials | 99 | 99 | 93 | 89 | 97 |
| B. Market share analysis | 99 | 98 | 96 | 98 | 97 |
| C. Determination of market characteristics | 99 | 99 | 93 | 99 | 98 |
| D. Sales analysis | 98 | 99 | 82 | 89 | 90 |
| E. Establishment of sales quotas, territories | 93 | 95 | 19 | 80 | 81 |
| F. Distribution channel studies | 89 | 83 | 26 | 66 | 68 |
| G. Test markets, store audits | 88 | 36 | 89 | 31 | 49 |
| H. Consumer panel operations | 87 | 31 | 90 | 63 | 53 |
| I. Sales compensation studies | 83 | 73 | 16 | 56 | 61 |
| J. Promotional studies of premiums, coupons, sampling, deals, etc. | 82 | 36 | 77 | 47 | 57 |

Source: Dik Warren Twedt, *1983 Survey of Marketing Research*, American Marketing Association, Chicago, 1983, pp. 40–44.

how well the firm's current or proposed offerings meet these desires. Thus, in the marketing concept, marketing research finds itself in the role of a "feedback mechanism" for management guidance.

   In the final chapter we'll return to the marketing concept and examine some of the broader implications of marketing research activities. As you will better appreciate after reading this text, marketing research can encompass more than just the innocent, objective collection and analysis of consumer information. Instead of helping to make the consumer a king, marketing research is looked at by some as reducing him to a mere servant.

> **EXHIBIT 1-1**
>
> *Supporting the Shuttle*
>
> On January 28, 1986, the space shuttle *Challenger* exploded, killing all seven astronauts aboard. Later that year, the results of a survey of 1200 adults were reported. The survey, commissioned by Rockwell International, makers of the space shuttle, reported that nearly 9 of 10 Americans would like shuttle flights to continue.
>
> *Source:* Jack Kelley, "Poll: 9 in 10 Want Shuttle to Fly Again," *USA TODAY*, September 18, 1986, p. 3A. Copyright 1986, *USA TODAY*. Excerpted with permission.

### Research and Marketing Decisions

As suggested by many of the applications shown in Table 1-2, a major function of marketing research is to help managers make decisions. Pricing, product and package design, product distribution, and promotion are typical of the areas in which research contributes to decision making, a topic discussed more fully in Chapter 2.

### Research and the Marketing Information System

Marketing research plays a key role in the larger scheme of marketing information, and its collection and use. In Chapter 2 we'll examine the **marketing information system** (MIS) and its four major components, including marketing research.

## Careers in Marketing Research

For readers interested in entering marketing research, employment opportunities in this field are as diverse as the academic and practical experience of the individual, and his or her quantitative, interpersonal, and communicative skills. Table 1–3 describes 11 typical job titles in marketing research, along with the responsibilities generally expected of each position.

Average salaries reported in this study ranged from $51,000 (research director) to $13,100 (full-time interviewers). Junior analysts, the most likely entry-level position for bachelor's degree holders, averaged $18,800, with analysts and statistician/data processing specialists (the typical entry level for MBA holders) averaging $25,100 and $30,700, respectively.[22] If you find yourself negotiating with a potential employer during the months before graduation, keep in mind two factors that tend to offset each other: (1) these are 1983 salaries that have

---

[22] Twedt, *1983 Survey*, p. 57.

**TABLE 1-3.** *Typical marketing research job titles and responsibilities.*

*Research Director.* The senior person in research, the director is responsible for the company's entire research program. Accepts assignments from superiors or clients, or may, on own initiative, develop and propose research undertakings to company executives. Employs personnel and exercises general supervision of research department. Presents research findings to company executives or clients.

*Assistant Research Director.* This position usually represents a defined "second in command," a senior staff member having responsibilities above those of other staff members.

*Statistician/Data Processing Specialist.* Duties are generally those of an expert consultant on theory and application of statistical techniques to specific research problems. Usually responsible for experimental design and processing of data.

*Senior Analyst.* Generally in larger research departments, participates with superior in initial planning of research projects, directs execution of projects assigned. Operates with minimum supervision. Prepares or works with analysts in preparing questionnaires. Selects research techniques, makes analyses, and writes final report. Budgetary control over projects and primary responsibility for meeting research time schedule.

*Analyst.* Usually handles the bulk of the work required for execution of research projects. Often works under senior analyst supervision. The analyst assists in questionnaire preparation, pretests them, and makes preliminary analyses of results. Handles most of the library research or within-company data collection.

*Junior Analyst.* Working under close supervision, junior analysts handle routine assignments. Editing and coding of questionnaires, statistical calculations above the clerical level, simpler forms of library research. Much of junior analyst's time is spent on tasks assigned by superiors.

*Librarian.* Builds and maintains a library of reference sources adequate to the needs of the research department.

*Clerical Supervisor.* In larger departments, oversees central handling and processing of statistical data. Duties include work scheduling and responsibility for accuracy.

*Field Work Director.* Usually employed only by larger departments. Hires, trains, and supervises field interviewers.

*Full-Time Interviewer.* Conducts personal interviews and works under direct supervision of field work director. Few companies employ full-time interviewers.

*Tabulating and Clerical Help.* Perform the routine, day-to-day work of the department.

Source: Dik Warren Twedt, *1983 Survey of Marketing Research,* American Marketing Association, Chicago, 1983, Appendix.

probably increased substantially since then, and (2) they combine entry-level individuals with more experienced (i.e., more highly paid) personnel.

Opportunities for instant research involvement are probably brighter than ever for well-trained entry-level personnel in marketing research, and the kinds of persons considered for such positions has changed considerably over the years. In the past, marketing researchers were often hired with relatively little research expertise, then trained on the job. An officer of a New York personnel firm specializing in marketing research observes, "Years ago, people were not educated specifically for marketing research. Exposure to it began after their careers began. . . . Today's trainees are better educated to the relevant technology of the field and are more capable of immediate productivity."[23]

One of the most important factors in obtaining an entry-level position in marketing research is the possession of an MBA degree. However, many bachelor's degree holders also enter marketing research. In either case, your chances are greatly increased if you possess at least a few of the following characteristics: a strong background in marketing, social science, and quantitative courses; computer literacy and familiarity with statistical analysis techniques; good interpersonal and communicational skills; and a basic curiosity about consumers and their behavior.

If your college or university is one of many that have a student chapter of the American Marketing Association, this can also prove beneficial as a source of advice and contacts (e.g., through activities such as monthly luncheons with area businesspersons). In addition, the American Marketing Association publishes an annual marketing services guide and membership directory that might prove useful in your personal-marketing efforts. The 1986 edition of this publication contains over 100 pages listing marketing research firms that might be able to utilize your talents.[24] Naturally, you should also explore opportunities with consumer and industrial companies, advertising agencies, publishers and broadcasters, and financial services, many of whom have research departments of their own.

## RESEARCH TECHNIQUES: TOOL KIT OR BAG OF TRICKS?

Earlier, we examined the variety of organizations using marketing research, and some of the purposes for which research is conducted. In actually carrying out a marketing research study, a broad range of specific tools and techniques are employed. Research techniques comprise a formidable tool kit for the marketing researcher. Regardless of what marketing question you wish to answer, chances are that one or more of these techniques will serve you quite well. Appropriately, the major orientation of the book is to acquaint you with the various research techniques and, within the constraints of a single course, to develop your proficiency with them.

However, as we will see throughout the text, research techniques can be misused. In this regard, the book is also designed to make you an informed "consumer" of claims and findings offered by others, especially those inevitable sources who are either (1) downright unethical, or (2) well-meaning but unscientific in their approach. Whenever we discuss any technique that offers the opportunity for abuse, we will examine one or more possibilities for purposely

---

[23] Marcia Fleschner, "Attracting a New Breed of Researcher," *Advertising Age*, November 14, 1985, p. 20. Copyright © 1985 by Crain Communications, Inc. Reprinted with permission.

[24] *1986 Marketing Services Guide and The American Marketing Association Membership Directory* (Chicago: American Marketing Association, 1986).

distorting research findings. As we enter such discussions, remember that the goal is a constructive one—that is, for your own information and self-defense, not to help you use marketing research as a tool for manipulation.

As one example of the kinds of "offenses" we'll discuss in the various chapters, consider a newspaper headline that seems to occur with increasing regularity these days: "Survey Shows That. . . ." Typically, the sponsors of a survey do not include specific question wordings in the news releases they distribute to describe their findings. Even if the exact wording *is* released, newspaper space constraints often preclude a detailed description of the survey and its questions. With this in mind, let's look at a hypothetical possibility.

For each of the following question wordings, judge for yourself how the wording might tend to bias the responses in either a "yes" or "no" direction (i.e., the blank space in the headline might be "Support" or "Oppose," depending on how the question is worded).

---

*SURVEY SHOWS THAT AMERICANS* ——————— *LIMITS ON JAPANESE IMPORTS*

Possible question wordings that could strongly influence respondents' answers are the following:

1. "To help keep America working, do you favor limiting imports from Japan?"
2. "Considering that foreign products are putting millions of Americans on unemployment benefits supported by your tax dollars, do you favor limiting imports from Japan?"
3. "At the risk of undermining free trade and international relations with our friends overseas, do you think that government should impose arbitrary limits on imports that happen to come from Japan?"

---

Naturally, different organizations may have a vested interest in whether or not such limits are imposed or continued, and it's *possible* that they could "lean" one way or the other in carrying out their study. Since newspaper editors are generally not skilled in the techiques of sample selection and questionnaire design (if they see the questions at all), the message in the headline may be the primary communication that reaches the public.

## ORGANIZATION OF THE TEXT

The flow of our discussion in the text will approximate the order of activities involved in a typical marketing research study. In Chapter 2 we will examine the vital role of research in marketing decisions. In Chapter 3 we'll consider the various types of research projects and their implementation, including the many data sources from which the researcher may choose.

Chapters 4 and 5 examine the notion of sampling and the sample-size decision, while Chapters 6 and 7 explore the basic notion of measurement and its attitudinal applications. Chapters 8 through 11 focus on the actual collection of information, ranging from survey research to experimentation.

Once we've obtained information, the next step is to analyze it, and Chapters 12 through 16 provide a wide range of techniques for this purpose. Chapter 17 examines market analysis, an important research function not always oriented around specific projects, and discusses a number of popular forecasting techniques employed by marketing research.

An important step in the research process is the communication of our findings to marketing management, and this is the subject matter of Chapter 18. Finally, in Chapter 19, we'll step back a few paces and take a look at the "big picture" of marketing research, examining some thought-provoking social and ethical issues that are an inevitable part of the research function.

At the end of each section of the text, cases will supplement the end-of-chapter questions to provide further opportunity to "operationalize" the materials presented in the chapters. In addition, there will be a variety of real-world exhibits and examples presented throughout the book for the purpose of enhancing your awareness of marketing research applications and (in some cases) honing your skepticism as a future "consumer" of research findings.

## ☐  SUMMARY

Marketing research, the "systematic design, collection, analysis, and reporting of data and findings relevant to a specific marketing situation," finds application in a wide variety of business and nonbusiness settings.

While there were scattered applications of marketing research techniques early in U.S. history, it was not until the early 1900s that more formal approaches came into being. In 1911, the Curtis Publishing Company established the first formal marketing research department.

Over the years, marketing research has evolved through phases that have combined innovations within the discipline with knowledge and experience gained from a wide range of other fields. This evolution has been accompanied by a continuing increase in the number of formal marketing research departments.

The biggest users of marketing research are manufacturers of consumer and industrial products. Publishers, broadcasters, advertising and public relations agencies, financial institutions and services, consulting agencies, retailers, wholesalers, government agencies, and nonprofit organizations are also among the key users of marketing research.

Marketing research facilitates the marketing concept by helping firms identify and satisfy consumer needs. It also provides valuable input for marketing decision making and serves as a vital component of the marketing information system. Career opportunities in marketing research are as diverse as the academic and practical experience of the individual, and his or her quantitative, interpersonal, and communicative skills.

Research techniques comprise a formidable tool kit for the marketing researcher and make it possible to answer a broad range of marketing questions. While the major orientation of the text is on introducing these techniques and developing proficiency in their use, emphasis is also placed on making the reader an informed "consumer" of claims and findings offered by others. Misuse of marketing research can be difficult to detect, and even subtle abuse can lead to distorted research findings and the potential for manipulation.

☐ **QUESTIONS FOR REVIEW**

1. Select any two recent television commercials you have seen, briefly describe each, then suggest possible marketing research findings that may have led to the specific verbal and nonverbal communications in each.

2. "A good marketing executive knows his customers and doesn't need marketing research to tell him what they like or don't like." Discuss.

3. An example in the text described a study in which researchers observed television programs and noted the characteristics of TV families versus those in real life. The TV mothers tended to be rather affluent and involved in highly adventurous occupations compared to their real-life counterparts. In conducting an observational study of television programming, what other sexual, occupational, ethnic, or product ownership characteristics might be observed in the "TV world" that are not typical of the real world?

4. A text example involved a study by the National Bowling Council in which it was found that there were 64,000,000 bowlers in the United States. Although this is an interesting finding, what was the underlying purpose of the study, and to what extent was this purpose achieved?

5. In a text example, consumers were given what they thought were three different deodorants for their evaluation. Considering that the deodorant inside all three was the same, and only the package designs were different, do you feel that researchers were ethical in not telling study participants the truth? Why or why not?

6. Select an organization (profit or nonprofit) that markets ideas, beliefs, or physical products that you think may be detrimental to our society. How might this firm benefit from the use of marketing research? Do you think it is ethical for marketing researchers to help such an organization achieve its goals? Why or why not?

7. For what purposes might each of the following organizations be interested in using marketing research?
   a. A local YMCA in your area.
   b. The National Rifle Association.
   c. The National Safety Council.
   d. Your local Pizza Hut restaurant.
   e. General Motors Corporation.

8. Assume that the American Red Cross is interested in using marketing research to increase the number of units of blood donated to the local hospital each year. What specific questions might they wish to answer through the use of marketing research?

9. What is meant by the "industrial statistics phase" of the development of marketing research, and why was this phase beneficial?

10. What was the "management awareness phase" of the development of marketing research, and why was this phase beneficial?

11. What role does marketing research play in making the marketing concept work?

12. In what ways might marketing research prove useful to your own college or university?

13. For the bachelor's degree holder, what are the most likely entry-level positions to marketing research, and what types of responsibilities would members of each position tend to have?

14. "Survey shows that . . ." newspaper articles are sometimes the result of press releases from specific companies or organizations, and summarize the findings of a given study done or commissioned by the company or organization. Assuming that legislation were proposed that such articles include research methodology details such as the exact wording of questions, what are some of the pros and cons of such legislation?

15. A local investor owns a home for the elderly that happens to be across the street from several social fraternities at a large university. The investor intends to commission a study of how community members perceive the university and the appropriateness of the behavior of its students. Speculate on some specific findings the investor might wish to see, and explain her reasoning.

# 2

# RESEARCH AND MARKETING DECISIONS

**Research Helps Put Mercedes 190 on Road to Success**

**Figure 2-1.** Marketing research helped ensure a warm welcome for the Mercedes-Benz 190 when it was introduced to U.S. customers. (Photo courtesy of Mercedes-Benz of North America, Inc.)

Mercedes-Benz, long known for its engineering orientation, also relies heavily on marketing research to achieve success in the marketplace. In the case of its down-sized 190 series, the company conducted an extensive research program to help formulate marketing and advertising decisions for the new model. The so-called "Baby Benz," introduced in 1983, was targeted toward young, affluent customers, drivers often found behind the wheel of a Saab, Volvo, or BMW instead of a Mercedes. Although smaller and less expensive than its other models, the 190 was engineered to traditional Mercedes performance and quality standards.

Research efforts included focus group interviews, product clinics, customer test-drive reactions, and studies of advertising impact and awareness. In addition, early-buyer and follow-up surveys were undertaken. According to David M. McCall, of McCaffrey and McCall, Inc., Mercedes' advertising agency, the information from this research "helped guide the most successful and exciting new-model launch Mercedes has ever staged in the United States."[1] The 190 now accounts for almost 40% of Mercedes production, with sales through 1986 nearly as high as the company's entire car output during the two years preceding the model's introduction.[2]

## INTRODUCTION

The dynamic world of today's marketing decision maker is beset with a combination of opportunity, peril, and perplexity that lends a certain degree of adventure to even the simplest marketing decision. Competitive pressures, government involvement, and environmental concern join an often capricious marketplace in providing marketers with slippery footing on the road to organizational prosperity.

Although faced with such sources of uncertainty, American marketers annually spend billions of dollars in the development, promotion, and distribution of the goods they have produced. Considering the collective magnitude of their activities, it is not surprising that marketing decision makers are deeply concerned with the gathering and utilization of information that promises to improve the quality of their decisions.

However, despite the very best efforts of marketing research practitioners, wrong decisions are made every day—for example, a study by one consulting firm found the overall success rate for new products to be just 65%.[3] This is not the result of faulty or incompetent marketing research, but rather is inherent in

---

[1] "Research Played Role in Launch of 'Baby Benz,' " *Marketing News*, January 4, 1985, p. 21, published by the American Marketing Association.

[2] Thomas F. O'Boyle, "Small Luxury Car Is Success for Daimler," *The Wall Street Journal*, September 19, 1986, p. 22.

[3] *New Products Management for the 1980's* (New York: Booz Allen & Hamilton, Inc., 1982).

the role of marketing research as a vehicle for the *reduction* of uncertainty associated with the complex interaction between present decisions and future events. Total elimination of uncertainty, although desirable as a goal, is generally impossible to achieve in real-world decisions.

In this chapter we'll first consider the larger informational context in which marketing research functions. This is known as the ***marketing information system,*** and marketing research plays a key role in its operation. We'll then examine the nature of the marketing decision situation, along with nonprobability and expected-value approaches to its resolution. In the latter case, we'll see how an upper limit can be placed on how much to spend on a single research study intended to reduce uncertainty in a given decision setting.

Finally, since research and marketing decision makers are necessary partners in the conduct and implementation of marketing research, we'll consider some of the conflicts a researcher can expect to encounter in this sometimes awkward relationship. Our presentation will be arranged according to the following topics:

 I. The marketing information system
 II. Structuring the decision situation
 III. Nonprobability approaches to marketing decision making
 IV. The expected-value approach: how much to spend on research
 V. Research and the marketing decision maker

## THE MARKETING INFORMATION SYSTEM

We live in an age where the generation and proliferation of information has truly become an explosion. Author John Neisbitt points out that the United States is in the midst of a "megashift" to an information-based economy, and that more than two-thirds of our work force is engaged in either the production or processing of information.[4] Organizing and selecting from the resultant sea of data must set the stage for even thinking about types of decisions to be made, let alone making the crucial selection of a course of action to be taken in a given situation. The *marketing information system* is an organized approach increasingly being utilized by firms to help them organize and use this universe of information without becoming overwhelmed by its sheer magnitude:

> A marketing information system is a continuing and interacting structure of people, equipment, and procedures to gather, sort, analyze, evaluate, and distribute pertinent, timely, and accurate information for use by marketing decision makers to improve their marketing planning, execution and control.[5]

---

[4] John Neisbitt, *Megatrends: Ten New Directions Transforming Our Lives* (New York: Warner Books, 1984); in Kotler, *Principles of Marketing*, 3rd ed., p. 86.

[5] Philip Kotler, *Principles of Marketing*, 3rd ed. (Englewood Cliffs, N.J.: Prentice-Hall, Inc., 1986), p. 87. Much of the discussion in this section is based on Kotler's treatment of the MIS.

Figure 2-2 illustrates the key components of the marketing information system, which serves as a link between the marketing environment (target markets, marketing channels, competitors, publics, and macroenvironmental forces) and marketing management. These components, or subsystems, are (1) the internal records system, (2) the marketing intelligence system, (3) the information analysis system, and (4) the marketing research system.

### The Internal Records System

The internal records component involves collecting and summarizing the many kinds of reports (e.g., sales, accounting, production, inventory) generated within the company. For maximum value, this information must be current, easily available, and in a form that is readily understood by the executives who will be using it. For example, Sears marketing managers make use of computerized information on the company's 40 million customers for the promotion of special product and service offers based partially on the types of past purchases customers have made from the firm.[6]

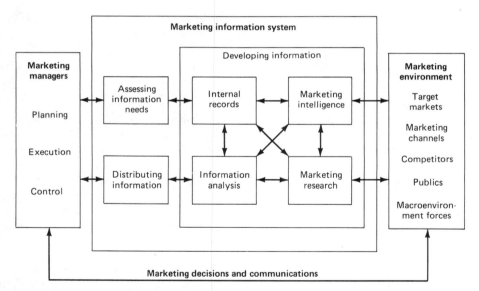

**Figure 2-2.** Key components of the marketing information system (MIS), which includes marketing research and serves as a link between marketing management and the firm's marketing environment. [*Source:* Philip Kotler, *Principles of Marketing, 3rd Edition* (Englewood Cliffs, N.J.: Prentice Hall, 1986), p. 87.]

---

[6] Ibid., p. 89.

### The Marketing Intelligence System

Information in the marketing intelligence system can be described as "happenings data, everyday information about important environmental events—new laws, social trends, technological breakthroughs, demographic shifts, competitor maneuvers—that helps managers prepare and adjust marketing plans."[7] Such sources might include radio or television broadcasts, newspapers, trade or financial publications, or informal conversations with sales personnel, customers, service technicians, and channel intermediaries. In general, executives obtain this type of information simply by keeping their eyes and ears open, and encouraging those with whom they come into contact to do the same. The locales in which such data are collected may range from industry trade shows to the electronic entertainment media in the executive's own living room.

---

**EXHIBIT 2-1**

*Cabbies Tell Dealer How He Fares*

In Madison, Wisconsin, it's not unusual for service customers of a certain large dealer to drop off their cars for repair during the day. The customers are then treated to free taxi service, courtesy of the dealership. Twice a year, the cab drivers are also treated—to a free dinner, also courtesy of the dealer, who proceeds to pump them for information about customer comments.

(See "Intelligence Gathering," *The Wall Street Journal*, May 29, 1986, p. 1.)

---

Information about competitors is particularly valuable to the marketing intelligence system. In one survey, responding companies reported spending an average of $450,000 per year for tracking their competition.[8] In discussing how companies gain information on competitors, *Fortune* magazine listed more than 20 specific techniques, including obtaining information from recruits and from competitor employees, sometimes at conferences or trade shows; from customers doing business with the competition; from published materials and public documents; from buying and analyzing competitors' products; and from observing either current activities or physical evidence of past activities (e.g., obtaining and examining garbage discarded by the competitor, observing trucking or other shipping/receiving volume).[9] At least one marketing intelligence

---

[7] Ibid., p. 90.

[8] "Study: Many Firms Foolish with Intelligence Funds," *Marketing News*, January 3, 1986, p. 44, published by the American Marketing Association.

[9] Steven Flax, "How to Snoop on Your Competitors," *Fortune*, May 14, 1984, pp. 29–33. Copyright © 1984 Time, Inc.; in Kotler, *Principles*, pp. 91–92.

consultant even gathers competitive data on the basis of container-manufacturer information stamped on the bottom of the cardboard boxes companies use to ship products to retailers[10] (see Figure 2-3).

### The Information Analysis System

The information analysis system consists of two components: (1) a ***statistical bank*** that includes advanced methods for statistical analysis (for example, regression, correlation, factor, discriminant, and cluster analysis techniques) and (2) a ***model bank***, consisting of computer models designed to mathematically represent real-world entities of marketing interest. The model bank may include mathematical models designed to help the marketing executive with such decisions as allocating the advertising budget, evaluating the progress of new products, or assigning sales representatives to their territories.

**Figure 2-3.** Seemingly insignificant, even the container manufacturer identification and numerical labels on cardboard shipping boxes can help collectors of marketing intelligence get information about the competition. (*Source:* Based on Bernie Whalen, "Marketing 'Detective' Reveals Competitive-Intelligence Secrets," *Marketing News*, September 16, 1983, sec. 1, p. 1, published by the American Marketing Association. Photo courtesy of Jim Wakefield.)

---

[10] Bernie Whalen, "Marketing 'Detective' Reveals Competitive-Intelligence Secrets," *Marketing News*, September 16, 1983, sec. 1, p. 1, published by the American Marketing Association.

*The Marketing Research System*

The marketing research system is the one emphasized in this book and is geared to answering specific marketing questions that arise from time to time. It typically involves survey research, attitude studies, experimentation, and other project-oriented methods that we'll be exploring in the chapters ahead. A key role of marketing research is to help managers make pricing, product and package design, product distribution, and promotion decisions such as these:[11]

> *Pricing.*   When we're deciding the price of a product, research can help by providing information concerning the *price elasticity of demand*—that is, the effect that different prices might have on sales.
>
> *Product and package design.*   By finding out what product features are liked or disliked, marketing research can assist in the development of new products and the redesign or improvement of current offerings. In the typical applications presented in Chapter 1, we saw how a toiletries manufacturer used a marketing research experiment in choosing the color scheme to be used for packaging a new deodorant.
>
> *Product distribution.*   Marketing research can be used in selecting from alternative channels of distribution, deciding on geographic areas and specific sites for retail outlets, and determining what types of inducements might work best for motivating and rewarding channel middlemen.
>
> *Promotion.*   In addition to helping generate and evaluate alternative advertising plans, marketing research is sometimes used for providing documentation to support specific product claims—for example, "In actual consumer tests, 9 out of 10 preferred the new taste of Stickum Peanut Butter." In the personal selling area, marketing research can help managers in selecting, improving, evaluating, compensating, and setting performance objectives for salespersons.

## STRUCTURING THE DECISION SITUATION

### Decision Variables and States of Doubt

The marketing decision maker faces a two-sided dilemma: (1) the need to make decisions, and (2) the degree to which the future will be a favorable environment for the courses of action selected. The variables involved are of two types, controllable and uncontrollable. In addition, there can be several levels of doubt regarding the environment that will follow the decision.

---

[11] The discussion in this section is based largely on Donald L. Thompson, "Uses of Research Findings," in Robert Ferber (ed.), *Handbook of Marketing Research* (New York: McGraw-Hill, 1974), pp. 1.96–1.106. Used with permission of McGraw-Hill Book Company.

## Controllable and Uncontrollable Variables

### Controllable (Should We . . . ?) Variables

Controllable variables are primarily alternate decision strategies that are under the control of the decision maker. This category also includes other closely related marketing decisions—for example, the selection of target market, distribution channel, promotional, pricing, manufacturing, and packaging strategies that may be crucial to each of the alternate courses of action available to the marketing manager.

### Uncontrollable (What If . . . ?) Variables

Variables assumed to lie beyond the control of the marketing decision maker are of two types, involving either (1) states of nature, or (2) competitive actions.

*States of nature.* States of nature are relatively passive but nevertheless very important environmental factors that are under the control of neither the decision maker nor any of his or her active competitors. Legal, technological, and societal variables are generally considered to be uncontrollable from the standpoint of the individual marketing decision maker.

*Competitive actions.* The decisions of active competitors in the marketplace are generally difficult to anticipate or predict, but often play an important part in determining the success or failure of a given course of action taken by your firm. Analysis of situations involving competitive actions is primarily carried out through the application of *game theory*, a topic reserved for discussion in the appendix to this chapter.

The following example illustrates the controllable and uncontrollable variables that might be faced by a domestic bicycle manufacturer considering the national introduction of an expensive, mechanically sophisticated model retailing in the over-$500 price range. Although the major decision may be whether or not to come out with the new model, other controllable and uncontrollable factors might also require consideration:

*Primary controllable variable.* Possible introduction of the new bicycle model.

*Other controllable variables.* Price, product features, channel of distribution decisions, promotional emphasis, and level of expenditures for marketing of the new model. For example: Should we include a tool kit and tire pump as standard equipment? Should we limit distribution to present dealers or expand to include discount department stores? To what extent should we emphasize various purchase appeals such as economy of operation, physical fitness, environmental concern, riding pleasure, and dependability?

*Uncontrollable variables—state of nature.* Possible government-sponsored bicycle-only lanes for commuting from suburbs to major cities. Potential enactment of strict safety requirements such as mandatory rider training and licensing, bicycle registration, and helmet usage laws. Uncertainties regarding the future price and availability of fuel required for operation of conventional, gasoline powered short-trip vehicles. Possible changes in world competitive position due to upward or downward valuation of the dollar relative to foreign currencies. Continuation of the propensity of Americans toward energy conservation and physical fitness. The future state of the national economy and its effect on discretionary personal income. The increasing popularity of the 150-mpg moped as a low-investment alternative to bicycles in the higher price ranges.

*Uncontrollable variables—competitive actions.*   Key competitor may also introduce a new model with similar price and features. Competition might cut price or expand features of comparable model currently on the market. A leading moped manufacturer may introduce a special, bottom-of-the-line model featuring engine-powered operation with a purchase price only slightly greater than that of your bicycle.

## States of Doubt

A decision maker operating in a state of *certainty* would have little difficulty selecting the best course of action, since she or he would know exactly the consequence that would result from each available strategy. For example, under complete certainty, a hypothetical marketing manager would have no problem in selecting advertising appeal II in the following decision situation:

| Advertising appeal | Next year's profit |
|:---:|:---:|
| I | $300,000 |
| → II | 500,000 |
| III | 250,000 |

Naturally, such a situation is extremely rare, if not totally nonexistent, in the complex world of marketing decisions. The real-life decision maker nearly always faces some degree of doubt regarding the anticipation of possible future states and the probability that each will occur.

The possible degrees of doubt present in a marketing decision situation are briefly summarized in Table 2-1, and include the categories of (1) risk, (2) uncertainty, and (3) ignorance.

### Risk

At the risk level of doubt, we know both the possible states of nature that may arise and their respective probabilities of occurrence. Insurance underwriters and gamblers are frequently called upon to make decisions that fall into this category.

**TABLE 2-1.** *Three states of doubt with which decision makers may be faced. Most marketing decisions involve the "uncertainty" situation.*

|                      |         | State-of-nature probabilities | |
|----------------------|---------|-------------------------------|-------------|
|                      |         | *Known*                       | *Unknown*   |
| **Possible states of nature** | *Known*   | Risk                  | Uncertainty |
|                      | *Unknown* | Ignorance           | |

### Uncertainty

In a situation of uncertainty, we know in advance the possible future events that may follow our decision, but we don't know their respective probabilities of occurrence. Most marketing decisions fall into this category. For example, if we were to decrease our prices by 10%, we could identify possible reactions by our customers and competitors, but would find it impossible to determine in advance the exact probabilities of their potential responses. While the decision maker might make a fairly good *subjective* estimate of the probabilities involved, these would not be as precise as the objective and exact probabilities found in the *risk* situation just described.

### Ignorance

Extremely unique or unusual situations may be impossible to analyze in terms of anticipating the range of future events following a decision. In this case, we have no knowledge of either the event possibilities or their probabilities of occurrence. In marketing, this kind of situation is relatively rare and generally involves an unprecedented course of action such as the introduction of an entirely new product or concept, the consequences of which are nearly impossible to anticipate at the time the decision must be made.

## The Payoff Matrix

Once we've identified a marketing decision problem and enumerated our decision strategy possibilities, our next step is to consider the various states of nature that might be encountered. We might also estimate the respective probabilities of these states of nature. In this way, the alternatives and their possible outcomes will be in a form that can be more easily visualized by the decision maker and more easily analyzed by the marketing researcher. Such a structured description of the decision problem may be referred to as a *payoff matrix*, and it contains the following elements:

1. *Alternatives:* strategies from which the decision maker will choose
2. *States of nature:* uncontrollable events that will affect the outcome from selecting a given strategy

**3.** *Consequences:* outcomes resulting from the intersection of each strategy with each possible state of nature

The entries in Table 2-2 are estimated company profits for various intersections of strategies and states of nature. In this situation, a tennis racquet marketer must select a product spokesperson for its tennis line, and will be deciding between two well-known athletes: (1) Johnny Goodscout, a bit bland, but a polite and steady performer both on and off the court, and (2) Jeremy Cosworth III, a fiery superstar whose tennis excellence is sometimes marred by immature, abusive treatment of opponents, judges, and media.

The states of nature are the relative degrees of preference that tennis product purchasers will have for the volatile Cosworth during the endorsement contract period. (Naturally, neither potential spokesperson's future popularity is actually known at this point.) The payoffs represent estimated company profits for the contract year for each combination of decision alternative and state of nature. For example, if we select Jeremy Cosworth III and the public has a low degree of preference for him, company profits for the year are estimated to be just $10,000.

The values of the payoffs entered in a matrix and the probabilities of the various states of nature are estimates based on experience, judgment, and available research, and are often subjective. Marketing research can be utilized both in estimating the value of a particular consequence and in helping us arrive at approximate probabilities for the various states of nature. In addition to reflecting estimated payoffs for the intersections between decisions and states of nature, Table 2-2 assumes a probability of $p = 0.5$ that Jeremy Cosworth III will have a "low" degree of preference, with $p = 0.3$ for "moderate" and $p = 0.2$ for "high."

It's quite possible that, for the same states of nature, different observers might assign entirely different sets of probabilities. However, despite their often subjective nature, such probabilities can be highly relevant to the decision-making situation because they explicitly recognize and quantify management's

**TABLE 2-2.** *Payoff matrix for selection of tennis star to be promotional spokesperson in racquet ads. Payoffs are estimated company profits during contract period.*

|  |  | State of nature: Consumers' degree of preference for Jeremy Cosworth III | | |
|---|---|---|---|---|
|  |  | *Low* ($p = 0.5$) | *Moderate* ($p = 0.3$) | *High* ($p = 0.2$) |
| *Alternative:* spokesperson choice | *Johnny Goodscout* | $70,000 | $50,000 | $40,000 |
|  | *Jeremy Cosworth III* | $10,000 | $70,000 | $100,000 |

knowledge, thus providing an avenue for its inclusion into the decision-making structure.

The resulting payoff matrix contains all of the essential ingredients for the decision process: (1) the alternatives, (2) the states of nature and their estimated probabilities, and (3) the consequences of each alternative for each state of nature. Its ability to combine all of these important factors, both visually and conceptually, makes the payoff matrix a useful structure on which to base decision-making deliberation as well as action. In the next two sections, Table 2-2 will be central to our examination of two very different approaches to decision making.

## NONPROBABILITY APPROACHES TO DECISION MAKING

There are always decision situations in which a marketing manager is either unable or unwilling to develop and use probability estimates for the various states of nature that might occur. In addition, some managers and companies tend to be very conservative in selecting courses of action while others in similar decision circumstances readily accept the risks involved. The point is that not all executives feel the same about facing uncertainty—on a TV game show, for example, some would accept with relief the prize they've already won, while others anxiously seek what's "behind the curtain." As a result, some decision criteria will appeal to the conservative marketer, while others may be more attractive to the person who is more willing to take risks. Since different criteria tend to appeal to different decision-making "types," their use will generally lead to different evaluations of which is the "best" course of action to be selected.

### The Worst-Case Criterion

This strategy depends heavily on Murphy's Law: "If something can go wrong, it will." The decision maker assumes that regardless of the alternative selected, the worst possible state of nature will occur.[12] As shown in Table 2-3, the worst result that could occur if we select Johnny Goodscout is a profit of $40,000. Should we select Jeremy Cosworth III, the worst thing that could happen would be a profit of just $10,000. Since this criterion assumes that nature is "out to get us," and $40,000 is better than $10,000, our choice for company spokesperson would be Johnny Goodscout.

Because any new venture or product will nearly always include the possibility of a highly unfavorable payoff, consistent application of this strategy will tend to squelch new marketing developments. However, it may sometimes be necessary for a firm to protect itself from even the slight chance of financial

---

[12] The worst-case and best-case criteria in this section are sometimes referred to as "minimax-maximin" and "maximax," respectively. Although there are other nonprobability approaches to decision theory, we have limited our discussion to these approaches in order to concentrate on the probability-based criterion in the next section.

*TABLE 2-3.* *Application of worst-case and best-case strategies in selection of tennis spokesperson. Neither approach considers probabilities of the possible states of nature.*

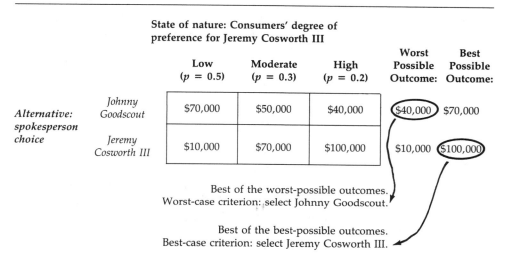

| | | State of nature: Consumers' degree of preference for Jeremy Cosworth III | | | | |
| | | Low ($p = 0.5$) | Moderate ($p = 0.3$) | High ($p = 0.2$) | Worst Possible Outcome: | Best Possible Outcome: |
| Alternative: spokesperson choice | Johnny Goodscout | $70,000 | $50,000 | $40,000 | $40,000 | $70,000 |
| | Jeremy Cosworth III | $10,000 | $70,000 | $100,000 | $10,000 | $100,000 |

Best of the worst-possible outcomes.
Worst-case criterion: select Johnny Goodscout.

Best of the best-possible outcomes.
Best-case criterion: select Jeremy Cosworth III.

disaster by playing its marketing cards very close to the vest. Whenever a corporation is relatively small compared to the magnitude of the possible consequences it faces, marketing management may find this conservative, pessimistic approach to be desirable.

### The Best-Case Criterion

Like the strategy just discussed, this one focuses on an extreme outcome for each alternative—in this case, the best payoff that might be achieved. Regardless of which alternative the decision maker chooses, he optimistically expects that the best possible state of nature will occur. Table 2–3 shows these possibilities for our tennis endorsement example. Our profit could be as high as $70,000 if we select Johnny Goodscout, and as high as $100,000 if we select Jeremy Cosworth III. Because this strategy is eternally optimistic, assuming that nature will smile on us regardless of what we do, our choice would be Mr. Cosworth.

In this approach the alternative with the best possible payoff is selected even though the necessary state of nature may be extremely improbable. For example, a picnic committee employing this strategy might insist on planning an outdoor picnic even if the weather service were predicting a 99% chance of rain. The reason for this would be the *possibility* (although slim, at 1%) of their preferred picnic situation occurring. Although such total optimism may be a bit extreme, a firm already facing financial extinction may decide that the "go for it" philosophy this strategy represents may be their only hope.

## THE EXPECTED-VALUE APPROACH: HOW MUCH TO SPEND ON RESEARCH

In the nonprobability criteria we've just discussed, the role of marketing research is simply to help estimate the consequences in the payoff matrix. However, in the expected-monetary-value (EMV) criterion examined here, marketing research is important in another way: helping to estimate the probability of occurrence for each possible state of nature.

### The Expected-Monetary-Value Criterion

The expected value of a particular decision alternative is just a weighted average of all the possible payoffs to which the course of action might lead. The "weights" used are the personal or objective probabilities associated with the various states of nature. In our tennis endorsement example, we've assumed these probabilities to be 0.5, 0.3, and 0.2 for the respective states of nature shown in Table 2-4. We can now proceed to calculate the expected payoff for each alternative by means of the following formula:

$$\text{EMV for alternative } i \text{ facing } k \text{ states of nature} = \sum_{j=1}^{k} \text{Prob}(s_j) \times (\text{payoff})_{ij}$$

where

$\text{Prob}(s_j)$ = probability that state of nature $j$ will occur

$(\text{payoff})_{ij}$ = payoff you'll receive if you select alternative $i$ and state of nature $j$ occurs

Applying this formula to the payoff matrix and probabilities of Table 2-4,

**TABLE 2-4.** *Expected monetary value approach to selection of tennis star to be promotional spokesperson in racquet ads.*

|  |  | State of nature: Consumers' degree of preference for Jeremy Cosworth III | | | |
|---|---|---|---|---|---|
|  |  | Low ($p = 0.5$) | Moderate ($p = 0.3$) | High ($p = 0.2$) | Expected monetary value (EMV) |
| Alternative: spokesperson choice | Johnny Goodscout | $70,000 | $50,000 | $40,000 | $58,000 |
|  | Jeremy Cosworth III | $10,000 | $70,000 | $100,000 | $46,000 |

Highest expected monetary value.
EMV selection: Johnny Goodscout.

[e.g., 0.5 (70,000) + 0.3 (50,000) + 0.2 (40,000) = $58,000]

we would calculate the expected value of each alternative as follows:

EMV (Johnny Goodscout) = 0.5(70,000) + 0.3(50,000) + 0.2(40,000) = $58,000

EMV (Jeremy Cosworth III) = 0.5(10,000) + 0.3(70,000) + 0.2(100,000) = $46,000

On this basis, steady Johnny Goodscout would be selected if we wish to maximize our expected payoff. Remember that the EMV of $58,000 will not actually occur but is an expectation based on a weighted combination of the estimated consequences. As we discussed earlier, a very conservative decision maker would also choose Mr. Goodscout, while a person willing to take greater chances might decide to "go for it" and select the talented-but-volatile Mr. Cosworth. However, because of his superior EMV, Mr. Goodscout would be chosen by the decision maker who uses expected value as the basis for his selection.

## How Much to Spend on Research: The Expected Value of Perfect Information

Based on our *present* level of information, we would choose Mr. Goodscout, with an expected monetary value of $58,000. But suppose that we now have the opportunity to conduct a marketing research study to help us better determine the true degree of preference that tennis product consumers will have for Jeremy Cosworth III. Should we (1) forget about gathering further information and go ahead with our decision, or (2) carry out the marketing research project? If we do undertake research, how much should we be willing to spend?[13]

In attempting to answer the preceding questions, we should first consider how much we would be willing to pay for a *perfect* research study—that is, one that would tell us for sure how the market was going to react to Mr. Cosworth. Although there is no such thing as a "perfect" study, calculating its worth will give us an upper limit on how much we should spend on a real-world study conducted by fallible human beings in a shifting environment.

> *Note to the reader:* Keep in mind that we are still at the "present" point on the time scale and that even if we had the opportunity to obtain perfect information about the future, we don't know right now what that information would be. Unfortunately, though, "right now" is when we have to decide whether or not to perform additional research.

With perfect information, we would be sure of making the best decision regardless of which state of nature were to occur. For example, if we knew that

---

[13] Approaches to decision making that rely on expected values and initial or revised probabilities for the states of nature are known as **Bayesian**. Since the nonprobability criteria in the preceding section do not utilize either, they are classified as **non-Bayesian**. Although it's possible to calculate the expected value of imperfect information, this technique is beyond the scope of this book and interested readers may wish to cover this topic from a more advanced statistical source. Our major point here is to point out the importance of the expected value of perfect information (EVPI) to marketing research expenditure decisions and describe the ease by which it can be calculated.

**Figure 2-4.**   This ad says a lot about the wisdom of making important decisions without the benefit of marketing research. The expected value of perfect information (EVPI) can help us place an upper limit on how much we should be willing to spend to reduce our reliance on "luck." (Courtesy of Chilton Research Services.)

the market had a high degree of preference for Jeremy Cosworth III, we would sign him to an endorsement contract and realize a payoff of $100,000. Based on our initial set of probabilities, there is a 0.2 chance that a perfect research study would lead us to this consequence. Similarly, there is a 0.5 chance that the perfect research study would tell us that Cosworth's degree of preference is "low," which would result in our retaining Mr. Goodscout and receiving $70,000. (Remember, we're assuming that we *will* have perfect information, but we don't know at this point exactly what that information will be.)

Using this logic, we can then calculate our *expected value with perfect information* by applying this formula to our $k$ states of nature:

$$\begin{matrix} \text{expected value with} \\ \text{perfect information} \end{matrix} = \sum_{j=1}^{k} \text{Prob}(s_j) \times \begin{pmatrix} \text{best payoff if state} \\ \text{of nature } j \text{ occurs} \end{pmatrix}$$

Applying this formula to the payoff matrix and probabilities of Table 2-4, we find that the promise of perfect information would enable us to expect a profit of $76,000:

$$\begin{matrix} \text{expected value with} \\ \text{perfect information} \end{matrix} = 0.5(70,000) + 0.3(70,000) + 0.2(100,000) = \$76,000$$

We would then determine, as illustrated in Figure 2-5, a value of $76,000 − $58,000 = $18,000 as the expected value of perfect information (EVPI). Note that the word *of* is especially critical in this context—although EVPI is expected value *of* perfect information, some mistakenly refer to it as the expected value *with* perfect information. Based on this calculation, we should consider any research study costing $18,000 or more as not being worth its expense. Depending on its accuracy, a real-world (i.e., imperfect) marketing research study would be worth somewhere between $0 and $18,000.

As the accuracy of a study deviates from perfect, the value of the study decreases quickly. For example, if the true state of nature is "high degree of preference for Cosworth," a random guess would have a 33.3% chance of correctly identifying this condition—but a random guess would obviously be worth $0. Thus, as a rule of thumb, it's not a bad idea to multiply EVPI by a small

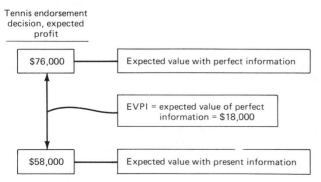

Tennis endorsement
decision, expected
profit

$76,000 ——— Expected value with perfect information

EVPI = expected value of perfect
information = $18,000

$58,000 ——— Expected value with present information

**Figure 2-5.** The expected value of perfect information is the difference between the expected monetary value with *perfect* information and the EMV with *present* information.

fraction such as $\frac{1}{4}$ or $\frac{1}{5}$ in order to get a more realistic idea of the upper spending limit for a real-world study.

## RESEARCH AND THE MARKETING DECISION MAKER

As with any other tool, marketing research will be of little value if it is either misunderstood or not used at all. Unfortunately, there are a number of areas of conflict that often occur between research and the decision makers who are to utilize it, and these conflicts end up reducing the potential effectiveness of research in the decision-making process. Although these problems are not insurmountable, they frequently require that the researcher be nearly as adept at handling human nature as he or she is with techniques of the research trade.

### Conflicts between Researcher and Manager

In general, researchers and managers tend to be different kinds of people. They often have divergent backgrounds, interests, and skills, as well as different organizational responsibilities. More important to this discussion, they frequently differ in terms of their appreciation for marketing research and their expectations of what research can and can't do. These are several of the reasons why researchers and managers tend to approach marketing research from different perspectives. Table 2-5 elaborates on their probable areas of conflict and provides a summary of the viewpoints they tend to exhibit.

### A Typology of Marketing Managers

Managers vary considerably in terms of how much they respect or use marketing research. Nancy M. Flinn, a former researcher who has moved into marketing management, observes that there are three types of marketing managers,[14] shown in Figure 2-6:

1. *Information lovers*, who have a "highly developed sense of curiosity and a mind open to new information. They generally embrace marketing research with true love. . . . They may press the researchers to overload questionnaires to get more information or want cross tabs that are beyond the quality of the data. . . . They challenge interpretation of research and motivate researchers to stretch for their maximum contribution to the business, even if occasionally it's painful to the researcher."[15]

---

[14] "Marketers Are Information Lovers, Expediters, or Manipulators When Interfacing with Researchers," *Marketing News*, January 22, 1982, sec. 2, p. 12, published by the American Marketing Association.

[15] Ibid.

**TABLE 2-5.** *Potential areas of conflict between the researcher and marketing management. Researchers and decision makers often have divergent backgrounds, interests, and skills, as well as different organizational responsibilities.*

| Area | Top management positions | Marketing research positions |
|---|---|---|
| 1. Research responsibility | a. Marketing research lacks accountability<br>b. Marketing research should provide information | a. Responsibilities not clearly defined<br>b. Authority not given to researchers<br>c. No decision-making involvement with top management |
| 2. Research personnel | a. Are poor communicators<br>b. Lack enthusiasm, salesmanship, and imagination<br>c. Need to have more empathy for other people | a. Researchers should be judged on performance<br>b. Top management does not understand staffing needs |
| 3. Budget | a. Research costs too much<br>b. Difficult to measure contributions to profit<br>c. Some "fat" in marketing research | a. "You get what you pay for" attitude<br>b. Inadequate financial support<br>c. Needs to be continuous |
| 4. Assignments | a. Too technical<br>b. Not done quickly enough<br>c. Doesn't solve management's needs | a. Not given all the facts<br>b. Don't appreciate scientific process<br>c. Do not help in the problem stage<br>d. Not given enough time |
| 5. Research reporting | a. Dull presentation<br>b. Not decision oriented<br>c. Too often reported after the fact<br>d. Too lengthy; irrelevant data | a. Good research demands thorough reporting and documentation<br>b. Do not give undivided attention when presentation is given<br>c. No desire to understand research process |
| 6. Use of research | a. Free to use it as we please<br>b. Needs changes which makes previous research useless | a. Used to confirm or excuse past actions<br>b. Isn't used after it was requested and conducted |

*Source:* From John G. Keane, "Some Observations on Marketing Research in Top Management Decision Making," *Journal of Marketing*, October 1969, pp. 10–15, published by the American Marketing Association. Reprinted with permission.

**Figure 2-6.** Marketing managers can be classified as (1) information lovers, (2) expediters, or (3) manipulators depending on their appreciation and use of marketing research. (*Source:* This is a dramatization of the marketer types discussed in "Marketers Are Information Lovers, Expediters, or Manipulators When Interfacing with Researchers," *Marketing News,* January 22, 1982, sec. 2, p. 12, published by the American Marketing Association.)

2. *Expediters,* who rely heavily on research and tend to be less aware of the limitations of research and to depend too much on researchers and their data in making decisions. "They rarely if ever challenge research findings, they hate to make recommendations that conflict with research. These marketers are expediters whose thinking lacks personal conviction and creativity. They are only as good as their research counterparts, who probably have very limited experience in assessing a proposition within the context of total business considerations."[16]

3. *Manipulators,* who "have little respect for the contribution of an individual researcher or the discipline of marketing research. In many cases, they don't understand the role of research or the techniques available. Their inflated ego or lack of smarts drives them to see research as a potential threat to being able to execute their plans as *they* see fit. . . . The marketers who don't respect research can be dangerous because they will attempt to manipulate study design, questionnaire format, and findings to heighten the probability that they will achieve data to support what they want to do."[17]

As a researcher, you can expect numerous encounters with one or more of these marketer "types." It will be up to you to make the relationship as effective as possible. Success also depends on both parties seeing corporate performance as a common goal toward which both must strive. According to Pat Pecorella, research manager of Quaker Oats, Inc., successful researchers "want to be part of the marketing team and see themselves as marketing people who just happen to be in research because they are particularly skilled in data analysis and the application of quantitative analytical methods to data."[18]

### The Research Generalist

To help bridge the gap between research and marketing decision makers, it can be helpful either to utilize a ***research generalist*** or to be one yourself. The research generalist is someone who provides a link between research and management, helping each to understand the perspective and concerns of the other.[19] Although this may not be the type of job description you find in the Sunday classifieds, the opportunity to serve in this capacity is available to any researcher who cares enough to try just a bit harder. Hopefully, top management will appreciate and reward efforts to bridge the gap.

As we proceed through the project planning, data collection, analysis, and

---

[16] Ibid.

[17] Ibid.

[18] "Successful Marketing Researchers Are Engendered by Corporate Management," *Marketing News,* June 10, 1983, p. 16, published by the American Marketing Association.

[19] For a more complete discussion of the research generalist, see Joseph W. Newman, "Put Research into Marketing Decisions," *Harvard Business Review,* March–April 1962.

presentation chapters that follow, you should obtain a better understanding of the technical nature of marketing research and the need for cooperation and close communication with marketing decision makers, who must be considered as partners in the process.

## □ SUMMARY

Marketing decision makers face many competitive, governmental, and other environmental factors that lie beyond their control. In addition, they have a wide variety of alternative marketing strategies that can be implemented in response to a decision situation.

The marketing information system serves as a link between the marketing environment and marketing management, and facilitates the gathering and utilization of information to improve the quality of marketing decisions. The MIS has four components: the internal records system, the marketing intelligence system, the information analysis system, and the marketing research system. It is with the latter system that the book is primarily concerned.

Marketing decisions are made in various states of doubt, which include risk, uncertainty, and ignorance. Most marketing decisions involve uncertainty, a setting where the possible states of nature are known but their exact probabilities are not. The marketing decision situation can be structured by means of a payoff matrix describing possible states of nature and the outcome resulting from the intersection of each with available decision alternatives.

Nonprobability approaches to the decision situation do not consider the probabilities of the states of nature. The expected-value approach takes state-of-nature probabilities into consideration, enables the decision maker to identify the alternative with the greatest expected payoff, and allows the calculation of the expected value of perfect information. The EVPI serves as an upper limit for how much should be spent on a real-world research study to reduce uncertainty.

Marketing research is of little value in decision making if it is either misunderstood or not used at all, and its potential effectiveness is sometimes reduced by conflict between research and marketing management. Members of these groups frequently differ in terms of their appreciation for marketing research and their expectations of what research can and can't do. The research generalist helps to fill the gap, assisting each to understand better the perspective and concerns of the other.

## □ QUESTIONS FOR REVIEW

1. What is meant by the "marketing information system," and what role does marketing research play within this system?
2. In the marketing information system, what is the difference between the internal

records system and the marketing intelligence system? Provide a brief description of each.

3. What are some of the controllable and uncontrollable variables that might be faced by an electronics manufacturer considering the introduction of a new pocket-sized video game?

4. What is the difference between the nonprobability and expected value approaches to decision making? In which type is marketing research more likely to be employed?

5. Under what conditions might a decision maker elect to choose an alternative other than the one that has the highest expected monetary value? Provide a real or hypothetical example in which this could be expected to occur.

6. Claude faces a decision relative to the Hower University homecoming parade. He has the choice of selling either ice cream or hot chocolate from his small vending wagon. If the weather is cold on the day of the parade, he estimates that his profit will be $200 for hot chocolate, and only $10 for ice cream. If the weather is fair, he anticipates a loss of $50 with hot chocolate and a profit of $100 if he sells ice cream. Assuming that the probability of a cold day is 0.6:
   a. If Claude tries to maximize his expected profit, what decision will he make, and how much profit can he expect?
   b. What is the expected value of perfect information?

7. For the decision situation of Question 6, what decision would Claude make if he were to utilize the "worst-case" criterion? The "best-case" criterion?

8. In considering three different strategies for a new soft drink, our profits will depend on the choice we make and the market condition that occurs. The following payoff matrix summarizes our profit picture (amounts are in millions of dollars):

|  |  | Market condition | | |
|  |  | I | II | III |
| Flavor selection | Sweet, cola | $12 | $14 | $18 |
|  | Nonsweet, cola | 16 | 12 | 12 |
|  | Fruit flavored | 4 | 8 | 30 |

   a. If we feel that the probabilities for the different market conditions are 0.2, 0.5, and 0.3, respectively, what choice would we make based on expected monetary value?
   b. If we feel that the probabilities for the different market conditions are 0.2, 0.5, and 0.3, respectively, what is the most that we should be willing to pay for a perfect market forecast?
   c. What strategy would we choose if we were to employ the "worst-case" criterion? The "best-case" criterion?

9. For each of the following activities, indicate whether the decision maker is using "worst-case," "best-case," or expected value as a criterion:
   a. Roy plays the state lottery.
   b. Mary buys homeowner's insurance for her new house.
   c. Charlie bets on the San Diego Chargers to win their next game. Nevada oddsmakers list the team as favored by 15 points.

10. Since there is no such thing as a "perfect" research study, what is the practical value of calculating the expected value of perfect information?

11. A decision situation involves two possible states of nature, and the expected value of perfect information is calculated to be $2000. A consultant promises a 70% probability of correctly identifying the actual state of nature which will occur, and requests $1400 (0.70 × $2000) for his research study. The manager of marketing research turns down the consultant's proposal. Why?

12. Is it possible for the expected value of perfect information to be zero? (i.e., you wouldn't be willing to pay anything to know which state of nature is actually going to occur). If so, provide a real or hypothetical example of such a situation.

13. In the text, three "types" of managers were discussed in terms of their respect for, and use of, marketing research. Briefly describe each type. If you were a researcher, how might you try to work with each without compromising the quality, practicality, and objectivity of your research efforts?

14. What are some of the kinds of conflicts that can occur between marketing management and marketing researchers, and how might these conflicts be reduced or resolved?

15. Who is the "research generalist," and what function does he or she serve in the marketing research arena?

# APPENDIX

## Marketing Decisions Involving Competition

### INTRODUCTION

In our discussion in the main part of the chapter, we concentrated on states of nature as the source of uncertainty for our payoff matrix. However, the consequence of a marketing decision may also depend heavily on the actions of a competitor. Analysis of such decision situations is part of a body of knowledge called *game theory* in which our competitor, unlike "nature," is a decision-making entity looking out for its own best interests. As just two examples, consider the following competitive situations:

- In their bitterly contested race for the governorship of Pennsylvania, candidates William Scranton and Bob Casey each engaged heavily in airing negative ads about the other. At least one political expert seems to feel that if a candidate engages in negative advertising, his or her opponent is forced to respond in kind. According to David Doak, an advisor to Mr. Casey, "People may not love the ads, but they crave the information, and if you don't use negative ads and your opponent does, it's a sure way to lose."[1]

---

[1] David Shribman, "Scranton's Shift to High Road in Governor's Race in Pennsylvania May Test Effect of Negative Ads," *The Wall Street Journal*, November 3, 1986, p. 3.

- In an open letter to Wendy's franchisees, Chairman Robert L. Barney used a full-page ad in *The Wall Street Journal* to advise them of the company's response to PepsiCo's acquisition of Kentucky Fried Chicken. PepsiCo already owned Pizza Hut and Taco Bell, both well-known competitors of Wendy's. Mr. Barney informed franchisees that Coca-Cola products would soon be replacing Pepsi in Wendy's restaurants across the United States.[2]

The concept of carrying out "marketing research" to determine what a competitor will do is sometimes considered to be an improper research function, especially since some unscrupulous firms may employ industrial espionage or spying for this purpose. For this reason, and because competitors are generally less cooperative than "nature," the contribution of marketing research to a competitive decision situation is largely toward the identification of (1) the possible actions of a competitor, and (2) the consequences associated with the intersection of each of our strategies with each of theirs.

Because of the rather specialized nature of *game theory*, we will discuss it only briefly here. By means of examples, we will consider two kinds of competitive situations:

1. *Zero-sum.* Whatever one opponent "wins," the other opponent "loses."
2. *Non-zero-sum.* Both competitors can "win" or "lose," depending on which strategy each selects.

**Zero-Sum Games**

In a zero-sum game, your gain is your opponent's loss, and vice versa. The rows of the payoff matrix represent your alternatives and the columns those of your competitor. The entries of the matrix are viewed from your standpoint, representing how much *you* will gain or lose in a given consequence.

As an example of a zero-sum game situation, consider the payoff matrix of Table 2A-1. We're assuming that Family Theater and Porny Palace are competing for a fixed market of movie goers and will have different degrees of

**TABLE 2A-1.** *Example of payoff matrix for a zero-sum game with a strategy equilibrium point. Payoffs represent Family Theater's share of the market and strategy equilibrium occurs at "G"-"X" intersection.*

|  |  | Porny Palace | | |
|---|---|---|---|---|
|  |  | ↓ "X" | "R" | "PG" |
| **Family Theater** | "PG" | 20% | 30% | 50% |
|  | →"G" | 30% | 40% | 60% |

[2] See "An Open Letter from Robert L. Barney, Chairman of the Board, Wendy's International," *The Wall Street Journal*, October 16, 1986, p. 29.

success depending on which kind of film each shows during a given week. The payoffs are seen from Family Theater's viewpoint—for example, if Family shows a PG-rated movie and Porny's movie is X-rated, Family will obtain a market share of just 20%, the other 80% going to Porny for their evening entertainment. (These figures could be based on either research-based estimates or past attendance data.)

One advantage of setting up a decision situation in game theory form is that you may be able to "eliminate" certain of your or your opponent's strategies as being unwise. Depending on how many are so eliminated, you may even be able to determine in advance an "equilibrium" that might otherwise take expensive time to reach naturally through periodic decisions. For example, in Table 2A-1 Family Theater's "G" strategy is superior to "PG" regardless of what Porny decides to do. (For each column, the "G" payoff is greater than that for "PG.")

Having thus eliminated the first row and reduced the payoff matrix to one row and three columns, we see that Porny will be able to select from "X" (100 − 30 = 70% market share), "R" (100 − 40 = 60% market share), and "PG" (100 − 60 = 40% market share). Remember that the payoff entries are seen from Family's point of view. Given this choice, Porny would naturally prefer 70% of the market and will show X-rated movies while Family shows G-rated films. The Family ("G") and Porny ("X") intersection is called an *equilibrium* point because if either competitor decides to move away from it, his market share will drop.

Such equilibrium points don't always happen, but are useful if they can be predicted in advance. More often, a matrix may be reduced by eliminating some rows and/or columns, but will end up comprising two or more rows and two or more columns. In this case, we may wish to rely upon one of our nonprobability criteria to guide us toward a strategy selection. Table 2A-2 shows such a situation—neither competitor can automatically eliminate a strategy from consideration. For competitor A, neither strategy is superior to the other and the same is true for competitor B.

## Non-Zero-Sum Games

In the non-zero-sum situation, both competitors can win, one can win and the other lose, or both can lose, depending on the combination of strategies selected.

**TABLE 2A-2.** *Example of zero-sum game with no strategy equilibrium point. Payoffs are as seen by competitor A.*

|  |  | Competitor B's alternatives | |
|---|---|---|---|
|  |  | I | II |
| Competitor A's | 1 | 75% | 40% |
| alternatives | 2 | 30% | 60% |

Consider, for example, two neighborhood food stores facing the decision of whether or not to give trading stamps to their customers.

The competitors, Mom & Pop, Inc., and Ajax Grocery, face the profit payoffs shown in Table 2A-3. In each cell of the payoff matrix, the profit on the left represents Mom & Pop, while that on the right represents Ajax. For example, if Mom & Pop give stamps, but Ajax doesn't, their respective profits will be $10,000 and $1000.

As with the zero-sum game, we assume that each competitor will look at the information relevant to his own interests and attempt to eliminate inferior alternatives. For this reason, Mom & Pop are better off giving stamps regardless of what Ajax does. (In the first column, $3000 is better than $1000 and in the second column, $10,000 is better than $7000, so giving stamps is the best decision for Mom & Pop.)

Similarly, Ajax finds that they are better off giving stamps regardless of the Mom & Pop decision. (In the first row, $3000 is better than $1000 and in the second row, $10,000 is better than $7000.)

Thus, if the two competitors reach their decisions independently, both will give stamps and make a profit of $3000 each. However, if they decide to enter into (illegal) collusion, they may decide to drop the stamps (since they're essentially neutralizing each other and enhancing the profits of the trading stamp company) and increase their profits to $7000 each, as shown in Table 2A-4.

**TABLE 2A-3.** *Example of a non-zero-sum game. In each cell, entry at left represents Mom & Pop profit, entry at right Ajax profit. If independent decisions are made, both will give stamps.*

|  |  | Ajax Grocery | |
|---|---|---|---|
|  |  | ↓ | |
|  |  | *Give stamps* | *Don't give* |
| **Mom** | →*Give stamps* | $3000, $3000 | $10,000, $1000 |
| **&** |  |  |  |
| **Pop** | *Don't give* | $1000, $10,000 | $7000, $7000 |

**TABLE 2A-4.** *If grocery competitors discussed in text decide to "collude" instead of making independent decisions, equilibrium will move to lower right cell, with neither giving stamps and each making more profit.*

|  |  | Ajax Grocery | |
|---|---|---|---|
|  |  | | ↓ |
|  |  | *Give stamps* | *Don't give* |
| **Mom** | *Give stamps* | $3000, $3000 | $10,000, $1000 |
| **&** |  |  |  |
| **Pop** | →*Don't give* | $1000, $10,000 | $7000, $7000 |

As indicated earlier, *game theory* is an extensive body of knowledge and these examples are only intended to give you an idea of how this kind of analysis works.[3] A key point is that not all situations can be handled by simply identifying an unknown factor as a "state of nature." When the possible actions of a competitor dominate a decision situation, it may be worthwhile to try to view the scenario from this competitor's standpoint as well as from your own.

---

[3] For a more detailed examination of game theory, the reader may wish to refer to R. D. Luce and H. Raiffa, *Games and Decisions* (New York: John Wiley & Sons, Inc., 1957).

# 3

# PLANNING THE MARKETING RESEARCH PROJECT AND IDENTIFYING POTENTIAL DATA SOURCES

**Finding Funds for Lady Liberty**

In 1985, the Statue of Liberty–Ellis Island Centennial Foundation was about $60 million short of the $230 million it needed from private donors in order to finish renovations in time for the July 4, 1986, centennial celebration. To raise the necessary funds, the foundation, advertising agency Kenyon & Eckhardt, and CACI, a private data company, joined forces in a research study to identify potential contributors and design promotional appeals to reach them.

Central to the project was CACI's ACORN (A Classification of Residential Neighborhoods) system, which classifies all American households into 44 market segments based on neighborhood demographic, socioeconomic, and housing variables. The system was used to categorize 8 million contributors, with categories having the heaviest concentration of donors to be the targets of an intensive final campaign. The types of categories identified were also to play a role in determining the types of ad appeals to be used in the campaign.

According to Mr. Mitchell Glatt, in charge of Kenyon & Eckhardt's Statue of Liberty account, the ACORN profile of contributors constituted "a tremendous opportunity to find out where our money is coming from. . . . This campaign is not like Smokey the Bear, where you have 20 years to reach

*Source:* "The Statue of Liberty Raises Funds," *American Demographics*, November 1985, p. 19.

**Figure 3-1.** This lucky lady was the beneficiary of marketing expertise that was key to her being refurbished in time for her 100th birthday. In one important research project, contributor categories were identified in preparation for a final, intensive fund-raising campaign aimed at those most likely to give. (Photo courtesy of the New York Convention & Visitors Bureau.)

people. . . . We have to work fast. And if we can identify 10 or 20 geographic concentrations of donors, then we can target certain media outlets and lean on them to run more public service ads." (*A postscript:* Considering that both Kenyon & Eckhardt and CACI donated their services, the successful staging of the centennial celebration suggests that these marketing firms were two of the most important donors to the cause.)

## INTRODUCTION

In Chapter 2 we examined the important role of research in reducing the uncertainty with which a marketing decision maker is faced. Naturally, as a decision involves either more uncertainty or more importance, the potential contribution of a marketing research study will be more significant. In this chapter, we're going to assume that the decision to conduct research has in fact been made, and we will examine some of the steps involved in planning, conducting, and controlling the research project itself.

It is tempting to present a "universal" set of research design instructions that will presume to apply to all marketing decisions, all market situations, and for all levels of managerial and researcher expertise. However, it is probably not in the best interest of either truth or practicality to even attempt such a grand endeavor within the limits of a single textbook. At this point, it is sufficient for us to view the overall research process as a matter of determining satisfactory answers to questions such as the following:

1. What problem or decision do we face?
2. How can we restate our problem in terms of information that is either in existence or available at reasonable cost?
3. What strategies and procedures can we employ in order to acquire the necessary information?

While discovering answers to such questions represents the general goal of research design, it is nevertheless somewhat like telling the manager of an electronics store to "go out there and sell some TVs." There must naturally be some attention given to particular strategies on a more workable level. Within the chapter, we will examine the marketing research project further in terms of the following, more specific topics:

I. Types of marketing research studies
II. The research process and common research errors
III. Types of marketing information
IV. Secondary data: internal sources
V. Secondary data: government sources
VI. Secondary data: published sources
VII. Secondary data: commercial sources
VIII. Evaluation and control of the marketing research effort

In approaching the topics that follow, keep in mind that research design is simply a plan of action for the collection and analysis of information pertinent to the problem or decision at hand. Without such a plan, it is likely that the resulting research will be inefficient because of the number and cost of midstream changes in direction necessitated by a shortsighted horizon.

## TYPES OF MARKETING RESEARCH STUDIES

There are a number of ways by which we might classify research designs. For example, a study may be either *quantitative* or *qualitative*, depending upon the form of the data generated and the degree of mathematical rigor to which it is subjected. Similarly, research may be either *applied* or *basic*, depending on whether the results are expected to contribute directly to a managerial decision (applied) or are intended to provide answers to questions of a theoretical nature (basic). Probably the most useful categorization of research designs is based on the functional objective of the investigation. Using this method of classification, we can identify four major designs: (1) exploratory, (2) descriptive, (3) causal, and (4) predictive.

## Exploratory Studies

It's not unusual to get a "that's what you do when you're at square number one" response when you mention the possibility of exploratory research with regard to a marketing problem. After all, exploratory research is often the very first step taken in the pursuit of many research efforts. Basically, exploratory studies are intended to help you become familiar with the problem situation, identify important variables, recognize alternate courses of action, suggest rewarding avenues for further research, and help establish which of these avenues should have the highest priority in competing for your limited budgetary resources. In short, exploratory studies are for the purpose of helping you obtain, relatively quickly, ideas and knowledge in a situation where you may be a little short on both.

However, it's not quite fair to tag the exploratory study with the "square number one" label. This type of research can be highly useful as an initial step in even the most extensive marketing research plans. As a matter of fact, failure to carry out an exploratory study may well lead to a misdirected research effort, a higher research cost than would otherwise be required, or even to a lengthy research effort that wasn't needed in the first place. Although generally carried out on a small scale, an exploratory study alone may well be sufficient to meet the informational needs of marketing management with regard to the problem under investigation. Figure 3-2 emphasizes the importance of an exploratory study in approaching a marketing problem, and illustrates its relationship to the other research designs discussed in this section.

Procedurally, the exploratory study is highly flexible, intuitive, and informal. The creativity and judgment of the researcher are very important, since at this stage, you're still attempting to get a "handle" on the exact nature of the problem as well as the potential usefulness of various research strategies in solving it. As a practical matter, you may have to resist some pressure from others to cut short the exploratory phase (remember that it's often perceived as the "we're at square one" degree of progress) and get on with the "actual" study. While the inherent flexibility of the exploratory study precludes setting forth firm procedural guidelines, there are two approaches—the literature survey and the experience survey—that can prove especially useful in exploratory research.

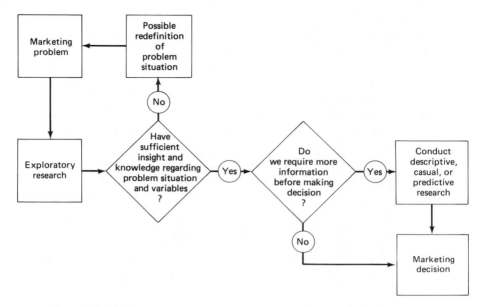

**Figure 3-2.** Exploratory research is especially important in the early stages of a marketing study.

### The Literature Survey

The literature survey is simply a search through available data. After all, if someone else has already investigated one or more aspects of your marketing problem, it doesn't make sense for you to spend money traveling the same path. Available literature (which we will expand upon shortly under the more proper label of "secondary data") is in general abundance from various corporate, commercial, private, and governmental libraries, services, documents, and publications. In a very short time, and at precious little expense, you can usually gain the benefit of insight from a truly vast amount of data from sources such as these.

### The Experience Survey

As admitted exploratory researchers, we can always profit by seeking the guidance and advice of persons who are experienced in the subject being investigated. Note that *experience* should not be equated with *status*. For example, if you're concerned about possible reasons for sagging sales of your company's hosiery, you may gain valuable insight by talking with salespersons as well as with acknowledged marketing experts in the field. This dimension of exploratory research is especially informal, and may include purposive "conversations" with people who have been identified as potential contributors. The approach should be as unstructured as possible, since it is to your advantage to allow each "expert" to elaborate his or her opinions on the topic to the maximum degree. Even if such opinions are inconsistent with each other, this allows you to gain the benefit of being able to identify a range of possible problem solutions or explanations that can be individually explored through subsequent research. Remember that the goal of exploratory research isn't to find *answers*, but rather to gain ideas and insight into the problem as well as its potential solutions. Chances are that exploratory research may end up generating more questions than answers, but at least such questions will assist you in reaching the ultimate information you are seeking.

### Descriptive Studies

The majority of marketing research studies are of the descriptive type—as the name suggests, they have as their purpose the description of something. The "something" that is described may take a wide variety of forms. For example, a company may be extremely interested in descriptive research that involves the following kinds of marketing information:

1. The characteristics of the users of a given product. How old are they? Are they predominantly male or female? Are they married or single? Do they tend to possess college degrees? How do they compare along these demographic dimensions with people who use competing products?

2. The percentage of the target market that recognizes your company's trademark or brand name. How do they perceive your product compared to others with regard to quality, price, durability, and other features? On an even more basic level, which product features do customers value most, and how much are they willing to pay for various levels of improvements in these features?

3. New developments that have been taking place in the field. For example, it may be most beneficial to conduct periodic price surveys at the retail level in order to detect as quickly as possible any changes in the pricing strategies of key competitors.

4. The more attractive market areas to be considered whenever expansion of the marketing effort is contemplated. How do the alternatives compare in terms of population, per capita income, family size, home ownership, or other characteristics that may be deemed important to the successful entry of your product into a new territory?

Compared to exploratory research, descriptive studies demand that the researcher identify in advance the specific research questions that are to be asked, how they might be answered, and the implications that likely potential answers may have for the marketing manager. In other words, a useful descriptive study must have a definite purpose. Naturally, it is probable that a descriptive study may provide results that lead to additional descriptive or other research.

## Causal Studies

The goal of a causal study is relatively simple—to determine the cause-effect relationship, if any, between variables. For example, the marketers of at least one dietary supplement claim that the fat in fish, known as Omega-3, may have a healthful effect on one's arteries and longevity. A Dutch study of 852 men over 20 years found that men who ate more than 1 ounce of fish per day were half as likely to have a heart attack than those who ate fish only rarely. In another study, it was found that Omega-3 pills reduced fat blockage in the arteries leading to the heart. Viewed in experimentation terms, the independent variable, $X$ (Omega-3), is seen as having an effect on a dependent variable, $Y$ (heart attack incidence or artery blockage).[1]

Causal studies are important to marketing decision makers in many ways—for example, finding out to what extent a price reduction might improve sales, evaluating alternative ads to see which one is more likely to change consumer attitudes, or determining if a package redesign will lead to a more attractive product. The application of experimentation techniques is a significant topic in itself, and is discussed in further detail in Chapter 11.

## Predictive Studies

The purpose of the predictive study is to arrive at a forecast or prediction of some measurement of interest to the researcher. Quite often, the ultimate target of such a study is the future sales level of the firm. Other goals of predictive research may involve industry sales levels, projections of future growth or decline of age groups to which the firm's products appeal, or the use of a test market to predict the likely success of a new product. The overlap between the predictive study and those previously discussed is not insignificant. For example, the prediction of sales may be viewed as a causal study in which the independent variables are simply "time" and marketing strategy decisions. Similarly, the predictive study might be considered a type of descriptive study—albeit one that "describes" not the present, but rather what is likely to occur in the future. Figure 3-3 summarizes the four types of marketing research studies, including their principal goals and a sampling of the types of management questions that would be likely to precipitate each approach.

---

[1] Michael Waldholz and Trish Hall, "Fish Oil Pills: An Aid to a Longer Life, or the Object of a New Marketing Hype?" *The Wall Street Journal*, September 10, 1986, p. 33.

**Figure 3-3.** A summary of the types of marketing research studies and the kinds of questions that could initiate each.

## THE RESEARCH PROCESS AND COMMON RESEARCH ERRORS

Once you've completed the exploratory phase of your investigation and have a clearer view of the research road ahead, it is now advisable to outline further steps in a more formal manner. This will not only benefit you in terms of better structuring your own efforts, but will also provide dividends in the form of improved communications and relations with marketing management. Clearly, the cooperation and support of management is essential to a good research study, the results of which are likely to be respected and used. To this end, the existence of a written plan of action serves as a basis for agreement on what you are going to do, how you are going to do it, and what potential results and recommendations may accrue from the research. Thus the early construction of a research plan will serve a variety of technical and public relations purposes.

### Planning the Study

In planning for a specific research project, it is necessary to anticipate your activities and informational requirements in order to avoid inefficiency and misdirection. However, rather than being a neatly packaged "connect the dots" set of directions, the activities involved are very much interrelated and difficult to structure in the manner we would like. As a result of (1) the need for structure, and (2) the complexity of obtaining such structure, it is prudent to recognize that the plan for any given study will certainly be characterized by the individuality of the circumstances that led to its formulation. The following six steps, although not applicable to every imaginable research study, provide a general prescription for planning the research project.

   *1. Formulate the marketing problem.* Try to state the problem as a question that can be answered by research. Define the problem situation and important variables as well as possible—exploratory research, which hopefully you've already done, can be of great assistance in this regard. Perhaps the most important part of solving a problem is taking the time and effort to define it clearly in the first place. At this point, it is very important to work closely with the marketing manager in order to arrive at a problem statement that both satisfies his or her decision-making requirements and is a relatively clear target for your research efforts.

   *2. Determine information requirements.* Once you've prepared a satisfactory problem statement, complete with specific research objectives, make a listing of the information you will need in order to satisfy these objectives. In so doing, keep in mind that some information may simply not be available to you. As a result, you may wish to go back and undertake a slight downward revision of the project objectives. Try to avoid the specification of information that, although interesting, may not contribute to the marketing decision that should be the focal point of your research.

    *3. Identify information sources.* Begin by determining if the information you need is already available as secondary data, either within your firm or from an outside source. If not, you may have to generate your own information by means of a survey or an experiment. While possible sources of secondary information are discussed in this chapter, the procurement of original data in the field is discussed later in the book. In considering the sources of research information, it will be necessary to determine exactly how and by whom the information will be collected. In addition, the information sources selected, and the form of the information itself, should be consistent with the type of analysis (e.g., quantitative, qualitative, or both) that you intend to use in processing the information after it has been collected.

    *4. Examine the decision implications of potential findings.* This part of the research plan may be somewhat difficult. After all, how can you make recommendations based on results that you haven't yet discovered? However, such "what do we do if . . ." deliberation is not just idle speculation, but a crucial check on the pertinence of the information and analyses that you are proposing. If the answer to a particular research question will have no influence on the ultimate decision reached, then resources should not be expended on attempting to answer the question.

    *5. Estimate time and cost requirements.* As with any other project, a marketing research study must fall within permissible time and cost constraints. If you are faced with constraints that are not realistic, it is advisable to make this known to management at the earliest possible stage of the project deliberations. Otherwise, you will either badly exceed the project completion deadline or run out of money without having completed the study—either way, you will lose both respect and credibility. It is sometimes possible, upon encountering adverse conditions that were not anticipated at the outset of the study, to obtain additional time or funding. However, unless you enjoy the security of an alternative source of employment, such extensions should never be counted upon.

    *6. Prepare the research proposal.* Even if exploratory studies have already been conducted, it is generally required to submit a written research proposal on behalf of the anticipated project. At this stage of planning, the project has not yet been "sold" to marketing management, and your potential "customer" will wish to reserve approval until it is clear how much the study will cost, how long it will take, exactly how you're going to conduct it, and (most importantly) what contribution it can be expected to make toward one or more important marketing decisions for which she or he is responsible. The content of the research proposal will include a discussion of planning items 1 through 5 presented above. In addition, a good research proposal will recognize some of the study limitations with regard to such areas as the applicability of possible findings and the effect of the time and cost constraints imposed on the researcher. Far from a simple ploy to squeeze more funding from the manager, the recognition of such potential limitations can go a long way toward helping to avoid possible misunderstanding and disagreement upon completion of the project.

**Study Execution and Implementation**

The actual performance of the study consists primarily of following the blueprint that the study plan represents. The only remaining steps in the process will then be (1) the analysis and interpretation of the information which has been collected, and (2) the formal presentation of the study findings and recommendations. Figure 3-4 describes the flow of research activities involved in conducting an image study for a banking institution.

Implementation of your research involves more than simply conducting the study and reporting its results. There is, not surprisingly, an element of human relations involved if you intend to see the product of your hard work collect respect and usage instead of dust. For example, it's a good idea to test early or tentative findings informally in order to determine the reactions of your research "customers." Such information may easily be obtained through informal conversations during the normal course of business. This strategy not only alerts you to potential objections that you must handle sooner or later, but also tends to make those concerned feel like "insiders" who are sharing in the research effort.

If the research findings suggest that a sudden change in marketing strategy is in order, be sure to exercise both caution and patience in advancing your recommendations. Some marketing managers and clients simply possess a great deal of strategic "inertia," and may require extensive convincing in a firm but courteous manner. Another strategy of implementation involves the degree of optimism that you express on behalf of your research. If you tend to overstate the potential benefits of your recommendations, your proposals are more likely to be accepted, but you will lose credibility in the long run. Some believe that the best strategy is to slightly understate potential benefits. In this way, when the eventual results are favorable, you will not only look good, but your future credibility will be enhanced. However, be careful not to understate too greatly the potential benefits of adopting your recommendations—if you do, they may not be adopted at all.

**Common Research Errors**

There are a wide variety of errors capable of reducing the accuracy and usefulness of a marketing research investigation. They are categorized here as (1) problem definition error, (2) informational error, (3) experimental error, and (4) analysis error.

### *Problem Definition Error*

As we discussed previously, it is highly important to begin consideration of a marketing research project with a well-defined, researchable statement of the marketing problem faced by the firm. If the problem has not been well

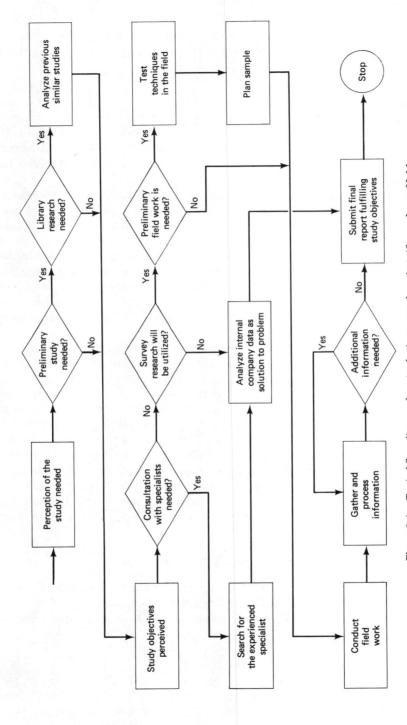

**Figure 3-4.** Typical flow diagram for a marketing research project. (*Source:* James H. Myers and Coskun Samli, "Management Control of Marketing Research," *Journal of Marketing Research*, 6, no. 3 (August 1969):272, published by the American Marketing Association.)

defined in the very beginning, the result is likely to be a research project intent on seeking information other than that required for the solution or alleviation of the problem.

### Informational Error

In the generation of primary data through the use of surveys, there are two types of errors—*sampling* and *nonsampling* errors.

*Sampling errors.* Sampling errors arise because the researcher has taken a sample instead of a complete census of the population. With an appropriate sampling strategy, these errors can be reduced by simply using a larger sample size in your study. However, though such error may be statistically recognized, it cannot be avoided without actually "sampling" every member of the population of interest. For a representative sample, the presence of sampling error may be recognized by a statement such as, "Based on our study, we are 95% sure that between 63% and 67% of the adult residents of Pittsburgh watched Channel 4 News last Saturday night." Had the sample size been larger, this interval may have been reduced (e.g., to 64.5 to 65.5%), but probably at the expense of an exorbitant research expenditure not worth its high cost.

*Nonsampling errors.* Nonsampling errors are those with which you would be faced even if you could afford to include a much larger sample of the population of interest. *Frame* errors are of this type, and are the result of the sample (however large it may be) not being representative of the population from which it was drawn. *Response bias* errors are also of this type, and may occur because of a tendency for subjects to exaggerate their incomes, understate their liquor consumption, misinterpret the question or, in some instances, take advantage of an interview situation to demonstrate their own creativity. Similarly, *nonresponse* errors may occur even if your selected sample is highly representative

---

**EXHIBIT 3-1**

*The Checkouts That Didn't Balance*

What consumers do is often not the same as what they *say* they do. Comparing actual purchases electronically monitored by BehaviorScan at the checkout aisle with what consumers said they bought, Information Resources Inc. found that only a third of those who reported buying Kellogg's Frosted Flakes during a three-month period had actually done so. Of those who said they had purchased Pledge furniture polish, only 10% had actually bought the product.

*Source:* Michael Davis, "Wired Consumers: Market Researchers Go High-Tech to Hone Ads, Weed Out Flops," *The Wall Street Journal*, January 23, 1986, p. 31.

of the population—that is, the people who do not respond to your survey may not have characteristics similar to those who do. Response and nonresponse errors are especially crucial to the successful development of a survey, and each will be discussed further in a later chapter.

### Experimental Errors

Experimental errors occur whenever confusion exists regarding whether the independent variable (X) caused the observed effect, or whether the result was also partly due to the influence of one or more other variables that were not controlled as part of the experimental design. For example, if a competitor were to reduce its regional prices at a time when you were test marketing a new product variation, a lack of sales success for your product might be due to the competitor's action instead of to an inherent marketing deficiency in the product offering. Experimental errors and their avoidance will be discussed in more detail in a later chapter.

### Analysis Errors

Analysis errors may result from applying improper analytical techniques to a particular set of data or from procedural mistakes in the tabulation or transformation of the data itself. A related problem is the forging of artificial "data" by unscrupulous field researchers who find it easier to obtain false data than the real thing. Particular techniques for the proper collection and analysis of research data will be discussed in a number of later chapters.

## TYPES OF MARKETING INFORMATION

Every marketing research study must rely on information in one form or another. From the perspective of examining the marketing research process, it is appropriate to categorize such information into two types—primary and secondary.

### Primary Data

Very simply, *primary data* comprise information collected or generated by the researcher for the purposes of the project immediately at hand. For example, the manager of a local Pizza Hut franchise may conduct a survey of area college students to determine their perceptions of the quality of her products and the courtesy of her personnel. Similarly, an automobile dealer may telephone a sampling of service customers to determine the extent to which they are satisfied with the treatment they received during their last visit to his shop. (Perhaps, in this situation, the dealer might be better advised to contact new-car purchasers who have *not* seen fit to trust their routine maintenance and service to his shop.) In any case, primary data are best characterized by their uniqueness to a particular research study. There will obviously be no published information available that elaborates the attitudes of customers and noncustomers toward Cedric's Chevy City.

Surveys and experiments constitute the principal sources of primary data. Both are covered in later chapters of the text. However, as with any primary data, the advantage of applicability to the research problem may be offset by the disadvantage of relatively high cost when compared to available secondary data sources.

Because primary data tend to be expensive in terms of both time and money, it is advisable to resist the initial impulse of the novice (i.e., "Let's print up some questionnaires and do a survey") in favor of the more reasonable approach of first eliminating or exhausting all possible secondary data sources of the information that is desired. For many, the definition of marketing research is "survey." Although this is a key source of primary data, such means should not be explored unless you have first determined that available secondary data alone will not satisfy your information needs.

### Secondary Data

*Secondary data* consist of information that has been collected, by someone other than the researcher, for purposes other than those involved in the research project at hand. Such data may be either *internal* or *external*, depending on whether or not the information was generated from within the firm. While accounting information is a common source of internal secondary data, the sources of external secondary data are seemingly infinite—government reports, commercial services, and published materials constitute but a few of the many sources.

Compared to primary data, secondary information has the advantage of lower time and cost requirements, but may not be particularly relevant to the marketing problem under consideration. Other possible difficulties with secondary data include lack of recency (due to the time lag between the occurrence of an event and your discovery of its published description in the library) as well as the possible bias that the original researchers may have brought to their collection, analysis, interpretation, or reporting of the information. Remember that all secondary information was *primary* information for the firm that originally generated it, and that this firm may have had a research objective that was far different from your own. Table 3-1 summarizes the relative merits of utilizing primary versus secondary information in a marketing research project. Keep in mind that these are general strengths and weaknesses, and that exceptions (e.g., a published study that is highly relevant to your particular marketing problem) may sometimes be encountered.

### Precautions

As shown in Table 3-1, economy and quickness are the two principal advantages involved in the use of secondary data sources. However, because secondary

**TABLE 3-1.** *Comparative advantages of primary versus secondary data sources (+ indicates relative strength).*

| | Information type | |
| --- | --- | --- |
| | *Primary* | *Secondary* |
| **Relevance to marketing problem** | + | |
| **Recency of information** | + | |
| **Objectivity of information** | + | |
| **Economy of information acquirement** | | + |
| **Speed of information acquirement** | | + |

data are collected for purposes other than your particular research study, such information may be unsuitable for use. More so than primary data, the evaluation of secondary data should be approached with a great deal of caution, and should include questions such as those discussed below.

### Is the Information Relevant to the Problem?

Do the definitions and reporting classifications meet our needs? Remember that *family, consumer, automobile* and other seemingly simple terms may be defined quite differently from one source to the next. Similarly, numerical units of measurement and classification should be in a form consistent with our requirements—for example, if family recreation expenditures are reported in $1000 increments ($0–$999, $1000–$1999, etc.), the data may be of little use to us if our purposes require a finer breakdown and the information is not available in a less aggregated form. Another potential problem is the lack of relevance of the data to the time period in which we are interested—for example, census data may be as much as 10 years behind the times.

### Is the Information Likely to Be Biased?

If the information were collected and published by an individual or organization with the possible intention of promoting selfish interests, it would naturally be suspect. For example, the author once received a publication from the National Highway Traffic Safety Administration that had the intention of informing readers of the activities and progress of the NHTSA over the years since its formation. Included in the publication was a chart describing the number of highway deaths per miles of vehicle travel since 1967, the year in which the agency was founded. The graph clearly indicated that, since 1967, the trend in deaths per vehicle mile was consistently downward, suggesting that the NHTSA had been highly successful in its efforts toward highway safety. However, had the graph been extrapolated backward in time, it could have been seen that the trend in deaths per vehicle mile had been steadily downward for at least several decades prior to the NHTSA's existence. Sometimes, what is *not* presented can be equally important to that which is.

Also, as we'll see later, the wording of a survey question can bias the results that are obtained. However, when survey results are reported (especially to the general public through the mass media), the original questions may be either omitted or paraphrased while the possibly biased result is presented in large headlines for all to see. If an item of secondary data stems in any way from an organization or an issue that is controversial, such information should be subject to the most severe scrutiny before being trusted and used in an objective research study. This is not to suggest that all research conducted by special-interest groups be ignored, but rather that such information be approached with an extra degree of caution.

When considering possible bias in secondary data, determine who sponsored the study. Research organizations often depend on contacts and "requests for proposals" for their funding and, ultimately, their very existence. In some instances, a research firm, through purely informal correspondence with the funding agency, may determine that the agency would be very pleased if the results of the study were to support a possibly preselected course of action.

In a later chapter, we'll examine some of the potential uses which marketing research has as a "weapon" (e.g., applied to legislation or litigation) as well as an objective tool for facilitating marketing decisions. However, suffice it to say at this point that an unethical research firm may "bend" its objectivity ever so slightly in order to reach the proper conclusion and increase its probability of procuring future business from the same contracting agency.

### Was the Research Carried Out Correctly?

In some cases, a very well-meaning research investigation may arrive at improper conclusions or data simply because the study was improperly conceived or implemented. Appropriate questions to help determine the presence of such weakness would include the following: Was the sample representative? Was the questionnaire or other measurement device properly constructed? Were possible biases in response or nonresponse corrected or accounted for? Were the data properly analyzed using correct statistical procedures? Was the sample size large enough to warrant confidence in the findings? Are the raw data available for your review? To what degree were field interviewers supervised and follow-ups carried out to ensure that their data were not "self-generated"? These are but a few of the many possible questions that could be asked and they should emphasize the desirability of collecting secondary data with open eyes as well as an open mind. Figure 3-5 presents a summary of procedures that can be followed in the evaluation of secondary data.

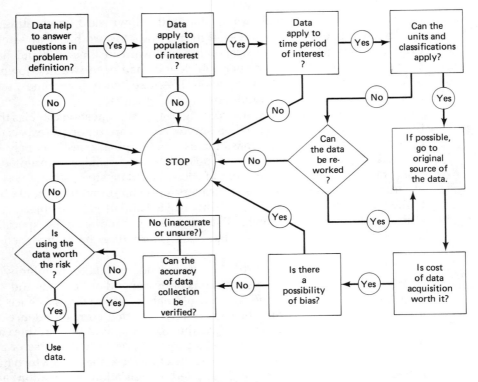

**Figure 3-5.** A suggested procedure for the evaluation of secondary data. (*Source:* From *Designing the Marketing Research Project* by Robert W. Joselyn. Copyright © 1977 by Mason/Charter Publishers. Adapted by permission of Van Nostrand Reinhold Company.)

## SECONDARY DATA: INTERNAL SOURCES

Internal secondary data exist within the firm but were collected for reasons other than the marketing research project being undertaken. Such information is often available from the accounting department in the form of sales and cost data. To the extent that the firm maintains a formal marketing information system, the data are more likely to be present in a form that satisfies the needs of marketing management in addition to the record-keeping requirements of the accounting function.

Besides the traditional financial and accounting records, other sources of internal secondary information include previous marketing research studies, periodic reports from field sales personnel, customer correspondence, warranty cards, and pertinent documents from other functional areas within the firm: for example, engineering, manufacturing, and long-range planning. Remember that some internal information may not exist in written form but may be present in collective experiences and observations mentally recorded over the years by executives, sales personnel, buyers, dealers, and others.

Sales invoices can be an especially useful source of internal secondary data. Upon analyzing its sales information over the previous three years, one company found that 60% of its customers represented a total of just 2% of its business. Further, almost all of these customers had come to the firm as the result of directory advertising—it became obvious that the company was paying to attract business it really didn't want. In this case, internal secondary data were both applicable and economical in providing insight to the marketing decision maker. As the consultant working with this client observed, "Simple questions don't always have expensive answers."[2]

## SECONDARY DATA: GOVERNMENT SOURCES

Federal, state, and local governments constitute the single most important source of external secondary data. Of these, the U.S. Department of Commerce, through the Bureau of the Census, is an especially massive collector and distributor of statistical information of interest to marketers.

- To reduce costs, a marketing consultant suggested that his client target a direct-mail campaign to higher-income households instead of the entire community. Using 1980 census data, the consultant identified census tracts with median incomes of $30,000 or above and those where at least 25% had incomes of $50,000 or more. It was judged that such households were the most likely to have an interest in the client's product.[3]

- A national insurance company was faced with the need to redistribute its sales force in a midwestern state. A specialist in insuring commercial firms, the company wanted to know where potential customers could be found, their size, and sales volume. Using *County Business Patterns* data and enterprise statistics from the Economic Census, the company was able to reallocate its sales territories and make more efficient use of its sales force.[4]

These cases exemplify the usefulness of census data to marketing decision makers. The following publications are representative of the wide variety of information available from the U.S. Department of Commerce:

*Census of Population.* The Census of Population provides detailed breakdowns of demographic information on the U.S. population according to location,

---

[2] Arthur S. Katz, "Inexpensive Research: Analyze Sales Data Hidden in Your Files," *Marketing News,* September 17, 1982, sec. 1, p. 6, published by the American Marketing Association.

[3] Arnold A. Goldstein, "Use Census Bureau Resources in Marketing Classes," *Marketing News,* July 20, 1984, p. 4, published by the American Marketing Association.

[4] Ibid.

age, sex, marital status, income, employment, education, and other criteria shown in Table 3-2. The population census is conducted every 10 years.

*Census of Housing.* Conducted in combination with the Census of Population since 1940, the Census of Housing provides data on home ownership or rental, type of structure, source of water, fuel used for heating and cooking, telephones, market value, and numerous other facts, such as ownership of dishwashers, radios, clothes dryers, and other major appliances. Data are available not only on a national basis, but broken down into states, urban and rural areas, counties, and even city blocks.

---

**EXHIBIT 3-2**

*Guardians of Privacy*

Census takers and Census Bureau employees are unyielding in protecting the identities of participating individuals and using data only in summary statistical form. During World War II, the Secretary of War asked the Census Bureau to provide names, ages, and addresses of all Americans of Japanese heritage who lived on the west coast. In 1947, during a period of fear of communist infiltration, the FBI asked for census information about certain individuals. In both cases, the Census Bureau held firm.

*Source: How America Studies Itself: The U.S. Census* (Washington, D.C.: Population Reference Bureau, Inc., February 1980), p. 4.

---

*Economic censuses.* An economic census program is conducted every five years (in years ending in 2 and 7) and includes the following information at national, state, and other levels of aggregation:

1. *Retail trade.* Includes sales, payroll size, sales by merchandise line and other characteristics for over 100 different retail business classifications belonging to 8 major groups.
2. *Wholesale trade.* Contains data on wholesale trade for 118 business classifications, including establishment size, operating expenses, inventories, and other characteristics.
3. *Construction industries.* Enumerates the number of home, industrial, and other contractors, along with their business volume and other characteristics.
4. *Transportation.* Includes information on commercial and private transportation volume and vehicle characteristics.
5. *Service industries.* Reports firm characteristics and receipts for over 150 service classifications, such as hotels, garages, and recreation parks.

**TABLE 3-2.** *Topics covered during the 1980 census. Items marked with an asterisk were newly introduced for this census.*

| Population | Housing |
|---|---|
| **Items collected at every household** | |
| Household Relationship | Number of units at address |
| Sex | Complete plumbing facilities |
| Race | Number of rooms |
| Age | Whether unit is owned or rented |
| Marital status | Condominium identification |
| Spanish/Hispanic origin or descent | Value of home |
| | Rent |
| | Vacant for rent, for sale, and period of vacancy |
| **Items collected at sample households** | |
| School enrollment | Type of unit |
| Educational attainment | Stories in building and presence of elevator |
| State or foreign country of birth | Year built |
| Citizenship and year of immigration | Year moved into this house |
| Current language and English proficiency* | Acreage and crop sales |
| Ancestry* | Source of water |
| Veteran status and period of service | Sewage disposal |
| Presence of disability or handicap | Heating equipment |
| Children ever born | Fuels used for house heating, water heating, and cooking |
| Marital history | Costs of utilities and fuels |
| Employment status last week | Complete kitchen facilities |
| Hours worked last week | Number of bedrooms |
| Place of work | Telephone |
| Travel time to work* | Air-conditioning |
| Persons in car pool* | Number of automobiles |
| Year last worked | Number of light trucks and vans* |
| Industry | Homeowner shelter costs for mortgage, real-estate taxes, and hazard insurance* |
| Occupation | |
| Class of worker | |
| Work in 1979 and weeks looking for work in 1979* | |
| Amount of income by source and total income in 1979 | |
| **Other topics** | |
| Families | Persons per room ("crowding") |
| Family type and size | Household size |
| Poverty status | Plumbing facilities |
| Population density | Institutions and other group quarters |
| Size of place | Gross rent |
| | Farm residence |

*Sources:* Bureau of the Census, U.S. Department of Commerce; *How America Studies Itself: The U.S. Census,* Population Reference Bureau, Inc., Washington, D.C., February 1980, p. 3.

6. *Manufactures*. Presents detailed information on the number, size, output, employment, and other characteristics of factories at national, state, and local levels. Includes about 450 lines of manufactured goods.

7. *Mineral industries*. Involves measurement of nearly all domestic raw materials that are converted into fuel and description of the size and operational characteristics of related establishments.

**Statistical Abstract of the United States.** An annual publication of the Bureau of the Census, the *Statistical Abstract* contains extensive social, political, and economic data. It is excellent both as a source of secondary data and as a guide to further information sources.

**Survey of Current Business.** The *Survey of Current Business* is a monthly publication dealing with population, trade, transportation, general business indicators, and other statistical topics. It includes over 2500 updated statistical series.

**County Business Patterns.** Published annually, *County Business Patterns* provides state and county information regarding the number, size, and type of business establishments. Information like that shown in Figure 3-6 is especially useful in estimating and comparing the market potential of economic areas.

**U.S. Industrial Outlook.** Another annual publication, *U.S. Industrial Outlook* reports on trends and projections for about 200 industries. In addition to providing detailed information on the industries, 10-year projections are made for each.

For additional information regarding these publications, as well as others available from this very prolific federal agency, write, call, or visit your local field office of the Bureau of the Census. To help your information search, you may wish to refer to the Department of Commerce publication, *Measuring Markets: A Guide to the Use of Federal and State Statistical Data*. Also, the government publishes the *Monthly Catalog of U.S. Government Publications*, which provides a listing of publications of all branches of the federal government. Most of these publications are available at extremely reasonable costs. For example, the Department of Agriculture commissioned a study of the fast-food industry, paid a research firm $100,000 to carry it out, then made the study available to aware members of the general public for just 25 cents.[5]

Among other worthwhile federal publications is the Bureau of Labor's *Monthly Labor Review*, containing information on employment, wages, and prices. The Federal Reserve System publishes the monthly *Federal Reserve Bulletin*, an excellent source of statistics relating to banking, interest rates, savings, international trade, department store sales, and industrial production. The Economic Statistics Bureau publishes the *Handbook of Economic Statistics* each year,

---

[5] "The Federal Government Is a Treasure Trove of Valuable, Free Data for the Marketing Researcher," *Marketing News*, August 19, 1983, p. 10, published by the American Marketing Association.

# Table 2. Counties—Employees, Payroll, and Establishments, by Industry: 1982

(Excludes government employees, railroad employees, self-employed persons, etc.—see "General Explanation" for definitions and statement on reliability of data. Size class 1 to 4 includes establishments having payroll but no employees during mid-March pay period. "D" denotes figures withheld to avoid disclosure of operations of individual establishments, the other alphabetics indicate employment-size class—see footnote.)

| SIC code | Industry | Number of employees for week including March 12 | Payroll ($1,000) First Quarter | Payroll ($1,000) Annual | Total | 1 to 4 | 5 to 9 | 10 to 19 | 20 to 49 | 50 to 99 | 100 to 249 | 250 to 499 | 500 to 999 | 1000 or more |
|---|---|---|---|---|---|---|---|---|---|---|---|---|---|---|
| | **BELKNAP** | | | | | | | | | | | | | |
| | **Total** | **14 384** | **41 472** | **185 411** | **1 222** | **730** | **207** | **136** | **93** | **30** | **20** | **5** | | **1** |
| | Agricultural services, forestry, fisheries | 25 | 50 | 270 | 10 | 8 | 2 | | | | | | | |
| | Mining | (A) | (D) | (D) | 1 | | | 1 | | | | | | |
| | Contract construction | 1 100 | 4 028 | 24 525 | 162 | 121 | 13 | 19 | 6 | 1 | 2 | | | |
| 15 | General contractors and operative builders | 373 | 1 472 | 6 629 | 54 | 43 | 1 | 5 | 4 | 1 | | | | |
| 151 | General building contractors | (E) | (D) | (D) | 24 | 13 | 1 | 5 | 4 | 1 | | | | |
| 16 | Heavy construction contractors | 227 | 1 114 | 10 794 | 19 | 9 | 5 | 2 | 2 | 1 | | | | |
| 161 | Highway and street construction | (C) | (D) | (D) | 10 | 5 | 2 | 1 | 1 | 1 | | | | |
| 162 | Heavy construction, except highway | (B) | (D) | (D) | 9 | 4 | 3 | 1 | 1 | | | | | |
| 17 | Special trade contractors | 500 | 1 443 | 7 102 | 89 | 69 | 7 | 12 | | 1 | | | | |
| 171 | Plumbing, heating, air conditioning | 184 | 625 | 2 704 | 15 | 10 | | 4 | 1 | | 1 | | | |
| 173 | Electrical work | 88 | 272 | 1 358 | 16 | 11 | 2 | 3 | | | | | | |
| 179 | Misc. special trade contractors | 81 | 168 | 772 | 13 | 11 | 1 | 1 | | | | | | |
| | Manufacturing | 4 844 | 16 265 | 66 071 | 120 | 48 | 20 | 9 | 17 | 10 | 11 | 5 | | |
| 22 | Textile mill products | 89 | 223 | 709 | 8 | 4 | | 2 | 2 | | | | | |
| 225 | Knitting mills | (B) | (D) | (D) | 6 | 3 | 1 | | 2 | | | | | |
| 2253 | Knit outerwear mills | (B) | (D) | (D) | 3 | 1 | | | 2 | | | | | |
| | ...el and other ...ducts | 260 | 696 | 2 776 | 9 | 2 | 1 | 2 | 2 | | | | | |

**Figure 3-6.** *County Business Patterns*, published by the Bureau of the Census, provides annual economic information at the state and county levels. Shown is a portion of the data describing Belknap County, New Hampshire. (*Source: Guide to the 1982 Censuses,* Bureau of the Census, U.S. Department of Commerce, p. 55.)

a publication summarizing economic data collected by a variety of government agencies.

At the state and local levels of government, the amount and quality of secondary information for marketing research is somewhat more variable, and certainly much less in quantity than that produced by the federal government. State and local chambers of commerce are useful sources of data, but remember that their primary concern is with the economic health of their areas, and that the information available may not be in the form or of the type you are seeking.

## SECONDARY DATA: PUBLISHED SOURCES

### A Selection of Useful Publications

Published sources include a variety of periodicals, handbooks, abstracts, news media, and others that may relate to your research project. The following are but a sampling of potential sources of useful information:

*Business Periodicals Index.*  A monthly publication containing a bibliography of articles in business periodicals according to specific subject areas.

*Reader's Guide to Periodical Literature.*  Similar to the *Business Periodicals Index*, but includes many other publications in addition to those specifically concerned with business.

*Dun & Bradstreet Million Dollar Directory.*  Annual publication that lists companies, products, sales, employment, SIC (Standard Industrial Classification) codes, and corporate officers for all businesses with a net worth in excess of $1 million.

*Dun & Bradstreet Middle Market Directory.*  Similar to the *Million Dollar Directory*, but covers firms with assets between $500,000 and $1 million.

*Moody's Manuals.*  Annual publication containing balance sheet and income statements for industrial, banking and finance, public utility, transportation, and governmental units.

*Sales & Marketing Management Survey of Buying Power.*  Annual publication that estimates retail sales and provides demographic information for cities, counties, and metropolitan areas as well as for the nation. Includes indices of relative buying power and retail sales.

*Rand McNally Commercial Atlas and Marketing Guide.*  Annual publication containing statistical items describing each U.S. county and approximately 100,000 cities and towns.

*The World Almanac and Book of Facts.*  An annual publication that is not specifically oriented to marketing, but which contains a wide variety of information that could be of use in carrying out marketing research.

In addition to the preceding published sources, there are a number of scholarly periodicals available; examples include *Harvard Business Review, Public Opinion Quarterly, Journal of Marketing, Journal of Marketing Research, Journal of Advertising Research*, and *Journal of Consumer Research*. Other popular sources include *The Wall Street Journal, Fortune, Business Week, Advertising Age, Sales and Marketing Management*, and *Industrial Marketing*.

Most industries are associated with one or more trade associations that collect and distribute data relating to the industry. These groups may be identified in the *Encyclopedia of Associations*, an excellent publication available in most libraries. Because trade associations work closely with their respective industries, they may be able to obtain information that would be difficult or impossible to get from other sources. The statistics and special reports generated by trade associations are often contained in the form of regular reports published by the association or published in trade journals related to the industry. The *Encyclopedia of Associations*, besides identifying trade associations and their publications, also describes a wide variety of other special-interest groups and organizations. As suggested by the diversity of Table 3-3, there seems to be a special-interest group for practically anything and everything.

### On-Line Bibliography Searches

There are now about 3000 database services available to personal computer owners, up from 600 in 1980.[6] Able to search electronically for published materials on a given topic, such databases constitute an approach that is a quantum leap beyond the library card catalog and other paper-dependent avenues for the identification of published secondary information. For example, Dialog Information Services, one of the largest on-line systems in the world, includes hundreds of bibliographic and statistical databases that cover business, science, and the humanities. Subscribers simply enter key words describing the topic of interest, then peruse the video display for articles on the subject.[7]

The experience of the New York Public Library is suggestive of the promising future of this technology. In 1985, the library replaced its card catalog system, all 8973 drawers and 10 million cards of it, with a central memory bank and 50 access terminals. Patrons need only type in a title or a topic, then wait for the computer to display the desired information on the screen before them.[8]

Table 3-4 lists some of the more popular on-line databases, several of which provide the bibliography-search function just discussed. Other firms shown in the table offer a variety of more specific informational services, such as those we'll examine in the next section.

---

[6] Jennifer Bingham Hall, "The World Beyond," from "A Special Report: Personal Computing," *The Wall Street Journal*, June 16, 1986, p. 34D.

[7] Diane Crispell, "The On-Line Search," *American Demographics*, February 1986, p. 46.

[8] "Terminals among the Stacks," *Time*, February 25, 1985, p. 92.

**TABLE 3-3.** *The Encyclopedia of Associations has one or more organizations for just about any interest or activity.*

| Organization and when founded | Purpose |
|---|---|
| Trade and industry-related associations | |
| Motor Vehicle Manufacturers Association (1913) | Makers of passenger and commercial cars, trucks, and buses; compiles and distributes industry data |
| Highway Loss Data Institute (1972) | Auto insurance companies; gathers, processes, and provides public with data concerning human and economic losses from highway crashes |
| Independent Automotive Damage Appraisers Association (1961) | Professional automotive damage appraisal firms that evaluate damaged automobiles for insurance companies, self-insured fleets, and rentals |
| Special-interest groups | |
| National Vietnam Veterans Coalition (1984) | Supports maximum relief for Agent Orange victims; seeks return of POWs and accountability for MIAs |
| Share (1978) | Parents who have suffered the loss of a newborn; provides comfort and support beyond hospital stay |
| American Running and Fitness Association (1968) | Individual runners and groups interested in running; promotes running and other aerobic activities |
| National Rifle Association (1871) | Target shooters, hunters, gun collectors, and enthusiasts; promotes shooting, hunting, gun collecting, firearm safety, and conservation |
| American Lung Association (1904) | Physicians, nurses, and laypersons interested in prevention and control of lung disease |
| Miscellaneous | |
| Tall Club International (1938) | Promotes tall awareness, happiness and welfare of tall (men, 6'2" +; women, 5'10" +) people |
| Three Stooges Club (1959) | Purpose is to keep alive the comedy of The Three Stooges and to provide memorabilia information |
| Society for the Restoration and Preservation of Red M & M's (1982) | Sought restoration of red M & M's to the color assortment of the plain chocolate and chocolate-covered peanut candies |
| Royal Association for the Longevity and Preservation of the Honeymooners (RALPH) (1982) | See Three Stooges Club, above; substitute "Honeymooners" TV series broadcast 1955–1956 on CBS |
| International Organization of Nerds (1984) | People who have volunteered or been nominated for membership as nerds |

*Source:* Selected from *Encyclopedia of Associations,* 1986, edited by Katherine Gruber (copyright © 1959, 1961, 1964, 1968, 1970, 1972, 1973, 1975, 1976, 1977, 1978, 1979, 1980, 1981, 1982, 1983, 1984, 1985, 1986 by Gale Research Company; reprinted by permission of the publisher), 20th edition, Gale Research, 1985.

*TABLE 3-4. Some of the more popular on-line databases available to microcomputer users.*

| Database | Description | Updates | Prices |
|---|---|---|---|
| **ADTRACK**<br>The Kingman Consulting Group, Inc. Energy Park Business Center 1421 Energy Park Drive St. Paul, MN 55108 (612)646-6558 | References to advertisements bigger than ¼ of a page in 160 major U.S. consumer and business periodicals. | Monthly | Connect time, $45/hour; does not include other Dialog charges |
| **Advertising and Marketing Intelligence Service**<br>Mead Data Central, Inc. P.O. Box 1830 Dayton, OH 45401 (800)227-4908 | Abstracts from more than 60 publications on advertising, marketing, and media. Covers new products, market research, consumer trends, and so on. Many are offered full text through Mead Data's Nexis service. | Daily, Monday–Friday | Requires Nexis subscription—$165 one-time software charge; monthly $50 for Nexis-only subscribers; connect-time charge $30–$35 an hour (depending on telecommunication method), and $9 peak, $6 off-peak per search. |
| **Consumer Spending Forecast**<br>Chase Econometrics 150 Monument Road Bala Cynwyd, PA 19004 (215)896-4843 | Part of the Consumer Forecasting service of Chase Econometrics. Includes monthly historical information and forecasts data, demographics, analysis, seminars, and so on. | Monthly | Based on individual client request. |
| **FIND/SVP Reports and Studies Index**<br>Information Products Department 500 5th Avenue New York, NY 10101 (212)354-2424 | Contains more than 10,000 citations with abstracts to publicly available market-research reports and studies. Covers more than 450 U.S. and non-U.S. publishers. | Quarterly | Connect time, $79/hour; off- and on-line remote-printing charges, $25/hour; user manual, $39 |
| **Frost and Sullivan Research Report Abstracts, Index to Frost and Sullivan Market Research Reports**<br>Frost & Sullivan, Inc. 106 Fulton Street New York, NY 10038 (212)233-1080 | Contains 1500 citations to Frost & Sullivan market-research reports. | Monthly | Open access (non-subscription), $35/hour; four levels of subscription pricing available; on-line citation charges, 5 cents a citation or less |

TABLE 3-4. (continued)

| Database | Description | Updates | Prices |
|---|---|---|---|
| **Magazine Index, Magazine ASAP Trade and Industry Index, Trade and Industry ASAP** Information Access Company 11 Davis Drive Belmont, CA 94002 (415)591-2333 | Contains citations to hundreds of consumer (magazine) and specialized (trade and industry) publications. ASAP contains citations and full text of many of the articles listed in the indexes. | Monthly | Various—based on provider. Example is $84/hour connect-time charge on Dialog |
| **Market Potential** Donnelley Marketing Information Services 1351 Washington Blvd., Fourth Floor Stamford, CT 06902 (203)965-5400 | Data-retrieval and - analysis system that contains data from the 1980 census. Focuses on market definition/ research. | Annually | Based on analysis and usage. |
| **Nielsen Retail Index** A.C. Nielsen Company Nielsen Plaza Northbrook, IL 60062 (312)498-6300 | Contains point-of-sale (POS) measurements of the effects on consumers of major marketing efforts and the flow of goods. | Monthly or every two months | Based on individual client request. |
| **Roper Reports** The Roper Organization A subsidiary of Starch INRA Hooper, Inc. 205 East 42nd Street New York, NY 10017 (212)559-0700 | Contains information on attitudes and opinions of U.S. adults. | Ten times a year | Subscription, $21,000/ year, connect-time charges based on information requested and analysis. |
| **Sales Prospector** Prospector Research Service, Inc. 751 Main Street Waltham, MA 02154 (617)899-1271 | Identifies companies likely to acquire goods and services or hire employees based on corporate expansion or relocation. | Monthly | $15/monthly; subscribers to Sales Prospector, $24/ hour; nonsubscribers, $60/hour |
| **SAMI** Selling Areas- Marketing, Inc. Time and Life Building Rockefeller Center New York, NY 10020 (212)484-5800 | Contains information on product movement and sales in the consumer- package-goods industry. | Monthly | Based on individual client request. |
| **VU/TEXT** VU/TEXT Information Services, Inc. | Provides 17 newspapers and news-wire services on-line. Specializes in | Daily | $60–100/hour; depends on usage and information accessed. |

**TABLE 3-4. (continued)**

| Database | Description | Updates | Prices |
|---|---|---|---|
| 1211 Chestnut Street Philadelphia, PA 19107 (215)665-3300 | regional and business news. | | |
| **Western Union InFact** Contact your local Western Union sales office | Gives access to more than 650 databases without making you learn the commands for each one and subscribe to each one individually. | | Subscription for Western Union Easylink, $25/year; connect time, $9/hour; various search charges. |

*Source:* From Ken Landis, "Sales and Marketing Database Strategies," *A+ Magazine*, June 1986, p. 47. Reprinted with permission.

## SECONDARY DATA: COMMERCIAL SOURCES

Commercial sources of secondary data are often an inexpensive supplement to the capabilities of a firm's own marketing research department, with both syndicated and custom information available from a wide variety of sources. *Syndicated* data are produced for the needs of a number of users, while *custom* information is collected for the study of a particular problem. The 1986 edition of the American Marketing Association's *Marketing Services Guide and Membership Directory* includes 109 pages describing commercial suppliers of research information, many of whom provide both syndicated and custom information.

### Syndicated Information

#### Panels

Panels are cooperating individuals or households that supply consumption and behavioral information on a continuing basis. Panel members may be asked to record their behavior in diaries like the Arbitron form shown in Figure 3-7. At periodic intervals, information from the panel members is reported to the syndicated commercial service, which in turn provides it in the form of secondary data to subscribers. Most of us have heard of A.C. Nielsen's panel of households, which provides valuable information to advertisers and program planners regarding television audience size and composition. Other popular consumer panels include those maintained by the Market Research Corporation of America, National Family Opinion, Inc., the Consumer Mail Panels division of Market Facts, Inc., and the National Purchase Diary, Inc.

Panel information is especially useful in evaluating promotional strategies, identifying differences between customers and noncustomers, measuring brand loyalty and brand-switching habits, testing the effect of various changes in mar-

This is your Arbitron Ratings diary.
Please fill it in yourself. Throughout
the seven days of the survey,
beginning on Thursday, please
keep this diary with you . . .

. . . at home

. . . in your car

. . . at work

. . . or wherever you go

Each time you listen to radio (whether you yourself turn it on or not), please fill in the following information:

**1** Time
Fill in starting and ending times in the time period.

If listening continues into another period, draw a line from the start to the stop time.

**2** Call Letters
Fill in the "call letters" of the station you are listening to. If you don't know the call letters, fill in the name of the program — or the dial setting.

Start a new line each time you change stations.

**3** AM or FM
Check whether AM dial or FM dial.

**4** Place
Check "At Home," "In a Car," or "Some Other Place."

**5** No Listening All Day?
Any day you do not listen to radio, check the box at the bottom of the page.

| TIME | | STATION | | | PLACE | | | |
|---|---|---|---|---|---|---|---|---|
| | | Fill in station "call letters" (If you don't know them, fill in program name or dial setting) | Check One (✓) | | Check One (✓) | Away From Home | | |
| From | To | | AM | FM | At Home | In a Car | Some Other Place | |
| **Early Morning** (5AM to 10AM) | 5:45 7:15 | WWTM | ✓ | | ✓ | | | |
| | 7:15 7:40 | WJL | ✓ | | | ✓ | | |
| | 9:30 | PIERCE SHOW | ✓ | | | | ✓ | |
| **Midday** (10AM to 3PM) | 12:10 2:00 2:05 | KADV | ✓ | | | ✓ | | |
| **Late Afternoon** (3PM to 7PM) | | | | | | | | |
| **Night** (7PM to 5AM) | 11:30 12:15 | 88.1 ON THE DIAL | ✓ | ✓ | | | | |

IF YOU DID NOT LISTEN TO RADIO TODAY PLEASE CHECK ✓ HERE ➡ ☐

**Important:** Many stations broadcast on both AM and FM. For this Arbitron Ratings survey, it is important to correctly identify whether you are listening on AM or FM (even though the station may use the same call letters and broadcast the same thing on the air).

© 1986 Arbitron Ratings Company

To keep your Arbitron Ratings diary from getting mixed up with others in your household — please fill in your initials (or first name) here . . .

**Figure 3-7.** Panel members may be asked to record their purchases or behavior in a diary like this one used by Arbitron for radio listening. (*Source:* Courtesy of Arbitron Ratings Company.)

keting strategy, and for similar purposes. While panel information is faster and less expensive than would be possible if the firm were to carry out an equivalent long-term study, there are also some disadvantages to the use of panel data. For example, panel memberhip is voluntary, and those who don't join (or who drop out) may affect the representativeness of the panel to the population at large. Panel members also age over time and must be replaced by suitable individuals or households in order to maintain the proper overall composition of the panel. In addition, panel members may become conditioned to behave and report in certain ways that may not be typical of the population they are presumed to represent. However, because of the low cost (since subscribers share what would otherwise be an exorbitant fee), immediacy of feedback, and a relatively consistent sample composition, consumer panels are an excellent source of secondary marketing information. We'll discuss them further in Chapter 10.

### Retail Store Audits

Retail store audits provide a measurement of product sales activity at the retail level. A large sample of stores may be visited periodically for the purpose of collecting inventory and recent purchase data that combine to describe product sales since the last audit. Such data also can be collected electronically through the use of scanning devices at the check-out aisle. In addition to its consumer panel activities, A.C. Nielsen also furnishes periodic information on product movement at the retail level in a large sampling of food and drug outlets. The Nielsen subscriber receives periodic reports that include the sales of the subscriber's own brand, sales of the total product class, and sales of key competitive brands.

Just as consumer panels help reveal the ultimate effects of adjustments in the firm's marketing strategy variables, retail sales audits also provide valuable information on activity at this important final step in the channel of distribution. Such data can be especially vital in the early identification of market trends relative to newly introduced products for which a timely evaluation of success or failure may be essential. In addition, the information obtained through retail store audits can prove beneficial in evaluating the firm's channel of distribution strategies and leading to the identification and solution of inventory management problems.

### Other Sources of Syndicated Data

There are a wide variety of other sources of syndicated secondary data. For example, at the wholesale level, Selling Areas Marketing, Inc., supplies information regarding the movement of products from wholesaling warehouses to retail outlets. The Starch Readership Service uses personal interviews to determine the effectiveness (in terms of the degree to which an ad was read or noted) of advertisements placed in business and consumer publications. Other firms, such as the familiar Gallup, Inc., conduct public opinion surveys that may contain questions of a marketing nature. Standard Rate and Data Service provides advertising cost rates along with a variety of other information for all major advertising media.

Marketing Evaluations/TVQ sells its "Q score" ratings to advertisers. The Q score measures the attractiveness of potential spokespersons who might be considered for an ad, and is a function of two variables: the number of people surveyed who describe a celebrity as "one of their favorites," and the number who know of the person. For example, professional football player William "Refrigerator" Perry has had the good fortune of possessing one of the top 10 Q-

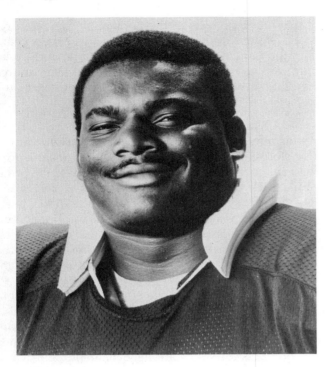

**Figure 3-8.** Marketing Evaluations/ TVQ sells its "Q score" ratings to advertisers. The Q score is based on (1) the number of people surveyed who describe a celebrity as "one of their favorites," and (2) the number who know of the person. William "Refrigerator" Perry's standing in the top 10 of the athletic world helps explain why companies seek him to endorse their products. (Photo courtesy of the Chicago Bears.)

scores in the world of athletics[9] (see Figure 3-8). It is no coincidence that Mr. Perry, the first 300-pound lineman to score a rushing touchdown and to catch a pass for another, has been able to convert his visibility into lucrative endorsement contracts with marketers of a wide variety of consumer products.[10]

In general, due to the unique expertise they have developed over the years, and because of their ability to spread the cost of information gathered over a large number of subscribers, syndicated sources of secondary data are typically capable of providing quality information at a relatively reasonable cost.

### Technological Advances and Syndicated Information

As described earlier, on-line computer databases provide an efficient way of providing or accessing both literature-search and syndicated data. With continuing advances in the capabilities and applications of microcomputers, the future is likely to include some amazing possibilities. An example of the present is the videotex system through which business and home subscribers can access news, weather, sports, financial, and consumer information; utilize banking and

---

[9] See Roger Lowenstein, "Many Athletes Have a Tough Time Playing in the Endorsement Game," *The Wall Street Journal*, August 29, 1986, p. 15.

[10] See Rick Telander, "Stocking Up the Fridge," *Sports Illustrated*, March 17, 1986, pp. 41–43.

shopping services; make reservations and obtain travel information; and send or receive electronic mail.[11] The combination of centralized database, home or business microcomputer, and telephone line will continue to amaze as well as serve us in the years ahead.

A second breakthrough is the UPC (Universal Product Code) technology and the information it makes possible. By the end of 1985, nearly 12,000 grocery stores had scanners, and during that year scanner-equipped outlets registered 45% of all grocery store dollar sales.[12] National Brand Scanning, Inc., which first used scanning research in 1975, maintains a nationwide sample of 1000 supermarkets with 10,000 checkout scanners, allowing subscribers to track purchases within 10 to 12 days after they occur.[13] The use of scanners is not limited to retail stores; for example, in the 1986 edition of Pittsburgh, Pennsylvania's "The Great Race," over 10,000 runners were monitored for identification and time at the finish line by UPC labels on their entry tags. Details of the UPC and its data-collection capabilities will be examined more completely in Chapter 10.

### Commercial Sources of Custom Information

Regardless of the marketing research function to be performed, there are reputable custom research firms that can either provide assistance or do the entire job themselves. Some companies specialize in focus group interviews, surveys, or data analysis, while others offer expertise in all of these areas and more. The American Marketing Association's *1986 Marketing Services Guide and Membership Directory* lists over 200 "full-service" research firms, identifies those specializing in various types of products, and lists companies whose specialty lies in such functions as data collection, personal interviewing, direct mail, focus groups, in-store testing and research, telephone/WATS services, test marketing/sampling, name testing, and field services.[14] Because the commercial supplier of custom information may be viewed as little more than an extension of the client firm, we have concentrated in this section on the commercial suppliers of syndicated information.

## EVALUATION AND CONTROL OF THE MARKETING RESEARCH EFFORT

In Chapter 2 we discussed the concept of expected value of perfect information, noting that this described the upper limit to be considered in allocating funds for a given research project. In addition, we noted that the expected value of

---

[11] A more complete description may be found in "Videotex: What It's All About," *Marketing News*, November 25, 1983, sec. 1, p. 17, published by the American Marketing Association.

[12] "UPC Scanners Used in Nearly 12,000 Groceries as Over 70,000 Supermarket Items Bear Codes," *Marketing News*, October 24, 1986, p. 16, published by the American Marketing Association.

[13] *Check It Out*, booklet published by National Brand Scanning, Inc., p. 2.

[14] *1986 Marketing Services Guide & The American Marketing Association Membership Directory* (Chicago: American Marketing Association, 1986), pp. 110–15.

imperfect, real-world information was likely to be substantially less. In this section we will examine two levels at which marketing research must be evaluated and controlled: (1) the individual research project, and (2) the firm's overall marketing research function.

## The Individual Research Project

One approach to controlling the individual marketing research project is the *checklist*, which may contain numerous standard questions (e.g., "Is the required information available within the firm?" "Is the research likely to be used by management?") applicable to the general conduct of research in marketing. In addition, based on a firm's past experience with specific research projects, it may be desired to include checklist questions that are especially applicable to the firm and its industry. While a management tool of long descent, the checklist can nevertheless prove useful in helping the researcher avoid mistakes that should have been obvious at the time they were made. As in other areas of management, the use of a checklist offers the advantages associated with what might be described as "hindsight in advance."

Another excellent technique for the evaluation and control of the individual research project is the PERT (Program Evaluation and Review Technique) network. Basically, this approach involves the construction of an arrow network of research subactivities, their orders of performance, and their estimated times for completion. The use of the PERT network allows the determination of required overall project completion time and provides the opportunity to compare the actual progress of the study with that projected at the planning stages in which the network was constructed. The PERT network also makes it possible to identify the set of related activities that are critical (i.e., on the *critical path*) to the timely completion of the project; hence management can better determine the most efficient allocation of personnel and monetary resources towards meeting the study completion deadline.

## The Total Marketing Research Function

While proper guidance and control of the individual research project is certainly important, such attention must be coordinated with the larger marketing research function in order to avoid the danger of having brilliant individual projects at the expense of a weak overall program. Myers and Samli have identified three formal systems—(1) the research advisory committee, (2) the research audit, and (3) the research budget—for guidance of the overall marketing research effort.[15]

---

[15] James H. Myers and Coskun Samli, "Management Control of Marketing Research," *Journal of Marketing Research,* August 1969, p. 272.

## The Research Advisory Committee

The advisory committee consists of representatives of all departments that utilize marketing research: for example, advertising, sales, product planning, and brand management. The purpose of the committee is to provide overall direction for the marketing research program by identifying problem areas that are of greatest importance to the company and directing the attention of marketing research toward informational needs in these areas. The committee does not concern itself with individual research projects and their methodology, but rather meets at quarterly or semiannual intervals to avoid becoming mired in "putting out fires" to the detriment of its ability to provide objective guidance from a larger perspective.

## The Research Audit

A periodic audit can be a useful supplement to the marketing research advisory committee. Conducted every two to five years, the purpose of the audit is to provide a fresh perspective (generally from an outside firm or observer) toward evaluation and control of the marketing research program. The use of an independent auditor helps to avoid internal friction problems that stem from the vested interests of those within the firm whose functions (and careers) may depend on the activities and objectives of the marketing research program. In addition, the use of an outside auditor is likely to bring to the analysis a variety of experience with and knowledge of various industries and research programs that does not exist within the firm itself. In general, the audit will follow the general direction taken by the advisory committee, and is likely to involve the pursuit of questions such as the following: Is research providing information relevant to the firm's decisions? Is research being utilized in decisions? What are the future information needs of the firm? Are sound research methodologies being employed? Is the marketing research staff adequately trained and experienced? What position should marketing research occupy in the structure of the firm? Is the research budget sufficient? Is the marketing research department organized for maximum efficiency and effectiveness? About six months after the audit has been conducted, it's a good idea to follow up on the results in order to determine to what degree, if any, the marketing research program has been altered to reflect the recommendations made.

## The Research Budget

The total research budget, because it becomes a natural constraint on marketing research program activities, is most effective as a means of controlling costs. However, by imposing cost constraints, budget limitations can also lead to serious evaluation of both individual projects and the overall research function. The research budget may be based on the total amount of research activity planned for the coming year, and proposed research may be evaluated on a project-by-project basis in which the overall objectives and capabilities of the firm are central to a research decision. Another alternative is to rely upon individual functions within the firm to provide research funding from their own budgets, effectively making the research department an internal consulting organization selling its services to various of the other departments. Possible problems with sole reliance on the budget approach include a less than optimum degree of coordination within the total research effort, a difficulty that may be at least partly resolved with the guidance of a research advisory committee.

☐ **SUMMARY**

Research design is a plan of action to assist the researcher in collecting and analyzing information relevant to the problem or decision at hand. Studies may be categorized as quantitative versus qualitative, applied versus basic, or classified according to the functional objective of the investigation. Using the latter method, we can identify four major designs: exploratory, descriptive, causal, and predictive.

While the plan for any given study depends on the individual circumstances that led to its formulation, a typical research study will involve (1) formulating the marketing problem, (2) determining information requirements, (3) identifying information sources, (4) examining the decision implications of potential findings, (5) estimating time and cost requirements, and (6) preparing the research proposal. Actual performance consists primarily of following the blueprint that the study plan represents.

There are a variety of errors capable of reducing the accuracy and usefulness of a marketing research investigation. Among the most common are problem definition error, informational error, experimental error, and analysis error.

Marketing research information may be categorized as primary or secondary. Primary data are collected by the researcher for the specific project at hand, while secondary data have already been collected by someone else for another purpose. Secondary data can be internal or external, depending on whether the information was generated from inside or outside the researcher's firm.

Primary data are generally more expensive and time consuming to collect, but have the advantage of direct applicability to the problem at hand. Secondary data are faster and less costly to obtain, but may either be ill suited to the problem or biased in favor of the firm or organization that has generated the information. There are numerous sources of external secondary data, including government agencies, published sources, and commercial suppliers.

Evaluation and control of the marketing research effort is exerted on two levels: (1) the individual research project, and (2) the total marketing research function of the organization. Checklist and PERT (Program Evaluation and Review Technique) approaches are among those taken at the project level, while the advisory committee, research audit, and research budget are used to monitor and control the firm's overall research effort.

## ☐ QUESTIONS FOR REVIEW

1. Under what conditions would one wish to use exploratory research—that is, when is exploratory research likely to be preferable to other approaches, such as causal, descriptive, and predictive?

2. Differentiate between applied research and basic research. Which type is likely to be more useful to the marketing firm?

3. What is the "experience survey," and how can it be useful as a form of exploratory research?

4. What are some of the key steps involved in planning the marketing research project? Why is each important?

5. Identify the following research efforts as exploratory, descriptive, causal, or predictive in nature, then briefly explain your reasoning.
   a. Determining the demographic characteristics of subscribers to *Reader's Digest*.
   b. Conducting a test market for a new juice product.
   c. Determining which of two package designs is perceived by consumers as being more modern.
   d. Identifying reasons for the recent decline in membership for a local PTA.

6. What is the difference between sampling error and nonsampling error in survey research?

7. What are some of the advantages and disadvantages of secondary data relative to primary data for a marketing research study?

8. Provide a real or hypothetical example of a situation in which a supplier of secondary data may have had something to gain by either obtaining or interpreting information in such a way as to better reflect on the goals or status of the supplying firm.

9. Using the *Encyclopedia of Associations*, identify at least one organization or group that might be able to supply information regarding:
   a. Recreational boating.
   b. Bicycling.
   c. Solar home heating.
   d. Pet ownership.

10. Using the *Business Periodicals Index*, identify at least three relatively recent articles on the marketing of home computers.

11. Differentiate between internal and external secondary data. What are some of the common sources of each?

12. What is the difference between syndicated and custom information as obtained from outside suppliers? What are some of the research approaches typically taken by commercial suppliers of syndicated information?

13. What are some of the weaknesses inherent in using consumer panels for the collection of marketing research information?

14. What is the Marketing Evaluations/TVQ "Q score," and how could it be useful to a marketer of home stereo equipment?

15. Describe the major approaches that companies typically use for exerting control over their overall marketing research effort.

# CASES FOR PART ONE

## CASE 1-1

### Cape Hatteras Lighthouse

Located on the North Carolina barrier islands known as the Outer Banks, the Cape Hatteras Lighthouse was activated in 1870 and, at 208 feet in height, is both a landmark of the Carolina coastline and the tallest lighthouse in the United States. When constructed, it was 1500 feet from the Atlantic Ocean, but in recent years has been threatened by a variety of forces, including storms, the gradually rising sea level, and the westward migration of the barrier islands themselves. By 1919, the ocean had advanced to within 300 feet of the lighthouse; by 1935, 100 feet. Since then, it has been practically on the water's edge and is in danger of being lost forever. (*Note:* The current lighthouse replaced an original structure that was built 1 mile inland in 1803, at a location now under water.)

The Cape Hatteras Lighthouse is (in more ways than one) a focal point of the Cape Hatteras National Seashore. According to the National Park Service, "Because of its historical importance to the region and the nation, the lighthouse and its associated station buildings have been designated a National Historic Landmark." However, because of the inevitable westward migration of the North Carolina barrier islands, "stationary structures built on them, such as the Cape Hatteras Lighthouse, are inevitably threatened."

Over the years, a number of projects have been proposed or carried out for the purpose of preventing the lighthouse from being claimed by the relentless Atlantic. Among other measures, barrier sand dune systems have been constructed, sand has been trucked to the beach, reinforced concrete groins have been extended into the sea, polypropylene tubes have been dropped offshore to catch and hold the drifting undersea sand, and protective sandbags have been liberally placed around the base of the lighthouse itself. In 1982, Senator Helms and Governor Hunt sponsored a statewide "Save Cape Hatteras Lighthouse Committee," which has helped fund sandbags, snowfencing to front the lighthouse, and the placement of the plastic "Seascape" tubes. None of the efforts has been very successful, and the lighthouse continues to be at the mercy of an unkind and unpredictable sea, as well as precariously positioned on an island that persists in obeying the lays of nature by migrating toward the mainland.

Expert Orrin Pilkey, a geology professor and coauthor of *The Beaches Are Moving,* has evaluated a number of alternatives regarding the lighthouse: (1)

allow nature to have its way and let the structure disappear into the sea; (2) bring in sufficient sand to construct and maintain an artificial beach; (3) build a structure around the lighthouse that would result in its eventually being transformed into an island as the shoreline continues to move westward; and (4) construct rails on which to lift the lighthouse and move it to a more secure inland location. In his article, "Don't Stop the Ocean, Move the Lighthouse," published in the Greensburg (Pa.) *Tribune Review* of February 15, 1987, he recommends alternative 4 as the best long-term solution. Alternatives 2 and 3 would be stop-gap measures at best, and there is much engineering precedent for the movement of structures of this size.

Considering (1) the tourism and historical value of the Cape Hatteras Lighthouse, and (2) the virtual certainty that it will be doomed if nothing is done, briefly discuss what roles marketing could play in helping to "Save the Lighthouse." Also, how could marketing research contribute to this cause; that is, what kinds of information might the Save the Lighthouse Committee wish to collect, from whom, and how might this information be utilized to help prevent this historic structure from becoming a lighthouse for submarines instead of surface vessels?

## CASE 1-2

### Optechnics Photo Company

The Optechnics Photo Company, a manufacturer of cameras and photographic supplies, has developed a pocket-size 35-mm camera that combines small size with excellent picture quality. According to photography experts, its pictures are comparable to those previously possible only with larger, conventional 35-mm equipment. The new camera is about the same size as an audio tape cassette holder, and it may offer significant advantages for the amateur or professional photographer who finds it awkward to carry a camera everywhere in order to record the interesting and unusual scenes that always seem to present themselves whenever one's camera is not handy. Like a personal radio, the camera even features a belt clip that allows the owner to carry it without occupying either hands or pockets.

Unfortunately, at its current level of development the camera is relatively expensive (estimated retail price of $450) and, because of size constraints, capable of taking only eight pictures before the film cartridge must be replaced with a new one (estimated retail price of approximately $10 and allowing conventional film-developing procedures). Although the camera is currently in the prototype stage, management is confident that actual production of the camera and film cartridges could be carried out with sufficient quality and efficiency to ensure that the retail prices mentioned would lead to both profitability and consumer satisfaction.

Management feels that this technological breakthrough in combined size and picture quality would be a big winner in the marketplace. Before proceeding further with the new camera, what types of primary and secondary information might the company wish to collect by means of marketing research?

## CASE 1-3

### Gannett Company[16]

According to a story in *Advertising Age*, when Gannett Co. got together with General Mills in a cooperative promotional venture, the result was somewhat unexpected. The promotion offered consumers free six-month subscriptions to *USA TODAY* and Gannett anticipated that between 10,000 and 20,000 would take them up on the offer. Far beyond this expectation, 450,000 people signed up for the free subscriptions. Being as specific as possible, what marketing research efforts might have helped the companies to predict more accurately the eventual popularity of their offer?

## CASE 1-4

### Kingston National Bank[17]

Valerie Lucas has been working for a year and a half as a loan processor. When she began her training period, she found that she had to work extra evening and weekend hours to keep up with her work load. She felt that as she became accustomed to her job, the extra hours would cease. However, because of the increase in loan applications, Valerie still finds herself working extra hours. Valerie enjoys working for the Kingston National Bank in Fort Wilson, and she gets along well with the other employees. Yet she is upset about the unreasonable demands she feels are being placed on her.

Lucas believes her loan quota is not being set by reasonable standards. She thinks the parent company basically just picks the number of loans they would like to see processed, then assigns a number to each branch. "They don't take things into consideration, such as the demographics of the branch location, or even how much the interest rates have changed. Another thing, how can they expect us to process loans efficiently if they won't give us enough room in which to do our job? It's hard to talk with a client while your office mate is also conducting an interview or even typing. I'm not the only one who is tired of the pressure. If it were not for my boss, I would have seriously considered leaving earlier."

Valerie's boss rates the current departmental employees as top-notch and

---

[16] (See "Gannett Pays for Success," *Advertising Age*, December 16, 1985, p. 3.)

[17] (*Source:* This case was prepared by Elizabeth Bonds, Research Associate, and Thomas Bertsch, Professor of Marketing at James Madison University. It was designed as a basis for class evaluation rather than to illustrate either effective or ineffective handling of a management situation. Confidential information has been disguised.)

does not want to lose any of them. What information should the boss gather in an effort to convince company officials that the branch location desperately needs either increased office space and personnel or lower quotas? What research evidence could the boss provide to officials that would show how valuable the staff is and how hard the workers would be to replace?

# 4

# PRINCIPLES OF SAMPLING

**Sampling and the Nielsen Retail Index System**

The United States has some 233,000 retail food, drug, and mass merchandise stores, a mass of outlets that makes it impossible to measure the retail sales in every one of them. As a result, the A.C. Nielsen Company relies heavily on sampling in producing its Retail Index System that reflects U.S. sales activity for these kinds of stores.

Using sampling techniques discussed more specifically in this chapter, Nielsen scientifically selects a sample of stores whose sales are to be measured. Naturally, once selected, these outlets must be approached by Nielsen for the purpose of achieving their cooperation in allowing access to inventory and accounting records as well as to the stores themselves.

Using auditing and, as possible, UPC (Universal Product Code) scanning, sales are measured and analyzed, and the resulting data are then projected to the nation as a whole. In the case of retail food outlets, the Retail Index System sample includes 1300 stores representing the purchases of 1,850,000 households—about 5,100,000 persons—who spend about $5.4 billion each year in these sample stores.

The result is a timely and reliable index of retail sales activity that provides clients with up-to-date marketplace information on which they can rely

---

*Source:* "Management with the Nielsen Retail Index System," brochure published by A.C. Nielsen Company, Northbrook, Ill.

in making marketing decisions. Companies are supplied with data not only on their own sales, but also sales of competitors, inventories, days-supply, in-store displays, average prices, merchandise purchased, and more. These data are available on either a monthly or bimonthly basis at both regional and national levels. Without sampling, it would be virtually impossible to supply sound information of this type at anything approaching a reasonable cost.

## INTRODUCTION

Sampling is an integral part of our daily lives. We are engaged in sampling every time we buy a new car, hear a television commercial, travel south for spring vacation, seek the social attention of a member of the opposite sex, or visit a new restaurant. For example, during your first few weeks at the college or university where you're reading this text, you may have ordered pizza from a number of local establishments before you determined the one that best satisfied your taste buds and budget. Nevertheless, there may still be a member of the local pizza-making population who hasn't yet had the good fortune to be included as a member of your "sample."

Because of the nature of samples, they aren't always representative. Chances are that you have either uttered or heard someone else say something like "I've had two of these #@%&$ Fords, and I'll never own another one," or "That's the last time I'll ever go out on a blind date!" (The author is acquainted with the manager of an automotive repair shop who absolutely refuses to accept checks from customers who own a certain make—best left unnamed—of foreign car.) Like the mass-produced good and the blind date, samples are not perfect, but they are a very necessary part of the marketing research function.

In this chapter our emphasis will be on the principles and methodologies of sampling, with the next chapter being devoted to the determination of sample size. As we discuss sampling in these two chapters, the following basic concepts will tend to appear rather frequently:

> *Population.* Sometimes known as the "universe," but we'll be a little more humble in our description. The population is the total collection of elements (e.g., consumers, roller bearing manufacturers, accountants, universities, fraternity members, motorcycle owners, etc.) about which we wish to make an inference based on sample information.
>
> *Sample.* The part of the population that we select and measure or observe.
>
> *Parameter.* The population characteristic in which we are interested. The true value of the parameter will be unknown, since this is what we're trying to determine through our sampling procedure.

*Estimate.*   The measurement, or "statistic," that results from the sample we have selected, and is our best estimate of the true value of the population characteristic. There is a good chance that the estimate will differ from the true value, depending on the degree of presence of sampling and nonsampling error.

*Sampling error.*   Results from our having taken a sample instead of a census. Sampling error is unavoidable in the sampling process.

*Nonsampling error.*   Sometimes described as "bias," or a tendency toward directional error (upward or downward estimation of the population parameter). It can be present even if we take a complete census instead of a sample.

*Accuracy.*   Sometimes termed "precision," this represents the closeness of our sample estimate to the true value of the population parameter, and is often expressed as an interval—for example, $200 ± $15.

*Confidence.*   The degree of certainty we have regarding the accuracy of our sample estimate. A trade-off exists between our level of confidence and the degree of accuracy to which it refers.

These are the major topics we'll be examining in our discussion of sampling in this chapter:

   I. Sample versus census
  II. The sampling procedure
 III. Types of samples
 IV. Nonprobability samples
  V. Probability samples

## SAMPLE VERSUS CENSUS

The president of a large automotive dealership once expressed concern to the author regarding his firm's performance in the eyes of its service customers. At the time, service feedback consisted primarily of knocks on the president's door, kind and unkind letters written by customers, and occasional responses to the "How were you treated?" cards available in an obscure corner of the service counter. When it was suggested that he merely contact customers by phone or mail and ask them a few relevant questions, his reaction was (1) with several thousand past and present customers, the cost would be exorbitant, and (2) they might react adversely to being contacted at home by the dealership, and be lost as customers. This person, although a highly successful businessman, was nevertheless unaware of the potential benefits that sampling held for the possible improvement of his service operation.

In the preceding situation, the executive involved was thinking "census" to the exclusion of sampling. While a complete census of the population may be desirable in some instances (e.g., when the population is very small or the cost of error very high), this was obviously not one of those cases. For example, if a population is comprised of just five manufacturers of an industrial product, a complete census would be in order whenever the population is subjected to a research study. However, in the case of the dealership, the businessman could have obtained a great deal of insight into his service clientele for the small investment of materials needed for the mailing and return of 200 to 300 questionnaires.

## Advantages of Sampling

Compared to a complete census of the population, sampling has a number of advantages: First, and perhaps most important, it's a lot less expensive—yet, if properly carried out, yields results that are just about as accurate. When one considers that, in many cases, the time required for a complete census would be so great as to render useless any conclusion reached, the swiftness of a sample is another important advantage. Imagine, for example, the time it would take for a manufacturer to conduct personal interviews with 50,000 individual customers—by the time the last one was interviewed, the first would probably be in a nursing home.

In addition, as the dealership executive expressed, measurement can be a destructive process. Such "destruction" is obvious when quality-control inspectors test the lifetime of light bulbs or the tensile strength of steel tubing—the product so "sampled" is lost in the process. However, though research questionnaires and interviews may not do physical harm, they may have a slight effect on the respondent's attitudes, knowledge, perceptions, or behavior. Thus, if the same person is sampled again, circumstances will not be the same. In most research studies, it is desired to *measure* changes in the population rather than to induce such changes by means of the measurement process itself. For example, it would certainly not be informative to call the same 100 people each

---

### EXHIBIT 4-1

#### It's a Tough Job, but . . .

Before a truckload of catfish is permitted into the Delta Pride processing plant in Indianola, Mississippi, a sample of its cargo must satisfy the discerning taste buds of inspector Stanley Marshall. After taking a fish from the truck, Mr. Marshall removes the head, puts the body into a plastic bag, and heats it up in a microwave oven. The truckload is accepted if the sampled fish tastes "sweet like a pecan," rejected if it has the flavor of "green grass or wet dirt." Mr. Marshall, who may sample as many as 150 to 200 fish in a day, admits that on some days "I don't generally feel like eating much for dinner."

*Source:* Matt Moffett, "Looking to Lure New Diners, Promoters of Catfish Work to Spruce Up Its Image," *The Wall Street Journal*, June 2, 1986, p. 17.

week and ask them if they know who won last year's Super Bowl game. Thus, if we were attempting to measure the success of a National Football League public relations campaign, we would naturally wish to include different (but comparable) members of the population in our periodic samples.

When considering the advantages of sampling over census, an important consideration is how accurate you can be with the amount of money you have to spend. Compared to foolishly trying to stretch your budget in order to conduct either a census or a sample of maximum possible size, it may be a far wiser move to invest the research funds toward obtaining a smaller, more represen- tative sample that is measured by fewer but better-trained interviewers or field- workers. Remember that nonsampling errors caused by poorly worded ques- tions or inexperienced interviewers will be present even if you "sample" the entire population. Figure 4-1 illustrates how nonsampling errors persist as the sample continually grows to the point of being a census.

### Sampling Error Revisited

As Figure 4-1 shows, a census will exhibit no sampling error. However, this is not necessarily desirable, because such a study will almost certainly lead to a greater amount of *total error* than could be obtained under more thoughtful planning with the same amount of resources. The following statement may be startling, but it's true: *It is possible to conduct a sample that is more accurate than a census!* Such a result may be accomplished by simply approaching the research situation with an eye toward total error and attempting to reduce each of its components instead of only one. By improved selection and training of field personnel, it may be possible to decrease the amount of response bias that results from respondents distorting the truth. By using monetary incentives, follow- ups, collection instrument pretesting, and other strategies, nonresponse bias (remember that people who don't respond may not be comparable to those who do) can be reduced. Also, careful selection of a representative sample will help avoid the frame bias that results from a mismatch between the population de-

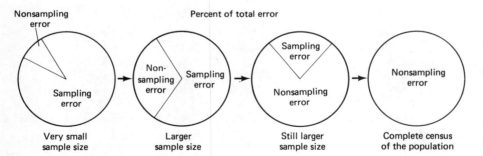

**Figure 4-1.** Even when "sampling" the entire population, nonsampling error remains to haunt you. The money required for a very large sample or census would probably be better spent on a higher quality study of a smaller sample.

sired and the sample actually chosen. All of the preceding nonsampling errors are very important to the accuracy of a study, and each will be discussed in the chapters ahead. However, for the time being, remember that sampling error (compared to nonsampling error) has the advantage of being subject to statistical estimation through analysis, and to reduction through the simple mechanism of an increased sample size. As we will see shortly, these characteristics of sampling error lend themselves well to certain types of sampling designs, known as probability samples.

## THE SAMPLING PROCEDURE

Given that the choice has been made to take a sample instead of a complete census of the population, we may now proceed to examine the various steps involved in the sampling process. A summary of these steps is presented in Figure 4-2. While the steps will be discussed briefly here, a more detailed treatment will be provided in later sections of this chapter.

*1. Determine relevant population and parameters.* The initial step in any sampling process is the selection of an appropriate target population and the

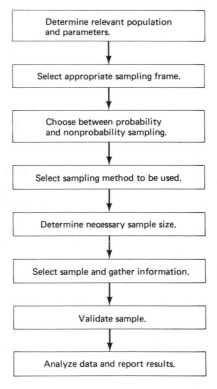

**Figure 4-2.** Steps in the sampling process.

identification of population parameters in which we are interested. For example, it may be desired to examine a population that consists of U.S. students in their senior year of college, owners of Honda Civic automobiles, Pittsburgh Steelers season ticket holders, registered voters in Soda Springs, Idaho, or other collections of people or units about whom we wish to make generalizations based on our sample results. The determination of the target population will always depend upon the particular objectives of the study in which we are involved. In addition, the target population must be well defined if we are to be successful in implementing the measurement process at the field level. For example, if we are concerned with the population of motorists in the state of California, there are a number of related questions that must be considered: Are we interested in motorists who possess a valid California driver's license, or are we to include tourists, commuters, and others who drive through the state? Should *motorists* be defined as anyone driving any vehicle any distance within the state, or might we be interested only in automobiles operated by persons who drive more than 3000 miles per year? If so, does the 3000-mile cutoff refer to miles driven last year or to expected miles to be driven during the coming year? Whether conducting a sample or a census, the population must be defined in terms that can be readily distinguished by field researchers charged with the actual collection of the sample units.

In addition to identifying the population, we must also determine the population parameters that we are attempting to measure. Again, definition of such parameters must be as detailed as possible. While variables such as "ownership of a color TV" or "vacationed in Vermont last year" are relatively straightforward, others—such as "attitude toward sports violence," "favorite brand of beer"—may require a more precise definition. For example, "favorite brand of beer" might be taken to mean the brand that the respondent would most prefer to drink (perhaps Michelob or Löwenbrau), or the brand that she or he drinks most frequently (perhaps Budweiser or Rolling Rock). In addition, the "favorite" brand may depend upon whether the respondent is drinking in a tavern or attending a cocktail party. Because of possible misinterpretations of the parameter definition at various stages of the sampling process, careful planning and forethought are necessary if a breakdown in communication is to be avoided. Many parameter definitions are not as simple as they first appear.

*2. Select appropriate sampling frame.* The sampling frame is intended to represent the members of the population, and the ideal sampling frame is a complete listing of all members of the population. Unfortunately, such a listing is rarely available and the sample frame actually used is likely to differ somewhat from the theoretical target population. For example, a widely used sampling frame is the telephone directory, which many persons view as being representative of the general population. While it is true that most households are listed in the telephone directory, there are a number of problems that cause this particular sampling frame to be less than perfect: First, some households elect to have unlisted telephone numbers, and hence are not represented in the directory. This would not be a problem, except that such households are likely to possess different characteristics from those who are listed—for example, higher-income households are more likely to be unlisted, as are single females. A second, related problem is the underrepresentation of families "on the move," since some may have a listing without a local residence, while others will have set up housekeeping and not be listed until the next edition of the directory is published. A third problem is that some households may have multiple listings in the directory, whereas others may not even own a telephone. The latter are especially likely to be of lower income or in rural locations.

A particularly frequent violation of the sampling frame concept is the presentation on evening television news programs of "person on the street" opinion and viewpoints. Quite often, such sidewalk interviews are extremely nonrandom, are conducted during the noon hour in a downtown area, yet are presented and perceived as the "voice of the people." In such situations, office workers, shoppers, and the unemployed are likely to be chosen, since steelworkers, truckers, and housewives are generally not found in abundance during the noon hour in large cities. Frame errors are practically unavoidable whenever we attempt to sample in the real world of marketing and consumers. Nevertheless, we should attempt to recognize potential sources of such error and minimize them whenever possible.

**3. Choose between probability and nonprobability sampling.** The differences between probability and nonprobability sampling will be discussed in greater detail in the section immediately following. However, at this point, it should be mentioned that probability sampling offers the advantage of our being able to calculate the sampling error of our measurement, whereas the nonprobability sample does not offer this possibility. In other words, after conducting the probability sample, we may be able to say that we are "95% sure that between two-thirds and three-fourths of the population identifies the Craftsman brand with quality." As will be examined shortly, the major drawbacks of nonprobability sampling are the resulting inability to determine sampling error and the subjectivity introduced by the judgment of the researcher in selecting the sample.

**4. Select the sampling method to be used.** At this stage, we must decide in what manner we will select the actual members of the sample—that is, exactly which probability or nonprobability procedure will be used. The possibilities are discussed further in the next section, and are summarized in Figure 4-3.

**5. Determine necessary sample size.** Methods for determining the size of both probability and nonprobability samples are discussed in Chapter 5.

**6. Select sample and gather information.** At this stage, we follow or delegate the rules of choice that have been determined earlier in the process. The use of such collection devices as interviews, mail questionnaires, telephone surveys, and observation is examined later in the text.

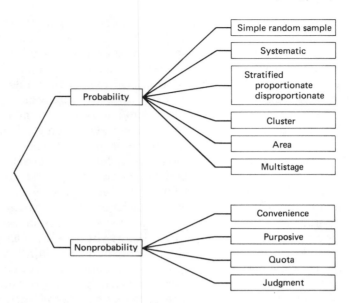

**Figure 4-3.**   Summary of probability and nonprobability sampling methods.

*7. Validate sample.* In order to determine if the sample we've selected is a representative cross section of the population, we may wish to compare the characteristics of the sample with those known to exist within the population from which the sample was drawn. Such comparisons may be based on census or other "benchmark" data. For example, if 45% of a department store's credit customers also carry an Exxon credit card, but only 21% of our sample of the

---

**EXHIBIT 4-2**

*No Strength in These Numbers*

In the 1930s, a magazine by the name of *The Literary Digest* produced what may well be the all-time Edsel of marketing research. Attempting to predict the winner of the 1936 presidential election, the magazine mailed 10 million questionnaires to readers and to persons identified from automobile registrations and telephone directories.

Altogether, over 2 million persons responded, making this one of the largest samples in history. Unfortunately, the sample's representativeness was far less than its considerable size, and the results were off by the proverbial mile. Instead of candidate Alf Landon soundly defeating Franklin Roosevelt as predicted, the exact opposite occurred. The culprit in this case was the use of a totally inappropriate sampling frame. It seems that those who read the magazine, owned an automobile, or had a telephone tended to be of the Republican persuasion, and the distorted survey result was due largely to their being grossly overrepresented in the sample.

credit customer population carry the Exxon card, then our sample may not be representative of the population from which it was presumably drawn.

 **8.** *Analyze data and report results.* The final stage of the sampling process actually overlaps somewhat with the validation of the sample, since such validation also requires analysis. While both data analysis and the reporting of research results are covered later in the text, it should be observed here that both the sampling procedure and the form of the data itself must be consistent with the techniques of analysis that are to be employed.

## TYPES OF SAMPLES

Sample designs can be categorized in a number of ways, including fixed versus sequential, probability versus nonprobability, and attributes versus variables. Some firms (see Figure 4-4) specialize in sample design decisions and the generation of samples for their clients.

**Figure 4-4.** To help avoid samples that don't represent the target population, it may be useful to retain the services of a specialty firm that specializes in the generation of samples for survey research. *The Literary Digest* certainly could have used their help. (Courtesy of Survey Sampling, Inc., Fairfield, Ct.)

## Fixed versus Sequential Sampling

Fixed samples involve a predetermined sample size, and all sample data are collected before the results are analyzed. On the other hand, in sequential sampling, the number of units to be sampled is not decided upon in advance, but is determined by a decision rule. After each sample is taken, the decision is made whether to (1) continue sampling, or (2) reach conclusions or take actions based on the information collected so far. The result of sequential sampling is often a combination of greater accuracy and lower cost, since at each stage further observations are not taken if their value is deemed marginal. A difficulty with sequential sampling is the mathematical complexity that characterizes the procedure. For this reason, in addition to the fact that most sampling is of the fixed type, we will concentrate on the fixed sampling approach.

## Probability versus Nonprobability Sampling

Probability samples involve selection methods in which the members of the sample are chosen through some random process. The most notable characteristic of the probability sample is that each member of the population has a known (or calcuable) probability of being included in the sample. Each member of the population may not have an *equal* chance of being included in the sample, but everyone has some chance of inclusion. The randomness of the probability sample should not be confused with a haphazard or aimless approach, for it is in fact quite rigorous in its adherence to selection rules that do not allow subjectivity or arbitrary judgment on the part of the researcher.

Nonprobability samples, on the other hand, do not provide an opportunity to determine the chance that a given population element has of being included in the sample. For this reason, we cannot be sure that the sample is representative of the population. Compared to the rigor of probability samples, nonprobability samples rely on the judgment of the researcher and are only as representative as the researcher's luck and skill permit.

Theoretically, probability sampling is the superior of the two possibilities here, and has the primary advantage that, because each unit of the population has a known chance of inclusion in the sample, it is possible to estimate objectively the amount of sampling error present. This advantage includes the opportunity to mathematically determine the necessary sample size if a given level of accuracy is desired. Principal disadvantages of probability sampling include greater time, cost, and complexity compared to the nonprobability approaches. In addition, we may not wish to be able to project the sample results with a known degree of accuracy to the population at large. Perhaps, as in the case of an exploratory study, the researcher merely wishes to gain familiarity with the population, and may even be interested in a sample that is purposely selected as being unrepresentative of the population.

A relative advantage of the nonprobability sample is that, for a given expenditure of time and money, we should be able to obtain a larger sample size than would be possible with the probability techniques. As a result, we might obtain a nonprobability sample that is more representative than the smaller probability sample that would have been possible. In addition, the monetary savings of using a nonprobability sample may provide funds for the payment of a token amount to reduce nonsampling error by helping secure the cooperation of respondents or subjects. However, despite these possible advantages, nonprobability sampling is generally an inferior approach because of the representation and generalizability difficulties noted.

### Attributes versus Variables Sampling

Sampling may also be categorized according to the type of population parameters that we are trying to estimate. Such parameters may be classified as either attributes or variables. An attribute is a qualitative or descriptive characteristic that a population member does or does not possess. Attribute sampling is generally concerned with the population proportion who possess the characteristic of interest. As such, we would attempt to use the sample proportion as an estimate of the population proportion having the same attribute. Examples of attributes include owning an RCA television set, having gone to a movie within the last week, having voted in the last presidential election, and other characteristics that may be of concern to a particular marketing research study.

Variables sampling attempts to estimate a population mean, rather than a proportion. For example, a study may have the goal of determining the average years of formal education, frequency of product purchase, age, or other arithmetic measure of the population. Note that a given parameter of interest may be expressed either as a variable or as an attribute. For example, frequency of purchase may be expressed in terms of a variable (purchases in the past year) or an attribute (0–4, 5–9, or 10 or more purchases in the past year). As we will see later, determination of the necessary sample size for a given degree of accuracy depends upon whether we are sampling for a mean (variable) or for a proportion (attribute) of the object of our research.

## NONPROBABILITY SAMPLES

As we've indicated, the nonprobability sampling approach may be described as "quick and dirty" because of its inherent weaknesses compared to the probability sample. However, should the research situation be of a type that might benefit from the cost and time advantages of a nonprobability sample, the techniques involved in (1) convenience samples, (2) purposive samples, (3) quota samples, or (4) judgment samples may be considered.

### Convenience Sample

"Because they're there" is the rallying cry best associated with the convenience sample, which is selected primarily for the convenience of the researcher. We have all seen newspaper stories where a reporter will ask a "random sampling" of passers-by to comment on what they think of the town's new paper mill, whether they favor beer sales in supermarkets, or if they would support converting the downtown area into a parking lot. The stories are often accompanied by photographs and partial quotes attributed to each respondent pictured. Such stories certainly have news value, but at the cost of possessing very little scientific value. Other examples of convenience sampling abound, some which are given high credibility simply because of the large sample sizes that accompany the "research." Radio call-in programs are a form of convenience sample, where listeners telephone their opinions on the subject of the day. What is often lost here is that the respondents are self-selected individuals who may have a more vital interest in the issue and more spare time in which to listen to the radio and talk on the telephone, and may be of a different personality type than the rest of us. Such samples are not representative, and any increase in the sample size will only focus more closely on an inaccurate conclusion.

As you've probably gathered to this point, convenience sampling is strenuously not recommended for descriptive, predictive, or causal studies in which the ability to project sample findings to the population is of great importance. Despite its weaknesses, however, the convenience sample is a useful tool in the exploratory phase of a research project, a phase in which ideas and insights are more important than scientific objectivity. For example, in an early stage of studying consumer perceptions of the Defensive Driving Course of the National Safety Council, the author held focus group interviews with two convenience samples from a local steel firm—one group that had taken the course when it was offered through the company, and another group that had elected to pass up the same opportunity. While the samples were certainly not representative of national students and nonstudents, they did assist toward the development of further hypotheses, variables, and ideas that proved extremely valuable in subsequent phases of the research.

**Purposive Sample**

A purposive sample is one in which the sample members are chosen in order to meet some predetermined criteria that have been deemed important. The researcher may select such a sample even though he knows that it is unrepresentative of the population. For example, a toy manufacturer may conduct an observational study in which children who have been selected because of their tendency to break toys play with the firm's products. Similarly, the marketer of a new pocket calculator may submit the product to engineers and other scientific people for their reactions before finalizing the design of the product. A political candidate, in formulating her strategies for an upcoming campaign, might like to obtain the viewpoints of persons who are known to be adverse to her candidacy. In conducting the exploratory group interviews for consumers' perceptions of the Defensive Driving Course, the author purposely selected members of one group who had known about the course but turned it down when it was made available to them. In addition to being a convenience sample (because their employer was conveniently located and the sample was readily available), this was also a purposive sample (because members were selected on the basis of *not* being representative of the population).

## Quota Sample

The quota sampling technique is a common approach that at least makes an attempt to systematically ensure that the sample bears some resemblance to the population. As an initial step, the population is divided into subcategories, then the sample members are selected according to established quotas that force the sample composition to be proportionally similar to that of the population with regard to membership in these categories. The categorization used may be one-dimensional (e.g., by age), two-dimensional (e.g., by age and sex), or three-dimensional (e.g., by age, sex, and educational level) or more. Table 4-1 illustrates how a quota sampling procedure might be applied to a sampling of students at a hypothetical university. As the table shows, since 1400 (14%) of the total student population consists of male freshmen, then 14 (also 14%) of the 100 sample members must be male freshmen. In actual practice, the required proportion of members in a sample category will generally call for a noninteger number of persons (e.g., 14.8). In this case, we would include 15 people in the sample category and round all figures upward or downward so that the total sample size requirement is met.

When conducting a quota sample study, selection errors may play an important role in the outcome. For example, in the sample described in Table 4-1, an interviewer might be positioned in a relatively high-traffic area of the campus and be reluctant to stop students who appear to be in a hurry, who are 6'6" tall and look angry, or who otherwise just don't look as if they would care to be interviewed. Another problem is that the categorization may not be appropriate to the problem under investigation. For example, if the research study

TABLE 4-1. *Hypothetical quota sample specifications with the population categorized two ways—by sex and by level of study.*

|  |  | Finehower University student population of 10,000 | | Two-way quota sample of 100 Students | |
|  |  | Sex | | Sex | |
|  |  | *Male* | *Female* | *Male* | *Female* |
| Level of study | *Freshman* | 1400 | 1200 | 14 | 12 |
|  | *Sophomore* | 1300 | 1100 | 13 | 11 |
|  | *Junior* | 1100 | 1000 | 11 | 10 |
|  | *Senior* | 1000 | 900 | 10 | 9 |
|  | *Graduate* | 600 | 400 | 6 | 4 |

is concerned with attitudes toward fraternities and sororities, it may be desired to set up a third dimension of classification that establishes appropriate quotas calling for a certain number of the sample members to be persons belonging to such organizations.

Because of time and cost considerations, quota sampling is often used by public opinion researchers and for the "stocking" of consumer panels. It must be remembered, however, that categorization of the sample into proportions that resemble the corresponding proportions of the population does not mean that the sample is representative of the population. Although it represents the population with regard to *these* characteristics, other similarities may be sadly lacking.

### Judgment Sample

The judgment sample is one that is, in the *judgment* of the researcher, representative of the population. The important distinction here is not that the sample *is* typical, but that the researcher *thinks* it is. With this introductory discussion, it should be apparent that the judgment sample is only as good as the judgment of the researcher or expert who has selected its members. This is not to say that a judgment sample cannot be representative—there may be cases in which the judgment of a specialist in the field may yield a more representative sample than would have been obtained through a probability sampling method. This is especially likely to occur if sample sizes are small—for example, in the selection of several test cities for a marketing experiment.

One approach to the judgment sample is the **snowball sample**, in which the researcher asks the respondent for the names of other individuals who might also be surveyed. This method is most useful when the population is very small, as might be the case if our population happens to consist of microbiologists specializing in the development of organisms to clean up oil spills. One difficulty of this technique is that respondents may tend to recommend close friends or colleagues, and subsequent interviews may involve persons who tend to think or behave in a fashion similar to the individual who recommended them.

As with all nonprobability samples, it is not possible to ensure that a judgment sample will be representative of the population. Also, we cannot use statistical techniques to determine the sample size required for a given level of accuracy, nor can we statistically project the sample results into a confidence level for the population parameter of interest.

## PROBABILITY SAMPLES

As you have been reminded several times, probability samples are the only kind from which you can statistically estimate the likely amount of sampling error. In this section we will examine the following probability sampling techniques: (1) simple random sampling, (2) systematic sampling, (3) stratified sampling, (4) cluster sampling, (5) area sampling, and (6) multistage sampling.

## Simple Random Sampling

The simple random sample is by far the most familiar type of probability sample. It is unique in that each member has an *equal* probability of being included in the sample. In concept, the idea of such a sample is quite simple—it is the equivalent of drawing names from a hat.

Since selecting names from a hat is rather cumbersome, an easier way to generate a random sample is to assign consecutive numbers to members of the population, then use a random number table to identify those who will become members of the sample. In a random number table, there is the same probability that a given digit will be a 0 as a 1, or a 2, and so on. Random number tables are available from a variety of sources, including that presented in the statistical appendix at the end of this book. Table 4-2 shows a portion of that table and will serve as the basis for the following example.

Table 4-3 shows a hypothetical telephone directory with 12 listings, from which we'll use the random number table of Table 4-2 to generate a simple random sample of five individuals. Since the population size of 12 is a two-digit number, we'll have to employ a series of two-digit random numbers to select members of our sample. Arbitrarily beginning with the first two-digit number in the shaded area of Table 4-2, we'll proceed in order until we obtain five nonduplicative (i.e., repeats are ignored) random numbers between 01 and 12. Beginning with 70, we proceed through slightly more than three columns, during which the first five nonduplicative numbers between 01 and 12 are 04, 12, 03, 10, and 11; these listings are marked with an asterisk (*) in Table 4-3 and constitute our simple random sample of five. Because our population size, 12, is rather small for a two-digit number, it was necessary for us to skip over about seven of every eight random numbers in order to obtain the sample.

*TABLE 4-2.* *A portion of a random number table. The shaded portion shows the series of two-digit numbers used in generating the simple random sample described in the text.*

| Row | Column | | | | |
| --- | --- | --- | --- | --- | --- |
| | *1* | *2* | *3* | *4* | *5* |
| 1 | 48461 | 14952 | 72619 | 73689 | 52059 |
| 2 | 76534 | 38149 | 49692 | 31366 | 52093 |
| 3 | 70437 | 25861 | 38504 | 14752 | 23757 |
| 4 | 59584 | 03370 | 42806 | 11393 | 71722 |
| 5 | 04285 | 58554 | 16085 | 51555 | 27501 |
| 6 | 77340 | 10412 | 69189 | 85171 | 29082 |
| 7 | 59183 | 62687 | 91778 | 80354 | 23512 |
| 8 | 91800 | 04281 | 39979 | 03927 | 82564 |
| 9 | 12066 | 24817 | 81099 | 48940 | 69554 |
| 10 | 69907 | 91751 | 53512 | 23748 | 65906 |

*Source:* From F. James Rohlf and Robert R. Sokal, *Statistical Tables*, 2nd ed., W.H. Freeman and Company, Publishers, San Francisco. Copyright © 1981 by W.H. Freeman and Company.

**TABLE 4-3.** *Hypothetical telephone directory. Listings with an asterisk are members of the simple random sample of five that is based on the sequence of shaded random numbers in Table 4-2.*

| Numbers assigned to population members | Directory | |
|---|---|---|
| 1 | Barr, Clark 19 Main | 307-4192 |
| 2 | Brustenaut, Carl 3 Main | 307-4932 |
| 3* | Clayer, Aubrey 31 Main | 307-0527 |
| 4* | Coyne, Iva 14 Main | 307-6817 |
| 5 | Croud, Theresa 20 Main | 307-1328 |
| 6 | Homyet, Arnie 17 Main | 307-7329 |
| 7 | O'Fessor, Eghad, Ph.D. 10 Academian | 307-2413 |
| 8 | O'Hara, Emilio 27 Main | 307-4205 |
| 9 | Shuze, Jim 15 Main | 307-2136 |
| 10* | Tba, Ruth, Ph.D. 20 Academian | 307-2589 |
| 11* | Vailable, Irma 15¼ Main | 307-1425 |
| 12* | Veeten, Sven R. 25 Main | 307-8888 |

Although the simple random sample is the picture of simplicity, there are a number of possible problems associated with its use. Perhaps the greatest disadvantage is the necessity of having a complete listing of the members of the population. While such a listing is feasible for the Smallville telephone directory or the Dow Jones Industrials, it is generally difficult to obtain a complete and accurate list of most populations. A second, related problem is the cost of determining the sample membership and gathering research information from each element of the sample. For example, the sample may contain elements that are widely dispersed, hence requiring extensive travel costs if personal interviews are to be conducted. A third problem is that the simple random sample is not as efficient (in the statistical sense) as other techniques, such as the stratified random sample. For example, if 30% of a population consists of college graduates, it is unlikely that a simple random sample would contain exactly 30% college graduates. While this would be the *expected* percentage, it would not occur in a typical simple random sample. This would be especially troublesome if college graduates differed significantly from the rest of the population with regard to the population parameter under investigation.

Despite these difficulties, however, a simple random sample may be quite useful whenever we sample a population that is small, for which a suitable listing is available, and where the geographical dispersion of the sample elements is not a problem.

### Systematic Sampling

The systematic sampling method is very similar to the simple random sample and is a lot easier to apply. Basically, it involves selecting a random starting point, then picking every *k*th element on the list. For example, if we have a listing of 5000 names and wish to select a random sample of 100 persons, we would first select a random number between 1 and 50, then select that individual and every 50th person thereafter. Because the population of 5000 is 50 times as large as our desired sample, we select every 50th person after our random starting point. The reason for the random starting point is to ensure that every member of the population has an equal chance of being selected in the sample.

Other variations from this theme include the specification of name locations from the telephone directory. For example, if a telephone directory listing contains 50 pages and we wish to obtain a systematic sample of 100, we may elect to simply choose the 5th person down in the first column and the 12th person up on the third column for each page. While the purist might argue that Amos Aardvark, being first on the list, has no chance of selection, we could use such an approach to obtain a fairly representative sample of the directory listing.

Another possible application of systematic sampling is the personal interview on the street, where a fieldworker can avoid the introduction of personal bias by simply selecting every 20th person walking by. This helps to reduce the potential problem of the interviewer avoiding inebriates and pedestrians walking Doberman pinschers, or otherwise shying away from contact with persons with whom an interview might not seem attractive. In both this and the preceding example involving the selection of two persons from each page of the telephone directory, the systematic sampling procedure simply describes a mechanical selection rule for the researcher to follow in order to reduce the chance of selection bias occurring.

When the population is arranged in a listing, and a systematic sample including every $k$th individual is selected, the result may be either more representative or less representative than a simple random sample of the same population. For example, if the population list is arranged in some order which is relevant to the parameter of interest (e.g., from larger store sizes to smaller store sizes), the systematic sample is likely to be more representative of the population than would be the case for a simple random sample. On the other hand, if there are periodic variations in the listing (especially if these variations occur with a period equal to $k$), the systematic sample is likely to be less representative than a simple random sample of the same population. Examples of the latter situation could occur if, for some reason, the $k$th house visited ends up being a corner lot, or if the $k$th day of sales is always a Wednesday. While problems associated with such "periodicity" within the population listing are quite uncommon, they should be considered whenever the use of a systematic sample is contemplated.

## Stratified Sampling

In stratified sampling, the population is divided into categories that are mutually exclusive (don't overlap) and collectively exhaustive (all members are included). The logic behind such stratification is that the categories may vary widely from one to another with regard to the parameter of interest, yet exhibit a high degree of similarity within each category. Stratified sampling involves the sampling of each stratum, or category, as if it were a separate population. Within each stratum, we may employ a simple random sample, systematic sampling, or other probability sampling technique to measure the characteristics of the subgroup. To the extent that some relationship exists between the strata chosen and the population parameter, the stratified sample will provide us with a better estimate of the value of the parameter. For example, if we were undertaking a study of attitudes with regard to the legalization of marijuana, we might wish to stratify our population into age categories, since it is not unlikely that younger persons are more liberal with regard to the substance and limitations on its use. The basic strategy of the stratified sample is similar to quota sampling but employs probability selection techniques in choosing the sample members of each stratum. Again, the advantages of stratified sampling are strongly dependent on the existence of strata within the population who differ widely with regard to the parameter being measured. For example, in Figure 4-5, the greater homogeneity of the strata at the left reflects the fact that stratified sampling would not be much more effective than a simple random sample. However, the diversity of the strata at the right of the figure suggests a situation in which stratified sampling would offer a better estimate of the population parameter, perhaps even with a smaller overall sample size.

The superiority of the stratified sample over the simple random sample will depend on how different the strata are compared to each other and how homogeneous each is within itself. In addition to the relative complexity and inherent cost of stratified sampling, however, it is also necessary that we have some advance information about the population for the basis of structuring the stratification design. For these reasons, the stratified sampling technique should not automatically be used in lieu of a simple random sample or systematic sample.

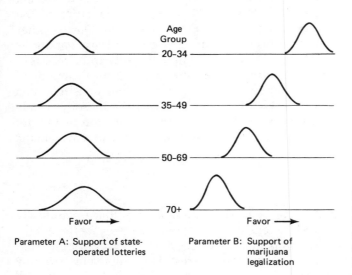

**Figure 4-5.** Given the hypothetical distributions, greater variability between age groups would cause stratified sampling to provide a better estimate of parameter B than would be possible with a simple random sample.

In designing a research study that utilizes the stratified sampling technique, it is necessary to consider a number of related questions. These relate to the bases and number of strata chosen, and whether the sample sizes of the various strata should be proportional or disproportional to the larger population.

### Bases of Stratification

As with the quota sample, there may be one or more bases of stratification of the population. We may wish to create strata divisions that are based either on available information or on the judgments of experts regarding the relevance of geographic, demographic, economic, and other variables to the population parameter we are trying to estimate. The general strategy is to have strata in which the members are as alike as possible, but who differ as much as possible from the members of other strata with regard to the parameter. In determining the bases of stratification, the results of a prior exploratory study, or related data presented in secondary sources, may be especially useful as a supplement to the commonly used "judgmental" strata approach in which the researcher has some (not necessarily unfounded) reason to believe that a certain stratification approach will be successful.

### Number of Strata

Diminishing returns set in rapidly as you attempt to break the population down into a large number of strata. In general, the same strategy applies as when determining the bases of the stratification—that is, don't have so many different strata that there is not much difference from one stratum to the next with regard to the parameter in question. Naturally, the more strata used, the greater the degree of homogeneity within strata, but this may occur at the expense of exorbitant cost that is not repaid by increased accuracy in the eventual estimate of the population parameter.

### Proportionate versus Disproportionate Stratification

The type of stratified sampling with which most of us are likely to be more comfortable is the proportionate variety. In this approach, as with the quota sample, the proportion of the sample possessing certain characteristics is the same as the proportion of the population who possess the same characteristics. For example, if 20% of the population are college graduates, then 20% of the stratified sample will also be college graduates.

However, there is an alternative to the proportionate stratification technique that may prove advantageous whenever the variability within some strata is much more or less than that of others. This alternative, called ***disproportionate stratified sampling***, takes into consideration that members of a particular stratum may be very much alike with regard to the population parameter; hence they will not need to be sampled as extensively as a stratum in which the parameter exhibits a great deal of variability. For example, in conducting a study regarding attitudes toward national health insurance, it may be desired to sample relatively fewer persons over the age of 65 (since we expect that they would be rather unanimously for the proposal), and relatively more persons from other segments of the population. Figure 4-6 provides an illustration in which disproportionate stratified sampling would be in order. In this case, because of the relative variability of the three strata, stratum A could be sampled less than proportionately, while the proportion of the sample from stratum C would be greater than their actual representation in the population. Because of the much smaller variability of stratum A, a relatively small sample size is sufficient to obtain an accurate estimate of its subpopulation mean.

From the standpoint of statistical efficiency in estimating a population mean with minimum sampling error for a given total sample size, disproportionate stratified sampling offers an advantage but requires that we know more about the characteristics of the strata we are studying; that is, we must have an idea not only of their relative means, but also of their relative degrees of variability around these means.

Figure 4-7 shows how A.C. Nielsen uses stratified sampling in their selection of retail outlets for the Nielsen Retail Index System. As illustrated in part (a) of the figure, Nielsen stratifies the universe according to geography, population, store type, and store size. Probability sampling is then employed to select sample outlets from each cell. Part (b) demonstrates Nielsen's dispro-

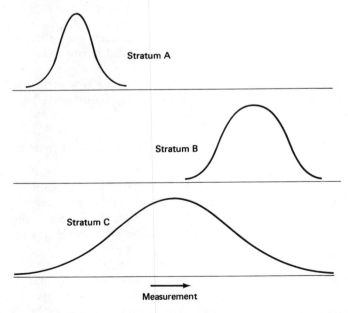

**Figure 4-6.** Because of its small degree of variability, stratum A may be underrepresented (i.e., lower percentage of members in sample than in population), while stratum C will be overrepresented (higher percentage of members in sample than in population) in a disproportionate stratified sample.

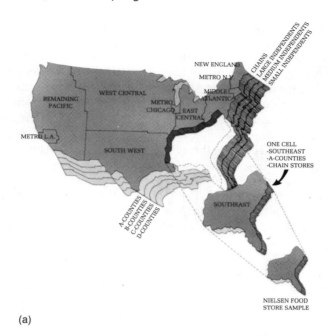

(a)

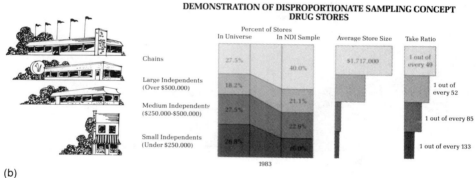

(b)

**Figure 4-7.** A.C. Nielsen uses the disproportionate stratified sampling approach in selecting sample stores for the Nielsen Retail Index System. (*Source:* "Management with the Nielsen Retail Index System," brochure published by A.C. Nielsen Company, Northbrook, Ill., pp. 10, 11.)

portional approach in selecting types of stores in either greater or lesser proportion to their presence in the population. For example, whereas small independent drugstores constitute 26.8% of the population, they are only 16% of the stores in the total sample; although large chains are just 27.5% of the store population, their representation in the sample is much greater, 40%.[1]

---

[1] See "Management with the Nielsen Retail Index System," brochure published by A.C. Nielsen Company, Northbrook, Ill., pp. 10, 11.

## Cluster Sampling

Unlike the previous sampling designs we've considered, cluster sampling is primarily oriented around the selection of groups, rather than individuals within the population. The first step in cluster sampling is to break the population down into groups that are (as in stratified sampling) mutually exclusive and collectively exhaustive. The next step, however, is where cluster sampling takes on its unique dimension: A random sample *of the groups* is selected for further sampling. At this point, the actual sample members are probabilistically chosen from the sampling of groups selected in the previous step. The procedure is summarized in Figure 4-8, in which the population has been categorized into eight strata, A through H. The strata are then sampled, by random number table or other probabilistic means, to obtain a sample of the strata groups—for example, A, C, E, and H. Concentrating on these strata, the researcher will then

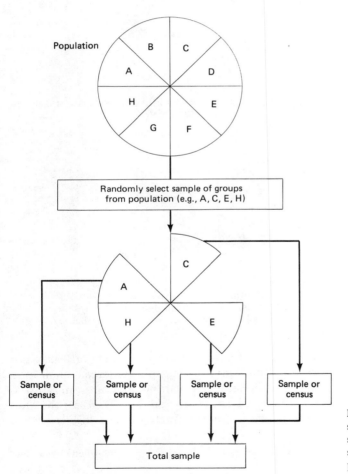

**Figure 4-8.** Unlike stratified sampling, in which all strata are sampled, cluster sampling involves sampling from a *sampling* of the population strata.

conduct a sample or census of each (generally a sample, for reasons of economy) in order to obtain the total sample.

As an example, let's suppose that we wish to sample the employees of a large manufacturing organization for the purpose of determining their attitude toward certain alternative benefit packages that may be offered during the coming year. A first step in using cluster sampling might be to list the various departments within the organization. This would be followed by randomly selecting a sampling of departments, which in turn would lead to a sample or census of the employees within each of the selected departments.

While cluster sampling yields a probability sample, it is not as statistically efficient as a simple random sample of the same size. However, the cluster sample will generally require a smaller cost in order to obtain a given sample size, thus making it possible to obtain a larger sample for a given expenditure. Cluster sampling is especially useful whenever the cost of reaching sample members in the field may be significant.

## Area Sampling

Area sampling is a form of cluster sampling in which geographic areas serve as the basis for determining our population strata. These geographic clusters are described in terms of counties, city blocks, and other area definitions. In taking an area sample of a particular city for the purpose of conducting personal interviews, we might first divide the city into blocks, then randomly select a sampling of city blocks from this listing. We could then have the interviewer visit a sample of the houses on the blocks selected. Figure 4-9 illustrates the common levels of geographic detail that are available for use in research involving area sampling. Information such as that shown is available from the U.S. Department of Commerce through the Bureau of the Census.

A problem with area sampling is that persons who are similar with regard to such demographic characteristics as income and education may tend to live in the same neighborhood, leading to reduced statistical efficiency for this method compared to a simple random sample of the same size. However, as with the cluster sample, the reduced cost of interviewer time and travel can make possible an increased sample size, which helps to offset this potential loss of accuracy.

## Multistage Sampling

Samples may be either single-stage or multistage, depending on the number of levels at which a probability selection procedure is used. By using multiple stages, with probability selection procedures at each stage, the end result is still a probability sample; that is, every member of the population has a known (or determinable) probability of being included in the final sample. The levels shown in Figure 4-9 could each be the object of probability selection in an area sampling study. In proceeding from standard metropolitan statistical area (SMSA), to cen-

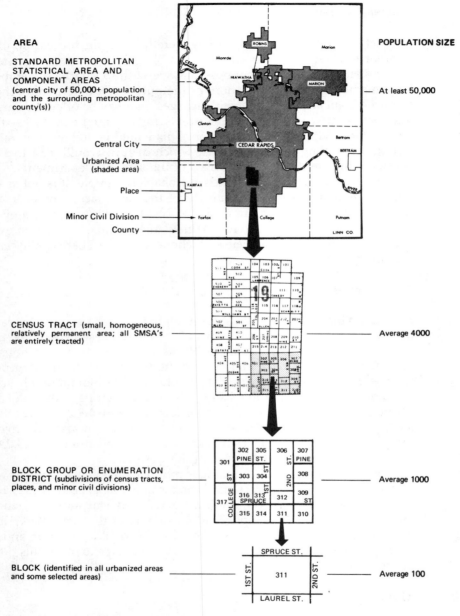

**AREA**

**STANDARD METROPOLITAN STATISTICAL AREA AND COMPONENT AREAS** (central city of 50,000+ population and the surrounding metropolitan county(s))

**POPULATION SIZE**

At least 50,000

Central City

Urbanized Area (shaded area)

Place

Minor Civil Division

County

**CENSUS TRACT** (small, homogeneous, relatively permanent area; all SMSA's are entirely tracted)

Average 4000

**BLOCK GROUP OR ENUMERATION DISTRICT** (subdivisions of census tracts, places, and minor civil divisions)

Average 1000

**BLOCK** (identified in all urbanized areas and some selected areas)

Average 100

**Figure 4-9.** Common geographic areas available from the Bureau of the Census for use in area sampling.

sus tracts, to block groupings or districts, to blocks, then to particular households, we would have a four-stage sampling procedure.

The multistage method reflects the beauty of cluster and area sampling possibilities, since it helps to convert a population for which no practical or accurate list may be available into one for which a pictorial (map) listing is extremely valuable. Thus it helps to bring the advantages of probability sampling to a sampling situation that might otherwise appear difficult or impossible to approach.

## Mailing Lists and Sample Selection

A number of firms offer lists that can be utilized for research purposes. For example, Alvin B. Zeller, Inc., maintains *compiled* mailing lists that include doctors, lawyers, homeowners, investors, students, engineers, scientists, and other "types" for the entire United States. These data are available by geographic area, sex, professional specialties, and disciplines. Families are categorized by

| QUANTITY | | PRICE |
|---|---|---|
| 2,300 | Music Department Chairmen, Colleges | $40/M |
| 23,000 | Music Professors, College | $40/M |
| 27,100 | Music Teachers, High School | $40/M |
| 3,900 | Music Instruction, Private | $35/M |
| 7,600 | Musical Instrument Dealers | $35/M |
| 65,000 | Musicians (Select Instrument) | $40/M |
| 425 | Mutual Funds | $75 |
| 1,750 | Mutual Fund Executives | $75 |
| 465 | Mutual Savings Banks HQ | $75 |

**N**

| QUANTITY | | PRICE |
|---|---|---|
| 17,000 | National Advertisers | $35/M |
| 76,000 | National Advertisers Executives | $35/M |
| 2,100 | Naturalists | $75 |
| 5,900 | Naval Engineers | $35/M |
| 235,000 | Narcotics & Drug Abuse Centers | Inquire |
| 3,950 | Navy Officers, Retired & Reserved | $35/M |
| 8,600 | Needlework & Yarn Shops | $35/M |
| 16,350 | Neon Sign Dealers | $35/M |
| 5,260 | Neuroscientists | $35/M |
| 2,400 | Newsdealers & Newsstands | $35/M |
| 3,175 | Newsdealers, Wholesalers & Distributors | $40/M |
| 3,900 | Newsletter Publishers | $35/M |
| 22,130 | Newspaper Executives | $35/M |
| 1,740 | Newspapers, Daily | $75 |
| 520 | Newspapers, Daily with circulation of 25,000 or more | $75 |
| 1,040 | Newspapers, daily with circulation of 10,000 or more | $75 |
| 7,300 | Newspapers, Weekly | $35/M |
| 675 | Newspapers, Weekly with circulation of 10,000 or more | $75 |
| 9,200 | Night Clubs, Discos | $35/M |
| 220,000 | Non-Profit Tax Exempt Organizations | $35/M |
| 8,600 | Notaries, Public | $35/M |
| 8,275 | Novelties (Advertising) Jobbers | $35/M |
| 1,900 | Novelty & Souvenir Shops | $75 |
| 22,500 | Nuclear Industry Executives | $35/M |
| 640 | Nuclear Medicine Specialists | $75 |
| 1,900 | Nuclear Physicists | $75 |
| 150 | Nudist Clubs | $75 |
| 13,750 | Nurseries & Greenhouses | $35/M |
| 45,700 | Nursery Schools & Kindergartens | $35/M |
| 3,300 | Nurses, Directors of | $45/M |
| 230,000 | Nurses, Hospital | Inquire |
| 6,500 | Nurses, Private Duty | $40/M |
| 1,530,000 | Nurses, Registered | Inquire |
| 3,950 | Nurses, Registries | $35/M |
| 23,170 | Nursing Homes | $35/M |
| 11,400 | Nursing Homes, 50 beds or more | $35/M |
| 5,650 | Nursing Homes, 100 beds or more | $35/M |
| 15,000 | Nursing Homes, Private | $35/M |
| 1,300 | Nursing Schools | $75 |
| 1,765 | Nutritionists | $75 |

**O**

| QUANTITY | | PRICE |
|---|---|---|
| 21,710 | Obstetricians & Gynecologists | $35/M |
| 18,640 | Occupational Therapists | $35/M |
| 15,500 | Oceanographers | $35/M |
| 8,200 | Odd Fellows Lodges | $35/M |
| 5,500 | Office Building Management Companies | $35/M |
| 31,300 | Office & Building Cleaners | $35/M |
| 14,200 | Office Equipment & Supplies Dealers | $35/M |
| 9,300 | Office Machine Dealers | $35/M |
| 1,200 | Office Machine Manufacturers | $75 |
| 10,050 | Office (Commercial) Stationers | $35/M |
| 389 | Office Parks | $75 |
| 2,000,000 | Office Workers, Home Address | Inquire |
| 60,000 | Officers, Men's Clubs | $35/M |
| 73,000 | Officers, Women's Clubs | $35/M |
| 115,000 | Offices, Government, All Levels | Inquire |
| 7,850 | Officials, Government, Top Federal | $35/M |
| 5,160 | Officials, Government, State | $35/M |
| 7,450 | Officials, Government, State Legislators | $35/M |
| 51,000 | Officials, Government, County | $35/M |
| 37,370 | Officials, Government, City | $35/M |
| 85,600 | Officials, Government, Top, All Levels | $35/M |
| 19,000 | Oil Burner & Furnace Dealers & Distributors | $35/M |
| 17,400 | Oil (Fuel) Dealers | $35/M |
| 52,000 | Oil Industry Executives | $35/M |
| 15,500 | Oil (Petroleum) Bulk Stations | $35/M |
| 18,000 | Oil (Petroleum) Wholesalers | $35/M |
| 8,100 | Oil (Petroleum) Producers & Refiners | $35/M |
| 935 | Oil Pipeline Companies | $75 |
| 3,650 | Oilwell Drilling Contractors | $35/M |
| 6,200 | Oilwell Supply Companies | $35/M |
| 135 | Opera Companies | $75 |
| 300,000 | Opinion Leaders | $35/M |
| 210,000 | Opportunity Seekers (Male/Female) | Inquire |
| 11,200 | Ophthalmologists | $35/M |
| 1,900 | Optical Equipment & Supplies, Wholesale | $75 |
| 13,400 | Opticians | $35/M |
| 27,400 | Optometrists | $35/M |
| 3,500 | Oral Surgeons | $35/M |
| 1,700 | Orchestras, Symphony | $75 |
| 400,000 | Organizations & Clubs | Inquire |
| 850 | Orphanages | $75 |
| 6,000 | Orthodontists | $35/M |
| 11,250 | Orthopedic Doctors | $35/M |
| 18,500 | Osteopaths | $35/M |
| 6,600 | Otolaryngologists | $35/M |
| 2,335 | Outboard Motors Dealers | $35/M |
| 2,500 | Outdoor Advertising Firms | $35/M |
| 203,000 | Owners, Aircraft | Inquire |
| 400,000 | Owners, Small Businesses | $35/M |

**P**

| QUANTITY | | PRICE |
|---|---|---|
| 6,200 | Packers & Canners, Food | $35/M |
| 1,500 | Packers, Meat | $75 |
| 7,100 | Packaging Industry Executives | $35/M |
| 1,500 | Paint Manufacturers | $75 |
| 7,900 | Paint Shops, Automobile | $35/M |
| 33,500 | Paint & Wallpaper Stores | $35/M |
| 6,600 | Painters & Sculptors | $35/M |
| 18,000 | Painting Contractors | $35/M |
| 6,850 | Painting Equipment & Supplies | $35/M |
| 20,500 | Paper Industry Executives | $35/M |
| 18,800 | Paper & Paper Goods, Wholesale | $35/M |
| 5,500 | Paper Products Mfrs | $35/M |
| 90,000 | Parent Teachers Associations (PTA's) | $35/M |
| 2,050 | Park Superintendents, City | $75 |
| 4,250 | Parking Lots & Garages | $35/M |
| 7,650 | Party Supplies | $35/M |
| 11,500 | Patent Attorneys | $35/M |
| 37,000 | Pathologists | $35/M |
| 7,900 | Pathologists (MD's) | $35/M |
| 21,000 | Patriotic Organizations | $35/M |
| 16,200 | Paving Contractors | $35/M |
| 4,000 | Pawnbrokers | $35/M |
| 22,500 | Pediatricians | $35/M |
| 1,950 | Pension Actuaries | $75 |
| 60,000 | Pension Fund Managers | $35/M |
| 2,500,000 | Pension Plan Holders (Individuals) | Inquire |
| 10,500 | Pension Plan Portfolio Managers, Financial Institutions | $35/M |
| 300,000 | Pension & Welfare Plans, Corporations & Unions | Inquire |
| 800 | Perfume, Cosmetic & Toiletries Mfrs. | $75 |
| 22,300 | Perfume & Cosmetic Shops | $35/M |
| 24,500 | Periodicals & Newspapers | $35/M |
| | Periodicals & Newspapers, Executives & Editors | $35/M |
| 2,300 | Periodontists | $35/M |
| 1,500,000 | Personal Computer Owners (Select by Model, Brand) | Inquire |
| 21,850 | Personal Loan Companies | $35/M |
| 1,500 | Personnel Administrators, Gov't. | $75 |
| 24,400 | Personnel (Employment) Agencies | $35/M |
| 70,400 | Personnel Executives | $35/M |
| 19,500 | Personnel Training Directors | $35/M |
| 14,600 | Pest Control (Exterminators) | $35/M |
| 15,000 | Pet Hospitals & Clinics | $35/M |
| 10,100 | Pet Shops | $35/M |
| 600 | Petrochemical Manufacturers | $75 |
| 38,600 | Petroleum Engineers | $35/M |
| 15,900 | Petroleum Geologists | $35/M |
| 52,000 | Petroleum Industry Executives | $35/M |
| 11,000 | Petroleum Bulk Stations | $35/M |
| 18,000 | Petroleum Wholesalers | $35/M |
| 1,700 | Petroleum Refiners | $75 |

**12**   **ALVIN B. ZELLER, INC.**   475 PARK AVENUE SOUTH, NEW YORK, NY 10016   (212) 689-4900 **TOLL FREE** (800) 223-0814 (OUTSIDE NEW YORK STATE)

**Figure 4-10.** While primarily used for direct-mail selling or solicitation, mailing lists can be useful in generating samples for marketing research. Cost per thousand varies according to list type, but is less than a nickel per name for many categories. (*Source:* From "1986 Catalog of Mailing Lists," brochure published by Alvin B. Zeller, Inc., New York, p. 12. Reprinted with permission.)

income and number of children, and demographic and psychographic variables. In the case of firms, the list can be tailored according to such variables as SIC code and company size. The Zeller lists include such diverse categories as 298,000 private aircraft pilots, 16,800 high school athletic directors, 55,000,000 homeowners, 325,000 hobbyists, 450,000 ham radio operators, and 12,250 zoology professors.[2] As shown in Figure 4-10, the cost per thousand for such lists varies according to group, but tends to be quite reasonable. The company also maintains *response* mailing lists based on past activities or behavior. These lists include such individuals as mail-order buyers, magazine subscribers, contributors to fund-raising programs, and seminar attendees.

Such lists can be especially useful if the target population happens to possess special characteristics (e.g., having a commercial multi-engine aircraft pilot license). However, as with Bureau of Census data, some persons may be deceased or may have moved from the address indicated for them—as a result, some information may be outdated. Although these lists can be useful in generating samples for marketing research studies, they continue to be utilized primarily for their value in selling and soliciting via direct mail.

☐  **SUMMARY**

Sampling, a frequent activity in our daily lives, is a technique that is central to the success of many marketing research investigations. Among the basic concepts in sampling are the population of interest, the sample itself, the population parameter being estimated, the sample estimate of this parameter, errors of sampling and nonsampling, and the accuracy and level of confidence that sample results provide.

Sampling error results from our having taken a sample instead of a complete census of the population. With the proper sampling approach, the likely amount of the error can be estimated mathematically and sampling error can be reduced by increasing the sample size.

Nonsampling error, or bias, is a tendency toward directional error that would exist even if we did take a complete census of the population. Because of the ever-present threat of nonsampling error, it is quite possible for a sample to be more accurate than a census. This is due to a combination of time and resource limitations, and the ability to statistically estimate the maximum error of a large, well-planned sample utilizing skilled fieldworkers.

Sample designs can be categorized as fixed versus sequential, probability versus nonprobability, and attributes versus variables. Fixed samples involve a predetermined sample size, and all sample data are collected before the information is analyzed. In sequential sampling, the number of units sampled depends on decision rules applied during the sampling process itself.

---

[2] "1986 Catalog of Mailing Lists," brochure published by Alvin B. Zeller, Inc., New York.

Nonprobability samples are most appropriate for exploratory research and for other circumstances in which statistical generalizations to the population are not deemed necessary. Convenience, purposive, quota, and judgment samples are of the nonprobability type.

Probability samples involve selection methods in which the members of the sample are chosen through some random process in which each member of the population has a known (or calcuable) chance of being included. The simple random sample, the systematic sample, and the stratified, cluster, area, and multistage samples are of the probability type. This kind of sample design is necessary if we are to statistically extrapolate our findings to the population and estimate the amount of sampling error likely to be present.

Sampling may also be categorized according to the type of population parameter we are trying to estimate. An attribute is a qualitative or descriptive characteristic that a population member does or does not possess, and a typical parameter is the population proportion. Variables sampling is concerned with the amount of a characteristic possessed by the population members, and the parameter of interest is usually the population mean.

## ☐ QUESTIONS FOR REVIEW

1. "A sample can be more accurate than a census." Since a sample includes only a fraction of those in the overall population, how could such a statement be true?

2. Briefly define the following terms: population, sample, parameter, estimate, accuracy, and confidence.

3. "Do you agree that big business should be forced to pay more taxes to help run our schools, hospitals, and other vital public services?" What influence might this question have on sampling error in a research study? On nonsampling error?

4. Differentiate between fixed and sequential sampling. In general, how is sequential sampling carried out?

5. What is the difference between the sampling of attributes and variables? If our goal is to measure annual household income, how might this be expressed as a variable? As an attribute?

6. What principal advantage does a probability sample have over one of the nonprobability type? Under what circumstances might one elect to use a nonprobability sample instead of a probability sample?

7. What is meant by "sampling frame," and why is this concept important? Provide a real or hypothetical example in which the sampling frame is not appropriate for the goal of the study.

8. What is the difference between a judgment sample and a convenience sample? Give a real or hypothetical example of each.

9. What is a purposive sample, and under what circumstances might a researcher wish to employ this approach? Give an example of such a circumstance.

10. A researcher wishes to use systematic sampling to interview shoppers leaving a gift shop. How would you advise the researcher to proceed?

11. What is meant by "periodicity," and how could this phenomenon detract from the representativeness of a systematic sample? If periodicity is present, how might we overcome its effects while still utilizing a systematic sample?

12. Both the quota sample and the stratified proportionate sample involve samples that are proportional to the population in terms of one or more variables. What is the key difference between these sampling strategies?

13. Under what circumstances might a researcher wish to use each of the following?
    a. A proportionate stratified sample.
    b. A disproportionate stratified sample.

14. The sample size is very small ($n = 20$) for a poll being conducted by a local radio station. In addition, it is felt that respondent age is an important factor in how individuals will respond to the question being asked. Why would the simple random sample probably not be a good choice for this study?

15. What is the difference between a compiled mailing list and a response list? Provide an example of each.

# 5

# SAMPLE-SIZE DETERMINATION

## Probability Sampling and Polling Error

In any survey it's unlikely that the sample finding will be exactly the same as the actual population value which the study aims to identify. However, with the use of a probability sample, the likely amount of this error can be statistically estimated.

In 1986, *The Wall Street Journal* and NBC News conducted a telephone survey of 1599 adults across the nation, measuring their reaction to the upcoming tax reform bill. The study employed a probability sampling plan that gave all telephone numbers, both listed and unlisted, a proportional chance of being included in the sample. In response to the question, "And in general, do you think major tax reform would help or hurt you personally?", 47% of the respondents said "Help."

Because the sample design was of the probability type, the likely amount of error between the 47% figure and the actual population value (i.e., the value that would result if *all* telephone numbers in the nation had been called) could be determined. This likely error was described as:

> Chances are 19 of 20 that if all households with telephones in the U.S. had been surveyed using the same questionnaire, the results would differ from the poll findings by no more than three percentage points in either direction.

*Source:* Based on Ellen Hume, "Tax Overhaul: Public Is Optimistic but Fears Losing Many Deductions," *The Wall Street Journal,* June 6, 1986, p. 23.

Thus there is a 95% probability that the true population value for the question above is 47% plus or minus 3 percentage points, or somewhere between 44 and 50%. This sample size, and the resultant maximum likely error, are typical of the many surveys undertaken daily by a wide variety of organizations and institutions in today's society.

## INTRODUCTION

When sampling, we should have a plan for determining how large a sample we should draw from the population to fulfill our research objectives. A popular misconception is that a sample must be large if it is to be representative of the population—that a sample of 2000 is, by definition, not as good as a sample of 2 million. However, as we observed in Chapter 4 when discussing the 1936 *Literary Digest* fiasco, a sample size of 2 million might not enlighten you at all with regard to the population parameter of interest, but will surely be successful in lightening your bank account.

Nonprobability samples do not lend themselves to the calculation of sampling error. Accordingly, the majority of the chapter does not apply to these types of samples. The emphasis here is on probability samples of the simple random type from which we can (1) estimate a population parameter based on sample data, and (2) use statistical methods to calculate our likely error, the difference between our sample estimate and the actual population parameter value.[1] We will begin by reviewing some basic, but important statistical concepts, then go on to discuss the idea of a sampling distribution of sample means and proportions followed by an examination of the confidence interval and its role in the sample-size determination process. Having gone through these preliminaries, we'll see how the actual sample-size determination formulas are developed. Finally, we'll examine the resulting formulas, along with several others that are appropriate for more specific situations, and discuss their application to the sample size decision. Our discussion will be according to the following topics:

    I. Basic statistical concepts

   II. The sampling distribution of a mean or proportion

---

[1] The discussion in the majority of this chapter assumes a simple random sample has been (or will be) taken. For most practical purposes (i.e., precluding either periodicity or an ascending or descending order of arrangement in the population), the discussion can be applied to the systematic sample as well. However, stratified, cluster, area, and multistage probability samples involve greater mathematical complexity because of standard deviation or variability considerations that must be taken into account for each stratum, cluster, area, or stage. While the sample-size decision is briefly discussed for stratified samples, the reader is advised to refer to a more advanced text when dealing with probability samples not of the simple random type. An excellent source is Leslie Kish, *Survey Sampling* (New York: John Wiley & Sons, Inc., 1965).

## BASIC STATISTICAL CONCEPTS

In this section we will review several statistical concepts basic to the sample size decision. These include the sample mean, the sample proportion, the standard deviation of a sample, and the normal distribution.[2]

### The Sample Mean

The sample mean, sometimes referred to as the arithmetic mean or arithmetic average, is simply the sum of the sample values observed divided by the total number of items in the sample. For example, given the following sales information:

|        |               |
|--------|---------------|
| Store A | $1.5 million |
| Store B | 2.0 million  |
| Store C | 1.0 million  |
| Store D | 2.5 million  |
| Total   | $7.0 million |

the sample mean is 7.0 million/4 = $1.75 million.

The sample mean $(\overline{X})$ is our estimate of the population mean $(\mu)$, and is computed whenever we are concerned with variables sampling involving dollar income, age, volume of purchases, sales, and similar population parameters.

### The Sample Proportion

The sample proportion describes the percentage (actually, the percentage divided by 100) of the sample who possess a given characteristic such as the ownership of a Craftsman lawn mower. For example, if we survey 100 persons and 65 recognize a picture of actor Jimmy Stewart, then our sample proportion $(P) = 0.65$, and is our estimate of the population proportion $\pi$. The sample proportion is appropriate in attributes sampling and is calculated by

$$P = \frac{\text{number in sample who possess the characteristic}}{\text{total number in sample}}$$

### The Standard Deviation of a Sample

The standard deviation of a set of data represents the variability of the sample data and is our estimate of the standard deviation of the population. The standard deviation is especially useful in the sampling procedure because of its

---

[2] Use of the normal distribution in this chapter assumes that the sample sizes with which we'll be dealing are relatively large, statistically speaking, or at least 30.

important role in allowing us to make use of the bell-shaped normal distribution. The formula for the calculation of the standard deviation ($s$) of a set of sample data is

$$s = \sqrt{\frac{\sum (X - \overline{X})^2}{n - 1}}$$

where

$X$ = each individual observation or measurement
$\overline{X}$ = sample mean
$n$ = sample size

As an example, if we have the following daily sales figures for a retail outlet:

| Day | Sales |
|-----|-------|
| 1 | $ 130 |
| 2 | 250 |
| 3 | 319 |
| 4 | 256 |
| 5 | 435 |
| 6 | 251 |
| 7 | 145 |
| 8 | 110 |
| 9 | 215 |
| 10 | 405 |
| Total | $2516 |

then the mean ($\overline{X}$) is calculated as

$$\overline{X} = \frac{2516}{10} = \$251.60$$

and the standard deviation ($s$) is

$$s = \sqrt{\frac{\sum (X - \overline{X})^2}{n - 1}}$$

$$= \sqrt{\frac{(130 - 251.60)^2 + (250 - 251.60)^2 + \cdots + (405 - 251.60)^2}{10 - 1}}$$

$$= \$110.19$$

## The Normal Distribution

The normal distribution is a standardized bell-shaped probability curve in which the areas under the curve represent the probability of an observation occurring within the limits of the area. The center point on the normal distribution is the mean, while distances from the mean are expressed in terms of standard deviations. Standard tables are available that describe the exact areas associated with various standard deviation distances from the mean. Such a table is presented in the statistical appendix at the end of this text. Figure 5-1 illustrates the shape of the curve and the areas that correspond to standard deviation multiples to the left and right of the mean. (Note that Z represents the number of standard deviations. Thus if the standard deviation is equal to 5, a distance of 10 would be $Z = 2$ standard deviation units.) The total area under the normal curve is 1.0, and as we get out past $Z = +3$, the area becomes extremely small. Useful reference values for use in statistical sampling are the following:

from $Z = -1$ to $Z = +1$, area $= 0.683$

from $Z = -2$ to $Z = +2$, area $= 0.954$

from $Z = -3$ to $Z = +3$, area $= 0.997$

Thus, approximately 68% of the observations will occur between $Z = -1$ and $Z = +1$, 95% between $Z = -2$ and $Z = +2$, and 99.7% between $Z = -3$ and $Z = +3$. The 95% interval is one that is often used in the determination of sample size and the subsequent analysis and projection of sample findings to the population. Because of the popularity of the 95% confidence level, it should be pointed out that this actually corresponds to the area from $Z = -1.96$ to $Z = +1.96$, but is rounded to 2 here for purposes of simplicity.

Table II in the statistical appendix provides the areas under the normal curve that correspond to various values of Z. Since the curve is symmetrical (one side is the mirror image of the other), the table provides only areas for one side. In using Table II, we look up the Z value in which we are interested, then refer to the table value to determine the area between the mean and that value of Z. For example, if we wish to find the area between the mean and the value $Z = 2.58$, we would first look down the first column to the $Z = 2.5$ value, then over to the 0.08 column, where we would find the area 0.4951. Thus, from the mean to $Z = +2.58$, the area is 0.4951, meaning that from $Z = -2.58$ to $Z = +2.58$, the total area on both sides of the mean is 2(0.4951), or about 99% of the total area under the curve.

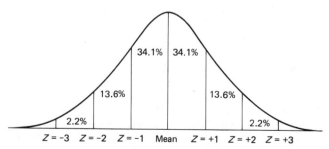

Z = number of standard deviations away from the mean

**Figure 5-1.** Approximate areas under the normal distribution curve.

## *THE SAMPLING DISTRIBUTION OF A MEAN OR PROPORTION*

If we were to take a number of simple random samples from the same population, we would end up with the same number of estimates for the population parameter that happens to be the object of our research. Thus 15 different samples from a population might yield as many as 15 different sample means or sample proportions. The larger our sample size, the more closely our sample means or proportions would cluster around the true value of the population parameter.

### Sampling Distribution for the Mean

The sampling distribution for the mean is the distribution of possible values of the sample mean, given the population mean and variability and the sample size. The sampling distribution of the mean for large (i.e., $n \geq 30$) samples will be normally distributed and may be described by the following[3]:

$$E(\overline{X}) = \mu$$

and

$$\sigma_{\overline{X}} = \frac{\sigma}{\sqrt{n}}$$

where

$E(\overline{X})$ = mean of the sample means
   $\mu$ = population mean
   $n$ = sample size
   $\sigma$ = standard deviation of the items in the population
   $\sigma_{\overline{X}}$ = standard deviation (standard error) of the sample means (when applied to the sample mean, we will use the term *standard error* instead of standard deviation)

For example, suppose that we have a population with a mean income of $15,000 and a standard deviation of $4000, as shown in the upper portion of Figure 5-2. If we were to take samples of size 100 from this population, the mean and standard error of our sampling distribution would be

$$E(\overline{X}) = \mu = \$15,000$$

and

$$\sigma_{\overline{X}} = \frac{\sigma}{\sqrt{n}} = \frac{4000}{\sqrt{100}} = \$400$$

---

[3] The discussion here is based on what is called the *central limit theorem*, which says that, for random samples of size $n$ from a population with mean ($\mu$) and standard deviation ($\sigma$), the sample means will tend to be normally distributed with a mean of $\overline{X} = \mu$ and $\sigma_{\overline{X}} = \sigma/\sqrt{n}$ and that the approximation to the normal distribution will be greater as $n$ increases.

as shown in the center distribution of Figure 5-2. In other words, as we repeatedly took samples of 100 from this population, our average sample mean would be $15,000 and the standard error of our sample means would be $400.

If we were to take larger samples, say $n = 400$, from this population, we would end up with a sampling distribution with the same expected value ($15,000), but with a smaller amount of variability; that is, the resulting standard error of the sample means would be just $4000/\sqrt{400}$, or $200. This tighter cluster around the population mean is shown in the lower part of Figure 5-2.

Based on our knowledge of the normal distribution, 95% of the sample means would be within 1.96 standard error units of the population mean. In other words, the probability is 95% that the mean of any given sample of size 400 will be within 1.96 ($200), or $392 of the population mean.

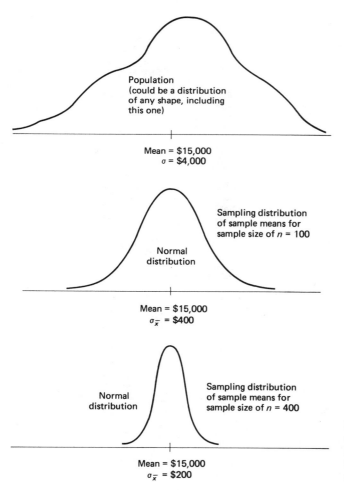

Population
(could be a distribution
of any shape, including
this one)

Mean = $15,000
$\sigma$ = $4,000

Sampling distribution
of sample means for
sample size of $n$ = 100

Normal
distribution

Mean = $15,000
$\sigma_{\bar{x}}$ = $400

Normal
distribution

Sampling distribution
of sample means for
sample size of $n$ = 400

Mean = $15,000
$\sigma_{\bar{x}}$ = $200

**Figure 5-2.**  Given any population, means of large random samples will be normally distributed. As $n$ increases, the standard error of the sample means will decrease.

## Sampling Distribution for the Proportion

The basic idea for the sampling distribution of a proportion is the same as that for the sample mean; that is, as larger samples are taken, the sample proportions will tend to have less variability and will tend to be closer to the actual population proportion. The sampling distribution of a proportion for random samples from the population will be a normal distribution described by

$$E(P) = \pi$$

and

$$\sigma_P = \sqrt{\frac{\pi(1 - \pi)}{n}}$$

where

$P$ = sample proportion
$\pi$ = population proportion
$n$ = sample size
$\sigma_P$ = standard error of the sample proportion

For example, if 40% of a certain population favor socialized medicine, and we were to take samples of 100 from this population, the sampling distribution

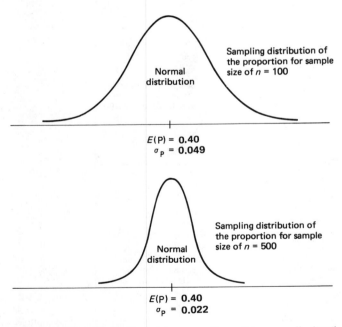

Normal distribution

Sampling distribution of the proportion for sample size of $n = 100$

$E(P) = 0.40$
$\sigma_P = 0.049$

Normal distribution

Sampling distribution of the proportion for sample size of $n = 500$

$E(P) = 0.40$
$\sigma_P = 0.022$

**Figure 5-3.**  Sampling distribution of the proportion will be normally distributed and will have a smaller standard error as $n$ increases.

would have

$$E(P) = \pi = 0.40$$

and

$$\sigma_P = \sqrt{\frac{0.40(1 - 0.40)}{100}} = 0.049$$

This distribution is illustrated in Figure 5-3, along with a comparison of the sampling distribution of the proportion if the sample sizes were 500 instead of 100. As with the sampling distribution of the mean, increasing the sample size will decrease the variability of the sampling distribution. If, in this example, the sample size of 100 were used, there would be a 95% probability that our sample proportion would be between $0.40 - 1.96(.049)$ and $0.40 + 1.96(0.049)$, or between 0.304 and 0.496.

## CONFIDENCE INTERVALS

The *confidence interval* is just a statistical way of expressing how close we think we've come to the actual population value we've tried to estimate. Although the term *confidence interval* may not appear in newspaper articles reporting Gallup, Roper, and other major polls, there is often a mention of the "likely error" or a warning that the sample result may be slightly different from the population value. If confidence intervals were stated in purely mathematical terms, they would appear in a form somewhat like this one:

> Based on our sample of 1500 U.S. adults, we are 95% sure that the proportion of the population who believe in flying saucers is somewhere between 0.28 and 0.32.

### Interval for the Mean—Large Samples

We would use the following method to estimate the interval for a population mean when our sample size is large (i.e., 30 or over):

1. Use the sample mean as the center of the interval.
2. Determine the confidence we'd like to have in the population mean actually falling into that interval, and choose the appropriate value of $Z$:

$$\text{for 90\% confidence, } Z = 1.65$$
$$\text{for 95\% confidence, } Z = 1.96$$
$$\text{for 99\% confidence, } Z = 2.58$$

If we'd like some other confidence level, we can use the normal distribution table and find the $Z$ that corresponds to this level. For example, if we'd like to be 99.4% sure that the population mean will be within our interval, the appropriate $Z$ value would be 2.75.

**3.** Construct the interval by substituting values into the formula

$$\text{Confidence interval} = \overline{X} \pm Z\frac{s}{\sqrt{n}}$$

where

$\overline{X}$ = sample mean
$Z$ = Z value that corresponds to the level of confidence we'd like to have
$s$ = standard deviation of the sample
$n$ = sample size

As an example of the preceding, let's assume that we've surveyed 1000 persons, and the average person in the sample spends $8.37 per week on entertainment, with the sample standard deviation equal to $5.25. If the desired confidence level is 95%, a typical figure, we could determine our confidence interval by calculating the following:

$$\text{Confidence interval} = 8.37 \pm 1.96\frac{5.25}{\sqrt{1000}}$$

$$= 8.37 \pm 0.33$$

or a confidence interval of $8.04 to $8.70. Thus we would be 95% sure that the population mean is somewhere between $8.04 and $8.70. In reporting our results, we might state that we are 95% sure of being within 33 cents of the actual population mean, or that our "probable error" is 33 cents or less.

**Interval for the Mean—Small Samples**

We would use the following method to estimate the interval for a population mean when our sample size is small (i.e., under 30):

**1.** Use the sample mean as the center of the interval.
**2.** Again, determine the confidence we'd like to have in the population mean actually falling into that interval. However, because of the small sample size, proper use of statistics requires that we use the so-called "student's *t* distribution" instead of the normal distribution. The appropriate value of *t* will depend on the sample size. First, we compute the value of "d.f.," or "degrees of freedom," by computing $(n - 1)$. Then we subtract our desired confidence level from 1.00 to determine the total tail area that will be left over. That is, if we'd like 95% confidence, we refer to the "0.05" column in the *t* table in the statistical appendix. Thus, if we have a sample size of 20, and would like 95% confidence, the appropriate *t* value would be 2.093.
**3.** Construct the interval by using the formula:

$$\text{Confidence interval} = \overline{X} \pm t\frac{s}{\sqrt{n}}$$

where everything is the same as with the larger sample size, except that now we're using $t$ instead of $Z$.

As an example of the preceding, assume that we've surveyed 15 households and found that their average telephone bill is $25 per month, with a standard deviation of $7.65. If we'd like to have 90% confidence that our interval will contain the real population mean, we'd use the $t$ distribution table with d.f. = $(15 - 1)$, and refer to the 0.10 (i.e., $1.00 - 0.90$) column. Our value of $t$ would be $t = 1.761$ and the confidence interval would be calculated as:

$$\text{Confidence interval} = 25.00 \pm 1.761 \frac{7.65}{\sqrt{15}}$$

$$= 25.00 \pm 3.48$$

or a confidence interval of $21.52–$28.48. Based on this result, we would be 90% sure that the population mean is somewhere between $21.52 and $28.48. Our reporting would be of the same format as with the larger sample size—the only difference is our use of the $t$ distribution instead of the normal ($Z$) distribution.

### Interval for the Proportion

We would use the following method to estimate the interval for a population proportion:

1. Use the sample proportion as the center of the interval.
2. Determine the amount of confidence we'd like to have that the interval will include the actual population proportion. Use the appropriate $Z$ value of the normal distribution:

$$\text{for 90\% confidence, } Z = 1.65$$

$$\text{for 95\% confidence, } Z = 1.96$$

$$\text{for 99\% confidence, } Z = 2.58$$

3. Construct the interval by using the formula

$$\text{Confidence interval} = P \pm Z \sqrt{\frac{P(1 - P)}{n}}$$

where

$P$ = sample proportion
$Z$ = Z value that corresponds to the desired level of confidence
$n$ = sample size

As an example of the construction of a confidence interval for a population proportion, assume that we've observed a random sample of 100 drivers passing a given point on the Pennsylvania Turnpike, and that 60% of them were wearing their three-point seat belts. If we'd like to have 95% confidence that our interval contains the actual proportion of drivers who wear their belts, we would have an interval described by

$$\text{confidence interval} = 0.60 \pm 1.96 \sqrt{\frac{0.60(1 - 0.60)}{100}}$$

$$= 0.60 \pm 0.096$$

or a confidence interval of 0.504 to 0.696. As a result, we would be 95% sure

**Figure 5-4.** In describing the results of public opinion polls, some researchers include confidence interval measures, others do not. If you know the poll result and the sample size, you can use the formula in the text and calculate the probable error for yourself.

that the percentage of the population who are wearing their seat belts is between 50.4 and 69.6, giving us an "error factor" of slightly less than 10 percentage points.

Published public opinion polls typically use sample sizes in the vicinity of 1000 to 1500, depending on how accurate the sponsors would like to be. For example, assuming a sample of 1250, and a sample proportion equal to 0.42, the 95% confidence interval would give us an error term of about 0.027 (or 2.7 percentage points). Like the viewer in Figure 5-4, you will probably notice such polls in newspapers and other media, and will see sample sizes and error terms that are in this general vicinity.

## DEVELOPING THE SAMPLE-SIZE FORMULAS

In deciding on the sample size, what we are actually doing is planning in advance the confidence interval we are seeking. Since the maximum likely error ($E$) is one-half the confidence interval, this interval is the basis from which our sample-size formulas are determined.

### Sample Size Required for Estimating the Population Mean

The formula for sample size when we are estimating a population mean is dependent on the expressions shown in Figure 5-5, which involve the following variables:

$\overline{X}$ = sample mean (unknown, but will be the center of our confidence interval)
$\sigma$ = known or estimated standard deviation of the population
$E$ = allowable error we are willing to accept
$Z$ = number of standard error units corresponding to desired level of confidence
$n$ = sample size (unknown, but we will determine this before the study is undertaken)

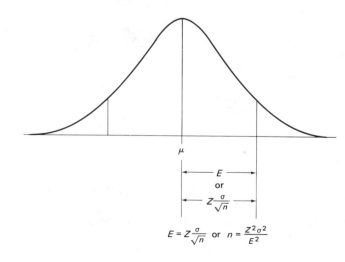

$$E = Z\frac{\sigma}{\sqrt{n}} \quad \text{or} \quad n = \frac{Z^2\sigma^2}{E^2}$$

**Figure 5-5.**   Confidence interval half-width (accuracy) represents two expressions shown. By setting them equal and solving for $n$, we may derive the formula presented in the chapter for determining sample size necessary to estimate the population mean.

As Figure 5-5 shows, we can construct a confidence interval for the population mean even though we don't yet know what sample size will be used. In the diagram, we can describe the half-width (or sampling error) of the confidence interval in two different ways: (1) as $E$, the maximum error we wish to accept; and (2) as $Z$ times the standard error of the sample mean. Since these two quantities represent the same distance on the scale beneath the curve, we can set them equal and solve for $n$, as follows:

$$E = Z\frac{\sigma}{\sqrt{n}} \quad \text{or} \quad E^2 = \frac{Z^2\sigma^2}{n}$$

and

$$n = \frac{Z^2\sigma^2}{E^2}$$

### Sample Size Required for Estimating the Population Proportion

The approach used in determining the sample-size formula when estimating the population proportion is similar in concept to that used for the mean. In this case, the key variables are:

$n$ = necessary sample size (unknown)
$Z$ = number of standard error units corresponding to desired level of confidence
$\pi$ = proportion of population who possess the characteristic of interest
$E$ = error, or maximum difference between sample proportion and population proportion that we are willing to accept

The distance between the population proportion (estimated by $P$, but we'll use $\pi$ in our calculation) and the upper confidence limit can be described in two different ways: (1) as $E$, the maximum error we will accept; and (2) as $Z$ times the standard error of the sample proportion. As with the sample mean situation, we set these quantities equal and solve for $n$:

$$E = Z\sqrt{\frac{\pi(1 - \pi)}{n}} \quad \text{or} \quad E^2 = \frac{Z^2(\pi)(1 - \pi)}{n}$$

and

$$n = \frac{Z^2(\pi)(1 - \pi)}{E^2}$$

## APPLYING THE SAMPLE-SIZE FORMULAS

In this section we'll see how the formulas we've just developed can be used in determining sample size. In addition, we'll examine several other formulas for more specific applications; these will include settings where the population is

---

**EXHIBIT 5-1**

*PR Puts This Census ahead of Sample*

When determining the required sample size for a research study, it's sometimes necessary that statistical considerations and sound research design take a back seat to other factors. In a project undertaken for a university client, a consultant was to survey the incoming freshman class to identify key factors in their college choice. For public relations reasons, administrators decided that every one of the 1400 freshmen was to receive a questionnaire. They were concerned that some students might feel alienated if their classmates got a questionnaire and they did not. The result was a sample size that was both excessively large and excessively expensive for its intended research purpose. However, the public relations purpose may have been achieved—a number of respondents indicated they were pleased about the university's being sufficiently interested in them to seek their opinions.

*Source*: Benjamin Sackmary, "Deciding Sample Size Is a Difficult Task," *Marketing News*, September 13, 1985, p. 30, published by the American Marketing Association.

---

considered to be finite and situations where we are using stratified sampling techniques.

## Sample Size When Estimating Population Mean

By anticipating the confidence interval resulting from a particular sample mean and standard deviation, it is possible to apply the normal distribution toward determining in advance how large the interval will be and the degree of confidence we will have in it. What we are doing is, in effect, examining the construction of the eventual confidence interval *before* we have conducted the study and determined the sample mean and standard deviation.

The formula for the calculation of the necessary sample size for the estimation of the population mean is

$$n = \frac{Z^2 \sigma^2}{E^2}$$

where

$n$ = necessary sample size
$Z$ = number of standard error units in the normal distribution that will produce the desired level of confidence (note that for 95% confidence, $Z = 1.96$; for 99% confidence, $Z = 2.58$)
$\sigma$ = population standard deviation (either known or estimated based on previous studies)
$E$ = error, or maximum difference between sample mean and population mean that we are willing to accept for the confidence level we've indicated

For example, let's assume that we are interested in determining the average yearly recreation expenditure of a certain population, and that we estimate (based on previous studies) that the standard deviation for the population is approximately \$300. In addition, we would like to be 95% sure that our sample mean is within \$50 of the true population mean. In this case, $Z = 1.96$, $\sigma = \$300$, $E = \$50$, and we would apply the preceding formula as follows:

$$n = \frac{(1.96)^2(300)^2}{(50)^2} = 139 \text{ persons to be included in the sample}$$

The greatest difficulty in determining the sample size necessary for estimating the population mean is in the estimation of the population standard deviation. After all, if we had complete knowledge about the population, there would be no need for us to conduct any research concerning its parameters. If we cannot rely on former studies to estimate the population standard deviation, alternatives include either judgment or the use of exploratory studies with small samples to help us gain some knowledge of its value.

If we wish, we can approach this same type of problem from the standpoint of *relative allowable error*, instead of absolute. In this case, the standard deviation ($\sigma$) and the allowable error ($E$) are expressed in terms of their percentage of the true population mean ($\mu$). The appropriate equation in this case is similar to that just presented, and would be

$$n = \frac{Z^2(\sigma \text{ as a } \% \text{ of population mean})^2}{(E \text{ as a } \% \text{ of population mean})^2} = \frac{Z^2 \left( \dfrac{\sigma}{\mu} \times 100 \right)^2}{\left( \dfrac{E}{\mu} \times 100 \right)^2}$$

where $\mu$ = population mean, the value of which doesn't matter here because it is cancelled out by appearing in both numerator and denominator of the equation.

For example, suppose that we wish to determine how much the average student at Finehower University earns upon graduation from the school's MBA program. Further, assume that we roughly estimate that the standard deviation of the population is about 40% of the population mean and that we want to be 95% sure that our sample mean is within 10% of the population mean. We could apply the preceding equation to these requirements and obtain the necessary sample size:

$$n = \frac{(1.96)^2(40)^2}{(10)^2} = 62 \text{ graduates to be surveyed}$$

Therefore, if we were to survey 62 graduates of Finehower's MBA program, we would be 95% certain that our sample mean would be within 10% of the actual mean starting salary for the population of MBA graduates from this fine school.

## Sample Size When Estimating Population Proportion

Determining the necessary sample size in this case is similar in concept to the procedure we followed in the preceding section, except that here we are dealing with a proportion instead of a mean. The appropriate formula is

$$n = \frac{Z^2 \pi (1 - \pi)}{E^2}$$

where

$n$ = necessary sample size

$Z$ = number of standard error units in the normal distribution that will produce the desired level of confidence (for 95% confidence, $Z = 1.96$; for 99% confidence, $Z = 2.58$)

$\pi$ = proportion of population who possess the characteristic of interest (if you can estimate the proportion, do so and use your estimate as $\pi$; if not, be conservative and use $\pi = 0.5$ in the formula)

$E$ = error, or maximum difference between sample proportion and population proportion that we are willing to accept for the confidence level we've indicated

In applying this formula, we should first determine if we can roughly estimate the value of the population proportion, $\pi$. If we can confidently say that $\pi$ differs very much from 0.5 in either direction, we will be able to obtain our desired accuracy with a smaller (and less expensive) sample size. As the formula illustrates, the sample size will be proportional to the product of $\pi(1 - \pi)$, and this product is the greatest whenever $\pi = 0.5$. Note the following products of $\pi(1 - \pi)$:

| $\pi$ | $(1 - \pi)$ | $\pi(1 - \pi)$ |
|-------|-------------|----------------|
| 0.5 | 0.5 | 0.25 |
| 0.4 | 0.6 | 0.24 |
| 0.3 | 0.7 | 0.21 |
| 0.2 | 0.8 | 0.16 |
| 0.1 | 0.9 | 0.09 |

As you can see, the product gets a lot smaller whenever a population proportion is either very small (e.g., the proportion of U.S. teenagers who have Abner Doubleday as their favorite sports personality) or very large (e.g., the proportion of U.S. households who drink milk). Thus, if we can at least narrow down the likely value of the population proportion, we can save money by being able to use a smaller sample size. The procedure is summarized in Figure 5-6.

As an example, assume that we wish to determine the proportion of the U.S. population who believe that UFOs (unidentified flying objects) are real, and that we wish to be 95% sure that our sample proportion is within 3 percentage points of the population proportion. Following the flow diagram of Figure 5-6, we first consider whether the true proportion is likely to be much greater or less than 0.5. We know little about how the public feels about this

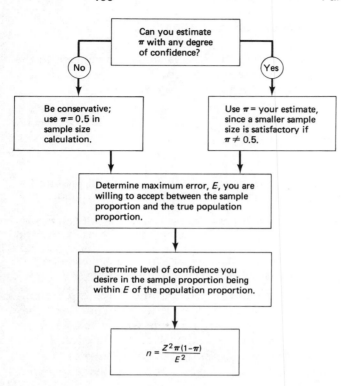

**Figure 5-6.** Procedure for determining necessary sample size when estimating a population proportion.

topic, so we remain conservative and use $\pi = 0.5$ in our formula:

$$n = \frac{(1.96)^2(0.5)(0.5)}{(0.03)^2} = 1068$$

Our sample would thus consist of 1068 persons (actually, 1067.1 rounded up to 1068 to ensure the accuracy we desire at the 95% level). Using Table 5-1, we could also have determined the sample size required, but without the necessity of calculations. As Table 5-1 indicates, we can save a lot on our sample

**TABLE 5-1.** *Sample sizes required for 95% confidence level, given allowable error (E) and value of population parameter (π).*

| | | $\pi$ = Population proportion | | | | | | | | |
|---|---|---|---|---|---|---|---|---|---|---|
| | | *0.1* | *0.2* | *0.3* | *0.4* | *0.5* | *0.6* | *0.7* | *0.8* | *0.9* |
| | *0.01* | 3457 | 6147 | 8067 | 9220 | 9604 | 9220 | 8067 | 6147 | 3457 |
| *E = maximum* | *0.02* | 865 | 1537 | 2017 | 2305 | 2401 | 2305 | 2017 | 1537 | 865 |
| *error allowable* | *0.03* | 385 | 683 | 897 | 1025 | 1068 | 1025 | 897 | 683 | 385 |
| *for 95%* | *0.04* | 217 | 385 | 505 | 577 | 601 | 577 | 505 | 385 | 217 |
| *confidence* | *0.05* | 139 | 246 | 323 | 369 | 385 | 369 | 323 | 246 | 139 |
| | *0.10* | 35 | 62 | 81 | 93 | 97 | 93 | 81 | 62 | 35 |

size if we are able to narrow down the probable range in which the true proportion lies. For example, if we had been attempting to measure the proportion
of U.S. housewives who hold the black belt in karate, we could have assumed
a proportion of 0.10 or less and used a sample size of only 385. In our UFO
example, however, we would not be justified in venturing to assert that the
proportion is different from 0.5.

If we are attempting to measure the value of a population proportion, but
have little idea regarding our likely results, we may wish to take an exploratory
survey for the purpose of getting a rough idea of what the true proportion is.
If the resulting proportion is very much different from 0.5, we can plan for a
smaller sample size in the principal phase of the study. In Table 5-1, note how
drastically the required sample sizes decrease as the population proportion deviates from 0.5. If the true proportion for which we're looking is less than 0.10,
we may be sampling more than three times as many persons as we would need—
note the 9604 ($n$ for $\pi = 0.5$) versus the 3457 ($n$ for $\pi = 0.1$) in the first row of
the table.

## Sampling When the Population Is Finite

So far, we have assumed that our sample will be relatively small compared to
the total population. Our sample size would be the same whether the population
consisted of 50,000, 100,000, or even 240 million members. This situation is
typical of most research studies involving sampling, and there generally is no
cause to be concerned about the size of the population.

However, there may be instances where the sample is 5% or more of the
population, in which case we must change the procedure slightly. After all, if
we sample 900 persons out of a population of 1000, we should have a pretty
fair idea of the population mean or proportion. In other words, as the sample
size ($n$) approaches the size of the population ($N$), sampling error disappears
and we eventually have a complete census of the population. The 5% cutoff
point is just a rule of thumb, but is sufficient for most practical purposes. If in
doubt, assume that the population is finite and apply the correction formulas
that follow.

### *Sample Size When Estimating Mean of a Finite Population*

$$n = \frac{\sigma^2}{\dfrac{E^2}{Z^2} + \dfrac{\sigma^2}{N}}$$

where other terms are as described earlier, and $N$ = population size.

For example, in the recreation expenditures problem we discussed earlier,
suppose that the population involved consisted of just 2000 persons. Applying
the preceding finite population formula, we obtain

$$n = \frac{(300)^2}{\dfrac{(50)^2}{(1.96)^2} + \dfrac{(300)^2}{2000}} = 130 \text{ persons to be included in the sample}$$

Note that this decrease in population size from "very large" to 2000 caused our required sample size to decrease very slightly, from 139 to 130 persons. Were the population of size 200, a sample of only 82 would have been required for the confidence level and accuracy that we were seeking.

### Sample Size When Estimating Proportion of a Finite Population

$$n = \frac{\pi(1 - \pi)}{\dfrac{E^2}{Z^2} + \dfrac{\pi(1 - \pi)}{N}}$$

where other terms are as described earlier, and $N$ = population size.

For example, in the UFO belief survey we examined earlier, suppose that the population, instead of being very large, consisted of only 2000 persons. Using our previous formula, we would have sampled 1068 people, or nearly half the population. Applying the finite population formula just presented, we would obtain

$$n = \frac{(0.5)(1 - 0.5)}{\dfrac{(0.03)^2}{(1.96)^2} + \dfrac{(0.5)(1 - 0.5)}{2000}} = 696 \text{ persons to be included in the sample}$$

The decrease from a large population to one of only 2000 caused our required sample size to decrease from 1068 to 696. Had we been studying a population of just 500 persons, the required sample size would have dropped still further, to 341.

## Sample Size for Stratified Sampling

Up to this point, we have been concerned with determining the required size of a simple random sample taken from the population. However, when employing the stratified sampling technique, the decision must be made regarding how many sample units to include from each stratum. Depending upon whether the stratification is proportionate or disproportionate, the answer to this question will be different. Remember that the reason for disproportionate sampling is to take advantage of situations in which some strata have less variability than others.

### Proportionate Stratified Sampling

In proportionate stratified sampling, the strata are represented equally in both the total sample and the population. As with quota sampling, if a certain stratum constitutes 20% of the population, it will make up 20% of the total sample.

### Disproportionate Stratified Sampling

In disproportionate stratified sampling, we can obtain the smallest possible sampling error by applying the following formula for optimal allocation of the total sample size:

$$n_A = \frac{nN_A\sigma_A}{(N_A\sigma_A + N_B\sigma_B + N_C\sigma_C + \cdots)}$$

where

$n_A$ = optimum sample size to take from stratum A
$n$ = total sample size
$N_A$ = number of items in stratum A
$\sigma_A$ = standard deviation of items in stratum A
$N_B$ = number of items in stratum B
$\sigma_B$ = standard deviation of items in stratum B

For example, suppose that we are interested in determining how much the average homeowner in a certain town spends on home maintenance each year, and that we have broken the population down into three strata, each with an estimate of the variability within the stratum:

|  | **Number of items in stratum** | **Standard deviation of stratum items** |
|---|---|---|
| Stratum A | 5000 persons | $20 |
| Stratum B | 3000 persons | 50 |
| Stratum C | 2000 persons | 80 |

If we should decide to sample 200 persons from this total population of 10,000, we may apply the formula for optimal allocation of the total sample size as follows:

number to be sampled from stratum A

$$= \frac{200(5000)(20)}{(5000 \times 20) + (3000 \times 50) + (2000 \times 80)} \cong 49$$

number to be sampled from stratum B

$$= \frac{200(3000)(50)}{(5000 \times 20) + (3000 \times 50) + (2000 \times 80)} \cong 73$$

number to be sampled from stratum C

$$= \frac{200(2000)(80)}{(5000 \times 20) + (3000 \times 50) + (2000 \times 80)} \cong 78$$

Total sample = 200

Note that stratum A, though 50% of the town's population, constitutes only about 25% (49 persons) of the total sample. This is because stratum A had the least amount of internal variation, and therefore did not require as large a subsample in order to estimate its mean. On the other hand, stratum C, though only 20% of the population, comprises 39% of the sample, in this case because of its very high variability compared to the other strata.

## DETERMINING THE SIZE OF NONPROBABILITY SAMPLES

With the exception of the preceding discussion of stratified sampling, this chapter has assumed that we're using a simple random sample and that we have specified a maximum error regarding likely differences between our sample mean or proportion and the actual value of the population parameter under investigation. However, when we're using a nonprobability sampling technique, such formulas are not applicable. For this reason, sample-size determination when using nonprobability approaches requires a slightly different set of strategies.

One way to approach the sample-size decision under these conditions is to determine how large a sample we can afford. (*Note:* As a practical matter, this can prove to be a constraining factor for probability samples as well.) In taking the *affordability* approach to the selection of a sample size, it may be necessary to take into consideration not only the available budget for the project, but also estimates for the costs of other required activities (e.g., postage, telephone, hiring of field workers, data collection forms and duplicating, travel, and data analysis).

Other possibilities include using a sample size about the same as past studies on the same topic. This approach assumes that the other studies have been suitable for their intended purpose. If our sample is of the quota type, we may plan our overall sample size so that a minimum number of individuals are included in each cell; for example, we might specify that no cell be smaller than 100 persons. Finally, we can use one of the formulas in the preceding section to see how large the sample would have to be *if* it were a simple random sample instead of a nonprobability sample. The resulting calculation should serve as no more than a guide, since the nonprobability sample is not suitable for making statistical generalizations about the population from which it is drawn. Although these strategies may seem rather arbitrary, keep in mind that nonprobability sampling is most likely to be employed in exploratory research, where sample size and statistical generalization to the population tend not to be major considerations.

## ☐ SUMMARY

When sampling, it is important to have a plan for determining how large a sample is necessary to fulfill research objectives. The larger the probability sample, the closer the sample estimate will be to the actual value of the population parameter. In addition, the probability sample makes it possible to use statistical methods to calculate the maximum likely error between the sample estimate and the parameter's actual value.

Nonprobability samples do not facilitate closer estimates for larger sample sizes, and they do not lend themselves to the calculation of likely sampling error. Sample-size determination for simple random samples is the primary focus of the chapter.

Development of sample-size formulas for estimating the population mean or proportion relies heavily on the concepts of (1) the sampling distribution of the sample mean or proportion, and (2) the confidence interval describing the range of values likely to contain the population parameter. Application of sample-size-determination formulas for simple random samples includes specification of the maximum desired error ($E$) between the sample estimate and the population parameter value and selection of the level of confidence we wish to have in this level of accuracy.

The necessary sample size will increase drastically as the desired error becomes smaller; for example, to cut error in half requires that the sample size be multiplied by 4. When the sample will be a substantial portion of the total population, the sample-size procedure is changed slightly. Application of the so-called "infinite" population assumption under these conditions would result in a sample size larger than that really needed for given levels of accuracy and confidence. For such situations, "finite population" sample-size determination formulas can be used.

The quantitative techniques in the chapter are not applicable to nonprobability sampling. For such samples there are a number of other ways to decide sample size, including affordability, the use of a sample size approximately the same as employed in successful comparable studies, and the use of simple random sample calculations to serve as a rough guide to the number selected. Nonprobability sampling is most likely to be employed in exploratory research, where sample size and statistical generalization to the population tend not to be major considerations.

## ☐ QUESTIONS FOR REVIEW

1. A systematic sample of passengers about to fly to Hawaii finds the following weights, in pounds, for the baggage of 10 persons: 40, 53, 41, 65, 80, 38, 59, 73, 95, and 78.
   a. Calculate the mean and standard deviation for this sample.
   b. What proportion of the passengers have baggage weighing 50 pounds or more?
2. In the normal distribution, what value of $Z$ is necessary for the area from $-Z$ to $+Z$ to be 0.80?
3. The average annual home heating bill for residences in a suburban section of town is $500, with a standard deviation of $225. If a simple random sample of 100 homes is selected, what is the probability that the resulting sample mean will be greater than $545?
4. In a recent year, 22% of the U.S. population visited an art museum or gallery at least once. What percent of simple random samples of $n = 100$ would have estimated the population proportion as 0.15 or more?

5. In a simple random sample of 900 persons, the average checking account balance is found to be $850, with a standard deviation of $415. What is the 95% confidence interval for the population mean?

6. A simple random sample of 600 persons includes 375 individuals who own a 10-speed bike. What is the 90% confidence interval for the proportion of people in this population who own a 10-speed bike?

7. A random survey of community members finds that 56% own a pet. The survey is claimed to have an error of no more than 5 percentage points. Assuming the 95% confidence level, what sample size was used?

8. We would like to determine, within 4 percentage points, the proportion of Americans who have eaten a Burger King Whopper within the past month. Assuming that a confidence level of 90% is satisfactory:
   a. Without making any assumptions about the true value of the population proportion, what sample size would be required?
   b. If we were to assume the true proportion to be no more than 0.30, by how many individuals would it be possible to reduce the sample compared to the total calculated in part a?

9. In Question 8, what would be your answers if the population consisted of students at a college with an enrollment of 1800?

10. In a study involving the estimation of a population proportion, your client has suddenly decided that he wants to be accurate to within 1 percentage point instead of the 3 percentage points originally agreed upon. To what extent will the required sample size increase?

11. In determining the necessary sample size for a study, a researcher used $\pi = 0.5$ as her estimate of $\pi$ for calculation purposes, then carried out the study and found a sample proportion of 0.37. She originally wanted to be within 3 percentage points of the true population value. Given her study outcome, will her probable error now be greater than or less than 3 percentage points? Why?

12. A research firm wishes to determine, within $200, the average total of credit purchases last year for MasterCard holders residing in the 07632 zip code area. Based on past experience, it is estimated that the standard deviation for this population is about $1600. Assuming a confidence level of 95%, what sample size is required?

13. In Question 12, what sample size would be necessary if the population consisted of the 1097 residents of Alpine County, California? Assume that other factors are unchanged.

14. A population consists of four strata: *A*, with 25,000 members and an estimated standard deviation of $1900 for automotive-related expenditures per year; *B*, with 45,000 members and an estimated standard deviation of $1200; *C*, with 2000 members and an estimated standard deviation of $7500; and *D*, with 50,000 members and an estimated standard deviation of $2500. For a disproportionate stratified sample of 1000, how many persons would be sampled from each stratum?

15. In conducting a study involving nonprobability sampling, how would one go about deciding how large the sample should be?

# 6

# CONCEPTS OF MEASUREMENT

**Drivers Compliant on Questionnaires, Scofflaws on the Road**

Following a two-year study that ended in 1984, the Transportation Research Board of the National Research Council recommended continuation of the 55-mph national speed limit in existence at the time. Measuring support for and compliance with the national speed limit had been the focus of several types of investigations.

According to survey research, the population as a whole strongly favored continuing the 55-mph limit, by a margin of 3 to 1. While high-mileage drivers (30,000 or more miles per year) were a little less enthusiastic, even they were said to favor the limit, by a margin of 2 to 1.

Authorities credited the limit with saving 2000 to 4000 lives, $2 billion of imported oil, and $65 million of medical and welfare payments each year. The average driver had to spend an extra seven hours per year in his car, but the societal benefits were judged to be well worth this small investment of time.

In observational studies using measurement devices such as traffic radar, compliance was found to be less than desirable. On highways posted with the 55-mph limit, the average speed was a whopping 59.1 mph. Since

*Source:* Geoff Sundstrom, "Speed Limit Retention Is Favored," *Automotive News*, December 3, 1984, p. 6.

**Figure 6-1.**   Ten years after its enactment, the 55-mph national speed limit received varying levels of support from different types of studies. Drivers tended to behave quite differently when responding to a questionnaire than when "voting with their feet." (Photo courtesy of Jim Wakefield.)

this was only an average, about half the drivers measured were going even faster than 59.1 mph.

The inconsistencies between the measurements described here is evident to any of us who spent much time on interstate highways when "55" was the national speed limit. In this setting we personally (and dangerously) observed that drivers seemed to vote much differently with their feet than when responding to questionnaires. The moral of the story: What is measured depends at least partly on how it is measured.

## INTRODUCTION

When presented with the word *measurement*, many tend to conjure up visions of such things as the latest reading on their bathroom scale, the height of the Boston Celtics' center, or the number of miles their car gets to the gallon. While all of the preceding are examples of measurement, they tend to focus on a length, weight, or distance associated with physical objects. In marketing research, we are concerned not only with these kinds of measurements, but also with measures of attitude, behavior, and other marketing variables that the layperson does not generally identify in terms of numerical values. In general, for the purposes of marketing research, **measurement** may be defined as the *assignment of numbers to objects or phenomena according to predetermined rules*.

In this chapter, our purpose will be to examine the "basics" of the measurement process in order to provide a foundation for later chapters that deal with the construction and application of specific instruments for the measurement of marketing variables. In our later discussion of the various techniques for the measurement of attitudes, we will adopt the more appropriate and specialized term, *scaling*, when dealing with this particular type of measurement objective.

Both measurements and the means by which we obtain them are vital to marketing research, and the way in which we choose to measure will often have an effect on the accuracy with which we are able to make our measurements. In Chapter 5 we examined how sampling error can affect our measurement effort when we are attempting to estimate a population parameter based on sample information. As we will see, there are other sources of error in the measurement process—just as clocks, fuel gauges, rulers, and circus knife throwers aren't perfect, neither are the measurement procedures we use in marketing research. However, with an awareness of possible sources of error, and a commitment toward minimizing their collective effect, we can provide marketing management with dependable and useful information to improve the quality of their decisions. In this chapter, our discussion of measurement and the measurement process will focus on the following topics:

   I. Marketing variables and concepts
  II. Scales of measurement
 III. Components of measurements
 IV. Validity and reliability concepts
  V. Validity assessment
 VI. Reliability assessment

## MARKETING VARIABLES AND CONCEPTS

### Types of Variables

As the goal of our measurement efforts, we will generally have one or more of the following kinds of variables in our research sights:

1. *State-of-mind variables:* Variables that are internal to the individual being studied, and hence difficult both to measure and to verify in terms of whether or not the subject is really telling the truth. Attitudes, personality characteristics, levels of product awareness, and product preferences are among the many variables that fall into this category.

2. *State-of-being variables:* Variables that are external to the individual and eas-

ier both to measure and to verify. Age, income level, product ownership, sex, and educational level are examples of this type of variable, which is probably the most common object of marketing research studies.

3. *Behavioral variables:* Variables that are concerned with *action*—past, present, or future—rather than a temporary state. Intentions are especially important in this category, because they relate to probable future courses of action by the consumer. Naturally, of these possible future courses of action, the purchase of our product is the one in which we're most highly interested. Behavioral variables are sometimes measured mechanically. Figure 6-2 shows a typical eye-movement pattern during the viewing of a TV commercial.

To the extent that we can identify and determine relationships among these three kinds of variables, our marketing research efforts will be increasingly fruitful. For example, if we are able to find out that persons of a certain income and educational level (state of being) have a positive attitude toward a certain activity or celebrity (state of mind), we can use this knowledge to help design our advertising and promotional efforts to help increase the likelihood that they will

**Figure 6-2.** Eye movement while viewing a TV commercial is an important and informative behavioral variable that can be measured by a special device called the eye camera. Shown is a typical viewing pattern for a consumer watching an advertisement. (*Source:* Courtesy of Applied Science Group, Inc.)

become customers (future behavior) of our firm's products. In Pittsburgh, the utilization of former all-pro Steeler linebacker Andy Russell as a spokesman for United Way promotional campaigns is an example of using information about the potential donor's state of mind to help bring about a desired behavior in the form of monetary contributions.

## Concepts

A *concept*, or *construct* (since, for practical purposes, the terms are interchangeable) is a symbol that we attach to some aspect of reality. Concepts are often expressed as word labels, and they are fundamental to thinking about and examining marketing questions that can be answered by research. In their role of representing reality, concepts are necessarily abstract. However, some concepts are more abstract than others—for example, the word *attitude* is more abstract than the word *Chevrolet*, although even the latter may have different meanings to different observers.

To the General Motors stockholder, *Chevrolet* may represent a division of the corporation; to production employees, it may be a physical collection of labor and parts from which they derive their income; to customers, it may be a source of pride and prestige or merely a means of personal transportation; to dealers, it may be just another commercial object to be stocked, sold, and serviced. Thus a concept may have vastly different meanings which depend on the perspective of the observer.

In marketing research, we frequently are concerned with concepts such as *brand loyalty, attitude, market segmentation, product positioning*, and *social class*. Compared to relatively clear concepts such as *dog* and *book*, those with which we must deal in marketing research are often more abstract and difficult to define in a physical sense such that there will be little disagreement as to exactly what is meant by the term. At the risk of sounding like an ancient philosopher (one of whom undoubtedly made such a statement at one time or another), we could say, "Nothing is what it is, but only what people 'think' it is." In these times of mass media, of distance between people and their leaders and idols, and the practical necessity of our formation of perceptions from electronic and printed media, such a statement is especially applicable to attitudes, product images, and modern consumer behavior in the economic, political, and entertainment marketplaces.

As we've discussed, it is not easy to define a concept in such a way that it can be the subject of an objective research effort. Much of the reason for this is that concepts are generally (as in the dictionary) defined *in terms of other concepts*. This circular reasoning may be useful when compiling a dictionary, but falls short when we wish to investigate the relationship between such variables as *brand awareness* and *social class*. For example, does brand awareness refer to whether or not the consumer has ever heard of a particular brand? Is the person who knows some of the particular features of the brand to be considered more "aware" than someone who does not? Does brand awareness mean that the respondent simply answers affirmatively when asked if she has ever heard of the brand, or must the respondent mention the brand on her own when asked about the product type? In the case of social class, on what basis do we categorize individuals into the various classes—from their own opinion of the class in which they belong; based on their occupation, income, and education; by means of identifying the clubs, associations, and activities in which they take part; or by relying on subjective categorizations provided by friends and associates?

For the purpose of marketing research, it is important that we be able to consistently define the concepts that we are attempting to measure. For example, if we are conducting periodic studies to determine consumers' awareness of IVY brand panty hose, we could run into severe measurement problems if, in January, we categorize consumers as "aware" only if they can mention the brand name without cue, then in February, we categorize them as aware only if they know that the brand is especially designed so that it doesn't itch. For purposes of comparison, such measurements would be akin to saying something like "The average adult male is bigger than he used to be—in 1950, he was 5'8"; today he's 165 lb." Just as we can't equate height with weight, we also cannot equate awareness of a brand's existence with knowledge of its particular attributes. For the objectivity that good marketing research requires, we must define concepts in such a way that the definition is not only practical in terms of measurement, but consistent in terms of avoiding disagreement over its meaning.

---

### EXHIBIT 6-1

#### Definitions Pave Way for Lemon Owner Aid

Operational definitions help determine whether a toothpaste gets the American Dental Association's Seal of Acceptance and if an automobile is officially a "lemon."

The American Dental Association puts some teeth into its Seal of Acceptance by defining a plaque-fighting toothpaste as one that contains "antibacterial agents, agents that affect (tooth) surface or enzymes that affect plaque metabolism." Products relying on abrasive qualities to prevent plaque buildup need not apply.[1]

An automobile might be defined as a lemon based on the simple criterion that its owner *thinks* it is a lemon. However, this circular definition isn't good enough for the legal process, in which 40 states now have a so-called "lemon law" to protect car buyers. Such laws can require the manufacturer to provide the owner with a new car or to refund the vehicle's purchase price. In most cases, "lemon" refers to a car that has been in the shop four or more times for the same problem, or out of service for over 30 days during the first 12 months or 12,000 miles after purchase.[2]

[1] Laurie Freeman, "Plaque Fighters Cool Pursuit of ADA Seal," *Advertising Age*, January 20, 1986, p. 36.

[2] Bridgett Davis, "Car Buyers Discover 'Lemon Laws' Often Fail to Prevent Court Trip," *The Wall Street Journal*, October 21, 1986, p. 35.

## Operational Definitions

Whereas the conceptual definition of a concept describes it in terms of other concepts (e.g., *customer* is someone who buys products from our company), the *operational definition* translates it into terms that are both precise and measurable—for example, *customer* is someone who is listed in our warranty card records as having purchased one or more of our products within the past 12 months. While the exact form of the operational definition may be subject to the judgment of the researcher and the informational needs of the marketing manager, the definition should be consistent within any given research study.

For example, if we define *loyal customer* as one who, in a telephone survey,

**TABLE 6-1.** *Examples of concepts and possible operational definitions that could facilitate their use in a marketing research study.*

| Concept | Possible operational definition |
|---|---|
| Customer | Based on company warranty card records, any individual or group who has purchased one or more of our company's products within the past 12 months. |
| Ford Escort driver | Any individual observed to be driving a Ford Escort automobile past mile marker 207 in the east-bound lane of the Pennsylvania Turnpike between 12:00 noon and 4:00 P.M. next Tuesday afternoon. |
| Small sailboat | Sailboats manufactured in the United States that are less than 13'7" in length and have a manufacturer's suggested retail price of $900 or less. |
| Educational level | Highest level of formal education achieved: (a) grade school or less, (b) high school graduate, (c) some college, (d) graduate of four-year college, (e) graduate degree, or (f) postgraduate work beyond a graduate degree. |
| Exposure to point-of-sale display | Stopped and visually examined display for five seconds or more as determined by hidden observer with stopwatch. |
| Brand loyalty | Based on consumer panel data, number of consecutive months in which a reporting household purchased our brand one or more times. |
| Product awareness | When asked to mention five brands of beer, subject mentions our brand in a personal interview situation. |
| Product attitude | When asked to mention five brands of beer that taste good, subject mentions our brand in a personal interview situation. |

claims to have purchased our brand in two or more of the past three purchases, we should adhere to this definition throughout our study. In another study, we may wish to use a different operational definition of this concept—for example, someone who, in a personal interview, claims to have purchased our brand the last two times he made a purchase.

Because so many of the concepts we study in marketing research cannot be seen or felt, it is crucial that we be able to operationally define them for purposes of measurement and analysis. Even such an abstract concept as *attitude* can be operationally defined—for example, one possible operational definition of a customer's attitude toward *Time* magazine may be the numerical score that results from the administration of a specific Likert summated scale instrument (a useful technique which we'll cover in the next chapter.) While the actual number and types of stimuli in the measuring instrument are still subject to researcher judgment, at least they are a "constant," which contributes toward the completeness of this particular operational definition. Naturally, other versions of this and other attitude measuring instruments could have been specified; however, the important thing is that one particular instrument was designated as pertinent to this unique operational definition. Table 6-1 illustrates a variety of marketing concepts along with possible operational definitions that might be used in defining them for research purposes.

## SCALES OF MEASUREMENT

Once we have operationally defined a concept, the next step is usually to collect data that can be used to quantify it for purposes of mathematical expression and analysis. The form the data take will be one of four types: (1) nominal, (2) ordinal, (3) interval, or (4) ratio. Each of the preceding represents a different kind of number assignment rule, or "scale" of measurement. As we proceed from the weakest (nominal) to the strongest (ratio), two things happen: First, the numerical requirements for scale membership become more stringent; second, the permissible modes of data expression and analysis become more liberal (i.e., more types of statistical operations are permissible).

### Nominal Scale

The nominal scale is the most primitive of the four, and is so mathematically weak that some purists may feel that it isn't even a scale of measurement at all. In essence, the nominal scale simply consists of categories that are collectively exhaustive (every individual or object must belong to one of the categories) and mutually exclusive (the categories don't overlap). To the extent that numbers are assigned to individuals or phenomena, their purpose is merely to identify the category into which each individual or phenomenon will be classified. The numbers themselves have no mathematical value, as they might just as well be letters of the Greek alphabet or pictures of fruit. As the preceding suggests, numbers aren't even necessary in the nominal scale of measurement.

Examples of nominal scale numbers include social security numbers, license plate numbers, and the numerals on football jerseys. We've become somewhat used to the idea of football linemen having numbers in the fifties, sixties, and seventies; ends and wide receivers in the eighties; running backs in the twenties, thirties, and forties; and quarterbacks in the single digits and teens. Naturally, since the numbers are there only for identification purposes, they needn't be numbers at all. But imagine the confusion that would result if professional football players had pictures of apples, oranges, and other fruit on their jerseys instead of numbers.

Application of the nominal scale to marketing measurement is generally for the purpose of coding questionnaire responses in which the data collected place the respondent into a particular category. For example, to facilitate tabulation and computer analysis, owners of imported cars may be identified with the number "1," while those who own domestic automobiles may be coded with a "0." The numbers are used strictly for convenience, and there would be no justification for claiming that imported car owners are more important because they have a "1" code—it would have been just as easy to assign the code numbers so that domestic owners were "1's" and import owners were "0's." The numbers assigned simply make it possible for a computer—which doesn't recognize the Greek alphabet or pictures of fruit—to cross-tabulate and count the number of persons in each category.

Such frequency counts are the basic reason-for-being of nominal data. Further analysis of the identification numbers, such as the averaging of social security numbers or category codes, is beyond the scope of nominal data and is totally meaningless. As an example of the use of nominal data, consider the case of a tavern owner whose establishment is located next to a major university. Assuming that the owner wishes to determine if a relationship exists between (1) frequency of patronage and (2) membership in a social fraternity or sorority, he may wish to pose the following questions to a sampling of his customers:

---

1. How often do you usually patronize the Tipsy Tavern?
   ☐ Less than      ☐ Once or      ☐ Three or
   1  once a        2  twice a      3  more times
      week             week            a week
2. Do you belong to a social fraternity or sorority?
   ☐ Yes            ☐ No
   1                2

---

In the recording of question responses, if respondent number 1 patronizes the tavern three or more times per week, but does not belong to a social fraternity or sorority, her code data may begin with the digits "132," which have no numerical significance except to denote her identification and question responses.

While the numbers that represent group membership cannot be further analyzed, the actual frequencies observed for the various categories can be the object of further mathematical analysis. For example, the tavern owner may wish to summarize the information he has collected in a manner similar to that shown in Table 6-2. When such data are presented in a frequency-based format such as this, they may be statistically analyzed to determine the likelihood that some relationship does in fact exist between the frequency of patronage of the tavern and membership in a social fraternity or sorority. Such analysis will be one of the topics in a later chapter. At this point, it is important to remember that the frequencies shown are not nominal data, but rather represent the number of times that a particular nominal number was assigned to members of the sample. For example, in Table 6-2, the "80" in the third column indicates that the nominal number "3" was assigned 80 times for the variable "frequency of patronage."

## Ordinal Scale

The *ordinal* scale goes beyond the simple identification capabilities of the nominal scale, and allows the possibility of "greater than" and "less than" as additional descriptors of marketing phenomena. The numbers assigned to objects or concepts simply represent the order in which they are arranged. For example, a consumer may be asked to rank a number of recreational possibilities in the order in which he would prefer to participate in them. Such a ranking would involve the assignment of ordinal numbers according to the ranking that each of the alternatives has from the perspective of this particular individual. Another person may have an entirely different ranking for the activities, as illustrated by the following stimulus question and resultant rankings:

---

If you had the following choices for making use of your spare time on a Saturday afternoon, what would be your order of preference for the following activities? (Place a "1" next to the activity you would most prefer, a "2" next to your second choice, etc.)

---

*Rankings provided by two respondents*

| Brutus's ranking | Activity | Cecil's ranking |
|:---:|:---|:---:|
| 1 | Go for a walk with Emmy Lou | 5 |
| 2 | Vandalize parking meters | 9 |
| 3 | Go to the movies | 6 |
| 4 | Play basketball | 7 |
| 5 | Play tennis | 3 |
| 6 | Listen to records | 1 |
| 7 | Watch television | 4 |
| 8 | Read a novel | 2 |
| 9 | Go fishing | 8 |

TABLE 6-2. Example of frequency table resulting from collection of nominal data.

| | | Frequency of patronage | | | |
|---|---|---|---|---|---|
| | | (1) Less than once a week | (2) Once or twice a week | (3) Three or more times a week | Total |
| Membership | (1) Yes | 10 | 45 | 50 | 105 |
| in social | (2) No | 20 | 65 | 30 | 115 |
| fraternity | Total | 30 | 110 | 80 | 220 |
| or sorority | | | | | |

The numerical rankings provided by these two respondents are ordinal numbers that reflect their individual preferences for the activities listed. Based on these data, we conclude that Cecil would prefer watching television (4) to going to the movies (6), and that Brutus would prefer going for a walk with Emmy Lou (1) over any of the other activities.

Remember that ordinal numbers simply reflect "greater than" or "less than" relationships, and that we cannot infer anything beyond this. For example, Brutus's ranking for playing basketball (4) is lower than his ranking for going to the movies (3). However, we don't know whether this would be a close decision or an easy choice for Brutus, since the only information we have is that he prefers one over the other. Thus, we don't know whether Brutus's difference between playing basketball (4) and going to the movies (3) is the same as between playing basketball (4) and playing tennis (5). It would be a mistake to conclude that these two distances are the same just because $(4 - 3) = (5 - 4)$; rankings cannot be added, subtracted, or multiplied, since they only represent an ordering of the items. We can, however, use such measures of position as the median, which is for each person the activity that has just as many above it as below. For Brutus, the median activity is playing tennis (5), with four activities that are more preferred and four others that are lower in preference. For Cecil, the median is going for a walk with Emmy Lou (5). Note that we cannot infer that a "1" for Brutus is the same as a "1" for Cecil, since it may be possible that Brutus doesn't really care for any of the activities listed, while Cecil may be highly interested in all of them. Because of the structured nature of the list, we have omitted many of the wide variety of activities that could have been included—perhaps Brutus's favorite activity is collecting stamps.

The ordinal scale is a frequent source of marketing data, since consumers are often asked which of several competing brands they prefer, or how they would rank the brands in terms of quality, price, durability, attractiveness, or any other characteristic or combination of characteristics. For example, a consumer may be presented with a listing of products and asked to rank them in terms of which are the "best value for the money." However, ordinal numbers only indicate that one object possesses more or less of a characteristic than another object; the relationship is strictly directional in terms of listing the objects in decreasing or increasing order with regard to the basis on which they are being judged.

## Interval Scale

The *interval* scale of measurement is one step more powerful than the ordinal scale, and includes not only "greater than" and "less than," but the ability to determine *how much* more or less of a characteristic is present. Thus the interval scale makes use of a constant unit of measurement that allows us to describe the distances between the various measurements. However, this unit of measurement is arbitrary and the interval scale has no absolute zero point where *none* of the characteristic being measured is present.

The most common example of the interval scale is a nonmarketing application—the Fahrenheit and Celsius temperature scales. Both scales measure temperature in constant units (°F and °C, respectively), but each has a zero point that describes a different level of temperature—that is, 0°F corresponds to −17.8°C and 0°C corresponds to 32°F. (As you may recall from high school physics, the zero point on the Celsius scale is arbitrarily defined as the freezing point of water.) Both scales use constant units of measurement, but the degrees on the Fahrenheit scale are 5/9 as large as those on the Celsius scale with regard to describing differences between any two levels of temperature. Thus, from the freezing point to the boiling point of water, the Celsius scale goes from 0 to 100°C while the Fahrenheit scale goes from 32 to 212°F. In addition, because of the arbitrary zero point, multiples may not be expressed if they refer to absolute values—for example, it is not appropriate to say that 80°F is "twice as hot" as 40°F.

With regard to marketing, theoretically appropriate interval scales are a rarity. However, the use of measurements that are assumed to come from an interval scale is neither uncommon nor impractical in marketing research. For example, the questions posed in Figure 6-3 require the respondent to select

| *"The Volkswagen Jetta is . . .* | Strongly disagree | | Neutral | | | Strongly agree | |
|---|---|---|---|---|---|---|---|
| | −3 | −2 | −1 | 0 | +1 | +2 | +3 |
| 1. well engineered." | ☐ | ☐ | ☐ | ☐ | ☐ | ☐ | ☐ |
| 2. too expensive for its size." | ☐ | ☐ | ☐ | ☐ | ☐ | ☐ | ☐ |
| 3. a lot of fun to drive." | ☐ | ☐ | ☐ | ☐ | ☐ | ☐ | ☐ |
| 4. good for taking long trips." | ☐ | ☐ | ☐ | ☐ | ☐ | ☐ | ☐ |
| 5. not very safe to drive." | ☐ | ☐ | ☐ | ☐ | ☐ | ☐ | ☐ |
| 6. inexpensive to service." | ☐ | ☐ | ☐ | ☐ | ☐ | ☐ | ☐ |
| 7. very economical to drive." | ☐ | ☐ | ☐ | ☐ | ☐ | ☐ | ☐ |
| 8. good for commuting to work." | ☐ | ☐ | ☐ | ☐ | ☐ | ☐ | ☐ |

**Figure 6-3.** Example of question-response format that assumes approximately equal intervals between possible responses.

the block that best describes his or her attitude with regard to the Volkswagen Jetta. Because the possible responses are physically located at equal intervals on the questionnaire, they are assumed to represent equal intervals in terms of the measurement process. While such data are theoretically of the ordinal form, the assumption that they are approximately interval in nature makes possible the application of more powerful statistical techniques without excessive risk to scientific "purity."

The use or assumption of interval scale data allows the use of a broad range of statistical methods for the description and analysis of information collected. For example, such descriptive measures as the mean and standard deviation become appropriate for summarizing the data, while analysis of variance, correlation, and various multivariate techniques are available for analysis of research variables and the subsequent drawing of conclusions from the study. The various types of statistical analysis, and their applicability to the examination of marketing research data, are sufficiently important to be the subject of several later chapters in this text.

## Ratio Scale

As the "ultimate" scale of measurement, the *ratio* scale has both an absolute zero point and equal intervals of measurement. All of the statistical techniques just discussed for the interval scale apply to the ratio scale as well. Marketing research information that qualifies as ratio scale data would include such measures as age, income, price, and market share. Note that each of these items has a very definite zero point at which absolutely none of the characteristic is present. In addition, variables in the ratio scale can be viewed in terms of multiples. For example, a person earning $40,000 per year has twice the income of a person earning $20,000, and a 45% market share is three times a 15% market share. While the ratio scale is the top of the line of the scales of measurement, and is applicable to a number of marketing variables such as those just mentioned, it is a fact of life that most of our marketing research information will be in nominal, ordinal, or interval (generally by assumption) form.

## Measurement Scales and Techniques of Analysis

In general, data from a higher-level (i.e., closer to ratio) scale allow the use of more powerful methods of statistical analysis, which in turn allows a smaller and more economical sample size during the data collection phase of the research study. In addition, the use of such techniques permits the formation of more definitive conclusions and recommendations upon completion of the analysis of the data. Statistically, it isn't very efficient to collect data from a higher scale (e.g., interval or ratio) and then proceed to analyze them by means of a technique that has a lower scale (e.g., nominal or ordinal) as the limit of its applicability. To do so means that you are wasting valuable information that could be put to better use. For example, if you were to collect income information from various market segments, you might have the data in the form of dollars per year for each household. This information is in ratio scale form and suitable for expression in terms of means and standard deviations for various household groups. If you proceeded to take these raw data and simplify them into "high income" and "low income" categories, you would be descending to the nominal level of analysis and, in effect, discarding information that may have been expensive to collect at that level of detail. This is not to say that data should never be combined into a higher level of aggregation, but that you should anticipate, before collecting the data, the scale of measurement they will represent and the type of analysis to which they will be subjected.

While more detailed discussion of statistical techniques for marketing research is deferred until later in the book, it seems appropriate at this point to at least mention some of these techniques in the context of summarizing key

**TABLE 6-3.** *Summary of scales of measurement and applicable statistical techniques.*

| Scale | Marketing examples | Typical methods for: | |
|---|---|---|---|
| | | *Describing* | *Analyzing* |
| Nominal (identification or categorization) | Owns or does not own a Chevrolet<br>Male or female<br>Season ticket holder or non–season ticket holder for Los Angeles Rams | Frequency<br>Percentage<br>Mode<br>Cross-tabulation | Chi-square test |
| Ordinal (greater than or less than) | Prefers Michelob over Budweiser<br>"Compared to brand X, Peter Pan tastes more like real peanuts"<br>Has more positive attitude toward political candidate A than toward B | Median<br>Mode<br>Percentile | Rank-order correlation<br>Sign test<br>Nonmetric multidimensional scaling |
| Interval (greater than or less than, constant unit of measurement, but arbitrary zero point) | Selects "disagree slightly" alternative in equal-appearing interval instrument question for attitude measurement<br>Attitude toward socialized medicine is + 1.5 on a given Likert scale instrument | Mean<br>Standard deviation | Correlation analysis<br>Discriminant analysis<br>Analysis of variance<br>Metric multidimensional scaling |
| Ratio (all of the above plus an absolute zero point) | Age<br>Income<br>Pounds of detergent purchased each year | Same as interval | Same as interval |

characteristics, marketing examples, and appropriate methods of description and analysis for the four scales of measurement that we've just discussed. This summary is presented in Table 6-3.

## COMPONENTS OF MEASUREMENTS

In any effort we make to measure a marketing variable, our (generally unattainable) goal is to determine the exact numerical value of that particular variable. Such an ideal measurement would have no error of any kind, and would provide us with a "true" measure. However, in the unkind real world of the marketing researcher, the "true" value of what we are trying to measure is obscured by a variety of factors, many of which lie beyond our control. In general, we can describe the measured value as

$$\text{value measured} = \text{actual value} + \text{error}$$

Some of the error we experience will be systematic (resulting from a directional tendency, or bias), while the rest will be nonsystematic (resulting from random causes). In the preceding chapters, we described sampling error as a type of nonsystematic error that could, when a probability sample is used, be reduced through the use of a larger sample size. In this section, we will examine a number of possible sources of the error component of a measurement, including some that are random, but that are not necessarily reduced through the use of a larger sample size. (Remember that sampling error is *a type of* nonsystematic error.) For example, the attitude or mood of a respondent and the enthusiasm of an interviewer will vary from one day to the next, as will the circumstances in which they interact. Even cities or larger geographical units can have ups and downs, as evidenced by the effect of World Series championships, natural disasters, or other abnormal events on the collective state of mind of the populace. For these reasons, even if a complete census were taken, it would still be a sampling of how these individuals normally feel and behave, since another (hypothetical) census conducted the day before or the day after would probably yield different measurements.

To this extent, nonsystematic (random) error is representative of short-term variations in the measurement procedure or in the person being measured. However, unlike systematic error, there is no directional tendency—it is simply a lack of consistency in which the error has just as much chance of being positive as negative with regard to the characteristic under investigation.

When collecting data, we may experience or invite both systematic and nonsystematic error in many ways. For the purpose of discussion, we will break down the sources of error into the following components: (1) the respondent, (2) the measurement procedure, and (3) the situation in which the measurement is taken.

### The Respondent

The respondent, in addition to possessing the true measurement value we are seeking, may knowingly or unknowingly be a source of error with regard to our earnest attempts to measure this value. The respondent is a combination of stable and transitional characteristics that join to affect the response that he provides in the research situation. As a product of his past experiences and present environment, he will have a tendency to draw upon this relatively firm foundation for what could be a fair approximation of the true value for which we are searching. Typical of such characteristics are such variables as personality, social class, occupation, ethnic group membership, and other descriptors that do not vary in the short run. It is reasonable to expect that these factors will contribute toward the "actual value" component of the equation presented at the beginning of this section.

However, the respondent is not a permanent, computerized entity who will provide the same answers every time you ask the same questions. There are many transitional factors that contribute toward the "error" term of our equation. For example, if he is in a bad mood, is in a hurry, has not slept sufficiently the night before, or if he is called during the first quarter of the Super Bowl, the response you will get is likely to be quite different from the value you are trying to determine. A respondent may also provide false answers in order to impress you with what he knows or earns; or he may not even know or remember the answer to one or more of the questions. If the research topic is controversial, he may simply be too close to the subject matter and find himself unable to provide objective responses, though he will probably never admit his bias. If the questionnaire or interview is lengthy, or if the respondent wishes to minimize the time he is contributing to your cause, he may just provide simplistic or unduly brief answers (e.g., his response to the question, "How would you compare the features of the new Radio Shack stereo receiver with other brands you've seen?" may be simply "OK."). Similarly, if the respondent has not yet eaten lunch, his evaluation of the taste of a new brand of steak sauce (steak included) is probably going to be somewhat in excess of the product's true contribution to dining excellence (Figure 6-4).

### The Measurement Procedure

The measurement procedure, which we'll assume to include both the overall research plan and the data collection instrument itself, is another component of the eventual measurement that we observe. In previous chapters, we discussed the impact that improper sampling procedures can have on our research results—for example, if the sample is not representative of the population, our estimate of the population parameter will be in error.

The data-collection instrument, often a questionnaire or a personal or telephone interview, will also affect the value of the measurement observed. Written questionnaires may suffer from confusing or improper wording of questions,

**Figure 6-4.**  Possible sources of measurement error include the respondent, the measurement procedure, and the situation in which the measurement is taken.

excessive length, sloppy physical appearance, positional bias in the ordering of questions, or a lack of sufficient space for replies by the respondent. These and other problems of questionnaires will be covered in the more specialized topics included in Chapter 9, which deals specifically with the construction and use of questionnaires to collect marketing information.

When there is personal or telephone communication between the respondent and an interviewer, possible interaction effects between these individuals also comprise a component of the measurement. The age, sex, personality, and style of dress of the interviewer can have an influence on the response, as can conscious or unconscious verbal and nonverbal expressions of approval or disapproval. In addition, the relative strengths and weaknesses of telephone, personal, and observational data collection media, to be discussed later, will also contribute to the ultimate success or failure of the measurement effort. The same question asked through different media is likely to elicit different responses, especially if the subject matter is of a personal nature, such as whether or not an individual has ever engaged in shoplifting.

In addition to the preceding sources of error, a researcher or interviewer may purposely bias questions, misinterpret (or even falsify) data, and otherwise exhibit unprofessional behavior in an unethical attempt to obtain research results that are to be used for other than purely informational purposes. Such purposely induced errors serve only to compound the natural propensity for human beings to make honest mistakes in their coding, tabulation, and analysis of data. While the relative occurrence of such dishonest "errors" is small on the part of marketing researchers, knowledge of how to avoid measurement errors is inevitably accompanied by an awareness of how to purposely cause them to occur in your favor. This is an important issue in marketing research and in the interpretation of research results presented to you by others, and is one of the ethical issues that we'll examine in Chapter 19.

### The Measurement Situation

The situation in which the data are collected is an additional factor that contributes to the measurement observed, and overlaps somewhat with the two components just discussed. However, this factor refers to the particular "mini-environment" in which the information is gathered, and includes such items as the presence or absence of other persons when the subject is responding to the questions of the interviewer or collection instrument. For example, if a friend or spouse is present, the response is likely to differ from what would have been obtained under more isolated conditions. In addition, ambient temperature, background noise, the availability of coffee and doughnuts, or the comfort of the seating arrangements may all affect the measurement. If our interviews are conducted on a busy urban sidewalk, we cannot expect respondents to elaborate to the same extent as they would in more comfortable surroundings. While we often have little opportunity to optimize interview conditions in the real world, we must consider that part of our measurement consists of the respondent's reaction to the situation as well as to the questions we are asking.

The measurement errors we've just considered may be controlled to some extent by the researcher, but only within practical limits—neither we nor our employer would want a simple brand preference study to turn into a lifetime project. However, we must still be concerned with the evaluation of our measurements in terms of how they compare with the true values that were our goal. Since we have no way of knowing for sure exactly what these true values are, we must rely on two potential sources of support for the soundness of our research—these criteria are known as *validity* and *reliability*.

## VALIDITY AND RELIABILITY CONCEPTS

Validity and reliability are two concepts frequently associated with both research theory and marketing research as practiced in the real world. Very briefly, they may be defined as follows:

> *Validity.*   A measuring instrument is *valid* when it measures what it is supposed to measure. The instrument is valid to the extent that its measurements are free from systematic error (bias).

> *Reliability.*   A measuring instrument is *reliable* when the results it delivers are consistent. The instrument is reliable to the extent that its measurements are free from nonsystematic (random) error.

Naturally, it is desirable for the marketing information we collect to have both validity and reliability. Of the two, validity is probably the more important, especially if the research is being conducted for the purpose of making a one-time decision. If, on the other hand, a research instrument is to be used repeatedly (e.g., the design and administration of a consumer panel purchase reporting form), reliability takes on an added dimension of importance. However, validity, because of its more basic concern for the measurement of what we really *want* to measure, may be viewed as the more critical of two criteria which are both very important to the execution of good marketing research.

Figure 6-5 illustrates the concepts of validity and reliability in a more graphic sense, and the divers shown in each frame may be considered to be four different researchers using the same measuring instruments in their respective attempts to determine the actual value of the characteristic that is the subject of their research. Alternatively, we may view the four daredevils in the figure as representing a single researcher applying the same measuring instrument on four different occasions.

Validity is present in frames A and B, as the results tend to center on the actual value of the characteristic. Reliability is present in frames A and C, since the measurements obtained are quite consistent with each other. Frame C is a rather pitiful case, because it represents the kind of research study that utilizes an immense sample size, yet ends up with the wrong conclusion because the questionnaire items were biased. In frame B, the instrument is not biased, but the results are not reliable, possibly because of an insufficient sample size. Note, however, that the "average" diver in this frame hits the target, even though all four missed.

In general, a study that is both valid and reliable is analogous to an accurate target rifle (reliability) aimed in the proper direction (validity). On the other hand, a study that is neither valid nor reliable may be considered to be the

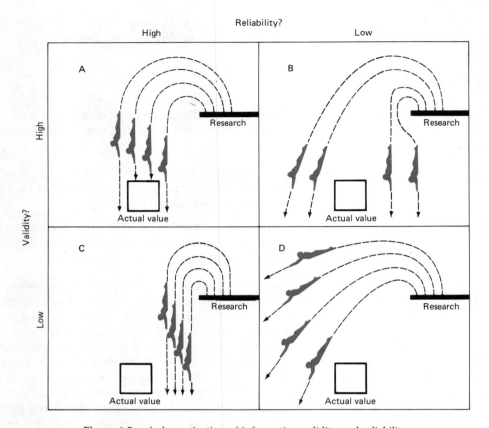

**Figure 6-5.**  A dramatization of information validity and reliability.

equivalent of aiming a sawed-off shotgun in the wrong direction, a mishap that is visually similar to the situation shown in frame D of Figure 6-5.

In considering types of studies that could lead to the four combinations of high and low validity (remember that these should not be considered as absolutes that are either completely present or absent), suppose that a political candidate for mayor is intent on gathering information to determine the proportion of the city's population who will vote for her in the coming election. The possibilities that would lead to the four categories of Figure 6-5 are described below.

1. *High validity and high reliability*. The candidate selects a random sample of 1000 registered voters who are subsequently surveyed by telephone interviews with follow-up calls or other appropriate means utilized to compensate for not-at-homes or unlisted numbers.

2. *High validity and low reliability*. The candidate does the same thing as in (1), above, but uses a sample size of only 20 registered voters, which makes the random error component very great.

3. *Low validity and high reliability*. The candidate walks through the park on a typical afternoon, hands out campaign buttons, and personally interviews everyone who comes up to speak with her. This procedure introduces considerable upward bias into the measurement, which reduces the validity to near zilch, but is reliable because she would very likely obtain the same (biased) results in repeating this scene on any other typical afternoon in the park.

4. *Low validity and low reliability*. The candidate does the same thing as in (3), except that the park happens to be the scene of a rock concert that afternoon and most of the people lying around on their blankets don't know or care who she is. The unusual circumstance involving the rock concert crowd introduces more random error into the picture and reduces reliability. Similarly, the atypical nature of the afternoon, combined with the candidate's campaign-button-plus-interview approach, does nothing to help the already low validity described in (3).

## VALIDITY ASSESSMENT

The problem of determining the validity of a particular research effort or measuring instrument lies with the basic definition of validity itself—that is, are we really measuring what we are trying to measure? If we did know the true value of the characteristic involved, there would have been no reason to conduct research in an attempt to measure it. Therefore, we have no solid basis for comparison and it would appear that we are traveling a somewhat circular path of reasoning. As a result, we must rely on other methods to determine the validity of the measurements we obtain. The major approaches to the assessment of validity are the following: (1) content validity, (2) predictive validity, (3) concurrent validity, (4) construct validity, (5) convergent validity, and (6) discriminant validity.

### Content Validity

*Content validity*, sometimes referred to as *face validity*, concerns the extent to which the measurement instrument "appears to be" measuring the characteristic it is intended to measure. Assessment of content validity is necessarily subjective, and usually involves the judgment of experts. For example, consider a questionnaire designed to measure students' attitudes regarding the college or university they attend. If the questionnaire has omitted any reference to such items as the quality of instruction, the availability of extracurricular recreation activities, and the suitability of student housing, one would suspect that the intrument lacks content validity. Such variables are very important to most students, and their omission indicates that at least some important components of the characteristic under study are conspicuously absent from the investigation.

Because of the judgment aspect of content validity, we can never be sure on this basis alone that our study will be valid. Despite this weakness, however, the content validity approach is very commonly used, especially in the formative stages of instrument design when the judgment of experts regarding the representativeness of the instrument is often a source of constructive input and suggestions for getting the instrument better "aimed" in the direction of the characteristic we are attempting to measure.

It is a good idea to initially define as best we can the variable we are studying and to include more items than we may feel are necessary for coverage of the various dimensions that we have identified. More often than not, we will delete some of them at the suggestion of those whom we consult, and we will probably add others that the judgment of the experts deems necessary to more fully represent the characteristic under investigation. One word of caution: Although tempting and convenient, it is not advisable to rely on yourself as the sole "expert." Don't hesitate to obtain a richer perspective by relying on the judgments of others who may be either more knowledgeable or able to approach the task with a viewpoint that is fresher than your own.

### Predictive Validity

*Predictive validity* refers to the ability of our measurement to predict some future value associated with the variable we have presumed to measure. For example, we may conduct a study that attempts to measure consumers' "intent to buy" a product in the class of which our brand is a member. The predictive validity of our measurement will thus be dependent upon how closely we can use our study results to predict the actual product sales that occur during this future time period. In conducting such a study, we are hopeful that there is in fact a relationship between the "intents" we measure and future purchase behavior. If our measurements are not successful in predicting the approximate level of future product sales, either (1) we are not really measuring "intent to buy," or (2) there is little relationship between "intent to buy" and actual future behavior in the marketplace.

### Concurrent Validity

*Concurrent validity*, like predictive validity, is concerned with comparing our measurement with some external criterion of success. These two approaches differ primarily from a time perspective. Whereas predictive validity involves comparing a predicted value with the future value which actually occurs, determination of concurrent validity involves the comparison of our measurement with other measures that have been made at about the same point in time. In this case, the criterion against which we are comparing our measurement is a value obtained by an alternate (and, by implication, more established) measure of the same characteristic. For example, in our "intent to buy" research study, we may wish to compare our own results with those obtained by a well-regarded professional polling organization in order to obtain an indication of the concurrent validity of our measurements.

## Construct Validity

Compared to the preceding approaches, *construct validity* is more abstract and theoretical in nature, and is concerned with the underlying concepts that lead to our numerical measurements. However, to the applied researcher, knowing that a measurement instrument seems to work is probably of more immediate concern than knowing exactly *why* it works. In general, construct validity is present whenever our measure of a particular concept is related to measures of other relevant concepts in a theoretically expected way. For example, we might expect "attitude toward X-rated movies" to be inversely related to "attendance of X-rated movies." If subsequent measurement finds that one's attitude has little to do with the frequency of attending X-rated movies, we will not be able to assume that our research has achieved construct validity.

## Convergent Validity

To the extent that a concept exists, we should be able to measure it by means of different measurement approaches. This is the basis for the notion of *convergent validity*, which is reflected when results obtained by means of two or more independent measurement techniques "converge" on a single numerical value (see Figure 6-6). For example, if the object of the survey is to determine the proportion of the population who favor coin-operated television sets in their home, a mail survey may reveal 15% in favor, while simultaneously conducted telephone survey and personal interview studies may show results of 13% and 16%, respectively. Since each of these survey techniques has its own particular strengths and weaknesses (which we will explore later), it is encouraging if they converge on a common measurement value. Actually, multiple methods of re-

**Figure 6-6.** Telephone interviews and automated polling machines, like the one shown here, were used in two separate studies of consumers' perceptions of local supermarkets. The two methods yielded similar results. If the two techniques are judged to be of equal research value, this represents convergent validity. If the telephone approach is viewed as a more proven measure, the similarity of findings could be categorized as concurrent validity, supporting automated polling as a research medium. (*Source:* Paul A. Suneson and Ernest R. Cadotte, "Research Suggests Automated Polling Machines Yield Reliable and Valid Data," *Marketing News,* January 6, 1984, p. 8, published by the American Marketing Association.)

search are often applied so that the strengths of each will tend to compensate for their various weaknesses, and convergent validity (if present) will lend support to their common conclusion.

Although it is, of course, possible for two methods of approaching the same measurement to result in the same incorrect conclusion, the presence of convergent validity helps to support the contention that the findings of each effort were more than an accident or random occurrence.

## Discriminant Validity

Related to the idea of convergent validity is that of *discriminant validity*, which is present to the extent that a measurement procedure does not measure characteristics it is not supposed to measure. While different methods of measuring the same concept *should* correlate with each other (convergent validity), methods used to measure *different* concepts should *not* (discriminant validity).

Both convergent validity and discriminant validity may assist in determining the construct validity of a measurement. They hold, in effect, that the measure must correlate with measures with which it should correlate, but must not correlate with those with which it is not supposed to correlate. From the standpoint of this text, we will be primarily concerned with the idea of convergent validity, since we will be considering in later chapters the relative strengths and weaknesses of various methods of collecting primary data. The important thing to remember at this point is that different research methods can complement

---

**EXHIBIT 6-2**

**Dueling Polls**

When polls disagree, they confuse politicians and voters alike. During the same week, three different polls were taken during the 1986 Florida Senate campaign. One gave Governor Bob Graham a margin of 52% to 38% over Senator Paula Hawkins; another showed the race as nearly even, 48% to 43%; the third indicated that Hawkins was the leader, with a 48% to 40% margin. Also, in the Missouri Senate race, each candidate could point to a poll indicating his or her front-runner status, with two other polls placing the politicians as even.

According to *USA TODAY* poll expert Tony Casale, one explanation could be the selection of respondents. For example, the poll showing Hawkins to be the leader utilized only those who said they would vote. In addition, voter sentiment can change quickly, and "even a time difference of a few days can make a difference." However, some attribute the disparity of such polls to research ineptness; as Democratic pollster Peter Hart puts it, "Anyone can hang out their shingle and start doing polls."

(*Source:* Based on "Polls Often Puzzling If Results Don't Jibe," *USA TODAY*, October 13, 1986, p. 11A. Copyright 1986 by *USA TODAY*. Excerpted with permission.)

each other and increase the likelihood that their combined results will have validity.

## RELIABILITY ASSESSMENT

A reliable measurement is one that will deliver consistent results and be relatively free from random error. Although "consistent results" is a characteristic exhibited by a reliable measure, this should not lead you to believe that reliability is important only when a measure is to be repeated over a period of time. Even if a study is to be undertaken just once, freedom from random error is important because we wish to have confidence that our results are close to the actual value that we are trying to measure. This concern was central to our discussion of sampling error in Chapter 5, since a smaller sample size increases the amount of random error that we can expect to experience. In addition, as pointed out previously, the use of a probability sampling technique allows statistical determination of the likely amount of sampling error present in the results we obtain.

However, remember that sampling error is not the only source of random error, as even a complete census involving a given measurement instrument will tend to yield different results from one time to the next as the result of random personal and situational changes in both the population and the measuring process. While reliability is not quite as valuable as validity, it is more easily measured and has historically been more greatly emphasized, especially with regard to attitude measurement instruments. There are two major approaches to the assessment of reliability: stability and equivalence.

### Stability

The *stability* approach to the assessment of reliability involves application of the measuring instrument to the same people or objects at two different points in time, then determining if the resulting measures are correlated with each other. If the instrument is reliable, *and* if the individuals or objects have not changed during the time between measurements, the first measurement for each individual or object should correspond very closely to the second. This method is also known as *test–retest reliability*, and is something you have probably engaged in whenever you have stepped on your bathroom scale two or more consecutive times. Chances are that, depending on the quality of the scale and the manner in which you position yourself upon it, you will obtain different readings that are obviously not the result of expending calories through the physical exercise involved in getting on and off the scale.

The test–retest assessment of reliability is not appropriate whenever there is reason to believe that the first measurement will have an effect on the second, in which case the second measurement will include factors other than the characteristic presumed to be measured. For example, if the measurement involves the subject's attitude toward some topic or product, the first measurement may cause him to become more sensitive to media presentations, publicity, or advertisements regarding the object of the research—thus, the second measurement will not only include the measures taken by the first, but will also contain the effects of the added knowledge and sensitivity imparted by the initial measure. If a "first impression" is involved in the measuring instrument, the second measurement will automatically be inappropriate because first impressions, by definition, happen only once. In addition to the possible effects of increased knowledge and sensitivity from the first measurement, it is possible that a measurement procedure (especially if it involves a lot of the subject's time, or attention) may result in subjects who are bored, tired, alienated, or otherwise uncooperative when they are being measured for the second time.

Thus, if a particular measuring instrument does not show a high degree of consistency between observations recorded during the first and second measurements, we are not certain whether the instrument is unreliable or whether the changes we have seen are due to such factors as the passage of time between measurements or the effect of the first measurement upon the second. However, if the observations from the two separate measurements do exhibit consistency, we will have support for the reliability of our measurement device, especially if such support is also obtained from alternate means of reliability assessment.

### Equivalence

The *equivalence* approach involves two measurements taken at the same point in time, and is generally referred to as *split-half reliability*. In this technique, we are concerned with the internal consistency of the instrument rather than its stability over time. In assessing split-half reliability, we divide the measuring instrument into two or more sets of items (e.g., by using random selection or odd- versus even-numbered questions) and determine if the score of an individual or object on one set of items will be comparable with the score on the other set or sets of items. If the separate breakdowns tend to produce similar measures, split-half reliability is said to be present.

An alternative approach that is similar in purpose is the *equivalent-forms* technique, in which we design two measurement devices with the intention of having two instruments that are "equivalent." If, when applied to the same persons or objects, these two instruments deliver comparable results, the reliability of each is supported. For example, we may construct two different lists of attitude measurement stimuli aimed at measuring consumer attitudes toward Timex watches. If there is a high correlation between the scores recorded by the two instruments (e.g., persons having very positive attitudes toward Timex on one form also score high on the other form), the reliability of each is supported. The major problem of this approach is the designing of forms that are truly equivalent, as the absence of similar results could result from either a lack of reliability or a lack of equivalence, and we aren't able to determine which was the culprit.

Split-half and equivalent-forms reliability assessment techniques are especially useful in the design and evaluation of attitude measurement instruments and can complement both each other and the test–retest approach, since as we've discussed, some measurement devices will have a destructive effect that precludes or obscures stability-over-time measures of reliability.

## ☐ SUMMARY

Measurement is the assignment of numbers to objects or phenomena according to predetermined rules. Measurements, and the means by which we make them, are vital to the practice of marketing research. The types of variables typically measured are state of mind, state of being, and behavioral.

A concept, or construct, is a symbol that we attach to some aspect of reality, and is often expressed in the form of a verbal label. While the conceptual definition of a concept describes it in terms of other concepts, the operational definition translates the concept into terms that are precise and measurable. For objective marketing research, concepts must be operationally defined to ensure both practicality and consistency of measurement.

Once a concept has been operationally defined, its quantification will fall into one of four scales of measurement: nominal, ordinal, interval, or ratio. As we proceed from the weakest (nominal) to the strongest (ratio) scale, requirements for scale membership become more stringent and permissible modes of data expression and analysis become more liberal.

Measurement errors may be systematic (directional) or nonsystematic (random). In data collection, these errors may be due to the respondent, the measurement procedure, or the situation in which the measurement is taken. Reliability represents freedom from nonsystematic (random) error, and a measuring instrument is reliable when it delivers consistent, repeatable results. Validity is the extent to which measurements are free from systematic error, or bias. It is possible for a measuring instrument to have a high degree of reliability, or consistency, yet have very low validity.

Validity may be established through content validity, predictive validity, concurrent validity, construct validity, convergent validity, and discriminant validity. The reliability of an instrument can be supported by stability (test–retest) or equivalence (split-half) techniques.

## ☐ QUESTIONS FOR REVIEW

1. What is meant by *measurement*, and why is this process important to marketing research?
2. Differentiate between (a) state of mind, (b) state of being, and (c) behavioral variables, and give an example of each.

3. Provide (a) a conceptual definition, and (b) an operational definition for each of the variables you supplied in Question 2. Why is it important for variables to be operationally defined?

4. We might operationally define a movie celebrity as "wholesome" if he or she has never appeared in an R-rated film. Using your own judgment, suggest a meaningful operational definition for each of the following.
   a. Good student.
   b. Tall.
   c. High income.
   d. Too far to walk.
   e. A large beer.

5. Charlie was accepted to UCLA for the coming academic year and, because he scored 1400 on the SAT exam, his uncle gave him $1000 to help defray expenses. He was pleased to be accepted, because he likes UCLA better than DePaul and Notre Dame, the other schools to which he applied. Having gone to high school in Green Bay, he looks forward to the 70 to 80-degree weather of sunny California. Given the preceding description of Charlie's situation, identify at least one piece of information that falls into:
   a. The nominal scale of measurement.
   b. The ordinal scale of measurement.
   c. The interval scale of measurement.
   d. The ratio scale of measurement.

6. Sam has indicated that he likes Pepsi "a million times better than Classic Coke."
   a. Technically, in what scale of measurement can his statement be classified?
   b. Practically, in what scale of measurement can his statement be classified?

7. Mary says she'd be willing to pay $500 more for a used '86 Toyota than for a used '85 Chevy. This comparison between the two cars represents what scale of measurement?

8. In the chapter it was claimed that "value measured" is the sum of "actual value" plus "error." Provide an example, real or hypothetical, in which a researcher purposely creates a data-collection setting likely to generate errors that are beneficial to his or her firm.

9. What is the difference between systematic error and nonsystematic error? Provide an example of each.

10. For each of the following situations, indicate whether the error is systematic or nonsystematic.
    a. A candidate for political office walks through the park, greets voters and gives them a free coupon for a McDonald's Big Mac, then asks if they intend to vote for him.
    b. Tom's bathroom scale is broken. Regardless of who gets on it, the scale says they weigh 136 pounds.
    c. An interviewer asks respondents, "Do you agree that pet owners should be made to shoulder their responsibilities by being required to get their pets spayed or neutered in order to avoid the cruelties of animal overpopulation?"
    d. To avoid running up more than 12,000 miles before the time portion of his auto warranty expires, a technical sales representative disconnects the odometer for his first three months of ownership.

11. Is it possible for a marketing research study to be valid but not reliable? If so, provide a real or hypothetical example of a situation in which this may occur.

12. Is it possible for a marketing research study to be reliable but not valid? If so, provide a real or hypothetical example of a situation in which this may occur.

13. Is it possible for a marketing research study to be neither reliable nor valid? If so, provide a real or hypothetical example of a situation in which this may occur.

14. What is the difference between content validity, convergent validity, concurrent validity, and predictive validity? Briefly explain and give an example of each.

15. Under what research conditions might the test–retest method of reliability assessment not be appropriate? Why?

# 7

# ATTITUDE MEASUREMENT

**Dull Image Inspires "Raisin Shuffle"**

Concerned with slow sales growth, the California Raisin Advisory Board asked their advertising agency, Foote, Cone & Belding, to find out why raisins weren't more popular. According to Veronica Kludjian, supervisor of the agency's raisin account, "We found that people understood what raisins were good for, but that people didn't have a positive emotional image of them." Words like "dull," "uninteresting," and even "wimpy" seemed to describe the consumer's attitude toward raisins.

Ad writer Seth Warner, faced with the task of reversing the poor raisin's stodgy image, describes the agency's solution: "We thought, 'Why not give raisins a personality of their own?'" Warner created an animated ad with two dozen "hip" raisins strutting to the Motown sound of "I Heard It Through the Grapevine." After five weeks and 720 hand-arranged scenes, the super-cool raisins exuded both personality and rhythm as they shuffled to a tape of the "Grapevine" song.

The dancing raisins made an immediate impact. Robert Phinney, director of advertising and promotion for the California Raisin Advisory Board, says: "We know from the letters and the phone calls that we are getting

*Source:* "Grapevine Commercial Has Teens Doing Raisin Shuffle," *TV Magazine, The Pittsburgh Press*, November 23, 1986, p. 2. Copyright by Associated Press. Photo courtesy of the California Raisin Advisory Board, Fresno, CA.

**Figure 7-1.**   The California raisins strut to the Motown sound of "I Heard It Through the Grapevine." The commercial, which followed research revealing consumers' lukewarm attitude toward raisins as dull and uninteresting, inspired high school students to dance the "Raisin Shuffle." (*Source:* "Grapevine Commercial Has Teens Doing Raisin Shuffle," *TV Magazine, The Pittsburgh Press,* November 23, 1986, p. 2. Copyright Associated Press. Photo courtesy of the California Raisin Advisory Board, Fresno, CA.)

attention—people see the commercial and they like it." Following the raisins' premier, children were asking for raisin costumes for halloween, high school students were doing the "Raisin Shuffle," and, the Advisory Board hopes, they were all eating more raisins.

## INTRODUCTION

Attitudes are a pervasive component of both personal lives and marketing research activities. As consumers, we are bombarded daily with communications intended to improve or reinforce our attitude toward commercial and noncommercial offerings of all types. As marketing researchers, we deal with attitudes in two general ways: (1) we measure the attitudes that customers or respondents have toward the object of our marketing efforts; and (2) having discovered these attitudes, we help devise, and compare the effectiveness of, alternative potential strategies for improving or otherwise shaping them.

We'll be concentrating here on the first of these two relationships between attitudes and marketing research—that is, on how to measure or quantify attitudes. While our initial emphasis will be on the *unidimensional* (one attitude dimension at a time), we will also examine the *multidimensional* (objects examined as points in multidimensional attitudinal space) approach to attitude measurement. Our discussion of attitude measurement will be arranged according to the following topics:

   I. Attitudes and their measurement
  II. Attitude rating scales
 III. Attitude scaling techniques
 IV. Multidimensional scaling

## ATTITUDES AND THEIR MEASUREMENT

### Attitudes in Marketing

For our purposes, *attitude* can be defined as a mental state that predisposes the individual to respond in a certain way when he or she is subjected to a given stimulus. Attitudes can be considered as having both strength and direction. For example, a consumer may have a highly favorable attitude toward Michelob, a slightly favorable attitude toward Schlitz, and a highly unfavorable attitude toward Dr. Pepper.

Attitudes are generally viewed as having three components—cognitive, affective, and behavioral. The *cognitive* component refers to our knowledge or beliefs with regard to an object, the *affective* component refers to our positive or negative feelings with regard to an object, and the *behavioral* component refers to our predisposition toward action in a given situation. The following examples illustrate each component in a hypothetical situation where an attitude measurement study might be helpful to the marketing decision maker.

*Cognitive.* A domestic automobile manufacturer wishes to learn the extent to which consumers believe that Japanese cars are of higher quality than domestic models.

The management of the Pizza Cove restaurant would like to know what proportion of the local population is aware that the restaurant sponsored a Little League team in last summer's recreation program.

*Affective.* The Hooterville Town Council wishes to determine what proportion of the townsfolk are in favor of granting a construction permit for a combination discotheque and self-service gas station.

The Crinkle Cab Company wants to find out if its recent advertising campaign has been successful in improving the negative image that the public has of the company's safety performance.

*Behavioral.*    Chicken City wants to learn if customers would be likely to purchase steak hoagies and burritos if these items were added to the menu.

The new service manager of Myopic Motors wants to find out how many recent service customers intend to return to Myopic for their next repair job.

The key reason for the importance of attitudes in marketing is the link that is generally assumed to exist between attitudes and consumer behavior. While the notion of such a link is a straightforward idea, the exact manner in which it operates is not universally agreed upon by marketing theoreticians. However, as a practical matter, we are relatively safe in assuming that consumers having a more favorable attitude toward a product or service will tend to be more likely to purchase it in the marketplace.

### The Measurement of Attitudes

The measurement techniques of this chapter tend to be of the self-administered variety, in which the consumer is largely on his or her own in responding to the situation or questions posed. A number of other useful approaches for at-

---

**EXHIBIT 7-1**

***Consumers Link Sausage Preference with Low-Salt, but Taste Tests Disagree***

In a study of 10 sausage products, consumers were asked to rate the products and scale them along a number of attributes, including greasiness and saltiness. Subjects were also asked to rate what they considered the ideal product on the same attributes. The ratings revealed that consumers preferred low levels of saltiness and greasiness; thus it would appear that the ideal product would have little of these attributes.

In the transition from rating scales to actual product testing, however, a different story emerged. The two sausages ranked highest in taste tests had ranked first and second in saltiness, and were among the most greasy as well. Some of the least greasy products were among those with the bottom taste ratings in the study. According to the researchers, sensory results must be considered along with the consumer's preference as revealed on rating scales: "Low salt and grease content may be positives in the consumer's attitude bank, but actual preference did not support that. In some cases, consumers are not able to articulate or are not aware of their actual preferences."

(*Source:* Howard R. Moskowitz and Barry E. Jacobs, "Combine Sensory Acceptance, Needs/Values Measures When Researching Food Products," *Marketing News,* January 22, 1982, sec. 2, p. 6, published by the American Marketing Association.)

titude measurement, involving other strategies and mentioned briefly here, will be discussed in greater detail in Chapter 10. These techniques, and their implications for attitude measurement, can be categorized as (1) personal and mechanical observation of behavior, and (2) indirect questioning and projective techniques.

### Personal and Mechanical Observation of Behavior

Observational approaches assume that one's behavior is reflective of attitude toward some object related to the behavior. For example, an observational study in which drivers are observed not wearing seat belts suggests that these individuals may not have a highly favorable attitude regarding automotive seat belts and the accident protection they afford. (On the other hand, subjects could have a favorable attitude regarding the value of seat belts in an accident, but might just perceive the probability of *their* being involved in an accident as infinitesimally small. As this suggests, inferring attitude from behavior alone is not a foolproof research approach, and could often benefit from supplemental information obtained through other means.)

### Indirect Questioning and Projective Techniques

Indirect methods assume that one's responses to unstructured or partially structured stimuli, such as sentence completion, word association, story completion, and cartoon tests, will reveal one's attitude towards the object of the study. When using these techniques, a major problem can arise if the researcher tends to misinterpret the responses that subjects have provided—that is, if the researcher does not share the same frame of reference as the respondents.

While the observational and projective approaches to attitude measurement are often useful, they generally take a back seat to self-reporting methods. These rely on relatively direct questions that the respondent answers in such a way as to indicate both the strength and direction of his or her attitude regarding the object of interest. These approaches may also use an attitude scale for the purpose of measuring the response provided. It is with these types of scales that the next two sections are primarily concerned. The various types of scales and scaling techniques are all examples of *measurement*—the assigning of numbers to objects or phenomena according to predetermined rules—as discussed in the introduction to Chapter 6. They are all measurement techniques, but the *rules* differ from one approach to another.

## ATTITUDE RATING SCALES

There are many types of rating scales used in marketing research, but those included here—graphic, itemized, rank order, paired comparison, constant sum, and fractionation—are among the most popular. A rating scale typically requires that the respondent indicate his attitude toward an object by (1) indicating a position along a continuum or series of ordered categories that best describes his attitude, (2) selecting one object over another with regard to a given attribute, or (3) assigning numerical values to one or more objects as a reflection of their relative strengths in possessing an attribute.

## Graphic Rating Scale

In the *graphic rating scale*, the respondent is asked to indicate his attitude by placing a mark at some point along a continuum that includes the entire range of possible ratings. Because of the continuum of alternatives, a theoretically infinite number of responses are possible. The following are examples of the graphic rating scale:

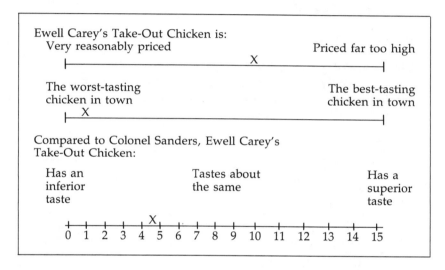

Based on the responses above, it appears that the respondent would much rather visit the Colonel than Ewell Carey. Graphic scales can be arranged horizontally, as above, or vertically. In addition, the continuum can be supplemented by hatch marks, with or without accompanying numbers. Similarly, verbal descriptions can be used either along the continuum or just at the extremes.

As with the itemized scale, which follows, the graphic scale can be either *noncomparative* or *comparative*. The first two of the preceding examples are noncomparative—that is, the respondent judges Ewell Carey's Take-Out Chicken in an absolute sense, without being explicitly asked to compare Ewell with the infinitely more famous Colonel Sanders. In the absence of a comparative instruction, the respondent is free to compare the stimulus with any other stimulus that comes to mind, a possibility that should be considered if it seems likely that respondents may be using a frame of reference that is not relevant to the purpose of the study.

In constructing a graphic scale, one should be careful not to make the ends of the continuum too extreme—this will tend to force respondents into the center of the scale, thus losing information. Also, if the ends of the scale are too mild, the extremes will tend to be too frequently used.

The graphic rating scale is easy to set up and analyze. If the scales are not described by numeric intervals, one need only physically measure the distance from the left extreme to the respondent's mark and assign a score that reflects that distance. When the respondent has been assisted by a scale already marked for distance, the researcher need only read the position of the response. For example, in a question such as the third example here, a respondent may be measured as 12.5 or 13.6. Generally, it is not useful to take a scale that is already finely divided and measure attitudes to extremes such as 12.51 and 13.64 (some might even argue that the difference between 12 and 13 is too close to call).

## Itemized Rating Scale

The *itemized rating scale* is similar to the graphic approach except that the respondent is asked to choose from a limited number of categories instead of placing a mark on a continuous scale. The following are examples of itemized rating scales:

---

Overall, how do you like your new Snowchucker snowblower?

| Very dissatisfied | Somewhat dissatisfied | Somewhat satisfied | Very satisfied |
|:---:|:---:|:---:|:---:|
| ☐ | ☐ | ☐ | ☐ |
| 1 | 2 | 3 | 4 |

What do you think of the food at Chung Ho's Burrito Palace?

| Terrible | | | | | | Terrific |
|:---:|:---:|:---:|:---:|:---:|:---:|:---:|
| ☐ | ☐ | ☐ | ☐ | ☐ | ☐ | ☐ |
| −3 | −2 | −1 | 0 | +1 | +2 | +3 |

---

In addition to having an importance of its own, the itemized rating scale is useful in the development of some of the attitude scaling techniques presented in the next section. In general, the following are important considerations to keep in mind when creating a rating scale of the itemized type:

*1. How do we handle respondents who either don't know or are not sure?* In the first of the two examples given here, the respondent has no choice but to answer either favorably or unfavorably with regard to her new Snow-chucker—that is, she is forced to take one side or the other and does not have neutrality as an alternative. Similarly, the respondent who has not yet had the opportunity to use her Snowchucker may be forced to invent an answer because a "don't know" category has not been provided. When an odd number of categories are used, the central category is usually identified as a neutral position.

Practitioners are not unanimous in their recommendations regarding the inclusion of a neutral category, with some claiming that everyone has some degree of attitude regarding the object and that this attitude should be forced from them. In order to handle as accurately as possible those respondents who are truly neutral or who don't know how they feel about the object, it's generally best to use an odd number of categories (with central position neutral) and an additional category ("don't know" or "no opinion") whenever it is likely that a significant number of respondents may not be aware of the object or have never tried it.

   **2. *To what extent should we identify the categories?*** Decisions regarding category descriptions include (1) numbers versus no numbers, (2) descriptions for all categories versus descriptions for the extremes only, and (3) extensiveness of verbal descriptions that are presented (see Figure 7-2). The use of ***numerical designations*** for categories enhances the soundness of treating the results as interval-scale data. One can have more confidence that the distances from $+1$ to $+2$ and from $+3$ to $+4$ are equal than that the psychological distance from "somewhat" to "moderately" and from "moderately" to "very" are equal. The combination of equally spaced categories and ordered numerical designations lends itself well to situations where interval-scale assumptions are to be made about the data obtained. Regarding the use of ***verbal descriptions*** for all categories instead of just the extremes, such complete labeling can be helpful to the respondent in making his or her choice, but such descriptions may not be psychologically equidistant from each other. Thus, there may exist a tradeoff between aid to the respondent and interval-scale assumptions for analysis. When deciding on the extensiveness of individual verbal descriptions, use those that are clear, precise, and unlikely to be confused with each other. For example, a scale containing the descriptions "somewhat pleased" and "fairly pleased"

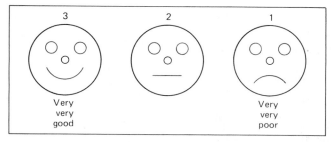

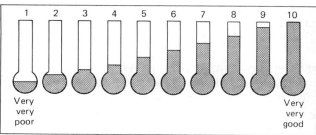

**Figure 7-2.** When children's attitudes are being measured by a rating scale, visual cues like these can facilitate communication. (*Source:* Fred Cutler, "To Meet Criticisms of TV Ads, Researchers Find New Ways to Measure Children's Attitudes," *Marketing News,* January 27, 1978, p. 16, published by the American Marketing Association.)

might lead to difficulties because respondents could disagree over which of these two descriptions represents the greater amount of satisfaction.

*3. Should the scale be balanced or unbalanced?* In a balanced scale, the number of favorable categories is the same as the number of unfavorable categories. An unbalanced set of response categories can lead to biasing of the respondent. However, if it is believed that the overall attitude of respondents will be largely favorable or largely unfavorable (i.e., that the attitudes you're measuring are concentrated in one direction or the other), then an unbalanced scale would be appropriate.

*4. How many categories should the scale have?* Theoretically, the greater the number of response categories, the greater will be the precision of the scale. However, it is not likely that most respondents can differentiate meaningfully between 10 or 15 different categories that are separated by verbal descriptions such as "very much satisfied" and "extremely satisfied." In some studies (e.g., when one wishes to determine voters' sentiments towards a proposed piece of legislation), a simple scale with just 2 categories—"in favor of" and "not in favor of"—will tend to suffice. Though it's difficult to generalize on what number of categories is best, it should be pointed out that practitioners typically use scales of 5 to 7 categories, and that these work quite well for most research situations.

### Rank-Order Rating Scale

For a *rank-order* rating scale, the respondent is required to arrange a number of objects according to some criterion—for example, quality, good taste, or attractiveness. The result is a purely ordinal scale that describes the objects from most favored to least favored, but says nothing about the distance between any of the objects. The following is an example of a question calling for a rating scale obtained by ranking:

---

Please rank the following restaurants according to the quality of their food. Place a "1" beside the restaurant you believe has the highest quality food, a "2" next to the second best establishment, then continue until you've placed a "5" next to the one with the lowest-quality food:

_____Ewell Carey's Take-Out Chicken
_____Colonel Sanders' Kentucky Fried Chicken
_____Wolfgang Schmidt's Genuine Italian Pizza
_____Harold's Hoagie Heaven
_____Chung Ho's Burrito Palace

---

Compared to the *paired-comparison* approach in the next section, the rank-order rating scale has the advantage of being more realistic in representing the actual shopping situation, where the consumer must make direct comparisons among all competing alternatives at the same time. In addition, ranking is a familiar activity that many people know from such nonconsuming pursuits as watching televised political debates or reading college football poll reports. A principal difficulty is that it becomes arduous for a respondent to meaningfully rank many more than a half dozen objects at the same time. However, since rank-order rating is a familiar activity to most respondents, and since the directions are usually easily understood in a self-administered questionnaire, the rank-order approach continues to be a popular and useful technique.

### Paired-Comparison Rating Scale

In the rank-order technique just discussed, it was necessary for the respondent to consider all objects simultaneously in arriving at an ordinal scale describing her attitude toward them. In the *paired-comparison* rating scale, the respondent makes a number of comparisons in which she selects between objects presented to her two at a time. As with other rating scales, the respondent uses (or is provided with) a relevant criterion along which to make the comparisons. In order to rank all of the objects, it is necessary to present the respondent with all possible pairs. The number of pairs ($N$) needed can be calculated as $N = [n(n - 1)]/2$, where $n$ is the total number of objects. For example, if there are six objects to be evaluated, $N = [6(6 - 1)]/2$, or 15 comparisons to be made. The number of comparisons required goes up quite rapidly as more objects are added. For example, with just three more objects, a total of 36 comparisons will be necessary. It is this rapid escalation of the comparison task that limits this approach to relatively small sets of objects.

The following represents a hypothetical set of data for a respondent who has been asked to evaluate five restaurants with regard to the criterion "a good place to take a date." With five objects, $N = [5(5 - 1)]/2$, or 10 different comparisons.

| | |
|---|---|
| _____ Chung Ho's Burrito Palace | vs. _√_ Harold's Hoagie Heaven |
| _____ Chung Ho's Burrito Palace | vs. _√_ Wolfgang Schmidt's Genuine Italian Pizza |
| _____ Chung Ho's Burrito Palace | vs. _√_ Ewell Carey's Take-Out Chicken |
| _√_ Chung Ho's Burrito Palace | vs. _____ Fred's Frog Leg Factory |
| _____ Harold's Hoagie Heaven | vs. _√_ Wolfgang Schmidt's Genuine Italian Pizza |
| _____ Harold's Hoagie Heaven | vs. _√_ Ewell Carey's Take-Out Chicken |
| _√_ Harold's Hoagie Heaven | vs. _____ Fred's Frog Leg Factory |
| _____ Wolfgang Schmidt's Genuine Italian Pizza | vs. _√_ Ewell Carey's Take-Out Chicken |
| _√_ Wolfgang Schmidt's Genuine Italian Pizza | vs. _____ Fred's Frog Leg Factory |
| _√_ Ewell Carey's Take-Out Chicken | vs. _____ Fred's Frog Leg Factory |

If we were to combine 100 hypothetical respondents who have compared the same combinations of these five restaurants, we might end up with a matrix such as that represented in Table 7-1. The matrix entries represent the proportion of the sample who preferred the column restaurant (vertical entries) to the row restaurant (horizontal entries). For example, the table shows that 59% of the respondents rated Wolfgang Schmidt's Genuine Italian Pizza over Chung Ho's Burrito Palace when comparing these two restaurants.

In order to convert Table 7-1 into an ordinal scale along which the restaurants are positioned, we can convert the proportions in the table to "wins" (value = 1) and "losses" (value = 0) as seen from the perspective of the restaurant at the top of each column. For example, from examining Table 7-1, it can be seen that respondents didn't exactly jump at the chance to go to Fred's Frog Leg Factory—this establishment scored below 0.50 against every competitor, thus earning a complete column of 0's.

The result of this conversion is Table 7-2, which can be transformed into an ordinal scale by simply adding each of the columns. (*Note:* Since the proportion of the respondents favoring Ewell's over Wolfgang's was 0.50, we awarded one-half point to each of these competitors.) Based on the column totals, the ordinal ranking of the five restaurants is as follows:

1st (tie)  Wolfgang Schmidt's Genuine Italian Pizza
           Ewell Carey's Take-Out Chicken
3rd      Chung Ho's Burrito Palace
4th      Harold's Hoagie Heaven
5th      Fred's Frog Leg Factory

### Constant-Sum Rating Scale

In the *constant-sum* rating scale, respondents are required to allocate a given number of points among a number of objects according to some criterion. When the questionnaire is administered in person, it is useful to use a round number (e.g., 100) of physical objects such as pennies. Respondents are told to allocate their points or pennies in proportion to their preferences for the objects. For example, if object A is valued twice as much as object B, then object A should receive twice as many points. The assumption is that the ratio-scale nature of the instructions will yield results that are also of a ratio-scale nature. (However, this might sometimes be difficult to justify. For example, it's possible that a respondent could award zero points to an object, implying that the others have a relatively infinite amount of the criterion.) An example of the constant-sum approach:

---

Please divide 100 points among the following television brands so as to reflect how much overall quality you believe each one has:
RCA     _____ points     Sears     _____ points
Zenith     _____ points     Magnavox   _____ points
Sony     _____ points

---

**TABLE 7-1.** *Matrix shows proportion of respondents favoring column restaurant over row restaurant as "a good place to take a date."*

|  | Ewell Carey's Take-Out Chicken | Chung Ho's Burrito Palace | Wolfgang Schmidt's Genuine Italian Pizza | Fred's Frog Leg Factory | Harold's Hoagie Heaven |
|---|---|---|---|---|---|
| Ewell Carey's Take-Out Chicken | — | 0.28 | 0.50 | 0.20 | 0.32 |
| Chung Ho's Burrito Palace | 0.72 | — | 0.59 | 0.38 | 0.12 |
| Wolfgang Schmidt's Genuine Italian Pizza | 0.50 | 0.41 | — | 0.40 | 0.19 |
| Fred's Frog Leg Factory | 0.80 | 0.62 | 0.60 | — | 0.82 |
| Harold's Hoagie Heaven | 0.68 | 0.88 | 0.81 | 0.18 | — |

If a respondent assigns 30 points to RCA and only 15 to Sears, it is assumed that he or she feels that RCA has twice the quality of Sears. The technique is best used for relatively small numbers of objects—otherwise, respondents will encounter difficulty in making their scores add up to the required number of points. Naturally, this difficulty is overcome if pennies or other objects are used in personally administering the question to the respondent.

### Fractionation Rating Scale

The *fractionation*, or reference alternative, rating scale requires that respondents rate an object by comparing it with a reference object. The goal is a ratio-scale representation of attitudes toward the complete set of objects. The following is

**TABLE 7-2.** *After converting original preference matrix to "wins" (1) and "losses" (0), column totals are obtained to arrive at an ordinal ranking of the restaurants.*

|  | Ewell Carey's Take-Out Chicken | Chung Ho's Burrito Palace | Wolfgang Schmidt's Genuine Italian Pizza | Fred's Frog Leg Factory | Harold's Hoagie Heaven |
|---|---|---|---|---|---|
| Ewell Carey's Take-Out Chicken | — | 0 | $\frac{1}{2}$ | 0 | 0 |
| Chung Ho's Burrito Palace | 1 | — | 1 | 0 | 0 |
| Wolfgang Schmidt's Genuine Italian Pizza | $\frac{1}{2}$ | 0 | — | 0 | 0 |
| Fred's Frog Leg Factory | 1 | 1 | 1 | — | 1 |
| Harold's Hoagie Heaven | 1 | 1 | 1 | 0 | — |
| Total | 3.5 | 2 | 3.5 | 0 | 1 |

an example of this approach:

> If the Volkswagen Jetta is assumed to score 100 points in terms of being "fun to drive," how would you compare each of the following cars to the Jetta?
>
> | | | | |
> |---|---|---|---|
> | Volkswagen Jetta | 100  points | Ford Escort | _____ points |
> | Buick Regal | _____ points | Porsche 928 | _____ points |

A hypothetical respondent could rate the Buick at 80, the Ford Escort at 90, and the Porsche 928 at 150 points. However, these results could depend on which vehicle is used as the reference object. For example, if the Buick were the reference object, it is unlikely that this same respondent would have awarded 100 × (100/80), or 125 points to the Volkswagen Jetta. In addition, this takeoff from the paired-comparison approach makes it possible for extreme individuals to express ratings that, for all practical purposes, are ordinal in nature. For example, consider a devout Porsche fanatic, who may rate the Porsche at 1 million to the Jetta's 100. Does she really believe that the Porsche is 10,000 times as much fun to drive? Assuming that she could afford both, would she turn down a brand new Jetta for $3 in favor of a brand-new Porsche for $30,000? Not likely. The million points awarded to the Porsche simply says that she believes it to be very much more fun to drive. Provided that the objects are at least remotely similar, and that respondents are realistic in expressing their ratings relative to the reference object, fractionation can be a useful tool to the marketing researcher. However, because the constant-sum approach provides much the same information with less risk of such highly extreme ratings, it is to be preferred.

## ATTITUDE SCALING TECHNIQUES

The rating scale approaches just discussed require the respondent to react to a stimulus that typically consists of a single statement or question. To this extent, the response is a very limited sample of a person's attitude toward the object or objects being examined. The techniques in this section involve a battery of questions or statements in order to provide a more complete view of the respondent's overall attitude. In this section, we will examine several of the more popular scaling approaches employed in marketing research.

### Likert Scale

Sometimes referred to as the *summated scale*, the *Likert scale* is one of the most widely used attitude scaling techniques. In this approach, the respondent is asked to indicate his degree of agreement or disagreement with each of a series of statements that are related to the object in question. The responses are scored so that they are consistent in terms of directionality, then added to obtain the respondent's total attitude score toward the object.

Figure 7-3 summarizes the major steps in the development and administration of a Likert scale instrument. For purposes of illustration, let's assume that we're trying to measure the attitudes of students towards a hypothetical school called Hower University.

As Figure 7-3 indicates, the first step is to generate a number of favorable and unfavorable statements with regard to the school. The number of statements at this stage will be relatively large, perhaps 50 statements or more. Among the possible statements we might use are:

> Hower U. is a terrific place to go to school.
>
> This school has a very attractive campus.
>
> If I had it to do over again, I'd have gone someplace else.
>
> As a graduate of Hower University, I'll probably get a lot of good job offers.
>
> There are a lot of exciting things to do on campus.
>
> The school administration tends to ignore student needs.

As these few statements indicate, there are a lot of possibilities. The key at this point is to generate ***attitude-revealing*** statements, the kind that people tend to argue about, and to avoid statements that are almost universally regarded as facts. For example, if the football team hasn't won in five years, "Hower's football team has an outstanding record" would not be an appropriate statement— since every honest respondent would disagree with it, the statement would be useless. Similarly, statements such as "The library is of brick construction" and "The campus is five miles from the nearest liquor store" would not be wise choices.

The next step is to test and refine the instrument by using a sample of persons who are similar to the eventual respondents. The purpose of this is to eliminate statements that contribute very little to the eventual attitude score a respondent receives. The eventual statements should be those that discriminate best between high and low attitude scores toward the school. At this stage, the sample responds to the entire, unrefined instrument by selecting one of the following for each statement:

$$
\begin{array}{ll}
\text{Strongly agree} & (+2) \\
\text{Agree} & (+1) \\
\text{Neutral} & (\ \ 0) \\
\text{Disagree} & (-1) \\
\text{Strongly disagree} & (-2)
\end{array}
$$

The numbers in parentheses are for scoring purposes, and need not be shown to the respondents. Assuming that there are 20 statements, the poorest possible attitude toward Hower would be $-40$, that is, someone had given the least favorable response for each of the 20 statements. After administration, it is nec-

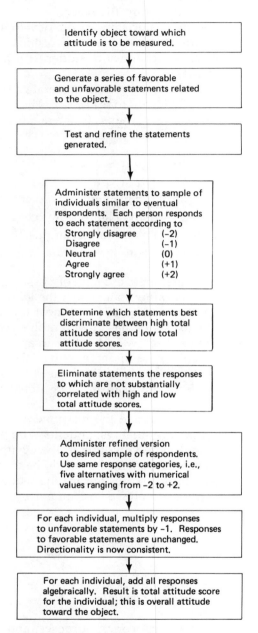

**Figure 7-3.**    Steps show the general procedure for setting up and administering Likert scale instrument for attitude measurement.

essary to eliminate statements of the following types:

1. Statements for which most respondents tend to provide the same response.
2. Statements that do not discriminate between those who have favorable and those who have unfavorable attitudes towards the university—for example those generating responses that are somewhat randomly distributed and unrelated to total attitude scores.

Once the instrument has been refined and the number of statements reduced to those that are most meaningful, the final version is administered to the respondents of interest. Each person responds to each statement according to the "strongly disagree," "disagree," "neutral," "agree," "strongly agree" format, then the responses are translated to their numerical counterparts.

At this point, each individual's responses to unfavorable statements must be multiplied by −1 for purposes of directional consistency—that is, so that positive responses will reflect favorable attitudes and negative responses will reflect unfavorable attitudes. For example, someone who answers "strongly agree" (+2) to the statement, "The school administration tends to ignore student needs," is really voicing an unfavorable attitude about the school and the −1 multiplication only changes the directionality of the response to be consistent with the idea that plus is favorable and minus is unfavorable.

Following correction for unfavorable statements, each individual's responses are algebraically added to provide a total attitude score for that respondent. Figure 7-4 provides a numerical example of the scoring for a hypothetical respondent on a small-scale version of such a Likert instrument.

The main strengths of the Likert technique are related to its ease of construction and the simplicity of the directions required for respondent self-administration. While the output of this scaling approach is, from a purely technical standpoint, no stronger than an ordinal scale, practitioners routinely treat the Likert total attitude score as an interval-scale result.

### Semantic Differential

The *semantic differential* approach to attitude scaling is fascinating, simple and very widely used in marketing research. In this technique, the respondent is asked to express his or her feelings relative to an object by selecting a position along a scale bounded by bipolar adjectives or phrases. The following is an example of the semantic differential approach:

*Chung Ho's Burrito Palace*

Modern __ __ __ __ ✓ __ __ Old-fashioned
Fast __ __ __ ✓ __ __ __ Slow
Bright __ __ __ __ ✓ __ __ Dark
Happy __ ✓ __ __ __ __ __ Sad

|  | Clyde's Responses | | | | |
| Statements | Strongly disagree (−2) | Disagree (−1) | Neutral (0) | Agree (+1) | Strongly agree (+2) |
|---|---|---|---|---|---|
| 1. "Hower U. is a terrific place to go to school." | ☐ | ☐ | ☐ | ☒ | ☐ |
| 2. "The school administration tends to ignore student needs." | ☐ | ☐ | ☐ | ☐ | ☒ |
| 3. "There are a lot of exciting things to do on campus." | ☐ | ☒ | ☐ | ☐ | ☐ |
| 4. "It's very difficult to make friends here." | ☐ | ☐ | ☐ | ☐ | ☒ |

*Note:* Statements 2 and 4 are unfavorable statements with regard to the university. Responses to these statements must be multiplied by −1 to ensure consistent directionality so that the eventual sum will be a meaningful reflection of Clyde's attitude.

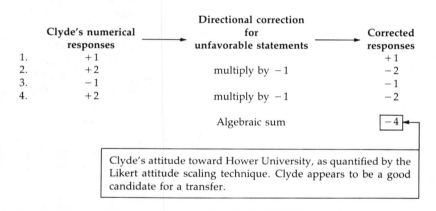

| | Clyde's numerical responses | → | Directional correction for unfavorable statements | → | Corrected responses |
|---|---|---|---|---|---|
| 1. | +1 | | | | +1 |
| 2. | +2 | | multiply by −1 | | −2 |
| 3. | −1 | | | | −1 |
| 4. | +2 | | multiply by −1 | | −2 |
| | | | Algebraic sum | | −4 |

Clyde's attitude toward Hower University, as quantified by the Likert attitude scaling technique. Clyde appears to be a good candidate for a transfer.

**Figure 7-4.**   Illustration of scoring technique for Likert scale instrument.

The semantic differential is frequently used in conducting corporate and brand image studies through the use of bipolar adjectives and phrases that sometimes don't make immediate sense when they are seen on the questionnaire. As an example of this facet of the approach, consider the following situation: The author, in attempting to convey the possibility that seemingly meaningless adjective pairs could make sense (even though after the fact), asked his class members to think of two adjective pairs that had absolutely nothing to do with beer. From the suggested pairs, the two that seemed most meaningless at the time were (1) loud-quiet, and (2) fast-slow. After all, unlike Rice Krispies, beers are generally not noisemakers—and they remain still unless one happens to upset the glass. A small-scale study was then conducted in which class mem-

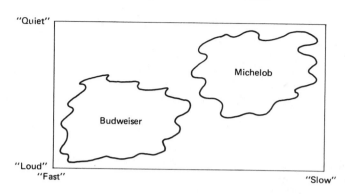

**Figure 7-5.** The results of applying two "meaningless" adjective pairs in a semantic differential study of two well known beers. The positioning of the brands suggested that the adjective pairs weren't so meaningless after all. As with multidimensional scaling, the semantic differential places objects in multidimensional perceptual space, although the results are generally presented in a *profile analysis* instead of graphically depicted.

bers rated each of two popular beers along each of the bipolar adjective scales. The results, which were quite pronounced, are described in Figure 7-5. Michelob tended to be identified with "slow" and "quiet," while Budweiser tended to be identified with "fast" and "loud."

Much to the amazement of both class and instructor, the "meaningless" adjective pairs had revealed a consistent pattern in the positioning of the two brands. In an after-the-fact analysis, the positioning seemed consistent with the images of the beers—Budweiser (action, parties, music) and Michelob (quiet, dignified, special occasions) are promoted in ways that fit well with the semantic differential results uncovered in this very small-scale test. The moral of this story is that a *truly* meaningless adjective pair will tend to exhibit either a random pattern of responses, or responses that do not change much regardless of which object is being evaluated. However, should consistent patterns arise (even if you can't interpret them very well at first), they are worth further investigation to determine what aspect of the object's image may have caused them to occur. The presentation in Figure 7-5, looking very similar to the multidimensional scaling approaches we'll be examining later, also reflects the value of semantic differential results in providing input data for multidimensional scaling studies.

In carrying out a semantic differential study, it is typical to have at least two brands or objects subjected to the same series of adjective pairs, with the data from all respondents averaged (the median position can also be used) for each question. The result is a *profile analysis* similar to the following:

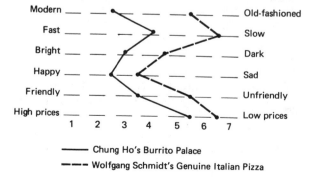

As indicated by the preceding profiles, Chung Ho's is perceived as being more modern, higher priced, and happier than Wolfgang Schmidt's establishment. Overall, considering the age group that typically frequents fast-food restaurants, Chung Ho appears to have the better image. In contrast, Wolfgang may be well advised to hire more efficient, friendly employees. While this analysis is quite brief, it is suggestive of the type of thinking that accompanies the analysis of semantic differential results.

Semantic differential scaling may include as many as 20 or 30 different adjective pairs that have been selected for various reasons. Some adjective pairs will be quite concrete. For example, in studying the image of a retail store, pairs such as convenient hours–inconvenient hours, friendly salespersons–unfriendly salespersons, high prices–low prices, good value for the money–poor value for the money, and high-quality goods–low-quality goods are obviously going to be of interest. In addition, "fishing" with some adjective pairs that are more abstract (e.g., hot–cold, strong–weak, good–bad) could be quite revealing. While a pattern arising from such adjective pairs may be difficult to interpret based on the adjectives alone, it could suggest something important that consumers perceive about the store. Such findings might well be pursued in greater detail through other methods—for example, by means of projective techniques or focus group interviewing.

Osgood and his associates, in their original work with the semantic differential, identified three factors that tended to contribute the most to the judgments being made by respondents: (1) *evaluative* (e.g., good–bad, positive–negative), (2) *potency* (e.g., strong–weak, masculine–feminine), and (3) *activity* (e.g., fast–slow, active–passive).[1] While the evaluative kinds of adjective pairs are often the most useful for marketing research studies of companies and brands, potency and activity-related pairs tend to be more abstract and helpful in uncovering aspects of an object's image that can be quite important, but not very obvious.

Because of its ease of construction, simplicity of administration and coding, and the great amount of image information that can be obtained from a single, brief questionnaire, the semantic differential is easily one of the most popular scales used by practitioners of marketing research. The nature of the approach is such that it is a "natural" for examining many different dimensions of the images that consumers have of companies, brands, and other objects of marketing efforts.

## Stapel Scale

The *Stapel scale* is essentially a slight modification of the semantic differential, replacing the adjective pair with a single adjective or phrase. In addition, points

---

[1] C.E. Osgood, G.J. Suci, and P.H. Tannenbaum, *The Measurement of Meaning* (Urbana: University of Illinois Press, 1957).

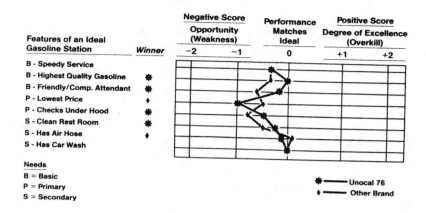

**Figure 7-6.** Stapel-scale profile of the performance of Unocal 76 attendants. (*Source:* "Actionable Research Needed When Markets Change," *Marketing News,* January 3, 1986, p. 53, published by the American Marketing Association.)

on the scale are numerically identified, and there are typically 10 scale positions instead of the 7 generally used in the semantic differential.

Construction, administration, and analysis are similar to their counterparts in the semantic differential, although instructions may differ slightly to correspond to the single adjective or phrase being used to describe the scale. Figure 7-6 illustrates the result of a Stapel scale applied to the performance level of Unocal 76 attendants compared to a major competitor.[2]

## MULTIDIMENSIONAL SCALING

In the previous approaches to attitude measurement, (1) we looked at a product or object in terms of only one dimension at a time, and (2) each dimension examined was, of necessity, identified prior to the measurement process. In contrast, multidimensional scaling makes no assumption with regard to the dimensionality of the objects being examined.

Multidimensional scaling is performed by a wide variety of computer programs, with the goal of

1. Beginning with a relatively simple set of data that describe similarities and differences between objects as reported by one or more respondents, then
2. Generating a multidimensional spatial configuration in which the relative

---

[2] "Actionable Research Needed When Markets Change," *Marketing News,* January 3, 1986, p. 53, published by the American Marketing Association.

positions of the objects closely resemble those suggested by the input data, and

3. Identifying the meaning of the dimensions of the spatial configuration in order to discover along what dimensions the respondents tend to differentiate between the objects.

## Direct versus Derived Multidimensional Scaling

Multidimensional scaling involves configurations that have been generated from either (1) *direct* similarity or preference judgments by respondents, or (2) *derived* positions described by the scores of each object on dimensions that have been predetermined and measured. Most of our discussion in this section will be relative to the direct judgments approach to multidimensional scaling. In this type of study, respondents simply provide information regarding the objects they believe are "most alike" or "most different." In the derived approach, the objects have already been measured along a number of predetermined dimensions. For example, in Figure 7-5, Budweiser and Michelob had already been measured by semantic differential along the dimensions "fast–slow" and "loud–quiet." If the beers had been located according to their means on each dimension, the result would have been two object points located in two-dimensional space, and would have been, in effect, a multidimensional scaling configuration of the derived type.

## Fundamental Principles

An important concept in multidimensional scaling is the notion of *interpoint distance*. This is the distance between any two points, and is the basis on which the rank order of distances is determined in a configuration.

Figure 7-7 summarizes the major steps of a multidimensional scaling analysis of direct judgments data. The input to the program contains the rank order of object interpoint distances—that is, which pair is most similar, next most similar, and so on. The computer first generates an initial configuration, which may or may not exhibit the same rank order of distances as the input data. The computer then proceeds to compare the rank order of input distances with the rank order of distances in the configuration it has just generated. If they are excessively different, the program will generate an improved configuration that more closely matches the input data. The evaluation is repeated, and the process continues until the configuration is a good "match" to the input rank order of distances. (*Note:* There are two major approaches to multidimensional scaling— *metric* and *nonmetric*. The metric procedure makes the assumption that data are of the interval scale or stronger. Nonmetric assumes that data are only of the ordinal scale. The output of both techniques is a metric, or interval, configuration of objects. Because of its popularity and its lesser assumptions regarding the nature of the data, our discussion here will concentrate on the nonmetric approach.)

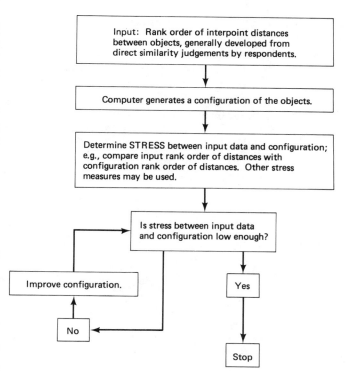

**Figure 7-7.** The major steps in a multidimensional scaling program.

## How Multidimensional Scaling Works: The Road Map Problem

As an illustration of how multidimensional scaling works, and how well it works, the following example is an excellent demonstration. The purpose of the study was to evaluate the multidimensional scaling procedure by applying it to a problem that already had a known solution.[3]

Imagine Rand McNally's probable dismay if there were no such things as mileages, and some cities were simply "farther away" than others. Well, this is what the multidimensional scaling program was given as input data—a rank order of distances for 15 U.S. cities. The 105 intercity distances were simply arranged in order of closest together (New York and Boston) through farthest apart (Miami and Seattle). At this point, mileages were completely forgotten—the only thing the computer was told was the ***rank order*** of distances between

---

[3] Marshall G. Greenberg, "A Variety of Approaches to Nonmetric Multidimensional Scaling," paper presented to the 16th International Meeting of the Institute of Management Sciences, New York (March 1969); discussed in Lester A. Neidell, "The Use of Nonmetric Multidimensional Scaling in Marketing Analysis," *Journal of Marketing*, October 1969, pp. 37–43, published by the American Marketing Association.

the objects, much as would be the case if toothpastes, politicians, or household detergents were the objects being scaled.

The results not only supported the validity of the multidimensional scaling technique, but did so quite dramatically. The configuration arrived at is shown in Figure 7-8, along with the actual geographic locations of the cities. Despite the lack of actual mileage figures, the program nevertheless succeeded in placing the cities at (or very near) their actual geographical locations. While several cities are out of position by a few hundred miles (e.g., Miami's slight offshore location), this is largely due to the fact that the cities' interpoint distances were ranked according to *road mileages* rather than "as the crow flies." Also, as far as

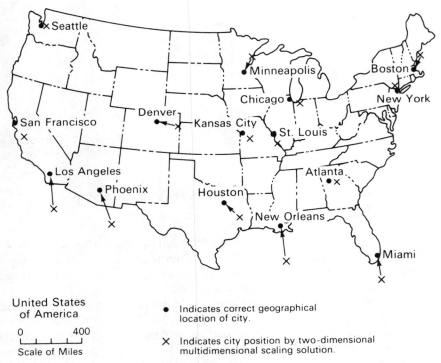

United States
of America

0            400
Scale of Miles

● Indicates correct geographical
location of city.

X Indicates city position by two-dimensional
multidimensional scaling solution.

**Figure 7-8.** Armed only with a *rank order* of intercity distances (no mileage information), a multidimensional scaling program was able to position these 15 U.S. cities very close to their actual geographic locations. Purpose was to lend support to the validity of multidimensional scaling as a research technique. [*Source:* Marshall G. Greenberg, "A Variety of Approaches to Nonmetric Multidimensional Scaling," paper presented to the 16th International Meeting of the Institute of Management Sciences, New York (March 1969); discussed in Lester A. Neidell, "The Use of Nonmetric Multidimensional Scaling in Marketing Analysis," *Journal of Marketing,* October 1969, pp. 37–43, published by the American Marketing Association.]

the computer was concerned, the two most distance cities (Miami and Seattle) could have been on different planets instead of just at opposite ends of a continent—the input data indicated only that they were farther apart than any other pair of cities. Given the strength of the results versus the nonmileage nature of the input, multidimensional scaling came out looking very good as a valid research technique for describing spatial configurations based on rank-order-of-distance data.

### Dimensionality and the Identification of Axes

Given the nature of the data in the "road map" example, it is obvious that (1) the most appropriate configuration is two-dimensional, and (2) the axes are north-south and east-west. However, things aren't always that easy when we are examining consumer perceptions by means of multidimensional scaling. As a matter of fact, determining the number of important dimensions is often a key purpose in conducting a multidimensional scaling study. The greater the number of important dimensions, the more attributes consumers are considering when they differentiate between two products or other objects. Once dimensionality is decided upon, the next step is to identify the dimensions, or axes, in terms of their meaning to the respondents. The three principal methods of axis identification are expert judgment, property fitting, and experimental design.[4]

*Expert judgment.* Expert judgment is a popular approach, though subjective and dependent on the amount of expertise and/or intuition possessed by the researcher. In some cases, the researcher may augment his or her own ideas with follow-up questioning of respondents to determine what criteria they used in making their similarity judgments of the objects.

*Property fitting.* The property fitting method relies on unidimensional attribute ratings which the respondents provide for each of the objects being scaled. For example, a respondent may be asked to rate each object by means of a scale like this one:

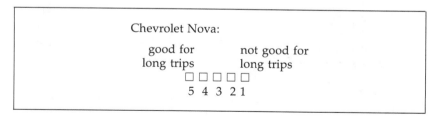

When the researcher measures attributes in addition to obtaining similar-

[4] Based on Paul E. Greene and Frank J. Carmone, *Multidimensional Scaling* (Boston: Allyn & Bacon, 1970), pp. 57–59.

ities data for the objects, he or she then has two sets of data that complement each other. Once the configuration is obtained, an attribute "vector" is constructed by the computer in such a way that the attribute vector is pointed in the same direction as the objects that tended to score highest on that property. For example, a "good for long trips" vector would be directed toward those cars that respondents tended to rate highest in that attribute. In statistical terms, each vector is oriented so there is a maximum correlation between (1) the objects' actual scores on that property, and (2) the objects' configuration positions along the direction of the property vector (see Figure 7-9).

*Experimental design.* With some objects, it may be possible to vary the extent to which the objects themselves possess various attributes—for example, the strength of different coffee mixtures or the sweetness of soft drinks.

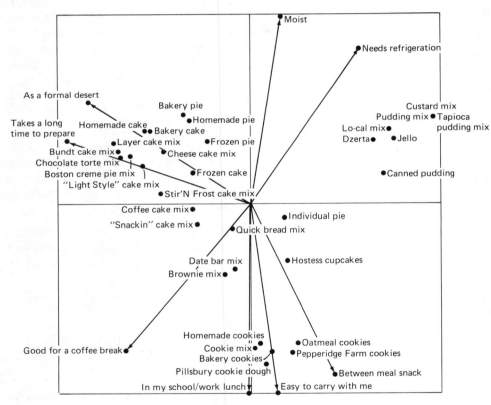

**Figure 7-9.** This MDS study identified the perceived positions of a variety of desserts. Arrows represent key usage occasions and product attributes, and products in close proximity tend to be good substitutes for each other. (*Source:* "CATALYST Measurement, Mapping Method Identifies Competition, Defines Markets," *Marketing News*, May 14, 1982, sec. 1, p. 3, published by the American Marketing Association.)

## Marketing Applications for Multidimensional Scaling

There is a wide variety of potential areas in which multidimensional scaling can be useful in marketing. The applications discussed below have already been identified for this fascinating technique.[5]

*Product life-cycle analysis.* With periodic multidimensional scaling studies, the equivalent of a series of "photographs" could reveal movement along performance and product attribute dimensions, extending the life-cycle idea from the traditional preoccupation with unidimensional measures, usually sales or market shares.

*Market segmentation.* With the inclusion of preference as well as similarities data, both brands and consumer ideal points could be located in the same configuration. Market segments could then be viewed as "subspaces" in which some consumers have similar perceptions of the brands and have "ideal points" that are close together. Combining this with the ideas in the preceding paragraph, a series of multidimensional scaling "photographs" could help the marketing manager measure the success of his product or advertising strategies in moving his brand toward a cluster of ideal points (or, conversely, in moving the ideal points toward his own brand).

*Vendor evaluations.* Just as consumers select from products that vary along numerous dimensions, so must the industrial purchaser—for example, he must consider factors such as quality, price, delivery, technical expertise, and support. Multidimensional scaling could help to determine how purchasing agents "collapse" these and many more supplier characteristics in deciding on who gets their business. Naturally, knowledge of how this simplifying process takes place would be valuable to industrial marketers as an aid to developing improved sales strategies.

*Advertising evaluation.* Multidimensional scaling could help describe the attributes that separate "good" ads from "bad" ads, contribute to the pretesting of alternative advertisement possibilities, and help determine which types of advertisements are best matched with various media.

*New products.* The combination of preference and similarity data sometimes leads to configurations where there are a lot of ideal points in a space occupied by no existing products. This indicates the possibility that a new product with appropriate attributes (i.e., it would have been positioned in that space had it been included among the input objects) would be well received by consumers.

---

[5] Discussion is based in part on Green and Carmone, *Multidimensional Scaling*, pp. 14–18.

---

**EXHIBIT 7-2**

**Traveling the Mind's Highway**

In the mid-1980s, General Motors encountered a problem in the close proximity of its Buick and Oldsmobile divisions. As shown in parts (a) and (b) of Figure 7-10, by 1986 these nameplates had drifted much too close together, tending to result in their competing too much against each other instead of taking on the products of other manufacturers. GM is not alone in facing this kind of dilemma—it has also happened to Chrysler Corporation with its Plymouth and Dodge nameplates.

Part (c) of the figure illustrates GM's goals for the late 1980s, as drafted in 1984, while part (d) shows more recent positioning plans. The 1984 plans were for Chevrolet to claim the low-price, functional location; Pontiac to regain the low-price "personal car" territory it had in the late 1960s; Oldsmobile to hold onto its higher-price, conservative area; Buick to move away from its traditional luxury position to attract "yuppies" in the higher-priced personal segment; and Cadillac to move even farther upscale.

In the two years following the 1984 plans, Chevrolet and Cadillac strengthened their positions at the top and bottom of the price range, Pontiac used the "We build excitement" theme while moving in the personal-expressive direction, and Oldsmobile moved slightly while continuing to enjoy strong sales. Buick, however, was not successful in its efforts to attract younger buyers interested in sportiness.

Comparing diagrams (c) and (d), the biggest change in plans has been the intended switching of positions for Buick and Oldsmobile for the late 1980s. Two other developments are also reflected in these illustrations: (1) Saturn, planned for introduction in 1989, and (2) Opel, being considered as either a "captive" imported version of other models, or as a separate model with its own dealer network. Regarding the Buick–Oldsmobile positioning switch, Robert T. O'Connell, GM's vice-president, Marketing and Product Planning Staff, expects the repositioning to move relatively fast, with "really significant progress in 2–4 years."

*Source:* Based on Jesse Snyder, "4 GM Car Divisions Are Repositioned in Effort to Help Sales," *Automotive News*, September 15, 1986, pp. 1, 49.

---

***Store and salesperson image research.*** As with the semantic differential, multidimensional scaling can help identify a store's image and the attributes that make it similar and different from various of its competitors. However, multidimensional scaling has the ability to proceed where no attributes have been predetermined, making it a potentially more powerful tool in this area. In addition to measuring store or company images, the images of various sales personnel can also be compared. Through multidimensional scaling of salespersons, it can be determined if the image projected by a salesperson is consistent with the larger efforts being made by the corporation on behalf of its company image.

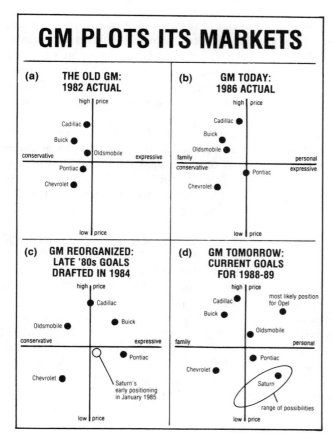

**Figure 7-10.**   Actual and planned product positions for General Motors nameplates. Biggest change involved the plan to reposition Buick and Oldsmobile between 1986 and late 1980s. (*Source:* Reprinted from Jesse Snyder, ''4 GM Car Divisions Are Repositioned in Effort to Help Sales,'' *Automotive News,* September 15, 1986, pp. 1, 49.)

## ☐  SUMMARY

Marketing research deals with attitudes in two ways: (1) we measure the attitudes that customers or respondents have toward the object of our marketing efforts, and (2) having discovered these attitudes, we compare the effectiveness of alternative strategies for improving or otherwise shaping them. The quantification of attitudes may be either unidimensional (one attitude dimension at a time) or multidimensional (objects are examined as points in multidimensional attitudinal space).

*Attitude* can be defined as a mental state that predisposes the individual to respond in a certain way when he or she is subjected to a given stimulus. Attitudes are generally viewed as having three components: cognitive (what we know or believe about an object), affective (our positive or negative feelings with regard to the object), and behavioral (our predisposition toward action in a given situation).

Rating scales require that the respondent indicate his or her attitude toward an object by (1) indicating a position along a continuum or series of ordered categories, (2) selecting one object over another with regard to a given attribute, or (3) assigning numerical values to one or more objects as a reflection of their relative strengths in terms of possessing an attribute. Popular rating scales include the graphic, itemized, rank-order, paired-comparison, constant-sum, and fractionation techniques.

While rating scales require the respondent to react to just a single statement or question, attitude scaling techniques involve a battery of questions or statements that provide a more complete view of the individual's overall attitude. Based on responses to a set of questions or statements, an attitude score may be computed that represents the individual's attitude toward the object of the investigation. Popular attitude scaling techniques include the Likert scale, the semantic differential, and the Stapel scale.

In multidimensional scaling, objects are positioned in multidimensional perceptual space based on the judgments or attitudes of one or more respondents. Multidimensional scaling may be either derived or direct. In the derived approach, the positions of the objects are described by their respective scores along dimensions that have been predetermined and measured.

In direct multidimensional scaling, the configuration of objects is based on similarity or preference judgments by the respondents. Input generally consists of a rank order of object interpoint distances, describing which two objects are most alike, next most alike, and so on, all the way to the two that are least alike. In this approach, there are no predetermined dimensions, and axis identification is typically carried out by expert judgment, the fitting of property vectors to the configuration, or by experimentation.

## ☐ QUESTIONS FOR REVIEW

1. Differentiate among the cognitive, affective, and behavioral components of attitude and provide an example of each.
2. Describe how one might construct and administer a question utilizing: (a) the constant-sum technique, and (b) the fractionation technique. Provide an example of each.
3. When would it be desirable to use a comparative rating scale instead of the noncomparative type?
4. Construct a five-question noncomparative graphic rating scale instrument to measure consumer attitudes toward a pizza establishment near your campus. Next, convert the instrument so that the questions are of the itemized scale type.
5. Construct a five-question Stapel-scale instrument to evaluate a local department store.
6. What is the primary difference between an attitude rating scale and the attitude scaling techniques described in this chapter?
7. What is the nature and purpose of the semantic differential technique? Provide an example of how the technique might be used in examining attitudes towards Sears.
8. With a convenience sample of 15 students, apply the semantic differential technique

to measure attitudes towards two products, celebrities, or other objects of your choice. Using the text's Budweiser–Michelob visual example as a guide, plot the perceived positions of the objects as they appear on two of the dimensions you have selected. Does there appear to be a significant difference between the positions of the objects?

9. Cyrus is compiling a series of favorable/unfavorable statements for use in a Likert summated scale measurement of students' attitudes toward Ben Thomas University. Evaluate the suitability of including each of the following statements.

   **a.** "The climate around BTU is uncomfortably hot in the summer."

   **b.** "BTU has a football team."

   **c.** "BTU's professors are well-qualified in their fields."

   **d.** "BTU doesn't offer a challenging educational experience."

10. Mortimer's responses to the following statements are:

    | | |
    |---|---|
    | "Reading in the library is my favorite pastime." | −2 [disagrees strongly] |
    | "Libraries are dull." | +1 [agrees] |
    | "You meet interesting people in the library." | −1 [disagrees] |
    | "I never go to the library unless I have to." | +2 [agrees strongly] |

    Using the Likert summated scale technique, what is Mortimer's numerical attitude rating toward the library?

11. Construct a Likert summated scale instrument to measure attitude toward an object of your choice. Include at least four statements in the instrument. Supply responses for a hypothetical respondent, then calculate the attitude score for that respondent.

12. Construct a two-dimensional multidimensional scaling configuration that will satisfy the following rank order of distances: A-B (closest), B-C, A-C (furthest apart). Are there any other configurations that would satisfy this input requirement? If so, what does this suggest about the wisdom of using MDS with a very small number of objects?

13. What was the purpose of the "road map" multidimensional scaling study described in the chapter? If the input rank order of distances had been based on air miles instead of road miles, how would the resulting configuration have been changed?

14. In the analysis of a perceptual configuration that has been obtained by means of multidimensional scaling, how can a researcher identify the "meaning" of each dimension, or axis, along which the objects lie?

15. Differentiate between the direct and the derived approach to MDS. What type of approach was the Michelob–Budweiser example mentioned in the text?

# CASES FOR PART TWO

## CASE 2-1

### Evergreen University (A)

The following hypothetical information describes the results of an observational study of the population of automobiles driven to school by Evergreen University professors and parked in the university's faculty parking area. All 280 faculty cars are included, and their characteristics arranged in order of sticker number. The observations are coded according to:

|  |  |
|---|---|
| C, country of origin | 0, imported |
|  | 1, domestic |
| T, transmission type | 0, automatic |
|  | 1, manual |
| B, body style | 0, two-door sedan or coupe |
|  | 1, four-door sedan |
|  | 2, station wagon |
|  | 3, convertible or two-seater |
| M, odometer reading, thousands of miles |  |

| | C | T | B | M | | C | T | B | M | | C | T | B | M |
|---|---|---|---|---|---|---|---|---|---|---|---|---|---|---|
| 1. | 1 | 0 | 1 | 25 | 36. | 1 | 0 | 1 | 26 | 71. | 0 | 1 | 0 | 52 |
| 2. | 1 | 0 | 0 | 29 | 37. | 0 | 1 | 3 | 29 | 72. | 1 | 1 | 0 | 44 |
| 3. | 0 | 1 | 0 | 53 | 38. | 1 | 1 | 1 | 21 | 73. | 0 | 0 | 3 | 29 |
| 4. | 1 | 1 | 0 | 38 | 39. | 1 | 0 | 1 | 34 | 74. | 1 | 1 | 0 | 46 |
| 5. | 1 | 0 | 2 | 23 | 40. | 1 | 0 | 1 | 37 | 75. | 1 | 0 | 1 | 32 |
| 6. | 0 | 1 | 0 | 35 | 41. | 1 | 1 | 0 | 54 | 76. | 1 | 1 | 0 | 38 |
| 7. | 1 | 0 | 1 | 37 | 42. | 1 | 0 | 2 | 22 | 77. | 1 | 0 | 0 | 30 |
| 8. | 1 | 0 | 0 | 35 | 43. | 1 | 0 | 0 | 32 | 78. | 1 | 0 | 0 | 35 |
| 9. | 0 | 1 | 0 | 38 | 44. | 0 | 1 | 2 | 33 | 79. | 0 | 1 | 0 | 27 |
| 10. | 1 | 0 | 1 | 24 | 45. | 0 | 1 | 0 | 45 | 80. | 1 | 0 | 0 | 50 |
| 11. | 1 | 0 | 2 | 23 | 46. | 0 | 1 | 0 | 40 | 81. | 0 | 1 | 0 | 26 |
| 12. | 0 | 1 | 3 | 19 | 47. | 1 | 0 | 0 | 20 | 82. | 0 | 1 | 0 | 31 |
| 13. | 0 | 1 | 1 | 33 | 48. | 1 | 0 | 1 | 25 | 83. | 1 | 0 | 1 | 26 |
| 14. | 1 | 0 | 2 | 30 | 49. | 1 | 0 | 2 | 32 | 84. | 1 | 0 | 0 | 29 |
| 15. | 0 | 0 | 2 | 39 | 50. | 1 | 1 | 1 | 26 | 85. | 0 | 1 | 1 | 27 |
| 16. | 1 | 1 | 0 | 43 | 51. | 1 | 0 | 1 | 30 | 86. | 1 | 1 | 0 | 31 |
| 17. | 0 | 1 | 0 | 37 | 52. | 1 | 0 | 0 | 36 | 87. | 0 | 1 | 0 | 22 |
| 18. | 1 | 1 | 0 | 33 | 53. | 0 | 1 | 1 | 26 | 88. | 1 | 0 | 0 | 37 |
| 19. | 1 | 0 | 0 | 33 | 54. | 1 | 0 | 1 | 35 | 89. | 1 | 0 | 0 | 38 |
| 20. | 1 | 0 | 1 | 34 | 55. | 0 | 0 | 1 | 37 | 90. | 0 | 1 | 2 | 43 |
| 21. | 1 | 0 | 0 | 30 | 56. | 0 | 1 | 3 | 41 | 91. | 1 | 0 | 1 | 19 |
| 22. | 0 | 0 | 0 | 40 | 57. | 1 | 0 | 1 | 27 | 92. | 0 | 1 | 1 | 33 |
| 23. | 1 | 0 | 0 | 30 | 58. | 1 | 0 | 0 | 38 | 93. | 0 | 1 | 1 | 34 |
| 24. | 0 | 1 | 1 | 28 | 59. | 1 | 0 | 1 | 27 | 94. | 1 | 0 | 2 | 53 |
| 25. | 0 | 0 | 0 | 50 | 60. | 1 | 0 | 2 | 28 | 95. | 1 | 0 | 1 | 34 |
| 26. | 1 | 0 | 1 | 40 | 61. | 0 | 1 | 2 | 44 | 96. | 0 | 0 | 1 | 43 |
| 27. | 0 | 1 | 0 | 25 | 62. | 1 | 0 | 2 | 27 | 97. | 0 | 1 | 0 | 38 |
| 28. | 1 | 0 | 0 | 35 | 63. | 0 | 1 | 1 | 47 | 98. | 0 | 1 | 0 | 49 |
| 29. | 0 | 1 | 0 | 50 | 64. | 0 | 0 | 1 | 10 | 99. | 1 | 0 | 0 | 16 |
| 30. | 1 | 0 | 0 | 44 | 65. | 0 | 1 | 0 | 27 | 100. | 0 | 1 | 0 | 68 |
| 31. | 0 | 1 | 0 | 53 | 66. | 1 | 0 | 0 | 24 | 101. | 0 | 0 | 0 | 36 |
| 32. | 1 | 0 | 1 | 36 | 67. | 1 | 0 | 0 | 26 | 102. | 0 | 1 | 2 | 42 |
| 33. | 0 | 1 | 0 | 34 | 68. | 0 | 1 | 0 | 38 | 103. | 1 | 0 | 1 | 41 |
| 34. | 0 | 0 | 1 | 43 | 69. | 1 | 0 | 2 | 35 | 104. | 1 | 0 | 0 | 21 |
| 35. | 1 | 0 | 3 | 38 | 70. | 1 | 0 | 2 | 34 | 105. | 1 | 1 | 0 | 37 |

| | C | T | B | M | | C | T | B | M | | C | T | B | M |
|---|---|---|---|---|---|---|---|---|---|---|---|---|---|---|
| 106. | 0 | 1 | 3 | 49 | 157. | 1 | 0 | 1 | 25 | 208. | 0 | 1 | 0 | 37 |
| 107. | 1 | 0 | 1 | 29 | 158. | 1 | 0 | 1 | 36 | 209. | 1 | 0 | 1 | 28 |
| 108. | 1 | 0 | 1 | 24 | 159. | 1 | 0 | 0 | 36 | 210. | 1 | 0 | 1 | 23 |
| 109. | 1 | 0 | 1 | 38 | 160. | 0 | 1 | 0 | 36 | 211. | 1 | 0 | 1 | 29 |
| 110. | 1 | 0 | 1 | 35 | 161. | 1 | 0 | 1 | 23 | 212. | 1 | 0 | 2 | 29 |
| 111. | 1 | 0 | 1 | 33 | 162. | 1 | 0 | 1 | 26 | 213. | 0 | 0 | 2 | 52 |
| 112. | 1 | 1 | 0 | 36 | 163. | 1 | 0 | 1 | 24 | 214. | 1 | 0 | 1 | 32 |
| 113. | 0 | 1 | 0 | 38 | 164. | 1 | 1 | 2 | 38 | 215. | 0 | 1 | 0 | 41 |
| 114. | 1 | 0 | 1 | 45 | 165. | 1 | 1 | 1 | 31 | 216. | 0 | 1 | 0 | 42 |
| 115. | 1 | 0 | 0 | 45 | 166. | 1 | 0 | 1 | 30 | 217. | 1 | 0 | 1 | 22 |
| 116. | 0 | 1 | 2 | 50 | 167. | 0 | 0 | 0 | 43 | 218. | 1 | 1 | 2 | 17 |
| 117. | 0 | 1 | 1 | 39 | 168. | 0 | 1 | 3 | 44 | 219. | 1 | 0 | 1 | 29 |
| 118. | 0 | 1 | 1 | 28 | 169. | 1 | 0 | 1 | 30 | 220. | 0 | 1 | 0 | 35 |
| 119. | 1 | 0 | 1 | 25 | 170. | 1 | 0 | 0 | 26 | 221. | 0 | 1 | 1 | 38 |
| 120. | 1 | 0 | 0 | 25 | 171. | 0 | 1 | 1 | 25 | 222. | 1 | 0 | 0 | 30 |
| 121. | 0 | 0 | 2 | 27 | 172. | 1 | 0 | 1 | 36 | 223. | 1 | 0 | 1 | 32 |
| 122. | 0 | 1 | 0 | 35 | 173. | 0 | 0 | 0 | 34 | 224. | 1 | 0 | 1 | 22 |
| 123. | 1 | 0 | 2 | 32 | 174. | 1 | 0 | 1 | 33 | 225. | 0 | 0 | 1 | 21 |
| 124. | 1 | 1 | 0 | 27 | 175. | 0 | 1 | 1 | 31 | 226. | 1 | 0 | 0 | 37 |
| 125. | 0 | 1 | 1 | 39 | 176. | 1 | 0 | 0 | 39 | 227. | 0 | 1 | 0 | 26 |
| 126. | 1 | 0 | 1 | 26 | 177. | 1 | 0 | 1 | 26 | 228. | 1 | 1 | 1 | 22 |
| 127. | 0 | 1 | 1 | 42 | 178. | 1 | 1 | 1 | 26 | 229. | 0 | 1 | 1 | 53 |
| 128. | 0 | 0 | 2 | 34 | 179. | 1 | 0 | 1 | 32 | 230. | 1 | 0 | 1 | 19 |
| 129. | 1 | 0 | 0 | 44 | 180. | 1 | 0 | 1 | 32 | 231. | 1 | 0 | 1 | 38 |
| 130. | 0 | 0 | 1 | 37 | 181. | 0 | 0 | 2 | 25 | 232. | 1 | 0 | 1 | 37 |
| 131. | 0 | 1 | 0 | 47 | 182. | 0 | 1 | 0 | 43 | 233. | 1 | 1 | 1 | 39 |
| 132. | 0 | 1 | 2 | 42 | 183. | 1 | 0 | 1 | 33 | 234. | 1 | 0 | 1 | 23 |
| 133. | 0 | 1 | 0 | 26 | 184. | 1 | 0 | 0 | 22 | 235. | 1 | 0 | 3 | 37 |
| 134. | 0 | 1 | 1 | 66 | 185. | 0 | 0 | 0 | 54 | 236. | 1 | 0 | 2 | 33 |
| 135. | 0 | 0 | 0 | 38 | 186. | 1 | 0 | 1 | 24 | 237. | 1 | 0 | 1 | 22 |
| 136. | 1 | 0 | 1 | 27 | 187. | 1 | 0 | 1 | 19 | 238. | 0 | 1 | 2 | 38 |
| 137. | 0 | 0 | 0 | 36 | 188. | 1 | 0 | 2 | 41 | 239. | 1 | 1 | 0 | 28 |
| 138. | 0 | 0 | 2 | 24 | 189. | 1 | 0 | 1 | 34 | 240. | 1 | 0 | 1 | 16 |
| 139. | 1 | 0 | 1 | 37 | 190. | 1 | 0 | 2 | 31 | 241. | 1 | 1 | 1 | 29 |
| 140. | 1 | 0 | 1 | 36 | 191. | 1 | 0 | 2 | 30 | 242. | 0 | 1 | 1 | 35 |
| 141. | 0 | 1 | 0 | 41 | 192. | 1 | 0 | 0 | 30 | 243. | 1 | 0 | 2 | 36 |
| 142. | 0 | 1 | 2 | 34 | 193. | 1 | 0 | 0 | 43 | 244. | 1 | 0 | 0 | 44 |
| 143. | 0 | 1 | 0 | 35 | 194. | 0 | 1 | 0 | 42 | 245. | 1 | 0 | 1 | 25 |
| 144. | 0 | 1 | 1 | 41 | 195. | 1 | 0 | 1 | 33 | 246. | 0 | 0 | 1 | 38 |
| 145. | 0 | 0 | 0 | 32 | 196. | 0 | 0 | 2 | 41 | 247. | 1 | 0 | 0 | 41 |
| 146. | 1 | 0 | 1 | 39 | 197. | 1 | 0 | 2 | 23 | 248. | 1 | 1 | 0 | 40 |
| 147. | 0 | 0 | 0 | 38 | 198. | 0 | 1 | 1 | 29 | 249. | 1 | 0 | 2 | 23 |
| 148. | 0 | 0 | 2 | 37 | 199. | 0 | 1 | 1 | 44 | 250. | 0 | 0 | 1 | 36 |
| 149. | 1 | 0 | 1 | 23 | 200. | 0 | 1 | 0 | 35 | 251. | 0 | 0 | 0 | 33 |
| 150. | 1 | 0 | 1 | 42 | 201. | 1 | 1 | 1 | 37 | 252. | 1 | 0 | 2 | 31 |
| 151. | 1 | 1 | 2 | 40 | 202. | 0 | 1 | 1 | 38 | 253. | 0 | 0 | 2 | 38 |
| 152. | 0 | 1 | 1 | 46 | 203. | 0 | 1 | 1 | 39 | 254. | 0 | 0 | 1 | 36 |
| 153. | 1 | 1 | 0 | 40 | 204. | 0 | 0 | 0 | 37 | 255. | 1 | 1 | 0 | 37 |
| 154. | 1 | 0 | 1 | 27 | 205. | 1 | 1 | 0 | 34 | 256. | 1 | 0 | 1 | 31 |
| 155. | 1 | 0 | 1 | 35 | 206. | 1 | 0 | 2 | 28 | 257. | 1 | 0 | 0 | 35 |
| 156. | 0 | 1 | 1 | 29 | 207. | 1 | 0 | 0 | 32 | 258. | 1 | 0 | 0 | 30 |

| | C | T | B | M | | C | T | B | M | | C | T | B | M |
|---|---|---|---|---|---|---|---|---|---|---|---|---|---|---|
| 259. | 1 | 0 | 1 | 35 | 267. | 1 | 0 | 2 | 18 | 275. | 0 | 1 | 1 | 50 |
| 260. | 0 | 1 | 1 | 26 | 268. | 1 | 0 | 1 | 40 | 276. | 0 | 1 | 1 | 49 |
| 261. | 1 | 0 | 1 | 27 | 269. | 0 | 1 | 0 | 29 | 277. | 1 | 1 | 0 | 34 |
| 262. | 0 | 1 | 0 | 35 | 270. | 1 | 1 | 0 | 42 | 278. | 0 | 1 | 1 | 44 |
| 263. | 0 | 1 | 2 | 43 | 271. | 1 | 1 | 0 | 38 | 279. | 1 | 0 | 0 | 29 |
| 264. | 1 | 0 | 1 | 34 | 272. | 1 | 1 | 2 | 22 | 280. | 1 | 0 | 0 | 27 |
| 265. | 1 | 1 | 0 | 39 | 273. | 0 | 1 | 0 | 43 | | | | | |
| 266. | 0 | 1 | 0 | 36 | 274. | 1 | 1 | 1 | 27 | | | | | |

Given the preceding data set for faculty automobiles:

1. Using the table of random numbers in the text, select a simple random sample of 35 faculty automobiles. Calculate the average odometer reading of the vehicles in the sample.
2. Using the systematic sampling technique, select a sample of 35 faculty vehicles, then calculate the average odometer reading for the sample.
3. Using the cluster sampling technique, select a sample of 35 faculty vehicles. In applying this technique, assume that the population consists of 56 clusters of 5 vehicles each. Calculate the average odometer reading for the vehicles in the sample.
4. Given that 60% of the vehicles in the population are dometic makes, with 40% being imported, select a proportionate stratified sample of 35 cars from the vehicle population. Calculate the average odometer reading for the vehicles in the sample. Also calculate separate means for the odometer readings of the domestic versus imported vehicles that comprise the overall sample. Does a comparison of these means suggest that a proportionate stratified sample based on country of origin would be advantageous for estimating the overall average mileage in the data set?

## CASE 2-2

### Cellular Phone Users

In a survey reported in *Automotive News*,\* AT&T and the Potomac Division of the American Automobile Association refuted the fears that some harbored regarding the safety of cellular mobile telephones. Just 7.4% of the 1000 cellular-phone users polled had an accident in the year prior to the survey, compared to a 10.2% accident rate for AAA Potomac members. At the time of the study, there were approximately 15,000 cellular phones in use in that area.

Based on this information alone: (a) comment on possible ways in which the phone user group and AAA group might not be representative of the overall

---

\* (See Geoff Sundstrom, "Cellular-Phone Users Called Safer Drivers," *Automotive News*, August 26, 1985, p. 24.)

cellular-phone-user and general driving populations, respectively, and (b) speculate as to possible sources of response and nonresponse error that, at least theoretically, could have influenced the results obtained.

## CASE 2-3

### Home-Builder Convention

Relying on attendees of a 1984 home-builders' convention, a home-insulation manufacturer conducted a survey on the outlook for the industry*. While most forecasters had been predicting that construction activity would be about the same as the preceding year, the company found members of their sample to expect a 30% increase in housing starts over 1983. Armed with this information, the firm set up a press conference, complete with panel of experts, to announce their findings.

One of the experts at the press conference, asked for his interpretation of the +30% forecast, was not very supportive of the survey finding. Following the press conference, company officials quickly pointed out that their study was not meant to be a scientific poll. On the basis of sampling representativeness, provide an explanation as to why this erroneous result probably occurred.

## CASE 2-4

### Consumerweek Magazine

In comparing several rotary lawn mowers for a lawn products issue, *Consumerweek* magazine has rated each product on 10 different attributes, as shown in the table below. Each of four staff experts has assigned a 0–10 score to each mower on each attribute, making possible a maximum additive score of 400 points for each product tested.

|  | Lawngopher | Bladewizard | Lawnchomper |
|---|---|---|---|
| Compactness for storage | 28 | 25 | 15 |
| Safety deflector effectiveness | 35 | 34 | 24 |
| Ease of changing cutting height | 29 | 37 | 12 |
| Quietness of operation | 27 | 29 | 23 |
| Ease of maintenance | 34 | 30 | 25 |
| Dealer service availability | 38 | 33 | 28 |
| Ease of starting | 29 | 32 | 26 |
| Ease of operation | 35 | 31 | 27 |
| Overall safety of operation | 36 | 37 | 22 |
| Overall level of quality | 34 | 30 | 19 |
| Total score | 325 | 318 | 221 |

---

* (See "Stupid Questions," *The Wall Street Journal*, February 7, 1984, p. 35.)

The editors of *Consumerweek* conclude that the Lawngopher was the "clear winner" in this comparison test, and go on to point out that it is now second only to the more expensive Lawngroomer model tested in a previous issue. From a measurement perspective, does this procedure appear to be appropriate for the scale of measurement of the data collected? Why or why not?

# 8

# SURVEY RESEARCH

**Survey Research Helps New Camera Click**

In the mid-1970s, having successfully introduced small, simple-to-use cameras that allowed consumers to take pictures in previously impractical situations, the Eastman Kodak Company was not content to rest on its laurels. Kodak began an extensive marketing research program to, as John J. Powers, vice-president and director of marketing communications puts it, "determine under what conditions consumers were and were *not* taking pictures; and second, once we determined where they *weren't* taking pictures, we set out to develop a photographic system which could function in those areas." The eventual result was the Kodak disc camera, a new concept combining small size, versatility, and film on a disc instead of a roll.

Survey research helped both in developing the new camera and in testing the effectiveness of promotional messages on its behalf. Following the manufacture of prototypes, Kodak conducted over 1000 in-home interviews to gauge consumers' reactions. To evaluate the effectiveness of the ads, two research firms were hired to see if ad viewers recalled key features of the product. Of consumers who were shown the ads, "100% remembered the disc film feature and the take-pictures-you-may-mave-been-missing theme. And 95% rated the camera's decision-free feature good to excellent . . .

*Source:* Based on "Credit Success of Kodak Disc Camera to Research," *Marketing News*, January 21, 1983, pp. 8–9, published by the American Marketing Association.

**Figure 8-1.** Over 1000 in-home interviews were conducted to evaluate consumer reactions to prototypes of the Kodak disc camera. (Courtesy of Eastman Kodak Company, Rochester, N.Y.)

Among all of our survey groups, the ads generated excitement and enthusiasm."

The marketplace, that ultimate arbiter of success, supported both Mr. Powers' own enthusiasm and the positive predictions of marketing research. Following the camera's introduction, "sales of film, cameras, and photofinishing equipment far exceeded our most optimistic expectations."

## INTRODUCTION

Basically, there are two methods we can use to obtain information from individuals—we can either ask them or observe them. The first of these possibilities, an approach that some mistakenly equate with marketing research itself, is known as *survey research*, whereby we communicate with a sampling of respondents in order to make generalizations about the population they represent. Every year, there are about 23 million survey interviews conducted in the United States alone.[1] In this chapter we will examine the "family" of survey research

---

[1] "Workshop Covers Response-Rate Formula, Phone Survey Bias, Other Research Issues," *Marketing News*, January 21, 1983, sec. 2, p. 22, published by the American Marketing Association.

methods and their implications for the acquisition of marketing information, focusing on the following topics:

I. Survey research methods and applications
II. Sources of error in survey research
III. The personal interview
IV. The telephone interview
V. The mail questionnaire
VI. Strategies for reducing nonresponse error
VII. Selection of a survey method

## SURVEY RESEARCH METHODS AND APPLICATIONS

### Types of Surveys

When conducting a survey, we have three basic methods of communication with respondents: (1) interview them in person, (2) interview them by telephone, or (3) ask them to respond to a mail questionnaire. In the personal interview, the questions are asked during a face-to-face encounter between the interviewer and the respondent. In the telephone interview, the situation is similar except that communication occurs by means of the telephone. In the mail questionnaire survey, respondents are usually asked to complete and return a questionnaire which they receive in the mail. In this method, however, the means of delivering the questionnaire may vary—for example, the questionnaire may be included within the body of a newspaper or magazine, attached to a product sample, or left with the respondent by workers in the field. Naturally, it is possible to "mix" these modes of communication in order to take advantage of their individual strengths and help compensate for their respective weaknesses. For example, we might use a brief telephone interview followed by a mail questionnaire sent to the same respondent. Such possibilities are discussed later in the chapter.

### Applications of Survey Research

Survey research is generally aimed at securing some piece of information about the (1) present, (2) recent past, or (3) short-term future value of a respondent variable of interest to the researcher. The nature of these variables may be, as discussed earlier, state of mind (e.g., "Do you approve of selling beer in supermarkets?"), state of being (e.g., "Are you watching 'Cagney & Lacey' on TV?"), or behavioral (e.g., "Do you normally shop more than one dealer before buying a new car?"). Because private behavior is often not observable, we must rely on communication with the respondent in order to answer many questions similar to the preceding.

Besides their information value to its originator, survey research data can be useful in facilitating marketing actions on the part of others as well. For

MR. BUBBLE'S BIRTHDAY BASH
25 years old & still cleaning up.

Also inside...
BODYBUILDER RACHEL McLISH
THE LATEST: HIGH-TECH TUBS
SPRINGSTEEN & THE COMMON MAN

**Figure 8-2.** Inspired by a survey pointing out that 31% of adults read in the bathroom, a Cleveland publisher rolled out this new publication. (Courtesy of Davis Communications, Cleveland, Ohio.)

example, *The Wall Street Journal* is typical of many publications in its surveying of subscribers for the purpose of obtaining income and other data that will attract other companies to use the publication as an advertising medium. According to a 1986 ad in the WSJ, subscribers "have an average income of $107,800. And an average household net worth of $767,800."[2] In a totally different direction, a Cleveland publisher became aware of a survey which showed that 31% of adults read in the bathroom, with *True Story, Seventeen,* and *Time* comprising the top three literary choices for this inspirational setting. The survey prompted Michael S. Cohen to come out with *Bathroom Journal,* a new publication specifically intended for bathroom reading. While targeted toward a mass audience, BJ includes editorial content especially designed for professionals in the 25–45 age group. The publication, the front cover of which is shown in Figure 8-2,

---

[2] Advertisement, *The Wall Street Journal,* October 14, 1986, p. 26.

offers a mixture of stories on health and fitness, money, sports, and other general-interest topics in addition to regular features that will include fiction, humor, games, and horoscopes.[3]

## SOURCES OF ERROR IN SURVEY RESEARCH

Incredible as it may seem to the layperson, asking questions and receiving answers is not the simple process it might initially appear to be. The procedure is subject to errors, often unpredictable, that may undermine the entire purpose and results of the survey. While taking a survey should not be compared to walking through a mine field, there are three types of errors we must recognize in conducting survey research of any kind: (1) sampling error, (2) response error, and (3) nonresponse error.

### Sampling Error

As we discussed in Chapter 4, *sampling error* is present whenever we take a sample, instead of a complete census, of the population. While unavoidable in sampling, the probable extent to which this error exists can be statistically estimated whenever our sampling procedure involves probability selection techniques.

### Response Error

Unlike sampling error, *response error* may be present even if we take a complete census of the population. Response error occurs whenever the true value of the variable under investigation is distorted during the communication process involved in the survey. An actual, though extreme example, of this type of error is shown in Figure 8-3. In general, the ability to obtain a true reply depends on the following sequence of possibilities:

*1. Does the respondent understand the question?* Naturally, if the respondent does not understand the question, any answer he or she provides will be meaningless. For example, we could not expect to interview members of the general public and ask, "Do you believe that the expected value of perfect information is a valid upper limit to the amount that should be expended on a marketing research study?" or "Do you generally frequent commercial sources of cinematic entertainment?" What we perceive as a relatively simple term may be interpreted in an entirely different manner by a respondent. It is very important that we word our questions in such a way that the respondent understands what we are asking and shares our meaning of the various terms that are used. We will examine this topic further in the next chapter, which deals with the content and wording of the questions we ask.

---

[3] "Roll Out Privy Periodical," *Marketing News*, August 29, 1986, p. 4, published by the American Marketing Association.

**Figure 8-3.**   Response error is a type of informational error possible whenever survey research is undertaken. Besides misinterpreting questions and knowingly providing incorrect responses, some subjects will attempt to impress you with their creativity. (*Source:* Based on an actual response reported in "Confessions of an Interview Reader," Lee Adler, *Journal of Marketing Research*, May 1966, p. 195, published by the American Marketing Association.)

Three interesting examples of respondents' inability to understand terms that may have been quite clear to the researcher are (1) the individual, involved in an advertisement copy test for what was referred to as a "bathroom sanitizer," who indicated that "I'm certainly for that. I think we so need sanity in the bathroom"; (2) an insecticide advertiser who found that "residual insecticide" was interpreted as meaning "has no residue," "for insects that reside," "more powerful," or "powder form"; and (3) the finding of a 1947 study that a "nuclear physicist" was someone who "studies eggs," "reads minds and tells things by the stars," "does something at an operation," or is an "assistant to a physic."[4]

[4] Lee Adler, "Confessions of an Interview Reader," *Journal of Marketing Research*, May 1966, p. 194, published by the American Marketing Association.

**2. *Does the respondent know the answer to the question?*** Even if the respondent understands the question and shares your meaning of the terms used, it is possible that he or she may simply not know the answer. For example, if we are interested in determining beer consumption among members of a particular market segment, we would not be well advised to ask, "How many ounces of beer did you drink during the past year?" or "How many bottles of beer did you drink in 1987 compared to 1986?" A better approach would be to ask the respondent approximately how many bottles of beer were consumed during the past week. We would not expect younger family members to know whether the tires on the family station wagon are Firestones or whether the battery under the hood is a Diehard.

**3. *Is the respondent willing to provide the true answer to the question?*** A respondent who understands the question and knows the answer may nevertheless be reluctant to provide you with the correct information. This is especially true for relatively sensitive topics. Some questions may threaten respondents' self-esteem, prestige, or pride, causing them to gravitate toward responses that support these important psychological possessions. Remember that the asking of a question may involve more than one level of communication. For example, asking a young subject whether he has seen the movie *Rocky IV* consists of more than a simple question involving attendance of a movie—the subject may feel that a "no" response will indicate that he is not socially active or popular with his peers. Similarly, asking an adult if she owns a Bible may involve the simultaneous (though not formally asked) question, "Are you religious?" In either case, the respondent will tend to react in such a way as to protect his or her prestige from what may be perceived as a threatening question. Another possibility at this stage of the response process is the respondent who simply dislikes questionnaires or interviews, and knowingly provides incorrect information. For example, a close friend once purchased a new Nissan automobile and subsequently received a routine questionnaire asking for demographic, product satisfaction, and other information. Being a member of the aforementioned antiquestionnaire group, he responded to "What is your current occupation?" with "Emperor of Japan." The remainder of the completed questionnaire included demographic and attitudinal information of a level of absurdity that no doubt short-circuited the computer at Nissan headquarters. Luckily for the marketing research profession, individuals like this are a distinct minority—but watch for them.

**4. *Is the wording of the question or the situation in which it is asked likely to bias the response?*** While the topic of wording is covered more completely in the next chapter, it should be noted at this point that undue bias in the wording of the question is likely to result in a distorted response. Consider, for example, the following possibilities for determining consumer attitudes toward the mandatory installation of safety equipment in the form of air bags designed to inflate and cushion the effects of a collison:

> A. To help protect the lives of your loved ones, do you favor the mandatory installation of air bags in new cars?
> B. Do you think that American car buyers should be forced to have air bags in their cars whether they want them or not?

If you were conducting the survey for a company that manufactures air bags or related equipment, would you be tempted to ask the question in form A? Also, if you were conducting the survey for an automobile manufacturer, would you be tempted to use form B? Hopefully, as an ethical practitioner of marketing research, you would select a more neutrally worded question as your means of collecting these attitude data.

In some cases, respondents might even purposely lie just to lend confusion to survey results. Displeased with election-day exit polls, one columnist has gone so far as to encourage such behavior on the part of voters approached by interviewers as they leave the polls.[5] Other sources of response error include the interaction that takes place between the interviewer and the respondent in personal and telephone survey efforts, and may include (depending on the medium used) the appearance, sex, age, personality, mode of dress, and general professional level of the interviewer. In addition, the interviewer may provide cues of a verbal or nonverbal nature (e.g., smiling or nodding) that might intentionally or otherwise encourage the respondent to provide certain replies to the questions asked. The interviewer as a source of error should not be under-

---

### EXHIBIT 8-1

#### Boosting a Bowl

Following the 1984 college football season, Brigham Young University was ranked as the number one team in the country. BYU went on to defeat Michigan in December's Holiday Bowl and finish its season with a 12–0 record.

On New Year's Day 1985, No. 2 Oklahoma was to play No. 4 Washington in the Orange Bowl, the game to be telecast by NBC. The network surveyed the 60 sportswriters and sportscasters who vote in the Associated Press football poll, asking them "Have you already determined to vote for BYU No. 1 regardless of the outcome of the Orange Bowl?" The results were 18 "yes," 42 "no," and NBC continued its promotion of the Orange Bowl as a game that "could decide the national championship."

*Source:* Rudy Martzke, "Voters Not Ready to Hand BYU the National Title," *USA TODAY*, December 31, 1984, p. 12C. Copyright, 1984, *USA*, Excerpted with permission.

---

[5] See Mike Royko, "How My Liars Ruined Polls," *The Pittsburgh Press*, November 11, 1984, p. B2.

estimated when you are planning a survey that involves personal or telephone communication.

Figure 8-4 summarizes the preceding sources of response error. Remember that it takes only one broken link in the chain to cause error to occur, and that some unethical researchers may purposely encourage such error if it suits the interests of their firm or client.

### Nonresponse Error

*Nonresponse error* occurs when the individuals who respond to your survey are different from those who do not. For example, in a personal or telephone interview survey, the "not-at-homes" are likely to differ in many ways from persons or families who are not away. Not the least of such differences might be such variables as age, income, number of children, employment status of the

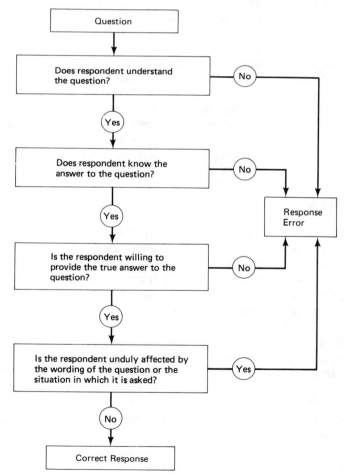

**Figure 8-4.** Response error may occur at any of these stages in the communication process upon which survey research depends.

husband and wife, and their level of participation in recreational, entertainment, and charitable activities.

In addition to the not-at-home problem, some persons will refuse to take part in a personal or telephone interview—such individuals can also be expected to differ in various ways from those respondents who do choose to cooperate. In the mail questionnaire survey, nonresponse is an especially crucial problem because of the normally low percentage of questionnaires that are actually completed and returned. It has been estimated that 38% of the people asked to participate in surveys refuse to comply.[6]

### Importance of Standardized Procedures in Survey Research

Regardless of the communication medium used—personal, telephone, or mail—it is advisable to use a standardized procedure in collecting data in the field. Because of unavoidable differences between interviewers (and in the same interviewer, from one situation to the next), a standardized approach can help to ensure that interviews are comparable, and that data are recorded both efficiently and accurately. In addition to reducing the likelihood of error, standardized procedures and reporting forms contribute to later ease of data summarization and analysis. A very important part of this standardization is the use of a well-planned and pretested data collection form. While such forms are generally referred to as *questionnaires* (and often associated with mail or personal interviews), they are equally applicable to surveys conducted by mail, telephone, or in person. Whenever a standardized data collection instrument is used in conjunction with a personal or telephone interview, it may be referred to as an *interview guide*.

### Consideration of the Potential Respondent

A sometimes overlooked factor in reducing both errors of response and nonresponse is the manner in which we treat the potential respondent to our survey. Unfortunately, some researchers approach this matter with the somewhat perverted assumption that the general public has a duty to cooperate in their survey. They view the potential respondent as a mere answer generator, rather than as a human being for whom the survey situation may create apprehension, suspicion, and curiosity, While it is both impractical and unwise to bring each respondent into our complete confidence with regard to the purpose, subject matter, and utilization of our survey results, we should recognize that the respondent must derive more from the interview experience than a simple "Excuse me . . ." and "Thank you" for his or her time and inconvenience. Although each individual survey technique has its own possibilities for courteous treatment of respondents that will increase the likelihood of obtaining their full co-

---

[6] "Study Determines 38% Refuse to Participate in Research Surveys," *Marketing News*, February 28, 1986, p. 1, published by the American Marketing Association.

operation, a few general notions should be kept in mind. First, we must consider the survey from the respondent's point of view and recognize the concerns that he or she may have regarding what may be a highly unique or bewildering experience. Such concerns are likely to include questions regarding who is doing the survey, for what purpose, how long it will take, and how the results will be used.

Having identified such natural reactions, we should then set out to satisfy these and other questions as best we can *without adversely affecting the objectivity of the survey itself*. Such attention to the respondent is not only scientifically advantageous (serving to reduce the extent of nonresponse and response errors), but also helps to generate good will towards marketing research in general and to increase the probability that the individual will respond favorably when asked to participate in a future survey conducted by you or another marketing researcher. The general public is the raw material upon which surveys depend, and a courteous and honest approach toward respondents will help to assure both their cooperation in a given research study and their continued existence as a valuable resource for future marketing information.

## THE PERSONAL INTERVIEW

The personal interview may be described as a purposeful conversation between interviewer and respondent—a conversation in which both subject matter and direction are provided by the interviewer, though the respondent will generally have the opportunity to expand on his or her views regarding the topic at hand.

### Procedure

In carrying out a personal interview, the first concern should be to ensure the full cooperation of the respondent in providing the information desired. In general, a professional appearance and "presence" on the part of the interviewer will facilitate such cooperation, as will a brief explanation of the study and the part which the respondent is expected to play in it. The respondent must be made to feel that both the study and her responses are important.

Having obtained the respondent's cooperation, attention should now focus on the interview guide or data collection instrument in order to standardize the procedure to the extent which the research requires. The interviewer should ask the required questions, in the proper sequence, and using the exact wording that is called for. In order to take advantage of the natural flexibility of the personal interview medium of communication, the interviewer may encourage the respondent to provide more detailed information if an initial response is either vague or unduly brief. Such stimulation of further response to a question can include a variety of techniques—for example, nodding, repeating the question or the answer, pausing in anticipation of a further response, or even actually asking for further clarification of the response are all possibilities. A statement such as "I'm not sure I understand. Would you tell me what you mean by that?" can be instrumental in evoking a more detailed response to a question.

The personal interview may take place practically anywhere, including the respondent's home, but shopping centers are among the most popular settings. In *mall-intercept interviewing* the respondent is (1) questioned "on-the-spot" while shopping, or (2) asked to accompany the interviewer to a special facility within the mall that is set aside for such purposes. Using this technique, an interviewer need not travel to find respondents and can efficiently obtain relatively large samples. A related technique is *purchase-intercept* interviewing, in which the consumer is approached immediately after making a purchase and questioned about his decision.[7]

Advances in microcomputers and their applications make it possible for the respondent either to be interviewed by an interactive computer that completely replaces the personal interviewer, or to respond to video-display questions that are under the interviewer's control. In one such development, Maritz Marketing Research, Inc. has come up with an interactive system based on microcomputers and laser videodiscs that allows a single interviewer to supervise five to seven interviewing stations. Shown in Figure 8-5, the computer features a touch-sensitive screen for the recording of responses and automatically makes use of previous answers to skip questions not applicable to a given respondent.[8]

### Advantages and Disadvantages

One of the greatest strengths of the personal interview technique is the degree of *flexibility* it affords the researcher. Questions that are not understood by the respondent may be clarified by the interviewer. Vague, interesting, or unusual responses may be probed in order to provide greater insight into the research topic. Questions may be easily bypassed whenever they are inappropriate for a given respondent or interview situation. In addition, visual displays (e.g., alternative advertisements) and actual products may be shown to the respondent for the dual purpose of better communication and increased motivation for participation in the survey. Because of the generally low rate of refusal, the personal interview tends to have *less nonresponse error* than do the other survey approaches. It's more difficult for a potential respondent to say no in a face-to-face situation than to hang up or refuse by telephone or to simply toss a mail questionnaire into the wastebasket. Another strength of the personal interview is the *ability to obtain more information* than might be gathered under circumstances in which the researcher has less control over the situation. Just as it's difficult for a potential respondent to personally say no, it isn't likely that he or she will cut short a polite and competent interviewer by saying "That's enough." The

[7] See "PIT Stop Discovers Reason behind Purchasing Habits," *Marketing News*, September 12, 1986, p. 1, published by the American Marketing Association.

[8] "Laser Disc and Computer Ask Respondents Questions," *Marketing News*, March 14, 1986, p. 17, published by the American Marketing Association.

**Figure 8-5.** Interactive microcomputers can replace or supplement the personal interviewer, and may even feature a touch-sensitive screen to facilitate the recording of responses. (Photo courtesy of Maritz Marketing Research, Inc., St. Louis, Mo.)

nature of the personal interview is such that a *short time period* will suffice in order to obtain the information desired, whereas another medium (e.g., mail questionnaire) may require several days or weeks until the data are eventually acquired. Finally, the personal interview permits the collection of different types of information, ranging from extremely short responses to the longer, open-ended variety that is characteristic of the unstructured questions often used in exploratory research.

With all of these strengths, one might wonder why personal interviews are not the sole means of collecting survey research information. However, as with any other technique, the personal interview is subject to certain weaknesses. First, the *high cost* of using trained interviewers in the field makes this approach a great deal more expensive than simply using the telephone interview (which obviously requires no travel time on the part of the interviewer) or the mail questionnaire. The cost disadvantage becomes even more pronounced whenever the respondents are dispersed over a large geographical area or if they are difficult to locate and must be interviewed during call-back visits to their places of residence. The second difficulty with the personal interview is the *greater possibility of response error* that results from the face-to-face interaction between interviewer and respondent, a problem that is compounded by poorly trained interviewers who may deviate from standardized procedures or unknowingly inject bias into either the questions they ask or the answers which the respondent provides.

### Interviewer Ability and Integrity

The interviewers we utilize in a personal interview survey should possess two very important characteristics—ability and integrity. The first of these attributes describes the interviewer's capability of following instructions and objectively collecting and recording respondent information. Depending on the complexity of the survey, the ability of the interviewer may have a significant influence over the results obtained. If, for example, the survey involves very short questions and answers regarding a topic that is noncontroversial, the negative effect of an inexperienced interviewer can be minimal. If, on the other hand, the survey involves a sensitive topic or requires probing beyond the respondent's initial reaction to a question, lack of interviewer experience can be disastrous. While employing trained and experienced interviewers may seem expensive at the time, to do otherwise represents a false economy that will be likely to undermine the success of the study. The educational background, personality, and physical characteristics of the interviewer are all crucial to his or her ability to carry out a research study in an objective manner without exerting undue influence over the respondents who are interviewed. Consider, for example, the difficulty that a highly educated interviewer might experience in a low-income neighborhood if he employs a vocabulary level or style of dress that prevents the establishment of satisfactory rapport between himself and potential respondents. It may be expected that the sex and age of interviewers could have a significant influence over the responses obtained. For example, consider the possible question, "Have you ever purchased a copy of *Playboy* magazine?" and the bias that might be presented by having the question asked by a grandmotherly woman versus an attractive young lady in her 20s. It seems likely that when interviewing young men, the former interviewer would introduce a downward bias, while the latter would tend to evoke a greater proportion of positive responses to the question. While both individuals may be trained and competent, their physical appearance is partly beyond their control. For this reason, the selection of interviewers for a particular study should be based on their appropriateness as well as their ability.

In addition to being concerned about the ability of our workers in the field, we must also consider the possibility that some interviewers may simply not be doing the job for which they were hired. Even if the interviewer knows how to follow our instructions and fully understands the nature of the information for which we are looking, this is to no avail if he invents answers to questions rather than actually posing them to the respondent, or "interviews" phantom respondents who don't exist. In some cases, especially if a question deals with sensitive information (e.g., age, income, sex habits), an interviewer will be tempted to make up an answer rather than risk the embarrassment of posing the question to the respondent. Also, an interviewer may collect actual data from friends or neighbors, then report that the interviews were the result of contact with the original sampling of individuals for which the survey was intended.

In all of the preceding cases, the use of experienced interviewers who are carefully supervised and adequately compensated will tend to reduce the incidence of cheating. However, to be more certain that such deception does not take place at your expense, it may be desirable to do a "real people" check— that is, to contact a small sample of the persons who were supposedly interviewed and establish whether or not they were actually contacted by the interviewer. An inexpensive alternative to this approach is to let it be known that you may be carrying out such a check upon completion of the interviews. This will discourage potential cheaters from taking unfair advantage of the freedom they experience in the field. Whenever specific respondents cannot be identified (e.g., in some "person on the street" interviews or when respondent anonymity requires the interviewer to avoid requesting the identity of the respondent), data from various interviewers may be closely checked for discrepancies that suggest cheating may have taken place. In any case, most honest interviewers will not be adverse to follow-up or other checks that are intended to evaluate either the existence or the quality of the interviews they conduct. After all, it is in their best interest to perform satisfactorily so they will have a greater chance of being retained whenever your next survey is conducted.

## THE TELEPHONE INTERVIEW

A popular alternative to the personal interview is the use of the telephone as a medium of communication. This approach is especially useful if we wish to obtain information regarding what the respondent is doing at the time of the call. For this reason, the telephone interview is frequently used in television and radio survey research dealing with audience size and composition, sponsorship knowledge, and related information. While the telephone interview is similar to the personal variety in terms of two-way conversation taking place between interviewer and respondent, the conversion from a face-to-face format to one that is merely voice-to-voice involves an entirely different set of problems, procedures, strengths, and weaknesses.

### Procedure

With regard to securing the cooperation of the respondent, clarifying questions that the respondent does not fully understand, and recording the data collected, the telephone interview is similar to the personal interview in terms of both problems and opportunities. However, compared to the personal interview, the telephone medium does not lend itself as readily to the collection of lengthy, detailed, or loosely defined information. The kind of data that can be collected by telephone is generally straightforward and concise.

A major procedural dilemma faced by the telephone interviewer is the problem of unlisted and obsolete telephone numbers. Especially near the end of the year of its application, a telephone directory will contain a significant portion of numbers that are no longer in use due to households having moved away during the year. Similarly, households that have moved into the area within the year are not yet listed. In addition, a significant proportion of telephone owners have elected to have numbers that are not listed in the directory. While their reasons are admirable (avoiding crank calls, salespersons, and unwanted business or personal calls), the fact remains that these individuals are likely to differ from those listed in the directory in terms of income and other demographic variables. The actual proportion of numbers that are unlisted varies widely—for example, in 1977, 28.1% of the Pacific Telephone Company numbers were unlisted, including a 37% unlisted rate for the city of Los Angeles.[9]

One approach to overcoming the problem posed by unlisted numbers is that of *random digit dialing*, in which the last four digits of the telephone number are generated by means of a random number table. For example, if we wish to call a random telephone in a given location, we dial the first three digits as they would normally appear in the telephone directory, then use random numbers to determine the other four digits. Although this procedure does generate a significant proportion of nonworking numbers (due to certain banks of numbers not having been assigned by the telephone company), those numbers that are reached will include both the listed and the unlisted variety. An alternative to random digit dialing is an approach called *plus-one dialing*, in which a number is selected from the directory by conventional systematic sampling just as we would do if we were taking a sample of the numbers listed in the directory. However, rather than dial the number that is listed, we add one to the final digit (e.g., 313-2483 becomes 313-2484) and dial the revised number instead. The result is less likely to be a nonworking number, since the existence of the first number increases the probability that the second, revised number will also exist. Although the telephone company may not be willing to tell you which banks of numbers have been assigned to customers, it is fair to presume that a number that is one digit away from an assigned number will also have been assigned. While the procurement of fewer nonworking numbers may increase the efficiency of the interviewing procedure in terms of number of completed calls per number of attempted calls, some bias may exist due to unforeseen factors such as the assignment rules utilized by the telephone company, the addition of new numbers (possibly from a new assignment bank), and related factors such as the growth rate and mobility of the area being sampled.

The telephone interview process can be facilitated through use of a microcomputer and a video display that shows each question that is to be asked. As with the application discussed in the preceding section, computer-assisted telephone interviewing (CATI) combines the efficient recording of responses with the ability to electronically skip over questions that are nonapplicable as the result of the respondent's answers to earlier questions. Since the data are being entered directly into the computer, this technique also reduces both the likelihood of errors in data manipulation and the time required for data analysis.

As with the personal interview, it is advisable to use only carefully selected and trained interviewers, to compensate them fairly for their work, and (for your own protection) to validate their interviews by calling a sampling of the numbers they claim to have reached. For the telephone interview, it is especially important that interviewers remain aware of the time differences between var-

---

[9] Clyde R. Rich, "Is Random Digit Dialing Really Necessary?" *Journal of Marketing Research*, August 1977, p. 301, published by the American Marketing Association.

ious parts of the country if long-distance calls are being used in the survey. The telephone is a relatively impersonal mode of communication in terms of (1) contacting individuals in their homes at times that may not be convenient for even a short interview, and (2) the absence of person-to-person contact which may serve to placate individuals who might otherwise be hostile and uncooperative as the result of being interrupted in the sanctity of their home.

## Advantages and Disadvantages

One of the primary advantages of the telephone interviewing technique is its *low cost* relative to the personal interview. Because all calls are made from the same location, travel time and expense are eliminated. This cost advantage is especially important when respondents are geographically dispersed or whenever call-backs are to be made. While the technique does require an interviewer's time, this time is spent very efficiently on the business at hand—that is, interviewing respondents. This is quite unlike the personal interview, where the interviewer may be employed for a large portion of the day as a pedestrian rather than as an interviewer. With WATS (Wide Area Telephone Service), centralized interviewing of respondents nationwide has become an economical proposition enabling researchers to exert a higher level of administrative control over the interviewers, hence improving the quality of the information generated. Under the WATS system, a subscriber is permitted to use a limited number of total hours to make an unlimited number of telephone calls to a given area of the United States for a fixed monthly charge.

Another advantage of the telephone interview is its *speed*. Compared to both the personal interview and the mail questionnaire techniques, the telephone interview is able to obtain information as the activities involved are actually taking place. Where the personal interview approach may involve the selection and training of interviewers as well as their travel time between interviews, the telephone medium of communication is able to generate considerably more usable interviews in a given period of time. Also, the quickness of telephone survey results is far ahead of the several days (minimum) that are required for the mail questionnaire to reach and be returned by even the most conscientious of respondents.

The telephone interview has the advantage of incorporating a sense of *importance* and *priority*, especially when a long-distance call is involved. Physicians, busy executives, and others have no way of knowing whether the long-distance call is using some faraway person's money during the expensive 8:00 A.M. to 5:00 P.M. time period, or if the call is really a "freebie" that has been made through the WATS system. In either case, the caller can legitimately claim that he or she is calling "long distance" from a location and telephone number which, if left with the secretary at the receiving end, serves as evidence that an important long-distance telephone call has indeed been received.

Among the disadvantages of the telephone interview technique is the *limited amount and detail of information that can be collected* when compared to the personal interview. Because it is easier for the respondent to break off the interview, questions must be relatively short, simple, and interesting. If the subject matter of the survey is not very appealing to the respondent, it is advisable to keep the interview as short as possible.

Another disadvantage is the *lack of representativeness* of available listings to the general population. Although this problem may be partly overcome through the use of random digit and plus-one digit dialing, these approaches are not perfect either, and may introduce biases of their own. Since unlisted subscribers are, by their own choice, not included in the directory, they may tend to be less than fully cooperative when they find that you have managed to reach them anyway. In addition, some households—especially in rural and lower-income areas—may not have telephones. A related problem is that some telephones may serve a large number of individuals (e.g., one phone may serve an entire fraternity or apartment house) while others may serve just one person (e.g., teenagers in an affluent family may each have their own personal telephone).

With regard to *response errors* induced by the interaction between interviewer and respondent, the telephone interview probably falls somewhere between the personal interview (higher response error) and the mail questionnaire (lower response error). Because of the more impersonal nature of the telephone interview, there is less likelihood that the effect of the interviewer on the respondent's replies will be an important component of the information obtained.

Finally, because of the nonvisual nature of the telephone interview, there is no possibility of using visual displays, product examples, or other props during the interview itself. However, this difficulty may be overcome by either using verbal descriptions (when applicable), or mailing the necessary visual aids prior to or following initial contact by telephone.

## THE MAIL QUESTIONNAIRE

In the mail questionnaire survey, there is no interviewer available to ask questions, clarify points that the respondent may raise, or guide the respondent through the data collection instrument. Because the questionnaire is actually administered to the respondent *by* the respondent, this approach to survey research has its own peculiarities with regard to strategies, strengths, and weaknesses.

### Procedure

Since we have no interviewer to explain the purpose of the study and encourage the respondent's participation, the actual construction of the questionnaire and related materials becomes highly important to the success of this approach. The quality, attractiveness, and persuasive powers of the envelope contents become our personal representative in the respondent's home or office, and it is vitally important that curiosity and a spirit of cooperation be aroused very quickly if our questionnaire is to avoid joining yesterday's newspaper in the respondent's "circular file."

The persuasive efforts of the interviewer in the personal or telephone survey are replaced in the mail questionnaire by a cover letter like the one shown in Figure 8-6. This accompanies the questionnaire and attempts to serve a variety of purposes. The cover letter, while being brief and readable, must deal with potential questions such as (1) the nature of the study, (2) why the materials happened to be mailed to the respondent, (3) who is sponsoring the study, (4) why the respondent's cooperation is important, (5) exactly what the respondent is being asked to do, (6) what use will be made of the information that he or she provides, and (7) whether he or she will remain anonymous.

A particularly important aspect of the cover letter is the attempt to convince the respondent why he or she should complete and return the questionnaire that is enclosed. As with the personal and telephone interview, the respondent should be made to feel important. The author once received, from a well-known university, a lengthy (about 40 pages) questionnaire accompanied by a cover letter that began with a paragraph containing a statement that explained that the recipient was "one of several thousand individuals selected at random to participate" in a study.

Another consideration when constructing a cover letter is the promise of anonymity to the respondent if the subject matter is somewhat personal or controversial. An ethical researcher will abide by this promise to potential respondents. However, for various reasons, even former Boy or Girl Scouts may be tempted to secretly code the questionnaires by using pinholes or dots in the questionnaire, or by writing with ink that is visible only under ultraviolet light. One of the reasons for such coding may be to identify nonrespondents so that postage is not wasted in sending follow-up questionnaires or reminder cards to *all* members of the sample. Another is to enable the researcher to identify individual respondents in the event that subsequent research is deemed necessary to acquire more detailed information which will be added to that originally collected from each person. However, regardless of the scientific benefit of respondent identification, it should be considered less than moral to promise anonymity when it is known in advance that such a promise will not be respected. It should be noted that this is an individual judgment, as some researchers may see no harm in identifying respondents in order to facilitate data analysis, further research, or subsequent sale calls on respondents who indicate a positive attitude that may be commercially exploited.

### Advantages and Disadvantages

The *low cost* of the mail questionnaire is a distinct advantage when compared to either personal or telephone interviews. While the WATS capability is helpful in minimizing the cost of a telephone survey, the mail questionnaire technique generally will have a cost advantage versus the other survey methods. The cost advantage of the mail survey will be especially great if respondents are geo-

**Decision Software**
**Research Associates**
P.O. Box 47007
Gardena, CA 90247-9988

Dear Honda Customer,

We need your help! You recently contacted American Honda's customer service office regarding a request. Your answers to the enclosed survey will be vital to Honda in evaluating current customer relations programs and procedures, and in providing direction for the future.

You will find that the questionnaire is easy to read and you will make progress quickly. It should only take a few minutes to fill out.

Please complete your survey carefully including written comments if desired, and promptly return it to us in the self-addressed, postage-paid envelope provided with each survey.

Your opinions are important to American Honda. Honda continually strives to refine their products and procedures. For your answers to be used in guiding future decisions by Honda, it is essential that you mail the completed survey soon, and if possible

**WITHIN 7 DAYS**

Why not complete yours right now? Thank you for your time.

Sincerely,

*S. Parsons*

DECISION SOFTWARE RESEARCH ASSOCIATES

**Figure 8-6.** An important part of the mail questionnaire is a good cover letter, such as the excellent example shown here. (Copyright © 1987 by American Honda Motor Co., Inc. All rights reserved. Reproduced by permission.)

graphically dispersed: Although postage isn't really cheap these days, it still costs the same to send a questionnaire to the other end of the country as it does to reach the other side of town.

Compared to the other methods, the mail survey will tend to have a *lower degree of response error*, since there is no interviewer with whom the respondent must interact either in person or over the telephone. This advantage is related to the anonymity that can be promised to (and believed by) the respondent. Such anonymity can be useful in obtaining confidential information that would otherwise be difficult or impossible to acquire.

Use of a mail questionnaire includes the advantage of allowing the respondent to *more carefully formulate and record* his or her responses at a pace that is more leisurely and free from distractions. By contrast, the personal or telephone interview request may be made at a time when the baby is crying, a favorite TV program is on the air, or the respondent is otherwise engaged in activities that are not favorable to the highest level of cooperation with the interviewer. This flexibility also allows the respondent to gather information that may not be immediately available at the time when an interview would take place—for example, the brand of tires on the family automobile may be unknown, but easily identifiable when the spouse returns from work or shopping.

Another advantage of the mail questionnaire is that of *eliminating interviewer bias* in the selection of sample members. In other words, the person delivering the mail will (as legend has it) endure snow, sleet, steep stairways, run-down homes, and Doberman pinschers. On the other hand, the typical interviewer will probably be less determined, and may avoid persons or dwellings that do not look attractive as an interview source.

The main weakness of the mail questionnaire survey is that of **nonresponse error**. Many of those receiving questionnaires will simply not return them, and respondents are likely to differ from nonrespondents in terms of many characteristics that are directly or indirectly important to the study. This disadvantage is related to some of the positive characteristics we have just discussed. For example, allowing respondents an opportunity to respond to the questionnaire at their convenience may not always work out to our benefit because some members of the sample will find it most convenient not to respond at all.

Another disadvantage of the mail questionnaire survey is the *limited amount and depth of information* that we are generally able to obtain through this medium of communication with the respondent. A lengthy questionnaire, unless dealing with a hobby or other attractive subject matter, will likely be discarded instead of completed and returned. For practical purposes, it is optimistic to expect that respondents will be willing to fill out a questionnaire that requires (or is perceived as requiring) more than 10 minutes of their time. In addition, the self-administration nature of the mail questionnaire eliminates the opportunity for an interviewer to assist the respondent with questions that are not clear, or to probe for more detailed responses to replies that are terse, vague, or potentially insightful into the subject matter of the research. A related problem with the mail questionnaire is the functional illiteracy of some members of the population with regard to being able to complete even the most simple questionnaire. While such illiteracy should be expected to decrease in this, the twentieth century, its incidence is probably in the range of 10% or more of the adult population of the United States. Another limitation on the amount of information that may be obtained by mail survey involves the concurrent observations that could have been made by an interviewer during a personal encounter with the respondent—such information, for example, as mode of dress, physical appearance, and other characteristics descriptive of the person being interviewed.

Another problem with the mail questionnaire is the *time required for the survey*. Not only must we take the time to prepare and mail the questionnaires,

---

(A)        Thank you for dining with us. We would appreciate your comments on our restaurant.

1. We came to the Red Bull Inn of _____
   for: ☐ lunch ☐ dinner ☐ _____
2. When we came we found the restaurant:
   ☐ crowded ☐ busy ☐ not too crowded ☐ slow
3. The personnel treated us:
   ☐ very friendly ☐ average ☐ not too friendly
4. The restaurant was:
   ☐ clean ☐ could be cleaner ☐ very clean
   Specifically _____
5. Service for our table was:
   ☐ slow ☐ prompt ☐ average ☐ too fast
6. Our meal was:
   ☐ average ☐ superior ☐ not too good ☐ above average
7. When served our food was:
   ☐ hot ☐ just warm ☐ hot enough ☐ too cool
8. How does the portion size for the price compare with similar places where you eat?
   FOOD:
   ☐ larger ☐ same ☐ slightly bigger. ☐ smaller
   DRINK:
   ☐ larger ☐ same ☐ slightly bigger ☐ smaller
9. We come to the restaurant around: ☐ ____ a.m.
   ☐ Noon ☐ 4 p.m. ☐ 10 p.m. ☐ ____p.m.

10. Waitress _____

Suggestions: _____
_____
_____
_____

---

**Figure 8-7.** Self-administered questionnaires may reach you in a variety of ways other than the U.S. Postal Service, as indicated by these examples which were available at a restaurant table (a) and at a state unemployment office (b). [*Sources:* (a) Courtesy of Red Bull Inns of America, Inc.; (b) Commonwealth of Pennsylvania, Bureau of Employment Security.]

(B)          PENNSYLVANIA STATE EMPLOYMENT SERVICE

In the interest of maintaining and improving our standards of service, we would appreciate your comments and suggestions. Please complete this postage-paid card and mail it to us at your convenience. Sign if you wish.                                                                        Thank you.

What service did you request?
☐ Employment                        ☐ Unemployment Compensation

                              EXCELLENT   SATISFACTORY  UNSATISFACTORY

Courtesy.........           ☐                ☐                ☐
Speed...........            ☐                ☐                ☐
Results ..........          ☐                ☐                ☐

Comments _____
_____
_____

Signature _____Occupation _____

**Figure 8-7.** (*continued*)

but we must also endure the delay of round-trip passage through the U.S. mail transportation and delivery system in addition to the amount of time the respondent allows to pass before deciding to complete and return the questionnaire to us. In short, if you need survey information within a matter of a few days, don't even consider a mail questionnaire survey.

The mail survey also suffers from the possibility that *a suitable mailing list* may not exist. Naturally, if the target population is described by a list (e.g., a business directory or magazine subscription list), this possible limitation will not be a problem.

### Alternative Methods of Administration

While the terms *mail questionnaire* and *self-administered questionnaire* are sometimes perceived as synonymous, it should be recognized that a variety of other methods exists for the delivery and return of questionnaires that are completed by the respondent without the assistance of an interviewer. For example, a questionnaire may be personally delivered to the respondent and returned through the mail or by other means, such as personal pickup by the researcher.

Another approach to self-administered questionnaires is the warranty card packaged with many consumer products, a common approach to measuring customer characteristics. Questionnaires may find their way to you in a number of other ways as well—for example, at the service desk of an auto repair shop, attached to your favorite newspaper or magazine, on the dresser of a motel room, on the back of a restaurant check (a Pizza Hut practice), or even at the unemployment office, as shown in Figure 8-7.

In addition, it is sometimes convenient to administer a questionnaire to an assembled group for the purpose of gaining information at very little time and cost. Most college students are familiar with the scene where the instructor, or perhaps another student, takes a few minutes of class time in order to hand out a questionnaire as part of a study being conducted. Whenever a group is already assembled, whether they be students, organization members, business people, PTA members, or conventioneers, the opportunity to generate a lot of data at very little cost may be very attractive. However, remember that such mass administration of a questionnaire will only be useful if the group members are in some way representative of the population about which you wish to make inferences based on your survey. Nevertheless, the ease and economy of this approach will surely maintain its popularity—especially when a questionnaire is being pretested or if the purpose of the research is exploratory in nature.

## STRATEGIES FOR REDUCING NONRESPONSE ERROR

In attempting to reduce the effect of nonresponse on our survey results, there are two general strategies that we may follow: (1) *reducing the number of nonrespondents*, and (2) recognizing that it is impractical to reduce the number of nonrespondents to zero, *attempting to compensate for their absence* from the data we obtain.

### Reducing Nonresponse in Personal and Telephone Interviews

In personal and telephone interviews (especially the former), person-to-person interaction helps to ensure that the rate of refusal will be relatively low. The personality and sales ability of the interviewer are highly influential in this regard, and it is reasonable to expect that the knowledgeable researcher will see fit to retain interviewers who possess each of these important attributes.

Because of the lower incidence of refusals in the personal and telephone interviews, the key to reducing nonresponse in these survey approaches is often in our ability to communicate successfully with potential respondents in the first place. In the event that the respondent is not at home, personal or telephone call-backs may be made in an attempt to eventually initiate contact with the respondent. However, diminishing returns will set in, and each wave of call-backs is likely to have a lower contact rate than the wave that preceded it. In general, unless the sample size is very small or each respondent is very important to the study (e.g., the survey may involve a small number of purchasing agents who represent substantial corporations), it is not advisable to make more than two or three call-back attempts. Naturally, this is just a rule of thumb, and you may wish to record the success rate of each call-back wave and discontinue your efforts only when it becomes obvious that the percentage being contacted is beginning to drop off drastically.

Once we have gained personal or telephone access to the respondent, it may require something more than selling ability and a pleasing personality to persuade her to participate in the survey. To this extent, we may profit from what experience has taught salespeople over the years—that a "foot in the door" will assist greatly in completing the sale. In the survey context, the equivalent of having one's foot in the door consists of achieving the respondent's cooperation with a smaller task prior to asking her to comply with a request that may be more demanding. For example, an initial telephone contact may be made for the purpose of identifying the respondent, asking a few questions, and securing her cooperation in supplying further information as part of a later survey by mail, telephone, or personal interview. Table 8-1 summarizes the results of a study that attempted to examine the foot-in-the-door strategy for improving the degree of cooperation with a telephone survey.[10] Two variables were studied: (1) the size of the initial request, in terms of the number of questions asked, and (2) the effect of a monetary incentive, in the form of a five-dollar gift certificate that was promised to some respondents. Depending on the group to which a respondent had been randomly assigned, he or she received an initial request for answering either 5 or 35 questions. The compliance rates of Table 8-1 describe the proportion of respondents who were willing to answer the 20 questions that were contained in the second request being made of them. As might be expected, the smaller "foot" had a much better chance of getting into the "door."

### Reducing Nonresponse in Mail Questionnaires

As we've discussed, nonresponse is especially troublesome whenever a survey is conducted by mail questionnaire. Because of the absence of the interpersonal verbal contact possible with the two interview approaches, successful motivation of the mail questionnaire respondent depends largely on his reaction to written materials and related items that comprise the survey "package" he has received. In addition, strategies that either precede or follow actual receipt of the mail questionnaire are often useful in reducing the amount of nonresponse experienced in the survey. Some of the techniques described here are also applicable to other survey approaches, but are discussed in this section because of their particular applicability to the more severe nonresponse problem associated with mail questionnaires.

#### *Strategies That Precede Receipt of the Questionnaire*

Advance communication with the respondent in the form of a telephone call, letter, or post card is a good method for increasing response rates. This is a variant of the foot-in-the-door approach, and often involves no more than

---

[10] Peter H. Reingen and Jerome B. Kernan, "Compliance with an Interview Request: A Foot-in-the-Door, Self-Perception Interpretation," *Journal of Marketing Research*, August 1977, pp. 365–69, published by the American Marketing Association.

**TABLE 8-1.** *As indicated by the compliance rate of group D, respondents are more likely to comply with a second request if the first request is not very demanding.*

|  |  | Size of initial request | |
|  |  | *High* *(35 questions)* | *Low* *(5 questions)* |
| --- | --- | --- | --- |
|  | *$5 gift certificate* | A = 0.44 | B = 0.48 |
|  | *No incentive offered* | C = 0.53 | D = 0.74 |
| **Monetary incentive** | *Control group receiving second request only* | 0.58 | |

*Source:* Adapted from Peter H. Reingen and Jerome B. Kernan, "Compliance with an Interview Request: A Foot-in-the-Door, Self-Perception Interpretation," *Journal of Marketing Research,* August 1977, p. 368, published by the American Marketing Association.

simply calling the potential respondent and asking for permission to mail the questionnaire to him. Such treatment of potential respondents can be highly successful. For example, in a survey conducted by the author, 30 out of 36 potential respondents contacted by telephone indicated their willingness to complete and return the mail questionnaire that was to follow. Of these 30, 24 returned questionnaires that were usable—an overall response rate of two-thirds of those initially contacted. In another study, 68% of those who had been prenotified by telephone returned the questionnaire compared to only 20.5% of a control group who had not been contacted in advance.[11] A sincere and courteous preliminary communication with the potential respondent can be a very effective device for enlisting his cooperation in your mail questionnaire survey.

### Strategies Associated with Receipt of the Questionnaire

**Questionnaire length.** The questionnaire should be perceived as not requiring very much of the respondent's time. To this extent, it is a mistake to squeeze all of your questions onto a single 8½-by-14-inch sheet just for the purpose of having a one-page questionnaire. Include only the questions that are really needed and do everything possible to make it appear to be simple to complete.

**Cover letter.** As discussed earlier, the cover letter should be honest, interesting, and persuasive, but not lengthy. Be sure to see it from the respondent's point of view as well as your own.

**Stamped, self-addressed envelope.** For the convenience of the potential respondent, it is strongly advisable to include a stamped, self-addressed envelope for the return of the completed questionnaire. Rather than use a business reply

---

[11] James E. Stafford, "Influence of Preliminary Contact on Mail Returns," *Journal of Marketing Research,* November 1966, pp. 410–11, published by the American Marketing Association.

permit, which may give the impression of junk mail, spend the extra money to use stamps on the return envelopes. Not surprisingly, people hesitate to throw away an unused stamp, even if it is attached to an envelope with your address on it. On the other hand, very few will take the trouble to steam it from the envelope and use Elmer's Glue to help it stick to an item of future personal correspondence. The result will be an increased likelihood that the envelope will be used for the return of the completed questionnaire that you are so anxiously seeking.

*Personalized address.* Instead of sending the questionnaire to "occupant," use the individual's name whenever possible. To add to this personal touch, avoid the use of mailing labels, even though the cost of typing may be a little higher. Similarly, a legitimate return address on the envelope will help to reduce the probability that the envelope will be perceived as containing junk mail.

*Sponsorship.* The sponsor of the survey should be legitimate, respected, and nonthreatening if the survey is to obtain maximum returns. Neither the cover letter nor the sponsorship identification should be such that anything remotely resembling a sales pitch is perceived by the respondent. For example, if the sponsor is a corporation, it is advisable to include the term "consumer research department," "department of consumer affairs," or some other identification that serves to separate the survey from the selling activities of the company. A natural sponsor for surveys is a respected college or university, from whom respondents can be relatively certain that there is no sales dimension to the questionnaire, and that the survey is being undertaken by a socially beneficial institution.

*Type of appeal.* Depending on the survey sponsor, it may be advisable to consider using a type of appeal that will be more likely to result in the respondent's cooperation with that sponsor. In one study, for example, it was found that the use of a social utility appeal ("your assistance is needed") was more successful for a university sponsor, while an egoistic appeal ("your opinions are important") was more effective for a commercial sponsor.[12] A summary of the results of this study, and the wording of the various appeals tested, is presented in Table 8-2. By using their most effective approaches to the respondent, the university and commercial sponsors were able to achieve comparable rates of response to the five-page questionnaire that had been mailed to a systematic sample of households listed in the telephone directory of a medium-sized town. The results of this study are of special interest to us because a great many surveys are conducted under university or commercial sponsorship.

*Monetary incentives.* The use of cash and other direct incentives has been found to greatly increase the rate of return of mail questionnaires. This has been

---

[12] Michael J. Houston and John R. Nevin, "The Effects of Source and Appeal on Mail Survey Response Patterns," *Journal of Marketing Research*, August 1977, pp. 374–87, published by the American Marketing Association.

**TABLE 8-2.** *As shown by the return rates in the following table, different appeals tend to work better for university versus commercial sponsors of mail questionnaires.*

|  |  | Sponsor | |
|---|---|---|---|
|  |  | *University* | *Commercial* |
|  | *Social utility* | 47.2% | 38.8% |
| **Appeal** | *Help-the-sponsor* | 44.8% | 36.8% |
|  | *Egoistic* | 35.6% | 46.8% |
|  | *Combined* | 41.6% | 39.2% |

Wording of appeals

Social utility — "Your assistance is needed!! Your attitudes and opinions can provide information that contributes to understanding how consumers can be better served by local retail shopping facilities. . . . Your cooperation is truly appreciated."

Help-the-sponsor — "We need your assistance!! Your attitudes and opinions are very important to our successful completion of this study. . . . We truly appreciate your cooperation."

Egoistic — "Your opinions are important!! It's important for you to express your opinion so Madison's retailers will know the types of products and shopping facilities you would like to have available. . . . Thanks for expressing your opinions."

Combined appeal — "Your opinions are important and useful!! Your attitudes and opinions are important for three reasons: (1) they can provide information that leads to an understanding of how consumers can be better served by local retail shopping facilities; (2) they will enable Madison's retailers to know the types of products and shopping facilities you would like to have available; and (3) they will help us successfully complete this study. . . . Thank you for your cooperation."

*Source:* Michael J. Houston and John R. Nevin, "The Effects of Source and Appeal on Mail Survey Response Patterns," *Journal of Marketing Research,* August 1977, pp. 347–87, published by the American Marketing Association.

true whether the respondents are typical consumers or corporate executives. In fact, the results of one study suggest the existence of a threshold value for increasing responses with monetary incentives, and that this threshold value appears to be lower for commercial populations than for the general public.[13] It must be remembered, however, that the enclosing of money with a cover

[13] Milton M. Pressley and William L. Tullar, "A Factor Interactive Investigation of Mail Survey Response Rates from a Commercial Population," *Journal of Marketing Research,* February 1977, pp. 108–11, published by the American Marketing Association.

letter or questionnaire is really just a *token of appreciation*, not an amount actually intended to monetarily compensate the respondent for his or her time required for the completion of the questionnaire.

The amount used should be at least somewhat commensurate with the task the respondent is called upon to perform, but will tend to be $1 or less. The effects possible within this range should be more than satisfactory—in one study, the inclusion of a dollar bill was found to double the response rate.[14] The key is to (1) reward and thank the respondent for her cooperation, and (2) make her feel slightly indebted without feeling that she has been "bought." Monetary incentives can be accompanied by or replaced with other items of value (e.g., McDonald's coupons or gift certificates). Another popular strategy is to offer a contribution to a charity of the respondent's choice, an approach utilized in the cover letter of Figure 8-8.

In considering the possible use of monetary incentives for the increase of mail questionnaire returns, remember that your objective *should not be to simply maximize the number of returns per dollar spent*. Because of the crucial nature of nonresponse error in the mail survey, it may well be advisable to spend 50% more money in order to obtain 30% more responses to a fixed number of mail questionnaires.

*Providing survey results.* In some instances, respondents will be more favorably inclined toward helping you with your survey if you offer to send them a summary of the research results. People tend to enjoy learning about themselves and how their opinions, attitudes, and behaviors compare with others, and such a promise may prove beneficial in improving your return rate. The cost of such compliance with the respondent's natural curiosity need not be excessive, especially if you summarize in one page enough information to satisfy his or her inquiry without going into great technical detail. As part of the cover letter, you may wish to include a statement such as "If you would like a short summary of the survey results, please write to me at the above address any time after March 25. Thanks again for your help." In the author's experience, only a small percentage of respondents will actually inquire regarding the results of the survey, since by the date given many will have either misplaced the cover letter or forgotten about the survey altogether. However, it is a friendly gesture that can enhance the perceived sincerity of you or your organization, improve the climate of communication between the respondent and yourself, and (most important, from an objective point of view) help to reduce the nonresponse that you experience in the survey itself. However, because too much emphasis on the "feedback" appeal for questionnaire completion may bias your results toward a sampling of respondents who are above average in education, intellectual curiosity, or self-interest, try not to overdo the "learn about yourself" possibilities of the survey.

---

[14] Sid Groeneman, "People Respond to Surveys When the Price Is Right," *Marketing News*, September 12, 1986, p. 29, published by the American Marketing Association.

# TIME
### INCORPORATED

TIME & LIFE BUILDING
ROCKEFELLER CENTER
NEW YORK 10020
586-1212
EXECUTIVE OFFICES

Dear Reader:

We need a little of your time.

We're conducting a survey which will help us make sure that TIME continues to meet _your_ needs.  So we want to know a few facts about you -- our reader.

To thank you for your assistance, we'll make a contribution to one of the charities listed below:

**RETURN YOUR QUESTIONNAIRE TODAY, AND WE'LL MAKE A VALUABLE CONTRIBUTION TO:**

**THE AMERICAN CANCER SOCIETY**

**THE UNITED WAY**

**THE AMERICAN HEART ASSOCIATION**

**FOUNDATION FOR CHILDREN WITH LEARNING DISABILITIES**

**STATUE OF LIBERTY ELLIS ISLAND FOUNDATION**

In the last 3 years TIME Magazine's contributions to worthwhile foundations have totaled $200,000.  Last year alone, we donated more than $95,000 in this manner.  That's because helpful, concerned people like you participated in our survey.

So won't you take a few moments now to fill out and return your questionnaire in the postpaid envelope?  We'll appreciate it, and so will the charitable organization of your choice. Just indicate on your form which foundation you'd like to help. It's that simple.

Thank you for being so generous.

Sincerely,

John A. Meyers
Publisher

JAM:tb

**Figure 8-8.**   As an alternative to a direct monetary incentive, a charitable contribution can be made to an organization of the respondent's choice. (Courtesy of Time, Inc.)

### Strategies That Follow Receipt of the Questionnaire

The third group of strategies generally involves one or more followups directed at those who do not respond to the questionnaire. As with the telephone and personal interview, we can expect each follow-up wave, whether conducted by telephone, mail, or in person, to provide a diminishing success rate compared to the wave that preceded. Again, the number of follow-ups to be undertaken is a subjective matter that is highly dependent on the individual survey and the importance of having a large percentage of the original questionnaires completed and returned. Keep in mind that your persistence in securing responses from individuals who may not be naturally inclined toward providing a response could lead to their careless or hasty completion of the questionnaire just to get you off their back. Hence, too much emphasis on following up on nonrespondents could reduce nonresponse error at the expense of introducing additional errors of the response type. Figure 8-9 shows the format of a typical reminder postcard used in survey research.

## Dealing with Nonresponse in Survey Research

Despite our best efforts, we will generally find it either impractical or impossible to totally eliminate nonresponse to our survey, be it by mail, telephone, or personal interview. Although follow-up mailings, call-backs, and other strategies may reduce the amount of nonresponse to a tolerable level, we may still wish to have some idea of the effect that nonresponse has had on the results we've obtained.

### Decision Influence Analysis

The first step in dealing with nonresponse is somewhat obvious—that is, to ask if we need to deal with it at all. If, for example, a legislator conducts a survey for the purpose of determining the proportion of her constituency who favors reducing trade barriers between the United States and Japan, she will probably not be very much concerned about nonresponse if 80% of the sample responds and 75% of these persons are in favor of reducing the barriers. This means that *at least* 60% (0.80 × 0.75) of the sample are in favor of the idea even in the unlikely event that *all* of the nonrespondents are opposed to it. Because of this outcome, the legislator would gain relatively little from pursuing the survey further in order to identify the nonrespondents and measure their attitude toward the issue at hand. Given the results of her survey, she would be politically unwise to vote against reducing the trade barriers, and this decision would be unchanged regardless of the disposition of the nonrespondents on this matter. Therefore, if we should find ourselves in a position where added knowledge about the nonrespondents would do nothing to change our decision, we should not waste our time or money in attempting to find out more about them.

Dear Amweek Subscriber:
A few weeks ago we sent you a short questionnaire asking
for your opinions on the articles and photographs featured
in our magazine. This information is important in helping
us best serve the needs of our readers. If you have not
already returned the questionnaire, we's appreciate your
reply as soon as possible.

If you happened to have misplaced the questionnaire or
forgotten about it, please call us at (999) 123-4567 and
we'll promptly send you another one. Thanks very much
for your help.

**Figure 8-9.** Typical format of a
reminder postcard used for soliciting
the questionnaires of nonrespondents.

### The "Ostrich" Approach

A simple approach to estimating the effect of nonrespondents is to assume
that they are the same as respondents—that is, that there is nonresponse, but
no nonresponse **bias**. This is a rather chancy proposition, however, especially
if the subject matter is controversial or if the questionnaire requires written
communication skills that are average or above. As we discussed earlier, factors
such as education, income, and degree of transience are just a few of the possible
differences that may exist between respondents and nonrespondents—and to
the extent that these are related to the variable under investigation, we will have
nonresponse error. In the preceding example regarding the legislator, she may
simply assume that three-fourths of the nonrespondents are also in favor of
lowering the trade barriers, thus reinforcing her political resolve to vote for the
issue.

### Sensitivity Analysis

In this approach, we determine exactly how different the nonrespondents
would have to be in order for this difference to have an effect on our decision.
For example, the legislator may have decided in advance that she would vote
for the proposed legislation only if at least 65% of her constituents were in favor
of it. Thus, in order for this to be true, at least one-fourth of the nonrespondents
would have to be in favor of the issue. At this point, she knows that the proportion of her total sample who are in favor of the issue is somewhere between
60% (if all nonrespondents are opposed) and 80% (if all nonrespondents are in
favor). If the legislator considers it unlikely that less that 25% of the nonrespondents are in favor of the trade barrier reduction, she will conclude that the
overall proportion is greater than 65%, and will be inclined to vote in favor of
the proposed legislation. Such calculation of an "indifference" (with regard to
changing a decision) point for a group of unknown nonrespondents may be
applied to other marketing variables. It may be decided, for example, that a new
product will be introduced only if a certain minimum percentage of the recipients
of a free sample and questionnaire report that they prefer the new brand over
a comparison brand that is already established. In any event, the key to this

approach is (1) to determine how different the nonrespondents would have to be in order for you to alter your decision, and (2) to estimate whether the nonrespondents are highly likely to exhibit less than this amount of difference from those who did respond.

### Subsampling of Nonrespondents

A scientifically more powerful approach to the nonrespondent problem is to expend a reasonable amount of time and money in order to study a sampling of the nonrespondents in order to use the data for making generalizations about *all* of the nonrespondents. For example, the legislator may have a separate telephone survey conducted for the express purpose of finding out how a sampling of the mail survey nonrespondents feels about the possible reduction of trade barriers. If the result of this sampling is a "favorable" proportion of 40%, she may proceed to assume that 40% of all the nonrespondents are also in favor, and revise her findings from 75% (of those who responded) to a level of 68% [based on her subsampling of the nonrespondents and calculated by $(0.75 \times 0.80) + (0.40 \times 0.20)$]. In other words, of the 80% who responded, 75% were in favor of the issue; and of the 20% who did not respond, only 40% were estimated as being in favor of it.

### Trend Analysis

Another method for dealing with nonresponse is to keep a record of the characteristics of those who respond in successive call-back or follow-up waves, then determine if a trend appears to exist. For example, we may find that each wave of responses presents a higher proportion of individuals who are in favor of a certain issue, such as the trade barrier reduction discussed in this section. In such a case, we may wish to extend this trend to estimate the characteristics of our nonrespondents, who would be assumed to constitute a nonexistent call-back or follow-up beyond those we have actually made. For the mail questionnaire, we have the option of using either follow-up number (1st, 2nd wave, etc.) or date of questionnaire return (identifiable by means of the return postmark) in order to describe our successive responses as a function of time. A variant of this approach is merely to assume that those who respond later are similar to those who don't respond at all, in which case we are assuming (perhaps wrongly) that a trend does exist from early respondents to later (and non-) respondents.

Your selection of one or more of the preceding strategies for dealing with survey nonresponse should be made on the basis of (1) whether or not you actually *need* to estimate the effect of nonresponse on your findings, (2) your time and financial resources, and (3) your willingness to take a chance on being wrong in your assessment of the characteristics possessed by the nonrespondents. If this last item is of special importance, it is advisable to take the time and money necessary to subsample the nonrespondents by means of a special survey. Because of the probable difficulty in locating and communicating with nonrespondents, such a follow-up survey is likely to be more expensive than the original in terms of cost per response. However, the increased knowledge you obtain regarding the nonrespondents may cause this additional effort to be well worth the extra cost, especially if there is a substantial difference between those who responded initially and those who did not.

## SELECTION OF A SURVEY METHOD

As we have discussed, each of the survey approaches—personal interview, telephone interview, and mail questionnaire—has its own distinct set of strengths and weaknesses. These are summarized in Table 8-3, where we must recognize that the evaluations listed are *general* in nature and will not be true

**TABLE 8-3.** *Relative strengths and weaknesses of the three methods of conducting survey research*[a]

| Criterion | Personal interview | Telephone interview | Mail questionnaire |
|---|---|---|---|
| Overall cost | − | + | + |
| Response rate | + | + | − |
| Ability to acquire complex information | + | | − |
| Opportunity to use visual aids or stimuli | + | − | |
| Ability to probe for more detailed response | + | | − |
| Ability to control situation in which response is made | + | | − |
| Ability to acquire lengthy information | + | − | |
| Ability to control phrasing of questions | | | + |
| Ability to offer anonymity to respondent | − | − | + |
| Ability to provide immediate monetary or other incentive for cooperation | + | − | + |
| Avoidance of errors caused by respondent-interviewer interaction | − | − | + |
| Time required for completion of survey | | + | − |
| Ability to reach a population which is geographically dispersed | − | + | + |

[a] + indicates relative strength; − indicates relative weakness.

for every possible research situation. Typically, it is advisable to consider the particular set of circumstances you face, evaluate the ability of each technique to provide you with the answers you seek, then select the method that is likely to satisfy your informational needs at the least possible cost. In addition, do not hesitate to consider a combination of two or more techniques applied simultaneously to the same research problem. Because each technique has its unique set of strong and weak points, the simultaneous application of two approaches can help you establish convergent validity and lend additional confidence to the results you obtain. On the other hand, if two or more approaches deliver markedly dissimilar results, convergent validity will be absent and it will be necessary to determine which, if any, of the approaches provided the correct answer to your research question. While the latter possibility may not enjoy a welcome reception on your desk, such a disparity between simultaneous measures of the same phenomenon will alert you to potential research errors that may be corrected in time to avoid the negative consequences of a decision based on erroneous survey results.

## A Closing Comment

"Hello, I'm calling from Fillintheblank. We're doing a survey of homeowners in your area. How long have you lived in your home? . . . Are you planning any home improvements during the coming year? . . . "Would you like a free estimate? . . . "Maybe a neat set of encyclopedias instead?" . . . "How about a furnace overhaul with a 300-year guarantee? . . . Hello? . . . Hello?"

Although most surveys are legitimate attempts to obtain information for marketing decisions, there are exceptions. For example, we have all been the targets of sales pitches that are only thinly disguised as surveys. This type of masquerade deserves special consideration, especially in these days when consumer-citizens are increasingly protective of their privacy and skeptical of strangers who ask them questions. Although worthy of mention here, it will be discussed more fully in the final chapter, Social and Ethical Issues in Marketing Research.

Another exception to the pure information-seeking goal is the "Survey shows that . . ." newspaper article headline that often highlights a study conveniently supportive of its sponsor's interests. Newspaper editors are generally not skilled in research methodology—thus it is not surprising that such articles often suffer from flaws of either commission or omission. For example, the next time you see such an article that happens to describe a mail survey, look for both the number of questionnaires mailed and the number returned; chances are you won't find both. As with the topic of the preceding paragraph, this one will be examined more fully in the final chapter of the text. Because the data collection instrument can play the role of accomplice in this travesty, the faulty survey is also fair game in the questionnaire chapter that follows.

> **EXHIBIT 8-2**
> **Your Lucky Day?**
>
> Upon returning from their mailboxes and opening an urgent-looking enve-
> lope marked "Dated Material, Open At Once," lucky recipients were informed that
> they had not only won a prize, but were invited to participate in a "Market Survey
> Test." All they had to do was return an "Award Order Form" and they would win
> between $500 and $5000 cash, or "one of the $10,000 worth of other prizes."
>
> Accompanying the combined Award Order Form and Market Survey Test
> was a colorful brochure displaying the company's line of bathing suits, available
> at the "Special Test price" of $19.95 each, or two for $38.00. For anxious respondents
> eager to participate in the Market Survey Test, the Award Order Form included
> two lines at the bottom where they could indicate the suits they liked best and
> second-best. To be sure of receiving their award, participants also had to return
> the Award Order Form card by the expiration date: "1 week from Tuesday."

## ☐ SUMMARY

In survey research, we communicate with a sampling of respondents in
order to generalize on the characteristics and behavior of the population they
represent. Three basic methods for this communication are the personal interview, the telephone interview, and the mail questionnaire.

Three main sources of survey error include sampling error, response error,
and nonresponse error. Sampling error is present to the extent that we've taken
a sample instead of a census, but can be statistically estimated if the sample is
of the probability type.

Response error occurs whenever the true value of the variable being measured is distorted during the communication process—for example, respondents
may knowingly exaggerate household income or frequency of church attendance. Nonresponse error occurs when the individuals responding to the survey
are different from those who do not respond.

The personal interview offers flexibility and low nonresponse error, but is
relatively expensive and poses the possibility of response error caused by interaction between interviewer and respondent.

The telephone interview is a fast, inexpensive survey approach, but not
all households have telephones or directory listings. This difficulty in obtaining
a representative sample can be reduced through the use of random digit and
plus-one dialing to reach unlisted telephones.

Mail questionnaires assure anonymity to respondents, are relatively inexpensive, and allow one to easily reach sample members scattered across a
wide geographic area. The greatest weakness of the mail questionnaire is nonresponse error, a difficulty that can be reduced by a variety of strategies.

Each of the three survey approaches has its own strengths and weaknesses.
Selection of a technique for a specific purpose will depend on our time and

monetary constraints, the type of information we need, and the likelihood that the potential respondent will be able and willing to provide it.

## ☐ QUESTIONS FOR REVIEW

1. Provide an example of each of the following.
   a. A survey question which is ambiguous.
   b. A survey question which may exceed the typical adult's ability to answer.
   c. A survey question which may unduly influence the respondent.
2. What are the strengths and weaknesses of the personal interview compared to the mail and telephone survey approaches?
3. Since the respondent doesn't get to read it, why is an interview form desirable in both telephone and personal interviews?
4. Differentiate between response error and nonresponse error in a survey. How can these difficulties be minimized when conducting survey research?
5. A survey is conducted to determine the popularity of bowling, and is carried out by means of telephone interviews made during the 7 to 10 P.M. time slot. There are no callbacks for sample members who aren't at home. Is the measured popularity likely to be (a) higher, (b) lower, or (c) about the same as that which actually exists? Why?
6. Describe how one would go about using random digit dialing and plus-one digit dialing in a telephone survey. Why are these techniques used, and what advantage does the plus-one approach have over the random-digit technique?
7. In what ways are persons not listed in the telephone directory likely to differ from those who are listed?
8. In carrying out a mail questionnaire survey, what are some of the strategies for:
   a. Reducing nonresponse?
   b. Compensating or adjusting for nonresponse?
9. Provide an example, real or hypothetical, in which the sex, appearance, or general manner of a personal interviewer might cause a considerable degree of response error.
10. Respondents who take part in public opinion surveys are usually not rewarded monetarily for their time. What other, perhaps intangible, gratifications and rewards may tend to compensate the respondent for the time he/she has spent answering the questions of a public opinion researcher?
11. How might the type of sponsor (university, corporation, charity), and the appeal used, influence the rate of return of a mail survey? Do you feel it is ethical to identify the survey as being carried out by someone other than the actual sponsor? Why or • why not?
12. Might it ever be advantageous to spend 80% more money on a mail questionnaire (i.e., through monetary incentives, etc.) in order to get a 50% greater response rate? Wouldn't it be more advisable to simply send out 50% more questionnaires in order to get back 50% more responses?
13. Restaurants often provide questionnaire cards at tables so that customers may provide information regarding quality of service, food, etc. Aside from being a channel for customer feedback to the restaurant, what other benefits might such an effort provide to the business?

14. Locate a "Survey shows that . . ." newspaper or magazine story, then evaluate the survey with regard to possible response and nonresponse error. If question wording, sample size, or response rate are missing from the story, speculate as to whether these omissions could have been advantageous to the sponsor of the survey. If the sponsor of the survey is identified, also speculate regarding possible benefits the sponsor may have gained from the specific survey results.

15. Presumably, a survey is done to collect sound information. However, this may sometimes not be the primary purpose of the effort. Provide an example, real or hypothetical, in which a survey might be carried out primarily for a purpose other than the simple generation of truthful, objective information.

# 9

# QUESTIONNAIRE DESIGN

**Question Wording Can Be "Hamburger Helper"**

Armed with the results of a survey showing that fast-food customers preferred flame-broiled hamburgers over fried by a wide margin, Burger King embarked on a comparative advertising campaign in its ongoing competition with McDonald's. Later, Leo Shapiro, president of a marketing research firm, decided to use his own survey to see how question wording might influence preference for the cooking methods used by these two chains.

Sending an interviewer to question 308 consumers, Shapiro showed the verbal description of a cooking method to make a big difference in the taste evaluation that resulted. His results, along with the earlier Burger King finding:

In Burger King's original survey, the question was "Do you prefer your hamburgers flame-broiled or fried?" Result: Burger King's flame-broiling beat McDonald's fried by a 3-to-1 margin.

Shapiro's interviewer inquired of customers, "Do you prefer a hamburger that is grilled on a hot stainless-steel grill or cooked by passing the raw meat through an open gas flame?" Result: 53% preferred McDonald's grill.

---

*Source:* Reprinted with permission from Christy Marshall, "Here's the Word on Surveys about Burger Favorites," *Advertising Age*, March 21, 1983. Copyright © 1983. Crain Communications, Inc. All rights reserved.

**Figure 9-1.**   Although Burger King's "flame-broiling" beat McDonald's "frying" in one survey, another showed that an "open gas flame" versus a "hot stainless-steel grill" made preferences a lot more even. The phrasing of the question can make a big difference when consumers are asked to choose between hamburgers. (Photo courtesy of Jim Wakefield.)

The Shapiro interviewer then asked: "The chain that grills on a hot stainless-steel griddle serves its cooked hamburgers at the proper temperature without having to use a microwave oven. And the chain that uses the gas flame puts the hamburgers after they are cooked into a microwave oven before serving them. Just knowing this, from which of these two chains would you prefer to buy a hamburger?" Result: McDonald's grill beat Burger King's flame by a margin of $5\frac{1}{2}$ to 1.

# INTRODUCTION

"Let's write up a questionnaire and get the facts we need" is a statement all too representative of the rather cavalier approach many take when faced with the need to design a data collection instrument for survey research. However, as we shall see, "writing up a questionnaire" is no less precarious than delivering groceries to Little Red Riding Hood's grandmother. Questionnaire design is beset with potential pitfalls, is a combination of art and science, and often involves *satisficing*; that is, the best data collection instrument is not necessarily one that is perfect. Instead of trying to develop the "ideal" questionnaire, circumstances usually demand that we proceed in timely fashion with one that is both workable and adequate for the job at hand. This is partly reflective of the artistic dimension of the task and represents the practical necessity of acquiring "fresh" marketing information by imperfect means rather than obtaining out-of-date data through the use of a "perfect" questionnaire.

Another important feature of questionnaire design is the opportunity it offers for "research on research." Rather than concentrating on the acquisition of information for immediate marketing decisions, **research on research** helps us to understand the basic underlying processes and to advance the state of the art regarding how best to undertake various research activities. Such items as the effect of positively worded versus negatively worded questions, the effect of various question sequences and the order of presentation of products to be compared are important and engaging examples where both practitioner and student may gain valuable insight about marketing research and potential avenues for its improvement as an objective source of data.

The design of an appropriate questionnaire involves no firm set of foolproof procedures, but consists of general advice that often includes rules of thumb and general advice. However, to help dispel any impressions that questionnaire design is a dark, mysterious art, we will identify a number of procedural steps that, if followed, should result in a questionnaire capable of satisfying your informational requirements. These procedures and guidelines are discussed under the following headings:

  I. Initial considerations
 II. Questionnaire types
III. Questionnaire development
IV. Pretesting the questionnaire

## INITIAL CONSIDERATIONS

In constructing the questionnaire itself, whether it is to be administered by mail, telephone, or in person, it is important that the instrument be designed in a manner that is consistent with the knowledge, interest, and intellectual level of

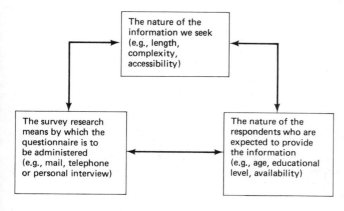

**Figure 9-2.**  Before constructing the actual questionnaire, consideration of potentially important interrelationships between these key elements is a necessity.

## CUSTOMER RELATIONS SURVEY

**PLEASE TELL US ABOUT YOURSELF: (OPTIONAL)**

1. Gender:  Male _____  Female _____

2. Age:  _____Years

3. Education:  Grade School _____  Some College _____  Graduate School _____

   High School _____  College Graduate _____

4. What is your total annual household income: $_____,000

**PLEASE TELL US ABOUT YOUR HONDA EXPERIENCE:**

5. Based on your overall ownership and service experience with this vehicle, how likely would you purchase the same make if you were going to replace this vehicle with another vehicle?

   Definitely Purchase Same Make _____     Probably **Not** Purchase Same Make _____

   Probably Purchase Same Make _____     Definitely **Not** Purchase Same Make _____

6. Would you recommend Hondas to a friend or relative?  Yes _____  No _____

**PLEASE INDICATE YOUR EXPERIENCE IN THE FOLLOWING AREAS WITH THE PEOPLE YOU CONTACTED. PLEASE LEAVE THOSE ITEMS BLANK WHICH DON'T APPLY TO YOU OR FOR WHICH YOU HAVE NO OPINION.**

**FOR THE REGIONAL CUSTOMER SERVICE OFFICE, PLEASE CONSIDER ONLY THOSE PERSONS WHO IDENTIFIED THEMSELVES AS CUSTOMER SERVICE AGENTS OR SUPERVISORS; PLEASE DO NOT INCLUDE RECEPTIONISTS, MANUFACTURER'S REPRESENTATIVES, OR OTHER PERSONNEL.**

| 7. ATTITUDE OF PERSONNEL HANDLING YOUR REQUESTS: | Dealership Personnel | Regional Customer Service Office |
|---|---|---|
| Did the Person You Contacted: | Yes No | Yes No |
| a. Have a friendly attitude? | __ __ | __ __ |
| b. Handle your request(s) with respect? | __ __ | __ __ |
| c. Allow you to say what you wanted to say? | __ __ | __ __ |
| d. View your request as important? | __ __ | __ __ |

Comments: _____

| 8. KNOWLEDGE AND UNDERSTANDING OF THE PEOPLE YOU CONTACTED: | Dealership Personnel | Regional Customer Service Office |
|---|---|---|
| Did the Person You Contacted: | Yes No | Yes No |
| a. Seem to understand your situation? | __ __ | __ __ |
| b. Seem to know what you were talking about? | __ __ | __ __ |
| c. Refer you to the right people? | __ __ | __ __ |
| d. Make you feel that you should have talked to someone else who knew what you wanted? | __ __ | __ __ |
| e. Seem knowledgeable about Hondas? | __ __ | __ __ |

2

**Figure 9-3.**  A self-administered questionnaire for measuring the effectiveness of customer relations programs and procedures. (Copyright © 1987 by American Honda Motor Co., Inc. All rights reserved. Reproduced by permission.)

| | Dealership Personnel | | Regional Customer Service Office | |
|---|---|---|---|---|
| | Yes | No | Yes | No |

**9. ACCURACY OF THE INFORMATION YOU OBTAINED:**

a. Was the information you obtained useful? —— —— —— ——

b. Was the information you obtained accurate? —— —— —— ——

c. Was the information appropriate for your request? —— —— —— ——

| | Dealership Personnel | | Regional Customer Service Office | |
|---|---|---|---|---|
| | Yes | No | Yes | No |

**10. LISTENING SKILLS OF THE PEOPLE YOU CONTACTED:**

a. Do you feel that the person was interested in what you had to say? —— —— —— ——

b. Do you feel that the person really listened to you? —— —— —— ——

| | Dealership Personnel | | Regional Customer Service Office | |
|---|---|---|---|---|
| | Yes | No | Yes | No |

**11. PROCESS BY WHICH YOU WERE REFERRED TO THE INFORMATION SOURCES:**

a. If they could not satisfy your request, did they supply you with a person and number or address to contact? —— —— —— ——

b. Were they prompt in supplying you this information? —— —— —— ——

| | Dealership Personnel | | Regional Customer Service Office | |
|---|---|---|---|---|
| | Yes | No | Yes | No |

**12. TIMELINESS (THE AMOUNT OF TIME IT TOOK TO TAKE CARE OF YOUR REQUEST):**

a. If you were put on hold, was the time you waited reasonable? —— —— —— ——

b. Did they tell you where and when to expect action? —— —— —— ——

c. Was that reasonable? —— —— —— ——

Comments: _____

_____

| | Dealership Personnel | | Regional Customer Service Office | |
|---|---|---|---|---|
| | Yes | No | Yes | No |

**13. SUMMARY OF YOUR EXPERIENCE:**

Did the Person You Contacted:

a. Handle your question in a professional manner? —— —— —— ——

b. If you were to contact Honda again, would you want the same person(s) to handle your request? —— —— —— ——

Comments: _____

3

14. Did you contact the <u>Dealership</u> before contacting the Customer Service Office?

    Yes _____            No _____

If yes, please complete the following box.

---

**IN GENERAL, BASED ON YOUR CONTACT WITH THE <u>DEALERSHIP</u>, PLEASE RATE THE FOLLOWING ITEMS:**

HOW GOOD?

| | VERY POOR | | | | EXCELLENT |
|---|---|---|---|---|---|
| A. Attitude of dealership personnel | 1 | 2 | 3 | 4 | 5 |
| B. Knowledge and understanding of dealership personnel | 1 | 2 | 3 | 4 | 5 |
| C. How well the personnel listened | 1 | 2 | 3 | 4 | 5 |
| D. The time it took to take care of your request | 1 | 2 | 3 | 4 | 5 |
| E. The accuracy of information you obtained | 1 | 2 | 3 | 4 | 5 |
| F. The degree of professionalism | 1 | 2 | 3 | 4 | 5 |
| G. Promptness in referring you to the right information source | 1 | 2 | 3 | 4 | 5 |

15. How satisfied were you with the manner in which your problem was handled by the <u>DEALERSHIP</u>?

      Very Satisfied _____                 Somewhat Dissatisfied _____

     Somewhat Satisfied _____                Very Dissatisfied _____

---

End of Dealership Box

4

16. Did you contact the <u>Regional</u> <u>Customer</u> <u>Service</u> <u>Office</u>?

       Yes \_\_\_\_\_              No \_\_\_\_\_

If yes, please complete the following box.

---

**IN GENERAL, BASED ON YOUR CONTACT WITH THE <u>REGIONAL</u> <u>CUSTOMER</u> <u>SERVICE</u> <u>OFFICE</u>, PLEASE RATE THE FOLLOWING ITEMS:**

HOW GOOD?

| | VERY POOR | | | | EXCELLENT |
|---|---|---|---|---|---|
| A. Attitude of the customer service personnel | 1 | 2 | 3 | 4 | 5 |
| B. Knowledge and understanding of customer service personnel | 1 | 2 | 3 | 4 | 5 |
| C. How well the personnel listened | 1 | 2 | 3 | 4 | 5 |
| D. The time it took to take care of your request | 1 | 2 | 3 | 4 | 5 |
| E. The accuracy of information you obtained | 1 | 2 | 3 | 4 | 5 |
| F. The degree of professionalism | 1 | 2 | 3 | 4 | 5 |
| G. Promptness in referring you to the right information source | 1 | 2 | 3 | 4 | 5 |

17a. How did you make the contact?

       By mail \_\_\_\_\_    In person \_\_\_\_\_

       By phone \_\_\_\_\_   Other (Please specify) _____

17b. How satisfied were you with the manner in which your contact was handled by the <u>Regional</u> <u>Customer</u> <u>Service</u> <u>Office</u>?

      Very Satisfied \_\_\_\_\_    Somewhat Dissatisfied \_\_\_\_\_

      Somewhat Satisfied \_\_\_\_\_    Very Dissatisfied \_\_\_\_\_

---

End of Regional Customer Service Office Box

5

18. Did you contact American Honda's National Office?

      Yes _____          No _____

      If yes, please complete the following box.

---

**IN GENERAL, BASED ON YOUR CONTACT WITH AMERICAN HONDA'S NATIONAL OFFICE, PLEASE RATE THE FOLLOWING ITEMS:**

HOW GOOD?

| | VERY POOR | | | | EXCELLENT |
|---|---|---|---|---|---|
| A. Attitude of the National Office's personnel | 1 | 2 | 3 | 4 | 5 |
| B. Knowledge and understanding of National Office's personnel | 1 | 2 | 3 | 4 | 5 |
| C. How well the personnel listened | 1 | 2 | 3 | 4 | 5 |
| D. The time it took to take care of your request | 1 | 2 | 3 | 4 | 5 |
| E. The accuracy of information you obtained | 1 | 2 | 3 | 4 | 5 |
| F. The degree of professionalism | 1 | 2 | 3 | 4 | 5 |
| G. Promptness in referring you to the right information source | 1 | 2 | 3 | 4 | 5 |

19a. How did you make the contact?

      By mail _____    In person _____

      By phone _____    Other (Please specify) _____

19b. How satisfied were you with the manner in which your contact was handled by American Honda's National Office?

      Very Satisfied _____        Somewhat Dissatisfied _____

      Somewhat Satisfied _____        Very Dissatisfied _____

---

End of American Honda's National Office Box

**EVALUATION OF FINAL OUTCOME**

20. What was the final outcome of your contact? (check all items that apply)

    _____ Obtained information regarding products or services.

    _____ Aired a complaint about products or services.

    _____ Received explanation regarding a problem with products or services.

    _____ Obtained desired repair or services.

    _____ Did not obtain desired repair or services.

    _____ Still waiting for a reply to my question/problem.

    _____ Other (please specify)_____

21. Please rate how satisfied you were with the outcome indicated above.

| Very Dissatisfied | | | | Very Satisfied |
| :---: | :---: | :---: | :---: | :---: |
| 1 | 2 | 3 | 4 | 5 |

22. Overall, how quick was the action in comparison to what you had expected?

| Slower | | About Right | | Faster |
| :---: | :---: | :---: | :---: | :---: |
| 1 | 2 | 3 | 4 | 5 |

23. How could we improve our actions to better serve you? _____

_____

_____


**HOW DO WE COMPARE?**

24. How many times have you contacted <u>some</u> <u>type</u> of customer relations or customer service office other than American Honda?

     _____ number of times     _____ never contacted

25. Have you ever contacted the customer relations or customer service office of a major national company other than American Honda (e.g. AT&T, IBM, Proctor & Gamble, etc.)?

     Yes _____          No _____

     If yes:

          a. Company's Name _____

          b. Please rate how American Honda's customer relations
             compares to this company.

Honda is . . .

| MUCH WORSE | | ABOUT THE SAME | | MUCH BETTER | | |
| :---: | :---: | :---: | :---: | :---: | :---: | :---: |
| 1 | 2 | 3 | 4 | 5 | | NEVER CONTACTED _____ ANOTHER COMPANY |

**THANK YOU FOR YOUR PARTICIPATION**

our potential respondents. We will probably fail to achieve success in our survey research effort if we either ignore or underestimate the importance of possible interactions between the factors shown in Figure 9-2—for example, by asking numerous and complex questions by means of a telephone survey, wording our questions at the college graduate level when many of our respondents have not finished high school, or sending interviewers into the field with a data collection instrument that leaves them "unarmed" against the inevitable difficulties they will encounter with both respondents and their responses in the unpredictable real world of survey research.

To introduce the reader to the general format of a questionnaire, Figure 9-3 is presented on the pages immediately preceding. This excellent questionnaire, the cover letter for which was shown in Chapter 8, is designed to measure the effectiveness of customer relations programs and procedures for a major auto manufacturer. Notice the clarity of the questionnaire, including understandable language and directions for the respondent to skip questions that may be inapplicable to her; for example, on items 14 and 16, the respondent is to answer the questions in the accompanying boxes only if the answer to an initial question is "yes."

## QUESTIONNAIRE TYPES

Now that you've had the opportunity to examine a contemporary questionnaire, as represented in Figure 9-3, we can proceed toward a more detailed level of discussion, the first portion of which deals with the various types of questionnaires used in survey research. In general, questionnaires may be categorized according to structure and directness. *Structure* refers to the degree to which the questions and possible responses are formal and standardized. For example, a highly structured questionnaire would include predetermined questions asked in exactly the same order each time and would provide each respondent with a choice of certain fixed responses. *Directness* refers to the degree to which the respondent is made aware of the purposes for which the questionnaire is being administered. For example, in some instances, it may be desirable to disguise the questionnaire in order to avoid possible response bias that may be the result of either adverse or favorable respondent attitude toward the product or issue that is the true objective of the survey. Of the four possible combinations of these two questionnaire characteristics, the unstructured-indirect approach is not applicable to marketing research situations and will not be discussed. The remaining combinations are described in the sections which follow.

### The Structured, Direct Questionnaire

The type of questionnaire most frequently used in marketing research generally involves both structured questions and responses, and does not attempt to hide the purpose of the survey from the respondent. It should be noted, however, that it is not uncommon to avoid identification of the true sponsor of the re-

search; as indicated earlier, this is often carried out by having the survey conducted by an independent organization or by using a fictitious sponsor identification. Nevertheless, even though the true sponsor may not be revealed, the
purposes of the survey are readily evident to the respondent. Figure 9-3 is an
example of a questionnaire that is both structured and direct.

Data collected by means of this type of questionnaire have the advantage
of being relatively easy to record, tabulate, and analyze, since the information
is received in a form that readily lends itself to coding and cross-tabulation
operations. The strong degree of standardization in this approach also tends to
provide reliable survey results. Since the respondents receive exactly the same
questions in the same order and with the same possible answers, interviewer
inexperience or bias are less likely to influence the results obtained. The structured and direct type of questionnaire is especially applicable if your purpose
is simply to obtain straightforward, factual information, if your interviewers are
not highly skilled, and if you wish to be able to easily record and analyze the
survey results.

Because of its relative formality and lack of flexibility, this survey research
approach is generally most useful in the later stages of a research study, after
you have already carried out exploratory research for the purpose of identifying
necessary questions and their possible answers.

## The Unstructured, Direct Questionnaire

The unstructured, direct questionnaire typically consists of general questions
directed at the research topic, allowing the respondent a great deal of freedom
in formulating his or her response. When this type of instrument is used in a
personal or telephone interview, the skill and competence of the interviewer
become especially important. In these settings, the interviewer can probe more
deeply into responses that are especially interesting as well as those judged to
be either superficial or implausible.

One of the first examples of an unstructured, direct question to which most
of us were subjected at an early age was when we eagerly sat upon the knee
of a department store Santa Claus and were asked what we wanted for Christmas. The following are also questions in which the objective is relatively obvious
and the respondent has complete freedom in formulating his response:

---

How do you feel about investors from foreign nations purchasing stock
in American corporations?

What goes through your mind whenever you see the "L.L. Bean" label
on a product?

How would you react if your wife were to tell you that she had just
registered both of you for a cardiopulmonary resuscitation (CPR) course
to be offered locally by the YMCA?

---

In some applications of unstructured, direct questioning, there is no formal line of conversation to follow, but rather a general direction is achieved by using the interviewer as a moderator who leads a small group in discussing the product or topic that is the object of the research. This approach is referred to as the *focus group interview*, and is covered along with the *depth interview* and other topics in the next chapter. Both of these are more specialized variations of the unstructured, direct questionnaire approach. While the former utilizes a moderator in conjunction with a small group, the latter involves a skilled interviewer who attempts to probe the attitudes of a single respondent at a time.

The inherent flexibility of the unstructured, direct questionnaire makes this approach especially useful in the exploratory stages of a study in which a later, more formal questionnaire is to be utilized. With the initial administration of the unstructured instrument, we can gain valuable insight into both the subject matter of the research and the potential problems and responses that are likely to be encountered in the later phases of the study. Depending on the amount and value of the information that is collected by means of the unstructured, direct instrument, it may even be decided to forego additional research in favor of making a timely decision based on the information that has already been collected.

One of the key areas of concern with the unstructured, direct questionnaire is the availability of competent interviewers when the instrument is to be administered in person or by means of the telephone. Because qualified interviewers are expensive to retain, we can expect our cost per interview to be somewhat higher than if a more structured approach were used. However, because of the ability of the interviewers to obtain information that might otherwise be lost in the formality of a highly structured data collection instrument, this greater expense is likely to be worthwhile, especially in an exploratory study where the strength of this approach is most evident. Another difficulty with this type of instrument is the relative complexity of recording, editing, and analyzing the responses that result from allowing interviewers to follow intuition in asking questions and permitting respondents to expand upon their points of view in providing the answers.

## The Structured, Indirect Questionnaire

Because of its rather unique nature and importance, the structured, indirect data collection approach is covered more thoroughly in the next chapter. At this point, however, we should recognize that individuals will often be unwilling or unable to provide us with meaningful answers to direct questions regarding various topics, and are more likely to be useful sources of information if we approach them in such a way that they are not aware of the purposes of our study.

For example, we might be interested in determining respondents' perceptions of the income characteristics of men wearing eyeglasses of various styles. However, if we were to directly present three styles of eyeglasses and ask the

---

**EXHIBIT 9-1**

**The Mythical Mr. Chapman**

When surveyed in a political poll, voters might well find a Mr. "Robert Chapman" among the candidates about whom they are asked. Although Mr. Chapman doesn't really exist, one marketing research firm finds it useful to include him as a control with whom to compare the candidate who happens to be their client. In polling New Yorkers for their awareness of various candidates, the researchers found Mr. Chapman to be twice as well known as their client, indicating that much work remained to be done before election time.

*Source:* "Research's Expanding Role Is Helping Elect Candidates, Improve Political Parties' Images," *Marketing News,* December 9, 1983, p. 1, published by the American Marketing Association.

---

respondent how much money was earned in the past year by the person wearing each style, the result would probably be a combination of comedy, confusion, and suspicion. Many respondents would undoubtedly think us foolish for even suggesting that they attempt to state the income of someone they know nothing about except the style of eyeglasses he happens to wear. On the other hand, if we approach the same situation indirectly by showing, to three comparable groups of respondents, a picture of the same individual wearing each of the eyeglass styles (i.e., each group views and reacts to only one picture), our degree of success is likely to be much greater. Whereas, in the first situation, some respondents might hesitate to associate income with eyeglass style alone, the indirect approach would involve their reaction to a complete individual, rather than to just two lenses and a frame. A comparison of the structured, direct and the structured, indirect approaches to this situation is presented in Figure 9-4. Because respondents in the second setting would not know the purpose of the study, they would be more likely to attribute varying incomes to the same individual posed in identical dress and circumstances, but wearing a different style of eyeglasses. The means of setting up such studies will be examined in Chapter 11, on *experimentation.* The particular approach taken in this example is one of several kinds of *projective techniques* that will be discussed in Chapter 10.

The strategy of structured, indirect questioning manifests itself in many ways. For example, a local kindergarten once sent the author a questionnaire requesting information on a child who was to enter school during the coming year. While most questions were straightforward queries on background, health, and special needs, one question asked *"Do your child's friends tend to get hurt often?"* Since few parents of bullies are going to admit that their children might be a threat to other kids, this was certainly a creative attempt to avoid response error and get at the truth.

A. Assuming that all you know about a certain individual is that he wears eyeglasses of a certain style, how much would you estimate that each of the following individuals earns each year?

Income: $____,000

Income: $____,000

Income: $____,000

B. Please fill in the blanks below in order to describe the characteristics that you think would apply to the individual in the picture.

(THIS FIGURE IS SHOWN TO ONE-THIRD OF RESPONDENTS.)

(THIS FIGURE IS SHOWN TO ONE-THIRD OF RESPONDENTS.)

(THIS FIGURE IS SHOWN TO ONE-THIRD OF RESPONDENTS.)

Age:_____

Income:

$___,000 per year

College graduate:
Yes____ No____

Age:_____

Income:

$___,000 per year

College graduate:
Yes____ No____

Age:_____

Income:

$___,000 per year

College graduate:
Yes____ No____

**Figure 9-4.** Comparison of structured, direct (A) and structured, indirect (B) approaches to determining perceived income associated with different eyeglass styles. In Approach B, the purpose of the study is not revealed to members of the three comparable groups involved in the study.

## QUESTIONNAIRE DEVELOPMENT

At this point, we can proceed to examine a series of decisions that serve to describe a general procedure for the actual construction of the questionnaire. These decision areas—involving question content, question type, question wording, question sensitivity, question sequence, and physical appearance of the questionnaire—are not only related to each other, but also to the three important interactive elements of Figure 9-2. In our examination of the following topics, we will attempt to recognize not only specific strategies applicable to each, but also potential pitfalls that the unwary researcher might encounter in his or her efforts to design a satisfactory questionnaire.

### Question Content

When evaluating possible questions for inclusion in the data collection instrument, we must consider each of the three issues discussed below.

*1. Is the question really necessary?* While some information may be of great personal interest to the survey sponsor or the individual researcher, it may have nothing to do with the objectives of the research study. For example, the manager of a store may be interested in how people feel about his running for a local public office, but this has no relevance to a study in which we are attempting to determine whether or not his customers would be interested in a new installment payment system that is being contemplated. If a research effort is intended to assist in the selection of a marketing decision alternative, potential questions must be evaluated in terms of whether different responses would tend to support different courses of action. Whenever the response to a particular question will have no effect on the eventual strategy selection, or if the content of the question does not represent the subject matter of the research, it is wasteful of both time and money to persist in asking the question.

*2. Will the respondent be willing and able to provide the information requested?* Even though a question may address the content area of interest, this will be to no avail if the respondent is either unwilling or unable to supply a meaningful answer. It is not at all unusual for respondents to attempt to impress the interviewer, to misinterpret terms they were expected to understand, and to generally provide responses that are more "acceptable" than truthful. A classic example of this survey research problem is the pattern of responses to the following question:[1]

---

Which of the following statements most closely coincides with your opinion of the Metallic Metals Act?
- ☐ It would be a good move on the part of the United States.
- ☐ It would be a good thing, but should be left to the individual states.
- ☐ It is all right for foreign countries, but should not be required here.
- ☐ It is of no value at all.
- ☐ No opinion.

---

[1] Sam Gill, "How Do You Stand on Sin?" *Tide*, March 14, 1947, p. 72.

Thirty percent of the respondents expressed "no opinion" with regard to this legislative stimulus. Of those who did voice an opinion, the results were distributed among the responses as follows: (1) 21%, (2) 59%, (3) 16% and (4) 4%. Nearly 6 out of 10 who expressed an opinion felt that the Metallic Metals Act "would be a good thing, but should be left to the individual states," a curious finding in view of the fact that *there was no such thing as the Metallic Metals Act.* This situation should serve to illustrate that respondents will often be more than willing to provide answers—but their responses (or the question to which they react) may be totally nonsensical, as in the case of the "Metallic Metals Act." If respondents will readily provide answers to any question, regardless of how much sense it makes, we should be forewarned to take the greatest of precautions in planning and evaluating the content of the questions we choose to ask in survey research.

*3. Does the question adequately cover the content area for which it is responsible?* A question may be extremely relevant to the subject matter of the research study, but may in itself be incapable of providing the information desired. It will sometimes be necessary to divide a question into two or more separate questions, instead of attempting to cover the content range in a single question that will produce confused and conflicting responses. For example, consider the question, "Do you frequently watch college and professional football on television?" A positive response to this question may mean that the respondent watches college football only, professional football only, or that she watches both levels of competition. In addition, the meaning of the word "frequently" may vary considerably from one respondent to the next. Some respondents could associate "frequently" with watching four or more games each weekend (and Monday night) during the season. Other respondents may define "frequently" as watching more than one game each week. In this case, we might well break the question down into a number of related questions that cover the content area:

---

How often do you generally watch televised college football games during the season?

- ☐ Never.
- ☐ Sometimes, but not every week.
- ☐ Usually watch one game every week.
- ☐ Usually watch two or more games every week.

How often do you generally watch televised professional football games during the season?

- ☐ Never.
- ☐ Sometimes, but not every week.
- ☐ Usually watch one game every week.
- ☐ Usually watch two or more games every week.

---

Because of our necessary closeness to the questionnaire we are developing, it is not surprising that we may be oblivious to possibilities where respondents will have differing frames of reference when confronted with a particular stimulus. Ideally, we would recognize all possible frames of reference when deciding upon the content of a given question, but as frail human beings ourselves, we tend to persist in our own mental "set" and often do not consider potential frames of reference that are different from our own. Based on numerous student marketing research projects over the years, the author has found that one of the most common errors is the inclusion of ambiguous first-draft questions such as "Why do you shop from the Sears catalog?" To some customers, the question will be interpreted as asking why they shop by means of catalog orders instead of personally selecting items from the retail department store. To other customers, the frame of reference will be why they shop through Sears' catalog rather than from J.C. Penney's or other catalog retailers. As with the football viewership question, this one begs to be divided into separate questions: "Why do you shop by catalog?" and "Why did you select Sears for your catalog shopping needs?" The assumption that others share our own frame of reference can be quite damaging whenever we attempt to develop a questionnaire. Even prior to pretesting the questionnaire, we should set it aside for at least a brief period of time, then give it a fresh look—with the resulting likelihood that we will see content dimensions that were not initially apparent to us.

## Question Types

In the development of a questionnaire, three basic types of questions may be utilized: (1) open-ended, (2) multiple choice, and (3) dichotomous. Each form tends to have its own set of advantages and disadvantages, which we will discuss in turn, and a given questionnaire is likely to contain a mixture of questions of the various types. In terms of the amount of structure involved, *open-ended* questions have the least and *dichotomous* questions the most structure. As the following examples demonstrate, we can often approach the same general subject area by means of any or all of the three types:

---

*OPEN-ENDED*
How do you feel about allowing female sports writers to enter professional football locker rooms for postgame interviews?

---

*MULTIPLE CHOICE*
Which of the following best describes how you feel about allowing female sports writers to enter professional football locker rooms for postgame interviews?
- ☐ Should not be allowed under any circumstances.
- ☐ Should be allowed only under limited circumstances (e.g., after players have had the opportunity to shower and dress before being interviewed).
- ☐ Should be afforded the same postgame privileges as male sports writers.
- ☐ No opinion.

---

> *DICHOTOMOUS*
> Do you feel that female sports writers should be allowed to enter professional football locker rooms for postgame interviews?
> ☐ Yes      ☐ No

Although each of the preceding questions deals with the same general subject matter (i.e., respondent attitudes toward allowing female sports writers into male locker rooms), don't be misled into thinking that they are equally capable of measuring this or any other variable of research interest. As we will see in the discussion and examples that follow, each approach has both strengths and weaknesses, and it can be a grave strategic error to use a particular type of question in a situation where it is inappropriate.

### Open-Ended Questions

The *open-ended* question offers the respondent freedom to answer in his own words and to express any thoughts which he feels are appropriate to the question. Unlike the other question forms, this approach does not force the respondent to select from a fixed set of alternatives. As a result, depending on the nature of the question and the interest of the respondent, answers may vary a great deal in their length and detail. In the female sportswriter question presented at the beginning of this section, we might expect open-ended responses to range all the way from a simple yes or no to a one-hour discourse on the merits of women's rights and equal opportunity. Other examples of open-ended questions are:

> What do you like best about your new RCA television?

> How do you feel about students who join fraternities or sororities?

> If you were the manager of the New England Aquarium, what would you do to improve attendance?

> Where do you like to go during family vacations?

As these examples suggest, one strength of the open-ended question is that it is the easiest for the researcher to formulate—that is, it is up to respondents to provide their own answers to the questions, so it is not highly important for the researcher to anticipate in advance the potential responses that may be obtained. Another advantage is that, because there is no fixed set of response alternatives from which to choose, respondents are less likely to be swayed toward a response that does not reflect their true opinion regarding the subject of the question. For these reasons, the open-ended question is especially useful in exploratory research, where we typically wish to obtain insights that may be helpful in further, more structured research. In general, the open-ended question will also provide respondents with the opportunity to "vent" possible strong or adverse feelings about the topic under investigation. To this extent, an open-ended question may serve the added purpose of placating the ill feelings of an unhappy customer or constituent.

Still another advantage of open-ended questions is that the responses obtained may tend to enrich the final research report through the inclusion of actual quotes from respondents who are judged to be representative. Such incorporation of selected quotes will help the client, research director, or other reader of the report to have a better feel for both the nature of the research and the attitudes of the respondents who participated.

Despite its strengths, the open-ended question has a number of disadvantages that may result in its being less than appropriate for certain applications. Although this type of question is generally short and easy to formulate, the responses evoked can be highly difficult to record and categorize. Because respondents are answering in their own words, each response will be slightly different from the next, and a personal or telephone interviewer may not be able to accurately record the precise sentiments expressed by the respondent. Inteviewers who possess great handwriting speed will thus be able to record more exactly what the respondent has said, while those who write more slowly may have to compensate by increasingly summarizing and interpreting what the respondent *seems* to be saying. The result will be a combination of what the respondent has said and what the interviewer *thinks* that the respondent has said. The use of tape recorders, if permitted by the respondent, may help alleviate this difficulty. Awareness of the presence of the recorder, however, is likely to cause some respondents to react in a different fashion than if the conversation were not being taped. Obviously, if the open-ended question is administered as part of a written questionnaire completed by respondents themselves, such interviewer effects will not be a problem.

Another difficulty with the open-ended question is that, even if answers are successfully recorded verbatim, someone must edit the collective responses for the purpose of summarizing the results and reaching general conclusions. While this is less important in exploratory research, where we are often more interested in the individual answers than in summarizations intended to reflect their range and type, such editing and categorization are both time-consuming and difficult in other types of studies. In addition, such analysis must be carried out in an objective manner by a trained researcher if biases of interpretation and personal attitude are to be minimized. Because open-ended questions are relatively demanding on the respondent in terms of requiring self-expression either verbally or in writing, the editor's problem is compounded by the tendency for those who are more articulate to expound more completely or effectively in formulating their response to a question. Such respondents, who are likely to be of higher income and possess a greater level of education, will tend to provide a greater depth of response, which can result in their being over-represented in the final tabulation of all responses. For example, if a question happens to concern the features that are most liked by owners of a new microwave oven, the more articulate respondent may cite a number of features (e.g., "convenience," "speed of cooking," "energy efficiency," "versatility," "compactness"), while a less articulate individual may only mention the feature that first comes to mind (e.g., "it cooks things fast"). As a result, for a given number of respondents, the majority of "most-liked" features will consist of those provided by higher-income, better-educated respondents.

### Multiple-Choice Questions

The *multiple-choice* format typically presents the respondent with a question and a set of alternatives that will be *mutually exclusive* (only one alternative can be selected) and *exhaustive* (the alternatives include all possible responses). From the choices provided, the respondent is to select the one that most closely describes him. The *checklist* is a variant of the multiple-choice approach, and asks the respondent to select all alternatives that apply to him. Figure 9-5 shows both approaches—the questionnaire consists mostly of multiple-choice questions, with one checklist item at the end.

Compared to the open-ended question, multiple-choice offers a number of advantages. In general, these two question types are nearly opposite in their strengths and weaknesses. For example, the multiple-choice approach ensures greater ease of data recording and tabulation, thus eliminating interviewer bias and editing subjectivity in the recording and summarization of data. Likewise, respondents who are more articulate are not as likely to be overrepresented in the answers that are obtained. Not the least of the advantages of the multiple-choice question is the simplicity afforded the respondent, who needs only to place check marks in the appropriate boxes rather than take the effort to speak or write at great length with regard to the question topic. For this reason, the use of a multiple-choice question format is extremely useful in obtaining the cooperation of potential respondents, especially in mail or other self-administered questionnaires.

Disadvantages of the multiple-choice question are largely related to the limitations of the fixed set of alternatives and their effect on the respondent. First, if the respondent is to select just one alternative, the possible responses must be both exhaustive and mutually exclusive. This may be difficult for us to achieve, especially in the exploratory stages of a study, where we are likely to have little idea of the possible range of responses that may be obtained. In addition, because the respondent has the opportunity to hear or view the alternatives prior to making his selection, he may select a response he would not even have thought of had the question been of the open-ended variety. Similarly, if the respondent doesn't really agree with any of the available alternatives, he

---

### EXHIBIT 9-2
### *This Candidate Really Is a Nobody*

In Nevada, voters have the opportunity to indicate "None of the above" as a response on their ballot. As a result, some politicians have been embarrassed by being "out-polled" by this mythical candidate.[2] In Nevada's 1986 primary election for state treasurer, "None of the above" received 24.3% of the votes cast, while the most popular real candidate got just 22.5%. Since the "None" choice is intended to serve as a forum for voter dissatisfaction, the election rules require that the real person with the most votes be declared the winner.[3]

---

is likely to take the easy way out and select one anyway, instead of writing in "None of the above" or selecting the "Other _____" or "No opinion" category (if included among the response alternatives).

Because of the need to anticipate potential answers and to formulate questions that are more easily adapted to a self-administered questionnaire, another disadvantage of the multiple-choice question is that a greater degree of effort is required in order to ensure that the question will be understood, that the frame of reference will not be uncertain, and that the vast majority of potential responses will be accommodated by the available selection of alternatives. Good multiple-choice questions are not easy to make up, and it is only appropriate that the additional resources expended in formulating good questions be compensated by greater economy and simplicity in recording, tabulating, and analyzing the responses that are obtained.

The number and range of responses to a multiple-choice question involve especially difficult decisions. If a large number of alternatives are listed for a given question, the tendency will be to reduce the number of responses to any single alternative. This could introduce the opportunity for an unethical researcher to intentionally bias the survey results in favor of his or her personal or organizational interests. For example, consider the following questions:

---

A. How would you rate the reliablity of your *Snowchucker* snowblower?
   ☐ Superior      ☐ Very good      ☐ Good      ☐ Poor

---

B. How would you rate the reliability of your *Snowchucker* snowblower?
   ☐ Extremely poor      ☐ Very poor      ☐ Poor      ☐ Good

---

[2] "A Perfect Candidate," *Time*, November 20, 1978, p. 47.

[3] Jean Becker and Laura Myers, "'None of the Above' Wins," *USA TODAY*, September 4, 1986, p. 1A. Copyright, 1986 *USA TODAY*. Excerpted with permission.

# ⦿PIONEER® PURCHASER'S RECORD

Model No: _____  Serial No: _____

Date of Purchase: _____

Dealer Name: _____

Dealer Address: _____

City _____ State _____ Zip _____

*Detach here and retain this section for your records.*

································································

*Seal card here.*

## Product Registration ⦿PIONEER®

**Congratulations on buying a PIONEER product. You made an excellent choice! Now . . . would you please help us by completing and returning this card within 10 days. While it is not required, the information requested will help us learn about our customers and their desires. We analyze our customer information to help plan our advertising, plan for new products, and guide our customer service efforts. THANK YOU!**

Car Stereo
27E

1. ☐ Mr.   2. ☐ Mrs.   3. ☐ Ms.   4. ☐ Miss

First Name                Initial   Last Name

Street                                            Apt. No.

City                              State    Zip

2. Date of Purchase: ☐☐ ☐☐ ☐☐  Mo Day Yr

3. Pioneer Model # ☐☐☐☐☐☐☐☐

**4. Store where product was purchased:**
1. ☐ Department store
2. ☐ Electronic store
3. ☐ Discount store
4. ☐ Record/Tape/Music
5. ☐ Car stereo specialist
6. ☐ Radio/TV/Appliance
7. ☐ Audio store
8. ☐ Military PX
9. ☐ Gift that I requested
10. ☐ Surprise gift
11. ☐ Car dealer
12. ☐ Other

**5. Check the two (2) most important factors influencing your selection of this PIONEER product:**
1. ☐ Recommendation by retailer
2. ☐ Recommendation by friend/family
3. ☐ PIONEER name and reputation
4. ☐ Sound quality
5. ☐ Design/appearance
6. ☐ Price
7. ☐ Reliability
8. ☐ Special features
9. ☐ Technical specs
10. ☐ Ease of installation
11. ☐ Value for the money
12. ☐ Guarantee

**6. Which three (3) features are the most important to you:**
1. ☐ Auto Reverse
2. ☐ Push Button/Preset
3. ☐ Supertuner
4. ☐ Electronic Tuning
5. ☐ Separate Bass/Treble
6. ☐ Fader
7. ☐ Music Search
8. ☐ Dolby
9. ☐ Matches interior of car
10. ☐ Fit into car
11. ☐ Other

**7. Which type of purchase is this?**
1. ☐ First time purchase
2. ☐ Replacement purchase
3. ☐ Additional purchase

**8. The make of my car in which my car stereo will be used is: (Example Make: Chevrolet)**
Make: _____

**9. The model of car in which my car stereo will be used is: (Example Model: Camaro)**
Model: _____

**10. The model year of this car is:**
1 9 __ __

**11. Who installed this product:**
1. ☐ Selling dealer
2. ☐ Another dealer
3. ☐ Myself
4. ☐ Friend
5. ☐ Other

**12. Price paid:**
1. ☐ Less than $99.99
2. ☐ $100.00-$149.99
3. ☐ $150.00-$199.99
4. ☐ $200.00-$299.99
5. ☐ $300.00-$399.99
6. ☐ Over $400.00

**13. Which other PIONEER products do you own?**
1. ☐ None
2. ☐ Car Stereo
3. ☐ Car Speakers
4. ☐ Progression IV
5. ☐ Portable Cassette
6. ☐ Syscom
7. ☐ Video/Disc Player
8. ☐ Projection TV
9. ☐ Home Components
10. ☐ Other

**14. Date of birth of person listed above:**
☐☐ 1 9 ☐☐  Mo Yr

**15. Occupation:**

| | You | Your Spouse |
|---|---|---|
| | | 0. ☐ NOT MARRIED |
| Homemaker | 1. ☐ | 1. ☐ |
| Professional/Technical | 2. ☐ | 2. ☐ |
| Executive/Administrator | 3. ☐ | 3. ☐ |
| Middle Mgt./White Collar | 4. ☐ | 4. ☐ |
| Sales/Marketing | 5. ☐ | 5. ☐ |
| Clerical | 6. ☐ | 6. ☐ |
| Craftsworker | 7. ☐ | 7. ☐ |
| Machine Oper./Blue Collar | 8. ☐ | 8. ☐ |
| Service Worker | 9. ☐ | 9. ☐ |
| Retired | 10. ☐ | 10. ☐ |
| Student | 11. ☐ | 11. ☐ |
| Military | 12. ☐ | 12. ☐ |

**16. Do you have any children living at home in any of the following age groups?**
0. ☐ None
1. ☐ Under age 2
2. ☐ Age 2-4
3. ☐ Age 5-7
4. ☐ Age 8-10
5. ☐ Age 11-12
6. ☐ Age 13-15
7. ☐ Age 16-18

**17. Which group describes your annual family income:**
1. ☐ Under $10,000
2. ☐ $10,000-$14,999
3. ☐ $15,000-$19,999
4. ☐ $20,000-$24,999
5. ☐ $25,000-$29,999
6. ☐ $30,000-$34,999
7. ☐ $35,000-$39,999
8. ☐ $40,000-$44,999
9. ☐ $45,000-$49,999
10. ☐ $50,000-$54,999
11. ☐ $55,000-$59,999
12. ☐ $60,000 & over

**(over)**

**Figure 9-5.** This warranty-card questionnaire is mostly multiple-choice, with one checklist item at the end. (Courtesy of Pioneer Electronics of America, Inc. and National Demographics & Lifestyles, Inc.)

# ⓂPIONEER®

**Pioneer Electronics (USA), Inc.**
**P.O. Box 17486**
**Denver, Colorado 80217**

**MARKET RESEARCH DEPARTMENT**
Please do not send any products or correspondence to this address

Please fold here

**18. Which types of credit cards do you use regularly?**
1. ☐ American Express, Diners Club, Carte Blanche
2. ☐ Bank card (MasterCard, Visa)
3. ☐ Department Store
4. ☐ None of the above

**19. For your primary residence, do you:**
1. ☐ Own a house?
2. ☐ Rent a house?
3. ☐ Own a townhouse/condominium?
4. ☐ Rent an apartment?

**20. To help us understand our customers' lifestyles, please indicate the interests and activities in which you or your spouse enjoy participating on a regular basis:**

1. ☐ Golf
2. ☐ Racquetball
3. ☐ Running/Jogging
4. ☐ Snow Skiing
5. ☐ Tennis

6. ☐ Bicycling Frequently
7. ☐ Boating/Sailing
8. ☐ Bowling
9. ☐ Gardening/Plants
10. ☐ Physical Fitness/Exercise

11. ☐ Camping/Hiking
12. ☐ Fishing Frequently
13. ☐ Hunting/Shooting
14. ☐ Motorbiking/Motorcycling
15. ☐ Recreational Vehicle/4–WD
16. ☐ CB Radio

17. ☐ Automotive Work
18. ☐ Electronics/Do-It-Yourself
19. ☐ Home Workshop/Do-It-Yourself
20. ☐ Photography
21. ☐ Stereo, Records & Tapes

22. ☐ Avid Book Reading
23. ☐ Bible/Devotional Reading
24. ☐ Crafts
25. ☐ Needlework/Knitting,
26. ☐ Sewing

27. ☐ Attending Cultural/Arts Events
28. ☐ Community/Civic Activities
29. ☐ Foreign Travel
30. ☐ Gourmet Cooking/Fine Foods
31. ☐ Home Decorating
32. ☐ Wines

33. ☐ Coin/Stamp Collecting
34. ☐ Collectibles/Collections
35. ☐ Fine Art/Antiques
36. ☐ Real Estate Investments
37. ☐ Stock/Bond Investments

38. ☐ Contests/Sweepstakes
39. ☐ Health/Natural Foods
40. ☐ Household Pets (dogs, cats, etc.)
41. ☐ Our Nation's Heritage
42. ☐ Wildlife/Environmental Issues

43. ☐ Science/New Technology
44. ☐ Personal/Home Computer
45. ☐ Video Games
46. ☐ Videocassette Recording (VCR)
47. ☐ Cable TV Viewing
48. ☐ Watching Sports on TV

Thanks for taking the time to fill out this questionnaire. Your answers will help us better serve you, and others who buy our products, in the future. They will also allow you to receive important mailings and special offers from a number of fine companies whose products and services relate directly to the specific interests, hobbies, and other information you have indicated above. Through this selective program, you will be able to obtain more information about activities in which you are involved and less about those in which you aren't. Please check here if, for some reason, you would prefer *not* to be included in this unique opportunity. ☐

In question B, not only is the order of possible responses different, but only one alternative is favorable to this hypothetical brand. The results of such a survey would probably be extremely well suited for use in an advertisement placed by a competing manufacturer. On the other hand, the results of question A would be more likely to indicate that the Snowchucker is a reliable machine. In each of the preceding questions, the alternatives are unbalanced in terms of there being a majority of response possibilities that are either favorable or unfavorable to the object of the question.

Selection of the range and number of available alternatives to multiple-choice questions is an important decision not limited to commercial organizations conducting surveys. Consider, for example, the following multiple-choice "question" appearing on a weekly collection envelope delivered to members of a certain church:

---

This week, my contribution is:
☐ $____    ☐ $20    ☐ $15    ☐ $10    ☐ $5

---

In addition to identifying the amount of the enclosed contribution, the alternatives on the envelope are decidedly biased in the upward direction, with the "$____" alternative appearing at the high end of the range. While it is difficult to criticize a worthy religious organization for arranging alternatives in this way, one can't help but wonder about the potential effect on contributions if the "open" alternative were to be moved to the lower extreme of the range of potential choices.

### Dichotomous Questions

The *dichotomous* question is really just a multiple-choice question that has only two alternatives from which to select. In practice, however, the two principal choices are often supplemented by an additional possibility of the "Don't know" or "No opinion" type. For some questions (e.g., "Do you own a tuba?") respondents are unlikely to be in doubt, and such a third alternative is not appropriate. For others, it may not even be desirable. Congressman Joe Kolter, in explaining the lack of a "No opinion" possibility in the legislative questionnaire of Figure 9-6: "While the questions were simply stated, the same is true of the way issues are voted on the House floor. Many times I would like to say 'Yes, if . . .'—but I do not have that option."[4]

The dichotomous question has the same basic strengths as the multiple-choice approach—that is, ease of acquiring, recording, tabulating, and analyzing data. With only two basic alternatives from which to choose, the dichotomous question makes it very easy for the respondent to reply, an advantage that is

---

[4] Mailing to constituents, Congressman Joe Kolter, U.S. House of Representatives, Autumn 1986.

# Congressman Joe Kolter's
## *1987 Legislative Questionnaire*

1. In this Congress, the President will most likely ask for additional dollars for the Contras in Nicaragua. Should America continue to fund this war?
   
   ____ **Yes**          ____ **No**

2. If forced to choose between the two, do you consider your beliefs:
   
   ____ **Conservative**          ____ **Liberal**

3. Which issue is the most important to resolve?
   
   ____ **Budget Deficit**          ____ **Economic Recovery**

4. The Administration is continuing to carry out plans for Star Wars. Should tax dollars be used to increase weapons or defenses in space?
   
   ____ **Yes**          ____ **No**

5. Do you favor a constitutional amendment that would require a balanced budget no matter what, including times of war, unemployment or economic depression?
   
   ____ **Yes**          ____ **No**

6. Do you support the President's plan to sell arms to Iran?
   
   ____ **Yes**          ____ **No**

7. Is mandatory unannounced drug testing a violation of a person's basic rights?
   
   ____ **Yes**          ____ **No**

8. Please use this space to indicate a specific issue about which you are also concerned. Please be brief and indicate how you think Congressman Joe Kolter should vote:

   _____

   _____

   _____

   _____

   _____

   _____

Please check the items that apply to you:

| | | |
|---|---|---|
| ____ Municipal Employee | ____ Business owner | ____ Veteran |
| ____ Professional | ____ Factory Worker | ____ Doctor |
| ____ Retired Citizen | ____ Educator | ____ Health Care Employee |
| ____ Federal Employee | ____ Farmer | ____ Construction Worker |
| ____ Steelworker | ____ State Employee | ____ Airline Employee |
| ____ Unemployed | ____ Senior Citizen | ____ Electrician |
| ____ Homeowner | ____ Attorney | ____ Other _____ |
| ____ Union Member | ____ Apartment Renter | _____ |

Please fill in name and address on other side.

**Figure 9-6.** This questionnaire, sent to constituents to get their feelings on legislative issues, consists mostly of dichotomous questions. (Courtesy of Congressman Joe Kolter.)

especially pronounced when the issue at hand clearly involves an "either-or" categorization. In addition, as with the multiple-choice question, there is less opportunity for the interviewer bias and tabulation subjectivity that are inherent problems when using questions of the open-ended type.

A major difficulty with using the dichotomous question is that some issues may not really involve "either-or" positions or categories, and the dichotomous responses that are obtained may be overly simplistic. For example, the seemingly straightforward question "Are you in favor of allowing girls to compete in Little League baseball?" may involve more complexity than would seem apparent at first glance. For many, the answer will be a simple "yes," but some may be in favor of the issue only under limited conditions—for example, provided that girls are not permitted to play at the catcher position. Others may not really be sure about the issue, but will select "yes" or "no" in order to avoid having the researcher think they have no opinion on the matter.

### Position Bias

When respondents are asked to select from a list of alternatives, the possibility of *position bias* exists. Depending on the nature of the question and its alternative answers, respondents may tend to select those presented in first, last, or central locations. This is a potential difficulty with both multiple-choice and dichotomous questions. Asking the same question, but with the alternatives arranged in a different order, will often result in a different set of response frequencies. The effect of position bias may be reduced by employing a "split ballot"—that is, on some questionnaires one sequence of alternatives is used; on others, the sequence is reversed. In some situations, where it is not important that the list be arranged in decreasing or increasing order with regard to some attribute, random ordering of the alternatives may also be used. Examination of the possible effects of position bias in a particular survey situation provides the opportunity to gain insight into both the phenomenon and its presence in a given setting—another excellent example of the *research on research* notion discussed earlier.

As with the location of individual questions and the order of presentation of possible alternatives in multiple-choice or dichotomous questions, the order of presentation of products in a *paired comparison test* can have an influence on the results. In the paired comparison test, respondents are asked to evaluate two products, then indicate which, if either, they prefer. Table 9-1 illustrates the influence of position bias in a product comparison test in which the "brands" tested are really the same brand, but disguised. As shown in the table, even though the two stimuli were actually identical, participants had a tendency to select the "brand" that was tested first.[5]

The basic notion of position bias in product comparison tests is not sur-

---

[5] Ralph L. Day, "Position Bias in Paired Product Tests," *Journal of Marketing Research*, February 1969, p. 100, published by the American Marketing Association.

**TABLE 9-1.** *In this product comparison test involving the same product identified as two different "brands," participants tended to reflect the presence of position bias by gravitating toward the "brand" they tested first.*

| Respondent preference | Brand E tested first | Brand F tested first |
|---|---|---|
| Preferred E to F | 51% | 42% |
| Preferred F to E | 33 | 48 |
| No preference | 16 | 10 |
| Total | 100% | 100% |
| *n* | 45 | 40 |

*Source:* Ralph L. Day, "Position Bias in Paired Product Tests," *Journal of Marketing Research,* February 1969, p. 100, published by the American Marketing Association.

prising, especially if the products being tested are either identical or very much alike. Imagine, if you were extremely thirsty, how much better the sip of Coca-Cola from cup A would taste than the subsequent sample from cup B. Here again, it seems appropriate to mention an opportunity for the misuse of marketing research by someone who wishes to take advantage of position bias in order to conduct a study in which it is desired that her product be perceived as better than a very similar competing brand. Depending on the nature of the position bias for the particular product type and situation, the unethical researcher might arrange to have her product tested either first or second. For example, in testing the riding quality of two luxury cars on a bumpy country road, participants in the study may tend to favor the second car tested—perhaps because they have already been bounced around during one test drive and are less surprised by the oscillations they experience the second time around. Conversely, if the rough-road test were to be carried out immediately following a heavy lunch of tacos and pizza, participants might very likely feel more comfortable during the first trip than during the second, assuming that their digestive systems react normally to the cumulative effects of rough-road driving at moderate speeds. In order to avoid the potential effects of position bias in a paired product comparison test, or in other situations where the order of presentation may be a factor, it is advisable to randomize the testing order.

## Question Wording

When actually formulating the question, we should make every effort to ensure that the wording is such that the question is (1) clear to the respondent, (2) stated in terms of a vocabulary and frame of reference shared between researcher and respondent, and (3) not likely to exert undue influence on the answer which the respondent provides. Such "rules of thumb" are usually more easily understood in theory than applied in practical situations. Even what seem at first to be very simple questions can be misunderstood by respondents, and this can be extremely frustrating to the researcher. For example, if you were to ask a sample of individuals the question, "What kind of shape are you in?" various respondents will assume frames of reference that differ from your own. Whereas you may have been interested in physical condition, some may respond with their estimate of the family's current financial situation, others with an outlook of their degree of optimism for the future, and still others may assume you're referring to their employment status. Even if you switch to the term *physical condition*, instead of *shape*, responses may include height and weight rather than the more athletic definition you may have originally intended to convey. Absence of shared vocabulary and frame of reference can be especially troublesome when you're trying to develop a question that provides real two-way communication between researcher and respondent. Considering the following two examples, note that a frame-of-reference problem exists in each case.

1. Interviewer: "What is your Church preference?"
   Respondent: "Gothic."
2. Immigration official: "Name?"
   Immigration applicant: "Olaf Swenson."

   Immigration official: "Occupation?"
   Immigration applicant: "Carpenter."

   Immigration official: "Age?"
   Immigration applicant: "Seventy-three."

   Immigration official: "Sex?"
   Immigration applicant: (thoughtful pause) "Oh, a little bit."

Even the slightest change in the wording of a question can make a significant difference in the response pattern that is obtained. For example, in the following set of questions, only one word is changed from one question to the next, with each question being posed to a comparable sample of respondents. At first glance, the words *should, could,* and *might* may not seem to be very much different in their content and meaning, but in the context of a given question, they may produce markedly different results. As the following responses indicate, they can be perceived quite differently and strongly influence the research findings:[6]

> Do you think anything should be done to make it easier for people to pay doctor or hospital bills?
> [Percent replying "Yes" = 82%]

---

[6] Stanley L. Payne, *The Art of Asking Questions*, copyright © 1951 and 1979 by Princeton University Press. Excerpts pp. 8, 9.

> Do you think anything could be done to make it easier for people to pay doctor or hospital bills?
> [Percent replying "yes" = 77%]

> Do you think anything might be done to make it easier for people to pay doctor or hospital bills?
> [Percent replying "yes" = 63%]

The preceding example helps to underscore the importance of question wording in its most simple sense, and is somewhat of a classic in the field. Further issues regarding question wording include deciding whether to use positive or negative statements, avoiding potentially biasing words or phrases, and ensuring that the respondent's vocabulary level will not be exceeded by the words you have chosen to use.

Naturally, the objective researcher will wish to avoid biasing statements or phrases that make a given answer more attractive or acceptable to the respondent. However, the closeness of the researcher or client to a certain perspective may nevertheless lead to an inadvertent question wording that promotes unintentional bias. Questionnaires from environmental groups, consumer advocates, political interest groups, sporting organizations, and others can (purposely or otherwise) tend to attract responses of a given type. Consider, for example, the following hypothetical questions relating to the requirement of automotive emission checks of the type now required in certain states:

> A. To help clean up the air we breathe, do you think that owners of cars that pollute excessively should be required to have them fixed?
> B. Do you think that the government should be allowed to force you to make potentially expensive auto repairs so that your car will meet their exhaust emission regulations?

It would be hoped that neither the Environmental Protection Agency nor the Motor Vehicle Manufacturers Association would resort to such biased questions as the preceding. However, it takes little imagination to visualize the vast difference in responses that would probably emanate from actual administration of each of these question alternatives.

## Questions Dealing with Sensitive Topics

As might be expected, questions dealing with age, income, sex, arrest records, vehicular accidents, and other sensitive topics are rather special in that they tend to bring about some degree of response bias on the part of the person being surveyed. In addition, some individuals may even decline to answer such ques-

## EXHIBIT 9-3

### Data and Dollars

Some questionnaires are designed to collect data as well as attract support.

```
                      Please return to:

                      Reed Larson
                      National Right to Work Committee
                      8316 Arlington Boulevard
                      Fairfax, Virginia  22038

SPECIAL QUESTIONNAIRE FOR:


Professor Ronald M. Weiers
Indiana Univ of Penn
Indiana, Pennsylvania  15701

Please answer the questions below and return this form at
once in the enclosed envelope. Your name will not be used
without your written permission.

1.  Do you feel there is too much power concen-
trated in the hands of labor union officials?     YES___NO___

2.  Are you in favor of forcing state, county,
and municipal employees to pay union dues to
hold their government jobs?                        YES___NO___

3.  Are you in favor of allowing construction
union czars the power to shut down an entire
construction site because of a dispute with a
single contractor...thus forcing even more
workers to knuckle under to union agents?          YES___NO___

4.  Do you want union officials to decide how
many municipal employees you, the taxpayer,
must support?                                      YES___NO___

5.  Should all construction workers be forced
into unions through legalized situs picketing
thus raising the cost of building your schools,
hospitals, and homes?                              YES___NO___

6.  Would you vote for someone who had forced
public employees to join a labor union or be
fired?                                             YES___NO___

TO HELP YOU COMPILE AND PUBLICIZE THIS SURVEY AND INCREASE
ITS COVERAGE ALL OVER AMERICA, I ENCLOSE MY CONTRIBUTION TO
THE National Right to Work Committee OF:

 $1000 _____, $500 _____, $100 _____, $50 _____, $25 _____,

Other Amount $_____

Mr. Larson,

You may_____may not_____use my name when contacting my Congress-
man and Senators with the results of this survey.

Signed_____
```

(Courtesy of National Right to Work Committee, Springfield, Virginia.)

tions, thus making nonresponse bias another common source of error—one that may be particularly problematic when answers to these types of questions are vital to our research effort. Responses to sensitive questions are often quite dependent on the wording of the question, the potential responses available, the circumstances under which the question is asked, and even on the form of the question itself. For example, people are generally more willing to indicate the category (e.g., "$35,000–$40,000") into which their income falls than to reveal the exact amount of their earnings.

Even in this case, however, the exact form of the question can have a significant effect on the responses obtained. In one study of question phrasing in telephone interviewing, the median reported income was 35% higher when income categories were presented in descending rather than ascending order.[7]

### The Randomized Response Technique

One very interesting approach to the procurement of sensitive information is known as the ***randomized response*** technique. Some who are not statistically inclined may view the method as especially curious because we are able to obtain the answer to a question *without really being sure that we've even asked the question!* While the technique is limited to questions which can be answered with a "yes" or "no" response, it is a promising approach to the attainment of information that would otherwise be difficult or impossible to obtain.[8] Essentially, the technique involves two questions: (1) an innocent type of question that would not cause the respondent to feel threatened or embarrassed regardless of his response, and (2) the question of interest, which would be very likely to evoke either a refusal or a purposely distorted response. The respondent, depending on the outcome of a coin flip or other randomizing device (the outcome is known only to the respondent), is instructed to answer the question that is associated with the random outcome, which he alone observes. As a result, the researcher receives only a "yes" or a "no" response, but does not know which question the respondent has answered.

Since all of this may seem rather unsettling even to those who are familiar with statistics and expected values, let's make a hypothetical example in which we are interested in determining the percentage of Snob Heights PTA members who have been in jail. Naturally, since few members of this elite population would take pride in having spent time in the "slammer," a direct approach to this question would very likely result in a landslide of "no" responses. However, relatively few members of the same population could be expected to distort the truth when confronted with a harmless, nonthreatening, or even meaningless

---

[7] William B. Locander and John P. Burton, "The Effect of Question Form on Gathering Income Data by Telephone," *Journal of Marketing Research*, May 1976, pp. 189–92, published by the American Marketing Association.

[8] For further discussion of the randomized response technique, the reader may be interested in consulting C. Campbell and B. L. Joiner, "How to Get the Answer without Being Sure You've Asked the Question," *The American Statistician*, December 1973, pp. 229–31.

question—for example, "Do you like pepperoni pizza?" A randomized response approach involving these two questions would proceed in a manner similar to the following:

1. A random sample of members are surveyed and, among other possible stimuli, are asked if they like pepperoni pizza.
2. A second random sample of members are surveyed in which the following procedure is followed:
   a. Each respondent is handed a card containing two questions:
      1. "Do you like pepperoni pizza?"
      2. "Have you ever been in jail?"
   b. Each respondent is asked to turn his back and flip a coin, then (without revealing the coin-flip result to the interviewer):
      Answer question 1 if the result was "heads."
      Answer question 2 if the result was "tails."
3. After the second random sample has been surveyed, the researcher has the information required to determine what percentage of the membership has been in jail.

How? Consider the numerical example demonstrated in Figure 9-7. First, the researcher either uses secondary data or conducts a survey in which she finds that 65% of the PTA respondents answer "yes" to the question, "Do you like pepperoni pizza?" The second step is to apply the randomized response technique to a second sample, consisting of 400 individuals. The result of the second survey is a total of 160 "yes" responses and 240 "no" responses—a seemingly discomforting situation because we have a lot of answers, but don't know to which question they refer. The solution is statistical and very straightforward. Because of the coin flip, we can expect that each person had a 50% chance of answering each question. Thus, we can expect that 200 persons (i.e., 0.5 × 400) answered the "pepperoni pizza" question, while another 200 answered the "been in jail" question. Based on our initial study, we found that 65% of those surveyed liked pepperoni pizza. Based on this information, we may estimate that 130 (0.65 × 200) of our "yes" responses came from those answering the "pepperoni pizza" question, while the other 30 "yes" responses came from those answering the "been in jail" question. The result is our finding that 15% (i.e., 30 of the 200 responding to that question) have been in jail.

The key to the success of the randomized response technique is that the respondent must realize that you don't know which question he answered. For this reason, you may wish to employ any randomizing device that you feel is appropriate to the population you are studying. For example, you may ask the respondent to use a spinner on a card or to answer the question that is determined by whether the last digit in his social security number is even or odd. In addition, the respondent may require a bit of special treatment or reassurance in order to gain his cooperation. He must be willing to provide his trust in an

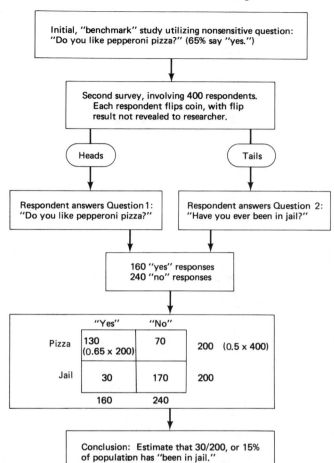

Initial, "benchmark" study utilizing nonsensitive question: "Do you like pepperoni pizza?" (65% say "yes.")

Second survey, involving 400 respondents. Each respondent flips coin, with flip result not revealed to researcher.

Heads

Tails

Respondent answers Question 1: "Do you like pepperoni pizza?"

Respondent answers Question 2: "Have you ever been in jail?"

160 "yes" responses
240 "no" responses

|       | "Yes"              | "No" |     |              |
|-------|--------------------|------|-----|--------------|
| Pizza | 130 (0.65 × 200)   | 70   | 200 | (0.5 × 400)  |
| Jail  | 30                 | 170  | 200 |              |
|       | 160                | 240  |     |              |

Conclusion: Estimate that 30/200, or 15% of population has "been in jail."

**Figure 9-7.** Numerical example of the randomized response technique for obtaining sensitive information.

unusual situation and his cooperation in a task which he may view as equally unusual, and perhaps even frivolous. You may wish to provide further explanation to the respondent in terms of your interest in the "overall answers" rather than his individual response.

### The Counterbiasing Statement

Recognizing that a given question or topic is likely to result in a biased response, we can attempt to neutralize this bias by prefacing the question with a statement that is intentionally biased in the opposite direction. For example, if we anticipate that responses will tend to be distorted in the "yes" direction, we can precede the question with a statement that makes the "no" response more acceptable for the respondent. Consider the following alternative approaches to a question involving church attendance:

1. Did you attend church services last Sunday? [Brief, direct question likely to evoke a bias toward "yes" response]
2. For various reasons, many people find it impossible to attend church every Sunday. Did you attend church services last Sunday? [Negative bias of prefacing statement designed to offset positive bias of question]
3. For various reasons, most people find it impossible to attend church every Sunday. Did you attend church services last Sunday? [Prefacing statement incorporates stronger negative bias by substitution of "most people" for "many people"]

Compared to approach 1, the two alternative questions ease the impact of the question on the respondent and make it easier for him to admit that he did not attend church services on the previous Sunday. However, as approaches 2 and 3 indicate, there are different levels of opposite bias that can be introduced by the counterbiasing statement. Ideally, the prefacing statement will contain just enough bias of its own to exactly offset the response bias that would result from the question itself. However, the danger exists that either too much or not enough countering bias will be introduced. For example, approach 3 would be likely to include a stronger degree of countering bias than approach 2, and perhaps more than enough bias to offset the initial question. If too much opposite bias is introduced in the prefacing statement, respondents may distort the truth by reacting to the counterbiasing statement instead of the question itself.

As with so many other facets of marketing research, the counterbiasing statement approach may enable the unethical researcher to arrive at findings that are purposely distorted to suit his or her personal or corporate interests. While such applications of research knowledge are certainly not to be encouraged, their potential existence should nevertheless be of concern to students, practitioners, and consumers of research. An awareness of the ability of a counterbiasing statement to offset the bias inherent in a given question may inspire the unobjective "researcher" to *compound* the natural bias of the question with a prefacing statement that is biased in the *same* direction. In the case of the church attendance subject just discussed, such distortion could take the form of:

Many people find that attending church regularly helps them in their daily lives and brings their family closer together. Did you attend church services lat Sunday? [Positively biased prefacing statement reinforces the positive bias already inherent in the question.]

Just as the wording of a question can have a great deal of influence on the results obtained, the strength and directionality of a prefacing statement can also be an important factor in either reducing or increasing the amount of bias included in your research findings. While the proper research goal of the counterbiasing statement is to reduce such bias, it is possible that some prefacing statements may cause more distortion instead of less.

### *Other Approaches to Sensitive Topics*

In addition to those just discussed, there are several other strategies for obtaining information that may be potentially embarrassing, ego-threatening, or otherwise likely to evoke a biased reaction from the respondent. For example, a question may be phrased in terms of other persons, such as "most people," "your friends," or alternative means by which respondents can reveal their attitudes by reflecting them indirectly through a third party. Instead of asking an individual if she attends hockey games because she enjoys the violence of the sport, it may be more useful to ask if *her friends* attend hockey games because *they* enjoy the violence of the sport. Likewise, rather than ask if an individual would contribute to air pollution by removing his car's emission controls for better gas mileage, a more truthful response might be obtained if the question dealt with whether or not "most people" or "many of your friends" would engage in the same activity.

Another approach is to "hide" the potentially sensitive question within a group of other, more innocuous questions. This strategy takes advantage of the respondent's momentum in proceeding through the data collection instrument. Having become accustomed to answering each question as it is asked, he is more likely to maintain his pace by not balking at a question that might stop him cold if it were asked in a vacuum.

## Question Sequence

The order in which the questions are presented to the respondent is another important factor in the design of the data collection instrument. However, as with so many other aspects of questionnaire design, it is not possible to set forth an unalterable set of rules that will automatically provide an optimum sequence in which the questions should be asked. The combination of common sense and a sensitivity for the respondent and his or her perspective will go a long way toward helping to avoid a great many sequencing errors. For example, in the following series of stimuli, it should be obvious that a serious mistake has been made in the sequence of the questions:

---

21. Have you ever tried IVY brand panty hose?
    ☐ Yes    ☐ No    ☐ Not sure
22. Have you ever heard of IVY brand panty hose?
    ☐ Yes    ☐ No    ☐ Not sure
23. Compared to other brands you've tried, IVY panty hose are:
    ☐ More comfortable        ☐ Less comfortable
    ☐ Equally comfortable     ☐ Not sure

---

The positioning of question 21, with its mention of the existence of IVY brand panty hose, practically assures that the response to question 22 will be "yes" for all respondents except those who happen to be struck with amnesia between questions. Likewise, question 23 will not apply to anyone who has answered "no" or "not sure" to question 21. Thus, for some respondents, question 23 should be bypassed in some logical fashion rather than presented as equally prominent compared to the others.

Compared to the preceding alternative, a superior order of presentation would be:

---

21. Have you ever heard of IVY brand panty hose?
    ☐ Yes    ☐ No    ☐ Not sure
22. Have you ever tried IVY brand panty hose?
    ☐ Yes       ☐ No      ☐ Not sure
    22(a) *If "Yes"*: Compared to other brands you've tried, IVY brand
          panty hose are:
          ☐ More comfortable        ☐ Less comfortable
          ☐ Equally comfortable     ☐ Not sure

---

In order to generate a question sequence that will provide useful data while being both clear and acceptable to the respondent, it is advisable that a number of general guidelines be followed:

**1.** Before asking any questions, provide a brief introduction that tells the respondent who is doing the research, for what purpose, and what is being asked of him or her in terms of time and cooperation. If the subject matter is potentially sensitive, some assurance may also be provided regarding the anonymity of the respondent or the confidential treatment of the information collected. In addition to being a positive, courteous approach to a member of the general public, such attention to the respondent will reduce the likelihood of his refusal to participate.

**2.** The initial questions should be simple and interesting, even if they may not be of primary concern in the purpose of your study. At this stage of the questionnaire, the motivation of the respondent is of prime concern. Short, interesting questions at the beginning will encourage the completion of those that remain.

**3.** Group related questions or issues together so that the respondent will be able to devote his or her full concentration to one topic at a time.

**4.** Within a given topic, ask general questions before proceeding to more specific questions. By asking the more general questions first, you can reduce the probability that answers to later questions will be biased by earlier questions or responses to them. For example, if we were to ask a respondent what he dislikes most about his car, then follow with an inquiry regarding his overall satisfaction with the product, we would be likely to obtain a negatively biased response to the second question. By proceeding from general to specific—in this case, asking about overall satisfaction before inquiring about particular likes and dislikes—we can reduce the effects of undesirable interaction between questions.

**5.** Place difficult or sensitive questions near the end of the questionnaire. In a personal or telephone interview, the interviewer will by this stage have had a chance to gain the trust and cooperation of the respondent. In the mail questionnaire, the respondent who has invested sufficient time to reach this point will be more likely to continue until the questionnaire has been completed.

**6.** To avoid both distraction and duplication of instructions, try to place questions together that are similar in format, especially if they are complex in nature. However, if too many complex questions are related, it may be advisable to separate them with one or more simpler questions in order to provide a mental change of pace for the respondent.

**7.** Place questions of a classificatory nature (e.g., age, income) at the end of the questionnaire. While some questions may be sensitive, others will be of little interest to the respondent. In either case, questions intended to classify respondents are best left until the end.

**8.** Be sure to thank the respondent for his or her cooperation. A simple "Thank you!" at the conclusion of the questionnaire takes little space and effort on your part, and is likely to be rewarded when you or another researcher happens to contact either the same respondent or someone to whom he has related his experience.

### Physical Appearance of the Questionnaire

The physical appearance of the questionnaire is especially important in mail surveys or in other instances where the data collection instrument is self-administered. In these cases, the questionnaire is "on its own," having no persuasive interviewer to encourage the respondent's cooperation. Remember that it is an imposing sight to receive a lengthy mail questionnaire, and such a questionnaire is very likely to be discarded instead of completed and returned. If possible, try to minimize the number of pages by not allowing excessive gaps between questions, especially on later pages that are less important as a factor in the respondent's first impression. Just as the initial questions should be short and simple, so should the initial page of a multiple-page questionnaire be relatively uncrowded in terms of allowing a generous amount of white space between questions.

The layout of the questions should facilitate the respondent's or interviewer's path of travel through the questionnaire by presenting either a physical flow diagram or a description of which question should be answered next after a given response has been recorded. Such directional advice was provided in the earlier questionnaire of Figure 9-3, making it easier for the respondent to bypass inapplicable questions. An example of the flow diagram alternative is presented in Figure 9-8.

Naturally, reproduction of the questionnaire should be neat and make use

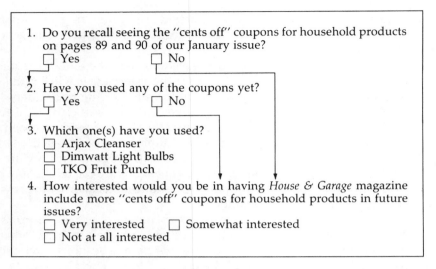

**Figure 9-8.**   Diagramming can help guide the respondent or interviewer through the logical flow of the questionnaire.

of a quality grade of paper. A mimeographed questionnaire will generally not be held in high esteem by respondents, who will perceive that the study is apparently of little importance and not deserving of their time and effort. Given the expenditures that are already being made for typing, postage or administration, and other materials, the slight additional cost of quality printing and reproduction is an excellent investment.

## Questionnaire Development and the Microcomputer

With recent-developed software packages, questionnaires cannot only be administered by the microcomputer, as discussed in Chapter 8, but can be developed on it as well. The following packages are among those currently available for questionnaire development:[9]

Sawtooth Software, Inc. has produced a microcomputer package that enables researchers both to develop and to administer questionnaires on the computer. Constructing the questionnaire involves building the computer screens that respondents will see, and allows the use of color as well as special characters. The researcher tells the computer in what order the questions are to be presented, the skip patterns that are to follow given responses, and whether the questions are to be presented in random order to avoid bias caused by order of presentation. The two versions of Sawtooth's C12 system allow up to 100 or 250 questions, respectively.

---

[9] Jim Minno, "Software Replaces Paper in Questionnaire Writing," *Marketing News,* January 3, 1986, p. 66, published by the American Marketing Association.

In another interesting development, Marketing Metrics has come out with Interviewdisk, which involves (1) placing the questionnaire onto the diskette, and (2) distributing the actual diskette to respondents, who use their own personal computers in answering the questions on it. The questionnaire construction capabilities include the ability to display graphics and to handle multiple-choice, dichotomous, semantic differential, constant-sum, and paired comparison questions. Skip patterns are programmed into the questionnaire and automatically followed during the interview. After completing the questionnaire, the respondent simply returns the diskette for analysis.

Naturally, the respondent must either own or have access to a personal computer. However, for many populations, this is not a problem. As with other approaches to computerized interviewing, data manipulation errors of recording and keypunching are minimized, since the data are already magnetically recorded and computer readable.

## PRETESTING THE QUESTIONNAIRE

After a first draft of the data collection instrument has been generated, it should be subjected to pretesting that simulates as closely as possible the actual research conditions under which it will be administered. Very often, the only pretesting a questionnaire receives involves its administration to friends, relatives, and colleagues—a practice that is satisfactory only if your research happens to involve friends, relatives, and colleagues. While such a convenience sample may be helpful as an initial step toward uncovering potential ambiguities and other problems, one or more additional pretests should be undertaken using the same kind of individuals who will be the object of your research.

Once you have selected a small subsample of the population in which you are interested, it is a good idea to administer the questionnaire in person. *This is true regardless of the medium which will actually be used later*. The presence of an interviewer during pretesting can result in valuable insights that might otherwise be lost. For example, subjects may request additional information regarding a question, may exhibit a different frame of reference from that which has been assumed, be unable to follow the directions provided, or find it impossible to supply the information in the form or detail that has been requested. Personal observation of respondent reactions to the questionnaire will almost inevitably result in useful revisions to the instrument.

After pretesting has identified necessary changes in question wording, sequence, information requirements, and other variables, further testing should be carried out to verify that a revised version has succeeded in overcoming the difficulties uncovered in the earlier testing. If subsequent personal testing reveals that the earlier problems have been corrected, it is wise to proceed toward still another pretest that involves both the questionnaire and the actual method of administration—mail, telephone, or personal interview. This will help to identify possible difficulties that may be peculiar to the combination of the data

**EXHIBIT 9-4**

**Pretesting the Census**

In 1986, the Bureau of the Census conducted a pretest of the 1990 Census of Population and Housing by mailing census questionnaires to 48,000 households across the United States. Members of the sample received one of eight different versions of the questionnaires—three short forms and five long. (The short form includes questions asked of everyone; the long form includes these plus added questions asked of just a fraction of participants.)

Along with the pretesting of questions, two different kinds of envelopes were used in order to determine if return rates differed according to envelope type. One envelope was an attractive, "commercial" design, with a red, white, and blue flag, the other a plain "official business" envelope. Recipients were asked to complete their questionnaires and return the completed form by April 1, with those not returning by April 22 being sent a second questionnaire and those not responding by May 12 receiving a personal visit by an experienced interviewer.

Approximately 40% of the respondents were asked to participate in the final phase of the pretest, which began in late June. The purpose of this stage was to make sure that respondents understood the original questions. To this end, interviewers personally asked more detailed questions about answers provided earlier.

Depending on results of the pretest, plans were to include a number of new or expanded questions in 1990. The additions included more detailed questions for persons with health or disability problems. One of the tested items on this topic is shown in Figure 9-9. Among other items tested: addition of "solar" to a question about types of fuel used for home heating; a question about the number of smoke detectors in the home; more detailed questions about level and type of education; and questions regarding second jobs, pension income, and motor vehicle ownership and annual mileage.

In his message to pretest participants, John G. Keane, Director of the Census Bureau, described the survey as "a key activity in preparing for the 1990 census . . . To do our job well, we need your help in determining what to ask in the 1990 census. . . . The census is more than just a count of the population. It is a chance for us to take stock of ourselves as a people and successfully meet future local and national challenges. The 1990 census will be your personal and national bridge to the 21st century."

*Source:* "'Sneak Preview' of 1990 Census Questions Mailed to 48,000 Households Nationwide," *Data User News*, June 1986, published by the Bureau of the Census, U.S. Department of Commerce, p. 1.

collection instrument and the medium to be used. Questionnaire pretesting offers many benefits, including the opportunity to experiment with various approaches to a given question or topic, examination of the effect of different question sequences, and potential insight into the existence of position bias in the location of either the questions or their possible answers. Such experimen-

**Does this person need the help of another person in order to —**

**(1) Shop, care for the house, or get around outside the home?**

1 ☐ Yes

2 ☐ No

**(2) Take care of personal needs such as bathing, dressing, or getting around inside the home?**

1 ☐ Yes

2 ☐ No

*If "Yes" is marked in 20a or 20b —*

**What is the main cause of this person's limitation?** *Mark (X) ONE box.*

1 ☐ Arthritis or rheumatism

2 ☐ Heart condition

3 ☐ Serious problem with back or spine

4 ☐ Limited use or absence of arm(s)

5 ☐ Limited use or absence of leg(s)

6 ☐ Muscular disease or impairment

7 ☐ Diabetes

8 ☐ Cancer

9 ☐ Serious stomach, kidney, or liver condition

10 ☐ Respiratory or lung problem

11 ☐ High blood pressure or hypertension

12 ☐ Hard of hearing or deafness

13 ☐ Poor vision or blindness

14 ☐ Serious speech impediment

15 ☐ Senility or Alzheimer's disease

16 ☐ Mental retardation

17 ☐ Mental or emotional disorder

18 ☐ Other condition

**Figure 9-9.** One of the potential new topics evaluated by the Bureau of the Census when pretesting 1990 census questionnaires. The Bureau mailed both short and long forms to 48,000 households four years before the official census was to commence. (*Source:* " 'Sneak Preview' of 1990 Census Questions Mailed to 48,000 Households Nationwide," *Data User News, June 1986,* published by the Bureau of the Census, U.S. Department of Commerce, p. 1.)

tation may be carried out by using alternative forms of the questionnaire, then comparing the responses obtained through each approach.

While pretesting is very important, resist the temptation to spend too much time and effort in its pursuit. Remember that your primary goal is not to develop the "perfect" questionnaire, but rather to objectively study a sample of respondents from a given population. Excessive pretesting, especially when time is an important factor in your study and the implementation of its results, may be almost as harmful as no pretesting at all. However, for even the most urgent research studies, some degree of questionnaire pretesting is highly advisable. It represents a cheap insurance policy against the potential calamity of incorrect marketing decisions based on distorted or misleading research findings.

## ☐ SUMMARY

The questionnaire serves as a guide for the communication between respondent and researcher. While often associated with written informational requests, it is applicable to all of the survey research techniques discussed in Chapter 8.

Before constructing the questionnaire, we must consider potentially important interrelationships between a number of key elements. These are (1) the nature of the information we seek, (2) the nature of the respondents who are expected to provide this information, and (3) the medium by which the questionnaire is to be administered.

Questionnaires may be categorized in terms of structure and directness. Structure refers to the formality and standardization of the questionnaire, while directness refers to the extent to which the respondent is aware of the purpose for which the questionnaire is being administered. The structured, direct questionnaire is the type most frequently used in marketing research.

The unstructured, direct instrument usually consists of only general questions directed at the research topic, and allows the interviewer a great deal of freedom in both formulating specific questions and probing for additional information as he or she deems necessary. The skill and competence of the interviewer are vital when such a questionnaire is to be administered by telephone or in person.

The structured, indirect instrument is unique in both nature and importance, and is typically used in the projective research techniques discussed in the next chapter. This type of instrument recognizes that individuals may be more willing or able to provide meaningful answers if they are not aware of the true purpose of our study.

A series of decisions must be made with regard to the actual construction of the questionnaire. Throughout these steps, it is crucial that we try to see the questionnaire from the respondent's point of view.

In evaluating each potential question, we must ask: (1) Is the question really necessary? (2) Will the respondent be willing and able to provide the information requested? (3) Does the question adequately cover the content area for which it is intended? It is especially important that the respondent share our frame of reference, as questions or terms that mean one thing to us could have quite another meaning for the respondent.

Three basic types of questions are used: open-ended, multiple-choice, and dichotomous. The open-ended question offers respondents freedom to answer in their own words and to express any thoughts they feel are appropriate to the question. In the multiple-choice and dichotomous approaches, the respondent is forced to select from a fixed set of alternatives.

When respondents are asked to select from a list of alternatives, the possibility of position bias exists. Depending on the nature of the question and its alternative answers, respondents may tend to select responses that are presented in first, last, or central locations. Position bias may also result from the order of the questions themselves, or from the order of presentation used in paired comparison tests evaluating two products or other stimuli.

Question wording must be in a form that is clear to the respondent, stated in terms of a vocabulary and frame of reference shared between researcher and respondent, and not likely to exert undue influence on the respondent. Questions dealing with sensitive topics, such as age, income, and driver accident records, must be approached with caution. Among strategies for handling such questions are the counterbiasing statement and randomized response techniques.

Another important factor is the sequence in which the questions are presented. Initial questions should be simple and interesting, even if they may not be of primary concern to the purpose of the study. Within a given topic, general questions should be asked before proceeding to more specific questions. Difficult or sensitive questions should be placed near the end of the questionnaire, as should questions of a classificatory nature.

The layout of the questions should facilitate the respondent's or interviewer's path of travel through the questionnaire. This can be aided by presenting either a physical flow diagram or a description of which question should be addressed next after a given response has been recorded. Such assistance makes it easier to bypass questions that may not be applicable to a given respondent.

After a draft of the data collection instrument has been prepared, it should be subjected to pretesting that simulates as closely as possible the actual research conditions under which it will be administered. This will help identify potential ambiguities and other problems, and should involve the same types of individuals who will be the object of the survey research.

## □ QUESTIONS FOR REVIEW

1. Questionnaire development was described in the text as providing the opportunity for *research on research*. What is meant by this concept, and how can it be useful to both current and future marketing research efforts of the firm?

2. Under what research circumstances might it be most desirable to use the following types of questionnaire?
   a. The structured, direct type.
   b. The structured, indirect type.
   c. The unstructured, direct type.

3. The sponsor of Hooterville's first annual tractor pull contest would like to know the seating preferences of potential customers so that he can price the tickets accordingly for the various reserved sections. Assuming that there are three different sections—starting line, midway, and finish line—how might he phrase:
   a. An open-ended question to identify seating preference?
   b. A multiple-choice question to identify seating preference?

4. What are the advantages and disadvantages of multiple-choice questions versus those of the open-ended type? Under what circumstances would each tend to be used?

5. Construct a set of five structured, indirect questions to measure what might be "communicated" by males wearing jewelry, such as neck chains, rings, and bracelets.

6. Provide an example of a multiple-choice question:
   a. In which the alternatives are unbalanced.
   b. In which the possible responses are not mutually exclusive.

7. Provide an example of a survey question that would have an upward bias—that is, people would be likely to give a "yes" response.
   a. Rephrase the question so that there would be a downward bias—that is, people would be likely to give a "no" response.
   b. Rephrase your original question so that respondents would be likely to provide a truthful response.

8. Multiple-choice and dichotomous questions may or may not include the "don't know" or "no opinion" option for the respondent. What should one consider when deciding whether to include such an option?

9. What is meant by "position bias" in a product comparison test? Give a real or hypothetical example of how an unethical marketing researcher might take advantage of this phenomenon.

10. A survey of a certain population showed that 80% of the members answered "yes" to the question "Have you ever eaten pepperoni pizza?" A comparable sample of 200 members of the same population were surveyed using the randomized response technique, in which question I (concerning pepperoni pizza) was accompanied by question II: "Have you ever hired someone to write a term paper for you?" The results of the randomized response survey were 125 "yes" and 75 "no" answers. Based on these results, what percent of the population had hired someone to write a term paper? Assume that a coin flip was used as the randomizing device.

11. What is the purpose of a counterbiasing statement in a marketing research questionnaire? Provide an example of such a statement as it might appear on the questionnaire. What is the principal danger in using the counterbiasing statement?

12. Provide an example in which a biased prefacing statement reinforces the bias already existing in a sensitive question.

13. What strategies should be followed in selecting questions to place:
    a. At the beginning of the questionnaire?
    b. In later stages of the questionnaire?
    c. At the end of the questionnaire?

14. Construct a 10-question instrument to measure the satisfaction of students with the services provided by your college library.

15. How might one go about pretesting a questionnaire which has been constructed for telephone administration to respondents? Why is such pretesting advisable?

# 10

# INTERVIEWING, OBSERVATION, AND PANELS

**Group Interviews Help Select Juries, Pretest Arguments**

When million-dollar sums are involved, today's trial attorney would like some idea in advance regarding the best jury composition for her case and the best arguments for winning their support. With the application of proven marketing research methods to jury selection and courtroom strategy, she can.

In 1976, SCM Corp. went to trial with an antitrust suit against Xerox. Part of SCM's preparation included hiring a public relations agency, Decision Research Corp., which ran over 20 mock trials using simulated juries.

In each simulation, the session leader would read about 30 facts likely to be presented during the actual trial. The leader then left, allowing the simulated jury to reach a decision. Deliberations were taped, observers recorded which individuals were for and against the SCM position, and jury members were probed further for the reasoning behind their decision.

Women were found more likely than men to be supportive of the SCM position and, when jurors were selected for the actual trial, men were rejected whenever possible. (The eventual jury consisted of nine women, three men.) On the other hand, long-time white-collar workers tended to favor Xerox,

*Source:* Based on Curt Schleier, "Lawyers Court Help in Jury Selection, Legal Cases," *Advertising Age*, November 14, 1985, p. 30. Copyright Crain Communications, Inc. All rights reserved. Reprinted with permission.

**Figure 10-1.** Before subjecting their case to the scrutiny of a real jury like this one, attorneys find it increasingly useful to apply the group interviewing techniques of marketing
research to simulated juries in order to select and fine-tune their arguments. (Photo courtesy of Court of Common Pleas, Allegheny County, Pa.)

possibly being sympathetic to the company for rescuing them from messy
carbon paper and mimeograph copies early in their careers. Thought was
also given to what types of persons were most likely to become leaders within
the jury, and hence worthy of more attention and eye contact during the trial
proceedings.

The result of the eventual trial was in SCM's favor and the jury awarded
the firm over $100 million in damages. However, the (male) judge overturned
the verdict, finding in favor of Xerox, a judgment that was upheld on appeal.

## INTRODUCTION

In Chapters 8 and 9 we examined survey research methods and data-collection
instruments for gathering information. However, in some instances, important
data are needed and we are not able to rely on these to get the information we
seek. In such cases, depth and focus group interviews, projective techniques,
and observation may provide a useful alternative. Along with discussing these
approaches here, we'll also explore the ability of panel information to provide
marketing data on an intermittent or continuing basis. As with the techniques
just mentioned, panels offer a number of strengths that often offset the problems
encountered in conventional survey research.

Our purpose here is not to discount or otherwise understate the importance of survey research, but rather to present a number of possibilities that can be used either on their own or as a complement to survey research. The chapter materials will be discussed under the following topics:

I. Depth interviewing
II. Focus group interviewing
III. Projective techniques
IV. Observation
V. Panels

## DEPTH INTERVIEWING

The *depth interview* is one in which the interviewer, generally a highly trained person with some background in psychology, interacts with an individual subject and encourages him to freely express his thoughts on the product or subject of interest. The general idea is to descend beneath the superficial answers that are often provided by respondents. In so doing, the interviewer must perform a careful balancing act between probing for additional response detail and avoiding the danger that such probing may influence the answers that are provided.

The interviewer must be able to recognize answers that are incomplete or superficial and to skillfully uncover attitudes, opinions, and motives of more basic meaning to the respondent. The following are some of the key phrases the interviewer may employ toward this end: "What do you mean by that?" "Can you give me an example?" "I'm not sure I understand what you mean." "What else does that product mean to you?" "Can you be more specific about that?" "That's very interesting; please go on." In addition, appropriate positive mannerisms (e.g., nodding of the head, smiling or other nonverbal expressions of approval, friendship, and sincerity), repeating of the answer just given, but in question form ("So you liked the way friends admired your new car?"), or even complete *silence* can be helpful in drawing more in-depth responses from the subject.

The depth interview—along with focus group interviewing and projective techniques—is often associated with *motivation research*, a term used to describe this family of research methods when they gained popularity in the 1950s. Although the "motivation research" label is less fashionable today, the depth interview and its related techniques are still widely used, and constitute a valuable tool for the marketing researcher.

### Applications of Depth Interviewing

The depth interview may be applied to any product, service, or idea. For example, the interviewer might encourage the respondent to express her feelings about encyclopedias, Porsche automobiles, country clubs, hardware stores, X-rated movies, or giving blood to the Red Cross.

As an example of the results that can be obtained by probing beyond the initial, often superficial answers provided by respondents, consider the following statements reported by the well-known motivation researcher, Dr. Ernest Dichter, in his studies regarding the seemingly straightforward practice of taking a bath.[1] Note especially how these responses differ markedly from the standard "keep clean," "smell good," "stay healthy" answers that individuals might be expected initially to provide:

> I always sing in the tub; for those few minutes I don't have to buy a steak, or scrub the floor, or mind the children.

> I lie on my stomach and play like a child. I blow bubbles and I drape my knees over the side of the tub and I sing. I have a wonderful time and like to move up and down and make waves.

> Bathing provides luxury for a dime. Even people who are not wealthy have to get a feeling of luxury once in a while, even if it's only from a cake of soap.

> I like to watch the dirt roll off.

As the preceding statements indicate, there is more to taking a bath than simply the washing, cleaning, rinsing, and drying of one's body as if it were a dish. Dichter observes that bathing often takes on a "special psychological function because it coincides with the beginning or ending of a day, or even a week." In addition, washing and bathing "give us a sense of accomplishment," allow us to shed our "adult dignity" by singing or playing in the tub, and provide us with the opportunity to "wash our troubles away."[2]

One of the classic applications of the depth interviewing technique was associated with a relatively undramatic product: prunes. While being well known for its laxative value, the unfortunate prune was found to have a distinctively negative image, being a "symbol of old age," "devitalized," "dried out," and having "nothing to offer." According to Dichter, "when prunes were changed to the California 'wonder fruit,' and their patent juiciness was publicized by introducing such things as the sunshine jar in which prunes were cooked beforehand and then chilled in the refrigerator, a considerable increase in sales was achieved."[3] In order to provide the prune with a new personality, children were used in advertisements in an attempt to counter the wrinkled, old-age associations that had prevailed.

Another particularly interesting product that has been the object of depth interviewing research is the cigarette, which involves a number of dimensions and attributes that might not be readily admitted during a brief interview or other survey research approach. For example, the following respondent com-

---

[1] Ernest Dichter, *Handbook of Consumer Motivations* (New York: McGraw-Hill Book Company, 1964), pp. 191–95. Copyright © 1964 by McGraw-Hill Book Company. Used with permission.

[2] Ibid., p. 195.

[3] Ibid., p. 60.

ments are typical of those provided during a study of smokers and their thoughts and feelings associated with their use of cigarettes:[4]

### Smoking as fun, measure of time

You sometimes get tired from working too hard, and if you sit back for the length of a cigarette, you feel much fresher afterwards. I wouldn't think of just sitting back without a cigarette. I guess a cigarette somehow gives me a good excuse.

### Smoking as oral pleasure

In school, I always used to chew my pencils. Whenever I try to stop smoking for awhile, I get something to chew on, either a pipe or a menthol cigarette. . . . I also chew a lot of gum when I want to cut down on smoking.

### Smoking as a self-reward

I nearly always smoke a cigarette before going to bed. That finishes the day.

### Smoking as a measure of time

Now I'll smoke one more cigarette and then I'm off.

### Cigarette as a companion

When I lean back and light my cigarette, and see the glow in the dark, I am not alone anymore.

Cigarettes, prunes, and bathing are just a few of the many interesting objects toward which in-depth research of respondents' feelings has been, and can be directed. Recognition of these underlying thoughts and attitudes can be extremely helpful in overcoming consumers' reluctance to purchase certain products, accept certain ideas, or adopt certain modes of behavior that we are trying to market.

## Advantages and Disadvantages of Depth Interviewing

The principal strength of the depth interview lies in its capability to uncover more complete and basic answers to questions that might be answered at a relatively superficial level if asked during conventional survey research. Compared to the focus group interview, described in the next section, the one-on-one depth interview has the advantage that it may sometimes facilitate a respondent's revealing of attitudes or motives that he or she would be reluctant to discuss in a group setting.

Despite its considerable strength, the depth interview has a number of weaknesses that have led to its decline in popularity as a research technique.

---

[4] Ibid., pp. 345–52.

First, with the interviewer spending approximately one hour with each subject, sample sizes are necessarily small and statistical extrapolation of research findings becomes a problem. A related difficulty concerns the individual interviewer, and the likelihood that the subjectivity she or he must exercise will lead to conclusions that differ very much from those obtained by another interviewer studying comparable respondents. Another problem is the difficulty of editing, coding, and analyzing the qualitative results, which are themselves the product of a highly subjective process.

The subjectivity inherent in the gathering and recording of the research results is thus compounded by questions involving the reliability and validity of the information obtained. The combination of subjective collection and subjective analysis probably causes many researchers to distrust depth interviewing on this basis alone. In addition, the speculative and psychological nature of some past research results may have had an adverse effect on the general acceptability of depth interviewing, resulting in a greater degree of difficulty for a researcher to "sell" the technique to colleagues, superiors, and clients. For example, the finding by some practitioners that women subconsciously associate baking a cake with giving birth to a baby is of a type that may have caused some to regard the entire concept of depth interviewing with suspicion.

Both the depth interview and the focus group interview are used primarily in exploratory research for the purpose of helping to define problems, generate hypotheses, and identify potential courses of action. However, unless a situation demands an extraordinary level of rapport between interviewer and respondent that can only be achieved through a close one-on-one relationship, the focus group interview is generally capable of providing the same information at a lower cost.

## FOCUS GROUP INTERVIEWING

Basically, the *focus group interview* is similar to the depth interview, with the exception that small groups are interviewed instead of one individual at a time. The group is generally selected so as to include about 10 to 12 persons who are chosen because of their common backgrounds or experience regarding the subject of the interview. The physical layout of a typical focus group facility is shown in Figure 10-2. Note the viewing area and one-way mirror next to each of the two conference rooms.

As with the depth interview, the key figure in the focus group interview is the interviewer, in this case referred to as the *moderator*. He or she must be sensitive to the group members and their feelings and comments, but possess the firmness necessary to successfully direct the group along the intended direction of discussion. In addition, unlike the depth interview, one or more of the individuals may tend to be domineering, which calls for skillful maneuvers if the moderator is to avoid having the group interview turn into a one-on-one discussion. While some individuals may persist in attempting to dominate the

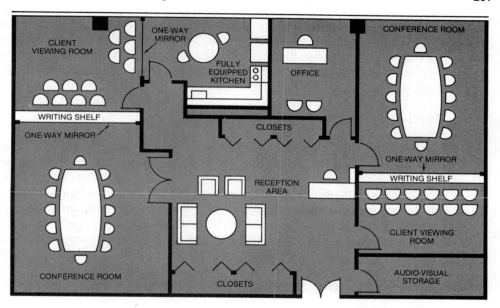

**Figure 10-2.** The physical arrangement of a focus group facility. Next to each conference room is a viewing area equipped with a one-way mirror to facilitate the observing and recording of interview proceedings. This facility also includes a kitchen for preparing and serving food products that might be the subject of the group interview. (Courtesy of O'Hare in Focus, Division of Irwin Broh & Associates, Des Plaines, Ill.)

interview, in most cases the moderator can reduce their effect by calling for the opinions of others, not looking in the direction of the offender, halting the interview flow by pausing to poll the feelings of all group members, looking at his watch or at the ceiling when the offender is speaking, or (short of violence or falling asleep) by other appropriate forms of verbal and nonverbal communication.

In general, it is a good idea for the moderator to indicate at the beginning of the interview the subject matter to be pursued. People are much more likely to be cooperative if they have a fuller understanding of why they have been assembled to take part in the interview experience. As part of the introductory stage of the interview, it may also be desirable to have individual participants introduce themselves. This is advantageous as an "icebreaker," which makes it a little easier for the more timid members to speak up later when a relevant thought or feeling comes to mind.

While the moderator should have an outline in mind for the interview session, inflexible formats and highly structured question sequences should be avoided. A simple list of questions may suffice for charting the course of the interview, especially since the purpose of the entire affair is to find out things that may well be unexpected and new. After all, if we already knew that we had included all relevant questions, there would be little need to go through the formality of conducting the interview. It is far better that the interview be flexible, flow (within reasonable limits) in the general direction in which the participants are leaning, then revert back to the main theme whenever the group or one of its members appears to be on the verge of getting too far from the topic of interest.

### Applications of Focus Group Interviewing

Focus group interviews are useful in exploratory research where the goal is to develop ideas and insights before proceeding toward further investigation into the topic of interest. The group interviewing approach can also be of more immediate value—for example, in identifying problems associated with existing products, in evaluating the attractiveness of alternative new products and their features, in probing the effectiveness of advertising and other forms of communication that reach the consumer, and in determining customer attitudes, perceptions, frames of reference, and behavioral patterns. Where it is decided to hold more than one focus group interview, the results of each effort can be helpful in identifying the topics most worthy of coverage in the interviews to follow.

In a study conducted by the author, focus group interviews were used in helping to determine the strengths and weaknesses of the Defensive Driving Course of the National Safety Council. In one interview, the group was comprised of a purposive sample of corporate employees who had decided to enroll in the course when it had been offered under company sponsorship. In a second interview, a sample of employees were selected because they had *not* enrolled in the course at the time of its availability. The results of these two interviews reflected both good and bad attributes of the course as they were either experienced (first group) or perceived (second group). In a third interview, group members were actual instructors of the course, who were encouraged to discuss the program from their own perspective and with regard to their perceptions of student and nonstudent reactions to it.

Syracuse University, planning for what was hoped to be a $10 million fund drive, held more than two dozen focus groups involving school alumni. As a result, previous enthusiasm for a promotional film stressing science and research was dampened. Instead of impressing potential donors, it was found to have the opposite effect. According to Harry W: Peter III, vice chancellor for university relations, "We were so proud of showing off our technology toys that we had underestimated the abiding interest [alumni] had in their undergraduate, humanistic education." The university no longer shows the film.[5]

In another application, long-distance company MCI learned from focus groups that people trusted the fact that businesses used MCI, even though the company was not mentioned by name during group interviews. Although par-

---

[5] Amanda Bennett, "Once a Tool of Retail Marketers, Focus Groups Gain Wider Usage, *The Wall Street Journal*, June 3, 1986, p. 27.

ticipants were not very supportive of big business, they had confidence in the businessperson's ability to make good judgments.[6]

## Advantages and Disadvantages of Focus Group Interviewing

Compared to the depth interview, which involves just one respondent at a time, the focus group interview has the efficiency advantage of allowing a paid moderator to interact with a greater number of persons at very little increase in either time or money. Each type of interview takes about the same length of time, but the focus group alternative may include a dozen or more participants in a given session. As with the individual depth interview, the focus group interview has the strength of allowing the researcher to probe beyond answers that are either superficial or incomplete, and offers a great deal of flexibility in the collection of meaningful reactions and ideas from those who participate. This capability places both interview alternatives at a distinct advantage compared to structured approaches in which a respondent is neither permitted nor encouraged to expand upon his or her feelings about a topic.

Another advantage the focus group interview enjoys over the individual depth interview is related to the natural interaction that takes place among members of the group being interviewed. There is likely to be a "domino" process whereby statements made by one person will lead to agreement, disagreement, a different perspective, or a related idea being expressed by other members of the group. To some extent, the presence of others may provide a greater stimulus for reaction than would be present in a purely one-on-one interview situation, and some persons who might be hesitant to reveal a personal feeling in privacy will do so more readily when comforted by the security of being among others who feel the same way.

Among the disadvantages of the group interview situation is the likelihood that persons who submit to the interview process may not be typical of the population they are presumed to represent. Naturally, this presents a problem in generalizing upon the results of the interviews, and is one reason why both focus group and individual depth interviews are frequently used in exploratory or other situations in which statistical extrapolation to the larger population is not of critical importance. However, given that we understand this "weakness," it should not undermine our overall research effort whenever we use the approaches in the context for which they are best suited—that is, in exploratory or informal research where statistical generalizations are not necessary. A related problem with the focus group interview is the inevitably small sample size that is required by the nature of the technique. Even if a sample *were* fully representative of the population, the accuracy of quantitative interview findings would not be great compared to the more statistically powerful survey research approaches. Another problem with the focus group interview is the inherent

---

[6] Larry Kahaner, "When MCI Tested the Ad Waters," *Advertising Age*, March 17, 1986, p. 56. Copyright Crain Communications, Inc. All rights reserved. Reprinted with permission.

subjectivity of the results and the corresponding likelihood that different researchers may well reach dissimilar conclusions based on the same set of interview data.

## PROJECTIVE TECHNIQUES

*Projective techniques* are derived from the methods of clinical psychology, and rely upon stimulus ambiguity to obtain a more free and open response from the study participant. The more ambiguity presented, the greater the degree to which the respondent must depend on his or her own background and beliefs to formulate a response. Projective techniques are indirect not only in the respondents being unaware of the true purpose of the question or situation posed, but also in terms of the respondents being provided with the opportunity to "indirectly" express their views through a third party or by interpreting the behavior of others. Figure 10-3 is a dramatization of the "third-party" communication phenomenon upon which many projective techniques are able to capitalize.

### Applications of Projective Techniques

As with depth interviews and focus group interviews, projective techniques are useful in determining respondents' attitudes, opinions, motives, and behavior, especially in cases where direct questioning would likely result in superficial or biased responses not reflective of the respondent's true state of mind or his or her actual behavior in the circumstances of interest.

Perhaps the best-known example of projective technique application is the famous study by Mason Haire, in which consumer attitudes about instant coffee were the subject of investigation.[7] The study was conducted during the very early stages of this product's appearance on the American market, and previous studies (surveys) had indicated that housewives did not use instant coffee because of its inferior flavor. This survey finding was in sharp contrast to actual taste tests in which subjects were generally not able to tell the difference between instant and regular coffee. Haire's approach consisted of preparing two shopping lists, identical in every respect except that one contained Nescafé instant coffee, while the other contained Maxwell House regular coffee. Each shopping list was then presented to separate, but comparable, samples of housewives who were asked to describe the shopper whose list they were given. The housewives, as expected, projected their own attitudes in describing the hypothetical housewife of each shopping list, and tended to view the "instant coffee" housewife as being lazy, a spendthrift, and generally a poor wife. On the other hand, the regular coffee purchaser was described in more positive terms as a thought-

---

[7] Mason Haire, "Projective Techniques in Marketing Research," *Journal of Marketing*, April 1950, pp. 649–56, published by the American Marketing Association.

**Figure 10-3.**  It's not unusual for people to attribute their own thoughts to someone else. Projective techniques use this phenomenon to help gain valuable marketing information.

ful, thrifty, and caring wife. Thus the projective approach uncovered an apparent guilt feeling about deviating from traditional, "made-the-hard-way" coffee and the love and care that were identified with its preparation. A summary of the results of the classic Haire study is shown in Figure 10-4.

### Types of Projective Techniques

The specific projective techniques that follow are suggestive of the methods available. They can be expanded upon or combined according to your research needs and level of imagination.

#### Word Association

In the *word association* approach, the respondent is presented with a series of words, some of which are "neutral," while others are closely related to the subject of the research. The words are read to the respondent in rapid sequence,

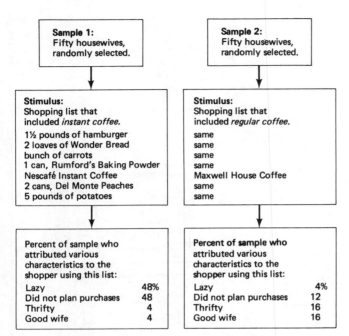

**Figure 10-4.** A summary of the methodology and results of Haire's classic projective study of instant versus regular coffee. (*Source:* Adapted from Mason Haire, "Projective Techniques in Marketing Research," *Journal of Marketing,* April 1950, pp. 649–56, published by the American Marketing Association.)

and he or she is asked to respond to each with the first word that comes to mind. Since the rapidity of response is crucial to this technique, personal or telephone interviews are the best media for its utilization. In a written questionnaire, the respondent would have excessive opportunity to consider each stimulus word and screen possible answers before settling upon a final choice. The general idea is that "first-thought" responses are more likely to reveal the respondent's strongest feelings regarding the stimulus. If a respondent does not respond to a stimulus word within a reasonable period of time, the eventual response should be either discounted or disregarded. The same general approach may also be applied to phrases, such as "visiting the museum," "having dinner at McDonald's," or "buying a Sears wedding ring." As an example of the word association technique, consider the following sequence where the key words (identified with an asterisk) are intended to help determine respondents' attitudes toward *advertising*:

| Stimulus word | Response |
| --- | --- |
| House | _____ |
| Book | _____ |
| *Television | _____ |
| Train | _____ |
| *Commercial | _____ |
| Automobile | _____ |
| Umbrella | _____ |
| *Advertisement | _____ |

### Sentence Completion

*Sentence completion* is an extension of the word association concept, and requires that the respondent finish an incomplete sentence with the first thought which comes to mind. As with word association, it is important that the respondent not devote excessive time to the formulation of answers that are not initial reactions to the stimuli being presented. Compared to word association, in which the opportunity exists for the inclusion of "neutral" words within the list, it is more difficult to disguise the purpose of a sentence completion question. Sentence completion stimuli may be worded in either the first person ("I smoke cigars because _____") or the third person ("Most people probably smoke cigars because _____"). However, especially with personal or threatening subjects, the use of the third person has the advantage of enabling the respondent to "project" his or her feelings onto another party, thus avoiding any direct personal association with the answer provided. Incomplete sentence stimuli may take a variety of forms. For example, in studying perceptions toward motorcycles, the following could be a few of the questions used:

> The thing I dislike most about motorcycles is _____.
> People who ride motorcycles are usually _____.
> Motorcycles are _____.
> Some people are afraid of motorcycles because _____.
> When I think of motorcycles, I become very _____.

### Story Completion

An extension of the sentence completion technique, *story completion* provides the respondent with the beginning of a story, then asks him to complete it. For example, if we were studying the extent to which children affect grocery shopping decisions, we might ask a respondent to complete a partial story such as the following:

> Mrs. Adams and her son Hobart, age 6, picked up a grocery cart and proceeded to shop for the family's supply of groceries for the week. After filling most of the cart, they came to the cereal aisle, where they encountered a wide variety of choices. . . .

In completing the story, the respondent will likely include some reference to the child's role (or lack of same) in selecting the brands of cereal that are purchased. Compared to the sentence completion technique, story completion provides a slightly greater degree of structure, but retains the freedom of imagination and stimulus direction enjoyed by the simpler approach. The greater versatility of the story completion approach allows the researcher to construct a story situation that conforms very closely to a unique problem or circumstance that would be difficult or impossible to explore by means of other techniques.

For example, if it is desired to evaluate brand images, promotional idea alternatives, or personal selling strategies, the story completion technique is an ideal approach. In the case of determining the probable success of a personal selling strategy, a story could be initiated in which an individual entered a store and, after browsing for a short time, was engaged in conversation by a salesperson and given the sales talk that is being evaluated. In completing the story, the respondent will tend to indicate the hypothetical customer's reactions to the selling effort, whether or not it was successful, and why.

The story completion approach, with its inherent versatility and imaginative opportunities for both researcher and respondent, tends to provide data which are even more qualitative than those resulting from word association and sentence completion. However, the ability to tailor the beginning of the story to describe very closely a real-world problem or decision alternative is a very strong point in support of this unconforming, but promising, projective research possibility.

### Cartoon Tests

The *cartoon test* involves a drawing of characters in an ambiguous situation that is of special interest to the researcher. As with the story completion approach, the cartoon test offers the opportunity to construct a stimulus that is very similar to the specific problem or question being addressed. The respondent is asked to complete one of the captions in the cartoon—a caption that is generally a response to a statement made by another cartoon character, but sometimes a reaction to an obvious situation presented by the drawing.

An example of the cartoon test is shown in Figure 10-5, containing one of two illustrations used to compare the images of two automobiles, the Chevrolet Corvette and a now-extinct American Motors sedan. The total sample was divided into two groups, with the first group responding to the cartoon as shown here. For the second group, the AMC model replaced Corvette in both the sketch and the question being asked. The following responses were typical of reactions to these two very different stimuli: "Hey Herman, where are you going in your new . . . ."

| Corvette"? | AMC"? |
|---|---|
| "Cruisin'." | "Nowhere. The #&*@% thing won't start." |
| "Pick up some chicks." | "To trade it in." |
| "To the drag strip." | "To buy some groceries." |
| "To the drive-in movie." | "To the laundromat." |
| "Got a big date tonight." | |

The contrast between response categories was very strong, with the Corvette heavily associated with sex, youth, and action. On the other hand, the AMC product was largely perceived as devoid of both personality and mechanical reliability.

**Figure 10-5.**    This cartoon test was used to compare the image of the Chevrolet Corvette with that of another, less exciting vehicle. The results were interesting, but not unexpected.

### Thematic Apperception Test

A very popular technique in both marketing research and clinical psychology is the *Thematic Apperception Test*, or TAT, in which the respondent is asked to react to a picture or series of pictures. For example, a picture may depict a man and woman walking into a Sears store. The respondent might then be asked to explain the situation, describe either the couple or the circumstances under which they are entering the store, and may even be asked to make up a story about the couple and their experience before, during, and after being at Sears that day. In the process, it is hoped that the respondent will reveal his or her own feelings about Sears, including thoughts that might not be communicated in more direct questioning.

The TAT may well be the most ambiguous of the projective research techniques, and is about one step short of the ultimate in ambiguity, the Rorschach ink blot test in which respondents reveal their inner selves by describing what they see in symmetrical blots of ink. If the TAT is the most ambiguous of the techniques we've discussed, it is also the most flexible, since the pictures can be constructed to depict nearly any type of marketing problem or situation in which images, perceptions, preferences, or attitudes are of importance. However, accompanying this flexibility is the inherent difficulty of administering the test, interpreting the results of some long and confusing stories, and generalizing the results of all stories in such a way that some light is shed on the marketing problem that initiated the application of the technique.

### Role Playing

In this approach, the respondent is usually asked to assume the role of another person (e.g., a salesperson, a shopper, a jogging enthusiast, a model railroading hobbyist, an employee, or a company president). More abstract possibilities also exist, such as having several individuals playing the role of objects such as fast-food chains, brands of cologne, or popular vacation spots. At first glance, it may seem odd to have three people involved in a role-playing scene in which one is masquerading as K-mart, another as Sears, and a third as Montgomery Ward. However, at first glance, practically all of these techniques seem odd to those who are unfamiliar with the unique capabilities they offer. Exhibit 10-1 illustrates a practical example of role playing applied to young children.

### Projective Techniques in Combination

A given questionnaire or other data collection instrument may utilize a combination of projective techniques in examining respondents' feelings regarding a particular subject. For example, in Figure 10-6, two different ap-

---

**EXHIBIT 10-1**

*Kids Give Data by Acting Grown-up*

A paper products manufacturer, considering a new bib/napkin concept for children aged 3 to 6, set up fantasy play sessions to help find out how kids might react to such a product. In each session, a small group of kids were put into a make-believe family meal scene, together with stuffed animals and dolls, who served as their "children."

After seating the make-believe children at the pretend dinner table, youngsters quickly equipped the mute diners with a variety of protective bibs and napkins, then created conversation and behavior on their behalf. It seems that the stuffed animals and dolls really wanted to be messy, but their make-believe parents sternly lectured them on the importance of cleanliness at the table.

Among the results of these fantasy sessions was the finding that children preferred having their chests covered by something, but did not like bibs around their necks because they were "itchy and babyish." Instead, they wanted to be more like grown-ups by having something on their laps. Following the fantasy play sessions, the company developed a prototype product incorporating these findings.

*Source:* "Projective Research Techniques Extract Valuable Market Data from Children," *Marketing News,* January 21, 1983, sec. 2, p. 19, published by the American Marketing Association. Originally published in "Topline," November 1982, newsletter published by McCollum/Spelman & Co., Inc., Great Neck, N.Y.

**Figure 10-6.** A combination of sentence completion and cartoon test projective techniques used in measuring nonstudents' perceptions of the National Safety Council's Defensive Driving Course.

proaches were used in attempting to determine individuals' perceptions of the Defensive Driving Course of the National Safety Council. The questionnaire was used prior to a focus group interview session as an icebreaker for subsequent discussion of the course. The two projective techniques used in this approach were sentence completion and the cartoon test.

Responses to the questionnaire helped to determine promising avenues for discussion during a group interview of non-DDC students. Many expressed the feeling that the DDC is a corrective course for those who either don't know how to drive or who have had excessive violations or accidents, that the course is a boring repetition of facts they already know, and that people simply don't sign up for it because they feel it to be unnecessary. The negative connotation of the "defensive" (described by some participants as "pondering one's way through life") portion of the course title was an item frequently mentioned in both the group interviews and the questionnaires.

One questionnaire response was especially revealing with regard to the image of the DDC. In projecting the stick figure's nonparticipation response to question 1 of Figure 10-6, the respondent simply filled in the words, "No, I gave at the office." Not intended to be a comical response, this represented the individual's feeling (clarified later in the interview) that taking the DDC resembles a charitable undertaking in which one gives but does not receive. (Such attitudes are unwittingly encouraged by the National Safety Council itself. For example, upon completion of the program, DDC graduates are awarded a "certificate of appreciation" thanking them for their personal effort toward helping to reduce the severity of our nation's traffic accident problem.) The combination of the projective questions and the focus group interview was quite useful in determining the image of the social product known as the Defensive Driving Course. As an example of the data obtained, and of the manner in which such data are generally analyzed and expressed, the response breakdown is shown in Table 10-1.

### Advantages and Disadvantages of Projective Techniques

The greatest advantage of projective techniques is that they can enable us to get information that would not be available through direct questioning or by other means. In addition, the types of data that these techniques generate are often useful in the exploratory stage of a research study—a stage in which ideas, insights, and hypotheses are of prime importance. From the standpoint of economy, a good exploratory study may well be sufficient in itself to provide the answers we are seeking, hence eliminating the need to allocate funds for further study of the problem.

On the minus side of the ledger, projective techniques are best carried out by trained interviewers and their results interpreted by experienced analysts, both of whom may be relatively expensive to retain. Also, samples used are usually of small size and of the nonprobability type, making it difficult to project results to the general population. However, despite these problems, projective

**TABLE 10-1.** Breakdown of responses to projective questions that were asked in questionnaire of Figure 10-6.

| Responses | Percent |
|---|---|
| **Question 1** | |
| Can drive well enough already. | 53 |
| Don't have time. | 23 |
| Already took it. | 12 |
| Other. | 12 |
| **Question 2** | |
| Are bad drivers/want to improve driving ability. | 40 |
| Want lower insurance rates. | 20 |
| They have to/need course for their job. | 18 |
| Had a close call or accident recently. | 10 |
| Are afraid of other drivers. | 7 |
| Other. | 5 |
| **Question 3** | |
| Already knew material. | 49 |
| Class was too long. | 20 |
| Class was boring. | 17 |
| Other (e.g., ". . . I wrecked the instructor's car"). | 14 |
| **Question 4** | |
| Bored statement/daydreaming. | 47 |
| Already knew material. | 35 |
| Positive statement or thought expressing interest in lecture. | 8 |
| Want to be in car instead of classroom. | 5 |
| Other. | 5 |

methods remain a solid research tool when used within their limitations, and are especially relevant to research of the exploratory type.

## OBSERVATION

Instead of asking people for information, it is sometimes cheaper and more effective to simply *observe* either their current behavior or the results of past behavior. For example, rather than questioning individuals regarding the brand of tires on their automobile, a better alternative may be to simply look at the tires. This approach to the collection of information is as old as the human race, and is a phenomenon that surrounds us every day, since most of our own knowledge about people and things comes from our own observation or from the observations of others.

While observation may be used by itself, it is frequently used along with other means of measuring the same phenomenon. To this extent, observation may be able to provide you with reassurance that your results are well founded by demonstrating convergent validity with other research approaches. However, in some cases, observation may be the *only* way to obtain marketing information that is desired. For example, if a store manager wishes to determine the current pricing and sales promotion activity taking place at her competitor's establishment, a personal visit or assignment of a lesser-known "shopper" to the task will be necessary.

There are five ways in which observational studies are generally classified: (1) whether the observation is made under natural or contrived circumstances, (2) whether the persons being observed are aware or unaware of their participation in the research process, (3) whether the observation process is structured or unstructured, (4) whether or not the behavior is observed as it actually takes place, and (5) whether the observations are made by people or by mechanical devices.

### Natural versus Contrived Observation

*Natural observation* occurs whenever we observe behavior as it is taking place in a normal setting—for example, watching customers entering a Roy Rogers Family Restaurant, observing the length of time that bookstore browsers spend in the store before they either leave or make a purchase, or watching automobile drivers from an overpass to determine whether or not they are wearing their safety belt. In natural observation, we make no attempt to manipulate the setting in which we are examining behavior. In the preceding examples, we could be interested in determining (1) whether the clientele of the Roy Rogers establishment tends to include a higher percentage of young couples compared to a competing restaurant across the street, (2) whether there is any relationship between the length of time an individual spends in the book store and the probability that he or she will make a purchase in excess of $10, and (3) whether safety-belt usage has increased following an intensive promotional campaign encouraging motorists to "buckle up."

In a study of parent–child interaction in the selection of breakfast cereals, observers dressed as supermarket clerks recorded the communication and behavior of parent–child combinations who were alone in the store.[8] Following the collection of field data, independent coders summarized the communications into a flow diagram descriptive of the behavior that was observed. This flow diagram is representative of the type of information that can arise from natural observation, and is presented in Figure 10-7.

The National Football League has been concerned about the greatly increasing length of NFL games. In 1970, the average game lasted 2 hours, 36 minutes, but during the 1986 season had increased to 3:12, up from 3:09 the

---

[8] Charles K. Atkin, "Observation of Parent–Child Interaction in Supermarket Decision-Making," *Journal of Marketing*, October 1978, pp. 41–45, published by the American Marketing Association.

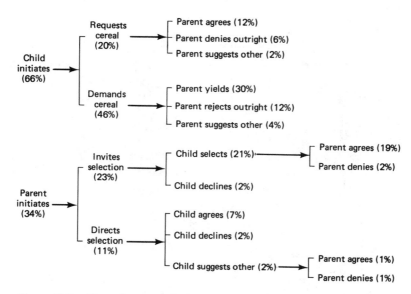

**Figure 10-7.** Flow of communication in natural observation study of parent–child interaction in the selection of breakfast cereal. (*Source:* Based on Charles K. Atkin, "Observation of Parent–Child Interaction in Supermarket Decision-Making," *Journal of Marketing*, October 1978, p. 43, published by the American Marketing Association.)

year before. In attempting to reduce this duration, a logical first step is to identify how the time is spent. Such a breakdown for a 1986 game between the Pittsburgh Steelers and Detroit Lions is shown in the direct observational results of Figure 10-8, describing the time breakdown for a contest lasting 3 hours and 23 minutes. Nonfans will be quick to point out that 56% of the minutes were spent in so-called "dead time," huddling, unpiling, and so on.[9]

*Contrived observation*, in which the researcher purposely alters the environment in order to create a particular situation to be observed, is often more efficient than waiting for the same situation to occur of its own accord. For example, the Los Angeles Motor Car Dealers Association used contrived observation in evaluating the quality of service provided by its members. A retired expert mechanic posed as an average customer in need of service advice on several typical mechanical problems. Service persons delivering exceptional service were given $100 on the spot, and an enthusiastic evaluation sent to the dealer. Subpar personnel were given nothing, but dealers were sent confidential evaluations detailing their performance.[10]

---

[9] Ron Cook, "Tick, Tick, Tick . . . ," *The Pittsburgh Press*, December 14, 1986, p. D3.

[10] "L.A. Service Checked by 'Mystery Shopper,'" *Automotive News*, September 12, 1985, p. 24.

**Figure 10-8.** Observation of a professional football game revealed this breakdown of time spent on various activities, including nearly 2 hours just huddling and unpiling the players. (*Source:* Ron Cook, "Tick, Tick, Tick . . . ," *The Pittsburgh Press,* December 14, 1986, p. D3. Illustration courtesy of *The Pittsburgh Press.*)

Because some behaviors occur so seldom, it becomes very inefficient to simply wait for them to happen. In such cases, contrived observation becomes an attractive alternative to the natural variety. On the other hand, natural observation is likely to provide data that better reflect how an individual really behaves in an everyday setting. The trade-off is essentially one in which we must balance the cost of waiting for the right situation to occur versus the representativeness of the behaviors we observe when it does occur.

## Disguised versus Undisguised Observation

Observation is *disguised* to the extent that the person being observed is unaware that he or she is being watched. The previous example in which the undercover mechanic evaluated dealer service personnel was disguised as well as contrived. In general, it is advisable to utilize the disguised observational study whenever the person being observed is likely to behave differently if he knows he is being observed.

Although in some cases we may not be able to disguise the observational process as well as we'd like, it is highly recommended that the observer either be hidden or that he or she blend into the environment to the maximum extent possible. However, with some observational approaches, including a few that involve mechanical devices (e.g., the "people meter" placed in the home to record TV viewing behavior), it will not be possible to disguise the fact that someone is in the process of being observed.

## Structured versus Unstructured Observation

In *structured observation*, we know in advance the types of activities and characteristics that we are to identify and record. This is only feasible if our marketing problem has already been well defined and the phenomena involved are neither highly ambiguous nor subject to excessive "judgment calls" by observers in the field. Structured observation is facilitated by the use of a data collection instrument that is also structured. For example, if we were to undertake an observational study of service station customers, items such as the following might be included:

> Service station name and location: _____.
> Date: _____.        Time of day: _____.
> Vehicle make and model: _____.
> Vehicle approximate year: _____.
> Weather conditions: ☐ Warm      ☐ Cool
> Precipitation: ☐ Yes      ☐ No
> Type of fuel purchased: ☐ None        ☐ Regular      ☐ Premium
>                                      ☐ Unleaded regular
>                                      ☐ Unleaded premium
>                                      ☐ Diesel
> Price per gallon: _____.        Total cost of fuel purchased: _____.
> Sex of driver: ☐ Male      ☐ Female      ☐ Not sure
> Approximate age of driver: _____. Number of passengers: _____.
> Dress of driver: ☐ Well-dressed      ☐ Casual      ☐ Sloppy
> Condition of vehicle: ☐ Clean      ☐ Dirty
> Underhood checks: ☐ None      ☐ Oil      ☐ Water
>                            ☐ Battery      ☐ Other _____.
> Direction of travel after leaving station:
>   ☐ North      ☐ South      ☐ East      ☐ West
> Other purchases made: ☐ Auto accessories or equipment
>                                      ☐ Snacks or drinks      ☐ Other _____.

In structured observation data collection forms, it is inevitable that some judgment must be exercised by the observer. For example, in the preceding items, the observer is called upon to approximate the age of the customer, his or her style of dress, and whether the vehicle is clean or dirty. Such judgments may not be consistent from one observer to the next, and perhaps not even consistent for the same observer from one day to the next. For these reasons, it is best to retain observers who are well qualified and who have been briefed regarding the objectives of the study and the desired bases for categorization of the behaviors and characteristics being observed.

In *unstructured observation*, the observer is free to note whatever he or she deems relevant to the situation being studied. This approach is highly applicable to exploratory research, in which ideas and hypotheses are to be generated for subsequent and more conclusive examination. Compared to structured observation, the unstructured variety is much more susceptible to bias on the part of the observer. However, this same freedom of judgment and interpretation serves as a strength when unstructured observation is used in its proper role.

### Direct versus Indirect Observation

In *direct observation*, we observe behaviors as they are actually taking place, whereas *indirect observation* involves observing the *results* of behavior that has already happened. Direct observation is relatively straightforward, is the type of observation that generally comes to mind whenever we think of observational techniques, and therefore does not require much explanation in this section. However, this is not meant to imply that direct observation is either mundane or unimaginative.

Indirect observation, with its orientation toward behavior that has occurred in the past, is a novel approach that enables the researcher to employ a great deal of ingenuity in obtaining information. The legendary Sherlock Holmes could be considered not only a detective, but also a master of indirect observation. Curiously, the same might be said for garbage collectors, who (at least until the popularization of plastic trash bags) have long known more about our purchasing habits than even the most determined survey researcher could ever learn.

Studies involving the collection and analysis of garbage have actually been carried out. For example, in one study, the amount of alcoholic beverages consumed in a community was estimated by counting the number of empty liquor bottles discarded in the trash.[11] This approach is sometimes referred to as the

---

[11] See H.G. Sawyer, "The Meaning of Numbers," speech before the American Association of Advertising Agencies, 1961, reported in E.J. Webb, D.T. Campbell, K.D. Schwartz, and L. Sechrest, *Unobtrusive Measures: Nonreactive Research in the Social Sciences* (Skokie, Ill.: Rand McNally & Company, 1966), pp. 41–42.

study of *physical traces*, or those things, clues, or other impressions that people leave behind. For example, the success of an antilitter campaign might be measured by counting the number of beer and soft-drink containers deposited along the highway before and after the campaign. Some other examples of indirect observation:

- A Washington lobbyist tells seminars his secret to making an ad campaign look bigger than it is. In one case, during a debate on Social Security, his aides stationed themselves at House parking garages, observing the time of arrival of members of the Ways and Means Committee, along with the positions of their radio dials. He uses such data in buying radio spots, a procedure he refers to as "narrowcasting."[12]

- As an index of business activity, the Conference Board monitors help-wanted ads in the nation's major newspapers.[13]

- Since 1983, R.L. Polk's Vehicle Origin Survey (VOS) program has reported over a million license plate numbers throughout the United States. Among other applications, the data are used to define trade areas and measure competitive customer bases.[14]

- In a much different application of vehicle observation, bumper stickers and window decals are replacing personal ads as a medium for singles to get together. For $20 to $50 a year, clubs such as Bumper Buddies will transmit introduction notes and phone numbers between members who happen to spot each other in traffic. New York City even has a pedestrian version featuring numbered buttons.[15]

- In 1985, U.S. officials accused the KGB of having used fluorescent "spy dust" to track the movements of U.S. diplomats in Moscow. Some have speculated that the dust was employed as shown in Figure 10-9.[16]

The *pantry audit* is another form of the physical traces approach, and relies upon gaining permission to examine participants' homes for the presence of certain predetermined products and brands. With the increasing use of panel data, this approach is less important than in the past, but remains a good source of convergent validity for the evaluation of panel information.

Secondary data and other published records constitute another source of information for studies involving indirect observation. A useful approach for

---

[12] See R. Jarslovsky, Washington Wire Column, "Trick of the Trade," *The Wall Street Journal*, March 21, 1986, p. 1.

[13] "National Trend Is Up for Help-Wanted Ads," *Pittsburgh Post-Gazette*, February 4, 1985, p. 25.

[14] Larry D. Crabtree and James A. Paris, "Survey Car License Plates to Define Retail Trade Area," *Marketing News*, January 4, 1985, p. 12, published by the American Marketing Association.

[15] Scott Kilman, "How to Meet Singles in Your Car, Or, It Was Love at First Light," *The Wall Street Journal*, August 14, 1985, p. 23.

[16] Mark Roth, "Superpowder," *Pittsburgh Post-Gazette*, August 25, 1985, p. 30.

# How the spy dust might work

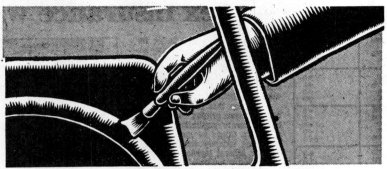

**1.** Agent puts "spy dust" on steering wheel.

Robert J. Patla/Post-Gazette

**2.** Diplomat drives to meeting.

**3.** Dust on diplomat's hand touches doorknob.

**4.** Agent detects dust with ultraviolet device.

**Figure 10-9.** Speculating on the possible use of "spy dust" to track the movements of U.S. diplomats in Moscow; scientists believe the technique could be employed as shown here. (*Source:* Mark Roth, "Superpowder," *Pittsburgh Post-Gazette,* August 25, 1985, p. 30. Illustration courtesy of the *Pittsburgh Post-Gazette*.)

> **EXHIBIT 10-2**
>
> **TV Events and the "Flush Factor"**
>
> As television networks commenced with so-called "big event" programming like the miniseries "Roots," the movie *Jaws*, and the first showing of *The Godfather*, city sanitation supervisors were among the first to realize that many viewers weren't watching the commercials. The phenomenon they observed nearly firsthand has been dubbed the "flush factor," reflecting a dramatic rise in water consumption during the commercial breaks of these and similar programs.
>
> *Source:* Bernie Whalen, "$6 Billion down the Drain," *Marketing News*, September 14, 1984, p. 1, published by the American Marketing Association.

making use of such sources is known as ***content analysis***, which involves systematically noting specified characteristics that exist or don't exist within the materials under examination. An example of this approach was a study in which the role of women was studied by means of analyzing the content of advertisements in general audience magazines. The study, conducted in 1971, revealed that only 9% of the women in the ads were portrayed in working roles, versus 45% for men.[17] It is interesting to note that in a later study, conducted in 1973, this percentage had risen from 9% to 21%, with the range of the women's occupations having increased, and the ads portraying a greater percentage of women in the professional job categories.[18]

## Human versus Mechanical Observation

It can sometimes be helpful to replace or supplement the human observer with one or more of the mechanical devices frequently used in marketing research. Compared to the human observer, such devices tend to offer lower cost, greater accuracy, and an ability to measure phenomena that lie beyond the observational limits of their human counterparts.

The *Audimeter* is one of the best-known mechanical observation devices and was developed by the A.C. Nielsen Company for recording the television viewing behavior of its panel of families. The device, mounted on the television set, records the times during which the set is in operation and the station to which it is tuned, thus providing the audience-share measurements we are used to reading about in the TV sections of our newspapers and other media. A related

---

[17] Alice Courtney and Sarah Wernick Lockertz, "A Woman's Place: An Analysis of Roles Portrayed by Women in Magazine Advertisements," *Journal of Marketing Research*, February 1971, pp. 92–95, published by the American Marketing Association.

[18] Louis Wagner and Janis B. Banos, "A Woman's Place: A Follow-Up Analysis of the Roles Portrayed by Women in Magazine Advertisements," *Journal of Marketing Research*, May 1973, pp. 213–14, published by the American Marketing Association.

device is the "people meter," also an electronic box connected to the TV set. In this case, there is a button for each member of the family so that individuals can register their presence at the TV.

The *eye camera* photographs eye movements, and is used to record these movements as a person responds to a visual stimulus, such as a television, newspaper, or magazine advertisement. Besides telling us the order in which the parts of an ad were viewed, the resulting picture can indicate the amount of time spent viewing each component of the stimulus, as shown in Figure 10-10.

The *pupilometer* is an interesting device that reflects emotional reactions by measuring changes in the diameter of the pupil of the eye. While the pupil typically expands or contracts as a function of changing light conditions, it has been discovered that the pupil will also change slightly in size as an involuntary reaction corresponding to the amount of interest an individual has in the stimulus she or he is observing.

The *psychogalvanometer* measures changes in the rate of perspiration, a physiological reaction that is a part of an individual's emotional response to a stimulus. The stimulus may be an advertisement, brand name, product design, or other verbal or nonverbal marketing entity. The general principle involved

**Figure 10-10.** Based on eye movement research, the sizes of the circles in this scene represent the proportion of time viewers spent looking at each segment. (Courtesy of Applied Science Group, Inc.)

---

### EXHIBIT 10-3
### *Lie Detector Has Ancient Roots*

Today's polygraph, or lie detector, typically monitors three different physiological functions: breathing rate, heart rate, and perspiration. These reactions are recorded on moving graph paper and monitored by the operator. When the average individual is under stress, as when lying, telltale changes tend to occur in the lines being traced by the machine. Some disagreement exists regarding the reliability of the device. For example, a number of studies have found that some people can lie without producing physical symptoms of stress.

Historically, other cultures have had their own version of the "lie detector." The ancient Chinese would "test" an accused person by requiring him to chew rice powder, then spit it out. If the powder remained dry, the individual was presumed guilty. The British, in a similar approach, had the suspect attempt to swallow a "trial slice" of dry bread. The inability to do this was a sign of guilt.

In Arabia, the Bedouins made the accused lick a hot iron. If he burned his tongue, the verdict was "guilty," and his suffering had probably just begun. Relying on the basic principle that stress is accompanied by physiological change, each of these three techniques also utilized the more specific phenomenon that stress tends to reduce the flow of saliva.

*Source:* John A. Belt, "The Polygraph: A Questionable Personnel Tool," *Personnel Administrator*, August 1983, p. 66. Reprinted from the August 1983 issue of *Personnel Administrator*, Copyright 1983, The American Society For Personnel Administration, 606 North Washington Street, Alexandria, Virginia 22314.

---

is not unlike the lie detector, which is also designed to measure involuntary physiological reactions.

The *hidden camera* is another of the photographic approaches to observation, but is little more than a mechanical answer to the problem of observers' being too large to hide behind pictures and in other inconspicuous locations. However, it has the advantage of allowing the same behavior sequence to be observed by a number of analysts during one or more replays.

*Brain wave analysis* measures the electrical patterns emitted from the brain itself, with separate measurements of activity for the left and right hemispheres. The left side of the brain is associated with logic and rationality, the right with emotion. One application of brain wave analysis is the testing of commercials; for example, an ad designed to communicate product information may not be very effective if it elicits activity mainly from the right hemisphere. Figure 10-11 shows the result of brain wave analysis for a primarily emotional commercial, with left–right-hemisphere activity levels shown for each 5-second segment of the ad. The commercial begins with a woman questioning a man about his moodiness, followed by her handing him something to read. Pausing before reacting, he smiles and a product jingle ensues. According to Sidney Weinstein, president of Neuro-Communication Research Laboratories, Inc., "the resolving

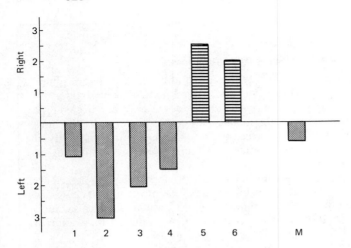

**Figure 10-11.** Brain wave analysis for an emotional TV commercial showed these levels of left and right hemisphere brain activity for each 5-second period during the ad. (*Source:* Sidney Weinstein, "Advances in Brain Wave Analysis Allow Researchers to Test Effectiveness of Ads," *Marketing News,* September 17, 1982, sec. 1, p. 22, published by the American Marketing Association.)

of the situation" caused the shift from left- to right-hemisphere activity in segments 5 and 6.[19] In another application, brain wave patterns were used in determining which scents were most calming for a new line of foaming bath oil and bar soap.[20]

*Voice pitch analysis* measures emotional response by monitoring normal voice frequency and changes in it. In an attempt to popularize this relatively new research technique, one firm went so far as to market a watch based on this concept:

> For those who have everything . . . A hidden device, a silicon chip, in a new $29.95 watch now makes it possible for the wearer to tell whether someone is lying or telling the truth by the amount of stress in the person's voice. The minipolygraph or lilliputian lie detector will retail by Christmas.[21]

While the functional wristwatch lie detector may be as far off as Dick Tracy's two-way wrist computer-TV-radio, one thing is certain: It would make political speeches and the evening news a lot more interesting.

Among other observation devices are such items as the breathalyzer, used by law enforcement agencies to measure blood-alcohol levels by the concentration of alcohol in the breath; chemical analysis of urine, blood (and even hair) samples for evidence of substance use; and electronic transmitters to monitor the movement of individuals. In the latter case, transmitters can be used for such purposes as keeping track of elderly patients[22] and in-home detention as

---

[19] Sidney Weinstein, "Advances in Brain Wave Analysis Allow Researchers to Test Effectiveness of Ads," *Marketing News,* September 17, 1982, sec. 1, pp. 21–22, published by the American Marketing Association.

[20] See Ronald Alsop, "Firms Push 'Aroma Therapy' to Treat Flat Fragrance Sales," *The Wall Street Journal,* April 24, 1986, p. 30.

[21] "Tattletale Timepiece," *Pittsburgh Post-Gazette,* April 14, 1979, p. 1.

[22] David Stipp and Jerry E. Bishop, "Elderly Wanderers," *The Wall Street Journal,* September 17, 1986, p. 33.

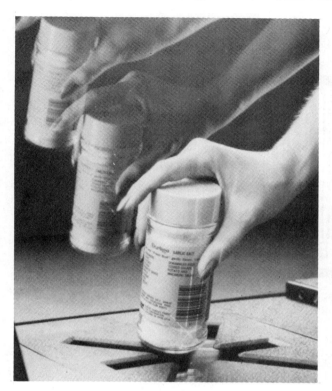

**Figure 10-12.** Quickly passing through the laser beam of a store scanner, this UPC-labeled product provides detailed information about itself, including manufacturer, size or weight, and more. The store computer "looks up" the price, making it unnecessary to change the label on each item when prices change or products are on sale. When consumer panel members are identified by scanner-readable cards, their shopping behavior can be instantly monitored as well. (Courtesy of NCR Corporation.)

a jail substitute for some prisoners.[23] Medical researchers are even working on a remarkable device that can measure heartbeat and respiration with a radar device located in the same room.[24]

## UPC Scanning

The availability of Universal Product Code (UPC) scanning has revolutionized mechanical observation. As shown in Figure 10-12, a UPC-labeled item need only be passed through the laser beam of the checkout counter in order to record information about the product and register its sale. Among the information contained in the code are such descriptors as brand, size or weight, color, and flavor. During scanning, the store's computer "looks up" the price and displays it on the register display. Store inventory data are automatically reduced to reflect the purchase.

A typical UPC symbol includes a pattern of bars and spaces of varying

---

[23] Earle C. Gottschalk, Jr., "Monitors Permit House Arrests Instead of Jail," *The Wall Street Journal*, March 17, 1986, p. 19.

[24] See Otis Post, "Watching over the Sick—From across a Room," *Business Week*, October 14, 1985, p. 104.

**Figure 10-13.** The UPC symbol relies on a pattern of bars and spaces of specified widths to communicate information about the product on which it is found. (Courtesy of Matthews, Pittsburgh, Pa.)

width that are accompanied by conventional numerals printed beneath. The parts of the UPC symbol shown in Figure 10-13 are:[25]

> *Quiet zones.*    Adjacent to the right and left guard bars, these areas have no marking except for the number system character.
>
> *Left and right guard bars.*    Signal the beginning and end of the symbol.
>
> *Number system character.*    The first numeral, this represents the product classification (e.g., 0 for grocery items, 3 for drug or health-related items).
>
> *Manufacturer's identification number.*    The five digits assigned to the manufacturer by the Uniform Code Council, these are encoded between the number system character and the center bar.
>
> *Center bar pattern.*    Separates the left and right sides of the symbol.
>
> *Item code.*    The five digits to the right of the center bar patterns, these

---

[25] "Some Answers to Questions You May Have about UPC Symbols," brochure published by Matthews, Pittsburgh, Pa., p. 4.

are assigned by the manufacturer. There are no other restrictions on this number.

*Modulo check character.*    This is based on 11 digits, including the number system character, the manufacturer's identification number, and the item code. To check for errors, the store scanner calculates this number and compares it with the value that is encoded in the symbol. The values must match in order to produce a successful scan.

UPC scanning is valuable in the collection of data from panels like the ones discussed in the next section. No longer is it necessary for consumers to keep detailed written records on their purchases. This not only contributes to accuracy, but also makes the panel member's job much easier. As described in Exhibit 10-4, scanner technology can even be combined with other observational measures to provide additional information on panel members and their behavior. Nielsen, Nabscan, and Behaviorscan are among those who rely heavily on scanner data to obtain panel information at the retailer or consumer level. Figure 10-14 shows the high level of detail made possible through the use of scanner data versus traditional four-weekly audit information.

### Advantages and Disadvantages of Observation

A principal strength of the observational approach is the avoidance of response error on the part of individuals who, for one reason or another, might not provide an accurate response to a question dealing with their attitudes or be-

---

### EXHIBIT 10-4
#### People Meter Instruments Panel

Electronically noting the program being watched and (with a "punch-in" button for each family member) the persons in the room at the time, the people meter is rapidly gaining popularity as an observation device for TV viewing. It even notices whether the program is being taped on a videotape recorder.

A.C. Nielsen began installing the meters in 1986, with plans to have 6000 people-metered households by 1988. According to William S. Hamill, executive vice president of Nielsen's Media Research Group, "This is the first step in the use of new technologies in the measurement of television viewers."

Another sign of things to come for the people meter is reflected in the plans of BehaviorScan, a unit of Information Resources, Inc. The company intends to combine existing electronic test-marketing capabilities with the device, planning to equip two-thirds of its panel homes with meters by the end of 1986. The resulting marriage of people meter data with UPC scanning information will be especially useful in helping researchers answer such questions as the extent to which viewing of commercials in the home is converted to product purchases at the store.

*Source:* "Pinpointing Who Is Watching What," *The New York Times,* June 15, 1986, p. F19. Copyright © 1986 by The New York Times Company. Reprinted by permission.

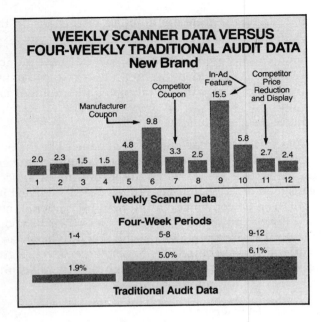

**Figure 10-14.** A lot of brand activity can occur beneath the surface of traditional four-weekly audit information. With the speed and accuracy of scanner data, these details are less likely to go unnoticed. (*Source:* "Introducing NabScan On Line," published by National Brand Scanning, Inc., p. 1. Courtesy of National Brand Scanning, Inc., New York.)

havior. In addition, if observation is carried out by some techniques, such as UPC scanning, data can be stored, summarized, and analyzed very soon after their collection, a feature not shared by conventional survey approaches.

Another advantage of observation compared to other techniques is that some data may simply not be obtainable by other methods—for example, product preference and usage information from small children who are not old enough to speak. In other instances, where data may be obtained from a variety of methods, observation may prove to be the most economical means available—for example, the use of mechanical counters for measuring highway usage and store customer traffic.

Unfortunately, observation is capable of measuring mostly short-term behaviors, mostly in the "present" time dimension. While indirect observation of physical traces has much to offer, other approaches are required in order to collect much attitudinal and behavioral information with which observation is unable to deal.

Observation is inherently a subjective approach to the collection of marketing information. While mechanical observation can help to alleviate this difficulty, most observation requires some degree of subjective judgment on the part of the observer. The selection of trained and experienced observers can reduce this problem to a minimum, but it will tend to exist whenever human observers are asked to watch and interpret the behavior of others. Another general problem with observation is its cost, a factor related to the expense of procuring and retaining skilled observers. The cost factor may be reduced by employing contrived observation instead of natural observation. This solution, however, may result in the inexpensive observation of unnatural behavior brought about by the "contriving."

## PANELS

Panels consist of persons, households, or business firms who report their purchasing activities at periodic intervals over time, and who are typically selected based on a combination of their willingness and representativeness. In addition, some panelists may be called upon to participate in a one-shot study involving one or more of the survey research approaches we've discussed. In return, they are compensated either monetarily or with gifts as a reward for their services (see Figure 10-15). Panels may be sponsored by a variety of organizations, including governmental bodies, corporations, research firms and universities. Among the best-known panels are those supported by the A.C. Nielsen Company, the Home Testing Institute, National Family Opinion, National Purchase Diary Panel, and National Brand Scanning. Panel members often provide information by means of a self-administered questionnaire, or *diary*, which is completed and returned to the sponsor at specified intervals. In some cases, panel members may simply be responsible for cooperating in surveys, but do not submit information on a continuing basis. Such panels, who provide a willing sample at a reasonable cost (including greatly reduced nonresponse), are referred to as *interval* panels as opposed to the *continuing* panel, which reports on a regular basis.

### Applications of Consumer Panels

Members of a consumer panel will usually be asked to provide information such as their exposure to various media, past and planned household expenditures, recreational and other behavior, and attitudes and opinions regarding consumer products and contemporary issues. In the case of industrial consumer panels (e.g., dealer panels), price information, sales data and inventory levels are among the informational requests most commonly made of panel members.

In the Pittsburgh area, the Guide-Post Consumer Mail Panel surveys 2000 female householders each month in order to provide information on their buying habits, activities, and opinions. A sample of the kinds of questions posed to panel members is presented in Figure 10-16, which is a portion of the panel reporting diary used during a two-week segment of the monthly reporting period. One of the key outputs of the Guide-Post panel is the annual *Grocery Expenditures* report for the Pittsburgh Standard Metropolitan Statistical Area (SMSA), a report that has been published each year since 1956. Consumer responses to diary and other informational requests provide data that allow analysis of (1) company market share, (2) shopping trends related to days of the week, (3) submarkets according to store and demographic information, and (4) motivations and behavioral patterns regarding grocery shopping habits.

The use of panel information allows marketers to measure the effectiveness of various marketing strategies, monitor the success of new products, identify customers or outlets that are the most profitable, and engage in field experimentation to determine the effect of planned or actual changes in one or more components of their marketing mix. For example, a panel subscriber may use two different subsamples of the panel in order to identify which of two pricing

# YOUR OPINION COUNTS!!

## IT'S AS EASY AS ... A · B · C

### AS A MEMBER OF NFO YOU WILL...

 Have the opportunity to express your opinions.

 Occasionally be selected to use a product at no cost to you.

 Receive periodic copies of my Digest publication, full of helpful hints, recipes, etc.

 Receive "Thank you" gifts for your help on lengthy or complicated question-naires.

 Rest assured that any information about you or your household will only be used for research purposes.

 Provide answers on my questionnaire studies which will be combined with replies from other participants. The final tabulated results will then be presented to our client.

 Join now by completing the attached questionnaire and returning it to me.

NATIONAL FAMILY OPINION. INC. P. O. Box 474  Toledo, Ohio 43691-9984

**Figure 10-15.** This part of an invitation to join a popular consumer panel describes the importance of belonging and the benefits received. (Courtesy of National Family Opinion, Inc., Toledo, Ohio.)

**Please keep a DAILY RECORD of all GROCERY PURCHASES from Monday, APRIL 3 through Sunday, APRIL 16**

**IMPORTANT: PLEASE READ CAREFULLY**
**Each Day** write in dollars and cents beside any store(s) listed where you purchased food/groceries. Also write in the names of any dairy stores, bakeries, delicatessens, meat, fish and vegetable markets and the dollars and cents spent at each store on food to eat at home. Don't try to anticipate your purchases. Your actual expenditure by store is very important.
**At the End of Each Week** write in the dollar value of any milk, eggs, bread, etc. **delivered** to your home. (Do not include this amount in your diary of daily food purchased at the store.)

| Monday, APRIL 3 | |
|---|---|
| 1 A&P $ | 5 Kroger $ |
| 2 Foodland $ | 6 Shop'n Save $ |
| 3 Giant Eagle $ | 7 Thorofare $ |
| 4 IGA $ | |
| Other (Write in) | $ |
| | $ |

| Tuesday, APRIL 4 | |
|---|---|
| 1 A&P $ | 5 Kroger $ |
| 2 Foodland $ | 6 Shop'n Save $ |
| 3 Giant Eagle $ | 7 Thorofare $ |
| 4 IGA $ | |
| Other (Write in) | $ |
| | $ |

| Wednesday, APRIL 5 | |
|---|---|
| 1 A&P $ | 5 Kroger $ |
| 2 Foodland $ | 6 Shop'n Save $ |
| 3 Giant Eagle $ | 7 Thorofare $ |
| 4 IGA $ | |
| Other (Write in) | $ |
| | $ |

| Thursday, APRIL 6 | |
|---|---|
| 1 A&P $ | 5 Kroger $ |
| 2 Foodland $ | 6 Shop'n Save $ |
| 3 Giant Eagle $ | 7 Thorofare $ |
| 4 IGA $ | |
| Other (Write in) | $ |
| | $ |

| Friday, APRIL 7 | |
|---|---|
| 1 A&P $ | 5 Kroger $ |
| 2 Foodland $ | 6 Shop'n Save $ |
| 3 Giant Eagle $ | 7 Thorofare $ |
| 4 IGA $ | |
| Other (Write in) | $ |
| | $ |

| Saturday, APRIL 8 | |
|---|---|
| 1 A&P $ | 5 Kroger $ |
| 2 Foodland $ | 6 Shop'n Save $ |
| 3 Giant Eagle $ | 7 Thorofare $ |
| 4 IGA $ | |
| Other (Write in) | $ |
| | $ |
| Sun. APRIL 9 (Write in) | $ |
| | $ |

| Monday, APRIL 10 | |
|---|---|
| 1 A&P $ | 5 Kroger $ |
| 2 Foodland $ | 6 Shop'n Save $ |
| 3 Giant Eagle $ | 7 Thorofare $ |
| 4 IGA $ | |
| Other (Write in) | $ |
| | $ |

| Tuesday, APRIL 11 | |
|---|---|
| 1 A&P $ | 5 Kroger $ |
| 2 Foodland $ | 6 Shop'n Save $ |
| 3 Giant Eagle $ | 7 Thorofare $ |
| 4 IGA $ | |
| Other (Write in) | $ |
| | $ |

| Wednesday, APRIL 12 | |
|---|---|
| 1 A&P $ | 5 Kroger $ |
| 2 Foodland $ | 6 Shop'n Save $ |
| 3 Giant Eagle $ | 7 Thorofare $ |
| 4 IGA $ | |
| Other (Write in) | $ |
| | $ |

| Thursday, APRIL 13 | |
|---|---|
| 1 A&P $ | 5 Kroger $ |
| 2 Foodland $ | 6 Shop'n Save $ |
| 3 Giant Eagle $ | 7 Thorofare $ |
| 4 IGA $ | |
| Other (Write in) | $ |
| | $ |

| Friday, APRIL 14 | |
|---|---|
| 1 A&P $ | 5 Kroger $ |
| 2 Foodland $ | 6 Shop'n Save $ |
| 3 Giant Eagle $ | 7 Thorofare $ |
| 4 IGA $ | |
| Other (Write in) | $ |
| | $ |

| Saturday, APRIL 15 | |
|---|---|
| 1 A&P $ | 5 Kroger $ |
| 2 Foodland $ | 6 Shop'n Save $ |
| 3 Giant Eagle $ | 7 Thorofare $ |
| 4 IGA $ | |
| Other (Write in) | $ |
| | $ |
| Sun. APRIL 16 (Write in) | $ |
| | $ |

**AT THE END OF EACH WEEK —**
Write in the dollar value of all the milk, eggs, bread, etc., DELIVERED TO YOUR HOME BY THE MILKMAN, BREADMAN, etc. Do not include this in your diary of daily food purchases.

| DELIVERED | DELIVERED |
|---|---|
| April 3-April 9 $_____ | April 10-April 16 $_____ |

**At the end** of the 2-week period (April 16) fill out this section:

1. Please write in the name and location of the one grocery store or supermarket where you have purchased most of your groceries within the last 2 weeks.
   Store name _____

   • Approximately how far away is this store from your home?
   ☐ Less than 1 mile    ☐ 2-3 miles    ☐ 5-8 miles
   ☐ 1-2 miles    ☐ 3-5 miles    ☐ Over 8 miles

2. Please "X" the most important reasons for shopping there:
   ☐ Neat and orderly    ☐ Many national brands
   ☐ Good quality meat    ☐ Open dating
   ☐ Convenient location    ☐ Unit pricing
   ☐ Open more/longer hours    ☐ Fresh produce
   ☐ Quick check out    ☐ Friendly personnel
   ☐ Good selections    ☐ Low prices
   ☐ Advertised specials available    ☐ Private (Store's own) Brands
   ☐ Other _____

3. Have you changed your favorite (primary) supermarket during the **past 12 months?**    ☐ Yes    ☐ No
   Why? _____

4. Where did you buy most of your meat within the past 2 weeks? _____

5. Which grocery chain would you say has the **best meat?** _____

6. Which grocery chain has the **best produce?** _____

7. "X" grocery stores whose ads you looked at in a Pittsburgh newspaper from April 3 thru April 16
   ☐ A&P    ☐ IGA    ☐ Thorofare   Other Stores:
   ☐ Foodland    ☐ Kroger    ☐ _____
   ☐ Giant Eagle    ☐ Shop 'n Save    ☐ _____

8. Have you purchased any grocery items using a coupon in the past 2 weeks?    1 ☐ Yes    2 ☐ No
   IF YES—"X" the way(s) you obtained these coupons:
   ☐ Clipped from a newspaper    ☐ Through the mail
   ☐ Clipped from a magazine    ☐ Included with or clipped from product package
   ☐ Other _____

9. Did you use a coupon to try a new product in the past 2 weeks?    1 ☐ Yes    2 ☐ No

10. Which grocery chain generally has the best **advertised specials?** _____

11. Which chain generally has the best **newspaper coupons?** _____

12. What influence would you say food ads in newspapers have on **where** you buy?    1 ☐ Considerable    2 ☐ Some    3 ☐ Very Little    4 ☐ None

13. Please "X" the newspapers you read Regularly:
    ☐ Pittsburgh Post-Gazette    ☐ Other(s) _____
    ☐ Evening Pittsburgh Press
    ☐ Sunday Pittsburgh Press    ☐ None

Any comments about grocery shopping? _____

**Figure 10-16.** Example questionnaire used in consumer mail panel survey. (*Source:* Guide-Post Research, Inc., Pittsburgh, Pa.)

alternatives (e.g., cents-off versus three for the price of two) is likely to be more successful as part of a special promotion campaign. In addition, with the opportunity to utilize interval panel capabilities, survey research may be conducted with a ready-made sample, thus avoiding the time and expense of generating a new and unique sample for a single study.

## Advantages and Disadvantages of Panels

Because the same people are reporting over time, it is possible to obtain a more detailed level of information than would otherwise be available. For example, we can identify specific households who have switched from our brand to that of a competitor, thus enabling us to focus more closely on these families and their characteristics. As a result, we may be able to make timely product or promotional changes before our market share suffers major, perhaps irreversible, losses. Having access to panel data from a consistent sample of consumers may also enable us to graphically depict the effect of our marketing efforts over time.

The greater dedication of panel members compared to the general public offers the chance to obtain greater amounts of information than would otherwise be the case. Panel members are generally willing to fill out questionnaires and undergo interviews that are longer and more demanding than those that members of the general public would find acceptable.

Compared to conventional survey research, panel information is likely to be more economical to obtain. Part of the reason for this is the existing nature of the sample, which eliminates the need to generate a one-time-only sample. In addition, the greater response rate means that fewer questionnaires or interviews are necessary for a given level of confidence in the results. Furthermore, the greater level of cooperation on the part of panel members is also likely to provide greater accuracy of results since these individuals are accustomed to recording and submitting purchase information, a habit that facilitates recall of the prices, brands, and behavior associated with their activities in the marketplace.

While interval panels offer many of the advantages of the continuous type generally identified with panel usage, they offer a number of advantages of their own. For example, since members of the interval panel are well known in demographic terms, we can readily identify and sample panel households who possess certain characteristics in which we are interested—for example, those with two or more cars, incomes over $30,000 per year, or who have spent more than $2000 on recreation during the past year. Such narrowing of the total panel to those in whom we are most interested for research purposes helps to reduce the number of extraneous sample members who would otherwise be the object of our postage, telephone, or personal visit expenditures. For example, if our objective is to evaluate the attractiveness of a university brochure to young persons nearing college age, we can easily have the brochure (or its alternative formats) evaluated by a sample (or subsamples) of the panel membership who have household members in the 17- to 18-year-old range.

One of the key problems with panels is the difficulty of maintaining a panel that is representative of the population from which the members are selected. Unfortunately, a substantial proportion of those contacted do not consent to being panel members; others either drop out after a short time or become lax in properly completing materials sent to them. A related difficulty is that panel members (as do the rest of us) tend to age over time, and must periodically be replaced with new (and younger) members in order to maintain a representative demographic profile for the entire panel. The way in which most panel sponsors attempt to maintain this representativeness is to adjust their membership so that important demographic characteristics are comparable between the panel and the general population. However, although panel members may have similar demographics compared to the overall population, the question inevitably arises as to whether the people who elect to participate are different (in non-demographic ways) from those who are not so cooperative.

Another question regarding panels is the possibility that members may gradually change their purchasing behavior because of increased sensitivity brought about by their continual recording of the goods and services they buy. To help alleviate the impact of this possibility, a number of strategies are available, including the more rapid turnover of panel memberships—for example, panel participants may be limited to just one or two years of membership, after which they are replaced.

☐  **SUMMARY**

For some research needs, depth and focus group interviews, projective techniques, and observation may provide a useful alternative to survey research. These approaches are often less direct, less structured, or both. Another alternative is the consumer panel, which can provide information on either an intermittent or a continuing basis.

The depth interview is a setting in which the interviewer, generally a highly trained person with some background in psychology, interacts with an individual and encourages him or her to freely express thoughts relevant to the product or subject of interest. In this approach, the interviewer probes beneath the superficial answers that are often provided by respondents in survey research. The depth interview is often associated with *motivation research*, a family of research methods that gained popularity in the 1950s.

The focus group interview is similar to the depth interview, except that small groups are interviewed instead of one person at a time. The key figure in this approach is the moderator, who must be sensitive to the group members and their feelings and comments, yet direct the group along the intended path of discussion. As with the depth interview, this technique allows probing beyond answers that are either superficial or incomplete. However, it requires less skill on the part of the interviewer, tends to be less expensive, and allows input from a greater number of individuals during a given session.

Projective techniques are derived from the methods of clinical psychology, and rely upon stimulus ambiguity to obtain a more free and open response from the study participant. The more ambiguous the stimulus, the greater the degree to which the respondent must depend on his or her own experiences and beliefs to formulate a response. These techniques often allow the respondent to "indirectly" express his or her views through a third party or by interpreting the behavior of others. As with depth interviews and focus group interviews, projective techniques are especially useful in cases where direct questioning would be likely to result in superficial or biased responses. Among the more popular projective techniques are word association, sentence completion, story completion, cartoon tests, and the Thematic Apperception Test.

Instead of asking people for information, it is sometimes cheaper and more effective to simply observe either their current behavior or the results of past behavior. There are five ways in which observation studies may be classified: (1) whether the observation is made under natural or contrived circumstances, (2) whether the persons being observed are aware of their participation in the research process, (3) whether the observation process is structured or unstructured, (4) whether the behavior is observed as it actually takes place, and (5) whether the observations are made by people or by mechanical devices. UPC (Universal Product Code) symbols provide manufacturer and product information that can be easily observed and recorded through the use of scanner technology. UPC scanning has been joined by the people meter in providing a combination of viewing and purchase data for panel members.

Panels consist of persons, households, or business firms who are typically selected based on a combination of their willingness and their representativeness. Panels may be sponsored by a variety of organizations, including governmental bodies, corporations, research firms, and universities. Panel information allows marketers to measure the effectiveness of various marketing strategies, monitor the success of new products, identify the most promising customers or outlets, and engage in field experimentation to determine the effect of planned or actual changes in the marketing mix.

## ☐ QUESTIONS FOR REVIEW

1. What is the depth interview, and how is it typically performed? What kinds of motivations do you think might be found if this technique were applied to the following consumer products? (Use your imagination.)
   a. Small personal portable stereo cassette players, such as the Sony Walkman.
   b. Video game arcades.
   c. Generic grocery products.
2. Discuss the purposes of a focus group interview and describe how such an interview would be carried out. What are the advantages and disadvantages of this technique compared to the depth interview?
3. What are some of the feelings and motivations that depth interviewers have found to be associated with cigarettes? Can you think of any possibilities in addition to those described in the text?
4. What are some of the difficulties that may be encountered during a focus group interview, and what strategies can the moderator employ to avoid them or minimize their effect?

5. Consumer panel members are selected for their demographic representativeness. However, members may differ from the general population in ways that are not so readily measurable. What social and psychological differences do you think may exist between: (a) persons or households who join a consumer panel and (b) those who turn down the opportunity?

6. What personal or behavioral variables might one be able to observe while watching shoppers in a K-Mart store?

7. Why is it sometimes advantageous to conduct observational research by means of exerting control over the observational setting (i.e., contriving to ensure that the situation you would like to study does, in fact, occur) instead of relying on natural situations to occur on their own?

8. Using the methodology of the classic Mason Haire instant coffee study, set up a research plan that would measure consumer perceptions of cigar smokers.

9. How might you use photographs of four male models clipped from magazine ads to measure the image of four different drinking, eating, or other retail establishments near your campus?

10. Although word association could be attempted in a mail questionnaire, it would probably not prove to be successful in this application. Why?

11. Projective techniques are often used to uncover the consumer's true feelings or perceptions. Using any product or brand of your choice, provide three examples of projective techniques that could be used to conduct research on that product or brand. Identify by name each technique you've included, and utilize the actual words or sketches you might use in carrying out the research.

12. Using the story-completion technique, formulate a short story beginning designed to measure consumer perceptions of door-to-door pollsters.

13. What are some of the commonly used mechanical and/or electronic observational devices and what advantages and disadvantages do they have compared to human observation?

14. How might one go about setting up an observational study to determine the incidence of car-pooling among faculty versus commuter students at your college or university?

15. What is the difference between direct and indirect observation? How could one employ indirect observation in identifying the relative popularity of various cigarette brands among spectators at a college football game?

# 11

# EXPERIMENTATION

**Experiment Supports Camping Trailer Efficiency**

In the early 1980s, The Coleman Company, Inc. was concerned that people might cut back on buying and vacationing in camping trailers because they thought the trailers used up too much fuel to pull. Coleman's Camping Trailer Division arranged for the author to conduct an on-the-road experiment to measure how much fuel the campers really used.

Using a sedan and a station wagon, the kinds of cars in which a family might vacation, this independent tester compared the fuel consumption of the vehicles with and without various Coleman campers attached behind. In addition, the Coleman Versatrailer, a small utility trailer, was compared with a typical rooftop carrier. For measurement accuracy, each towing vehicle was instrumented to measure every one-hundredth of a gallon of fuel consumed during the tests.

In highway tests involving the vehicles themselves, plus different configurations of vehicle and trailer, it was found that pulling a Coleman camper really didn't use much extra fuel: depending on the combination, the rate was just 0.82 to 1.38 extra gallons per 100 miles. Coleman proceeded to promote this efficiency with brochures like the one shown in Figure 11-1.

A bonus to the efficiency experiments was the finding that pulling the utility-minded Coleman Versatrailer used only 0.47 extra gallon per 100 miles,

*Source:* The Coleman Company, Camping Trailer Division, Somerset, Pa.

**Figure 11-1.** Using experimentation techniques, The Coleman Company found that pulling their fold-down campers required extra fuel at a rate of just 0.82 to 1.38 gallons of fuel per 100 miles. The Camping Trailer Division used these findings in promoting the efficiency of their products in brochures like this one. (Courtesy of The Coleman Company, Camping Trailer Division.)

while a lightweight rooftop carrier with much less capacity required more than twice as much fuel, 0.96 gallon per 100 miles. Coleman made use of this information as well, conducting a media blitz of Versatrailer press releases published in newspapers across the United States.

## INTRODUCTION

After carefully sampling wines from two different bottles, 60 of 100 tasters selected one of the two wines as crisper, smoother to the palate, and generally better tasting. What was the secret of this fine wine which was preferred by such a margin? Was it made from an especially exquisite grape? Was it served at a more tasty temperature? Was it an expensive "ringer" from France? No, none of these explains the preferred wine's margin of victory. In fact, the wines in the two bottles were *identical*, and only the labels on the bottles were different (see Figure 11-2).

**Figure 11-2.**   A dramatization based on wine taste test described in text. Results showed that new label design improved taste of the wine.

The purpose of this test was to evaluate the effect of a newly designed label described by the marketing vice president of the winery as having a lighter yellow color for "understated elegance," a redesigned drawing of the winery to look "more Jeffersonian," and the vintage year moved to a spot near the name of the wine variety, "the classic place for a wine year."[1]

In this study, the purpose was to determine causation—that is, does (did) X cause Y?—and the question was "Does the new label improve the perceived taste of the wine?" The apparent answer was "yes." *Experimentation*, the identification of cause–effect relationships between variables, is the primary choice of researchers involved with causal studies. To make decisions regarding products, advertising, pricing, and distribution, marketers often rely on experiments to determine the effect a particular strategy is likely to have on variables such

---

[1] "Wine Tasters Prefer New Label," *Indiana Evening Gazette*, September 24, 1981, p. 9.

as sales, market share, attitudes and more. The following examples all involve the cause–effect relationship central to experimentation:

- In a direct-mail test, responses were 15% higher when the envelope contained a self-adhesive token to be placed on the order form within.[2]
- In the face of increased customer resistance to software copy protection, a software marketer introduced a protected and an unprotected version of the same product. Although the unprotected software was priced $30 higher, it outsold the protected version by 5 to 1.[3]
- Mensa, a group for those with IQs in the upper 2%, uses IQ quizzes in mass-market publications to attract new members. In one instance, the organization received 75,000 inquiries following the appearance of an IQ quiz in *Reader's Digest*.[4]
- In a test of in-store broadcast commercials describing Sealtest as having "that ice cream parlor taste," sales rose 7.2% in Buffalo, New York, stores carrying the broadcast. In control stores without the broadcast, sales rose only 1.5%.[5]

In this chapter we'll examine the terminology and basic principles of experimentation, the notion of validity as it applies to experiments, and the strategies involved in setting up a number of popular experimental designs. In addition, we'll discuss popular approaches to the test marketing of new products or marketing strategies. Our exploration of experimentation in marketing will take us through the following sections:

---

[2] "Mail Order Response . . . ," *Collegiate Edition, Marketing News*, October 1986, p. 2, published by the American Marketing Association.

[3] Paul B. Carroll, "On Your Honor: Software Firms Remove Copy-Protection Devices," *The Wall Street Journal*, September 25, 1986, p. 37.

[4] Roy R. Bumsted, "How to Measure Effectiveness of PR Campaign," *Marketing News*, March 18, 1983, p. 13, published by the American Marketing Association.

[5] Ronald Alsop, "Companies Cram Ads in Stores to Sway Shopping Decisions," *The Wall Street Journal*, August 22, 1985, p. 23.

## EXPERIMENT TERMINOLOGY

At this point, let's prepare for the discussion to follow by taking a look at some of the key terms and symbols used in describing experiments. For the purpose of clarification, we'll assume that we're conducting this relatively simple experiment:

1. Using the Likert summated scale to measure the attitudes of a sample of consumers toward mobile home living
2. Showing the sample members a film that highlights the advantages of mobile home living
3. Using the same Likert instrument and the same sample of consumers, remeasuring their attitudes toward mobile home living

*Experiment.* An experiment is a research technique in which we control or manipulate one or more independent variables and determine the effect of such manipulation(s) on the dependent variable.

*Independent variable, or experimental treatment.* The independent variable is the variable the effect of which we're trying to determine. There may be one or more independent variables introduced or manipulated by the researcher. In the preceding experiment, the independent variable is the film on the advantages of mobile home living. Other examples of independent variables in marketing experiments could include price changes, product variations, alternative advertisements, or adjustments in the channel of distribution.

*Dependent variable, or measurement.* The dependent variable is the variable we expect may be influenced by the independent variable. In the mobile home experiment, the Likert scale measurement of attitude is the dependent variable that could be altered by the ad program. Other marketing examples of dependent variables could include sales, market share, brand preference, or

---

### EXHIBIT 11-1

#### Phone Poles Support State Law

Since the enactment of Pennsylvania's 1983 law ordering jail sentences for convicted drunk drivers, Duquesne Light Company reports that 30% fewer utility poles have been damaged in traffic accidents. According to company spokesperson Jean Grogan, "It may just be a coincidence, but before '83, we averaged 1000 broken poles a year. After that, it dropped to about 700 a year." She goes on to explain, "Most of the accidents involving our poles occur between 1 and 4 A.M., which is about the time when most bars are closing and the people are going home."

*Source:* "New Drunken Driving Law May Be Best News for Poles Since Creosote," *Pittsburgh Post-Gazette*, July 18, 1986, p. 8.

observed behavior in the marketplace. Measurements may take place at various times during the course of the experiment, but are typically made before and after the experimental treatment is applied—that is, there may be both *pre-* and *post-*measures of the dependent variable.

*Extraneous variables.* Extraneous variables are those that tend to confuse the issue—that is, they may influence the value of the dependent variable, but they lie beyond either our awareness or our control. In the preceding experiment, an extraneous variable might be a newspaper story about a mobile home fire. Much of the strategy involved in setting up an experimental design is concerned with eliminating or compensating for the effect of extraneous variables.

*Test units.* Test units are the entities to which the treatments are administered, and from which we make the measurements describing the effect the independent variable has had on the dependent variable. In the mobile home experiment, the test units could be members of a consumer sample selected to view the mobile home film. While test units are often people, they may also be physical entities such as stores or sales regions. When an experimental design involves more than one group, test units may be allocated to *experimental* and *control* groups.

*Experimental group.* Members of the experimental group are exposed to the treatment. In the experiment described above, we have just one experimental group. In experiments with multiple treatments, there will be multiple experimental groups, with each group receiving one treatment or combination of treatments.

*Control group.* In order to better determine the effect of the treatment, it helps to have a control group to whom you do absolutely nothing at all—that is, for this group, it's business as usual. Examples of control groups in your health books were the withered chickens who didn't get vitamin D, the toothless kids who brushed without the stannous fluoride additive, or the scurvy-ridden sailors who didn't receive their daily ration of citrus fruit. In marketing experiments, the control group typically receives the existing product design or the current advertising theme—that is, the standard fare from your present marketing mix menu.

Having examined the terminology of experimentation, let's proceed to summarize the popular symbols used to convert an experimental design into a shorthand description:

- $X$: The independent variable, or treatment. If multiple treatments are present, they are presented as $X_1$, $X_2$, and so on.
- $O$: An observation or measurement of the dependent variable, either before or after the treatment has been administered. As with $X$, this may also have subscripts when more than one is present.

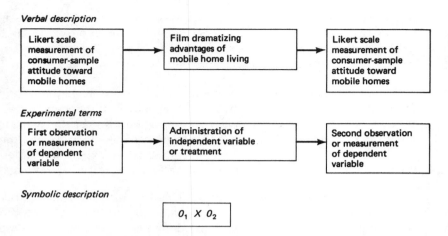

**Figure 11-3.** Summary of terms and symbols of mobile home experiment described in text.

    *R*:   Indicates *randomization*, or the random assignment of test units to experimental and control groups.

    Figure 11-3 illustrates the terms and symbols as they apply to the mobile home experiment described at the beginning of the section. Note that the time order of occurrence of events is from left to right—that is, symbols at the left represent activities that occur first.

## VALIDITY IN EXPERIMENTATION

    Now that we've covered the anatomy of an experiment, let's consider the critical bottom-line question associated with any experimental study: *Are the results valid?* There are two forms of validity to consider, internal and external, and each type can be described in the form of a question:

    *Internal validity.*   Did *X* really make the difference? Or might some other factor have been responsible for the effect we measured on the dependent variable?

    *External validity.*   So what if *X* did make the difference? To what extent can the results of the experiment be generalized?

### Internal Validity

*Internal validity* basically is concerned with alternative explanations for the experimental findings—that is, Did *X* really make the difference? Without internal validity, an experiment is virtually useless, because it has not succeeded in its goal of providing information of a cause–effect nature for the independent and dependent variables examined. This component of experimental validity faces a number of major threats, each of which is discussed in the following section.[6]

## Threats to Internal Validity

### History

*History* errors are the result of outside events that occur between the pre-measurement and the post-measurement and have an effect on the dependent variable. For example, in our mobile home experiment, a newspaper story about mobile homes being blown over by a tornado might cause the respondents to have a lesser opinion of mobile homes during the post-measurement than they had at the beginning of the experiment. An important thing to note here is that *history* is not used in the usual sense—that is, it does not refer to past events that have occurred prior to the experiment, but rather to events that occur during the experiment. The greater the time duration of an experiment, the more likely it will be for history to have an adverse effect on internal validity.

For marketing experiments, this internal validity factor is typically represented by such outside events as competitor price changes, favorable or adverse publicity in news media, governmental actions, labor difficulties, and numerous other possibilities. History is an ever-present threat that can manifest itself in many different ways.

### Maturation

As with history, **maturation** occurs between pre- and post-measures in an experiment. Unlike history, however, **maturation** refers to *changes within the test units* during this time. For example, in a mobile home film experiment, the pre-measurement may have been taken at 8:00 A.M. and the post-measurement at 5:00 P.M. During the interim, members of the consumer sample have put in a full day's work and could be somewhat fatigued. Thus, during the post-measurement, they may not feel very favorable toward *anything*, let alone mobile homes. When the test units in an experiment are people, maturation effects can appear in a variety of forms—for example, fatigue, impatience, being hungry, having just eaten. In longer-term experiments, subjects can also become more financially secure and more socially aware in addition to simply growing older.

### Testing

*Testing* is an internal validity factor concerned with the possible effects of a measurement taken prior to the experimental treatment. Results can be affected in two ways: (1) by the main testing effect, or (2) by the interactive testing effect.

---

[6] The discussion that follows relies heavily on the presentation of this material in Donald T. Campbell and Julian C. Stanley, *Experimental and Quasi-Experimental Designs for Research* (Skokie, Ill.: Rand McNally & Company, 1966). Copyright, Houghton-Mifflin Company.

---

### EXHIBIT 11-2
#### The Procrastinated Post-Measure

A marketer in one of the nation's foremost high-tech companies set out to measure the effectiveness of an advertisement promoting the company's corporate image among electrical engineers. Unfortunately, his good intentions were not accompanied by equally sound methodology.

In its pre-measurement, the company sent 10,000 questionnaires to subscribers of a widely read engineering magazine. Following this, the company ran the ad in a single issue of the publication. The post-measurement involved mailing 10,000 more questionnaires to another sample of subscribers—*12 months later!*

*Source:* Robert S. Lee, "Students Should Not Learn How to Do Research," *Marketing News*, July 18, 1986, p. 36, published by the American Marketing Association.

---

*The main testing effect.* The effect of $O_1$ on $O_2$, or the influence a measurement itself can have on subsequent measurements, is called the *main testing effect*. For example, consider the following hypothetical experiment:

$O_1$:   Before their monthly meeting, members of a PTA organization are asked, "Have you ever heard of IVY brand panty hose?" Result: 15% say yes.

$X$:   During the evening, a fashion film is shown in which one of the actresses happens to mention that her IVY brand panty hose never itch.

$O_2$:   At the end of the evening, members are again asked, "Have you ever heard of IVY brand panty hose?" Result: 95% say yes.

Although the purpose of the experiment was to determine the extent to which the film increased viewers' awareness of IVY, the pre-measurement alone virtually assured that everyone would be aware of the brand. Hence the improvement from 15% to 95% was probably due mostly to the pre-measurement rather than the incident during the film. In our mobile home experiment, the main testing effect could be present by virtue of respondents trying to fill out the post-measurement questionnaire by selecting the same answers they provided on the pre-measurement sheet. Such desire for consistency would tend to dampen the measured effect of the film, causing us to underestimate its impact.

*The interactive testing effect.* Any interaction between the pre-measurement process and the subjects' reactions to the experimental treatment may produce an *interactive testing effect*. For example, in our mobile home experiment, consider the possibility that (1) many sample members had little previous knowledge or experience with regard to mobile homes, (2) the pre-measurement experience awakened their curiosity to learn more about mobile homes, and (3) because of this aroused curiosity, they became intensely receptive to the positive facts and suggestions contained in the film. The result would be a measure of attitude improvement beyond that which could have been caused by the film alone. Internal validity would suffer because the improvement was caused by the film *plus* the "priming" of the pre-measurement. External validity would also suffer—that is, the sponsors of the film could not realistically expect the program to cause the same degree of attitude improvement if shown in a normal setting to the population from which the consumer sample was chosen.

### Statistical Regression

The **statistical regression** effect is a potential danger when members of a group have been selected for their extreme scores on some variable. As background, consider that a baseball player who is batting 1.000 will eventually make an out, and that a player currently batting 0.000 will eventually get a hit. In other words, the lofty can only move down, and those at the bottom have nowhere to go but up. Consider the following hypothetical situation:

A researcher selects the ten students who scored lowest on their mathematical achievement tests at the beginning of the school year:

$O_1$: Their average score on the test was 19% correct.

$X$: Each student receives a complimentary copy of the booklet, "Everything You Always Wanted to Know about Math Tests but Were Afraid to Ask."

$O_2$: Their average score at the end of the school year is 45% correct.

While part of the improvement can be attributed to retaking the same test, and part may be the result of the booklet's advice, it is also likely that some of the more random reasons for their poor showing on the first exam may not have been present for the second exam. For example, during the first exam three of the ten may have had head colds and been groggy from medication, four of the ten may have been sitting near the window and were distracted by cheerleader tryouts, and the other three may have just had a particularly bad day. Salespersons, teachers, students and brain surgeons all have good days and bad—this is a statistical fact of life. However, when we purposely select a group comprised of those at an extreme position, we are inviting the statistical regression effect.

### Instrumentation

The **instrumentation** effect refers to changes in the measuring instrument or process between $O_1$ and $O_2$. As a dramatization of this effect, consider the following experiment of the $O_1$ $X$ $O_2$ type:

$O_1$: A grandmotherly older woman politely stops college students on the street and asks, "What is your favorite magazine?" Result: 5% say "*Playboy*."

    $X$:    An advertisement for *Playboy* magazine appears in next issue of the school newspaper.

    $O_2$:    An attractive young lady stops college students on the street and asks same question. Result: 45% say *"Playboy."*

When approached by the first interviewer and her "grandmother" image, even the avid *Playboy* reader would be likely to respond with *"Reader's Digest"* or *"Christian Science Monitor."* While an extreme example of how different interviewers can influence the data they receive, this situation points out a question that exists whenever multiple measurements are made: Is $O_1$ comparable to $O_2$? Instrumentation can be a problem whenever the initial measurement method differs in any way from that of the follow-up (e.g., an initial measure by mail questionnaire and a post-measure by telephone interview).

### Mortality

Whenever people (or other test units) drop out of the experiment, the **mortality** factor should be suspected. In a single group, those who drop out may not be the same as those who choose to continue. In a multiple-group experiment, persons dropping out of one group may be different from those who have dropped out of others. If a treatment involves a substantial amount of time for the subject, dropouts from the experimental group are likely to exceed those from the control group. As a result, the experimental group—now consisting of people who may be more interested or who have more free time— may contain subjects who are different in many ways from those in the control group. In our mobile home experiment, it is possible that dropouts may have been those who had very unfavorable attitudes toward mobile homes and lost interest after viewing the highly positive film on mobile home living. The result of this situation would be an unrealistically high "attitude improvement" potential being credited to the film since $O_1$ would reflect the attitudes of the entire sample, while $O_2$ would reflect the attitudes of only those who remained.

### Selection Bias

The **selection bias** effect refers to assignments to experimental and control groups such that the test units are likely (1) to differ initially with respect to the dependent variable being measured, or (2) to differ in terms of the way in which they will respond to the independent variable being administered. Allowing individuals to select their own group will tend to result in this type of bias. For example, because control group membership typically involves less time and commitment, persons choosing this group might be younger, more occupied with business or personal pursuits, and less interested in the subject matter of the experiment.

Selection bias can best be prevented by randomly assigning matched sets of subjects to groups following pre-measurements on the dependent variable or on variables likely to be related to the dependent variable (e.g., age, sex, income, or education). Known as *matching*, this technique ensures better comparability between groups than would be possible with simple random assignment alone.

### Summary of Threats to Internal Validity

*History:*  The effect of outside events that occur between $O_1$ and $O_2$.

*Maturation:*  The effect of changes within the test units between $O_1$ and $O_2$.

*Testing:*  The main testing effect is the effect of $O_1$ on $O_2$. The interactive testing effect is the effect of interaction between $O_1$ and test units' reactions to experimental treatment, $X$.

*Statistical regression:*  The tendency for groups initially chosen because of their extremely high or low scores on a variable to gravitate toward the mean.

*Instrumentation:*  Changes in the measuring instrument or process between $O_1$ and $O_2$.

*Mortality:*  The effect of test units dropping out of the experiment and changing the composition of the experimental and control groups.

*Selection bias:*  Assignment of subjects to experimental and control groups such that test units (1) are initially different on the dependent variable being measured, or (2) differ in terms of their responsiveness to the experimental treatment, $X$.

## External Validity

While internal validity is concerned with whether or not it was really the experimental treatment, $X$, that made the difference in the measurements observed, *external validity* focuses on the extent to which the results of the experiment can be generalized to the real world. Can we be confident that the film which improved consumers' attitudes toward mobile homes in an experimental setting will work the same magic if distributed to PTA groups, fraternal organizations, schools, and universities?

Much of the difficulty in generalizing to the real world is created by the very control that must be exerted during the experiment to avoid the internal validity problems just discussed. When the experimental treatment makes the transition to the real world, consumers will not be selected, assigned to groups, and measured one or more times as were the subjects of the experiment. In general, external validity problems in experimentation are of two types: (1) interaction between $X$ and other aspects of the experiment, and (2) the artificial nature of the experimental setting.

As noted in the preceding section, interaction between the experimental

---

**EXHIBIT 11-3**

**Was Age a Factor?**

In reporting on a study examining the impact of fried food consumption on health, a newspaper article described how researchers measured the dietary habits of 422,094 men over a three-year period. Within this large group, some individuals were heavy consumers of fried foods, others ate none at all.

For those accustomed to warnings that fried foods might not be healthful, the results were surprising: Among those who ate fried foods more than 15 times a week, the death rate during the study period was 702 per 100,000 man-years. For those who ate *no fried foods at all*, the death rate was over 72% higher, 1208 deaths per 100,000 man-years. The article did not mention the relative ages of the individuals in the two groups.

See Betty Fier, "Science Finds Fried Foods Not Harmful," *Moneysworth*, November 24, 1975, p. 1.

---

treatment and pre-measurement (the interactive testing effect) can cause members of the experimental group to have an increased or decreased sensitivity to the treatment, thus making the experimental results different from what would occur in the real world. Other interactions involving the experimental treatment, $X$, could include interaction between subject selection and $X$ (persons more interested in the subject or the experimental treatment might volunteer).

The artificiality of many experimental settings adds yet another external validity question mark. In order to control for the many outside variables that could confound their results, researchers may have to set up their experiments in an artificial environment (e.g., conducting coffee taste tests in the firm's research laboratory or some other setting in which subjects are not accustomed to drinking coffee). The artificiality of the environment and the subjects' awareness of taking part in an experiment can combine to produce relationships that do not carry over to the real world. A classic experiment of the 1920s produced what has since been called the "Hawthorne effect." In this experiment, researchers attempted to discover the effect of different working conditions on productivity. However, regardless of the combination of working conditions tested, productivity still increased—largely because of the presence of the experiment itself and the resultant attention paid to the workers.

## LABORATORY VERSUS FIELD EXPERIMENTS

There are two kinds of settings in which marketing research experiments can be conducted: laboratory and field. In the *laboratory experiment*, the treatment is administered to the test units, typically consumers, in an artificial setting that has been contrived for the purpose of the experiment. The artificiality of the

**TABLE 11-1.** *Laboratory and field experiments tend to have opposite strengths and weaknesses with regard to internal and external validity.*

| | Experiment type | |
|---|---|---|
| | Laboratory | Field |
| Internal validity (control over outside variables) | Stronger | Weaker |
| External validity (ability to generalize results) | Weaker | Stronger |

setting helps the researcher to avoid or control for the unwanted effects of outside variables. In the *field experiment*, the test units are allowed to function in a more natural setting, such as their home or supermarket. As a result, consumers are less likely to react to the experimental situation itself (they may not even be aware that they're participating in an experiment), but control of outside variables may be diminished.

In general, the laboratory experiment will tend to have strong internal validity because of the control exerted over potentially confounding outside variables. However, the artificiality of the setting weakens the generalizability of results to real-world situations, causing external validity to be relatively weak. In contrast, the strengths and weaknesses of the field experiment are the exact opposite: Its natural setting lends itself to the generalization of results, while at the same time it allows outside variables to have a greater amount of influence. (See Table 11-1.)

Regarding other considerations, the laboratory experiment is less expensive and requires less time than the field experiment, though these advantages may not be worth the sacrifice in external validity. In selecting between laboratory and field experiments, the researcher must weigh their relative advantages for the situation at hand.

## PREEXPERIMENTAL DESIGNS

As a first step in examining the details of actual experimental designs, we'll take a look at several designs of the *preexperimental* type. These are so named because they afford the researcher very little control over the experimental situation. To make a long story short, the various threats to internal validity have a veritable field day, making the results of such experiments highly suspect. These designs are presented in the hope that, as a researcher, you will make minimal use of them, and that, as a consumer of research information, you will be rightfully suspicious when someone attempts to "sell" you the results of such experimental studies.

### After-Only Approach

The term *experimental design* is applied to the *after-only* approach primarily as a charitable gesture. However, it is an approach that is often used by those who are not highly concerned with the scientific strength of their results and who care relatively little about internal and external validity. Symbolically, this design can be described as:

$$X\ O$$

where

$X$ = experimental treatment
$O$ = follow-up observation or measurement

In this kind of experiment, a group is exposed to an experimental treatment, then measured with regard to some dependent variable of interest. Members of the experimental group are either self-selected or chosen by the researcher. Since the idea for an "experiment" may come up only *after* a group has already received some treatment, this design is sometimes called a *one-shot case study* or an *ex post facto* (after the fact) study. As an example of this approach, consider the following situation:

A researcher has surveyed 25 students who have had summer working internships with the Rustmaster Steel Corporation. Of the 25 students, 15 said yes when asked, "Would you consider a marketing career with Rustmaster Steel?" Thus, the symbolic description would be:

Can the researcher assume that $X$ (having an internship) tended to cause $O$ (considering Rustmaster for one's career)? Not necessarily—perhaps students selected Rustmaster because they already had a high opinion of the company. On the basis of the follow-up measurement alone, we simply can't tell whether the internship experience increased or decreased the attractiveness of this company as a potential employer.

### Before-After Approach

The *before-after* design overcomes some of the difficulties of the after-only design by including a pre-measurement of the dependent variable. Symbolically, this design can be described as

$$O_1\ X\ O_2$$

where

$$X = \text{experimental treatment}$$
$$O_1 = \text{pre-measurement}$$
$$O_2 = \text{post-measurement}$$
$$\text{Effect of treatment} = O_2 - O_1$$

This design is an improvement over the after-only approach because of the existence of a pre-measurement to help isolate the effect of the experimental treatment. Figure 11-4 shows a pre-measurement in process, with odor judges at a research facility judging the natural scent of paid volunteers prior to the application of the experimental treatment, a deodorant being evaluated. (In preparation for the pre-test, subjects use no deodorant and only nonfragrance soap for two weeks.)

Assuming that nothing else is responsible, the effect of the treatment in the before–after method is the difference between the post-measurement and the pre-measurement. However, in many cases, there *will* be something else at least partially responsible for the difference observed, especially if there is a long time duration between pre- and post-measures. Because there is no control group, it is hard to differentiate between the impact of the treatment and the effect of various internal validity factors.

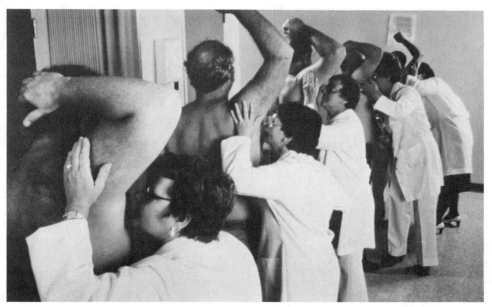

(LOUIS PSIHOYOS NY)

**Figure 11-4.** Without a pre-measurement, it's difficult to identify the effect of the experimental treatment. At this Cincinnati research facility, each subject's natural body scent is being judged prior to testing of a deodorant formulation.

As an example, let's consider the 1974 versus 1984 smoking habits of male smokers in Norway, a nation that banned all tobacco advertising in 1975:

| 1974: | 1975: | 1984: |
|---|---|---|
| 53.0% smoked daily | all tobacco ads banned | 41.6% smoked daily |

Can we conclude that the advertising ban caused this reduction in smoking? Not necessarily. For example, there had already been a downward trend evident before 1975. Also, the history effect may have played a role. As observed by the information director of the Norway National Council on Smoking and Health: "Our general impression is that the ad ban has played an important part in holding down tobacco consumption. . . . But it is impossible to single out the ad ban as the major cause since it was taken in connection with an intensive educational campaign and increased media attention to the hazards of smoking."[7]

Despite its weaknesses, this approach is popular with marketing decision makers who are typically involved with making what appear to be sound changes in their marketing mix, then observing whether a product's performance becomes better or worse as a result. To this extent, judgment is necessary in order to reject, with any degree of confidence, the possibility that outside variables are responsible for the difference in performance that has been observed. However, as with the after-only approach, this design is a favorite of those who would have you accept false or deceptive research results. Toward your improvement as an intelligent consumer of such results, the "fractured findings" in Figure 11-5 are presented.

## Static-Group Comparison

In the *static-group comparison* design, we have a control group in addition to the experimental group, but individuals are not randomly assigned to their groups. Symbolically, this design can be described as

$$\text{Experimental group: } X\ O_1$$
$$\overline{\phantom{------}}$$
$$\text{Control group: }\quad O_2$$

where

$X$ = treatment
$O_1$ = post-measurement of experimental group
$O_2$ = post-measurement of control group (------ indicates that subjects were not randomly assigned to groups)
Effect of treatment = $O_1 - O_2$

---

[7] Jack Burton, "Norway Up in Smoke," *Advertising Age*, April 14, 1986, p. 82. Copyright Crain Communications, Inc. All rights reserved. Reprinted with permission.

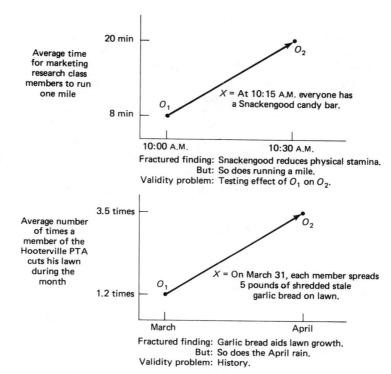

Fractured finding: Snackengood reduces physical stamina.
But: So does running a mile.
Validity problem: Testing effect of $O_1$ on $O_2$.

Fractured finding: Garlic bread aids lawn growth.
But: So does the April rain.
Validity problem: History.

**Figure 11-5.** These "fractured findings" illustrate the kind of internal validity problems with which the $O_1XO_2$ design is infested. While these errors are easy to spot, purveyors of false or deceptive research may someday rely on this design in an attempt to "sell" you findings containing errors that may not be quite so obvious.

A major problem with this design can be the self-selection of subjects into the two groups. For example, in a study of smoking habits and life span, a team of researchers found that age at death (the dependent variable) was an average of 75 years for nonsmokers, 65 for cigarette smokers, and 76 for pipe smokers.[8] Smoking habits were determined from interviews with relatives of the male subjects, and this portion of the study could be summarized as:

| | | |
|---|---|---|
| Experimental: | $X_1$ | $O_1$ |
| | (cigarette smoker) | (average age at death = 65) |
| Experimental: | $X_2$ | $O_2$ |
| | (pipe smoker) | (average age at death = 76) |
| Control: | | $O_3$ |
| | (nonsmoker) | (average age at death = 75) |

---

[8] "Smoking Study Debunks Theory Women Live Longer," *Pittsburgh Press*, October 12, 1975, p. 1.

While this three-group comparison provides no surprising results with regard to cigarette smokers versus nonsmokers, the finding that pipe smokers lived an average of one year longer than nonsmokers is initially puzzling. However, when one remembers that subjects chose their own groups, and that the type of person who smokes a pipe is generally a slower-paced, more relaxed, reflective individual, this person would probably have lived just as long if he chewed on a soda-pop straw instead of smoking a pipe. In addition, the person who smokes excessively is likely to mistreat his or her body in other ways, such as drinking, working, or doing anything else to excess. Although the tobacco effect is probably, if anything, detrimental to longevity, it seems that these age-at-death measurements were also a function of total personalities and life-styles that happened to include cigarette smoking, pipe smoking, or nonsmoking.

## TRUE EXPERIMENTAL DESIGNS

The main problem with the preceding designs was that the researcher could not be confident that the groups were actually comparable. Even when "matching" members to the groups, the researcher could not be sure that he or she had included all of the relevant variables that might contribute to successful matching. The designs in this section are said to be "true" experiments because of *randomization*, the random assignment of test units to the experimental and control groups.

### Before-After with Control Groups

A somewhat classical experimental design, the *before–after with control group* approach involves both experimental and control groups, with test units randomly assigned to each. Symbolically, it can be described as

$$\text{Experimental: } R \; O_1 \; X \; O_2$$
$$\text{Control: } R \; O_3 \;\;\; O_4$$
$$R = \text{random assignment of test units to groups}$$
$$\text{Effect of treatment} = (O_2 - O_1) - (O_4 - O_3)$$

With the use of two groups comprised of randomly assigned persons, it is assumed that history, maturation, testing, and instrumentation will have equal effects on the two groups, with regression having been eliminated entirely because of the randomization process. While these factors are largely taken care of, mortality could still be a problem, especially if the experimental treatment is demanding in terms of the subjects' time or energy. Similarly, the interactive testing effect (interaction between testing and the experimental treatment) could remain a problem, since only the experimental group is both pre-measured *and* subjected to the treatment. Figure 11-6 summarizes the results of a three-group experiment that examined the effectiveness of alternative educational programs in improving driver performance in the laboratory and on the road.

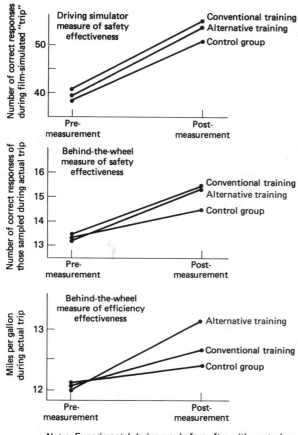

*Note*: Experimental design was before-after with control group:

       R O X₁ O
       R O X₂ O
       R O     O
where $X_1$ = conventional training program
     $X_2$ = alternative training program,
           including fuel efficiency segment.

**Figure 11-6.** In an experimental study, the author compared the effectiveness of two different versions of a popular driver improvement program.

## After-Only with Control Group

The *after-only with control group* design involves two groups, with random assignment to each, and requires that members of each group be measured only once. It can be symbolically represented as

$$\text{Experimental: } R \; X \; O_1$$
$$\text{Control: } R \quad\;\; O_2$$
$$\text{Effect of treatment} = O_1 - O_2$$

In applying this design to our mobile home film experiment, we would randomly assign individuals to the two groups,[9] then measure both groups after the experimental group had been exposed to the film. The effect of the film would then be the difference between the average attitude score of the experimental group and that of the control group.

Because there is no pre-measurement, there can be no interaction between pre-measurement and the experimental treatment. In addition, mortality is now less troublesome, since each group is measured only one time, which reduces the experimental group's number of responsibilities from three to just two ($X$ and $O_1$). Compared to the pre- and post-measurement approach, this design will tend to be both less expensive and less time consuming, and should be preferred whenever it is likely that the groups are not very much different on their initial values for the dependent variable.

### Solomon Four-Group Approach

The *Solomon four-group design* is probably the superstar of the true experimental designs discussed here. However, for most practical applications, using it instead of one of the others is something like renting a Rolls Royce to go camping. Symbolically, it is just a combination of the two preceding approaches:

$$\text{Experimental group 1: } R\ O_1\ X\ O_2$$
$$\text{Control group 1: } R\ O_3\ \quad O_4$$
$$\text{Experimental group 2: } R\ \quad X\ O_5$$
$$\text{Control group 2: } R\ \quad\quad O_6$$

Because of its expense and complexity, it is very rarely used in marketing research. For those who care, it is capable of isolating the effect of various internal validity variables—however, for most practitioners it is more important to control for these effects than to undertake the esoteric exercise of quantifying them.

## QUASI-EXPERIMENTAL DESIGNS

Thus far, we have examined the two extremes of experimental designs: (1) the preexperiments, which are the simplest to conduct, but horrendous in their susceptibility to the various threats to validity, and (2) the true experiments, which are very strong in terms of validity, but not always very practical to conduct in the real world of marketing and consumers. In this section, we'll discuss a number of designs that fall between these extremes. In the so-called *quasi-experiments*, we are not able to randomly assign test units to the exper-

---

[9] While randomization does *tend* to make the groups equal initially (i.e., if pre-measures *were* taken, one would expect the scores to be very similar), small sample sizes may lead to one group being higher or lower than the other by *chance alone*. If this is suspected as a problem, one should either increase the sample sizes, employ matching plus randomization, or switch to the pre- and post-measurement approach. However, before switching, be sure to consider that such a change may reintroduce the problem of interaction between pre-measurement and the experimental treatment.

imental and control groups, nor is it always possible to decide who gets the experimental treatment and when. However, we do have control over when and whom we measure. In essence, the quasi-experiment represents simply doing the best we can with what we've got available. The following designs are a few of the most popular quasi-experimental types.

### Time-Series Design

The *time-series design* involves a series of observations or measurements both before and after the experimental treatment, and can be symbolically represented as

$$O_1 \ O_2 \ O_3 \ O_4 \ X \ O_5 \ O_6 \ O_7 \ O_8$$

In this design, the treatment may either be introduced or allowed to occur naturally. The key is the series of pre- and post-measurements. The observations themselves can represent (1) separate samples from the population of interest, or (2) data from a single sample over time. The latter type is typical of consumer panel information or scanning data from a sample of retailers, such as undertaken by A.C. Nielsen's Scantrack service. Figure 11-7 is a time-series Scantrack view showing the impact of Thanksgiving on weekly sales of several food items popular during this seasonal event. All four of the product categories show a substantial increase from the base index of 100, then drop rapidly following the holiday.[10]

When Coca-Cola introduced New Coke in 1985, the new product was met with anger and controversy. However, as shown in Figure 11-8, the introduction also appeared to spark a greater awareness of Coke advertising. In addition, the figure reflects the increased awareness of Pepsi ads brought about by commercials featuring singer Lionel Richie, an increase that was short-lived following Coca-Cola's action.[11]

U.S. Presidents routinely have their approval ratings monitored over time to evaluate the success or failure of public statements, actions, or appearances. In 1981, President Ronald Reagan's approval rating peaked at 70% as the public rallied around him following the unsuccessful attempt on his life.[12]

Figure 11-9 shows some possible outcomes of a time-series experiment for evaluating the effect of a sales promotion event. Curves A and D indicate a short-term positive effect, while B reflects a short-term negative influence. Curves C and E suggest that the event had no sales effect at all, while F reflects what seems to be a longer-term positive result.

---

[10] "Management with the Nielsen Retail Index System," brochure published by A.C. Nielsen Company, p. 26.

[11] Scott Hume, "Marketers Find Bad News Does Some Good," *Advertising Age*, July 22, 1985, p. 6. Copyright Crain Communications, Inc. All rights reserved. Reprinted with permission.

[12] See Sally J. Suddock, "Following Dittman's Survey Success in Alaska," *Advertising Age*, November 14, 1985, p. 35. Copyright Crain Communications, Inc. All rights reserved. Reprinted with permission.

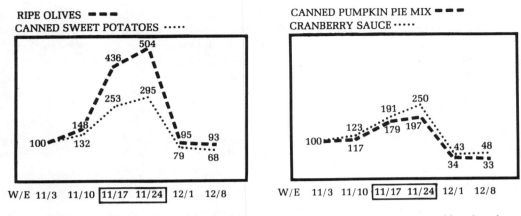

**Figure 11-7.** A time-series view showing the effect of Thanksgiving on weekly sales of selected food products, as measured by A.C. Nielsen Company's Scantrack service. Rapid rise from base index of 100 is followed by post-holiday drop to or below normal levels. (*Source:* "Management with the Nielsen Retail Index System," brochure published by A. C. Nielsen Company, p. 26. Courtesy of A.C. Nielsen Company.)

Although the time-series design is an extension of the preexperimental single group (*O X O*) design, it does not suffer as severely from the various threats to internal validity. Because the measurements are made over a broad span of time periods, factors such as maturation, testing, selection, and regression are not so critical as in the preexperimental counterpart. In addition, the frequency of data collection is likely to cause competent researchers or interviewers to settle into a somewhat consistent approach, so instrumentation is also less threatening to this design.

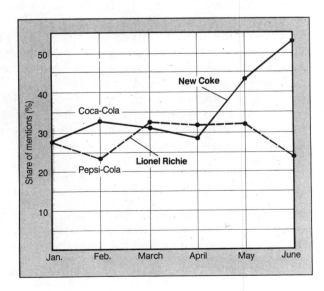

**Figure 11-8.** While Coca-Cola's introduction of New Coke in 1985 upset some consumers, it also brought a substantial increase in awareness of Coke advertising. (*Source:* Scott Hume, "Marketers Find Bad News Does Some Good," *Advertising Age,* July 22, 1985, p. 6. Copyright Crain Communications, Inc. All rights reserved. Reprinted with permission.)

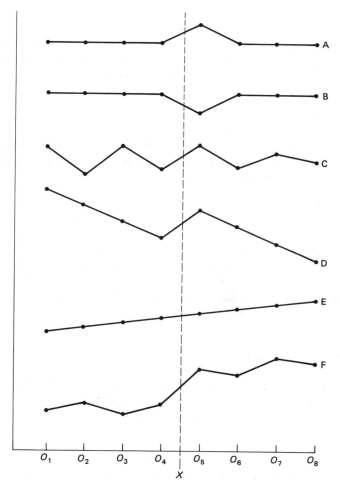

**Figure 11-9.** Measurements show some of the possible results from a special promotional event. Text discusses implications of each.

The major problem this design has is *history*, since it is always possible that some outside event may occur at about the same time as the experimental treatment, and that the outside event will be primarily responsible for an abrupt change in the series of measurements. Thus, in using the design, it is wise to be especially sensitive to outside events that could have an impact on the dependent variable.

## Multiple Time-Series Design

The *multiple time-series design*, except for the addition of a control group, is similar to that just described. A symbolic representation is

| Experimental: | $O_1$ | $O_2$ | $O_3$ | $O_4$ | X | $O_5$ | $O_6$ | $O_7$ | $O_8$ |
|---|---|---|---|---|---|---|---|---|---|
| Control: | $O_9$ | $O_{10}$ | $O_{11}$ | $O_{12}$ | | $O_{13}$ | $O_{14}$ | $O_{15}$ | $O_{16}$ |

In monitoring sales before and after a special event, we may wish to examine weekly sales in a control city where the event is *not* in effect. If sales in the control city are steady while sales in the test city increase, we will have greater confidence that the increase really is due to the promotion. Such selection of control units lessens the threat of *history* as an internal validity problem.

### Nonequivalent Control Group

The *nonequivalent control group design* is similar to the *before-after with control group* design, except that randomization is not used in the assignment of test units to groups. It can be symbolically described as

$$\text{Experimental:} \quad O_1 \quad X \quad O_2$$
$$\text{Control:} \quad O_3 \qquad\quad O_4$$

While the lack of randomization prevents this from being a true experimental design, it is nevertheless much better than having no control group at all. The researcher may be able to determine who gets the experimental treatment, but typically selects the control group from the standpoint of judgment or convenience.

### Separate-Sample Before-After Design

The *separate-sample before-after design* is similar to the preexperimental (*O X O*) approach, except that two groups are involved and members of *both* groups receive the experimental treatment. Symbolically, it is described as

$$\text{Sample 1: } R \; O_1 \; X$$
$$\text{Sample 2: } R \qquad X \, O_2$$

In the above diagram, since both groups receive the treatment, neither has been identified in terms of *experimental* and *control*. The measure of effectiveness of the experimental treatment is the difference between $O_2$ and $O_1$, as would be the case if only one group were used. However, since each group is measured only one time, there is no pre-measurement testing effect. Likewise, since members of the second sample are measured *after* receiving the treatment, there is no interactive testing effect in which a pre-measurement can influence sensitivity toward the experimental treatment. Thus, the quantity $(O_2 - O_1)$ is free from these validity errors. On the other hand, the threat of *history* is still present, because there is no real control group in the conventional sense.

As an example of its application, let's assume that a political candidate, "Honest Joe" Sampson, has scheduled a televised press conference for next Wednesday morning. Joe's campaign manager would like to measure the impact of this conference on voters' attitudes toward his candidate. Figure 11-10 summarizes how this experimental design could be utilized for this purpose.

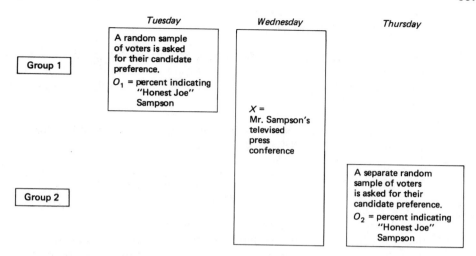

**Figure 11-10.**   An example of the separate-sample before-after experimental design. Effect of the press conference is expressed by $O_2 - O_1$.

As indicated in Figure 11-10, though members of both groups may be exposed to the televised press conference, the exposure of the first sample is purely incidental—that is, it can't be avoided, but this doesn't matter because members of this group aren't being measured again. Although we don't premeasure members of both groups, the combination of proper sampling techniques and sufficiently large sample sizes should ensure their comparability with regard to initial attitudes toward Mr. Sampson.

Although this design is susceptible to the effects of *history* (e.g., Mr. Sampson could be charged with public drunkenness on Tuesday evening), it is particularly simple to administer, and the ease of its application to a field situation provides it with exceptionally good external validity as well. As a quasi-experiment, it is certainly one cut above the others.

## ADVANCED EXPERIMENTAL DESIGNS

In this section, we'll examine four designs that are, in essence, extensions of the true experimental designs discussed earlier. Depending on one's selection from these designs, it is possible to (1) measure the effects of different levels of a treatment variable, (2) "control" for the effect of either one or two extraneous variables on the dependent variable being measured, or (3) determine the effect of two or more treatment variables, each at a number of different levels.[13]

---

[13] For a more complete discussion of these designs and their applications, see Keith K. Cox and Ben M. Enis, *Experimentation for Marketing Decisions* (Scranton, Pa.: International Textbook Company, 1969). Copyright Harper & Row, Publishers, Inc.

## Completely Randomized Design

In the *completely randomized design*, experimental treatments are randomly assigned to the test units, and it is assumed that outside variables will not affect one group any more or less than another. As an example of this design, consider the following situation:

An automobile manufacturer is considering possible incentives for enticing potential customers to visit dealerships for a test drive:

$$X_1 = \text{glove-compartment tool kit}$$
$$X_2 = \text{\$5 contribution to charity}$$
$$X_3 = \text{no test-drive incentive}$$

In applying the completely randomized design, the manufacturer might select a sample of nine dealerships, then randomly assign them to groups of three dealers, as shown in Table 11-2. Each group would then receive their treatment level for some period of time, perhaps one month, then the results would be analyzed by means of a statistical procedure called the *analysis of variance*. While this technique will be presented in Chapter 14, it is worth noting here that it involves comparing the average sales for the treatment groups to determine the likelihood that the differences observed could have simply occurred by chance, rather than as a result of the experimental treatments.

The completely randomized design is the least expensive and easiest to conduct of the experiments in this section. It is appropriate when we are confident that the test units are essentially similar, and that no group will differ

**TABLE 11-2.** *Application of the* completely randomized *design to test-drive incentive experiment discussed in text. Nine dealerships have been randomly assigned to the three treatment groups and the measure of effectiveness is the average sales for each group during the month of the experiment.*

| | Test-drive incentive | | |
|---|---|---|---|
| | $X_1$<br>Glove-compartment<br>tool kit | $X_2$<br>\$5 contribution to<br>charity | $X_3$<br><br>None |
| 9 dealers,<br>randomly<br>assigned<br>———→ | Sales,<br>dealer 7<br><br>Sales,<br>dealer 4<br><br>Sales,<br>dealer 1 | Sales,<br>dealer 3<br><br>Sales,<br>dealer 9<br><br>Sales,<br>dealer 6 | Sales,<br>dealer 8<br><br>Sales,<br>dealer 5<br><br>Sales,<br>dealer 2 |
| | Average sales,<br>treatment 1 | Average sales,<br>treatment 2 | Average sales,<br>treatment 3 |

greatly from another in terms of an important extraneous variable. However, it is not always possible to meet these assumptions. For example, cost constraints may dictate relatively small sample sizes, thereby making it more likely that test units will (by chance alone) not be highly similar. Likewise, there may be one or more outside variables that exert such great influence over the test units that they must be taken into consideration and controlled. In this instance, one of the following designs may be more suitable for the experiment.

### Randomized Blocks Design

The *randomized blocks design* makes it possible for the researcher to control a single extraneous variable that might otherwise confound the results of the experiment. The term *blocks* here refers to a stratifying of the test units in terms of an extraneous variable, such as customer education level, age or income, size of sales district, type of establishment, or any other variable that is judged to exert a major influence over the test units and the value of the dependent variable (e.g., sales level) that is measured for them.

In this design, test units are arranged into similar blocks before being randomly assigned to experimental and control groups. Employing the same rationale as the stratified sample, *blocking* makes it possible to better ensure similarity between test units, especially when small sample sizes are involved. Matching of test units before assignment to groups, discussed earlier, is another way to meet this objective.

In the test-drive incentive example just discussed, the auto manufacturer may feel that *dealership size* (in terms of preceding-year sales volume) is an extraneous variable that is important in determining sales level. In this case, we might do the following:

1. Select, for our overall sample, three large dealerships, three medium-sized dealerships, and three small dealerships
2. Within *each size category*, randomly assign the three dealers to the three treatment groups

Because we have three experimental treatments, there must be either three or a multiple of three dealerships of each type—that is, our total sample size could be 9, 18, 27, and so on. (Note: Because we are now being a little more "picky" about the kinds of dealerships allowed in the sample—three of each size category—we may not be able to use the same nine that would have been chosen randomly in the preceding section. For example, with purely random sampling, we could have ended up with two "small" dealers, four "medium" dealers, and three "large" dealers.) Table 11-3 shows how this experimental design would appear for the test-drive incentive experiment.

As with the preceding design, analysis of variance would be used as the analysis technique, although we could now identify two kinds of relationships: (1) if test-drive incentive type is related to sales during the month of the ex-

*TABLE 11-3.* Randomized blocks *design applied to test-drive incentive experiment. Dealership size category has been identified as a possible extraneous variable and is controlled by this design, which involves the same rationale as the stratified sample.*

| Dealership size categories | Test-drive incentive | | |
| --- | --- | --- | --- |
| | $X_1$ Tool kit | $X_2$ Contribution | $X_3$ None |
| 3 large, randomly assigned → | Sales, Colossus Motors, Inc. | Sales, Gigantus Motors, Inc. | Sales, Gulliver's Cars, Ltd. |
| 3 medium, randomly assigned → | Sales, Spectre Motorcars, Inc. | Sales, Medcenter Motors, Ltd. | Sales, Hazenfog Motors, Inc. |
| 3 small, randomly assigned → | Sales, Clyde's Car Corral, Inc. | Sales, Hooterville Auto Sales. | Sales, Sam's Fine Cars & Expert Lawnmower Repair. |
| | Average sales, treatment 1 | Average sales, treatment 2 | Average sales, treatment 3 |

periment, and (2) if dealership size category is related to sales during the month. As a result of the statistical "control" we have exerted over the dealership-size variable by means of this stratification, or blocking, we can now be more confident that the average sales for the treatment groups truly reflect the test-drive incentives offered.

In situations where small sample sizes are desirable for cost or other reasons, the randomized block design will be superior to the completely randomized design in much the same way that the stratified sample is superior to the simple random sample. However, if there happens to be more than one major extraneous variable, it will be necessary to use one of the following two designs.

## Latin Square Design

The **Latin square design** allows the researcher to control for the effects of *two* extraneous variables, thus making it a logical extension of the randomized blocks design. In the case of our test-drive incentive experiment, let's assume that the manufacturer has identified two extraneous variables that could have a major effect:

***Extraneous variable 1:*** dealership size, unit volume per year (large, medium, small)

***Extraneous variable 2:*** probable temperatures in dealership area during month of experiment (warm, moderate, cold)

In applying the Latin square design to this experiment, the manufacturer would set up test-drive incentive treatments according to a plan similar to the one of Table 11-4. Note that, since there are three different treatments, there must be three categories of each of the other two variables. This is a requirement for this design, and is a logical reason why it is called the Latin *square*. If we wished to evaluate four treatments, we would have to categorize the two extraneous variables into four segments each. Because of its size, the design in Table 11-4 is referred to as a 3 × 3 Latin square design.

As we did when making the transition to randomized blocks, we must again become more selective regarding the types of test units in our sample. Remember that we are now "stratifying" on the basis of two variables instead of one. Experimental treatments are again randomly assigned to the test units. However, the procedure must be one that ensures a given treatment will appear only once in each row and only once in each column. For the 3 × 3 table of this example, this could be carried out as follows:

1. Randomly select the treatment to be applied in the first row and first column. In Table 11-4, $X_2$ was chosen with the help of a random number table.

2. Randomly select, from the other two treatments, the one that will appear in the first column, second row. A coin flip decided in favor of $X_3$.

3. Randomly select, from $X_1$ and $X_3$, the one that will appear in the first row, second column. By a coin flip, $X_1$ was the winner.

At this point, the rest of the treatments have also been determined. For example, once the first row has $X_2$ and $X_1$, the only choice left is $X_3$ for the third column. The result is the configuration of treatments of Table 11-4, in which each combination of dealer size and area temperature receives only one treatment.

In the Latin square design, the effects of the extraneous variables (deal-

*TABLE 11-4. Application of the* Latin square *design to test-drive incentive experiment. This design allows researcher to control for two extraneous variables. Once 3 × 3 table has been set up, treatments are randomly assigned so that each appears only one time in each row and column.*

| | | Probable temperatures in dealership area during month of experiment | | |
| --- | --- | --- | --- | --- |
| | | *Warm* | *Moderate* | *Cold* |
| *Dealership* | *Large* | $X_2$ | $X_1$ | $X_3$ |
| *size* | *Medium* | $X_3$ | $X_2$ | $X_1$ |
| *category* | *Small* | $X_1$ | $X_3$ | $X_2$ |

$X_1$ = free tool kit with test drive
$X_2$ = charity contribution with test drive
$X_3$ = no special incentive for test drive

ership size and area temperature) on the dependent variable (sales during the month of the experiment) are controlled. However, there are two kinds of interactions that this design does not consider: (1) interactions between the two extraneous variables themselves, and (2) interactions between the extraneous variables and the treatment levels. For example, larger dealerships might tend to be located in warm weather areas, or smaller dealerships might find that the tool kit incentive is especially effective due to a lack of emergency road service in rural areas. Despite these potential weaknesses, the principal strength of the Latin square—its ability to control for two extraneous effects on the dependent variable—causes it to be a very popular design for marketing experiments.

### Factorial Design

The preceding designs have allowed us to measure the effects of just one independent variable. In the *factorial design*, we can measure the simultaneous effects of two or more independent variables, each at two or more treatment levels. The principal strength of this design is its ability to detect the result of **interactions** between the various treatments. In an earlier discussion of survey research, we examined what was an outstanding example of the factorial design and its usefulness. For convenience purposes, the key results of this experiment are summarized in Table 11-5. The two variables, and their treatment levels, are as follows:

$$X_1 = \textbf{Survey sponsorship}$$
$$\text{Level 1: University sponsor}$$
$$\text{Level 2: Commercial sponsor}$$

$$X_2 = \textbf{Type of appeal in cover letter}$$
$$\text{Level 1: Social utility}$$
$$\text{Level 2: Help-the-sponsor}$$
$$\text{Level 3: Egoistic}$$
$$\text{Level 4: Combined appeal}$$

**TABLE 11-5.** *The factorial experiment measures simultaneous effects of two or more treatment variables, allowing the identification of important interactions between treatment levels of each. In this 2 × 4 design, also discussed in our earlier coverage of survey research, mail questionnaire response rate showed strong interactions between appeal and sponsorship strategies.*

|  |  | Sponsor | |
|  |  | University | Commercial |
|---|---|---|---|
|  | *Social utility* | 47.2% | 38.8% |
| *Appeal* | *Help-the-sponsor* | 44.8% | 36.8% |
|  | *Egoistic* | 35.6% | 46.8% |
|  | *Combined* | 41.6% | 39.2% |

*Source:* Michael J. Houston and John R. Nevin, "The Effects of Source and Appeal on Mail Survey Response Patterns," *Journal of Marketing Research*, August 1977, pp. 374–78, published by the American Marketing Association.

If there were no interaction between these two variables, one appeal or another would tend to be superior *regardless of the type of sponsor*. Likewise, if one type of sponsorship were superior, it wouldn't matter which type of appeal was utilized. However, as the results show, there is a definite interaction between sponsorship and appeal: For the university, the social utility and help-the-sponsor approaches are best, while the egoistic ("express your opinion") appeal works best for the commercial sponsor.

This experiment is an example of a 2 × 4 factorial design because the first variable has two treatment levels and the second variable has four. If we were to add a third treatment variable—for example, type of postage—we would have a three-dimensional array. Figure 11-11 shows an example of a three-variable, 3 × 2 × 2, factorial experiment.

Analysis of the results of a factorial experiment leads to two types of measurements: (1) **main effects**, or the effects of each independent variable individually, and (2) **interactive effects**, resulting from two variables interacting to produce an effect that is greater than the simple sum of their individual effects. While detailed analysis is beyond the scope of this chapter, even a visual inspection of Table 11-5 shows a number of strong interactive effects between sponsorship and appeal type.

In most marketing experiments, there is likely to be at least some interaction between treatment variables, making the factorial design a particularly appropriate research approach. While the randomized blocks design assumes no interaction between the treatment variable and the outside variable being controlled, and the Latin square design assumes no interaction between the two

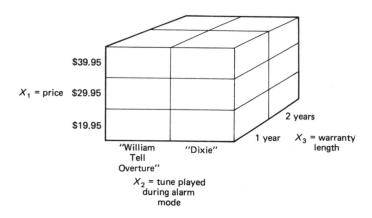

Dependent variable measured within each cell is the percent of consumer sample favoring new watch design over a popular competitor in a product comparison test. (Note: Because of 3 x 2 x 2 configuration, 12 different consumer samples would be selected for experiment.)

**Figure 11-11.** This factorial design could be used to measure consumer preferences in designing a new watch.

controlled variables, the factorial design makes no such assumptions. Thus, instead of merely trying to control one or two outside variables, it may be advantageous to actually invite them into the experiment as part of a factorial design. In this way we need not worry about the possibility of their being related, since the technique is readily able to handle this possibility.

## TEST MARKETING

*Test marketing* is the experimental testing of a new product or marketing mix in a trial setting.[14] In the context of marketing decision making discussed in Chapter 2, this constitutes the collecting of additional information to reduce the uncertainty of the decision situation.

### Who Does Test Marketing and Why?

Test marketing is undertaken by both consumer and industrial firms, and has two major goals: (1) to get an idea of the product's acceptability and potential sales, and (2) to test alternative marketing strategies. In addition, test marketing can sometimes provide early identification of problems that would be very costly to correct at a later date. For example, during test marketing of a pressurized can of barbecue sauce, a major company was fortunate to discover a flaw that could have been disastrous. According to a company spokesperson, "We thought we had a good can, but fortunately we first test marketed the product in stores in Texas and California. It appears as soon as the cans got warm they began to explode. Because we hadn't gotten into national distribution, our loss was only $150,000 instead of a couple of million."[15]

### Test Marketing of Consumer Products

#### The Standard Test Market

In this traditional approach, the company selects a number of cities or other test units in which the product is marketed as it would be in a national launch. Figure 11-12 shows the unique packaging of *Vital 15*, a high-calcium, low-fat milk which was test-marketed in San Diego using this method. Evaluation of such tests is based on audits of stores and warehouses, and on surveys of consumers, distributors, and retailers. Based on these data, sales and profit forecasts are made and the marketing mix fine-tuned for eventual distribution on a wider scale.

---

[14] Much of the discussion of test marketing experiments here is based on Philip Kotler, *Marketing Management*, 4th ed. (Englewood Cliffs, N.J.: Prentice-Hall, Inc., 1980), pp. 334–40.

[15] "Product Tryouts: Sales Tests in Selected Cities Help Trim Risks of National Marketings," *The Wall Street Journal*, August 10, 1962, p. 1, © Dow Jones & Co. Inc., 1962. All rights reserved.

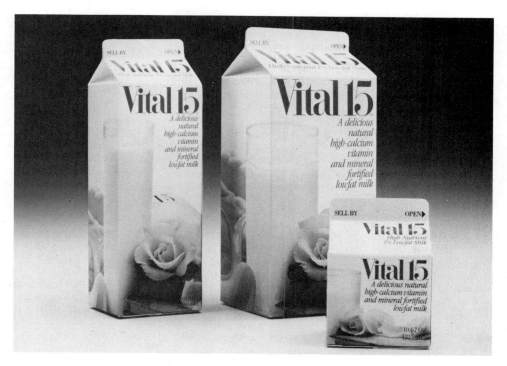

**Figure 11-12.** Market-tested in San Diego, this high-calcium, low-fat milk was packaged in a full-color printed carton and aimed at women in the 25–54 age group. (*Source:* "Marketing Briefs," *Marketing News,* October 24, 1986, p. 15, published by the American Marketing Association. Package design: Sidjakov Berman Gomez & Partners, San Francisco Marketing and Design Consultants.)

A major decision in this method is the number and choice of locations for the experiment. Cities should be representative of the larger population for which the product is eventually intended, and be typical with regard to such variables as media coverage, population demographics, and distribution channels. Table 11-6 lists 46 test-market cities recommended by Dancer Fitzgerald Sample, Inc.

Another important consideration is the duration of the test market. While longer tests allow more data to be gathered, they offer competitors greater opportunity to (1) interfere with the test, (2) come out with their own brands of the product, or (3) make early adjustments in their own marketing mix in anticipation of the product's eventual launch.

The principal strength of the standard test market is the external validity made possible by the real-world, "battlefield" conditions involved in the test. On the other hand, competitive actions like those of the preceding paragraph are possible due to the lack of secrecy inherent in a real-world setting. In addition, the time requirement for the test—a year or two is not unusual—can

**TABLE 11-6.** *An alphabetical listing of recommended test marketing cities, as compiled by Dancer Fitzgerald Sample, Inc. Test cities should have representative demographics and purchasing habits, along with a good distribution system for the product being evaluated.*

—Albany-Schenectady-Troy, N.Y.
—Boise, Idaho.
—Buffalo, N.Y.
—Cedar Rapids-Waterloo, Iowa.
—Charlotte, N.C.
—Chattanooga, Tenn.
—Cincinnati, Ohio.
—Cleveland, Ohio.
—Colorado Springs-Pueblo, Colo.
—Columbus, Ohio.
—Des Moines, Iowa.
—Erie, Pa.
—Evansville, Ind.
—Fargo, N.D.
—Fort Wayne, Ind.
—Green Bay, Wis.

—Greensboro-High Point-Winston-Salem, N.C.
—Greenville-Spartanburg, S.C.
—Indianapolis, Ind.
—Kalamazoo-Grand Rapids-Battle Creek, Mich.
—Kansas City, Kan.
—Knoxville, Tenn.
—Lexington, Ken.
—Little Rock, Ark.
—Louisville, Ken.
—Minneapolis, Minn.
—Milwaukee, Wis.
—Nashville, Tenn.
—Oklahoma City, Okla.
—Omaha, Neb.
—Orlando-Daytona Beach, Fla.

—Phoenix, Ariz.
—Pittsburgh, Pa.
—Portland, Ore.
—Roanoke-Lynchburg, Va.
—Rochester, N.Y.
—Sacramento-Stockton, Calif.
—St. Louis, Mo.
—Salt Lake City, Utah.
—Seattle-Tacoma, Wash.
—South Bend-Elkhart, Ind.
—Spokane, Wash.
—Springfield-Decatur-Champaign, Ill.
—Syracuse, N.Y.
—Tulsa, Okla.
—Wichita-Hutchinson, Kan.

*Source:* " 'Magic Town' Doesn't Exist for Test Marketers," *Marketing News*, March 1, 1985, p. 15, published by the American Marketing Association.

delay either the dropping of a poor product or the receipt of profits from a good one that is eventually launched. Finally, largely due to time duration and the need to employ the same marketing mix intended for later, expanded use, such tests can be quite expensive.

### The Controlled Test Market

In this approach, also referred to as the electronic mini-market test, a panel of participating outlets carries the tested product, and a research firm handles distribution, product stocking, and tracking of sales results. Electronic scanning methods are typically used for data collection. In the case of techniques like BehaviorScan, participating consumers are provided with ID cards that are scanned at the time of product purchase, allowing the gathering of such data as buyer characteristics and repeat purchase behavior.

At the cost of what some consider to be less realism, controlled test markets can be carried out much more inexpensively and quickly than the standard test market. While a full test market in two cities will often cost over $3 million for the first year, it has been estimated that an electronic mini-market test can reduce expenditures by about one-third.[16]

---

[16] Aimee L. Stern, "Test Marketing Enters a New Era," *Dun's Business Month*, October 1985, p. 85. Reprinted with permission, *Business Month* magazine (October, 1985), Copyright © 1985 by Business Magazine Corporation, 38 Commercial Wharf, Boston, MA 02110.

---

**EXHIBIT 11-4**

**A New Type of Market Test**

With the advent of the electronic mini-market test, it's no longer necessary to use different test cities to compare different marketing strategies. A marketer can now divide a sample of households into two demographically matched groups and test a separate strategy on each. Members of participating families receive electronic access cards to be scanned when they make purchases, and the family TV is equipped with a microprocessor that monitors the programs and commercials viewed and sends the information back to a central computer. In addition, a special signal tower can feed desired commercials for the new product into a designated subset of the homes.

Because companies are able to control the communications sent to each participating home in one locale, greater accuracy is possible than with a traditional test market involving a different city for each treatment. According to Tony Adams, director of market research for the Campbell Soup Co., "Now you can do, say, five experiments in four electronic test markets for a cost of about $450,000. Those same tests would have cost $600,000 before and you would have had more trouble reading the real differences between the markets."

Among current leaders in this field are A.C. Nielsen's Testsight, Information Resources' BehaviorScan, and Burke Marketing's Ad Tel. Portland, Oregon; Orlando, Florida; Rome, New York; Marion, Indiana; and Sioux Falls, Iowa, are among the cities where the firms have set up computerized mini-markets.

*Source:* Aimee L. Stern, "Test Marketing Enters a New Era," *Dun's Business Month*, October 1985, p. 85. Reprinted with permission, *Business Month* magazine (October, 1985), Copyright © 1985 by Business Magazine Corporation, 38 Commercial Wharf, Boston, MA 02110.

---

### The Simulated Test Market

In this laboratory approach to test marketing, consumers are placed in a simulated shopping environment, exposed to information on the tested product and others, and allowed to "purchase" items of their choice with funds provided by the sponsor. Follow-up interviews may be conducted to better explain the behavior and attitudes of test participants. The artificial nature of these tests enables them to be carried out relatively quickly and in highly controlled conditions. However, the same factors that provide this control tend to detract from the external validity of the results. Compared to other methods, this one provides a high level of secrecy from competitors. It can also be valuable as a preliminary screening step prior to engaging in one of the other approaches.

### The Sales Wave Approach

In this method, the product is given to consumers for trial use in their own homes. Participants are then offered, at reduced cost, the opportunity to receive additional supplies of either the tested product or its competitors in subsequent "sales waves." Extremely inexpensive and private, this method also enables the collection of detailed information from those who either choose or do not choose to receive more of the tested product. However, the small sample sizes tend to reduce generalizability to the larger population.

### Test Marketing of Industrial Products

For industrial products, testing may take a form generally similar to the standard or controlled test marketing methods used by consumer goods firms. In addition, trade shows may be used as a medium in which to present the product and measure the reactions of potential consumers to it. Similarly, the product may be placed in selected distributor or dealer showrooms to provide a measure of its attractiveness. In an approach especially useful for technical products, the product is placed with a sampling of potential customers who are closely monitored regarding their use of the product and their satisfaction with it.

### □ SUMMARY

Experimentation, the identification of cause and effect relationships, is the primary choice of researchers involved with causal studies. In making decisions on the marketing mix, managers often rely on experimental studies that describe the effect a particular strategy is likely to have on variables such as sales, market share, and consumer attitude.

In an experiment, we control or manipulate one or more independent variables in order to determine the effect of such manipulations on the dependent variable. Extraneous variables are those that may influence the value of the dependent variable, but may lie beyond either our awareness or our control. Test units are the entities to which the treatments are administered, and from which we make the measurements describing the effect the independent variable has had. When an experimental design involves more than one group, test units may be allocated to experimental and control groups.

Internal validity (did the experimental treatment really make the difference?) and external validity (to what extent can the results be generalized?) are both important to the experiment. Without internal validity, an experiment is virtually useless, because it has not succeeded in providing cause-effect information for the independent and dependent variables. Key threats to internal validity are the history, maturation, testing, statistical regression, instrumentation, mortality, and selection bias effects.

There are two kinds of settings in which marketing research experiments can be conducted: laboratory and field. In the laboratory experiment, the treatment is administered to the test units, typically consumers, in an artificial setting that has been contrived for the purpose of the experiment. The artificiality of the setting helps the researcher to avoid or control for the unwanted effects of outside variables. However, this same artificiality tends to weaken the external validity of the experimental findings.

In the field experiment, the test units are allowed to function in a more natural setting, such as their home or a supermarket. As a result, consumers are less likely to react to the experimental situation itself, but control of outside variables may be diminished, thus tending to reduce internal validity.

Preexperimental designs afford the researcher very little control over the experiment, making it likely that internal validity will suffer. The wise research consumer will be highly skeptical when someone attempts to "sell" the results of such studies. Among these designs are the after-only, before-after, and static-group comparison.

True experimental designs employ randomization, the random assignment of test units to experimental and control groups, a process that strengthens internal validity. These designs include the before-after with control group, after-only with control group, and the Solomon four-group. While strong in terms of internal validity, these designs are not always practical in the real world of marketing and consumers.

Quasi-experimental designs fall between preexperiments and true experiments in terms of desirability and practicality. In the quasi-experiment, we are not able to randomly assign test units to the experimental and control groups, nor is it always possible to decide who gets the experimental treatment and when. In essence, the quasi-experiment involves simply doing the best we can with the constraints we face. Popular quasi-experimental techniques include the time-series, multiple time-series, nonequivalent control group and separate-sample before-after designs.

Advanced experimental designs, which are essentially extensions of the true experiments, include the completely randomized, randomized blocks, Latin square, and factorial designs. Depending on our selection from these designs, it is possible to (1) measure the effects of different levels of a treatment variable, (2) control for the effect of either one or two extraneous variables, or (3) determine the simultaneous effects of two or more treatment variables, each at a number of different levels.

Test marketing is the experimental testing of a new product or marketing mix in a trial setting. In the context of marketing decision making, this constitutes the collecting of additional information to reduce the uncertainty inherent in the decision situation. Test marketing can help provide an estimate of a product's potential sales, test specific marketing-mix strategies, and can also provide unanticipated, but valuable, marketing information.

## ☐ QUESTIONS FOR REVIEW

1. What are some of the independent, dependent, and extraneous variables typically involved in marketing research experiments?
2. What are internal validity and external validity, and why is each important to the marketing research experiment?

3. Differentiate between *history* and *maturation* as factors that affect the validity of an experiment. Give an example of how each could influence the outcome of a real or hypothetical experiment of your choice.

4. How can the statistical regression effect exert an influence on the results of an experiment? Provide a real or hypothetical example of a situation in which this effect is likely to be present.

5. Provide a real or hypothetical example in which the sponsor of an experimental study employs the instrumentation effect to arrive at findings that are favorable to the firm or organization's objectives.

6. Is it possible for a marketing experiment to have high internal validity, but very low external validity? If so, provide an example of a situation in which this would be likely to occur.

7. What is randomization and why does it enhance the internal validity of an experiment involving more than one group?

8. What is the difference between the main testing effect and the interactive testing effect in experimentation?

9. Plan an after-only, with control group, experiment to measure the effectiveness of a college recruiting film in improving the attitudes that high school seniors have toward your school.

10. Provide an example of a 3 × 2 × 2 factorial experiment. Be sure to identify the independent and dependent variables.

11. Plan a time-series experiment to measure the sales effect of a "half-price" weekend at your favorite local eating or drinking establishment. What is the most serious internal validity problem which time-series experiments tend to encounter, and what are some possible ways in which this factor might adversely affect the experiment you have planned?

12. The Safety Products Company has come up with a new product: a running light to be placed on the front of cars for safety purposes. The light shines brightly whenever the engine is running and is thought to be a safety factor by virtue of its attention-getting qualities. In cooperation with the Crinkle Cab Company, the research manager of Safety Products posted a notice on the cab company's bulletin board asking for cabbies to volunteer for the experiment. The lights would be installed on their cabs free of charge and they would receive $25 for their cooperation. After a month of testing the effectiveness of the product, Safety Products came up with the following results: (1) 1000 taxicabs equipped with the Saf-T-Light incurred 10 accidents in April 1987 (2) the same 1000 taxicabs *not* equipped with light incurred 40 accidents in March 1987. (The lights were installed at the end of March 1987.) Safety Products is set to embark on a national advertising campaign stressing the ability of the light to reduce accidents by 75%. Criticize their findings on the basis of the internal and external validity of their experiment.

13. Under what circumstances might one wish to use:
    a. The completely randomized design?
    b. The randomized blocks design?
    c. The Latin square design?

14. Experiments may be conducted in a variety of settings, that are usually classified as laboratory or field.

**a.** What differences distinguish laboratory from field settings?

**b.** What concerns should the experimenter be particularly conscious of in each setting?

15. What are some of the benefits which test marketing experiments can provide for the marketing decision maker? What potential problems may be encountered in a test marketing effort?

# CASES FOR PART THREE

## CASE 3-1

### National Election Poll

Exercising his constitutional right of free speech, a citizen and observer of the American political scene has written the following letter to the editor of his local paper:

> As I'm writing this letter, which I know you'll never publish anyway, I'm thirsty since I couldn't stop for my usual beer and happy hour on the way home from work. Why couldn't I get a beer? Because today's election day and there's some law that says the bars can't be open until the polls close, that's why.
>
> What's all this big deal about us going out to vote? All these big-time public opinion pollsters have already figured out who's going to win anyway, and all we're doing is going through the motions. And I read someplace where only about half of the registered voters even bother to do that. Besides that, a lot of people, like my cousin Ernie and my neighbor Charlie, haven't even registered because they either don't know how or they're too busy.
>
> The other night on the TV, I tuned in the educational channel by mistake and watched a program about how to do surveys. I listened pretty good to what they said, and one guy had a pretty good idea. I guarantee it would save us millions of dollars every four years.
>
> One thing somebody mentioned was something called response error. The first thing that came to my mind was the mob of campaign fanatics who stick pamphlets in your face on your way into the voting place. Along with that, some of the candidates do things like list their name as Dick instead of Richard on the ballot, and I heard this helps them get more votes that way.
>
> I saw in the paper where a political research outfit invents a fake name just to see how many people say they favor the guy who doesn't exist over the candidate they're trying to sell. That wouldn't be so bad, but this guy who isn't even real often has a lot of people who say they like his policies and intend to vote for him.
>
> Then you've got this nonresponse error thing. When only half the people respond to a survey as important as this one that happens every four years, you've got a real problem. Just like in a survey, the people who vote might not have the same opinions and views as people who don't. And everybody knows that the turnout of older folks in the northeast isn't so good when there's a lot of snow or bad weather during that first week in November.
>
> One of the other survey guys on TV said that something called a simple random sample of just 40,000 people would be 95% sure of coming within one half of one

percentage point of what the entire country thinks. Just before the host asked him to leave, he suggested that we just do a large survey of registered voters instead of trying to ask over 100 million people and only getting an answer from half of them.

It seems to me that this guy had a good idea and should not have been asked to leave the show. Why don't we just hire a really good, professional polling firm to survey 40,000 registered voters, make sure we get answers from nearly all of them, then elect the president based on what they say? Wouldn't this cut down on this response and nonresponse error stuff and give us a better fix on who we really want for president? What do you think?

Q: What do you think?

## CASE 3-2

### Student Government Association

The Student Government Association of Scenic View University would like to conduct a survey to measure the opinions of undergraduate students toward their educational experience at the university. Permission has already been secured to distribute a questionnaire to a sampling of undergraduate classes during the first 5 minutes of class time, with the questionnaire passed out and collected by student volunteers.

The student leaders wish to obtain students' views on a wide variety of issues related to their undergraduate education, and would also like to be able to determine if there is any relationship between these viewpoints and such variables as one's sex, quality point average, major area of study, and year in school. After much discussion, officers of the SGA have identified the following as specific areas which the questionnaire should examine:

- Sex, class standing, quality point average, major, and if the person expects to graduate at the time that he or she initially expected upon entering the university
- Whether there are enough professors for the student's major and if sufficient sections are offered for major courses
- If class length is satisfactory for M-W-F and T-Th formats
- If classrooms physically facilitate a good environment for learning
- Whether professors seem to be qualified to teach their subjects, and if the grades they assign are reflective of course performance
- Professors' typical lecturing style, and whether this style is preferred by the student
- Whether professors tend to keep students' interest in a class, seem to be concerned with student progress, and adequately cover subject materials during the semester
- Whether the university requires too many general (nonmajor) courses for the undergraduate degree

- If students perceive courses in their major to be interesting, challenging, and likely to prepare them adequately for a career
- How students feel about the overall quality of a Scenic View education, whether they would still choose Scenic View if they were able to start college over again, and if they would recommend the university to others who are deciding which college to attend

For respondents' convenience and ease of filling out the questionnaire, and to facilitate analysis of the data, the SGA would like the instrument to be as structured as possible. They would also like a short introductory paragraph at the top of the questionnaire. Within these constraints, and with a maximum of 25 questions, develop a questionnaire that will allow the SGA to obtain the information desired.

## CASE 3-3

### Sears Camcorder

"Charlie bought a VHS camcorder on sale at a Sears store in Brooklyn so that he could take home movies of his family's camping vacation to Yellowstone Park. On their way out West, Charlie found that the camcorder was making a lot of funny noises and wasn't taking clear pictures. He substituted another brand of videocassette, but the problems continued. Along the Interstate, Charlie's wife happened to notice a Sears store near Omaha. . . ."

1. Administering the above partially completed story to one-half of a convenience sample of friends, use their completions to measure the extent to which Sears is perceived to stand behind its products.
2. Repeat step 1, but substitute K-Mart for Sears. Does there appear to be a different trend in the responses?

## CASE 3-4

### Homer Gumby

For the past year, Homer Gumby has been the anchorperson on the "Newscheck 6" 11 P.M. news. In recent months, Homer has been upset with management's plans toward more extensive coverage of state and national news at the expense of reduced attention to local events. Homer is currently exploring available announcing opportunities at other stations and has compiled some viewership information that he believes will support his value as a TV news personality. During the 12 months prior to Homer's first appearance on Newscheck 6, the average monthly viewership shares (March through February, percent of area sets tuned to channel 6 during the 11:00 news) were 15, 18, 17, 18, 18, 17, 19, 20, 18, 19, 20, and 21, for the 12 months. The corresponding monthly shares (also March through February) since Homer's first appearance as news anchor were 20, 22, 21, 23, 25, 24, 26, 25, 26, 24, 26, and 27 for this 12-month period.

Attached to Homer's résumé is a graphical portrayal of this monthly viewership information, along with his observation that viewership went from 15 percent (one year before his arrival) to 27 percent (one year after his arrival). Evaluate Homer's claim that he has been the key to the growing success of Newscheck 6. If you are skeptical of Homer's argument, what additional information might you wish to obtain in order to better evaluate his assertion?

# 12

# DATA PREPARATION AND SUMMARIZATION

**Census Bureau Serves up Massive Data in Bite-Sized Portions**

On the first day of April 1980, about 222 million persons living in 80 million housing units were asked to complete and return their questionnaires on population and housing. During the census, the Bureau of the Census temporarily became one of the nation's largest employers, retaining the services of a quarter of a million field enumerators, roughly equivalent to half the population of Vermont. While performing their data-collection task, they also delivered babies, put out fires, saved lives, and put up with uncooperative and cooperative respondents alike. In one case, an enumerator was asked to climb through the window because an ill resident was too feeble to get up and open the door. (The respondent, who had already dutifully completed his questionnaire, was eventually hospitalized.)

Since 250 surveys are taken each year in addition to the 10-year national census, the resulting data would constitute an insurmountable hurdle without a highly efficient approach to their preparation, summarization, and dissemination. Besides the great number of enumerators, the collection, analysis, and reporting of census information requires the services of statisticians, economists, demographers, writers, editors, artists, programmers, supervi-

*Source:* Based on *How America Studies Itself: The U.S. Census*, Population Reference Bureau, Inc., Washington, D.C., February 1980, p. 5.

sors, and accountants. Whenever one is momentarily overwhelmed by the avalanche of reports provided by the Bureau of the Census, he or she should find at least some solace in the major job of simplification they have performed for our benefit.

## INTRODUCTION

In even the fanciest gourmet restaurants, someone has to open the cans, chop the celery, and peel the potatoes. Basically, that is what this chapter is all about—taking the raw data we've collected and converting it into a form that facilitates analysis and reporting. Where most of the preceding chapters dealt with our collection of data, this one is concerned with what we do *after* it has been collected.

The data preparation process involves *editing* the data, *coding* responses into categories, then *tabulating* responses into frequencies or tables. Prior to further analysis and reporting, data may also be statistically or graphically summarized. Data analysis is often performed using a microcomputer and statistical software. Accordingly, our topics in this chapter will be:

I. Editing

II. Coding

**Figure 12-1.**   Raw data from a study are of little use until converted to a form suitable for analysis and eventual reporting.

III. Tabulation

IV. Statistical summarization

V. Graphical summarization

VI. Data analysis and the microcomputer

## EDITING

The first stage of data preparation involves examination of the raw data by a field or central editor for the purpose of ensuring that the information collected is as accurate, complete, and usable as possible. Among the considerations at this point are initial screening, establishing of response categories, and editing in the field and central settings.

### Initial Screening

As soon as possible after completion of a survey, an initial screening of the questionnaires should be carried out to determine if the responses are legible, consistent, and complete, and that the respondent has taken his or her responsibility seriously.

---

**EXHIBIT 12-1**

***Interviewer Consistency***

The Marketing Research Association, Inc. has published a number of very specific guidelines for interviewers to follow in recording and checking questionnaire data. Among their directives are the following items:

- "Be sure to get a female respondent's first name and also, in parentheses, how the respondent is listed in the phone book. (Have you ever tried to find a Mary Peterson or Jane Smith in the phone book and she's married and not listed by her name?)"
- "Always use an (X) or circle the computer code number to indicate the answer to a closed-end question: NEVER use a (✓) in a box."
- "*Check through your work* immediately after each interview to be sure it is neat, accurate and complete."
- "*Record the respondent's answers to open-end questions verbatim*, exactly in the respondent's words, including slang. Probe and clarify fully all answers to open-end questions unless otherwise instructed. Be sure the respondent's answers are clear, complete and meaningful. Use probing and clarifying symbols."
- "*Be sure to record any comments* that pertain to the subject matter of the interviewing situation."

*Source: The Unwritten Rules for Data Collection—A Guide for Interviewers*, Marketing Research Association, Inc., Chicago, Ill.

---

*Are the responses legible?* If the response to a question is not legible, we may have to (1) go back to the interviewer or respondent for clarification, (2) try to infer from other responses what the illegible answer *probably* is, or (3) discard the response altogether. Naturally, this type of problem is more likely to occur when open-ended questions are used and the respondent fills out his own questionnaire with no interviewer present.

*Are the responses consistent?* Inconsistency is demonstrated by the respondent who answers an educational-level question with "presently in the eighth grade," then later indicates his or her occupation as "college professor." Likewise, a respondent may be in favor of an issue or political candidate early in the questionnaire, then be opposed in a later response. In designing a questionnaire, we can purposely phrase the same question in two different ways in order to "catch" those who may be providing inconsistent answers. Responses that are inconsistent with each other indicate that the respondent has changed in some way during the course of the interview or questionnaire, has not understood one or more questions, or has simply not been very conscientious in fulfilling his or her role in the survey. In editing a questionnaire that contains inconsistencies, it's best to eliminate *all* inconsistent responses unless you're able to determine which ones are most likely to be true.

*Are the responses complete?* Nonresponse error can be present for individual questions as well as for entire questionnaires. The lack of a response to a question presents a special problem, since we can't be sure whether the individual just happened to skip the question, didn't know the answer to the question, or knew the answer, but didn't wish to let us in on the secret. With the anonymity offered by many self-administered questionnaires, the reason for the nonresponse may remain a mystery. When an interviewer has been present, however, it is sometimes possible to question this individual in order to obtain information about the missing response.

*Is the respondent a comedian?* While most individuals take seriously their role as respondent, others do not. For example, some may indicate "star short-stop for the New York Yankees" as an occupation, or "leaping tall buildings" as a hobby. Usually, the comedian is fairly easy to spot, and his or her questionnaire can safely be thrown out.

*Are the responses too consistent?* The presence of a highly consistent pattern within a questionnaire (e.g., every multiple-choice question has the first response category checked) suggests that the respondent may have done much more writing than thinking. Unusual similarities among a number of questionnaires can reflect the input of an unprofessional interviewer who may have either exerted a strong bias on the respondents or fabricated the responses altogether.

## Establishing Response Categories

While responses to well-formulated dichotomous and multiple-choice questions offer no difficulty for coding and summarization, those from sentence completion and other open-ended questions will often be difficult to anticipate. Hence, after observing the types of responses, it will be necessary to establish meaningful categories for use in coding and tabulation. For example, suppose that we've just asked a sample of recent television purchasers, "What do you like best about your new television set?"

After examining all of the responses, we would establish categories in which to code them. Some likely categories would be "picture quality," "attractive styling," and "good reception." In addition to these, we would also include other categories as the range of responses might require. Categories should be selected so that (1) they cover all responses, and (2) each response will fit into only one category. We'll be going over a more complete example involving category selection when we discuss the postcoding of survey responses.

## Field Editing

Editing at the field level occurs "in the trenches," where interviewers take a few minutes to finish incomplete sentences, expand on their abbreviations, and fill in other ideas or points that were relevant to the interview but couldn't be written down at the time. Because of the inevitable dimming of interview memories over time, it is particularly important that field editing be carried out as soon as possible after the interview has taken place. Both *field editing* and *central editing*, covered in the next section, are concerned with completeness, legibility, and other points discussed earlier under Initial Screening.

## Central Editing

After editing at the field level, questionnaires or interview forms typically are edited in a central office, thus providing the greater consistency made possible with a single editor. If the size of the survey makes it impossible for one person to do the entire central editing job, it is appropriate to divide the work so that each editor is responsible for a given section of the questionnaire. This helps ensure that each question will be treated consistently for each respondent.

## CODING

Coding is the assignment of responses to categories, and involves the identification of each response with a number associated with that category. There are two approaches to coding: precoding and postcoding.

### Precoding

*Precoding* is appropriate with dichotomous and multiple-choice questions, which have only a limited selection of responses. The nature of these question types allows the researcher to predetermine the ways in which numbers will be assigned to different responses. In the air travel questionnaire of Figure 12-2, numerical codes have been included on the instrument itself. For the completed driver improvement course questionnaire of Figure 12-3, numerical codes have not been included, but can be easily designated. As shown in the questionnaire, we have 14 different "descriptors" for each respondent:

1–10:   The degree of emphasis he would like to see placed on each of the 10 topics presented

11:   The topic he has identified as the one he would most prefer

12:   His degree of familiarity with the Defensive Driving Course

13:   Age

14:   Sex

Prior to tabulating the data, responses can either be coded onto a summary sheet or keyboarded directly into the computer, where they are stored on a magnetic medium such as a hard disk or floppy diskette. Regardless of whether the entries are placed on a summary sheet or directly entered into the computer, a coding scheme must be used to represent responses numerically.

Figure 12-4 illustrates the translation of responses into numbers for the first 16 people answering the questionnaire of Figure 12-3. Referring to the coding key at the bottom of the sheet, we can see that respondent number 9 is the person whose completed questionnaire appears in Figure 12-3. In the ninth row under the "Subject" heading, each of this individual's responses has been converted into a number. For example, he has given heaviest preference (7) to the state police officer presentation and adverse-conditions topics, and has indicated the latter as the one topic he'd most prefer. He is in the second of the four Defensive Driving Course awareness categories, giving him a "2" on that measure. This is not the only coding key that could have been constructed for translating responses into numbers. However, the important thing is to arrive at a logical key, then apply it consistently to all questionnaires.

## Postcoding

When responses are of the open-ended type, as occurs with a set of unstructured questions, it will be necessary to assign responses to categories that have been selected *after* the data have been collected. As an example of how postcoding works, consider the following question and the responses provided by a hypothetical sample of 15 persons:

### Question

"When I see a Porsche automobile, it makes me think of _____."

### Responses

1. "how much fun I'd have if I owned one."
2. "how unfair our social system is that only a few people have enough money to afford a car like that."

→ *MARKET PROBE INTERNATIONAL, INC.*
ONE PARK AVENUE, NEW YORK, N.Y. 10016

**AIR MARKETING RESEARCH DIVISION**

Dear Airline Passenger:

As part of our continuing effort to bring you better air service, we would like to give you this opportunity to let us know some details about your trip and how you enjoyed your flight. Please take a few minutes to complete this questionnaire and return it to us in the provided postage-paid envelope. Your cooperation will be greatly appreciated.

1.  **PLEASE GIVE US SOME INFORMATION ABOUT THE FLIGHT YOU WERE ON JUST BEFORE YOU RECEIVED THIS QUESTIONNAIRE . . .**

   a.  Where did you board your transatlantic flight?    | 6-1 |

   7-1 ☐ Los Angeles      -3 ☐ London         -5 ☐ Frankfurt      -7 ☐ Other city *(PLEASE SPECIFY)*
    -2 ☐ New York         -4 ☐ Paris          -6 ☐ Rome
   _____

   b.  Where did you get off and receive this questionnaire?

   8-1 ☐ Los Angeles      -3 ☐ London         -5 ☐ Frankfurt      -7 ☐ Other city *(PLEASE SPECIFY)*
    -2 ☐ New York         -4 ☐ Paris          -6 ☐ Rome
   _____

   c.  Which airline did you use for your flight?

   9-1 ☐ Air France       -3 ☐ British Airways  -5 ☐ Pan Am       -7 ☐ Not Sure
    -2 ☐ Alitalia         -4 ☐ Lufthansa        -6 ☐ TWA

   d.  What was the aircraft type used for your flight?

   10-1 ☐ 747             -2 ☐ DC10            -3 ☐ L1011         -4 ☐ Not Sure

   e.  What was your date of flight *arrival?*    Month_____(11)    Day_____(12,13)    Flight No._____(14-16)

   f.  In terms of occupied seats, how full would you estimate your section of the aircraft was?

   17-1 ☐ Less than one-quarter full                    -4 ☐ More than three-quarters full
    -2 ☐ One-quarter to one-half full                   -5 ☐ Appeared completely full
    -3 ☐ One-half to three-quarters full

   g.  In which section of the aircraft were you seated?

   18-1 ☐ First Class
    -2 ☐ Business Class (Clipper, Club, Ambassador, etc.)
    -3 ☐ Economy/Coach/Cabin

   h.  Did your plane depart from the gate on time?

   19-1 ☐ Yes             -2 ☐ No

   If no, how many minutes were you delayed in leaving the gate? *(CHECK ONLY ONE PLEASE.)*

   20-1 ☐ Less than 5 min.   -3 ☐ 15-29 minutes   -5 ☐ 45-59 minutes   -7 ☐ 2-3 hours
    -2 ☐ 5-14 minutes        -4 ☐ 30-44 minutes   -6 ☐ 1-2 hours       -8 ☐ over 3 hours

   i.  What was the primary reason for your trip? *(CHECK ONLY ONE PLEASE.)*

   21-1 ☐ Convention/trade fair                         -6 ☐ Personal business/moving/job interview/emergency
    -2 ☐ Accompanying family member on business trip    -7 ☐ Vacation/pleasure
    -3 ☐ Company business                               -8 ☐ Visiting friends or relatives
    -4 ☐ Military duty/leave                            -9 ☐ Travel to or from school/research/study
    -5 ☐ Government business                            -0 ☐ Other: _____

   j.  In the past 12 months, how many other transatlantic air trips have you made for business and for pleasure? Please count each roundtrip as one trip and include the trip on which you received this questionnaire.

   Number of transatlantic trips primarily for business:_____ (22,23)

   Number of transatlantic trips primarily for pleasure: _____ (24,25)

   k.  In the past 12 months, how many intra-European trips (trips between European cities) have you made primarily for business or for pleasure? Please count trips on which a number of different European cities were visited as single trips.

   Number of intra-European trips for business: _____ (26,27)

   Number of intra-European trips for pleasure: _____ (28,29)

**Figure 12-2.**    As shown on the first page of this pre-coded questionnaire administered to air travelers, the response categories have already been numerically designated. (Courtesy of Market Probe International, Inc.)

A well-known driver improvement program presently involves eight hours of classroom instruction in safe driving techniques and accident avoidance. If a redesigned version of the course were to become available, its designers would like to have the benefit of your input regarding its content.

I. Please indicate your reaction to each of the following course content possibilities by placing a check mark in the appropriate block:

**Degree of emphasis you would prefer:**

| Topic: | NONE | | | MODERATE | | | HEAVY | NO OPINION |
|---|---|---|---|---|---|---|---|---|
| Class discussion of personal driving experiences. | ☐ | ☐ | ☐ | ☒ | ☐ | ☐ | ☐ | ☐ |
| Class presentation by a bus driver or other professional driver. | ☐ | ☐ | ☐ | ☐ | ☐ | ☒ | ☐ | ☐ |
| Class presentation by a state policeman. | ☐ | ☐ | ☐ | ☐ | ☐ | ☐ | ☒ | ☐ |
| Behind-the-wheel driving instruction. | ☐ | ☐ | ☐ | ☐ | ☒ | ☐ | ☐ | ☐ |
| How to administer first aid to accident victims. | ☐ | ☐ | ☐ | ☒ | ☐ | ☐ | ☐ | ☐ |
| How to carry out a driveway safety check of your car. | ☐ | ☐ | ☐ | ☐ | ☒ | ☐ | ☐ | ☐ |
| Driving techniques to minimize wear and tear on your car. | ☐ | ☐ | ☐ | ☐ | ☒ | ☐ | ☐ | ☐ |
| Driving techniques for winter, wet and other adverse conditions. | ☐ | ☐ | ☐ | ☐ | ☐ | ☐ | ☒ | ☐ |
| Driving techniques to get the most miles per gallon from your car. | ☐ | ☐ | ☐ | ☐ | ☐ | ☒ | ☐ | ☐ |
| A review of your state's traffic laws and enforcement policies. | ☐ | ☐ | ☐ | ☐ | ☐ | ☒ | ☐ | ☐ |

II. If it were possible to include only *one* of the above topics in a revised program, which topic would you most prefer? Please draw a circle around this topic in the listing above.

III. Please place a check mark beside the statement which best describes your familiarity with the Defensive Driving Course of the National Safety Council:
\_\_\_\_\_ did not know of the course prior to receiving this questionnaire.
\_\_✓\_ aware of the course but never considered taking it.
\_\_\_\_\_ aware of the course and have considered taking it.
\_\_\_\_\_ have taken the course.

IV. To help us analyze the survey results, please provide the following information about yourself:

Age: \_36\_ Sex: Male ☒ Female ☐

THANK YOU

**Figure 12-3.** Text describes coding process for this completed questionnaire on which numerical codes have not been included.

| Subject number | 1 class discussion | 2 bus driver | 3 state police officer | 4 behind-wheel | 5 first aid | 6 safety check | 7 minimize wear | 8 adverse conditions | 9 miles per gallon | 10 law review | 11 preferred topic | 12 DDC category | 13 age | 14 sex |
|---|---|---|---|---|---|---|---|---|---|---|---|---|---|---|
| 1 | 4 | 4 | 6 | 7 | 4 | 7 | 7 | 7 | 7 | 7 | 4 | 2 | 62 | 0 |
| 2 | 3 | 1 | 3 | 5 | 4 | 6 | 3 | 6 | 1 | 7 | 10 | 2 | 26 | 0 |
| 3 | 2 | 2 | 2 | 9 | 1 | 4 | 6 | 7 | 4 | 7 | 8 | 4 | 51 | 1 |
| 4 | 4 | 4 | 4 | 4 | 7 | 7 | 4 | 7 | 4 | 7 | 6 | 2 | 62 | 0 |
| 5 | 5 | 3 | 4 | 7 | 4 | 5 | 7 | 7 | 6 | 4 | 4 | 2 | 30 | 1 |
| 6 | 4 | 7 | 7 | 7 | 9 | 7 | 7 | 4 | 5 | 4 | 7 | 2 | 52 | 1 |
| 7 | 4 | 4 | 7 | 4 | 7 | 7 | 4 | 7 | 4 | 7 | 8 | 1 | 45 | 0 |
| 8 | 3 | 4 | 6 | 2 | 3 | 6 | 5 | 7 | 5 | 5 | 8 | 4 | 32 | 0 |
| 9 | 4 | 6 | 7 | 5 | 4 | 5 | 5 | 7 | 6 | 6 | 8 | 2 | 36 | 1 |
| 10 | 3 | 7 | 5 | 7 | 5 | 4 | 5 | 6 | 5 | 6 | 2 | 4 | 18 | 1 |
| 11 | 4 | 1 | 1 | 7 | 4 | 6 | 7 | 7 | 7 | 7 | 9 | 2 | 23 | 1 |
| 12 | 9 | 4 | 4 | 7 | 6 | 3 | 2 | 7 | 2 | 3 | 8 | 1 | 62 | 1 |
| 13 | 7 | 5 | 5 | 7 | 9 | 7 | 6 | 6 | 7 | 7 | 4 | 3 | 51 | 1 |
| 14 | 4 | 4 | 7 | 7 | 7 | 7 | 5 | 7 | 5 | 7 | 6 | 2 | 61 | 0 |
| 15 | 2 | 4 | 7 | 4 | 6 | 4 | 6 | 5 | 7 | 6 | 9 | 2 | 31 | 1 |
| 16 | 6 | 6 | 6 | 4 | 5 | 5 | 6 | 7 | 5 | 6 | 8 | 3 | 27 | 1 |

CODING KEY:

| None | | | Moderate | | | Heavy | No opinion |
|---|---|---|---|---|---|---|---|
| □ | □ | □ | □ | □ | □ | □ | □ |
| 1 | 2 | 3 | 4 | 5 | 6 | 7 | 9 |

DDC Categories:
1 = did not know of prior to questionnaire
2 = aware of but never considered taking
3 = aware of and have considered taking
4 = have taken
Sex:
1 = male
0 = female

**Figure 12-4.** A data summary sheet can facilitate coding of survey responses. Coding key is shown at the bottom of this partial listing of results. The questionnaire of respondent number 9 was shown in Figure 12-3.

3. "racing."
4. "small cars and how dangerous they are."
5. "the U.S. balance of payments."
6. "what a ball it would be to drive."
7. "my brother, because he's a sports car nut."
8. "how much the insurance must cost to own one."
9. "rich people."
10. "how well I like my Nissan 300 ZX."
11. "all those Pittsburgh steelworkers who are laid off."
12. "what a pain they must be to work on."
13. "my wife fainting if I drove one home."
14. "going to a movie."
15. "sticking out my thumb and hitching a ride."

After selecting categories that account for all responses, we might postcode the preceding responses as follows:

Desire to drive or own one, responses 1, 6, 13, 15

Negative social/economic comment, responses 2, 5, 9, 11

Undesirability or ownership disadvantage, responses 4, 8, 10, 12

Other, responses 3, 7

Irrelevant or comic, response 14

Responses 9 and 13 present a bit of a problem, and were placed in their categories as a "judgment call." For example, further discussion with the person who provided response 9 may have revealed that he aspires to be wealthy and would like to have the Porsche for its status value. However, the coding of this response into the second category was carried out because of the negative connotation of the word "rich," when "wealthy" would have been a less derogatory descriptor of those who happen to be financially endowed. Likewise, placing response 13 into the first category was done under the assumption that the respondent would like to have such a car, but feels that his wife (and creditors) would be aghast at his buying one. Response 14 is listed separately from the "other" category because of its apparent irrelevance to the subject of the question.

If the sheer number of questionnaires makes it necessary to employ several coders, it's best to divide up the work so that each coder is responsible for all questions in a given portion of each questionnaire. This advice, and its consistency advantages, were discussed earlier in terms of the allocation of editing responsibilities when large numbers of questionnaires are involved. When such division of responsibility is required, it's also a good idea to let each coder "sample" some of the work of the others. In this way, they will be able to more closely approximate the results that would be attained if it were possible for a single coder to accomplish the task.

## TABULATION

Once we have the responses assigned to categories, the next step is to count how many we have in each category. This is *tabulation*, and it can take two basic forms: simple tabulation and cross-tabulation. Counting and summarization of responses can be carried out by hand or by computer, depending on the volume of the data and the availability of suitable computer statistical packages.

### Simple Tabulation

*Simple tabulation*, also called *marginal* or *one-way tabulation*, leads to a frequency distribution of how many responses were in each of the categories. As an example, let's assume that we have just surveyed the users of a hypothetical brand of weight-loss pill, with the following questions included in the questionnaire: (1) age, (2) number of months customer has used the diet pill, and (3) number of pounds customer has lost since beginning the diet pill program. A simple tabulation of the results might reveal data such as those shown in Table 12-1, with the entries being the number of persons in each category for the three questions.

### Cross-Tabulation

Although simple tabulation allows us to express our findings in terms of one variable at a time, many of the more useful results of marketing research studies represent important relationships *between* variables. In this case, a *cross-tabulation* is necessary. An example of a two-way cross-tabulation, again involving Dr. Helium's wonder tablet, is presented in Table 12-2. This cross-tabulation

**TABLE 12-1.** *Three simple tabulations of the responses in a hypothetical survey of 500 customers of Dr. Helium's Weight-Loss Tablets. Each is merely a frequency distribution of the number of responses in each category.*

| Age | Number of respondents | Number of months on Dr. Helium's Weight-Loss Tablets | Number of respondents | Number of pounds lost since first use of Dr. Helium | Number of respondents |
|---|---|---|---|---|---|
| Under 21 | 47 | Less than 2 | 90 | No loss | 113 |
| 21–30 | 104 | 2 | 80 | 1–5 | 104 |
| 31–40 | 132 | 3 | 80 | 6–10 | 130 |
| 41–50 | 118 | 4 | 60 | 11–15 | 88 |
| 51–60 | 61 | 5 | 50 | 16–20 | 47 |
| Over 60 | 38 | More than 5 | 140 | Over 20 | 18 |
| Total | 500 | Total | 500 | Total | 500 |

**TABLE 12-2.** *Example of a two-way cross-tabulation of two variables: (a) number of months on Dr. Helium's Weight-Loss Tablets, and (b) number of pounds lost since first use of the product.*

| | | Number of months on Dr. Helium's Weight-Loss Tablets | | | | | | |
|---|---|---|---|---|---|---|---|---|
| | | *Under* *2* | *2* | *3* | *4* | *5* | *Over* *5* | *Total* |
| | *No loss* | 17 | 10 | 15 | 18 | 14 | 39 | 113 |
| *Number of* | *1–5* | 24 | 17 | 10 | 14 | 11 | 28 | 104 |
| *pounds lost* | *6–10* | 19 | 30 | 28 | 13 | 9 | 31 | 130 |
| *since first* | *11–15* | 18 | 15 | 21 | 7 | 5 | 22 | 88 |
| *use of* | *16–20* | 8 | 5 | 5 | 6 | 9 | 14 | 47 |
| *Dr. Helium* | *Over 20* | 4 | 3 | 1 | 2 | 2 | 6 | 18 |
| | *Total* | 90 | 80 | 80 | 60 | 50 | 140 | 500 |

involves two of the three measurements shown in Table 12-1: (1) the number of months that the respondent has been using Dr. Helium's tablets, and (2) the number of pounds the respondent has lost since the first use of the product.

The two-way cross-tabulation of Table 12-2 takes on the appearance of a two-variable, 6 × 6, factorial experiment. Indeed, such a table could reflect the results of an experiment expressly designed for the purpose of determining if a relationship exists between the two variables shown. As with the factorial experiment, more than two variables can also be presented, though depicting them on a two-dimensional sheet of paper becomes somewhat of a challenge. For example, Table 12-3 shows the basic data of the Dr. Helium survey in a cross-tabulation including age, months since first tablet use, and number of pounds lost. In order to simplify Table 12-3, the age variable has been condensed into just two categories: 40 and under, and 41 and over.

**TABLE 12-3.** *Example of a three-way cross-tabulation of three variables: (a) age of respondent, (b) number of months on Dr. Helium's Weight-Loss Tablets, and (c) number of pounds lost since first use.*

| | | Age 40 or under Number of months on Dr. Helium's Weight-Loss Tablets | | | | | | | Age 41 or over Number of months on Dr. Helium's Weight-Loss Tablets | | | | | | |
|---|---|---|---|---|---|---|---|---|---|---|---|---|---|---|---|
| | | *Under* *2* | *2* | *3* | *4* | *5* | *Over* *5* | *Total* | *Under* *2* | *2* | *3* | *4* | *5* | *Over* *5* | *Total* |
| | *No loss* | 12 | 7 | 8 | 10 | 8 | 20 | 65 | 5 | 3 | 7 | 8 | 6 | 19 | 48 |
| *Number of* | *1–5* | 14 | 10 | 5 | 11 | 6 | 16 | 62 | 10 | 7 | 5 | 3 | 5 | 12 | 42 |
| *pounds lost* | *6–10* | 10 | 18 | 13 | 7 | 6 | 16 | 70 | 9 | 12 | 15 | 6 | 3 | 15 | 60 |
| *since first* | *11–15* | 11 | 10 | 13 | 4 | 3 | 10 | 51 | 7 | 5 | 8 | 3 | 2 | 12 | 37 |
| *use of* | *16–20* | 3 | 3 | 2 | 2 | 5 | 8 | 23 | 5 | 2 | 3 | 4 | 4 | 6 | 24 |
| *Dr. Helium* | *Over 20* | 3 | 1 | 0 | 2 | 1 | 5 | 12 | 1 | 2 | 1 | 0 | 1 | 1 | 6 |
| | *Total* | 53 | 49 | 41 | 36 | 29 | 75 | 283 | 37 | 31 | 39 | 24 | 21 | 65 | 217 |

Cross-tabulation is one of the most popular ways of summarizing marketing research data. It allows the analyst to identify statistically significant relationships between variables and offers the added benefit of presenting a logical "picture" of the data that the nonresearcher can visually examine and identify. While the most effective form of cross-tabulation is the two-way variety, little difficulty is presented when there are more than two variables being measured in a given study. All one needs to do is simply present the variables in a two-at-a-time fashion. Thus, if there are $n$ variables, this would involve $[n(n - 1)]/2$ different presentations (the combination of $n$ things taken two at a time). In the case of four different variables, there could be $[4(4 - 1)]/2$, or 6 different two-way presentations. Admittedly, limiting one's analysis to just two variables at a time is not wise. However, the two-way presentation remains one of the most powerful means of demonstrating between-variable relationships to the nonquantitative marketing decision maker. (After all, we wouldn't want Dr. Helium to be left up in the air with regard to knowing how effective his product is.)

## STATISTICAL SUMMARIZATION

In addition to being able to summarize our data in tabular form, as in the one-, two-, and three-way tabulations of the preceding section, we can also describe the data in statistical terms. In this section we'll review two of the principal ways in which data are statistically summarized—using measures of centrality and measures of dispersion. In addition, we'll take a look at an important statistical descriptor called the percentage.

### Measures of Centrality

The three most common ways to describe the centrality of a set of data are the *mode*, the *median*, and the *mean*. To illustrate each of these, let's assume that the manufacturer of a disposable razor has done a study to determine how many shaves the product is able to provide, with the following results from a sample of 11 men:

| Person number | Number of shaves |
|:---:|:---:|
| 1 | 11 |
| 2 | 9 |
| 3 | 6 |
| 4 | 14 |
| 5 | 12 |
| 6 | 8 |
| 7 | 14 |
| 8 | 10 |
| 9 | 7 |
| 10 | 14 |
| 11 | 9 |

## Mode

The *mode* is the value that occurs most frequently. It can be described as the "most typical" response. In the case of our shaving data, we might arrange the data in the following frequency distribution in order to identify the mode value:

| Number of shaves | Number of persons who obtained this many shaves |
|:---:|:---:|
| 6 | 1 |
| 7 | 1 |
| 8 | 1 |
| 9 | 2 |
| 10 | 1 |
| 11 | 1 |
| 12 | 1 |
| 13 | 0 |
| (14) | 3 |

Thus, for these data, the mode is 14 shaves, since this result was obtained from a greater number of individuals than any other. Given the preceding data, the razor manufacturer may have the company's advertising agency state that the product "in an actual consumer test, most typically provided users with 14 (yes, folks, count 'em, 14) shaves!" As this example demonstrates, a potential weakness of the mode is the possibility that the *most frequently recorded* measurement may not really be very typical of the entire set of results obtained. For example, in our data, 8 of the 11 persons got fewer than 14 shaves from the razor, yet 14 was the statistical mode. As a consumer of research information, it can pay to be a bit skeptical of the mode, especially if other measures of centrality are either far different or not provided at all.

## Median

The *median* value in a set of data is the value that has just as many responses above it as below it. If the responses are listed in a rank order from greatest to least, the median will be the one in the middle. For example, the shaving data could be listed as

14, 14, 14, 12, 11, (10), 9, 9, 8, 7, 6

The circled number, 10, is the median number of shaves obtained by the sample of 11 individuals. Five people got more than 10 shaves, while 5 others got fewer than 10 shaves.

In the event that there are an even number of responses (i.e., there is no truly middle response), it is necessary only to take the average of the *two* responses that together are in the middle. For example, the median of (6, 4, 2, 0) would be 3, since 4 and 2 represent the middle position. As a measure of central tendency, the median is generally more representative than the mode. In ad-

EXHIBIT 12-2

*Even a Median Can Mean Well*

In Chapter 1 an example was presented in which a study of bowlers revealed that the median income of bowlers was higher than the median income of the United States as a whole. The study was undertaken by an organization with a vested interest in bowling as a recreational activity.

Given the discussion of the mean and median in this chapter, one might speculate on whether this choice of the median as the income centrality measure could have been advantageous. While the mean is influenced by extremely high incomes, the median is not, and two pertinent questions arise: (1) To what extent do the proverbial "rich and famous" engage in bowling?, and (2) Would it be advisable to employ the median income instead of the mean if we wished to conduct a survey to promote tennis, golf, sailing, polo, or croquet instead of bowling?

dition, because it relies on an ordinal ranking of the data, it is less susceptible than the mean to extreme high or low scores.

### Mean

The *mean* is the most commonly used measure of the centrality of a set of data, and is known to the layperson as the *average*. Though used in a semifolk context in everyday language (e.g., the "average lumberjack," "average junior executive," etc.), it refers in statistics to the sum of the data divided by the number of data points, as described in Chapter 5. In the shaving example, this would be calculated by adding up the individual responses and dividing by 11, or

$$\text{sample mean} = \overline{X} = \frac{11 + 9 + 6 + 14 + 12 + 8 + 14 + 10 + 7 + 14 + 9}{11}$$

$$= 10.36 \text{ shaves}$$

Thus the mean for the data may be calculated as 10.36 shaves per person. An important characteristic of the mean is that we can calculate it without having to first arrange the data into a frequency distribution or to rank-order the scores from highest to lowest. Another attribute of the mean is its suitability for making statistical generalizations from the sample to the population—for example, when a simple random sample has been taken and the sample mean is used to estimate and construct a confidence interval for the population mean.

Probably the key weakness of the mean as a descriptor of a set of data is its susceptibility to extreme values. For example, suppose that our sample of testers had included one misinformed individual who made the mistake of using the wrong end of the razor, thus obtaining 935 "shaves" before wearing the plastic handle down to a stub. This would have raised the mean for the sample to approximately 95 shaves per person, definitely a false reflection of the true durability of the razor. While such an extreme occurrence is unlikely, lesser extremes often occur in common research situations. When measuring consumer incomes, for example, it is not unusual for the mean income to be higher than the median, reflecting the incomes of a few exceptionally well-paid individuals.

Before you begin to calculate any of the preceding centrality measures, be sure that data are in the proper scale of measurement. As with the scales of measurement themselves, these descriptors go from weakest to strongest (mode to mean). The appropriate scales of measurement are

*Mode:*  nominal scale data or stronger

*Median:*  ordinal scale data or stronger

*Mean:*  interval scale data or stronger

## Measures of Dispersion

In addition to describing the centrality of a set of data, it is also useful to determine the amount of dispersion, or "spread," that exists among a set of measurements. There are three major descriptors of dispersion: the range, the standard deviation, and the variance.

### Range

The *range* is the most elementary of the three measures, and is simply the distance between the two most extreme values. For example, in our razor study, one individual obtained only 6 shaves from the disposable razor, while another was able to shave 14 times before the blade became ineffective. Thus, the range was 14 − 6, or a difference of 8 shaves.

Because the range places sole emphasis on the most extreme values, it is unaffected by what we might describe as the *typical* spread in the data. For example, in the razor study, if one poor soul had indeed held the razor backwards and shaved 935 times before wearing out the plastic handle, the range would have been 935 − 6, or 929—not a very realistic picture of the typical spread of such data. As another example, consider a set of data reporting the annual income of residents of a small town: It would take only one unemployed person and one eccentric millionaire to stretch the range into a six-digit number and virtually destroy any meaningful description of the income spread among the many thousand more typical individuals falling between these two.

Nevertheless, the range remains a useful, though crude, measure of the amount of spread in the data. One disturbing note is its apparent popularity in describing the research results to be used in some advertisements. You've probably seen headlines such as "After installation of ____, the test cars got between 2% and 15% more miles per gallon." Remember that it takes only one extreme value to make the range a very impressive number.

### Standard Deviation and Variance

The standard deviation and variance measures of dispersion are more rigorous, but easily calculated. In addition, if our sample is of the *simple random* type discussed in Chapter 4, the standard deviation can also be used to statistically generalize from our sample to the population from which it was drawn. As presented in Chapter 5, the standard deviation of a set of data is calculated as

$$s = \text{sample standard deviation} = \sqrt{\frac{\sum (X - \overline{X})^2}{n - 1}}$$

where

$X$ = each observation in the data
$\overline{X}$ = mean of the observations
$n$ = number of observations
$\sum$ = "sum of"

In the case of the razor example, the standard deviation would be calculated as shown in Table 12-4, which also shows the calculation of the mean and the *variance* of the data. The variance is simply the square of the standard deviation. The calculations of Table 12-4, in addition to being available as part of "packaged" computer programs for the summarization and analysis of data, are available on several brands of pocket calculators as well.

When calculating the sample standard deviation and variance, it is standard procedure to use $(n - 1)$ as the divisor. When the sample $s$ and $s^2$ are calculated in this way, they are better "estimators" of the standard deviation and variance of the population from which the sample was taken. For large sample sizes (e.g., $n \geq 30$), the subtraction of 1 from $n$ makes very little difference.

If the data represent *every member of the population*, it is then appropriate to use only $n$ as the divisor. Since most marketing research studies deal with samples rather than complete populations, we will be using $(n - 1)$ as our divisor unless otherwise noted.

## Percentages

Another popular approach to summarizing the data is through the use of *percentages*, which represent the proportion of sample items that fall into various categories. The percentage is easily calculated and simple to understand, strengths that help explain its widespread use in the reporting of research findings. It is especially useful for surveys and public opinion polls. In the latter case, results are almost always expressed in terms of the percentage of respondents who favor one viewpoint or another, or who possess a certain characteristic.

**TABLE 12-4.** *Calculation of the mean* ($\overline{X}$)*, standard deviation* (s) *and variance* ($s^2$) *for hypothetical data representing number of shaves 11 respondents received from disposable razor.*

| Respondent number | X = number of shaves obtained by the respondent | $X - \overline{X}$ | $(X - \overline{X})^2$ |
|---|---|---|---|
| 1 | 11 | .64 | .41 |
| 2 | 9 | −1.36 | 1.85 |
| 3 | 6 | −4.36 | 19.01 |
| 4 | 14 | 3.64 | 13.25 |
| 5 | 12 | 1.64 | 2.69 |
| 6 | 8 | −2.36 | 5.57 |
| 7 | 14 | 3.64 | 13.25 |
| 8 | 10 | −.36 | .13 |
| 9 | 7 | −3.36 | 11.29 |
| 10 | 14 | 3.64 | 13.25 |
| 11 | 9 | −1.36 | 1.85 |
| | $114 = \sum X$ | (this total not needed) | $82.55 = \sum(X - \overline{X})^2$ |

$$\text{Mean} = \overline{X} = \frac{\sum X}{n} = \frac{114}{11} = 10.36$$

$$\text{Standard deviation} = s = \sqrt{\frac{\sum(X - \overline{X})^2}{n - 1}} = \sqrt{\frac{82.55}{10}} = \sqrt{8.26} = 2.87$$

$$\text{Variance} = s^2 = \frac{\sum(X - \overline{X})^2}{n - 1} = \frac{82.55}{10} = 8.26$$

**TABLE 12-5.** *Percentages are a popular way to summarize research results, especially when comparing groups that don't have the same number of members.*

| | | Number of months on Dr. Helium's Weight-Loss Tablets | | | |
|---|---|---|---|---|---|
| | | *4 months or less* | | *5 months or more* | |
| | | *Number* | *Percent* | *Number* | *Percent* |
| | *No loss* | 60 | 19.4 | 53 | 27.9 |
| *Number of* | *1–5* | 65 | 21.0 | 39 | 20.5 |
| *pounds lost* | *6–10* | 90 | 29.0 | 40 | 21.1 |
| *since first* | *11–15* | 61 | 19.7 | 27 | 14.2 |
| *use of* | *16–20* | 24 | 7.7 | 23 | 12.1 |
| *Dr. Helium* | *Over 20* | 10 | 3.2 | 8 | 4.2 |
| | *Total* | 310 | 100.0 | 190 | 100.0 |

Because percentages allow us to describe frequencies in a relative rather than an absolute sense, they make it easier to compare groups and distributions when sample sizes are not the same. For example, the percentage distributions of Table 12-5 allow us to compare a group having 310 members with one having only 190.

When using percentages to describe your data, remember that it's not appropriate to simply *average* percentages unless each one is based on exactly the same number of items. For example, suppose we did a study in which we found that:

1. 40% of 200 persons with a college degree said they favored socialized medicine, and
2. 55% of 300 persons without a college degree said that they favored socialized medicine.

For these data, we could not simply add 40 and 55, divide by 2, then state that 47.5% of our total sample favor socialized medicine. However, we *can* use a **weighted average** to weight each percentage by its relative sample size in order to arrive at the true overall percentage:

$$\frac{200}{500} \times 40\% + \frac{300}{500} \times 55\% = 49.0\%$$

Another potential problem when using percentages to summarize data is the possibility that some percentages will be based on a very small number of items. This can be somewhat misleading, since only a slight difference in frequencies can lead to a seemingly significant difference in percentages. For example, suppose that we've just observed four people leaving a bar, and three of the four (75%) were seen to be staggering. If just *one person* had consumed either more or less alcohol, the difference in percentages would be staggering as well. This could change the percentage from 75% to either 50% or 100% — quite a change, *in terms of percentages*.

## GRAPHICAL SUMMARIZATION

In addition to calculating statistical descriptors of the data, we may also wish to summarize our results in a more graphical sense. Such summarizations, as we will discuss further in Chapter 18, are extremely useful in getting important points across to your employer or client. In addition, as with statistical descriptors, they can be misused for unethical purposes. Such capacity for misleading the unwary reader is something shared by practically all aspects of statistics and research. However, we'll save the cloak-and-dagger treatment for Chapter 18 and concentrate here on simply describing the three major kinds of graphical summarization: graphs, bar charts, and pictorial displays.

### Graphs

*Graphical* approaches are useful for describing one or more variables over time or for visually depicting relationships between variables. These have long been popular in mathematics for describing how one variable changes in response to changes in another. As in the mathematics application, graphs in marketing research have a horizontal and a vertical axis, and the values of the displayed variables are plotted on this coordinate system.

### Bar Charts

The *bar chart* is one of the most popular ways of graphically representing the data of a frequency distribution. It typically shows the groups along one axis, with the frequencies or percentages described along the other, as shown in Figure 12-5. In addition to showing total frequencies, the bar chart rectangles can be divided into sections, as in Figure 12-6, to indicate how the frequency is broken down for each group.

### Pictorial Displays

Another way to visually summarize research data is the use of *pictorial displays*, which can take as many different forms as your imagination allows. Three of the most popular are the *pie chart*, the *pictogram*, and the *sketch*.

#### Pie Charts

The *pie chart*, as shown in Figure 12-7, actually involves a "pie" that is divided into portions based on the number of items that belong to a particular category. In constructing a pie chart without the assistance of computer graphics,

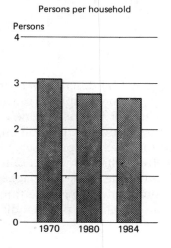

**Figure 12-5.** In the bar chart, or histogram, frequencies or percentages are reflected by the lengths of rectangles. (*Source: Statistical Abstract of the United States, 1986,* Bureau of the Census, U.S. Department of Commerce, p. xviii.)

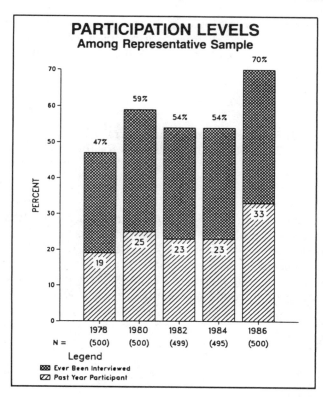

**Figure 12-6.** Bar charts can also be segmented to show the breakdown of frequencies or percentages within each category. In the most recent of this series of studies, 70% of the persons questioned had previously been interviewed in a marketing research survey, 33% within the preceding year. (*Source:* "Survey Participation Increases, Image of Research Is Still Good," *Marketing News*, January 2, 1987, p. 1, published by the American Marketing Association.)

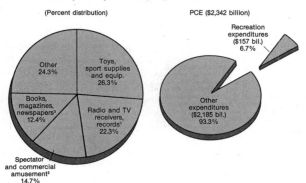

**Figure 12-7.** A pie chart describing personal consumption expenditures for recreation in 1984. (*Source: Statistical Abstract of the United States, 1986,* Bureau of the Census, U.S. Department of Commerce, p. 222.)

it's helpful to have a protractor for measuring angles, and just a little recall of trigonometry—that is, that there are 360 degrees in a complete circle. In calculating how many degrees wide a piece of the pie will be, just apply the following formula:

[number of degrees for a group]

$$= \text{[proportion of the total sample who are in this group]} \times 360°$$

In other words, if we find that 37% of our sample members fall into a certain category, we would allocate 0.37 × 360°, or 133.2 degrees for their "piece" of the pie chart.

### Pictograms

The *pictogram* is little more than a pictorial representation of the items that might otherwise be shown in a bar chart. In this approach, symbols are used to represent frequencies, as shown in Figure 12-8. Because the choice of symbols is largely up to the researcher, and since many symbols are extremely emotional in nature (e.g., grave markers, battered children, crashed automobiles, homeless persons, mushroom clouds representing nuclear weapons ex-

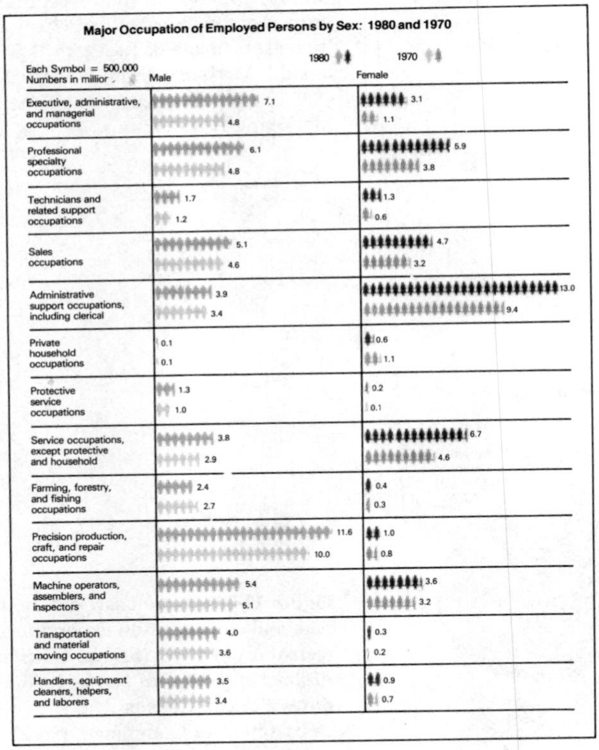

Figure 12-8.   A pictogram showing occupation according to sex in 1980 versus 1970. Each symbol represents 500,000 people. Within each job category, 1980 figures are above those for 1970. (*Source: General Social and Economic Characteristics, 1980 Census of Population*, Bureau of the Census, U.S. Department of Commerce, December 1983, p. 1–10q.)

**Figure 12-9.** In the *sketch*, the size of the figures is according to the underlying data. While the heights may be proportional to the data, larger figures become exaggerated because area is the product of both height and width. A figure that is twice as high will have an area *four times* as great.

penditures), the pictogram can be especially effective in reflecting a topic about which people may have strong emotional feelings.

### Sketches

*Sketches* that vary in size according to the value of a given variable are also used. An example of this approach is shown in Figure 12-9. This method has a particular ability to exaggerate differences. Note that in Figure 12-9 the drawing on the right looks much more than twice as big as the one on the left. This is because *the area is four times as great*. (Remember that both the height *and* the width have been doubled.)

The preceding are the major approaches to graphical displays. However, other possibilities seem to be unlimited (e.g., on the first page of each section

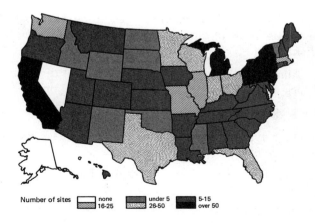

**Figure 12-10.** Maps with segments coded according to population, sales, or other characteristics are among the many alternatives available in the visual display of information. This map identifies states with the greatest number of hazardous waste sites. (*Source:* U.S. Environmental Protection Agency, Background Information, National Priorities List, September 1985, in *1986 Statistical Abstract of the United States,* Bureau of the Census, U.S. Department of Commerce, p. 205.)

of *USA TODAY*, the reader is apt to find numerical data being reflected by some extremely creative visuals). A more straightforward example of alternative displays is shown in Figure 12-10, which illustrates the proliferation of hazardous waste sites across the United States.

## DATA ANALYSIS AND THE MICROCOMPUTER

With increasingly powerful microcomputers and the proliferation of software packages for them, the world of data analysis has changed markedly since the days when the "mainframe" was the only practical way to carry out analyses of any magnitude or complexity. In this section we'll briefly discuss the basics of the microcomputer and its value in facilitating the analysis of research data and the interpretation of findings.

### Basic Components of the Microcomputer

Figure 12-11 illustrates the basic ingredients of the microcomputer, including the following:[1]

*System unit.* The box with the central processing unit, memory, disk drives, and device interfaces.

*Central processing unit (CPU).* Controls the computer, performing computations and logical operations.

*Memory.* The computer has read-only memory (ROM) and random-access memory (RAM), both measured in kilobytes containing 1024 characters each. A computer with 320K (320,000 kilobytes) memory can store the equivalent of about 170 pages of double-spaced text.

*Disk drives.* Electromechanical devices that can read information from floppy disks (diskettes) as well as transfer information onto them.

*Floppy disks.* Similar in concept to magnetic recording tape, a typical "floppy" can store at least 360K of data. Most software is provided in the form of a floppy disk.

*Device interfaces.* Allow for the connection of peripheral devices, such as printers or graphics plotters, telephone modems, and so on.

*Monitor.* Provides a visual display of text or graphics.

*Keyboard.* Looks like a typewriter keyboard and serves as a means by which instructions can be given to the computer.

*Printer.* Output device that generates text or graphical displays on paper.

---

[1] Based on Philip H. Dybvig, *Personal Computing for Managers with Lotus 123* (Palo Alto, Calif.: Scientific Press, 1986), pp. 3–5.

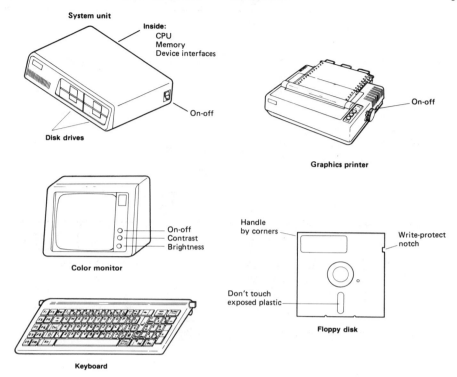

**Figure 12-11.**    Basic components of a microcomputer. (*Source:* Philip H. Dybvig, *Personal Computing for Managers with Lotus 1 2 3.* Scientific Press, Palo Alto, Calif., 1986, p. 4.)

## Software for Data Analysis

Some of the most popular mainframe statistical packages (e.g., SPSS and BMD) are now available for use on the microcomputer and the American Marketing Association regularly publishes updated listings of software for marketing and marketing research. For example, the February 14, 1986 issue of *Marketing News* includes descriptions, sources, and capabilities of 183 different packages indexed under 13 different applicational categories, including graphics, forecasting, questionnaire design, tabulation, survey data processing, statistics, statistical tests, and analysis.[2]

In the data analysis chapters to follow, examples of statistical software output will be presented along with explanatory discussion and worked-out examples for the techniques covered. As a marketing research student, you may be using a statistical analysis package as part of your course. One package for

---

[2] "Software for Marketing and Marketing Research," *Marketing News*, February 14, 1986, p. 9, published by the American Marketing Association.

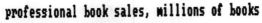

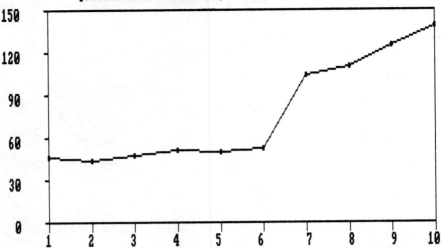

**Figure 12-12.** An example of a graphical display by microcomputer, this one was generated with the MARKSTAT software package and shows sales of professional books over a 10-year period.

(a)

MARKSTAT Statistical Analysis Program - Version 1.0

What do you want to do now?

1. ENTER new data from the keyboard
2. READ data from a disk file
3. SAVE data now in memory to disk
4. EDIT data now in memory
5. TRANSFORM data now in memory
6. CREATE new data series from mathematical functions
7. DISPLAY data in tabular or graphical form
8. ANALYZE data
9. CLEAR all data now in memory and restart MARKSTAT

(b)

What do you want to do now?

1. Basic statistics
2. Frequencies
3. Correlation analysis
4. ANOVA (one-way analysis of variance)
5. Regression analysis
6. Curve fitting
7. Cross-tabulation
8. Confidence intervals
9. Hypothesis testing

**Figure 12-13.** Many statistical analysis packages designed for use on the microcomputer feature "menus" from which the user can choose tasks to be performed. If the user selects "8" in the MARKSTAT menu of (a), he or she will then be provided with the more specific data analysis possibilities in (b). (*Source: MARKSTAT Student Manual,* Copyright © 1986 by Peter J. LaPlaca and the Futures Group, pp. 11, 31.)

Basic statistics for shaves

| | | |
|---|---|---|
| Number of data points | = | 11 |
| Number of valid points | = | 11 |
| Lowest value | = | 6.000 |
| Highest value | = | 14.000 |
| Range | = | 8.000 |
| Mean | = | 10.364 |
| Standard deviation | = | 2.873 |
| Coefficient of variation | = | 0.277 |
| Skewness | = | 0.264 |
| Kurtosis | = | −2.114 |
| Median | = | 10.000 |

Frequency distribution for variable shaves

| Value | Label | Absolute Frequency | Relative Frequency | Adjusted Relative Frequency | Cumulative Adjusted Frequency |
|---|---|---|---|---|---|
| 6 | 6 shaves | 1 | 0.0909 | 0.0909 | 0.0909 |
| 7 | 7 shaves | 1 | 0.0909 | 0.0909 | 0.1818 |
| 8 | 8 shaves | 1 | 0.0909 | 0.0909 | 0.2727 |
| 9 | 9 shaves | 2 | 0.1818 | 0.1818 | 0.4545 |
| 10 | 10 shaves | 1 | 0.0909 | 0.0909 | 0.5455 |
| 11 | 11 shaves | 1 | 0.0909 | 0.0909 | 0.6364 |
| 12 | 12 shaves | 1 | 0.0909 | 0.0909 | 0.7273 |
| 14 | 14 shaves | 3 | 0.2727 | 0.2727 | 1.0000 |
| | Missing Data | 0 | 0.0000 | ——— | |
| | Total | 11 | 1.0000 | 1.0000 | |

**Figure 12-14.**   If we were to call up selections 1 and 2 from menu (b) in Figure 12-13, MARKSTAT could provide us with basic statistical information and a frequency distribution for the shaving example discussed earlier in the chapter.

this purpose is MARKSTAT, and Figure 12-12 shows an example of the graphics capabilities offered by this software.[3] The illustration shown here happens to be a time-series plot of professional book sales over a 10-year span. Other graphical capabilities include the plotting of $Y$ versus $X$ graphs and histograms, or frequency distributions.

Many statistical analysis packages offer the user a "menu" for ordering up computer capabilities as needed. In the case of MARKSTAT, part (a) of Figure 12-13 shows the menu from which specific operations can be undertaken. If we were to select option "7," we would next be presented with a display menu from which to select the type of graph or chart to be generated. If our choice is "8," the menu in part (b) of Figure 12-13 would appear and inquire as to the type of analysis we wish to carry out. Each of these kinds of analysis will be

---

[3] *MARKSTAT Student Manual*, Copyright © 1986 by Peter J. LaPlaca and the Futures Group.

covered in the chapters to follow, and we'll occasionally present microcomputer output to complement examples relevant to our discussion of a statistical technique.

For the shaving example discussed earlier in the chapter, calling up items 1 and 2 from the second menu of Figure 12-13 would provide us with a quick summary of the descriptive statistics and a frequency distribution for the 11 data points. This information, shown in Figure 12-14, includes some items beyond our text: for example, in the basic statistics listing, the coefficient of variation refers to the relative magnitude of the standard deviation compared to the mean, skewness to the symmetry of the distribution (whether each side tends to be a mirror image of the other), and kurtosis to the levelness of the distribution. Since there are no missing data values, the adjusted relative frequency is the same as the relative frequency.

## □ SUMMARY

The data preparation process involves editing the data, coding responses into categories, then tabulating responses into frequencies or tables. Prior to further analysis and reporting, data may also be statistically or graphically summarized.

Editing involves examination of the data to ensure their accuracy, completeness, and usability. Initial screening is carried out to determine if the responses are legible, consistent, and complete, and that the respondent has taken his or her responsibility seriously. At this stage, response categories may be established for open-ended questions. Field editing is carried out as soon as possible after the interviews have taken place, with central editing taking place later to be sure that the questions are treated consistently for each respondent.

Coding is the assignment of responses to categories, and involves the identification of each response with a number associated with that category. Precoding is appropriate with dichotomous and multiple-choice questions, which have only a limited selection of responses available. When responses are of the open-ended type, as occurs with a set of unstructured questions, it may be necessary to assign responses to categories that are selected *after* the data have been collected. This approach is known as postcoding. Once the responses have been assigned to categories, tabulation is necessary to determine how many are in each category. Counting and summarization of responses can be carried out by hand or by computer, depending on the volume of data and the availability of suitable computer programs. Simple (one-way) tabulation leads to a frequency distribution of how many responses are in each of the categories, while cross-tabulation reveals the number of responses occurring in combinations of two or more categories. Data are typically summarized in statistical terms representing centrality and dispersion. Popular measures of centrality include the mode, the median, and the mean. Typical measures of dispersion are the range, the standard deviation, and the variance. Percentages are frequently used to represent the proportion of the sample who fall into various categories. The percentage is easily calculated and simple to understand, strengths that help explain its widespread use in the reporting of public opinion polls and other research findings.

In addition to calculating statistical descriptors of the data, we may also summarize results in a more graphical sense. Three major kinds of graphical summarization are graphs, bar charts, and pictorial displays. Among the more popular pictorial displays are the pie chart, the pictogram, and the sketch. Increasingly powerful microcomputers and a broad variety of software have enhanced the researcher's ability to process and analyze information as well as to easily generate graphical displays.

## ☐ QUESTIONS FOR REVIEW

1. Why is it necessary to edit survey questionnaires prior to analyzing the data collected? What are some of the difficulties that can be uncovered and resolved at this stage of data collection and analysis?

2. What advice would you provide to an assistant who is establishing response categories for an open-ended question for which the data have already been collected? What categories of responses would you anticipate for the question "What do you like best about going to college here?"?

3. If the responses on a number of personal interview forms seem either too consistent or too inconsistent, it's possible that the interviewer may have either exerted a strong bias on respondents or fabricated their responses altogether. What approaches might be taken to help ensure that interviewers in the field don't "cheat"?

4. Why is it important that central editing be carried out, if possible, by just one person?

5. "Many people don't enjoy professional football because it's _____" Code the following responses into categories of your choice.
   a. "too violent."
   b. "not fun to watch."
   c. "too difficult to understand the rules."
   d. "more enjoyable to watch a movie."
   e. "dumb."
   f. "not as much fun as playing scrabble."
   g. "too hard to find a parking place at the games."
   h. "boring."
   i. "hard for most people to afford tickets."
   j. "more enjoyable to watch college games."
   k. "not the kind of sport that most people can participate in."

6. Differentiate between precoding and postcoding of questionnaire-collected data, and explain under what conditions each would be most appropriate.

7. Explain the difference between simple tabulation and cross-tabulation, providing an example of each approach to data summarization.

8. In describing the centrality of a set of data, what possible problems may occur when using (a) the mean, (b) the median, and (c) the mode?

9. Determine the mean, median, mode, standard deviation, and range of the following data: 4, 3, 2, 7, 10, 12, 3, 56, and 3.

10. Provide an example, real or hypothetical, in which the range of a set of weight-loss data may provide a distorted view of the diet product involved. If the range were to be subsequently used in an ad promoting the product, would you consider this to be unethical? (After all, it might be argued that the ad is simply presenting a factual, statistical measure of the data obtained.)

11. In promoting each of the following activities to advertisers potentially interested in featuring that activity as an underlying theme within their ads, speculate as to whether the *mean* or the *median* income of participants would be the more desirable to report.
    a. Bowling.
    b. Yachting.
    c. Do-it-yourself auto repair.
    d. Tennis.
    e. Golf.

12. When calculating the standard deviation, how should one decide whether to use $n$ or $(n - 1)$ as the divisor in the formula?

13. A researcher finds that 40% of a sample of 200 prefer Brand A, and that 30% of a sample of 100 prefer Brand A. He "splits the difference", concluding that 35% prefer Brand A overall. What's wrong with his reasoning?

14. Of those who have been using Dr. Helium's product for at least 5 months, 27.9% have lost no weight; 20.5%, 1 to 5 pounds; 21.1%, 6 to 10 pounds; 14.2%, 11 to 15 pounds; 12.1%, 16 to 20 pounds; and 4.2%, over 20 pounds. Set up a bar chart which summarizes this information.

15. Sales have increased from 50,000 last year to 60,000 this year. With sales on the vertical axis, draw: (a) a graph that has a portion removed from the lower part of the vertical axis so sales will look more impressive, and (b) a graph that has a very large number at the end of the vertical axis, so sales will not look as impressive.

# 13

# UNIVARIATE DATA ANALYSIS

**Is it or Isn't it? Even Your Statistician Doesn't Know for Sure
(. . . but significance testing can help her decide)**

- Dunbar Wiggins, a previously unknown candidate for local office, has been heavily promoted in an ad blitz sponsored by his election committee. Following the campaign, the advertising firm tells Mr. Wiggins that he is now known by 75% of the electorate. In a poll conducted by an independent researcher, only 30% of the 200 voters surveyed had ever heard of Wiggins. Has Dunbar been duped?

- The instructions accompanying an electronics kit claim that the average assembly time from opening the box to having a working unit is 2.5 hours. Steve Fralik, host of a syndicated television program, distributes kits to 15 people, who end up requiring an average of 4.9 hours for kit assembly. Could this be a case of a contrived kit claim?

- During a news conference, the primary financial backer of rock singer Hubert Shubert tells media members that 55% of Hubert's fans are female teenagers. In a subsequent recording company survey, 63% of the 100 persons claiming to be Shubert fans are teenage females. Given these findings, does the creditor's claim continue to be credible?

- The owner of Frank's Franks typically sells 1200 hot dogs when the local baseball team has a home game at the nearby stadium. On a day following a graphic TV documentary on hot dog manufacturing, Frank sold just 1000 franks during the team's home game. Did the documentary make a difference?

## INTRODUCTION

Since the advent of taxation, wise persons have said there are only two things that are certain: death and taxation. The rest, like the cases in the preceding vignette, are subject to conjecture. For example, Mr. Wiggins might entertain some serious doubts about the performance of his ad agency, the TV host might question the kit's assembly time, Shubert may doubt his backer's knowledge of the music business, and Frank might blame his sales decrease on the TV documentary. However, none can say *with absolute certainty* that his suspicions are correct.

Matters like these, involving our degree of certainty regarding judgments based on data, are the topic of this chapter. For many research studies, mere processing and summarization of the data are not enough. There will remain questions to be asked about the conclusions that are most appropriate for the data we have collected.

Answering such questions is the goal of the statistical analysis techniques in this chapter and the two which immediately follow. In the discussions of this chapter, we will focus on *univariate* methods, those dealing with just one variable at a time. In the next two chapters, we'll examine *bivariate* techniques, involving two variables at a time. These basic methods, among the most popular tools of the marketing research analyst, are applied in a wide variety of settings. They can be classified into two major categories: parametric and nonparametric. *Parametric* techniques assume that the variables being studied are at least of the interval scale of measurement, and that the observations have been drawn from a population which is normally distributed. *Nonparametric* techniques assume that the variables are only of the nominal or ordinal scales of measurement, and make no assumptions regarding the shape of the underlying distribution from which the observations have been obtained.

With the exception of the *chi-square* and *Spearman rank correlation* techniques, which are nonparametric and rely only on nominal-scale data, the techniques in Chapters 13 through 15 will be of the parametric type. A detailed discussion of other nonparametric tests is available from a wide variety of statistical texts. Table 13-1 summarizes the statistical analysis techniques we will be discussing in these chapters, and provides guidelines for selecting an appropriate technique to satisfy most marketing analysis needs whenever one or two variables have been measured. Our discussion of univariate techniques

**TABLE 13-1.** *Summary of the statistical analysis techniques discussed in Chapters 13 through 15. Choice for a particular job depends on nature of the data and on the purpose for which the analysis is being conducted.*

| | Tests of significance | | Tests of association between two variables |
|---|---|---|---|
| | *For one sample* | *Between two independent samples* | |
| **Nonparametric** Nominal | Chi-square | Chi-square[a] | Chi-square |
| Ordinal | Sign test[b] Run test[b] | Mann–Whitney test[b] | Spearman rank correlation coefficent |
| **Parametric** Interval/ratio | Z test t test | Z test t test Analysis of variance[a] | Regression/ correlation analysis |

[a] Test is also applicable to more than two samples.
[b] Tests not included in text discussion.

for statistical analysis will be arranged under the following topics:

  **I.** Principles of significance testing
  **II.** Tests involving a sample proportion
  **III.** Tests involving a sample mean, large sample
  **IV.** Tests involving a sample mean, small sample
  **V.** P VALUES and significance testing
  **VI.** The chi-square test for goodness of fit

## PRINCIPLES OF SIGNIFICANCE TESTING

Once data have been converted into summary form, it's often desirable to reach some conclusion with regard to the significance of our results. For example:

1. If a population mean or proportion is thought (or claimed) to have a certain value, it's likely that an individual study may yield a sample mean or proportion that is not exactly the same. In this case, we may wish to consider whether (1) the observed difference is likely due to chance (i.e., sampling error), or if (2) the population parameter isn't really equal to the value originally believed. In this chapter we'll see how *significance tests involving a sample mean or proportion* can help us decide between these two possibilities.

2. If a population is said to exhibit a certain type of distribution (e.g., it is claimed that members are uniformly distributed in terms of income), this

assertion can be tested by comparing the distribution for a sample of individuals with the population distribution assumed to exist. This is one of
the goals that can be carried out by means of a technique called *chi-square
analysis*.

In this chapter our discussion will center on tests like those described
above. However, at this point it will be useful to present a general approach to
significance testing that will be applicable to all of the methods covered in this
chapter and the next two as well. The five basic steps, presented here in general
terms, will be followed whenever we carry out a significance test of any kind.

### Steps in Significance Testing

*1. Formulate the null hypothesis.* The *null hypothesis* is a statement that
is put up for testing in the face of numerical evidence. It is typically a negative,
skeptical statement that challenges you to prove it wrong. The philosophy of
statistical testing is such that the null hypothesis is accepted, and gets the benefit
of a doubt, until evidence to the contrary becomes statistically overwhelming.
Figure 13-1 is a dramatization of this philosophy. Until virtually battered by facts
that suggest otherwise, Mrs. Ferngreen will loyally adhere to her null hypothesis
that "my little Johnny's a good boy."

The null hypothesis, presented as $H_0$ ("$H$ sub zero"), is the statement
actually being tested. Along with its formulation, we also have what is called
an *alternative hypothesis*, written as $H_1$. If the null hypothesis is accepted, then
the alternative hypothesis must be rejected, and vice versa. Here are two examples of null and alternative hypotheses from the situations in the opening
vignette:

- "55% of Hubert Shubert's fans are female teenagers."
  Null hypothesis: $H_0$: $\pi = 0.55$, where $\pi$ is the population proportion
  assumed.
  Alternative hypothesis: $H_1$: $\pi \neq 0.55$. If the null hypothesis isn't true,
  then the population proportion must be something other than 0.55.
- "The average assembly time for the electronics kit is 2.5 hours."
  Null hypothesis: $H_0$: $\mu = 2.5$, where $\mu$ is the population mean assumed.
  Alternative hypothesis: $H_1$: $\mu \neq 2.5$. If the null hypothesis isn't true,
  then the population mean must be something other than 2.5 hours.

Significance tests may be either *nondirectional* or *directional*. Both of the
preceding examples are nondirectional, since the null hypothesis can be rejected
with a sample result that is either extremely low or extremely high. Nondirectional and directional tests may also be referred to as *two-tail* and *one-tail*,
respectively. The selection of a nondirectional test versus a directional test will
depend on the purpose for which the statistical test is being done. We will
concentrate here on nondirectional tests, leaving coverage of the directional type
to a separate appendix.

**Figure 13-1.** A dramatization of the philosophy of statistical testing. The null hypothesis always gets the benefit of the doubt, and continues to be accepted until evidence to the contrary becomes statistically overwhelming (i.e., if the null hypothesis were true, the observed results would have a very slim chance of occurring).

***2. Select the level of significance desired.*** Whenever the analysis leads to our rejecting the null hypothesis, there's a chance that we may be wrong in doing so—that is, we might make the mistake of rejecting a statement that is actually true. The probability of making such a mistake is called the **significance level**, and is generally represented by the Greek letter *alpha* ($\alpha$). In statistics, this is referred to as a "Type I" error, though there is also a "Type II" error (accepting a false hypothesis). These kinds of errors are illustrated in Table 13-2.

The researcher may use any desired level of significance in making a statistical test, but 0.05 tends to be the value most often used in practice. In other words, if you've done a test at this level and rejected the null hypothesis, there is no more than a 5% chance that your conclusion was a mistake. Numerically lower levels of significance (e.g., 0.01) mean that you will be less likely to reject a true hypothesis, but remember that there is a tradeoff involved. For example, the use of an extreme significance level in your test (e.g., 0.0000001) would make it meaningless to conduct any test at all, since you'd probably end up never rejecting *any* hypothesis.

If you subtract the significance level from 1.00, the result is the ***confidence level***, usually expressed as a percentage rather than a proportion. For example, if the level of significance you've chosen is 0.05, the corresponding confidence level will be 95%.

***3. Determine the observed value of the test statistic.*** In the third step, we determine the observed value of the statistic that will be used in the test. For the tests covered in this chapter, the test statistic could be any one of the following:

A sample mean, $\overline{X}$

A sample proportion, $P$

The calculated chi-square statistic, $\chi^2$

***4. Determine critical value(s) of the test statistic.*** At this stage, we find either one or two critical values that the test statistic would have to exceed in order for the null hypothesis to be rejected. Critical values are determined by consulting the table of the appropriate statistical distribution. In testing nondirectional hypotheses for a sample mean or proportion, there will be two critical values—one in each direction, as shown in part (a) of Figure 13-2. For the chi-square technique, there will be just one critical value, as in part (b) of Figure 13-2.

***5. Compare the observed value of the test statistic with the critical value(s).*** Critical values define the regions of acceptance and rejection of the null hypothesis. If the observed value of the test statistic falls outside the boundary described by a critical value, the null hypothesis is rejected. If not, the null hypothesis is accepted. The numerically smaller the level of significance, the more difficult it will be for a test statistic to succeed in reaching the "rejection"

**TABLE 13-2.** *The two kinds of mistakes we can make in a statistical test. We'll concentrate on the possibility of rejecting a true hypothesis. This probability is known as the* significance level *of the test.*

| | | The null hypothesis is really: | |
|---|---|---|---|
| | | *True* | *False* |
| **Statistical test says:** | *"Accept"* | Correct decision | Incorrect decision (Type II error). Probability of making this type of error = $\beta$. |
| | *"Reject"* | Incorrect decision (Type I error). Probability of making this type of error = $\alpha$. (This probability is the *significance level* of the test.) | Correct decision |

(a) Format when testing a sample mean or proportion

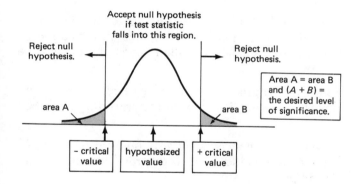

(b) Format for chi-square

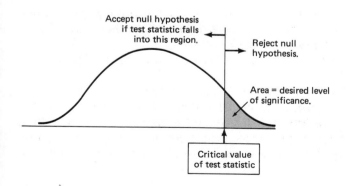

**Figure 13-2.** In the methods discussed in the chapter, tests of a mean or proportion will have two rejection regions, the chi-square technique just one.

**411**

region. For example, a critical value at the 0.01 level will be more distant than one at the 0.05 level.

## TESTS INVOLVING A SAMPLE PROPORTION

In research yielding a sample proportion, it's sometimes useful to compare this observed proportion with a value that has been hypothesized for the population as a whole. The following cases are typical of situations where this may be desirable:

- A city newspaper announces that 65% of weekday subway riders would be willing to pay a 50-cent higher fare in order to have more comfortable seats installed on the trains. In a study by the transit director, 43% of the 300 persons surveyed were in favor of this proposal.
- The owner of a local fast-food franchise, in attempting to sell the establishment to a prospective buyer, claims that 36% of her customers order the most expensive menu item during the dinner period. In observing a sample of customers, the potential buyer finds that 80 of the 350 persons observed chose this item.
- Our singing friend, Hubert Shubert, is still wondering about his financier's contention that 55% of the singer's fans are teenage females. In a record company survey, 63% of the 100 persons claiming to be Shubert fans were young ladies in their teens.

To demonstrate the testing of a sample proportion, let's evaluate Mr. Shubert's situation. In doing so, we'll apply the five steps in the procedure described in the preceding section:

**1.** *Formulate null hypothesis.* The financier's claim is nondirectional—that is, extreme results in either direction could tend to disprove his contention. Thus the null and alternative hypotheses are:

$H_0$: $\pi = 0.55$

$H_1$: $\pi \neq 0.55$        where $\pi$ = hypothesized value of the population proportion

**2.** *Select desired level of significance.* In this test we'll use the popular value of 0.05 in deciding whether to accept or reject the null hypothesis. As shown in Figure 13-3, the sum of the two tail areas will be 0.05.

**3.** *Determine observed value of test statistic.* The test statistic used here is the sample proportion, $P = 0.63$.

**4.** *Determine critical values of test statistic.* The normal distribution will be used, and there will be two critical values. To identify them, we use the hypothesized population proportion ($\pi = 0.55$) and the sample size ($n = 100$) in calculating the standard error of the sample proportion for samples of this size. The distribution in Figure 13-3 will be centered on 0.55 and have a standard

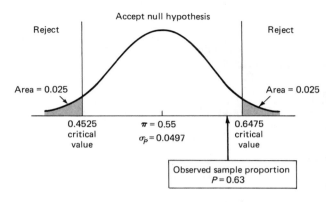

Null hypothesis, $H_0$: $\pi = 0.55$

Alternative hypothesis, $H_1$: $\pi \neq 0.55$

Accept null hypothesis

Reject                                      Reject

Area = 0.025                    Area = 0.025

0.4525          $\pi = 0.55$       0.6475
critical        $\sigma_p = 0.0497$  critical
value                            value

Observed sample proportion
$P = 0.63$

**Figure 13-3.** The result of this test of a sample proportion is our acceptance of the claim that 55% of rock singer Hubert Shubert's fans are teenage females. At the 0.05 level, the difference between the hypothesized and observed values could have occurred by chance.

error of

$$\sigma_P = \sqrt{\frac{(\pi)(1 - \pi)}{n}} = \sqrt{\frac{(0.55)(1 - 0.55)}{100}} = 0.04975$$

For the two tail areas in the normal distribution to add up to 0.05, the number of standard error units $(Z)$ must be $\pm 1.96$, and our critical values will be

$$\pi \pm Z(\sigma_P) = 0.55 \pm 1.96(0.04975)$$

$$= 0.55 \pm 0.0975$$

or critical values of 0.4525 and 0.6475.

5. *Compare observed value with critical values.* As shown in Figure 13-3, the observed value $(P = 0.63)$ falls within the acceptable limits. As a result, we should accept the financier's assertion that 55% of Hubert's fans are teenage females. At this level of significance, the difference between observed and hypothesized values is small enough to have happened by chance.

In the preceding test, we used the 0.05 level of significance. Had we used the 0.10 level instead, our conclusion would have been the same, but by a smaller margin. Again using the normal distribution, the required value of $Z$ for a two-tail area of 0.10 is $Z = \pm 1.65$. The standard error of the sampling distribution will stay the same, with $\sigma_P = 0.04975$. However, the critical values are now calculated as $0.55 \pm 1.65 (0.04975)$, or 0.4679 and 0.6321. At this level of significance, the observed value of 0.63 does not fall outside the critical values, and we continue to accept the null hypothesis—but just barely. For practice, you may wish to try the test again at the 0.20 level. (*Hint:* $Z = \pm 1.28$). If so, you'll find that the observed proportion falls outside the critical values and the null hypothesis will now be rejected.

For reference purposes, the critical value formulas we've used in this significance test are presented in Table 13-3. The table also describes the calculation of critical values for a sample mean, tests we'll be covering in the next two sections.

*Note:* In Table 13-3 the expressions for testing a sample proportion assume that $n \geq 30$ and both $\pi n$ and $(1 - \pi)n$ are $\geq 5$. This allows use of the normal distribution

**TABLE 13-3.** *Summary of critical values when testing a sample mean or proportion. For sample mean, t distribution is used only if sample size is less than 30 and population standard deviation is unknown.*

---

Testing a Sample Proportion:

Test statistic:  $P$, the sample proportion.

Standard error of sampling distribution:  $\sigma_P = \sqrt{\dfrac{\pi(1-\pi)}{n}}$

Critical values:  $\pi \pm Z\sigma_P$

$\pi$ = hypothesized population proportion
$n$ = sample size

---

Testing a Sample Mean:

---

If large sample ( $n \geq 30$) or if population std. deviation is known

Test statistic: $\overline{X}$, the sample mean.

Standard error of sampling distribution:  $\sigma_{\overline{X}} = \dfrac{\sigma}{\sqrt{n}}$

Critical values:  $\mu \pm Z\sigma_{\overline{X}}$

$\mu$ = hypothesized population mean
$\sigma$ = population standard deviation
$s$ = sample standard deviation (used above if $\sigma$ is unknown)
$n$ = sample size

---

If small sample and population std. deviation is unknown

Test statistic: $\overline{X}$, the sample mean.

Standard error of sampling distribution:  $s_{\overline{X}} = \dfrac{s}{\sqrt{n}}$

Critical values:  $\mu \pm t s_{\overline{X}}$

$\mu$ = hypothesized population mean
$s$ = sample standard deviation
$n$ = sample size

($t$ distribution is used, with degrees of freedom = $n - 1$)

---

as an approximation to the binomial, a distribution beyond the scope of this text. As noted in the table, in testing a sample mean we must choose between the normal distribution and the *t* distribution. The *t* distribution is used only when $n < 30$ AND the population standard deviation is not known; otherwise, the normal distribution is employed. An additional note: For convenience purposes, we're using "accept $H_0$" instead of the more technically correct (but more cumbersome) "fail to reject."

## TESTS INVOLVING A SAMPLE MEAN, LARGE SAMPLE

As in the preceding section, this discussion compares a sample statistic with a hypothesized value for the corresponding population parameter. In this case, the sample statistic is $\overline{X}$, the sample mean, and the population parameter is the assumed value for $\mu$, the population mean. As described in Table 13-3, the techniques in this section apply whenever the sample is large ($n \geq 30$) or (for any size sample) when the population standard deviation, $\sigma$, is known. Knowing the actual value of $\sigma$ in a practical situation is highly unlikely, so this tends to be simply a "large-sample" significance test for the mean. Of the situations presented below, we'll select one to demonstrate how the technique works:

- A national food company packages and freezes vegetables for subsequent distribution to wholesalers. The manager of the warehouse has told management that the average age of items in cold storage is 3 months. A com-

---

**EXHIBIT 13-1**

**Stars and Stripes Puts Wind in ESPN Sails**

ESPN found that about 1.1% of U.S. TV households watched their telecast of the first two races of the 1987 America's Cup challenge races in which *Stars and Stripes* (shown in Figure 13-4) defeated *New Zealand*. Taking place in Australia, the races were broadcast during the 11 P.M. to 3:30 A.M. EST time period, a slot when most people are sleeping and the network more typically has just 0.5% of TV households tuned in. *Assuming a sample size of 2000*, and using a nondirectional test at the 0.01 level, was the viewership significantly different from normal?

For these data, the observed proportion is $P = 0.011$ and the hypothesized proportion is $\pi = 0.005$. (Remember, this was aired in the middle of the U.S. east coast's night.) For the assumed sample size of $n = 2000$, the standard error of the sample proportion will be $\sigma_P = 0.0016$. In a nondirectional test at the 0.01 level, $Z = 2.58$ and the critical values are $0.005 \pm 2.58(0.0016)$, or 0.001 and 0.009. The sample proportion, $P = 0.011$, easily exceeds the upper critical value, and we can conclude that the yachting event attracted a percentage of viewers that was far different than could be expected by chance variation from one sample to the next.

*Source of data:* Rachel Shuster, "America's Cup Coverage Makes Splash in Ratings," *USA TODAY*, January 15, 1987, p. 3C. Copyright 1987, *USA TODAY*. Excerpted with permission.

**Figure 13-4.** As described in Exhibit 13-1, *Stars and Stripes* significantly increased ESPN's ratings during the first two races of the challenger series for the America's Cup. The swift 12-meter yacht went on to set ESPN viewership-share records during its four-race sweep of *Kookaburra III* in the final series. (*Source:* "ESPN's Cup Runneth Over," *The Indiana Gazette,* February 6, 1987, p. 20. Photo courtesy of Christopher Melhuish.)

pany inspector examines the processing date stamped on a sample of 100 items and finds their average age to be 4.2 months, with a standard deviation of 2.3 months.

- The manufacturer of a line of VCR equipment has told a news reporter that the average VCR owner has taped 5.7 movies from HBO. In a survey sponsored by a videotape rental firm, it is found that 200 VCR owners had an average of 7.5 movies taped from HBO broadcasts, with a standard deviation of 3.8.
- The vice-president of a finance company claims the average account has an outstanding balance of $3100. A consultant examining company records finds an average of $2950 and a standard deviation of $440 for a sample of 50 customers.

Examining the statement made by the vice-president of the finance company, we'll again apply the significance testing steps described earlier. The formulas used will be as presented in Table 13-3.

**1.** *Formulate null hypothesis.* For this case the null and alternative hy-

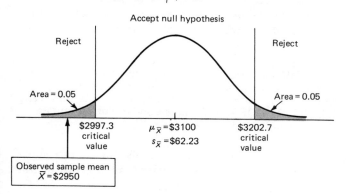

Null hypothesis, $H_0$: $\mu$ = $3100

Alternative hypothesis, $H_1$  $\mu \neq$ $3100

Accept null hypothesis

Reject

Reject

Area = 0.05

Area = 0.05

$2997.3 critical value

$\mu_{\overline{X}}$=$3100
$s_{\overline{X}}$=$62.23

$3202.7 critical value

Observed sample mean $\overline{X}$=$2950

**Figure 13-5.**  The vice-president of a finance company says the average outstanding balance for his customers is $3100. The sample mean from 50 accounts leads to our rejection of his claim.

potheses will be

$H_0$: $\mu$ = $3100

$H_1$: $\mu \neq$ $3100    where $\mu$ = hypothesized value of the population mean

**2.** *Select desired level of significance.* The 0.10 level will be used, and the sum of the two tail areas in Figure 13-5 will be 0.10.

**3.** *Determine observed value of test statistic.* The test statistic used here is the sample mean, $\overline{X}$ = $2950.

**4.** *Determine critical values of test statistic.* Using the normal distribution, two critical values are calculated. The center of the distribution of sample means for samples of this size will be the assumed population mean, $3100, and the standard error will be

$$s_{\overline{X}} = \frac{s}{\sqrt{n}} = \frac{\$440}{\sqrt{50}} = \$62.23$$

with critical values of

$\mu \pm Zs_{\overline{X}}$

or  $3100 \pm 1.65(62.23)$  or  $2997.3 and $3202.7

**5.** *Compare observed value with critical values.* Since the observed value ($\overline{X}$ = $2950) is not within the acceptable limits, we reject the vice president's contention that the average account has an outstanding balance of $3100. At the 0.10 level of significance, the gap between the observed sample mean and the hypothesized value is judged to be too great to have occurred by chance.

## TESTS INVOLVING A SAMPLE MEAN, SMALL SAMPLE

Significance tests of this type have the same goals as those already discussed, and are used whenever the sample size is less than 30 and the population standard deviation is not known. Because the sampling distribution of the mean can't be assumed to be normally distributed, the *t* distribution is used. Instead of the *Z* values we've used in other tests, a *t* value will be looked up in the statistical appendix. In referring to the table, the number of degrees of freedom (d.f.) will be *n* − 1. Our example of this technique is based on the following information:

> The manufacturer of a self-inflating emergency raft says it takes the compressed air system an average of 12.5 seconds to inflate the craft. Selecting a sample of rafts, a tester from a consumer magazine records inflation times of 15.0, 12.8, 11.9, 13.3, 14.9, 16.7, 10.8, 11.4, 13.2, 15.2, 17.1, and 14.3 seconds. (For these data, $\overline{X}$ = 13.883 seconds, *s* = 2.001 seconds, and *n* = 12.)

For this test, our null hypothesis will be $H_0$: μ = 12.5 seconds, our alternative hypothesis is $H_1$: μ ≠ 12.5 seconds, and we'll carry out the test at the 0.10 level of significance. Our test statistic, the sample mean, is $\overline{X}$ = 13.883. The assumed population mean, 12.5, is at the center of the distribution shown in Figure 13-6. For samples of this size, the standard error of the sample means is

$$s_{\overline{X}} = \frac{s}{\sqrt{n}} = \frac{2.001}{\sqrt{12}} = 0.578$$

Referring to the *t* distribution table, with degrees of freedom = $(n - 1)$ = $(12 - 1) = 11$, we find the *t* value for the 0.10 level to be 1.796. The critical values can now be calculated as

$$\mu \pm ts_{\overline{X}} = 12.5 \pm 1.796(0.578)$$

or   12.5 ± 1.04   or critical values of   11.46 and 13.54

Because our sample mean, $\overline{X}$ = 13.883, falls outside the range described by the critical values, the manufacturer's claim is rejected. At the 0.10 level, the

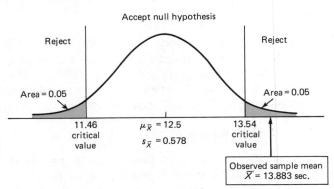

Null hypothesis, $H_0$: μ = 12.5 seconds
Alternative hypothesis, $H_1$: μ ≠ 12.5 seconds

**Figure 13-6.**   The maker of a self-inflating emergency raft says the compressed air system inflates the average raft in 12.5 seconds. Based on a sample mean of 13.883 seconds for 12 rafts tested, the null hypothesis is rejected at the 0.10 level of significance.

sample mean is too far away from the hypothesized value of 12.5 for this difference to have occurred by chance.

## P VALUES AND SIGNIFICANCE TESTING

If sample evidence enables you to reject a null hypothesis at a given level, you will also be able to reject it at all weaker levels as well. For example, if a sample mean differs significantly from the hypothesized population mean at the 0.05 level, it will be significantly different at the 0.10 level as well. This is because the 0.10 level is not quite so demanding. There are two strategies we can use in determining the significance of a statistical test result:

1. We can establish a cutoff point, using a critical value that corresponds to the desired level—for example, 0.05. This was the approach in the five steps described earlier in the chapter. In this method we establish a standard, then the test result is either significant or it isn't. As an analogy, in the high jump event of track and field, the crossbar may be positioned at 6'3" and a competitor will either clear it or he won't.
2. We can, by using different critical values (which correspond to different significance levels), determine the greatest critical value (i.e., the most demanding significance level) that the test statistic *is capable of exceeding*. In the high-jump analogy, this amounts to having no crossbar at all, allowing a competitor to jump as high as he can, then having the judges tell him how high he *could have cleared* if there had been a crossbar in place.

The first of these strategies has the advantage of simplicity and, to avoid unnecessary confusion, was the one selected during the significance tests conducted earlier in the chapter. However, it presents the possibility that you might understate the significance of a test because your selected significance level has been easily exceeded. As an example of the second approach, let's see what happens when we try a number of different significance levels for the small-sample test in the preceding section. Using the five levels available in the *t* distribution table in the Appendix, the following critical values and conclusions would result:

| Significance level for the test is: | Critical values for $\overline{X}$ are: | Observed value of $\overline{X}$ | Conclusion regarding null hypothesis, $H_0$: $\mu$ = 12.5 |
|---|---|---|---|
| 0.20 | 11.712 and 13.288 | 13.883 | REJECT ($\overline{X}$ outside limits) |
| 0.10 | 11.462 and 13.538 | 13.883 | REJECT ($\overline{X}$ outside limits) |
| 0.05 | 11.228 and 13.772 | 13.883 | REJECT ($\overline{X}$ outside limits) |
| 0.02 | 10.929 and 14.071 | 13.883 | ACCEPT ($\overline{X}$ within limits) |
| 0.01 | 10.705 and 14.295 | 13.883 | ACCEPT ($\overline{X}$ within limits) |

In this test, conducted at the 0.10 level of significance, we ended up re-

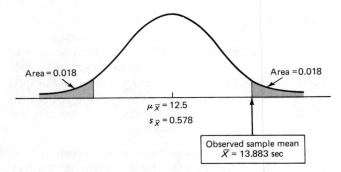

Null hypothesis, $H_0$: $\mu = 12.5$ seconds

Alternative hypothesis, $H_1$ : $\mu \neq 12.5$ seconds

Area = 0.018

Area = 0.018

$\mu_{\bar{X}} = 12.5$

$s_{\bar{X}} = 0.578$

Observed sample mean
$\bar{X} = 13.883$ sec

**Figure 13-7.** The P VALUE of a test is the level of significance where the observed sample statistic is exactly equal to the critical value. For the inflatable-raft test of Figure 13-6, the P VALUE is equal to 0.036. Since the null hypothesis could be rejected in either direction, the P VALUE is the sum of the two tail areas.

jecting the null hypothesis that the population mean was 12.5 seconds. As the preceding listing shows, we would have rejected $H_0$ at the 0.20 and 0.05 levels as well. At the more demanding 0.02 and 0.01 levels, the critical values are farther apart and $\bar{X}$ falls within them. As suggested in the possibilities just listed, *somewhere between 0.05 and 0.02, there will be a significance level where the observed sample mean is exactly equal to one of the critical values.*

In this approach, the most demanding level of significance that *could have been met* is known as the *P VALUE*. It is typically part of the output whenever a statistical software package is used in conducting a significance test. When you see "P VALUE," "≤ PROB," or "PROB =" as part of such output in the text, this will be *the maximum probability that such a great difference between the hypothesized population parameter and the observed test statistic could have occurred by chance.* The smaller the P VALUE, the more significant the test result. As shown in Figure 13-7, the P VALUE for the test just described is 0.036.

While this example involves a *t* test, the P VALUE is equally applicable whenever the normal distribution is used in testing the significance of a sample mean or proportion. It also applies to the chi-square technique of the next section as well as many of the techniques to be discussed in chapters to follow.

## THE CHI-SQUARE TEST FOR GOODNESS OF FIT

Chi-square analysis, one of the most popular techniques in marketing research, is used in a number of ways. In this chapter we'll examine how it can be applied to nominal (category) data in comparing a table of actual frequencies with one that has been hypothesized. Consider the following possibilities:

- In the past, the director of alumni contributions for a university has found that 40% of the contributors graduated from the College of Business, with 30% being from the College of the Arts, 10% from the College of Education, and 20% from other colleges within the university. In a sample of 180 persons who contributed during the most recent solicitation campaign, there were 70 business graduates, 45 arts graduates, 22 education graduates, and 43 graduates from other areas. Has there been a shift in the distribution of generosity?

- A spokesperson for a company selling "oldies" records through late-night TV ads claims the records sell equally well in Minnesota, Alabama, and North Carolina. For a sample of 120 orders from the past week, 35 of the orders were from Minnesota, 43 from Alabama, and 42 from North Carolina. Is the spokesperson's claim supported by these data?

In chi-square testing, the basic idea is to compare a table of observed data with one that assumes that a certain hypothesis is true. The former table will contain the actual frequencies observed; the latter, the frequencies that would be expected if the hypothesis were indeed true. If these tables differ too greatly from each other, we reject the possibility that the sample data came from a population with the hypothesized distribution. We'll use the university contribution situation to demonstrate how the technique works. As shown in the computer output of Table 13-4, the observed frequencies for the four groups are 70, 45, 22, and 43. The rest of the procedure is as follows:

**1.** *Identify null hypothesis.* Our null hypothesis will be $H_0$: "The population of contributors consists of 40% business grads, 30% arts grads, 10% education grads, and 20% other grads."

**2.** *Construct table of expected frequencies.* As shown in Table 13-4, our expected frequencies break down the 180 contributors according to the historical percentages on which the hypothesized distribution is based. While the data of the table were calculated by computer, the process isn't difficult; for example,

**TABLE 13-4.** *Chi-square goodness-of-fit example in text examined the breakdown of a university's alumni donors by college (1 = business grads, 2 = arts, 3 = education, 4 = others). Generated by Ecosoft, Inc.'s MICROSTAT, this chart summarizes the observed and expected frequencies and provides the calculated chi-square value and the P VALUE for the test. Results suggest that the "mix" of donors has not changed.*

| | CROSSTAB / CHI-SQUARE TESTS | | | |
|---|---|---|---|---|
| | GOODNESS OF FIT TEST | | | |
| | Alumni Contributors | | | |
| | FREQUENCIES | | PROPORTIONS | |
| CLASS | OBSERVED | EXPECTED | OBSERVED | EXPECTED |
| 1 | 70.00 | 72.00 | .3889 | .4000 |
| 2 | 45.00 | 54.00 | .2500 | .3000 |
| 3 | 22.00 | 18.00 | .1222 | .1000 |
| 4 | 43.00 | 36.00 | .2389 | .2000 |
| TOTALS | 180.00 | 180.00 | 1.0000 | 1.0000 |
| | CHI-SQUARE = 3.806, D.F. = 3, PROB. = .2832 | | | |

of the 180 persons, we would expect 0.30(180), or 54, of the contributors to be from the College of the Arts, and 0.10(180), or 18, to be graduates of the College of Education. (*Note:* To apply the chi-square technique, each expected frequency should be five or more. If this does not occur the first time you set up a table, combine categories until the requirement is met.)

**3.** *Determine calculated chi-square statistic.* This is our test statistic, $\chi^2$ (*chi* is a Greek letter that rhymes with "sky"), and reflects the amount of divergence between the observed ($f_o$) and expected ($f_e$) frequencies. It is calculated by the following formula:

$$\text{calculated } \chi^2 = \sum \frac{(f_o - f_e)^2}{f_e}$$

where

$$\sum = \text{"sum of"}$$
$$f_o = \text{observed frequency for each cell}$$
$$f_e = \text{expected frequency for each cell}$$

or

$$\text{calculated } \chi^2 = \frac{(70 - 72)^2}{72} + \frac{(45 - 54)^2}{54} + \frac{(22 - 18)^2}{18} + \frac{(43 - 36)^2}{36} = 3.806$$

**4.** *Determine critical value for the chi-square statistic.* The critical value of $\chi^2$ is obtained from the chi-square distribution in the statistical appendix to the text. As in previous tests, we must select a significance level—for this one, we'll use 0.10. It is also necessary to determine the number of degrees of freedom (d.f.) associated with the test; in this kind of test, d.f. = $k - 1$, where $k$ is the number of categories. Since there are four categories of contributors, d.f. = $k - 1 = 4 - 1 = 3$. In referring to the $\chi^2$ table in the statistical appendix, we will use the 0.10 column (significance level selected) and the third row (number of degrees of freedom). The resulting critical value is 6.25.

**5.** *Compare calculated chi-square with critical value.* If the calculated value exceeds the critical value, we reject the null hypothesis. If not, $H_0$ is accepted. In this case, the calculated value (3.806) does not exceed the critical value (6.25). As a result, we accept the null hypothesis, concluding that the "mix" of contributors has not changed.

In Table 13-4, note the P VALUE described in the preceding section. At the bottom of the chart, "PROB. = .2832" tells us that the observed versus expected frequencies don't differ a great deal [i.e., there is a high probability (up to 0.2832) that the divergence we see between the two frequency tables simply happened by chance]. Although the levels of significance in our statistical appendix do not go numerically higher than 0.10, statistical software packages aren't troubled by such limitations.

## □ SUMMARY

Basic techniques of statistical analysis are among the most useful tools of the marketing research analyst. These techniques fall into two major categories: parametric and nonparametric.

Parametric techniques assume that the variables being studied are at least of the interval scale of measurement and that the observations have been drawn from a population that is normally distributed. Nonparametric techniques assume that the variables are only of the nominal or ordinal scales of measurement, and make no assumptions regarding the shape of the underlying distribution from which the observations have been obtained.

Once data have been converted into summary form with statistical descriptors or frequency tabulations, it's often desirable to reach some conclusion regarding the significance of the results. One such instance involves testing whether a sample mean or proportion is significantly different from a population value assumed to exist, or whether the difference observed is more likely the result of random variation from one sample to the next. If data consist of frequencies, the chi-square goodness of fit method may be applied in testing the difference between observed frequencies and those expected if the sample had come from a population where values are distributed according to a hypothesized distribution.

In significance testing, the null hypothesis is a statement that is put up for testing in the face of numerical evidence. The philosophy of statistical testing is such that the null hypothesis is accepted, and gets the benefit of the doubt, until evidence to the contrary becomes statistically overwhelming. Typical null hypotheses are that the population mean or proportion has a given value or that observed frequencies have come from a population with the hypothesized frequency breakdown.

The significance level (designated by the Greek letter *alpha*, $\alpha$) is the probability that we might make the mistake of rejecting a statement that is actually true. The P VALUE of a test is the level of significance where the observed sample statistic is exactly the same as the critical value, and is the most significant level at which the null hypothesis could be rejected. It is usually part of the output whenever data have been computer analyzed.

## □ QUESTIONS FOR REVIEW

1. What is the difference between a null hypothesis and an alternative hypothesis, and how does each relate to the significance testing of a sample mean or proportion?

2. For a judicial situation where the defendant is presumed innocent until proven guilty:
   a. Formulate the appropriate verbal null hypothesis to which jury members should subscribe.

**b.** Point out how Type I and Type II errors might apply to the eventual outcome of the trial.

3. What is meant by the significance level of a hypothesis test?

4. An entertainment industry executive estimates that 65% of U.S. high school students rent one or more videotaped movies per month. In a sample of 200 students, 110 claim to have rented at least one movie during the previous month. For this situation:
   **a.** Formulate the appropriate null and alternative hypotheses.
   **b.** At the 0.10 level of significance, conduct a nondirectional test of the null hypothesis.

5. Overall, an insurance company's representatives have had a 15% success rate in obtaining a personal meeting with potential customers contacted by telephone. Fred has telephoned 300 individuals so far this year and has been able to meet with 32 of them. In a nondirectional test at the 0.05 level, is Fred's performance significantly different from the company's past experience?

6. Using the data of Question 5, repeat the test at the 0.01 level of significance.

7. The marketing director for a boat manufacturer has used a national sales conference as a forum to tell retailers that 35% of current recreational boat owners plan to buy a larger boat within the next two years. In a separate survey, 30% of the 150 boat owners questioned said they intended to purchase a larger craft during this period. At the 0.05 level, use a nondirectional significance test to evaluate the marketing director's claim.

8. The manager of a fast-food restaurant contends that customers spend an average of 11 minutes in the dining room during each visit to her franchise. In observing a sample of 75 customers, a researcher finds their average stay to be 9.9 minutes, with a standard deviation of 4.2 minutes. In a nondirectional test at the 0.10 level of significance, evaluate the manager's claim.

9. Using the data of Question 8, repeat the test at the 0.01 level of significance.

10. A resort owner has found that the average customer charges $120 worth of meals to his room during a weekend stay. During the past weekend, guests included 240 people participating in the annual convention of the National Magicians Association. They charged an average of $130 in meals, with a standard deviation of $65. In a nondirectional test at the 0.05 level, could the magicians' level of spending be considered abnormal?

11. For Question 10, if the sample size had been 16, could we conclude at the 0.20 level that the magicians' spending habits differed significantly compared to other guests?

12. A manufacturer's color TV models are labeled as consuming 120 watts of power. For a sample of 9 sets, the average power consumption is found to be 117 watts, with a standard deviation of 3.5 watts. In a nondirectional test at the 0.02 level, evaluate the label's accuracy.

13. Traditionally, a magazine's new subscribers have had the following as their highest level of education: 10%, less than high school; 35%, high school; 43%, college; 12%, postgraduate degree. A sample of 200 recent new subscribers has, respectively, the following numbers of people from these four groups: 22, 86, 70, and 22.
    **a.** At the 0.10 level, do these findings suggest that a change has occurred in the educational attainment of new subscribers?
    **b.** At the 0.05 level, does there appear to have been a change?

14. On the national level, telethon efforts for a public-service TV network have resulted in 48% of the pledges being for less than $50, with 37% between $50 and $200, and 15% for over $200. For a sample of 300 pledges among donations to a small local station, the corresponding percentages were 51%, 39%, and 10%.
    **a.** At the 0.10 level, did this station's performance differ significantly from those in the rest of the nation?
    **b.** At the 0.025 level, was the station's performance significantly different?

15. What is the P VALUE and what is its relevance to significance testing? Using the appropriate table in the statistical appendix, what is the most accurate statement that can be made about the P VALUE for the significance test of:
    **a.** Question 7?
    **b.** Question 10?
    **c.** Question 14?

# APPENDIX
## Directional Tests for a Mean or Proportion

In the chapter our statistical tests for a mean or proportion were nondirectional; that is, the null hypothesis could be rejected *in either direction*. However, occasions can arise where a directional test is called for. In this appendix, we will examine two such examples: one involving a sample mean, the other a sample proportion.

You will find that the general procedures and formulas are the same as the corresponding approaches discussed in the chapter. The main difference will be the acceptance-rejection decision regarding the null hypothesis; that is, in which sample-outcome direction should we accept the null hypothesis and in which direction should it be rejected?

### Directional Test for a Mean

To demonstrate the directional testing of a sample mean, we'll examine the following situation:

> Already beset with financial problems, the Chekzar Rubber Company is faced with legal action as the result of claims made in a recent advertisement. The company's claim was that "Chekzar tires run 40,000 miles on the interstate, then bounce back for more." A government agency has tested 25 Chekzar tires and found that the average life was only 38,500 miles in interstate use, with a sample standard deviation of $s = 3500$ miles. At the 0.05 level of significance, can the agency reject Chekzar's claim?

Although the company's statement is of a "greater than or equal to" nature, our null hypothesis will be $H_0: \mu = 40,000$ miles. This provides a central value for our sampling distribution. However, because the tires are claimed to last at least 40,000 miles, our alternative hypothesis is $H_1$: $\mu < 40,000$. This places the critical value to the left side of the distribution.

In deciding on the direction in which the critical value will be located, it helps to visualize what our conclusion would be if the sample result were extreme in each direction. For example, if the sample mean had been 98,000 miles, we would undoubtedly accept Chekzar's claim. On the other hand, if the sample result had been an average life of 15 miles per tire, we would clearly reject $H_0$. Since any outcome to the right of 40,000 would cause us to accept Chekzar's claim, the critical value must then be located at the left-side point where the 0.05 tail area begins.

Since $n$ is less than 30 and we don't have any idea regarding the population standard deviation, we must use the $t$ distribution in conducting the significance test. For $n = 25$ and a one-tail test at the 0.05 level, the appropriate value of the $t$ statistic is 1.711. This is obtained from the $t$ distribution table in the statistical appendix, and corresponds to $(n - 1) = 24$ degrees of freedom. (Note that this is the same $t$ value that would be used in a two-tail test at the 0.10 level, but we're interested in the tail area in just *one* direction.)

With $t = 1.711$ and the standard error of the sample mean $= 700$ miles, our critical value can be calculated as $40,000 - 1.711(700)$, or 38,802 miles, as shown in Figure 13A-1. Since the sample average was only 38,500 miles, we would reject the null hypothesis. Based on these data, it's very unlikely (less than a 5% chance) that the average tire life is 40,000 miles or more.

If we wished to give the company a little more benefit of the doubt, we could conduct the test at a more demanding level of significance, say 0.025. However, for this level, $t = 2.064$ and the critical value would be a sample mean of 38,555 miles. Since the actual sample mean, 38,500, is less than this critical value as well, we would also reject Chekzar's claim at the 0.025 level of significance.

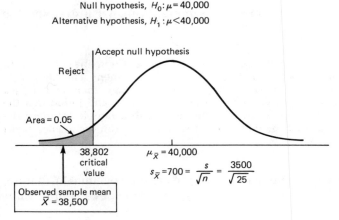

Figure 13A-1. Test for directional claim that average tire life is at least 40,000 miles. The observed sample mean, 38,500, falls short of critical value, so null hypothesis must be rejected.

In January 1987, the U.S. Veterans Administration announced the closing of cardiac surgery units at four VA hospitals doing fewer than 150 operations per year or where mortality rates were higher than 5%. Based on methods in this appendix, this exhibit presents significance-test results for two of the closed hospitals. Specifically, we'll test the significance of the difference between their cardiac operation mortality rates and the 5% cutoff figure used by the VA. Computer-generated P VALUES are included in our analysis.

Hospital A. 100 operations performed in 1986, 7% fatality rate.

Hypotheses and data:    $H_0: \pi = 0.05$    $H_1: \pi > 0.05$

$$P = 0.07 \qquad n = 100$$

Test:   $\sigma_P = 0.022$    At 0.01 level,

$$Z = 2.33 \text{ for directional test}$$

$$\text{Critical } P = 0.05 + 2.33(0.022)$$

$$= 0.05 + 0.05 = 0.10.$$

Conclusion:   Observed $P <$ critical $P$; accept $H_0$.

(P VALUE = 0.1794)

Hospital B. 96 operations performed in 1986, 10.4% fatality rate.

Hypotheses and data:    $H_0: \pi = 0.05$    $H_1: \pi > 0.05$

$$P = 0.104 \qquad n = 96$$

Test:   $\sigma_P = 0.022$    At 0.01 level,

$$Z = 2.33 \text{ for directional test.}$$

$$\text{Critical } P = 0.05 + 2.33(0.022)$$

$$= 0.05 + 0.05 = 0.10.$$

Conclusion:   Observed $P >$ critical $P$; reject $H_0$.

(P VALUE = 0.0076)

The preceding tests were performed as an additional example of the applicability of directional significance testing, and merely tested the possibility that either hospital may have been above the 5% rate due to chance variation. However, neither one satisfied the minimum requirement of 150 operations, and would have been dropped anyway.

Three important considerations: (1) For its 0.05 cutoff, the VA may have been relying on some lower historical rate, such as 0.03. No such figure was provided in this article. (2) Cardiac surgery patients who happen to live near some hospitals may tend to be higher or lower risk surgery candidates than those residing elsewhere. (3) Some hospitals or physicians may be more likely than others to accept patients for whom an operation offers very little hope.

*Source of data:* "VA Halts Some Heart Operations," *The Indiana Gazette,* January 13, 1987.

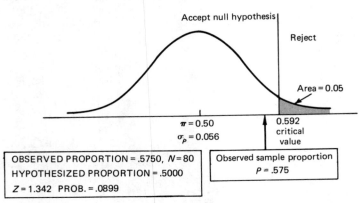

Null hypothesis, $H_0 : \pi = 0.50$

Alternative hypothesis, $H_1 : \pi > 0.50$

Accept null hypothesis

Reject

Area = 0.05

$\pi = 0.50$

$\sigma_p = 0.056$

0.592
critical
value

OBSERVED PROPORTION = .5750, $N = 80$

HYPOTHESIZED PROPORTION = .5000

$Z = 1.342$  PROB. = .0899

Observed sample proportion

$P = .575$

**Figure 13A-2.**   The developer of the food additive tested here has promised company officials that her product will "substantially improve" the taste of their instant coffee. In this preference test involving 80 subjects, the chemist's assertion cannot be accepted at the 0.05 level of significance. Listed below the distribution is the result of MICROSTAT analysis giving the exact P VALUE for the test.

## Directional Test for a Proportion

For the directional test of significance for a sample proportion, we'll use the following example:

> A prominent chemist has approached a food company and promised that a new additive she has developed "will substantially improve" the taste of the firm's instant coffee. In a taste test involving 80 persons, 46 prefer the test of the modified coffee over the standard formula. At the 0.05 level of significance, should the chemist's assertion be accepted?

If the new additive really has no favorable effect on taste, we would expect that no more than half of those trying both formulations would prefer the new one. This is the reasoning behind our null hypothesis, $H_0$: $\pi = 0.50$, which provides the central location for the sampling distribution in the significance test.

In deciding on the alternative hypothesis, keep in mind the chemist's boast that her additive would "substantially improve" the taste. By making such a strong directional statement, she has put the burden of proof on herself, and our alternative hypothesis will be $H_1$: $\pi > 0.50$. Thus we will accept her claim only if the sample outcome is *significantly greater than* 0.50.[1]

For the sample size ($n = 80$) and hypothesized population proportion ($\pi = 0.50$), the standard error of the sampling distribution is 0.056, as shown in Figure 13A-2. For a one-tail test at the 0.05 level of significance, the appropriate $Z$ value will be $Z = 1.65$ and the critical value will be $0.50 + 1.65(0.056)$, or 0.592. As Figure 13A-2 indicates, the observed sample proportion ($P = 46/80 = 0.575$) does not exceed the critical value, and the chemist's claim is not accepted.

Although the proportion of individuals preferring the coffee with her food additive was higher than 0.50, it *was not significantly higher* than 0.50. At the 0.05 level of significance, our conclusion is that the additive's good showing here was just due to chance. Figure 13A-2 also includes the MICROSTAT output for this test, showing the P VALUE ("PROB. = .0899") as well as the observed and hypothesized proportions and the actual $Z$ value corresponding to the observed sample proportion.

---

[1] As this example illustrates, in directional significance tests, the null hypothesis tested isn't necessarily the exact verbal statement that is made. The important thing is to (1) identify the central value of the sampling distribution, then (2) use the spirit in which the verbal statement was made to help select the direction where the critical value will be located. Although we could have placed the critical value for the Chekzar test in the right-tail direction (i.e., $H_1$: $\mu > 40,000$), to do so would not have been in the spirit of either the company's relatively modest claim or the government agency's intentions. Where Chekzar made an "at least as good as" statement, the chemist in this case has promised the food company a "substantial improvement."

# 14

# BIVARIATE TECHNIQUES
# FOR THE COMPARISON
# OF VARIABLES

## Much Ado About a Difference?

In mid-1986, a survey was conducted in which 1352 adult consumers were questioned about their spending plans for the future. Of those under 40, 8% said they were thinking of buying a color television. In the over-40 group, 13% were considering the purchase of a color TV set.[1]

Could it be that across the United States, both under-40 and over-40 consumers really had the same degree of interest in buying a color TV, and that they just happened by chance to differ by the 5 percentage points measured here? Using one of the techniques of this chapter, we can examine this question. Naturally, since we haven't yet covered the techniques of this chapter, let's just make some assumptions and reach a conclusion. After reading the chapter, you may like to return to this page and check out the answer for yourself.

Since no size breakdown for the age groups was given in the article, we'll assume (1) that an "adult" is at least 20 years old, and (2) that these 1352 adults had the same under-40/over-40 distribution as the 1984 adult U.S. population. In 1984, 47.71% of the adult population was under 40, 52.29%

---

[1] Source of total number surveyed and under-40/over-40 TV buying-intention proportions: Leo J. Shapiro and Dwight Bohmbach, "Future Looks Bright, Green for Americans," *Advertising Age*, July 21, 1986, p. 33. Copyright 1986, Crain Communications, Inc. All rights reserved. Reprinted with permission.

over 40.[2] Using this breakdown, we'd estimate that about 645 of those surveyed were under 40, and about 707 over 40.

> Q: Using the TV buying-intention proportions (0.08 and 0.13) given in the article, along with our estimated sample sizes of 645 and 707, could the population proportions really be equal?
>
> A: We'll put the details on horizontal hold for the time being, but using the techniques of this chapter, we would find that such a great difference between the sample proportions is significant at the 0.0029 level in a nondirectional test. In other words, if the population TV buying intentions really are the same, the probability would be 0.0029 or less that a difference this large would have been observed.

## INTRODUCTION

In Chapter 13 we discussed the basic principles of significance testing, then examined how marketing researchers could test whether a sample proportion ($P$) or a sample mean ($\overline{X}$) was significantly different from an assumed value for the corresponding population parameter (i.e., $\pi$ or $\mu$). In this chapter we'll see how the same basic ideas can be used in testing whether two samples are significantly different *from each other*. In marketing research it is often valuable to determine whether two independent random samples differ significantly with regard to some measurement or characteristic.[3]

In this type of test, the null hypothesis can be verbally expressed as $H_0$: *The population proportions (or means) are equal for the two groups.* As in Chapter 13, our tests here will be of the nondirectional type, in which the null hypothesis can be rejected by an extreme difference *in either direction*.

We will also examine two techniques that can be used to test more than two samples as well; for example, if we have three samples, could they have come from the same population? The first of these techniques is known as the *analysis of variance*, and it can be used to test two or more sample means. The second is an application of chi-square analysis to examine two or more sample proportions.

In describing each of the methods here, we will continue to follow the basic

---

[2] Source of estimated number of under-40 and over-40 respondents based on 1984 census data: *1986 Statistical Abstract of the United States*, Bureau of the Census, U.S. Department of Commerce, p. 26.

[3] *Independent* samples are those for which the selection process for one is not related to the selection process for the other. This precludes the use of these techniques, for example, in comparing "before–after" measurements for the *same* individuals.

steps of significance testing described in Chapter 13. We will also be referring occasionally to the P VALUE concept previously introduced. Our discussion will be according to the following topics:

I. Comparing two sample proportions
II. Comparing two sample means: large samples
III. Comparing two sample means: small samples
IV. Analysis of variance
V. Chi-square testing of sample proportions

## COMPARING TWO SAMPLE PROPORTIONS

In this test our null hypothesis is that the two populations from which the samples have been selected have the same population proportion. The following are among the many possible applications of this type of test:

- In comparing the effectiveness of two ads in an after-only experiment, agency researchers randomly divide 60 individuals into two groups. Of the 30 seeing ad A, 60% say "this product really works." For the 30 seeing ad B, only 40% make the same statement. At the 0.10 level, is there really a significant difference between these proportions, or could the better showing of ad A simply have occurred by chance?

- Ewell Carey, operator of the famous take-out chicken franchise, has surveyed customers in two different cities to find out if they would like to have roast beef sandwiches added to the menu. Two hundred of the 500 persons sampled in Pittsburgh said yes, while 150 of the 300 persons surveyed in Cleveland said yes. Ewell is interested in finding out if, at the 0.05 level, these results are significantly different.

Since we've already discussed the general process of testing hypotheses, we'll use the second of these cases to serve as an example.[4] Again, we'll follow the hypothesis-testing steps of Chapter 13. The following data summarize Mr. Carey's results:

$$P_1 = 200/500 = 0.40 \quad \text{and} \quad n_1 = 500$$

$$P_2 = 150/300 = 0.50 \quad \text{and} \quad n_2 = 300$$

**1.** *Formulate null hypothesis.* For this kind of study, our null hypothesis would be that the proportions are equal for both populations—that is, that $\pi_1 = \pi_2$, where $\pi_1$ and $\pi_2$ are the population proportions. Our alternative hypothesis is that they are not equal, or $H_1$: $\pi_1 \neq \pi_2$.

---

[4] In using this method to compare two sample proportions, we are assuming that $\pi_1(n_1)$, $(1 - \pi_1)(n_1)$, $\pi_2(n_2)$, and $(1 - \pi_2)(n_2)$ are each $\geq 5$. If any of these is less than 5, the normal distribution cannot be used and the necessary technique lies beyond the scope of our text. However, in the vast majority of marketing research applications, this constraint poses no problem.

**2.** *Select desired level of significance.* Ewell has specified what is probably the most commonly used level of significance, 0.05. If he ends up rejecting the null hypothesis, his chance of being incorrect will be 5% or less.

**3.** *Determine observed value of test statistic.* The test statistic used here is the difference between the sample proportions, $(P_1 - P_2)$. For the data of this study, the actual value of the test statistic would be $(0.40 - 0.50)$, or $-0.10$.

**4.** *Determine critical values for test statistic.* For this test, there will actually be two critical values, one negative and one positive, with both having the same absolute (i.e., without the sign) value. To find them, we first need to estimate the standard error of the difference between two such sample proportions:

$$s_{(P_1 - P_2)} = \sqrt{\overline{P}(1 - \overline{P}) \left( \frac{1}{n_1} + \frac{1}{n_2} \right)}$$

where

$$\overline{P} = \frac{n_1 P_1 + n_2 P_2}{n_1 + n_2}$$

$$= \frac{(500)(0.40) + (300)(0.50)}{500 + 300}$$

$$= 0.4375$$

$\overline{P}$ represents the overall proportion of both samples who said yes, and is equal to 350/800, or 0.4375. Using this value along with the sample sizes $n_1$ and $n_2$, we can calculate our estimate of the standard error of the difference between proportions as equal to 0.0362.

Next, we use the normal distribution table to find out what value of $\pm Z$ takes in 95% of the area under the curve. This is because we want the total of the tail areas to equal 0.05, the level of significance desired. As the normal distribution table indicates, the appropriate $Z$ value is $\pm 1.96$. Other $Z$ values would be appropriate for other levels of significance (e.g., $Z = \pm 1.65$ for the 0.10 level, or $Z = \pm 2.58$ for the 0.01 level).

The actual calculation of the critical values is according to the formula

$$\text{critical values} = 0 \pm Zs_{(P_1 - P_2)}$$

$$= 0 \pm (1.96)(0.0362)$$

$$= 0 \pm 0.071$$

and the critical values are $-0.071$ and $+0.071$. Thus, if the population proportions were really the same, and we were to do a great many studies of the type conducted by Ewell Carey, in 95% of the cases we would find the sample proportions to vary by no more than 0.071, or 7.1 percentage points.

**5.** *Compare observed value with critical values.* Carrying out this comparison shows that our observed difference $(-0.10)$ exceeds the left-hand, negative critical point $(-0.071)$, so we must reject the null hypothesis that the population proportions are really equal. Figure 14-1 summarizes the important values we've

*Null hypothesis: Population proportions are equal.*

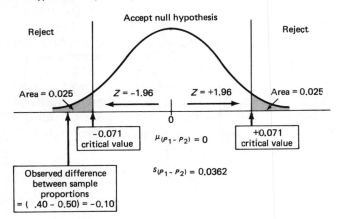

**Figure 14-1.** Graphical summary of text example comparing two sample proportions. Since observed difference was −0.10, hypothesis of "population proportions are equal" must be rejected in this two-tail test at the 0.05 level of significance.

calculated, and describes the acceptance and rejection regions for the test. Note that the midpoint of the distribution is zero, since the expected value of the difference would be zero if the null hypothesis were really true. In other words, if a great many such studies were done, the difference would sometimes be positive and would sometimes be negative, but would tend to average out to zero *if the population proportions were really equal*.

Thus, the observed difference between these sample proportions is significant at the 0.05 level. If we were to repeat the test at the more demanding level of 0.01, we would find the difference to be significant at this level as well. To check your understanding of the procedure, you might like to do this on your own. If so, you'll find that the critical values are ±0.093, which places the actual value of −0.10 slightly outside the acceptance range. (*Hint:* Since you'll be using the 0.01 significance level, Z must now be ±2.58.)

Computer analysis of this example leads to the results shown in Table 14-1. This enables us to identify the P VALUE, or exact level of significance of the

**TABLE 14-1.** *MICROSTAT output for Ewell Carey's test of proportions favoring addition of roast beef sandwiches to menu in Pittsburgh versus Cleveland. Because the computer assumes that we were doing a directional test, 0.002888 must be multiplied by 2 to arrive at the exact P VALUE for this nondirectional test.*

HYPOTHESIS TEST FOR TWO PROPORTIONS
FROM INDEPENDENT GROUPS

P1 = .4000,      N1 = 500
P2 = .5000,      N2 = 300

Z = −2.760      PROB. = 2.888E-03

difference between the sample proportions. This output assumes a directional test, giving the area in just *one* tail of the distribution, so we have to multiply by two to get the P VALUE for our nondirectional test. Thus, for this test, the P VALUE is 0.002888 times two, or 0.005776, and the difference between the sample proportions is significant at the 0.005776 level. (*Note:* In Table 14-1, "E-03" just means that the number in front is to be divided by 1000.)

## COMPARING TWO SAMPLE MEANS: LARGE SAMPLES

With this test, we can determine whether the difference between sample means is significant, or if the results are more likely the result of chance variation. The test assumes that each sample size is relatively large—that is, 30 or more.[5] As an example of its application, consider the following research situation:

> The Chekzar Rubber Company has done a study of the driving habits of various occupational groups. In a sample of 35 college professors, the average number of miles driven each year was 14,500, with a standard deviation of 3200 miles. In a sample of 40 dentists, the average mileage was 13,450, with a standard deviation of 1950 miles. In summary:

$$\overline{X}_1 = 14,500 \qquad s_1 = 3200 \qquad n_1 = 35$$
$$\overline{X}_2 = 13,450 \qquad s_2 = 1950 \qquad n_2 = 40$$

**1.** *Formulate null hypothesis.* Was the mean for the college professors significantly different from that extracted from the sample of dentists? The first step is to formulate the null hypothesis, which is that the population means are equal for the two groups (i.e., $H_0$: $\mu_1 = \mu_2$). The alternative hypothesis is $H_1$: $\mu_1 \neq \mu_2$.

**2.** *Select desired level of significance.* In this case, the company has not specified a level of significance, so let's use the popular 0.05 level in our test of the sample data. If we end up rejecting the null hypothesis, the probability that we're wrong will be 5% or less.

**3.** *Determine observed value of test statistic.* The test statistic here is the difference between the sample means, $(\overline{X}_1 - \overline{X}_2)$. For the data given, the observed value of the test statistic would be $(14,500 - 13,450)$, or $+1050$ miles.

**4.** *Determine critical values for test statistic.* For this test, as with that of the preceding example, there will be two critical values, since the hypothesis of equality could be rejected in either direction. However, they will have the same absolute value, with only the sign being different. In order to find the critical values, we must first estimate the standard error of the difference between two

---

[5] This section and the next are based on John E. Freund, *Statistics* (Englewood Cliffs, N.J.: Prentice-Hall, Inc., 1970), pp. 221–23.

## EXHIBIT 14-1
### Testing Drunk Driving Differences

In comparing the results of a 1973 survey with a similar study done in 1986, researchers concluded that drunken driving is on the decrease. In carrying out the more recent study, it was attempted to duplicate the 1973 effort as closely as possible. In the 1986 study, over 3000 drivers in randomly selected communities were stopped between 10 P.M. and 3 A.M. and asked to take voluntary roadside breath tests. Of those stopped, 92% complied with the request. In all states, a blood-alcohol concentration (BAC) of 0.10% or higher is the definition for driving under the influence. A few summary statistics:

|  | Females | | Males | |
|---|---|---|---|---|
|  | 1973 | 1986 | 1973 | 1986 |
| Percentage over 0.10% BAC | 2.6% | 1.4% | 5.4% | 3.7% |
| Approximate number tested[a] | 469 | 718 | 2291 | 2042 |

[a] Estimated from information in article; based on 3000 stopped, 92% compliance rate, and 17% women in 1973, 26% women in 1986.

Computer analysis compared 1973 with 1986 using a nondirectional test of $H_0$: $\pi_1 = \pi_2$ and was based on these reported proportions and the estimated sample sizes. The following results were obtained:

Females:
P VALUE = 0.1362 ($H_0$ can be rejected at the 0.1362 level of significance in a nondirectional test)

Males:
P VALUE = 0.0077 ($H_0$ can be rejected at the 0.0077 level of significance in a nondirectional test)

The significance of these nondirectional tests is especially striking in comparing the results of the two studies for the male drivers tested. The significance level for females is not as strong. However, even for the females, the difference between 1973 and 1986 would have been significant at the 0.0681 level if our test had been directional rather than nondirectional. (Directional testing is discussed in the appendix to this chapter, so don't worry about this right now.)

As you know only so well by now, no study is absolutely perfect. While not attempting to cast unnecessary doubt on this one, here are two points you may wish to consider: (1) Penalties for driving under the influence were much more severe in 1986 compared to 1973. (2) Could the previous point have had something to do with the 92% compliance rate of 1986; that is, could those who complied have differed in some important way from those who chose not to cooperate?

As we've discussed before, media coverage of research findings is, of necessity, often limited in terms of research details. Accordingly, this analysis (including sample size estimates) has been based solely on information as provided in the article and read by the general public.

*Source:* Based on "Drunk Driving Decreases Due to Changing Attitudes," *The Indiana Gazette,* January 31, 1987, p. 4.

such sample means:

$$s_{(\bar{X}_1 - \bar{X}_2)} = \sqrt{\frac{s_1^2}{n_1} + \frac{s_2^2}{n_2}}$$

$$= \sqrt{\frac{(3200)^2}{35} + \frac{(1950)^2}{40}}$$

$$= 622.6 \text{ miles}$$

Next, the normal distribution table is used to determine the Z value that takes in 95% of the area under the curve. As before, this will be $Z = \pm 1.96$. To calculate the critical values that define the acceptance and rejection regions, we use the following formula:

$$\text{critical values} = 0 \pm Zs_{(\bar{X}_1 - \bar{X}_2)}$$

$$= 0 \pm (1.96)(622.6)$$

$$= 0 \pm 1220.3$$

and the critical values are $-1220.3$ and $+1220.3$ miles. As with the proportions example, these critical values represent the largest differences that would occur by chance in 95% of such samples taken from the two populations.

5. *Compare observed value with critical values.* This comparison, shown in Figure 14-2, shows that our observed difference between the sample means (+1050 miles) falls within the two critical values, so we must accept the null hypothesis at the 0.05 level. In other words, although the sample means are more than 1000 miles apart, we must conclude that the population means could be the same, and that the difference between the samples occurred merely by chance.

While the difference is not significant at the 0.05 level, checking the same hypothesis at the 0.10 level (which is a little less "committed" to the null hy-

*Null hypothesis: Population means are equal.*

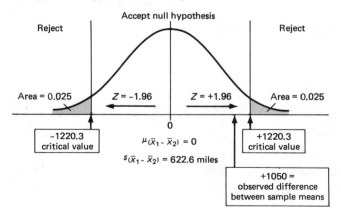

Accept null hypothesis

Reject

Reject

Area = 0.025     $Z = -1.96$     $Z = +1.96$     Area = 0.025

−1220.3 critical value

$\mu_{(\bar{X}_1 - \bar{X}_2)} = 0$

$s_{(\bar{X}_1 - \bar{X}_2)} = 622.6$ miles

+1220.3 critical value

+1050 = observed difference between sample means

**Figure 14-2.** Graphical summary of text example comparing means of two large (each $n \geq 30$) samples. Observed difference between $\bar{X}_1$ and $\bar{X}_2$ was 1050 miles, which fell into center region and allowed acceptance of the null hypothesis at the 0.05 level of significance.

pothesis), we would find the difference to be significant at this level. In this test, the Z value would be $\pm 1.65$ and the critical values for the difference between sample means would be $\pm 1027.3$ miles. Thus the actual difference of 1050 miles would fall into the "reject null hypothesis" region if this level were used. However, we would not be as sure of our conclusion, having a 10% chance of being incorrect.

Since the difference is not significant at the 0.05 level and significant at the 0.10 level, there will be some level at which it is *just barely significant* (i.e., the P VALUE). In this case, computer analysis determined the P VALUE to be 0.0920, which does indeed lie between 0.05 and 0.10. Thus 0.0920 is the exact level of significance of the difference between these sample means.

## COMPARING TWO SAMPLE MEANS: SMALL SAMPLES

Whenever at least one of the sample sizes is less than 30, we must take a slightly different approach to testing the significance of the difference between two sample means. Again, we are assuming that the samples are of the simple random type and are independent from each other. However, the technique requires two assumptions: (1) that the populations from which we are sampling have roughly the shape of the normal distribution, and (2) that the standard deviations of the populations are equal. Despite the latter assumption, the *sample* standard deviations may still be unequal, but this presents no problem.

In the previous two examples, we used Z values from the normal distribution. In this case we must use the $t$ distribution, with its corresponding values of $t$, to help describe distances from the midpoint of the hypothesized distribution. To illustrate this approach, we'll use the following set of sample results:

The Chekzar Rubber Company, trying to improve the company's image with its creditors and customers, has arranged a test to demonstrate that the durability of its tires is comparable to the best-selling competitor. Ten Chekzar tires are laboratory tested and show an average life of 24,227 miles, with a standard deviation of 4191.28 miles. Eight of the competitor's tires are tested, delivering an average life of 25,943.75 and a standard deviation of 2864.66 miles. In summary:

$$\overline{X}_1 = 24,227.00 \qquad s_1 = 4191.28 \qquad n_1 = 10$$

$$\overline{X}_2 = 25,943.75 \qquad s_2 = 2864.66 \qquad n_2 = 8$$

The null hypothesis will be that the population means are equal (i.e., that $\mu_1 = \mu_2$). As before, we'll assume a significance level of 0.05 for the test. The test statistic is the difference between the sample means, which is observed to be (24,227 − 25,943.75), or −1716.75 miles.

*Determining the critical values of the test statistic* is where the procedure differs from that used for large samples. In this test, the estimated standard error of the difference between the sample means will be calculated as

$$s_{(\bar{x}_1 - \bar{x}_2)} = \sqrt{\frac{(n_1 - 1)s_1^2 + (n_2 - 1)s_2^2}{n_1 + n_2 - 2} \left(\frac{1}{n_1} + \frac{1}{n_2}\right)}$$

$$= \sqrt{\frac{(10 - 1)(4191.28)^2 + (8 - 1)(2864.66)^2}{10 + 8 - 2} \left(\frac{1}{10} + \frac{1}{8}\right)}$$

$$= 1741.01 \text{ miles}$$

Our estimate of the standard error of the difference between sample means is then multiplied by the $t$ value that corresponds to the 95% area of the $t$ distribution. In looking up the $t$ value for this level, we refer to the column with total tail area of 0.05 and the row corresponding to $(n_1 + n_2 - 2)$, in this case $(10 + 8 - 2)$, or 16 degrees of freedom. Consulting the $t$ distribution table in the back of the book, we find that the two-tail value for the 0.05 level is $t = \pm 2.120$. Thus our critical values will be calculated as

$$\text{critical values} = 0 \pm ts_{(\bar{x}_1 - \bar{x}_2)}$$

$$= 0 \pm 2.120(1741.01)$$

$$= 0 \pm 3690.94$$

and the critical values are $-3690.94$ and $+3690.94$ miles.

A graphical portrayal of this test would be similar in appearance to that of the preceding test, for large samples. The result of the test would be accep-

**TABLE 14-2.** *From this MICROSTAT output for the Chekzar tire life comparison test, we can multiply 0.1694 (a one-tail area) by 2 in obtaining the exact P VALUE of 0.3388 for this nondirectional test. The difference in average tread life between Checkzar and Brand X tires tested was not very significant.*

CHEKZAR RUBBER CO. TIRE LIFE COMPARISON TEST
VERSUS BRAND X

|  | GROUP 1 | GROUP 2 |
|---|---|---|
| MEAN = | 24227.0000 | 25943.7500 |
| STD. DEV. = | 4191.2768 | 2864.6612 |
| N = | 10 | 8 |
| DIFFERENCE = | ********** | |
| STD. ERROR OF DIFFERENCE = | 1741.0067 | |

T = −.9861 (D.F. = 16)          GROUP 1: CHEKZAR:
GROUP 2: BRAND X:

PROB. = .1694

tance of the null hypothesis that the population means are equal, since the observed value of $-1716.75$ miles falls well within the acceptance region between the two critical values. While the results may not enable Chekzar to bounce back to profitability, this test suggests their tires are "in the ballpark" with the other manufacturer in terms of product durability. Although a better test comparison result would have been preferable, this one enabled them to accept the null hypothesis of product comparability.

The MICROSTAT output for this test is shown in Table 14-2, along with the descriptive statistics for each sample. As in Table 14-1, this result assumes that we've done a directional test, so the "PROB. = .1694" must be multiplied by 2 to get the combined area in both tails. Doing so, we arrive at a P VALUE of 2(0.1694), or 0.3388 as the exact significance level for the test. In other words,

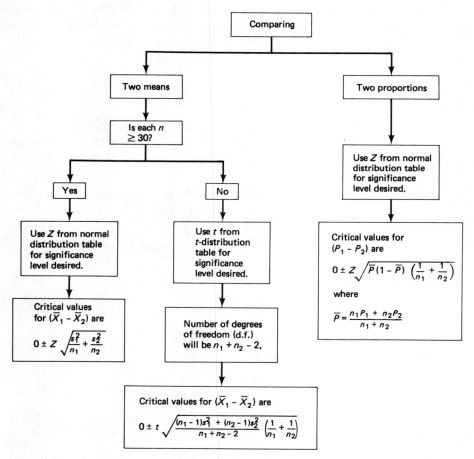

**Figure 14-3.** Summary of procedures for comparing means or proportions from two independent random samples. Detailed examples are discussed in text.

there was a fairly high probability (up to 0.3388) that such a difference could have occurred merely by chance.

### A Note on One-Tail Testing

The tests just described were all of the two-tail variety—that is, the null hypothesis was one of equality between the population means or proportions. In contrast, a one-tail test is used to examine the hypothesis that one population mean or proportion is greater than or equal to another. One-tail testing will be discussed further in the appendix to this chapter, but at this point it is appropriate to note that *any difference that is found to be significant in a two-tail test would be significant at one-half that level in a one-tail test.*

For example, in the test described in Figure 14-1, the proportion of Pittsburghers saying yes was found to be significantly different from the proportion of Clevelanders at the 0.05 level in the two-tail test. If we had set this up *from the very beginning* as a one-tail test, the difference could have been reported as significant at the 0.025 level. However, the test was not designed *from the beginning* for the purpose of testing a directional hypothesis, so it is a bit unethical—in after-the-fact fashion—to change our mind and test a different hypothesis from the one we were initially concerned with. After all, before the study, we may have neither suspected nor cared which sample showed the higher sample proportion.

It is not difficult for a researcher to make such a switch, from two-tail to one-tail, *after* the results are in. In addition, such a changeover may be buried in the midst of research jargon or in an obscure footnote, if it can be detected at all. As with so many other research and analysis strategies, this is another one that can be used as a weapon, either *for* or *against* you.

A flow diagram summarizing the approaches we've discussed for comparing two sample means or proportions is presented in Figure 14-3.

## ANALYSIS OF VARIANCE

Just as the chi-square technique (next section) compares two or more sample proportions, there is an analytical technique that enables us to compare two or more sample means. This approach is known as the ***analysis of variance***, commonly known as ANOVA. As an introduction to the technique, and how it works, consider the two sets of data in parts (a) and (b) of Figure 14-4. If asked which sample results are the most significant, you would probably indicate those in part (a), even though the respective sample means are the same. If pressed to explain your reasoning, you would likely point out that there is much more variability in the samples of result (b), making the differences among the sample means appear to be less important. If so, you've got the idea, because the basic

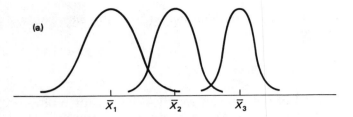

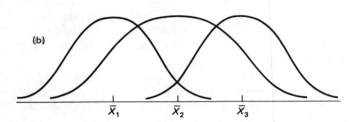

**Figure 14-4.** Visual examination suggests that the samples of (a) are more significantly different from one another than those of (b). Analysis of variance compares variability *between* samples with variability *within* samples to statistically determine whether the samples could have come from the same population.

principle of analysis of variance can be summarized by the following:

1. The null hypothesis is that all of the samples came from the same population (or from populations with equal means).

$$H_0: \mu_1 = \mu_2 = \mu_3$$

2. If the population means really are equal then

$$\begin{bmatrix} \text{variability } \textit{between} \\ \text{the samples} \end{bmatrix} \begin{matrix} \text{should} \\ \text{approximately} \\ \text{equal} \end{matrix} \begin{bmatrix} \text{variability } \textit{within} \\ \text{the samples} \end{bmatrix}$$

3. If the population means are not equal, then

$$\begin{bmatrix} \text{variability } \textit{between} \\ \text{the samples} \end{bmatrix} \begin{matrix} \text{should tend} \\ \text{to be greater} \\ \text{than} \end{matrix} \begin{bmatrix} \text{variability } \textit{within} \\ \text{the samples} \end{bmatrix}$$

The preceding summarization, which describes the case for three samples, could also be stated in terms of **between-column** variability and **within-column** variability, since each sample can be expressed by a column of data points. Statistically, the main assumption of analysis of variance is that the samples have been drawn from populations that are normally distributed and have the same population variance. Regardless of the number of samples being compared, the null hypothesis is always the same—that is, that their population means are equal. As with chi-square, we will calculate a measure of the discrepancy between our actual data and the null hypothesis. In this case, the amount of "stress" is reflected in a calculated ratio that describes the between-column variability divided by the within-column variability. This ratio is known as the **F ratio**, since it relies on the F distribution in the statistical appendix. In general, the larger this ratio, the more likely we will be to reject the null hypothesis that the samples came from populations with the same mean.

This method is called **one-way analysis of variance** because it considers only the treatment (column) effect. While it includes two variables, [group (nominal), and measurement (interval or ratio)], it is usually categorized as univariate since each group has just one sample mean. Chapter 16 examines the multivariate counterpart, where members of each group are measured by two or more variables.

> Rufus Leyken, the proprietor of Homer's Hardware, has devised three alternative sets of advertising copy to be considered for promoting the store during National Hardware Week. He's decided to test the effectiveness of these alternatives by using the Likert summated scale and a random sample of nine community adults in an after-only experiment of this type:

$$R\ X_1\ O_1$$
$$\text{Nine subjects randomly assigned: } R\ X_2\ O_2$$
$$R\ X_3\ O_3$$

There are three subjects in each group. $X$'s refer to the three ad copy alternatives, $O$'s refer to the Likert attitude scores of the subjects, which were:

| Ad treatment 1: "Homer's is where your heart is!" | Ad treatment 2: "Homer's Hardware: where prices are fair!" | Ad treatment 3: "Got a hardware need? Run to Homer's with speed!" |
|:---:|:---:|:---:|
| 12 | 15 | 7 |
| 9 | 16 | 11 |
| 15 | 20 | 9 |
| $\overline{X}_1 = 12$ | $\overline{X}_2 = 17$ | $\overline{X}_3 = 9$ |

As the preceding data show, the Likert scores for the three subjects exposed to ad treatment 1 were 12, 9, and 15, with an average of 12 for this group. The means for the three groups would, at first glance, appear to be quite different from each other. However, the samples are very small—only three individuals per group. Normally, there would tend to be larger sample sizes involved, but limiting each group to three will help provide an easier-to-follow demonstration of the analysis of variance procedure. As we go from one step to the next, the discussion will refer to the steps in the flow diagram of Figure 14-5. In addition, a summary table of calculations for this example has been provided in Table 14-3, which demonstrates the overall ease of carrying out an analysis of this type.

*1. Formulate null hypothesis.* At this stage, we assume that the ad treatments are no different in their effect, and that the differences we've observed in the sample means are simply due to chance variation. Appropriately, the null hypothesis is that the population means are equal for the three treatments.

*2. Calculate column means and grand mean.* The column means are the

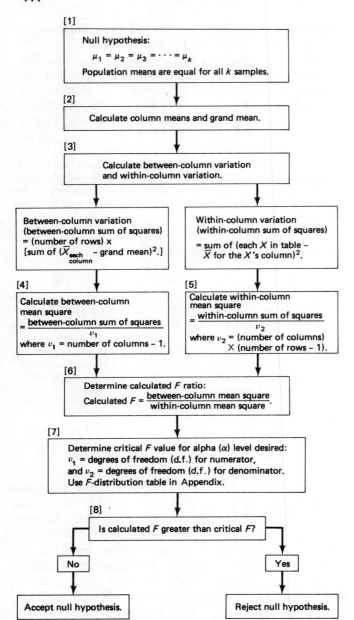

**Figure 14-5.** Procedure for one-way analysis of variance to compare two or more sample means. Step numbers are keyed to discussion and example in text.

means for each column, or sample, while the grand mean is the overall mean for *all* subjects in the experiment. Because the sample sizes are equal, the grand mean can be found simply by averaging the three sample means. Whereas the column means are expressed by $\overline{X}$, the grand mean is described as $\overline{\overline{X}}$ (the extra bar denoting its slightly higher level of importance).

**3. Calculate between-column variation and within-column variation.** The between-column variation is also known as the between-column "sum of squares," and is expressed here in relatively nonstatistical (though hopefully clearer) terms that don't rely on single and double subscripts. This quantity is

**TABLE 14-3.** *Calculations for analysis of variance example discussed in text. Since calculated F ratio is greater than critical value, we conclude that ad treatments differ significantly, and that sample means could not have come from the same population.*

| Raw data: | Treatment 1 | Treatment 2 | Treatment 3 | |
|---|---|---|---|---|
| | 12 | 15 | 7 | [1] Null hypothesis: $\mu_1 = \mu_2 = \mu_3$ |
| | 9 | 16 | 11 | |
| | 15 | 20 | 9 | |

[2] Column means     $\overline{X}_1 = 12$     $\overline{X}_2 = 17$     $\overline{X}_3 = 9$

Grand mean $= \overline{X} = \dfrac{12 + 17 + 9}{3} = 12.67$

[3] Between-column variation (between-column sum of squares)
= (number of rows)
× [sum of $(\overline{X}_{\text{each column}} - \text{grand mean})^2$]
= $(3)[(12 - 12.67)^2 + (17 - 12.67)^2 + (9 - 12.67)^2]$
= $(3)(32.67) = \boxed{98.0}$

Within-column variation (within-column sum of squares)
= sum of (each $X$ in table $- \overline{X}$ for the $X$'s column)$^2$
= $(12 - 12)^2 + (15 - 17)^2 + (7 - 9)^2$
$+ (9 - 12)^2 + (16 - 17)^2 + (11 - 9)^2$
$+ (15 - 12)^2 + (20 - 17)^2 + (9 - 9)^2 = \boxed{40.0}$

[4] Between-column mean square $= \dfrac{\text{between-column sum of squares}}{\nu_1} = \dfrac{98.0}{2} = \boxed{49.0}$

where $\nu_1$ = number of columns − 1
= 3 − 1 = 2

[5] Within-column mean square $= \dfrac{\text{within-column sum of squares}}{\nu_2} = \dfrac{40.0}{6} = \boxed{6.67}$

where $\nu_2$ = (number of columns)(number of rows − 1)
= (3)(3 − 1) = 6

[6] Calculated value of $F = \dfrac{\text{between-column mean square}}{\text{within-column mean square}} = \dfrac{49.0}{6.67} = \boxed{7.35}$

[7] Determine critical $F$ value for 0.05 level of significance,
$\nu_1 = 2$ degrees of freedom (d.f.) for numerator,     Critical value
and $\nu_2 = 6$ degrees of freedom (d.f.) for denominator.     is $F = \boxed{5.14}$

[8] Is calculated $F$ greater than critical $F$?

Yes, 7.35 is greater than 5.14. Reject null hypothesis (i.e., analysis shows that population means are *not* equal).

The means for the three ad treatments are significantly different from one another at the 0.05 level.

a measure of the variability among the sample means. In Figure 14-4, it would reflect how far apart the sample means lie.

The within-column variation, or within-column "sum of squares," is a measure of how much variability there is within each of the samples. In the expression used to calculate this quantity, the score for each subject is being compared *to the mean for his or her column*.

**4. Calculate between-column mean square.** For this calculation, we first need to find the value of $v_1$, which is the number of degrees of freedom associated with the numerator in the $F$ ratio. For this example, there are three columns and $v_1$ is simply (number of columns − 1), or 2.

**5. Calculate within-column mean square.** First, we must find the value of $v_2$, which is the number of degrees of freedom associated with the denominator of the $F$ ratio. This is (number of columns) × (number of rows − 1) and is equal to 6 for this example. Remember that the number of rows is the number of subjects or observations in each sample. This will come in handy in the shortcut method discussed in the next section.

**6. Determine value of calculated F ratio.** The $F$ ratio, based on our data and related calculations, reflects the between-column versus within-column variability and will be compared to the critical value in an approach not unlike our strategy in the chi-square technique.

**7. Determine critical value for F ratio.** The critical value is obtained from the $F$-distribution table in the statistical appendix, and is dependent on (a) the level of significance we desire—either 0.05 or 0.01; (b) the value of $v_1$, which will identify the appropriate column of the table; and (c) the value of $v_2$, which will identify the appropriate row of the table. In this example, we'd like to do the test at the 0.05 level of significance, and the values are $v_1 = 2$, $v_2 = 6$. Thus, we look in the second column and sixth row of the $F$-distribution table and find 5.14, the critical value.

**8. Compare calculated F with critical F.** If the calculated $F$ ratio does not exceed the critical value, we must accept the null hypothesis that the differences among our sample means are simply due to chance variation from one sample to the next. However, in this case, the calculated value (7.35) *does* exceed the critical value (5.14), so we can reject the null hypothesis at the 0.05 level of significance. Thus we conclude that there really is a difference from one ad treatment to another, and that the differences between the sample means are too large to have occurred by chance. (Note, however, that the critical value for the 0.01 level is 10.92, which means that the null hypothesis of "no difference" would have to be accepted at this more demanding level of significance.)

Table 14-4 shows the MICROSTAT output for the Homer's Hardware ad test, and you'll see that our earlier calculations match up with those performed by the computer. Naturally, using a computer software package is a lot easier, but your familiarity with the actual calculations in this small-scale problem will

**TABLE 14-4.** *Computer printout version of the one-way analysis of variance performed on Homer's Hardware ad effectiveness test. The null hypothesis of "population means are the same" was rejected at 0.05 level in text calculations. MICROSTAT output shows same figures calculated in text, plus the exact P VALUE for the test, 0.0244.*

ANALYSIS OF VARIANCE

HEADER DATA FOR: A:HOMER      LABEL: Homer's Hardware Ad
                                          Effectiveness Test
NUMBER OF CASES: 3            NUMBER OF VARIABLES: 3

ONE-WAY ANOVA

ANOVA COMPARISON OF MEAN AD EFFECTIVENESS SCORES,
3 TREATMENTS

| GROUP | MEAN | N |
|-------|------|---|
| 1 | 12.000 | 3 |
| 2 | 17.000 | 3 |
| 3 | 9.000 | 3 |
| GRAND MEAN | 12.667 | 9 |

| SOURCE | SUM OF SQUARES | D.F. | MEAN SQUARE | F RATIO | PROB. |
|--------|---------------|------|-------------|---------|-------|
| BETWEEN | 98.000 | 2 | 49.000 | 7.350 | .0244 |
| WITHIN | 40.000 | 6 | 6.667 | | |
| TOTAL | 138.000 | 8 | | | |

help you better understand exactly what the computer has done in producing the output shown in the table.

If you don't happen to have a computer handy, you can carry out one-way analysis of variance with a pocket calculator—it'll just take a bit longer. If you're doing this without aid of a computer, keep in mind that the technique described in the detailed calculations applies only when the sample sizes are equal for all groups—should one sample be slightly larger than the other, you can randomly remove cases from the larger samples until all sample sizes are equal. The alternative (aside from the computer) is to refer to a higher-level text or statistical reference.

### An Analysis-of-Variance Shortcut When You Have Summary Statistics for Groups

When the sample sizes are equal, and you have been given (or can readily calculate for yourself) the means and standard deviations for the various treatment groups, there is a slight shortcut you can take in order to save your time and calculator batteries. The basis of the shortcut is that calculation of the variance of a sample takes a form that is very similar to the within-column variation within each column (step 3 of the procedure in Figure 14-5).

Refer to step 3 of Table 14-3, where we calculated within-column variation for our example data, and you'll see that each column of squared terms resembles a quantity, $\sum (X - \overline{X})^2$, which is calculated in order to get the variance of the sample. As a reminder, remember that the formula for the variance of a sample is $s^2 = \sum (X - \overline{X})^2/(n - 1)$ for each column of data. Thus, if you know that a sample of three items has a variance of 9, then the sum of the squared deviations from the mean is equal to $(3 - 1)(9)$, or 18. If you check the first column of within-column sum of squares in step 3 of Table 14-3, you'll see that these squared deviations from the column mean add up to 18. This is column 1's "contribution" to the within-column sum of squares being calculated in step 3 of the table.

As an example, let's say that the data of our analysis of variance problem had been expressed as

|  | Treatment 1 | Treatment 2 | Treatment 3 |
|---|---|---|---|
| $\overline{X}$ | 12 | 17 | 9 |
| $s^2$ | 9 | 7 | 4 |
| $n$ | 3 | 3 | 3 |

Given this information, we can proceed to find the value of the within-column sum of squares "contribution" from each of the columns:

$$\text{column 1's contribution} = (n - 1)(s_1^2) = (3 - 1)(9) = 18$$

$$\text{column 2's contribution} = (n - 1)(s_2^2) = (3 - 1)(7) = 14$$

$$\text{column 3's contribution} = (n - 1)(s_3^2) = (3 - 1)(4) = \phantom{0}8$$

and total within-column sum of squares is 40.

Thus, armed with only the mean, variance, and sample size, we can carry out the same analysis as we did in the preceding section. The only difference in procedure is that step 3 becomes a little easier, especially if the treatment groups happen to have a very large sample size.

## An Ethical Consideration

Analysis of variance can be applied to the comparison of 2 sample means or 30 sample means, depending on the analysis situation you face. The "ethical consideration" in this subtitle comes in when you have the opportunity to do one of the following:

1. "Bury" the results of an exceptional treatment by including the treatment group in an analysis of variance comparing a large number of different samples

2. Purposely single out the "best" and the "worst" of a multisample comparison in a head-to-head confrontation via analysis of variance with just two samples

As an example of how this could work, consider the following data. From the experimental study on driver improvement programs discussed earlier in the text:

| Group | Mean improvement in correct responses |
|-------|---------------------------------------|
| 1 | $\overline{X}_1 = 1.67$ |
| 2 | $\overline{X}_2 = 2.50$ |
| 3 (control) | $\overline{X}_3 = 0.78$ |

The group that improved the most, group 2, could be "buried" in a multisample comparison including all three groups. On the other hand, group 2 could appear to be stronger if compared head-to-head with group 3, the control group. The following hypotheses represent the different analysis of variance replications that were performed for different combinations of the samples:

| Hypothesis tested | Can the hypothesis be rejected at the 0.05 level of significance? |
|-------------------|------------------------------------------------------------------|
| $\mu_1 = \mu_2 = \mu_3$ | No |
| $\mu_1 = \mu_2$ | No |
| $\mu_1 = \mu_3$ | No |
| $\mu_2 = \mu_3$ | Yes |

When combined with the other two groups, group 2 isn't "good" enough to cause the null hypothesis to be rejected at the 0.05 level. However, when group 2 is compared directly with group 3, this null hypothesis can be rejected at the 0.05 level. Thus an opponent of program 2 (or programs in general) could rely on the three-group analysis of variance, arguing that "there is no significant difference among the group means." On the other hand, a proponent of program 2 could compare group 2 directly with group 3, reject the null hypothesis of $\mu_2 = \mu_3$ at the 0.05 level; and argue that "program 2 is statistically superior."

This is probably nothing you'll lose sleep over tonight, but be wary whenever someone provides a multisample analysis of variance result that shows "no significance" as a result. Consider the researcher's motives and be alert to the possibility that either a "superstar" or a "bum" could be among the treatments that were found not to be significantly different.

## CHI-SQUARE TESTING OF SAMPLE PROPORTIONS

The chi-square method introduced in Chapter 13 can also be used to test the differences among two or more sample proportions. In this case the null hypothesis is that the differences observed between the sample proportions occurred simply by chance. Otherwise, the procedure is the same as that used to test goodness of fit in Chapter 13. To illustrate this application, let's assume we've collected the following information on television viewing habits in three communities:

| Community | Number of individuals surveyed | Percent who listened to the "Wake Up with Wilbur" show this morning |
|-----------|-------------------------------|--------------------------------------------------------------------|
| Smithton | 100 | 35 |
| Rock Island | 50 | 20 |
| Roosterville | 80 | 50 |

Using the chi-square approach, we'd first formulate the null hypothesis that $\pi_1 = \pi_2 = \pi_3$, that the population proportions are equal for all three communities. Our observed and expected frequencies would be as shown in the computer output of Table 14-5. Note that the "observed" cross tabulation relies on the sample sizes and percentages provided in the preceding description of the data—for example, in Rock Island, 20% of 50, or 10 individuals woke up with Wilbur, while 40 did not.

The expected frequencies are calculated under the assumption that the population proportions really are equal. For example, since there are 230 respondents altogether, with 100/230 of them from Smithton, 50/230 from Rock Island, and 80/230 from Roosterville, we'd expect that the 85 who listened to

**TABLE 14-5.** *Results of chi-square analysis applied to testing of three sample proportions. The chances are quite small (0.00269 probability or less) that such great variation among the sample proportions could have happened if the null hypothesis of "population proportions are equal" were really true.*

CROSSTAB/CHI-SQUARE TESTS
TESTING P1 = P2 = P3 FOR
"WAKE UP WITH WILBUR" LISTENERSHIP, 3 CITIES

OBSERVED FREQUENCIES

|       | 1   | 2  | 3  | TOTAL |
|-------|-----|----|----|-------|
| 1     | 35  | 10 | 40 | 85    |
| 2     | 65  | 40 | 40 | 145   |
| TOTAL | 100 | 50 | 80 | 230   |

EXPECTED FREQUENCIES

|       | 1      | 2     | 3     | TOTAL  |
|-------|--------|-------|-------|--------|
| 1     | 36.96  | 18.48 | 29.57 | 85.00  |
| 2     | 63.04  | 31.52 | 50.43 | 145.00 |
| TOTAL | 100.00 | 50.00 | 80.00 | 230.00 |

CHI-SQUARE = 12.176, D.F. = 2, PROB. = 2.269E-03

the show would be divided up proportionally. Thus the entries in the first row of the expected frequencies table are

$$\frac{100}{230}(85) = 36.96 \qquad \frac{50}{230}(85) = 18.48 \qquad \frac{80}{230}(85) = 29.57$$

From the observed and expected frequencies, we determine the value of the calculated $\chi^2$ statistic to get a measure of how much discrepancy exists between the two. As in Chapter 13, this is

$$\text{calculated } \chi^2 = \sum \frac{(f_o - f_e)^2}{f_e}$$

$$= \frac{(35 - 36.96)^2}{36.96} + \frac{(10 - 18.48)^2}{18.48} + \frac{(40 - 29.57)^2}{29.57}$$

$$+ \frac{(65 - 63.04)^2}{63.04} + \frac{(40 - 31.52)^2}{31.52} + \frac{(40 - 50.43)^2}{50.43}$$

$$= 12.17$$

For a data table in this application, the number of degrees of freedom is (number of rows $-$ 1) $\times$ (number of columns $-$ 1), or $(2 - 1)(3 - 1) = 2$. For the 0.005 level of significance, the critical value is $\chi^2 = 10.6$. Since our calculated value (12.17) exceeds this, we can easily reject the null hypothesis that the population proportions are the same. If the population proportions really were equal, there would be less than a 0.005 chance that our sample results would have been this different for the three communities. As shown in the MICRO-STAT results at the bottom of Table 14-5, the P VALUE of the test is 2.269E-03, or 0.00269. Since analysis of variance and chi-square tests are always directional, the 0.00269 one-tail area tells us the exact P VALUE for this test.

☐ **SUMMARY**

An important type of hypothesis test is the comparison of two independent samples to determine whether their respective sample proportions or sample means differ significantly. In this type of test, the null hypothesis $(H_0)$ is that the population proportions or means are really the same, and that the difference observed occurred simply through chance variation from one sample to the next.

Samples are independent whenever the selection process for one is not related to that for another. For example, this precludes the application of these bivariate techniques to "before" and "after" measures for the same individuals or objects. In such cases, there is really only one variable: the difference between the before and after measurements for each individual or test unit.

In the chapter, tests comparing two sample proportions or means were nondirectional, and the null hypothesis could be rejected by an extreme difference in either direction. Appropriately the alternative hypothesis ($H_1$) is that the population proportions or means are not equal.

One-way analysis of variance can be used to compare the means of two or more independent samples. In this case, the null hypothesis is that the samples have either come from the same population or from populations having the same value for the mean.

The chi-square technique presented in Chapter 13 can be used to compare the sample proportions for two or more independent samples. The null hypothesis being tested is that the samples have either come from the same population or from populations having the same value for the proportion. Both analysis of variance and chi-square analysis are directional tests where the null hypothesis is rejected if a calculated statistic (the $F$ ratio and chi-square, respectively) exceeds a single critical value for a desired level of significance.

## ☐ QUESTIONS FOR REVIEW

1. Two interviewers have each been assigned to survey a random sample of shoppers at two local malls. One interviewer is able to interview 53 of the 80 persons approached, the second gets interviews from 46 out of 83. In a nondirectional test at the 0.10 level, is there a significant difference between the success rates of these two individuals?

2. In attempting to measure the support they might expect from students attending a large urban university, an environmental group has asked students if they "would be willing to contribute one hour of time per week" in helping the organization achieve its goals. Of 200 sophomores who were surveyed, 31% said they would help, compared to just 20% of 120 seniors. At the 0.05 level, use a nondirectional test to examine the possibility that the population proportions for these two groups might really be the same.

3. A TV station is interested in viewers' reaction to two possible weather chart layouts. Of 40 persons exposed to version A, 25 say it is "easy to understand," while 24 of 50 individuals seeing version B make the same statement. In a nondirectional test at the 0.10 level, test the significance of the difference between these sample results.

4. The manager of a drive-through beer distributor is curious about the relative purchases of drivers of imported vehicles versus domestic models. For a sample of 120 customers driving imports, the average purchase is $15.21, with a standard deviation of $8.50. For 180 customers driving domestics, the corresponding figures are $13.50 and $7.35, respectively. In a nondirectional test at the 0.05 level, does the purchase behavior of these two samples differ significantly?

5. A demographic study reveals that the average income of 800 households owning pets is $39,000, with a standard deviation of $9500. In 290 households not owning a pet, the average income is found to be $33,100, with a standard deviation of $10,400. In a nondirectional test at the 0.05 level, is there a significant difference between these sample means?

6. The manufacturer of an automatic garage door opener is evaluating the effectiveness of two possible sets of instructions to help do-it-yourselfers install the product. For

35 persons reading one of the instruction booklets, the average time for installation is 93 minutes, with a standard deviation of 28.2 minutes. For 40 individuals relying on the other instruction booklet, the mean and standard deviation are 85 and 23.6 minutes, respectively. In a nondirectional test at the 0.05 level, compare the effectiveness of the booklets.

7. For the situation of Question 4, what conclusion would be reached if the test were conducted at the 0.20 level and the respective sample sizes were 12 and 15 for imported and domestic models?

8. For the situation of Question 5, what conclusion would be reached if the test were conducted at the 0.20 level and the respective sample sizes were 17 and 12 for households owning and not owning pets?

9. In testing the accuracy of the cheapest watch produced by two major manufacturers, a consumer group finds that seven watches from one manufacturer deviate from perfect accuracy by the following number of minutes over a two-month period: 3.1, 1.5, 4.3, 1.2, 5.3, 2.8, and 0.5 minutes. For nine watches from the second manufacturer, the deviations from perfect accuracy are 5.3, 3.4, 3.7, 3.0, 4.5, 3.9, 4.6, 5.1, and 4.3 minutes. In a nondirectional test at the 0.05 level, do the two models differ significantly in accuracy?

10. Each of three different ad treatments has been tested on five different subjects. The following are the attitude scores for individuals measured after exposure to each. At the 0.05 level, can we reject the hypothesis that the population means are equal for the three treatments? Would our conclusion be different if the test were conducted at the 0.01 level?

**Treatment**

| I | II | III |
|---|----|-----|
| 4 | 2 | 8 |
| 2 | 1 | 6 |
| 5 | 2 | 4 |
| 9 | 3 | 12 |
| 3 | 4 | 8 |

11. In measuring the strength of four different door-latch mechanisms, an appliance manufacturer tests three different examples of each. The number of pounds applied just prior to breakage is shown below. At the 0.05 level, can we reject the hypothesis that the population means are equal for the three designs? Would our conclusion be different if the test were conducted at the 0.01 level?

**Latch Design**

| I | II | III | IV |
|-----|-----|-----|-----|
| 700 | 730 | 840 | 640 |
| 740 | 680 | 750 | 460 |
| 715 | 770 | 925 | 510 |

12. The following results have been obtained for a one-way analysis of variance in which

the sample sizes happened to be different for the various groups:

| ONE-WAY ANOVA | | | |
|---|---|---|---|
| GROUP | MEAN | N | |
| 1 | 10.111 | 9 | |
| 2 | 15.714 | 7 | |
| 3 | 12.250 | 8 | |
| GRAND MEAN | 12.458 | 24 | |

| SOURCE | SUM OF SQUARES | D.F. | MEAN SQUARE | F RATIO | PROB. |
|---|---|---|---|---|---|
| BETWEEN | 124.141 | 2 | 62.070 | 3.487 | .0492 |
| WITHIN | 373.817 | 21 | 17.801 | | |
| TOTAL | 497.958 | 23 | | | |

For this output:
a. What is the exact P VALUE for this test?
b. At the 0.05 level of significance, can we accept the null hypothesis that the population means are equal?
c. At the 0.01 level of significance, can we accept the null hypothesis that the population means are equal?
d. Based on the information shown above, and using the F distribution tables in the statistical appendix, determine the critical values of F for the 0.05 and 0.01 levels of significance.

13. In the text, a discussion was devoted to the possibility of "diluting" the apparent effect of an exceptionally good or bad treatment by applying analysis of variance to a large number of more ordinary treatments along with the exceptional one. Provide an example, real or hypothetical, in which a firm or organization might be tempted to use this strategy.

14. In polling residents of three different sections of the city, a reporter finds that 40% of the 30 residents interviewed from area A are in favor of raising taxes to provide more frequent refuse pickup, compared to 50% of 20 in area B and 30% of 40 in area C. Using the chi-square technique and the 0.10 level of significance, test the possibility that the three areas really have the same degree of support for the proposed increase.

15. Studying viewership characteristics of four network news programs, researchers surveyed 100 "regular viewers" of program A, 50 of program B, 60 of C, and 80 of D. They find the percentage of females within each group to be 35%, 50%, 40%, and 52.5%, respectively. At the 0.10 level, are these percentages significantly different?

# APPENDIX

## Directional Tests for Comparing Two Sample Means or Proportions

In the chapter we tested the null hypothesis that two population means or proportions were equal, and our alternative hypothesis was that they were *not* equal (i.e., in comparing the two sample means or proportions, $H_0$ could be rejected by an extreme difference *in either direction*). In a directional test, the null hypothesis can be rejected if an extreme difference is observed in just *one* direction.

To demonstrate how directional testing works when we have two sample means or proportions, we'll carry out a directional test for the following situation in which two sample proportions have been observed:

> Iona Bewik, manager of the gift shop at a Florida beach hotel, has claimed that college students and others under age 21 are much more likely to buy postcards than persons who are older. In a sample of 100 younger customers, 40% were observed to buy a postcard during their visit, while just 30% of a sample of 50 older shoppers purchased postcards. At the 0.025 level of significance, do these data support Ms. Bewik's contention?

For this test, the appropriate null hypothesis is $H_0$: $\pi_1 = \pi_2$, where $\pi_1$ and

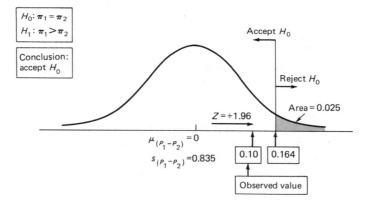

$P_1 = 0.40$    $P_2 = 0.30$

Observed $(P_1 - P_2) = (0.40 - 0.30) = 0.10$

$$s_{(P_1 - P_2)} = \sqrt{\bar{P}(1 - \bar{P})\left(\frac{1}{n_1} + \frac{1}{n_2}\right)} = \sqrt{(0.367)(1 - 0.367)\left(\frac{1}{100} + \frac{1}{50}\right)} = 0.0835$$

$$\text{where } \bar{P} = \frac{n_1 P_1 + n_2 P_2}{n_1 + n_2} = \frac{40 + 15}{100 + 50} = 0.367$$

---

HYPOTHESIS TEST FOR TWO PROPORTIONS FROM INDEPENDENT GROUPS

P1 = .4000,  N1 = 100
P2 = .3000,  N2 =  50

Z = 1.198   PROB. = .1154

---

**Figure 14A-1.** Graphical summary and computer output for directional test for difference in proportion of younger versus older gift shop customers buying postcards. Because the test is directional, there is only one rejection region instead of two. The null hypothesis of "no difference" is accepted at the 0.025 level. The exact level of significance, or P VALUE for the test is 0.1154.

$\pi_2$ are the population proportions of younger and older customers, respectively, who purchase postcards. Since Ms. Bewik's contention is directional, our alternative hypothesis will be $H_1$: $\pi_1 > \pi_2$. Although the observed purchase proportion is higher for the younger shopper than for the older shopper, our test will examine whether or not it is significantly higher; if not, we can conclude that the population proportions are equal, and that the higher rate of purchase observed for the younger persons could have happened by chance.

In examining our null hypothesis in a directional test at the 0.025 level, Z is +1.96 and the mean of the hypothesized distribution is $\mu_{(P_1-P_2)} = 0$, with a standard error of $s_{(P_1-P_2)} = 0.0835$. The standard error is calculated by the formula provided in Figure 14-3.

Examination of Figure 14A-1 shows that the observed difference, $(P_1 - P_2) = (0.40 - 0.30) = 0.10$, falls short of the rejection region that begins at the critical value of 1.96 (0.0835) = 0.164. Thus Iona must accept the null hypothesis that proportions are equal for the two populations, and conclude that the higher purchase rate for the younger customers was just the result of chance.

Also shown in Figure 14A-1 is the result of MICROSTAT analysis for this test. The P VALUE of 0.1154 is the area to the right of the observed difference between the sample proportions. Because this is a directional test, (i.e., we're interested in only one tail area), 0.1154 is the exact level of significance for the test.

If we were testing a directional hypothesis for the difference between two sample means, the same approach would be used. After noting the observed values of the sample means, $\overline{X}_1$ and $\overline{X}_2$, we would use the appropriate formula (as shown in Figure 14-3) in calculating the estimated standard error for the difference between sample means instead of proportions.

# 15

# BIVARIATE TECHNIQUES AND THE MEASUREMENT OF ASSOCIATION

## Is There a Statistician in the House?

In a survey of 2108 patients of single-specialty and multispecialty practices in three regions of the United States, Marketing Prescription asked respondents how they had selected their doctor. A primary purpose of the study was to examine the extent to which medical advertising plays a role in one's selection of a physician.

Of those surveyed, only 0.2% said they chose their physician as the result of seeing or hearing an advertisement. However, this particular finding may not represent an inherent weakness in this approach to marketing one's medical services. According to Tom Moody, vice-president and general manager of Marketing Prescription, "Medical advertising is such a recent phenomenon that many respondents may have been exposed to relatively little medical advertising at the time they chose their physician."

In addition, the role of advertising may have been understated for other reasons. For example, ads may have played a greater role than patients realized. As Mr. Moody puts it, patients "might have been much more likely to follow the advice of a family member or friend if they had seen or heard the name of the recommended physician's clinic in some form of advertising."

*Source:* Based on "Referrals Top Ads as Patient Influence on Patients' Doctor Selections," *Marketing News,* January 30, 1987, p. 22, published by the American Marketing Association.

**Figure 15-1.** In a study asking patients in three regions of the United States how they had selected their physician, researchers found that 34.2% of the 2108 respondents relied on the referral of a friend or family member. However, results varied from one region to another, suggesting a possible relationship between (1) method of selection, and (2) region of the country. (*Source:* Data from "Referrals Top Ads as Patient Influence on Patients' Doctor Selections," *Marketing News,* January 30, 1987, p. 22, published by the American Marketing Association. Photo courtesy of Jim Wakefield.)

Results showed that, overall, the most important basis for selection (given by 34.2% of respondents) was the referral of a friend or family member. However, even this varied by region, being less popular in the South, where the referral of another doctor (given by 59.9% of respondents in that region) was the most frequent explanation provided.

As implied above, two key variables in the study were: (1) method of physician selection, and (2) region of the country. Appropriately, a pertinent research question might be, "Do patients from these regions of the country really differ in how they chose their doctor—or, alternatively, might the differences from one region to another simply have been the result of chance variation?"

Since this chapter deals with bivariate (two-variable) measures of association, it's only fair that we include a technique through which we can examine whether the patient's method of physician selection might be related to the region of the country where he or she resides. The method constitutes another way of applying the chi-square technique we've used before. Does the Marketing Prescription study suggest a relationship between the two variables? We'll spend just a short time in pre-op before going into statistical surgery on this one.

## INTRODUCTION

Marketing research often involves the examination of two variables at the same time for the purpose of seeing if they are related in some way. In this chapter we'll examine several ."bivariate" techniques that can be applied to this end.

One technique, chi-square analysis, is a previously introduced method that will be used here to examine the possibility that two nominal (category) variables are not related to each other. It is typically applied whenever we have a two-way cross-tabulation where sample members have been categorized according to two different characteristics.

Another method, regression and correlation analysis, measures (1) the extent of, and (2) the nature of the relationship between two ratio or interval-scaled variables. Regression analysis describes the linear equation that "best fits" the values recorded for the two variables, while correlation analysis measures the strength of the relationship. A frequent purpose of this type of analysis is to predict or estimate what value of a dependent variable ($Y$) will be likely to occur for a given value of the independent variable ($X$). An important part of correlation analysis is testing whether the measured strength of the relationship differs significantly from zero.

When the two variables are of an ordinal, or preference nature, rank-order correlation can be used to measure the extent to which they might be related. Within the chapter, these topics will be discussed under the following headings:

I. Chi-square testing of variable independence
II. Regression and correlation analysis
III. The significance of a correlation coefficient
IV. Rank-order correlation for two ordinal variables

## CHI-SQUARE TESTING OF VARIABLE INDEPENDENCE

The test for the independence of two nominal variables has as its starting point a cross-tabulation of the two variables. The purpose is to determine statistically whether they are independent, and the general approach is similar to that used in Chapter 14. The details for this type of application are summarized in Figure 15-2. Remember that in chi-square analysis, each cell in the table of expected frequencies must have a value of at least five. If not, categories may be combined until this constraint has been satisfied.

To illustrate how the procedure works, let's assume we've collected observational data on age versus movie attendance—that is, we're interested in seeing if there might be a relationship between an individual's age and the selection he or she makes from the three movies available at a certain cinematic complex. These hypothetical data are shown in Table 15-1. As the table indicates, we have observed eight individuals who appear to be under 21 attending *Last*

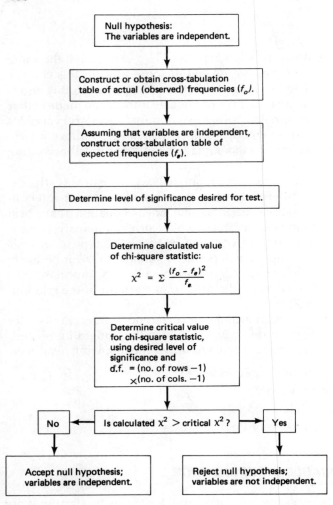

**Figure 15-2.** Procedure for using chi-square analysis to test the independence of two nominal variables.

**TABLE 15-1.** *Cross-tabulation of observed frequencies ($f_0$) from observational study discussed in text. Chi-square analysis is used to determine if these two nominal variables—age and movie selection—are independent.*

| | | Movie selection | | | |
|---|---|---|---|---|---|
| | | *Last Flight to Pittsburgh* | *Uncle Wiggily Goes to Prep School* | *Frankenstein Conquers UCLA (But Doesn't Get a Bowl Bid)* | *Total* |
| *Age* | *Under 21* | 8 | 18 | 13 | 39 |
| | *21–60* | 7 | 9 | 30 | 46 |
| | *Over 60* | 10 | 8 | 17 | 35 |
| | *Total* | 25 | 35 | 60 | 120 |

*Flight to Pittsburgh*, nine who appear to be 21–60 attending *Uncle Wiggily Goes to Prep School*, and so on.

**1. Identify null hypothesis.** Our null hypothesis for this analysis is, "There is no relationship between a moviegoer's age and the movie he or she will select." This is consistent with our previous chi-square tests, where the initial assumption was a skeptical "no significance" that challenged the statistical test to show us otherwise.

**2. Construct table of expected frequencies.** At this stage, we construct a second table, one that assumes the variables are unrelated. In this hypothesized table, the row and column totals will be the same as in the table of observed data. However, the distribution will be such that membership in the rows will be independent of membership in the columns. For example, 60/120, or one-half of all the moviegoers attended *Frankenstein Conquers UCLA*. Thus, our expected table would have one-half *of each age group* attending this movie. Likewise, 25 of all 120 moviegoers attended *Last Flight to Pittsburgh*. We therefore assume that, if the variables are independent, 25/120 of the 21–60 age group (or 9.58) would attend this movie. These calculations lead to the frequencies shown in Table 15-2.

**3. Determine calculated value of chi-square statistic.** Next, we find the value of chi-square represented by the discrepancy between the observed and expected frequencies. The larger this value, the more likely we will be to reject the idea that the variables are independent. As Figure 15-2 indicates, this statistic is calculated by summing the following terms:

$$\chi^2 = \sum \frac{(f_o - f_e)^2}{f_e}$$

$$= \frac{(8 - 8.13)^2}{8.13} + \frac{(18 - 11.37)^2}{11.37} + \frac{(13 - 19.50)^2}{19.50}$$

$$+ \frac{(7 - 9.58)^2}{9.58} + \frac{(9 - 13.42)^2}{13.42} + \frac{(30 - 23.00)^2}{23.00}$$

$$+ \frac{(10 - 7.29)^2}{7.29} + \frac{(8 - 10.21)^2}{10.21} + \frac{(17 - 17.50)^2}{17.50}$$

$$= 11.82$$

**4. Determine critical value for chi-square statistic.** The critical value for $\chi^2$ is obtained from the chi-square distribution table in the statistical appendix. However, before consulting the table, we need to determine the number of degrees of freedom (d.f.) associated with this test. For chi-square tests of this type, d.f. = (number of rows − 1) × (number of columns − 1), where the number of rows and columns refers to the size of the cross-tabulation table we are using. For this example, d.f. will be (3 − 1) × (3 − 1), or 4. Assuming that we'd like to test the hypothesis at the 0.05 level, we find the critical value to be 9.49 for this number of degrees of freedom.

## EXHIBIT 15-1

### Regions Differ When Prescribing Doctors

In the chapter-opening vignette, a survey was described in which respondents from three different regions indicated how they chose their physician. Based on the following summary findings, combined with our own estimates of the sample sizes from each region, we'll be using chi-square analysis to test the null hypothesis, "$H_0$: There is no relationship between method of physician selection and region of residence."

| | Patient responses:[a] How did you choose your doctor? (Percent) | | | |
|---|---|---|---|---|
| Selection method | South-western | North central | Southern | All respondents |
| 1. Referral, family/friend | 30.7 | 44.3 | 31.2 | 34.2 |
| 2. Referral, another doctor | 20.4 | 27.1 | 59.9 | 31.6 |
| 3. Referral, employer | 7.9 | 2.0 | 1.2 | 4.8 |
| 4. Consulted *Yellow Pages* | 3.5 | 2.9 | 2.6 | 3.1 |
| 5. Called MD referral service | 2.7 | 1.2 | 0.0 | 1.7 |
| 6. Direct contact with MD | 10.7 | 9.6 | 3.5 | 8.7 |
| 7. Referral, insurance/ HMO | 6.7 | 0.4 | 0.0 | 3.6 |
| 8. Other, including saw/ heard ad[b] | 12.5 | 5.5 | 0.6 | 7.8 |
| 9. Do not know | 5.0 | 7.0 | 1.0 | 4.5 |

[a] Since the actual number of respondents from each region was not reported in the article, this text's author had his computer try all possible combinations of proportional breakdowns among regions 1, 2, 3 until it found a set that best predicted the "total respondents" percentages, which are a weighted average of the individual region percentages. The resulting proportions were 0.51, 0.25, and 0.24, which led to estimated sample sizes of $n_1 = 1075$, $n_2 = 527$, and $n_3 = 506$. These assumed sample sizes were used in our hypothetical analysis.

[b] In carrying out our hypothetical analysis, we'll also combine the "saw/heard advertisement" category with "other method" because to do otherwise would lead to cells with an expected frequency less than five. (The three regional percentages for "saw/heard advertisement" were 0.5%, 0.0%, and 0.0%, respectively.)

*Source:* "Referrals Top Ads as Patient Influence on Patients' Doctor Selections," *Marketing News*, January 30, 1987, p. 22, published by the American Marketing Association.

Computer analysis comparing the "observed" and "expected" frequencies below strongly suggests that some relationship exists between the two variables. For 16 degrees of freedom and a 0.005 level of significance, the critical chi-square value from our statistical appendix is 34.3. This is far exceeded by the calculated chi-square, 428.217. The P VALUE for the test is, to four decimal places, 0.0000. In other words, given our assumed sample sizes, the probability is, for practical purposes, *zero* that physician selection method and region of residence are independent from each other.

CROSSTAB / CHI-SQUARE TESTS
TESTING INDEPENDENCE OF PHYSICIAN SELECTION METHOD AND REGION.

OBSERVED FREQUENCIES

|   | 1 | 2 | 3 | TOTAL |
|---|---|---|---|---|
| 1 | 330 | 233 | 158 | 721 |
| 2 | 219 | 143 | 303 | 665 |
| 3 | 85 | 11 | 6 | 102 |
| 4 | 37 | 15 | 13 | 65 |
| 5 | 29 | 6 | 0 | 35 |
| 6 | 115 | 51 | 18 | 184 |
| 7 | 72 | 2 | 0 | 74 |
| 8 | 134 | 29 | 3 | 166 |
| 9 | 54 | 37 | 5 | 96 |
| TOTAL | 1075 | 527 | 506 | 2108 |

EXPECTED FREQUENCIES

|   | 1 | 2 | 3 | TOTAL |
|---|---|---|---|---|
| 1 | 367.68 | 180.25 | 173.07 | 721.00 |
| 2 | 339.12 | 166.25 | 159.63 | 665.00 |
| 3 | 52.02 | 25.50 | 24.48 | 102.00 |
| 4 | 33.15 | 16.25 | 15.60 | 65.00 |
| 5 | 17.85 | 8.75 | 8.40 | 35.00 |
| 6 | 93.83 | 46.00 | 44.17 | 184.00 |
| 7 | 37.74 | 18.50 | 17.76 | 74.00 |
| 8 | 84.65 | 41.50 | 39.85 | 166.00 |
| 9 | 48.96 | 24.00 | 23.04 | 96.00 |
| TOTAL | 1075.00 | 527.00 | 506.00 | 2108.00 |

CHI-SQUARE = 428.217,   D.F. = 16,   PROB. = .0000

*5. Compare calculated chi-square with critical value.* Since the calculated value (11.82) exceeds the critical value (9.49), we are able to reject the hypothesis of independence at the 0.05 level of significance. Hence we can conclude that based on these data, there is some relationship between the age of a moviegoer and the movie that he or she elects to see. (*Note:* Although chi-square analysis has told us that a relationship exists, there is no indication of the *exact nature* of that relationship.)

While the calculated value of 11.82 is greater than the critical value for the 0.05 level, it does not exceed that for the 0.01 level. Accordingly, the exact level

**TABLE 15-2.** *Expected frequencies ($f_e$) corresponding to cross tabulation of Table 15-1. This table is constructed under the assumption that the variables are independent.*

| | | Movie selection | | | |
|---|---|---|---|---|---|
| | | Last Flight to Pittsburgh | Uncle Wiggily Goes to Prep School | Frankenstein Conquers UCLA (But Doesn't Get a Bowl Bid) | Total |
| Age | Under 21 | 8.13 | 11.37 | 19.50 | 39 |
| | 21–60 | 9.58 | 13.42 | 23.00 | 46 |
| | Over 60 | 7.29 | 10.21 | 17.50 | 35 |
| | Total | 25 | 35 | 60 | 120 |

$$\left(\frac{25}{120} \times 46\right) \qquad \left(\frac{35}{120} \times 35\right) \qquad \left(\frac{60}{120} \times 39\right)$$

of significance for this example lies between 0.05 and 0.01. Based on computer analysis of these data, the exact P VALUE was found to be 0.0189.

## REGRESSION AND CORRELATION ANALYSIS

In the chi-square technique, we examined an approach that allowed us to determine if two nominal-scaled variables were related. In this section, we will discuss *regression and correlation analysis*, which statistically measures: (1) the extent of, and (2) the nature of the relationship between two interval or ratio-scale variables.

In general, regression analysis describes the mathematical equation that "best fits" the values recorded for the two variables. While nonlinear equations may be used for this purpose, we will limit our discussion to regression equations of the linear (straight-line) type. Correlation analysis is used to measure the strength of the relationship between the variables.

The discussion here will be concerned only with regression and correlation for the analysis of two variables: the dependent variable ($Y$) and the independent variable ($X$). A frequent purpose of this type of analysis is to predict or estimate what $Y$ will be for a given value of $X$. Typical applications for these techniques in marketing include the identification of relationships between such dependent variables as sales or market share, and independent variables such as price, advertising level, number of salespersons, and other measures under the control of the marketing decision maker.

### Regression Analysis

Known as *simple regression* because it considers only two variables, this technique begins with a set of data values and determines a "best-fit" equation of the form $Y = a + bX$. In order to derive this equation, we must calculate the optimum values for *a* (the intercept on the *Y* axis) and *b* (the slope of the regression line).

   The typical starting point for the procedure may be represented by a *scatter diagram*, which visually describes the values of *X* and *Y*. Whether or not an actual diagram is used, regression analysis employs what is known as the *least-squares* criterion in fitting an equation to the data. This criterion ensures that the equation selected will minimize the sum of the squared deviations between (1) the actual value of *Y*, and (2) the value of *Y* predicted by the equation for each given value of *X*. As an example of how this works, refer to the two identical scatter diagrams in Figure 15-3. In each diagram, an equation has been fitted, and the value $(a^2 + b^2 + c^2)$ represents the sum of the squared deviations between the actual and predicted values of *Y*. Because this sum is smaller for line B, it is a better fit for this set of data.

   In fitting a line to a set of data, we can also rely on the *judgment*, or "eyeball" approach, and simply draw a line that *appears* to be a reasonable fit to the points in the diagram. Fortunately, we need not rely on judgment since there are mathematical formulas readily available for determining the values of *a* and *b* so that $Y = a + bX$ will be *the* least-squares equation for the data. As an example of how they work, let's consider the following data, which represent the unit sales of new and used cars in the United States over an eight-year period.[1]

| Y = sales of used cars by used-car dealers (millions) | X = sales of new cars (millions) |
|:---:|:---:|
| 4.15 | 8.98 |
| 4.18 | 10.64 |
| 4.39 | 11.31 |
| 4.29 | 11.18 |
| 3.98 | 10.10 |
| 3.36 | 8.63 |
| 3.23 | 8.85 |
| 3.89 | 11.43 |

   To identify the least-squares regression equation that describes these data, we'll need to calculate the appropriate values for *a* and *b* for substitution into $Y = a + bX$:

$$a = \frac{(\sum Y)(\sum X^2) - (\sum X)(\sum XY)}{n(\sum X^2) - (\sum X)^2}$$

and

$$b = \frac{n(\sum XY) - (\sum X)(\sum Y)}{n(\sum X^2) - (\sum X)^2}$$

---

[1] Data are from *Automotive News, 1981 Market Data Book Issue* (Detroit, Mich.: Crain Automotive Group, Inc., Division of Crain Communications, Inc. 1981), pp. 18, 38, 89.

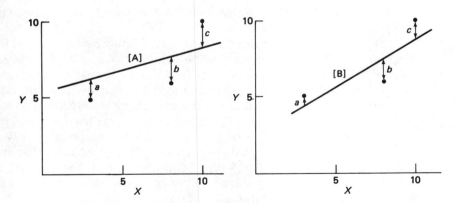

Note: In each diagram the (x, y) coordinates are (3, 5), (8, 6), and (10, 10), and the least-squares equation (which happens to be line B) is $Y = 2.69 + 0.62X$.

**Figure 15-3.** The least-squares method of regression mathematically ensures that the sum of squared deviations—in this case, $(a^2 + b^2 + c^2)$—*is minimized*. For the data shown here, line B would be a better fit than line A.

where

$$n = \text{number of data points}$$

$$\sum X = \text{sum of the } X \text{ values}$$

$$\sum Y = \text{sum of the } Y \text{ values}$$

$$\sum X^2 = \text{sum of all } X^2 \text{ values}$$

$$\sum XY = \text{sum of the products of } X \text{ times } Y$$

$$b = \text{slope of the least-squares equation}$$

$$a = Y \text{ intercept of the least-squares equation}$$

In applying these equations to the preceding data, the result is the least-squares equation $Y = 1.30 + 0.26X$, the calculations for which are shown in Table 15-3. (Note that Table 15-3 also includes, for purposes of efficiency, the calculation of the correlation coefficient that measures the strength of the relationship between $X$ and $Y$. This topic will be discussed in the next section.)

The auto sales regression equation, and the data on which it is based, is presented in the scatter diagram of Figure 15-4. The value of the intercept, $a = 1.30$, indicates that the line would intersect the $Y$ axis at 1.30 million cars (provided that the axes were not shortened, as these are). The slope, $b = 0.26$, represents the increase in used-car sales that could be expected with an increase of 1 unit in new-car sales. In other words, if new-car sales were to increase by 1 million cars, we would expect the used-car sales level to go up by 260,000 vehicles. If the slope were negative, this would mean that $Y$ would *decrease* with increases in $X$. (As a point of interest, it should be noted that the used-car data

**TABLE 15-3.** *Calculation of the least-squares regression equation for the auto sales data presented in text. Coefficient of correlation has also been calculated, and will be discussed in next section.*[a]

| Y = sales of used cars by used-car dealers (millions of cars) | X = sales of new cars (millions of cars) | $X^2$ | XY | $Y^2$ |
|---|---|---|---|---|
| 4.15 | 8.98 | 80.64 | 37.27 | 17.22 |
| 4.18 | 10.64 | 113.21 | 44.48 | 17.47 |
| 4.39 | 11.31 | 127.92 | 49.65 | 19.27 |
| 4.29 | 11.18 | 124.99 | 47.96 | 18.40 |
| 3.98 | 10.10 | 102.01 | 40.20 | 15.84 |
| 3.36 | 8.63 | 74.48 | 29.00 | 11.29 |
| 3.23 | 8.85 | 78.32 | 28.59 | 10.43 |
| 3.89 | 11.43 | 130.64 | 44.46 | 15.13 |
| 31.47 $= \sum Y$ | 81.12 $= \sum X$ | 832.21 $= \sum X^2$ | 321.61 $= \sum XY$ | 125.05 $= \sum Y^2$ |

Least-squares regression equation: $Y = a + bX$, where

$$a = \frac{(\sum Y)(\sum X^2) - (\sum X)(\sum XY)}{n(\sum X^2) - (\sum X)^2} = \frac{(31.47)(832.21) - (81.12)(321.61)}{8(832.21) - (81.12)^2} = 1.30$$

and

$$b = \frac{n(\sum XY) - (\sum X)(\sum Y)}{n(\sum X^2) - (\sum X)^2} = \frac{8(321.61) - (81.12)(31.47)}{8(832.21) - (81.12)^2} = 0.26$$

Least-squares equation is $Y = 1.30 + 0.26X$

Coefficient of correlation between X and Y:

$$r = \frac{n(\sum XY) - (\sum X)(\sum Y)}{\sqrt{n(\sum X^2) - (\sum X)^2} \sqrt{n(\sum Y^2) - (\sum Y)^2}}$$

$$= \frac{8(321.61) - (81.12)(31.47)}{\sqrt{8(832.21) - (81.12)^2} \sqrt{8(125.05) - (31.47)^2}} = \boxed{0.72}$$

[a] Because this example is for demonstration purposes, the results of calculations have been rounded to two decimal places. For greater accuracy, especially in the later calculations based on these values, we would have preferred at least four or five decimal places here. However, the improved accuracy would have been at the cost of reduced clarity for the reader.

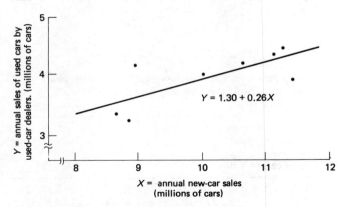

[Source: Data from *Automotive News, 1981 Market Data Book Issue,* (Detroit, Mich.: Crain Automotive Group, Inc., Division of Crain Communications, Inc., 1981), pp. 18, 38, 89.]

**Figure 15-4.** Scatter diagram showing data points and least-squares regression equation for auto sales figures presented in text.

here are only for those sold by *used-car dealers*, and do not include the millions sold by new-car dealers or by private owners. This is the reason for the large differences between the sales levels.)

## The Coefficient of Correlation

At this point, we've learned the basics of identifying the *nature* of a linear relationship that we have fitted to a set of data for two variables. In this section, we'll examine a way of expressing the *strength* of this same relationship.

In Table 15-3, we calculated a quantity called the **coefficient of correlation** (*r*) which was based on the auto sales data presented earlier. This is the measure of strength referred to here. The coefficient of correlation is a number that, for a given set of data, will be somewhere between $-1$ and $+1$ and tell us two things about the relationship between the two variables:

1. *Direction of the relationship.* If *r* is positive, this means that X and Y increase and decrease together—for example, if X increases, then Y will also tend to increase. If *r* is negative, the variables will tend to move in opposite directions—for example, if X increases, then Y will tend to decrease, as sales would tend to decrease when the price goes up.

2. *Strength of the relationship.* The larger the absolute value of *r*, the stronger the relationship between the two variables, and the better the least-square equation will "fit" the data in the scatter diagram. At the extremes (i.e., if *r* is either $+1$ or $-1$), the equation will actually contain *all* the data points, making it a *perfect fit* for the data. When $r = 0$, this means there is no linear relationship at all between the variables.

Figure 15-5 shows a variety of examples where the coefficient of correlation varies in both sign and magnitude according to the data being analyzed. Worthy

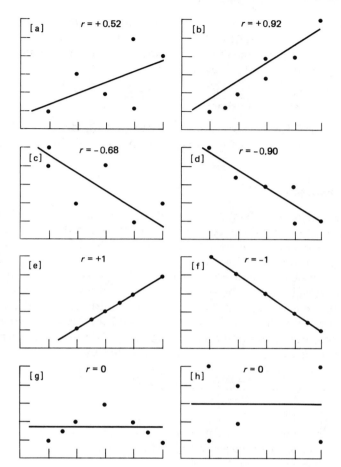

**Figure 15-5.** As a measure of the degree of linear relationships between two variables, the coefficient of correlation varies (1) in sign, according to the direction of the relationship, and (2) in magnitude, according to the strength of the relationship.

of special note is scatter diagram (g), where there is evidence of linear relationship, but in the form of *two* equations, not one. Thus, one linear equation, even if it is a "best fit," will tend to have a low correlation. For the data of diagram (g), the best-fit line is horizontal, which automatically means that r will be 0.

Besides the coefficient of correlation, there are two other measures deserving of mention in this section. They are the ***coefficient of determination*** and the ***standard error of estimate***.

### The Coefficient of Determination (r²)

The coefficient of determination is the square of the correlation coefficient, and takes on a special meaning because its value represents the proportion of the variation in Y that is explained by the independent variable, X, by means of the regression equation. For example, in part (e) of Figure 15-5, changes in Y are fully explained by changes in X, while in part (b) of the same figure, $(0.92)^2$, or

85% of the variation in $Y$ is explained by $X$. The dependent variable, $Y$, takes on many different values in a set of data—thus it has a variance. Some of this variance can be accounted for by changes in $X$, and some remains unexplained. The coefficient of determination simply expresses

$$r^2 = \frac{\text{variance in } Y \text{ that is explained by } X}{\text{total variance in } Y}$$

In the case of our auto sales of Table 15-3, we found that $r = 0.72$. Hence $(0.72)^2$, or 52%, of the variance in used car sales was explained by changes in the level of new car sales.

### The Standard Error of Estimate

The standard error of estimate is the standard deviation of $Y$ values for a given value of $X$. It is similar to other standard deviations, except that in this case our interval is in the vertical direction. For example, if we were to substitute $X = 10$ into the auto sales regression equation ($Y = 1.30 + 0.26X$), we would find the estimated value of $Y$ to be 3.9 million used cars sold. However, this is just a *point* estimate, and there is bound to be some uncertainty about how high or low $Y$ is likely to be when $X$ is equal to 10. Although we're fairly confident that used car sales will not be 100 million or 0 million, we need the standard error of estimate to help us compute an interval that is more "proper" in the statistical sense. The standard error of estimate ($s_{Y.X}$) can be calculated by

$$s_{Y.X} = \sqrt{\frac{(\sum Y^2) - a(\sum Y) - b(\sum XY)}{n - 2}}$$

where

$$a = \text{intercept calculated for } Y = a + bX$$
$$b = \text{slope coefficient calculated for } Y = a + bX$$
$$n = \text{number of data points}$$

$(\sum Y^2)$, $(\sum Y)$, and $(\sum XY)$ = column totals computed during calculation of the least-square regression equation

For the auto sales data, again using the regression equation and column totals calculated in Table 15-3, the standard error of estimate would be

$$s_{Y.X} = \sqrt{\frac{(125.05) - 1.30(31.47) - 0.26(321.61)}{8 - 2}}$$

$$= 0.295 \text{ million used cars}$$

### The Prediction Interval

The standard error of estimate is the first of two calculations necessary if we'd like to construct a ***prediction interval*** for the predicted value of $Y$. (The term ***prediction interval*** is used because we're trying to predict an ***individual value of Y***, not the mean of $Y$ for the given value of $X$.)

Because our regression line itself is based on sample data, and hence subject to error, we are going to be more sure of predictions that are made based on values of $X$ that are closer to the mean of $X$. For example, if our slope, $b$, is just a bit off from the "true" value, our regression line will be aimed in the wrong direction and will be less "trustworthy" at its extremes. Figure 15-6 visually describes how the prediction interval tends to widen as we get further away from the mean of $X$.

Once we have calculated our standard error of estimate, we need a "correction factor" before we can apply the $t$ distribution (appropriate for all sample sizes, especially small ones) to calculate the actual interval in which we predict the $Y$ value will lie. The formula used to construct the interval is

$$\begin{matrix} \text{prediction} \\ \text{interval for} \\ \text{an individual} \\ Y \text{ value} \end{matrix} = \begin{matrix} Y \text{ value} \\ \text{calculated from} \\ \text{the regression} \\ \text{line} \end{matrix} \pm t(s_{Y.x}) \sqrt{1 + \frac{1}{n} + \frac{(X \text{ value} - \overline{X})^2}{(\sum X^2) - \frac{(\sum X)^2}{n}}}$$

where

$t$ = $t$ distribution value for confidence level desired, and ($n - 2$) degrees of freedom

$s_{Y.x}$ = standard error of estimate

$X$ value = value of $X$ for which you're trying to predict $Y$

$\overline{X}$ = mean of the $X$ values in the sample data

$\sum X$ = sum of the $X$ values

$(\sum X^2)$ = column total for $X^2$, from regression equation calculations

$n$ = number of data points

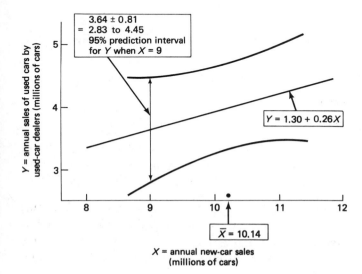

3.64 ± 0.81
= 2.83 to 4.45
95% prediction interval
for $Y$ when $X = 9$

$Y = 1.30 + 0.26X$

$\overline{X} = 10.14$

$Y$ = annual sales of used cars by used-car dealers (millions of cars)

$X$ = annual new-car sales (millions of cars)

**Figure 15-6.** As we make used-car sales predictions involving $X$ values to the left or right of $\overline{X}$, the 95% prediction interval tends to "stretch" slightly. Correction formula in text takes care of this problem, which is related to uncertainties regarding the location of the regression line itself. If next year's new-car sales are 9 million, we're 95% sure that sales by used-car dealers will be between 2.83 and 4.45 million cars. (*Source:* Underlying data from *Automotive News, 1981 Market Data Book Issue* (Detroit, Mich.: Crain Automotive Group, Inc., Division of Crain Communications, Inc., 1981) pp. 18, 38, 89.)

As an example of how this formula can help us express a prediction about $Y$, let's again consider the auto sales data, for which we already have the following information:

1. The least-squares regression equation, $Y = 1.30 + 0.26X$
2. The standard error of estimate, $s_{Y.X} = 0.295$ million cars
3. $\sum X = 81.12$
4. $(\sum X^2) = 832.21$
5. The mean of $X$, $\overline{X} = 81.12/8 = 10.14$
6. The number of data points, $n = 8$

Of the preceding, item 2 was calculated a few paragraphs ago, while the others are available from the regression calculations of Table 15-3. For our example, we'll assume the following:

A business forecaster has, after extensive study, projected that the sales of new cars next year will be 9 million units. Based on our regression study of used-car sales versus new-car sales, we'd like to use her projection in making a prediction of the number of cars that are likely to be sold by used-car dealers next year.

Applying our prediction-interval formula, a 95% interval requires a $t$ value of 2.447 (from the $t$-distribution table in the statistical appendix, with $(n - 2)$, or 6 degrees of freedom). The "$X$ value" in the formula will be $X = 9.0$, since this is the new-car level for which we're trying to predict what used-car sales will be. The "$Y$ value calculated from the regression line" is simply the sales level that would be predicted from our regression equation, $Y = 1.30 + 0.26X$. This is $1.30 + 0.26(9.0)$, or 3.64 million used cars. Substitution into the prediction-interval formula provides

$$\begin{array}{l} \text{95\% prediction} \\ \text{interval for} \\ \text{next year's} \\ \text{used-car sales} \end{array} = 3.64 \pm (2.447)(0.295) \sqrt{1 + \frac{1}{8} + \frac{(9 - 10.14)^2}{832.21 - \frac{(81.12)^2}{8}}}$$

$$= 3.64 \pm (2.447)(0.295)(1.12)^*$$

$$= 3.64 \pm 0.81$$

$$= \text{between 2.83 and 4.45 million used cars}$$

[Note at (*) that the expression beneath the square root sign has done its intended job. Because we're operating at $X = 9$ million new cars, instead of the mean (10.14 million), the standard error of the estimate will be "stretched" slightly via being multiplied by 1.12.]

Thus given that there will be 9 million new cars sold, we are 95% sure that the number of used cars sold will be somewhere between 2.83 million and 4.45 million. If we were to repeat the preceding calculations for a wide range of $X$ values, the result would be a 95% prediction interval "band" above and below the regression line calculated in Table 15-3. Such a band would tend to be wider at the ends of the regression line, as suggested by Figure 15-6.

## THE SIGNIFICANCE OF A CORRELATION COEFFICIENT

A high absolute value for the correlation coefficient (i.e., $r$ is close to $+1$ or $-1$) may not really be indicative of a very significant relationship. For example, it takes only two points to determine a straight line. Thus if you were to have only two data points, you would automatically have a correlation coefficient equal to $+1$ or $-1$, and a straight line would be a perfect fit for these "data."

For this reason, it is often desirable to test the null hypothesis that the "true" correlation coefficient (denoted by the Greek letter "rho," or $\rho$) might be equal to 0. This test is nondirectional and uses the $t$ distribution, with d.f. $= n - 2$. The test statistic is

$$t = \frac{r}{\sqrt{\dfrac{1 - r^2}{n - 2}}}$$

where

$$r = \text{coefficient of correlation}$$

$$n = \text{number of data points}$$

For our example involving sales of used versus new cars, we had $n = 8$ data points and calculated $r = 0.72$. Using these values in the preceding equation, we find the calculated value of the $t$ statistic to be

$$t = \frac{0.72}{\sqrt{\dfrac{1 - (0.72)^2}{8 - 2}}} = 2.54$$

Using the 0.05 level of significance and referring to the statistical appendix, the critical values are $t = \pm 2.447$. Since our calculated value falls outside these limits, we reject $H_0$ and conclude that the correlation coefficient is significantly different from zero at the 0.05 level. In other words, the probability is no more than 0.05 that an $r$ this large could have occurred by chance if the true value ($\rho$) were really equal to zero.

Table 15-4 shows the computer output for the used/new-car data, including the exact P VALUE of 0.0478 for the null hypothesis that $\rho = 0$. Because their respective statistical tests are equivalent (remember that a slope of zero always yields $r = 0$), this is also the P VALUE for the null hypothesis that the true value of the *regression equation slope* is zero—this is why ".04780" is seen twice in the output. Computer packages use analysis of variance and/or the $t$ distribution in arriving at these equal P VALUES. This one first used the $t$ test to examine the regression slope coefficient, then applied analysis of variance to come up with the same P VALUE in testing the coefficient of correlation.

Because the computer has carried out its calculations to a lot more than

**TABLE 15-4.** *Computer output for new/used-car sales data of this section. As explained in text, the more exact values here differ slightly from those presented earlier because our calculations were rounded to two decimal places for greater clarity of discussion.*

REGRESSION ANALYSIS

HEADER DATA FOR: A:USEDNEW      LABEL: SALES, USED/NEW
                                                      CARS.
NUMBER OF CASES: 8      NUMBER OF VARIABLES: 2

USED CAR SALES BY USED CAR DEALERS (Y) VS. NEW CAR SALES (X).

| INDEX | NAME | MEAN | STD.DEV. |
|-------|------|------|----------|
| 1 | NEW | 10.1400 | 1.1745 |
| DEP. VAR.: | USED | 3.9338 | .4261 |

DEPENDENT VARIABLE: USED

| VAR. | REGRESSION COEFFICIENT | STD. ERROR | T(DF = 6) | PROB. |
|------|------------------------|------------|-----------|-------|
| NEW | .2581 | .1041 | 2.480 | .04780 |
| CONSTANT | 1.3163 | | | |

STD. ERROR OF EST. = .3234
r SQUARED = .5062
r = .7115

ANALYSIS OF VARIANCE TABLE

| SOURCE | SUM OF SQUARES | D.F. | MEAN SQUARE | F RATIO | PROB. |
|--------|----------------|------|-------------|---------|-------|
| REGRESSION | .6434 | 1 | .6434 | 6.151 | .0478 |
| RESIDUAL | .6276 | 6 | .1046 | | |
| TOTAL | 1.2710 | 7 | | | |

the two decimal places we've used, the exact values of $r$, $r^2$, $a$, $b$, the standard error of estimate and $t$ in this output differ slightly from those calculated earlier. As we've discussed previously, the coefficient of determination ($r^2$) is equal to the explained variability of $Y$ divided by the total variability of $Y$. These are shown in the output as 0.6434 and 1.2710, respectively. The remaining, "residual" variability (0.6276) is the amount of variation not explained by the regression equation.

**Regression and Correlation: Closing Comments**

Before leaving the topic of regression and correlation analysis, let's consider a few ideas that can be important when using these techniques. As with other of our approaches to research and analysis, there can be pitfalls.

One thing to keep in mind is that strength of association does not necessarily mean *causation*. Just because changes in $X$ seem to explain a lot of the variation in $Y$, this does not automatically mean that $X$ *causes* $Y$. In fact, the reverse may be true, or both variables may be caused by a third variable that has not been identified. Sometimes high correlation values are recorded for variables that, on a common sense basis, would appear to have no direct relation to each other. For example, Figure 15-7 shows the data points for personal consumption expenditures on telephone service and alcoholic beverages between 1946 and 1970. While $r$ is an impressive 0.9868 and $r^2 = 0.9738$, there is no reason to believe that drinking causes people to spend more time on the telephone. Causation in either direction is extremely unlikely. Actually, each variable has simply increased in roughly linear fashion *as a function of time*. This type of situation is sometimes referred to as a *spurious*, or nonsense correlation.

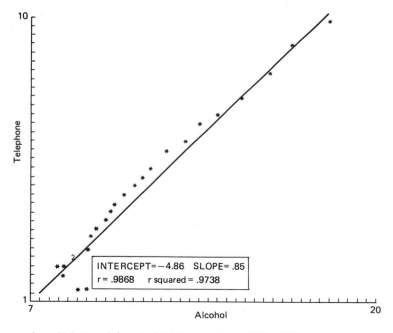

Annual telephone ($Y$) vs. alcohol ($X$) expenditures, 1946—1970

**Figure 15-7.**   Does drinking really cause people to spend more time and money talking on the telephone? Probably not, but these data on U.S. personal consumption expenditures on telephone service ($Y$) and alcoholic beverages ($X$) from 1946 to 1970 are nevertheless very highly correlated. This spurious or nonsense correlation is best explained by the fact that both variables simply tended to increase linearly as a function of time. (*Note*: The "2" in the scatter diagram indicates that two different years happened to have the same values for $Y$ and $X$.) Each variable is expression here in billions of dollars. (*Source*: Data from *Historical Statistics, Colonial Times to 1970*, Bureau of the Census, U.S. Department of Commerce, Series G 416–469, pp. 316–318.)

Another potential problem is trying to make predictions based on values of *X* that are *outside the boundaries of the data on which the regression line was based*. Simple extension of the regression line is mechanically very simple—all one needs is a ruler and pencil to make the line longer. However, the linearity of the relationship may not extend to this region, causing a prediction made from such an extension to be greatly in error. For example, registrations of Ford's ill-fated Edsel were 26,681 in 1957, 38,601 in 1958, and 40,778 in 1959, the only three years it was sold.[2] If we were to fit a linear regression equation to these data, then extrapolate forward to 1985, the estimate for Edsel registrations would be 225,669. At this volume, the Edsel easily would have been among the 10 most popular domestic cars of that year! As history demonstrates, be cautious about extrapolating a regression equation beyond the range of data from which it has been derived.

Finally, when a scatter diagram indicates that a relationship may not really be linear, but may involve an $X^2$ term somewhere in the equation, (e.g., $Y = a + bX + cX^2$), you may wish to break up the scatter diagram into different ranges of *X*, then calculate a least-squares equation for each of the ranges. The alternative is nonlinear regression analysis, which is beyond the scope of this book but generally included in computer statistical analysis packages.

## RANK-ORDER CORRELATION FOR TWO ORDINAL VARIABLES

When data are expressed in the form of preference, or ordinal information, the concept of correlation can still be applied—however, a different approach is required. In this section we'll examine how a statistic called the *Spearman rank coefficient* can be used in determining whether two preference rankings differ significantly from each other.

Like the correlation coefficient in the preceding section, the *Spearman rank coefficient* ($r_s$) will have a value between $-1$ and $+1$. For two sets of rankings, it can be calculated by

$$r_s = 1 - \frac{6(\sum d^2)}{n(n^2 - 1)}$$

where

$n$ = number of items ranked

$\sum d^2$ = sum of the squared differences between ranks for the *n* items

To illustrate this technique, let's consider a situation in which two travel editors have each ranked 12 countries as a "fun place to visit." These rankings, along with the values required to determine $r_s$, are listed in Table 15-5. As shown in the table, both editors seem to like country E, and both tend to place country

---

[2] Data as reported by R. L. Polk & Co., in *Automotive News, 1986 Market Data Book Issue* (Detroit, Mich.: Crain Automotive Group, Inc., Division of Crain Communications, Inc., 1986), p. 26.

**TABLE 15-5.** *Two travel editors have each ranked 12 countries in order of their desirability as a "fun place to visit." Using the Spearman rank coefficient method described in the text, we can determine the extent to which their rankings are related.*

| | Ranking | | Difference | |
| --- | --- | --- | --- | --- |
| **Country** | *Editor 1* | *Editor 2* | *d* | *d²* |
| A | 8 | 5 | 3 | 9 |
| B | 3 | 1 | 2 | 4 |
| C | 6 | 4 | 2 | 4 |
| D | 9 | 7 | 2 | 4 |
| E | 1 | 2 | −1 | 1 |
| F | 12 | 11 | 1 | 1 |
| G | 4 | 8 | −4 | 16 |
| H | 10 | 6 | 4 | 16 |
| I | 5 | 12 | −7 | 49 |
| J | 2 | 10 | −8 | 64 |
| K | 7 | 3 | 4 | 16 |
| L | 11 | 9 | 2 | 4 |

$$\sum d^2 = 188$$

F relatively low, but they appear to be less in agreement regarding the other 10.

To calculate $r_s$ for these data, we need both $n$ (already known to be 12 countries) and $\sum d^2$, the sum of the squared differences between the editors' rankings. To get the latter, we just compare the rankings for each country, square each result, then add them up. For example, $d_A$ will be $8 - 5$, or 3, and country A will contribute $(3)^2$, or 9 to the $\sum d^2$ total in the table. Adding the twelve $d^2$ values, we arrive at $\sum d^2 = 188$, and the Spearman rank coefficient for the two editors can be calculated as

$$r_s = 1 - \frac{6(\sum d^2)}{n(n^2 - 1)} = 1 - \frac{6(188)}{12(12^2 - 1)} = 0.343$$

The result, $r_s = 0.343$, indicates that the rankings are positively correlated (i.e., countries ranked higher by one editor tend also to be ranked higher by the other). The coefficient can be interpreted the same as the *correlation coefficient* of the preceding section.

When $n \geq 10$, we can use the $t$ distribution to test the null hypothesis that the true value of the coefficient is really zero (i.e., that our calculated $r_s$ has differed from zero simply by chance). In carrying out this test, the calculated $t$ statistic is

$$t = r_s \sqrt{\frac{n - 2}{1 - r_s^2}} = 0.343 \sqrt{\frac{12 - 2}{1 - 0.343^2}}$$

$$= 1.155$$

The number of degrees of freedom for this test is d.f. $= n - 2$, or 10. If we conduct our test at the 0.01 level, the critical values for $t$ will be $t = \pm 3.169$, as found in the statistical appendix. Since the calculated $t$ value of 1.155 falls within these limits, the null hypothesis is accepted and we conclude that $r_s = 0.343$ does not differ significantly from zero. From these data, it would appear that the two editors aren't in strong agreement as to what constitutes "a fun place to visit."

*Note:* Should the data contain ties, the *average* rank for the tied items would be assigned to each of them. For example, if one of the editors were to judge countries A and G as tied for third place, each country would receive $(3 + 4)/2$, or 3.5 as their ranking from that editor. If there are a great many ties, a correction factor can be applied to reduce their influence. However, its consideration here would lie beyond the scope of the text.

## ☐ SUMMARY

For some studies in which two variables are measured, it is useful to determine if they might be related in some way. In this chapter several methods are discussed that are applicable to such situations.

Chi-square analysis, also examined in Chapters 13 and 14, can be used to evaluate whether two nominal variables are independent of each other. It is typically applied when sample members have been categorized according to two different characteristics. If the calculated chi-square value exceeds the critical value at the level of significance chosen, the null hypothesis of "variables are independent" is rejected.

Regression and correlation analysis measures (1) the extent of, and (2) the nature of the relationship between two interval or ratio-scale variables. Regression analysis describes the linear equation, $Y = a + bX$, that "best fits" the values recorded, while correlation analysis measures the strength of the relationship.

The correlation coefficient $(r)$ will have a value between $-1$ and $+1$ and will be positive when the variables tend to increase or decrease together. The coefficient of determination $(r^2)$ describes the proportion of variation in $Y$ that is explained by the regression equation.

A correlation coefficient can be statistically tested to determine if it differs significantly from zero. If the test statistic falls within the two critical values for the test, it is assumed that the true correlation between the variables could be zero. The same test also reveals whether the slope $(b)$ of the regression equation differs significantly from zero.

Whenever two variables are ordinal, representing ranking or preference data, rank-order correlation can be employed to measure the strength of their relationship. The method discussed in the chapter for conducting such a test utilizes the Spearman rank coefficient. As with the coefficient of correlation, the

Spearman rank coefficient can be tested to determine if it differs significantly from zero.

## ☐ QUESTIONS FOR REVIEW

1. For a sample of shoppers leaving a local mall, a researcher determines how long they've been shopping and how much they've spent.

|  |  | Length of stay in mall | | |
|---|---|---|---|---|
|  |  | Less than 1 hour | 1–2 hours | More than 2 hours |
| *Amount* | *Under $20* | 24 | 12 | 5 |
| *spent* | *$20–$50* | 10 | 7 | 5 |
|  | *Over $50* | 6 | 11 | 10 |

   a. At the 0.05 level, examine the possibility that these two variables might be independent.
   b. Would your conclusion change if the test were conducted at the 0.01 level?
   c. Based on your calculated chi-square value, what is the most accurate statement you can make about the exact P VALUE for this test?

2. A sampling of students at a large university have been asked how they feel about the ethics of marketing practices in the United States:

|  |  | Major field of study | |
|---|---|---|---|
|  |  | *Business* | *Nonbusiness* |
|  | *Highly ethical* | 35 | 36 |
| **U.S. marketing** | *Mostly ethical* | 23 | 33 |
| **practices are:** | *Mostly unethical* | 15 | 26 |
|  | *Highly unethical* | 7 | 25 |

   a. At the 0.05 level, does there appear to be some relationship between a student's field of study and his or her attitude toward marketing?
   b. Would your conclusion change if the test were conducted at the 0.10 level?
   c. Based on your calculated chi-square value, what is the most accurate statement you can make about the exact P VALUE for this test?

3. For the following cross-classification of frequency data, use the 0.025 level in determining if the variables are independent:

|  |  | Preferred physical activity | | | |
|---|---|---|---|---|---|
|  |  | *Gardening* | *Bowling* | *Tennis* | *Walking* |
|  | *Under 30* | 10 | 13 | 23 | 6 |
| *Age* | *30–60* | 23 | 17 | 19 | 20 |
|  | *Over 60* | 17 | 5 | 18 | 14 |

4. For Question 3, combine the first two age groups and repeat your analysis at the 0.05 level.

5. The equation $Y = 10 + 5X$ is located on a scatter diagram that includes the following points: $(Y = 20, X = 3)$, $(Y = 60, X = 8)$, and $(Y = 30, X = 10)$. Calculate the sum of the squared deviations between actual and predicted values of $Y$.

6. For the following values of $Y$ and $X$, determine the regression equation describing $Y$ as a function of $X$, then calculate the correlation coefficient and the standard error of estimate.

| $Y$ | $X$ |
|-----|-----|
| 5 | 1 |
| 8 | 2 |
| 2 | 3 |
| 12 | 4 |
| 20 | 5 |
| 15 | 6 |

7. On the sales aptitude test they took when they were hired, Joe, Tom, Fred, and Mary had scores of 80, 70, 95, and 85, respectively. Their respective first-year sales volumes were 1050, 1000, 1200, and 1400 units.

   a. Calculate the regression equation describing $Y$ (units sold) and $X$ (score on the aptitude test) and determine the proportion of the variation in sales that is explained by this equation. Based on this information, does the test seem to be a good indicator of sales performance?

   b. At the 0.10 level, test whether the coefficient of correlation differs significantly from 0.

8. For 100 households in a community, the best-fit regression equation between $Y$ (annual expenditure on entertainment) and $X$ (household income) is found to be $Y = 200 + 0.01X$ and the coefficient of correlation is $r = 0.75$.

   a. What proportion of the variability in entertainment expenditures is explained by the regression equation?

   b. If a family has an income level of $30,000, what amount would be predicted for their entertainment expenditure?

   c. At the 0.01 level, test whether the coefficient of correlation differs significantly from 0.

9. For $Y$ = annual mileage driven in one's personal automobile, provide an example of:

   a. Two different $X$ variables that could be expected to have a positive correlation with $Y$.

   b. Two different $X$ variables that could be expected to have a negative correlation with $Y$.

   c. Two different $X$ variables that could be expected to have little or no correlation with $Y$.

10. Does a high coefficient of correlation necessarily mean that $Y$ is *caused* by $X$? Provide a real or hypothetical example of your choice in which a high coefficient of correlation might be expected, but for which direct causation between $X$ and $Y$ is highly unlikely. What common factor might better explain a high correlation between the variables you've cited?

**11.** Based on the information provided in Question 6, determine the 90% prediction interval for an individual $Y$ value when $X = 5$.

**12.** The output below is based on personal income ($X$) and expenditures on jewelry and watches ($Y$) for 1981 through 1984, with data in billions of dollars. (*Source: 1986 Statistical Abstract of the United States*, Bureau of the Census, U.S. Department of Commerce, pp. 435, 438.)

```
                    REGRESSION ANALYSIS

HEADER DATA FOR: A:EXAMPLE3     LABEL: PERSONAL INCOME
                                       AND EXPENDITURES
NUMBER OF CASES: 4     NUMBER OF VARIABLES: 2

JEWELRY/WATCH SPENDING V. PERS. INCOME (BILLIONS $), 1981–1984.

INDEX          NAME              MEAN        STD.DEV.
  1            INCOME          2692.5000     248.8112
DEP. VAR.:     JEWELRY           12.8000        .9933

DEPENDENT VARIABLE: JEWELRY

               REGRESSION
VAR.           COEFFICIENT     STD. ERROR   T(DF = 2)    PROB.
INCOME            .0037           .0010       3.652      .06749
CONSTANT         2.7764

STD. ERROR OF EST. = .4394

       r SQUARED = .8696
           r = .9325

              ANALYSIS OF VARIANCE TABLE

              SUM OF              MEAN
  SOURCE      SQUARES    D.F.    SQUARE    F RATIO   PROB.
REGRESSION    2.5739      1      2.5739    13.334    .0675
RESIDUAL       .3861      2       .1930
TOTAL         2.9600      3
```

**a.** What is the regression equation expressing jewelry and watch expenditures as a function of U.S. personal income?

**b.** What proportion of the variability in $Y$ is explained by the regression equation?

**c.** Rounded to four decimal places, at what P VALUE is the correlation coefficient significantly different from zero?

**d.** Rounded to four decimal places, at what P VALUE is the slope of the regression line significantly different from zero?

**13.** For a set of 10 data points, the regression equation explains 65% of the variability in $Y$. Calculate the coefficient of correlation, then use the 0.02 level in testing whether it differs significantly from zero.

14. Two local sportswriters have come up with the following rankings for the 10 high school basketball teams in their area:

| | Ranking | |
|---|---|---|
| *Team* | *Writer 1* | *Writer 2* |
| Sand City Cougars | 1 | 4 |
| Bay Bridge Bombers | 2 | 3 |
| Southfield Sandpipers | 3 | 5 |
| Brownsville Bobcats | 4 | 1 |
| Gila Bend Lizards | 5 | 6 |
| Portersville Panthers | 6 | 2 |
| Alcort Bandits | 7 | 10 |
| Cobstown Cobras | 8 | 9 |
| Laramar Wildcats | 9 | 7 |
| Tugsville Turtles | 10 | 8 |

   **a.** Calculate and interpret the Spearman rank coefficient for these data.

   **b.** At the 0.10 level, is the coefficient significantly different from zero?

15. Two wine tasters have each ranked 15 leading wines according to the criterion, "a good wine to serve at a party." The sum of the squared differences between their rankings is 754.

   **a.** Calculate and interpret the Spearman rank coefficient for these data.

   **b.** At the 0.01 level, is the coefficient significantly different from zero?

# 16

# MULTIVARIATE TECHNIQUES IN MARKETING RESEARCH

**Customs Agents Find the Variables That Find the Smugglers**

During 1984, 292 pounds of heroin were seized at New York's Kennedy International Airport. The next largest amount was only 66 pounds at Los Angeles International Airport, making the Kennedy haul all the more impressive.

In discriminant analysis, one of the techniques discussed in this chapter, we try to categorize individuals on the basis of things we observe or measure about them. As seen by the U.S. Customs Service agent, air travelers fall into two primary groups: (1) smugglers of drugs, and (2) nonsmugglers.

In deciding on the likely group to which an air traveler belongs, agents rely on variables found useful in identifying past smugglers, in the process spotting things that woud go unnoticed by the vast majority of observers. What variables are most valuable in finding the drug smuggler? As plainclothes customs inspector Sal Aloisio puts it, "There's no scientific method. The key thing is to be observant. Look for what's different."

Among the specific behaviors more likely to be displayed by the drug smuggler: nervousness, making a phone call right after debarking the plane, having either light or no luggage, and paying for the plane ticket in cash. Drug smugglers are also likely to be among the last to leave the plane.

---

*Source:* Based on Stanley Penn, "A Growing Band of Agents Stalks Drugs Flown into Kennedy Airport," *The Wall Street Journal*, August 22, 1985, p. 23.

**Figure 16-1.** U.S. Customs agents have learned that a number of physical and behavioral variables tend to be lin':ed with the smuggling of drugs in ) airports. Some smugglers are more easily identified than others. (Photo courtesy of Elliott Cramer and Bob Wittman.)

Plainclothes inspector Pedro Adorno points out that if passengers have difficulty bending over to retrieve their luggage from the conveyor belt, "it could mean that drugs are strapped around their waist." Also, if someone looks bloated or ill, it's not necessarily a poor reflection on the airline's food. In one instance, a woman who aroused suspicion wouldn't allow an x-ray of her stomach. A so-called "balloon swallower," the reason for her reluctance became obvious as time (and 88 bags of 80%-pure cocaine) passed during her detention.

## INTRODUCTION

In previous chapters, we focused on data analysis involving just one or two variables. These are the "meat and potatoes" of the techniques employed by the marketing researcher, and your ability to use them will take you a long way toward proficiency in the field. In this chapter you'll be introduced to a variety of techniques that are more the equivalent of lobster, almond shrimp, and roast duck.

This analogy is not to suggest that the methods covered here are frivolous or impractical. Just as gourmet foods are often nutritious and filling, these techniques can be very useful to the practicing marketing researcher. However, just as gourmet dining tends to demand more than our budgets allow, in-depth coverage of the approaches in this chapter would lie beyond the mathematical and statistical background that this book assumes.

*Multivariate* techniques are those that involve more than two variables at the same time. One such technique, multidimensional scaling, was discussed in our earlier chapter on attitude measurement because of its special relevance to that topic. This and other multivariate methods are useful because many marketing situations and research questions require that more than just one or two variables be considered. For example, consider the following possibilities:

- Instead of simply viewing sales as a function of advertising, a company wishes to undertake an analysis that considers sales as dependent on several variables—for example, advertising level, number of salespersons, price, and U.S. disposable personal income. For this application, *multiple regression analysis* would be appropriate.

- A life insurance company wishes to identify variables that will predict whether an applicant is likely to be (1) a good risk, or (2) a poor risk as a future policyholder. In this case, *discriminant analysis* could be helpful, with the company predicting group "membership" based on applicant age, sex, marital status, smoking and drinking habits, and past medical problems.

- We have designed a 100-question instrument intended to measure university attributes that students feel to be important when selecting a school to attend. Are we really measuring 100 different characteristics of a university, or is there a smaller number of more basic dimensions that these variables are describing? This is a situation in which *factor analysis* could prove useful.

In the next section we'll look at an overall categorization of the multivariate techniques that have found their way into marketing research, then we'll proceed to examine some of them on an introductory basis. As mentioned earlier, these methods are mathematically complex, and our level of discussion will not enable you to rush out and personally apply these research tools. However, you should come away with a greater understanding of the nature and purpose of these techniques, and a frame of reference from which to better communicate with and understand practitioners who employ them. Our treatment of the various multivariate methods will be organized according to the following topics:

I. Types of multivariate methods

II. Multivariate regression and correlation

III. Discriminant analysis

**IV.** Factor analysis

**V.** Cluster analysis

**VI.** Other multivariate techniques

## TYPES OF MULTIVARIATE TECHNIQUES

Multivariate techniques can be categorized by the structure shown in Figure 16-2. Basically, the selection of an appropriate analysis strategy depends on the answers to the three questions discussed below.[1]

*1. Are some of the variables dependent on others?* If we are assuming that one or more variables might be predicted or explained by the values of two or more other (independent) variables, *dependence* is involved. An example would be a study in which we are examining brand loyalty as a function of consumer age, income, and level of education. With *interdependence*, no variable is assumed to be dependent on, predicted, or explained by any other, and we are primarily interested in relationships that exist among the entire set of variables.

*2. Is there more than one dependent variable?* If the answer to question 1 is no, the answer to this one will also be no. However, some techniques (e.g., multiple regression) can handle only one dependent variable at a time, while others (e.g., multivariate analysis of variance) are capable of simultaneously considering more than one dependent variable.

*3. What is the nature of the data?* At this juncture, scale of measurement is considered—that is, whether the data are metric (interval or ratio scale) or nonmetric (nominal or ordinal scale). For approaches relying on *dependence*, we must first note the scale of measurement of the dependent variable(s), while for *interdependence*, all variables are considered at once. As shown in Figure 16-2, further subdivisions can be made on the basis of the scale of the independent variables.[2]

Before we proceed to a more detailed discussion of multivariate techniques in the sections that follow, let's briefly summarize some of the more commonly used approaches:

*Multiple regression analysis:*   Describes the best-fit linear relationship between one dependent variable ($Y$) and two or more independent variables ($X$'s).

*Multivariate correlation:*   Measures the strength of the linear association

---

[1] Jagdish N. Sheth, "The Multivariate Revolution in Marketing Research," *Journal of Marketing*, 35 (January 1971): 13–19, published by the American Marketing Association.

[2] Thomas C. Kinnear and James R.Taylor, "Multivariate Methods in Marketing Research: A Further Attempt at Classification", *Journal of Marketing*, 35 (October 1971): 56–59, published by the American Marketing Association.

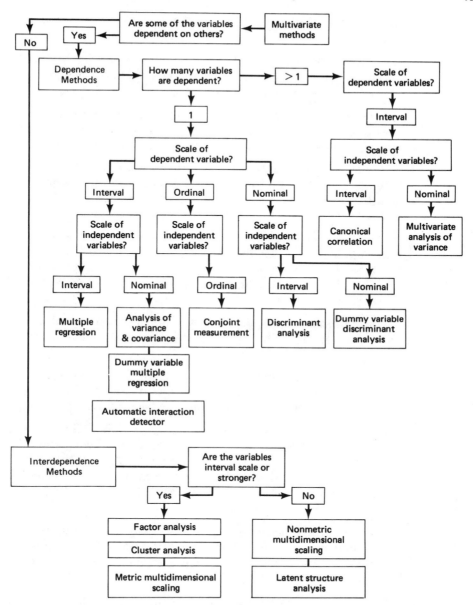

**Figure 16-2.**    A classification of the multivariates techniques used in marketing research. [*Sources:* Adapted from Thomas C. Kinnear and James R. Taylor, *Marketing Research: An Applied Approach,* McGraw-Hill Book Company, New York, 1979, p. 593 and Jagdish N. Sheth, "The Multivariate Revolution in Marketing Research," *Journal of Marketing,* 35 (January 1971): 13–19, published by the American Marketing Association.]

between one dependent variable (*Y*) and two or more independent variables (*X*'s).

*Discriminant analysis:*   Determines which variables best separate members of two or more groups. May also be used to predict group membership based on measurements of the independent variables.

*Factor analysis:*   Reduces a larger number of variables into a smaller set of variables (factors) that have a more basic meaning but contain most of the information of the original set.

*Cluster analysis:*   Based on measurements for each object in a large group, divides the objects into a number of smaller groups where the members tend to have similar measurements. May reduce a large number of consumers into smaller "clusters" of similar individuals, facilitating market segmentation.

*Multidimensional scaling:*   Based on similarities or preference data, "maps" a set of objects in multidimensional perceptual space, with dimensions representing important attributes possessed by the objects (covered earlier in the text).

*Multivariate analysis of variance:*   Similar to one-variable case, but each group is now described by two or more measurements instead of just one.

*Covariance analysis:*   Adjusts the value of a dependent variable by means of the regression relationship between the dependent variable and one or more independent variables. For experimental data, sometimes used to "remove" the effect of uncontrolled outside variables.

*Stepwise multiple regression:*   Similar to multiple regression, except that independent variables (*X*'s) are introduced into the equation one at a time, with the one selected first explaining the greatest amount of the variability in the dependent variable (*Y*). Subsequent introductions are also sequential, on the basis of which remaining *X* explains the greatest amount of the remaining variability in *Y*.

*Dummy variable multiple regression:*   Similar to multiple regression, except that some of the independent variables are of the nominal scale and are numerically represented as 0 or 1, depending on the category in which a given object or respondent lies.

*Automatic interaction detector:*   Using analysis of variance, sequentially splits a total sample into subsamples based on one variable at a time, taking the most powerful explanatory variable first. Useful in market segmentation and identification of the variables that distinguish the segments.

*Conjoint analysis:*   Based on a rank order of preferences expressed for various combinations of product features, determines underlying utility values for the features and assists in determining best "package" of features for a product offering.

*Canonical correlation:*    Similar to multiple regression and correlation, except that the dependent variable is really a linear combination of two or more dependent variables. Where ordinary regression-correlation involves just one $Y$ and a linear combination of $X$'s, canonical correlation involves both a *set* of $Y$'s and a *set* of $X$'s.

As suggested by Figure 16-2 and the preceding descriptions, these are a rich set of techniques in terms of their mathematical complexity and their overall versatility. However, the nature of their mathematical processes and statistical assumptions places in-depth coverage of each beyond the scope of this book. Because they're typically carried out by special computer programs, you'll never get involved in the actual calculations they require.

Chances are that your exposure to them will be in the form of a journal article, an advanced research class, or in a career situation where a specialist is discussing either the possibility or the results of their use in a specific research situation. In any of these eventualities, the combination of these minidescriptions and the chapter discussion should improve your chances of understanding and communicating effectively with regard to multivariate techniques in marketing research.

## MULTIVARIATE REGRESSION AND CORRELATION

In Chapter 15 we examined regression and correlation when only two variables were involved—one dependent ($Y$), and one independent ($X$). In this section, we'll look at the multivariate counterpart, in which there is still one dependent variable, but two or more independent variables are present to join in describing and predicting its value.

### Multiple Regression

The ability of multiple regression analysis to include more than one independent variable makes it possible to carry out a regression study that is more realistic because it reflects the fact that the value of a dependent variable is likely to be influenced by the values of a number of different independent variables. As with the bivariate case ($Y = a + bX$), the relationship is assumed to be linear, and the basic form is quite similar. For example, if there are three independent variables, the multiple regression equation would be

$$Y = a + b_1X_1 + b_2X_2 + b_3X_3$$

The dependent variable $Y$ is expressed as a function of the intercept $a$ plus a linear combination of the three independent variables $X_1$, $X_2$, and $X_3$. The coefficients $b_1$, $b_2$, and $b_3$ indicate how $Y$ tends to change when each $X$ changes, provided that the other $X$'s remain constant. For example, $b_1$ reflects how $Y$ would tend to change with changes in $X_1$, assuming that $X_2$ and $X_3$ remain unchanged. The $b$ coefficients are sometimes referred to as the ***partial regression coefficients***, and are calculated in a fashion analogous to the two-variable case of Chapter 15.

Multiple regression is typically used (1) to *describe* the nature of a linear relationship between one dependent variable and several independent variables, and (2) based on known values for several independent variables, to *predict* the value of a dependent variable. In the first case, we are attempting to better understand how the dependent and independent variables are related. The pizza establishment analysis that follows is an example of this kind of application. In the second usage category, the forecasting of sales based on multiple factors (e.g., advertising level, price, number of salespersons) is a common application of this technique.

As an example of how multiple regression works, let's consider a set of data for eight hypothetical off-campus pizza establishments. For each restaurant, we have three measurements: (1) the number of customers on a recent Friday evening, (2) the price of a large pepperoni pizza, and (3) the seating capacity of the establishment. In carrying out the multiple regression analysis, we would like to determine the linear relationship that best describes the number of customers ($Y$) as a function of price ($X_1$) and seating capacity ($X_2$).

| Establishment | $Y$ = Number of customers | $X_1$ = Price of large pepperoni pizza | $X_2$ = Seating capacity |
|---|---|---|---|
| Pauline's Perilous Pizza Palace | 180 | 5.00 | 50 |
| Ewell Carey's Chicken-Flavored Pizza | 120 | 6.00 | 34 |
| Granny's Old-Fashioned Pizza | 150 | 5.80 | 42 |
| Fred's Fine Pizza and Ambulance Service | 60 | 6.50 | 42 |
| Steve's Discount Pizza Place | 90 | 7.80 | 45 |
| A. Amos Aardvaark's AAAA Pizza | 20 | 7.40 | 22 |
| Wolfgang Schmidt's Genuine Italian Pizza | 50 | 8.00 | 30 |
| Dewey Yewtern's Ptomaine City | 60 | 5.20 | 24 |

If the data were presented in the form of a scatter diagram, it would look like Figure 16-3, where the number of customers is represented by the length of the vertical line from the "base" to the data point. Each point may be visualized as a helium-filled balloon anchored to the point indicated by the restaurant's combination of price and seating capacity, and the number of customers shown by the length of the "string" holding the balloon. As Figure 16-3 suggests, establishments with low prices and large seating capacities tend to be the most popular.

In two-variable regression analysis, we attempted to find the straight line that best fit a set of data. In this case, we're dealing with three dimensions, and the best-fit expression will be a two-dimensional plane. In Figure 16-3, this would take the form of a tilted "ceiling" over the base of the diagram. To avoid complexity in the picture, this plane has not been drawn. However, some data points would be above the best-fit plane, while others would be below, and the plane would be situated so as to minimize the sum of the squared deviations between the actual values of $Y$ and those predicted by the surface of the plane. If there were more than three variables involved, the best-fit "surface" would be a mathematical entity known as a *hyperplane*, difficult to visualize and impossible to draw.

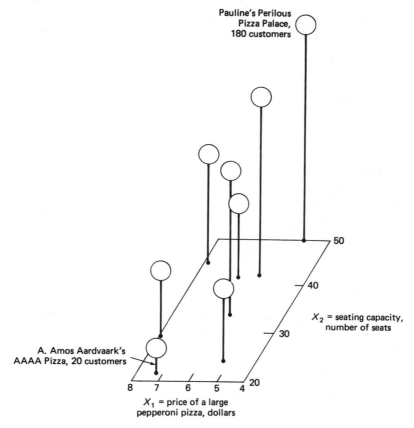

**Figure 16-3.**  Three-dimensional scatter diagram of multiple-regression data for pizza establishments discussed in text. Best-fit equation is $Y = 110 - 22.42X_1 + 3.49X_2$, where $Y$ is the number of customers observed on a recent Friday evening. The regression equation takes the form of a two-dimensional surface (not shown) passing through the data.

Analyzing the pizza data by means of a multiple-regression computer program, we would find that the best-fit equation for the data is

$$Y = 110 - 22.42X_1 + 3.49X_2$$

where

$Y$ = number of customers last Friday evening

$X_1$ = price of a large pepperoni pizza

$X_2$ = seating capacity of the restaurant

The partial regression coefficients, $-22.42$ and $3.49$, indicate how $Y$ is expected to change when either price or seating capacity is changed. For example, for a given seating capacity, we would expect the number of customers to decrease by 22.42 for each one-dollar increase in the price of a large pepperoni pizza. Likewise, for a given price, we would expect the number of customers to increase by 3.49 for each seat added to the establishment's capacity. Many of the estimates are not very different from the actual number of customers observed. For example, the regression equation predicts that the number of customers partaking of Pauline's Perilous Pizza will be $110 - 22.42(5) + 3.49(50)$ $= 172.4$, only 7.6 away from the actual value of 180.

When examining a regression equation, don't make the mistake of assuming that an independent variable is highly important simply because it happens to have the largest coefficient associated with it. For example, just because 22.42 is greater than 3.49, this does not mean that price is more important than seating capacity in determining the number of customers on a Friday evening. If the price had been expressed in pennies instead of dollars, the coefficient for $X_1$ would have been $-2242$ instead of $-22.42$, and if the price had been expressed in terms of the number of ten-dollar bills, the coefficient would have been $-2.242$.

## Multivariate Correlation

The job of multivariate correlation is to determine the strength of a linear relationship between the dependent variable and the set of independent variables. Thus, like multiple regression, it is also an extension of the two-variable case discussed in Chapter 15.

In addition to generating the regression equation, a computer analysis will also reveal $R$, which is the *coefficient of multiple correlation*. As in the two-variable case, this reflects the closeness of the actual values of $Y$ to the values predicted by the regression equation, and greater values of $R$ indicate a stronger relationship. For the data of our pizza establishments, the coefficient of multiple correlation is $R = 0.8891$, showing a good "match" between the actual and predicted number of customers for each establishment.

The *coefficient of multiple determination*, $R^2$, indicates the proportion of the variation in $Y$ that is "explained" by changes in the independent variables.

Thus $0.8891^2$, or 79.04%, of the variation in the number of customers for our pizza shops is explained by the price and seating capacity variables.

### Significance Tests for Multivariate Regression and Correlation

Table 16-1 shows the computer output for this example along with a "bottom line" interpretation of the printout. As with bivariate regression and correlation, there is a standard error of estimate and we can test whether a regres-

**TABLE 16-1.** *Computer output for pizza-customer example in text. Letters A through E refer to interpretation key beneath output.*

```
———————————REGRESSION ANALYSIS—————————————

HEADER DATA FOR: A: PIZZAEX  LABEL: Pizza Establishments
NUMBER OF CASES: 8  NUMBER OF VARIABLES: 3

——————————————————————————————————————————
#CUSTOMERS (Y) AS FUNCTION OF PRICE, LARGE PEPPERONI & #SEATS.

  INDEX       NAME          MEAN        STD. DEV.
    1         PRICE         6.4625       1.1600
    2         SEATS        36.1250      10.2042
  DEP. VAR.:  CUSTMRS      91.2500      54.6253

——————————————————————————————————————————
DEPENDENT VARIABLE: CUSTMRS

  VAR.        REGRESSION COEFFICIENT   STD. ERROR   T (DF= 5)   PROB.    PARTIAL r∧2
  PRICE           −22.4196              9.8902       −2.267     .07273     .5068
  SEATS             3.4914              1.1243        3.105     .02669     .6586
  CONSTANT        110.0078    (A)                                  (B)

  STD. ERROR OF EST. = 29.5898 — (C)

           R SQUARED = .7904 — (D)
           MULTIPLE R = .8891

              ANALYSIS OF VARIANCE TABLE

    SOURCE      SUM OF SQUARES   D.F.   MEAN SQUARE   F RATIO  PROB.
  REGRESSION       16509.7100     2      8254.8550     9.428   .0201 (E)
  RESIDUAL          4377.7900     5       875.5580
  TOTAL            20887.5000     7
```

(A) Describe the least-squares regression equation, $Y = a + b_1 X_1 + b_2 X_2$
Customers = 110.0078 − 22.4196 (Price) + 3.4914 (Seats).

(B) The first regression coefficient ($b_1 = -22.4196$) is significantly different from zero at the 0.07273 level.
The second regression coefficient ($b_2 = 3.4914$) is significantly different from zero at the 0.02669 level.

(C) Similar to its bivariate counterpart, the standard error of estimate for predictions when $X_1$ and $X_2$ are given.

(D) The regression equation explains 79.04% of the variation in Y.

(E) R is significantly different from zero at the 0.0201 level.

sion coefficient differs significantly from zero. In this case, we have two tests, one for $b_1$, another for $b_2$. Similarly, the coefficient of multiple determination ($R^2$) can be tested to see if it differs significantly from zero. The respective P VALUES, given in Table 16-1, are 0.07273 for $b_1$, 0.02669 for $b_2$, and 0.0201 for $R^2$. All three are significantly different from zero at the 0.10 level, although only $b_2$ and $R^2$ are significant at the 0.05 level.

Also shown in Table 16-1 are so-called "partial" coefficients of determination describing the relationship between $Y$ and just one $X$ at a time, with the effect of all other variables held constant. For example, 0.5068 tells us that $X_1$ explains 50.68% of the variation in $Y$ whenever the effect of $X_2$ on both $Y$ and $X_1$ is held constant. Note that "Seats" has a higher partial coefficient of determination than "Price," which is consistent with the more significant level at which $b_2$ differs from zero.

The sum of the two partial coefficients of determination (0.5068 + 0.6586) greatly exceeds the 79% of variation in $Y$ explained by the combination of $X_1$ and $X_2$ in the regression equation. This is because the two independent variables are not fully independent *of each other*. While the correlation between $X_1$ and $X_2$ is not especially large ($r = -0.22$), even such a small degree of relationship between the two indicates that they are not telling us two *entirely* different things about the pizza establishments.

## Multicollinearity

Whenever two or more of the independent variables are highly correlated with each other, a condition known as ***multicollinearity*** exists. When this occurs, the partial regression coefficients in the equation will be statistically unreliable and difficult to interpret. In our pizza shop example, we would have incurred a severe case of multicollinearity had we added a third variable, $X_3$ = the price of a large plain pizza. There would probably be a very high correlation between the price of a large pepperoni pizza ($X_1$) and that of a large plain pizza ($X_3$). Thus, if two variables are "saying" similar things about the dependent variable, the easiest solution is just to eliminate one of them from the analysis. Multicollinearity is not a problem when the sole purpose of our regression equation is to predict the value of $Y$. However, when we're trying to describe the *nature* of the linear relationship between $Y$ and the various independent variables, this condition should be avoided.

## Stepwise Regression

In the stepwise approach to multiple regression, the independent variables enter the analysis one at a time, with the first one entered being the variable that explains the greatest amount of variation in $Y$. The second variable entered is the one that explains the greatest amount of the remaining variation in $Y$. This continues until we either run out of significant independent variables, or have explained a satisfactory portion of the variability in $Y$. This approach helps to avoid the problem of multicollinearity, since each successive variable entered must be somewhat unique from the others in order to be "invited" into the regression equation. Because of its ability to judge the value of introducing each $X$ into the regression equation, the technique is especially useful when we have a large number of independent variables from which to choose.

### Dummy Variables in Regression Analysis

In some cases, we may have a dependent variable or one or more independent variables that do not meet the requirements of the interval scale of measurement. For example, in our pizza shop study, we could be interested in whether or not the establishment offers a home delivery service. This would be a nominal measure, but could be used in the regression analysis if considered a *dummy variable*—that is, if the shop had a delivery service, this variable would have a value of 1, and if it did not, the value would be 0. Dummy variables are *binary* (on-off, yes-no) since they have only two possible states. Typical dummy variables in marketing research relate to nominal measurements that describe a personal characteristic or group membership—for example, one's sex, or whether or not one subscribes to *Reader's Digest* or wears contact lenses. When $Y$ itself is a category and expressed as a (0,1) dummy variable, multiple regression becomes comparable to the two-group form of the discriminant analysis technique discussed in the next section.

## DISCRIMINANT ANALYSIS

*Discriminant analysis* is a technique which, like multiple regression, has one dependent variable and a set of independent variables. However, in discriminant analysis, the dependent variable is always of the nominal scale of measurement and represents group membership. The two principal uses for discriminant analysis are (1) classification of objects into groups, and (2) identification of the descriptive variables that best determine group membership.

   *Classification of objects into groups.* Based on measurements for the various independent ($X$) variables, discriminant analysis can be used to classify people or objects into one of two or more groups. As a consumer, you have probably found yourself "categorized" into groups many times, often by those who are using the idea of discriminant analysis without ever knowing it. For example, you may have gone through a "categorization" experience similar to the ones suffered by these poor souls:

* Clover Froshlevel and a few of her friends have gone to The Snobbery, an expensive local restaurant, to celebrate the close of their first year of college. The hostess, observing that the girls are young college students, and not expensively dressed, seats them in a brightly lit corner area of the dining room, between the kitchen entrance and the men's rest room. Perhaps

incorrectly, she has categorized Clover and her friends into the low-spending, low-tip category of patrons.

* Ralph Rumblestrip, upon applying for car insurance, discovers that his annual premium will cost nearly as much as his car. Although he hasn't had an accident or a traffic violation in over five years of driving, the insurance company observes that he is under 25, unmarried, and has not had driver training.
* Ace Magnumarm, Hower University's all-American quarterback, finds his telephone strangely silent during the National Football League draft of graduating seniors. A popular scouting service claims that Ace could never be a successful NFL quarterback because he is only 5'10", 165 pounds.

Whether we like it or not, individuals and companies are constantly categorizing us into groups on the basis of variables such as our age, level of education, income, marital status, physical height and weight, the kind of car we drive, our mode of dress, or quality point average. While the mathematical technique of discriminant analysis may not be specifically involved, its underlying ideas are present—that is, based on a set of observed measurements, we can attempt to classify an individual or object into a group.

*Identification of the descriptive variables that best determine group membership.* In this application of discriminant analysis, we examine members of *known* groups to determine which variables are most useful in helping us differentiate between members of each. For example, if we are in the business of loaning money to consumers, we may wish to identify the variables that best "discriminate" between (1) past borrowers who have paid us back on time, and (2) past borrowers who have not. Such variables might be age, income, number of years at current address, number of years at current job, health, and marital status.

Discriminant analysis generally assumes that the independent variables are of the interval scale of measurement. However, as with multiple regression, it is possible to include independent variables that are of the nominal variety. In this case, we would be using what Figure 16-2 describes as "dummy variable" discriminant analysis. While some of the preceding examples have included a few nominal-scale independent variables for purposes of illustration, the rest of our discussion will assume that we have independent variables of the interval scale or stronger.

## Two-Group Discriminant Analysis

In the *two-group* approach to discriminant analysis, we are interested in either classifying or describing membership in just two groups, and we may have more than two independent variables. However, our illustrations and examples will, for purposes of graphical representation, include only two independent variables, $X_1$ and $X_2$.

### Basic Principles and Terms

To illustrate the basic ideas behind discriminant analysis, let's assume that we have age and income information for (1) subscribers, and (2) nonsubscribers to three hypothetical magazines. Scatter diagrams for each magazine are shown in Figure 16-4. Let's consider each of these separately:

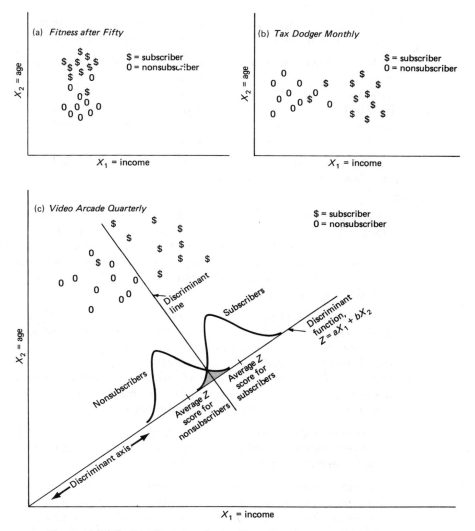

**Figure 16-4.** Scatter diagrams of subscribers ($) and nonsubscribers (0) to three hypothetical magazines. In diagrams (a) and (b), the two groups are separated along just one dimension. In diagram (c), both $X_1$ and $X_2$ help to differentiate between groups. Diagram (c) also illustrates key discriminant analysis terms discussed in text.

***Fitness after Fifty.***   For these data, shown in part (a) of Figure 16-4, it seems that $X_1$ (income) has very little to do with membership in the subscriber versus nonsubscriber groups. The groups are "spread apart" on the $X_2$ (age) dimension, suggesting that this variable is the only one that really separates the groups.

***Tax Dodger Monthly.***   For these data, shown in part (b) of Figure 16-4, the reverse of the preceding is true, with $X_1$ (income) being the only variable that appears to differentiate between the groups. Note that the groups are separated from each other only in the horizontal direction.

***Video Arcade Quarterly.***   For these data, shown in part (c) of Figure 16-4, the groups are different from each other along *both* dimensions, indicating that both variables play a role in differentiating between the members of the two groups. Note that, in this case, the groups are separated from each other along a line that would be, on a navigational compass, approximately in the northeast direction.

In addition to showing data for subscribers and nonsubscribers, part (c) of Figure 16-4 also illustrates a number of important terms used in discriminant analysis:

***Discriminant axis:***   This is the northeast line just mentioned—the line along which the groups are most separated. Mathematically, it's the direction along which a certain ratio (variation between groups divided by variation within groups) is maximized. Each of the data points can be projected onto this line, thus making possible the two normal-curve distributions shown on the line.

***Discriminant function:***   This is a mathematical function that describes the scores along the discriminant axis, and can be described as $Z = aX_1 + bX_2$, where $Z$ is the discriminant function score for an individual. Note that $Z$ is a *linear combination* (a weighted sum) of the $X_1$ and $X_2$ scores—this is how each data point is mathematically projected onto the discriminant axis. Depending on his or her discriminant function score, an individual would be predicted to be a member of one group or the other.

***Discriminant coefficients:***   These are the coefficients $a$ and $b$ in the discriminant function, and tend to reflect the relative importance of $X_1$ and $X_2$ in determining group membership.

***Centroid:***   For each group, this is a point corresponding to the intersection of the means of $X_1$ and $X_2$. The centroid can be thought of as a multidimensional mean. Projection of each centroid to the discriminant axis is carried out by the same linear combination approach applied to the individual data points.

***Discriminant line:***   This is a line, perpendicular to the discriminant axis, that is used to predict group membership or separate members of the two groups. Depending on an individual's scores on $X_1$ and $X_2$, he or she may fall on one side of the line or the other. The discriminant line represents a "cutoff" discriminant function score, above or below which any new individual will be "assigned" to one group or the other. The discriminant line is halfway between the two centroids.

*Misclassification:*   If, based on his $X_1$ and $X_2$ scores, we assign an individual to a group to which he doesn't really belong, we have misclassified him. In diagram (c) of Figure 16-4, the small shaded areas represent the two kinds of misclassification errors.

### An Example

To show how discriminant analysis works, let's look at how the technique might be applied to a hypothetical set of data. Consider the following research setting:

Since the death of his partner, Sam has been the sole proprietor of Sam & Ollie's Shoes, Inc. In an attempt to better identify serious shoe shoppers, Sam has collected observational data for three variables:

$X_1$:   the number of minutes a customer spends looking at the display window before entering the store

$X_2$:   the customer's approximate age

$X_3$:   whether or not the customer bought a pair of shoes before leaving the store

Sam's observational data are shown in the scatter diagram of Figure 16-5. Note that, as in part (c) of Figure 16-4, both $X_1$ and $X_2$ help to differentiate between the two groups, with nonbuyers tending to be older and to have spent less time looking at the display window. In this diagram, the centroids are shown for the two groups, and it can be seen that buyers, on the average, differ from nonbuyers on both dimensions.

With the help of two-group discriminant analysis, Sam can be a bit more rigorous in "classifying" individuals before they enter the store. While we won't go through the actual calculations (these are generally left to a computer program), we will examine the results of such an analysis. These are shown, both graphically and mathematically, in Figure 16-5.[3] In this summary, you should especially note the following key points:

The *centroid* for the buyers is ($\overline{X}_1$ = 3.0 minutes, $\overline{X}_2$ = 24.2 years), while that for the nonbuyers is ($\overline{X}_1$ = 1.9 minutes, $\overline{X}_2$ = 32.5 years). The *discriminant axis* is in approximately the "east-southeast" direction rather than vertical or horizontal. This indicates that both variables help to differentiate between mem-

---

[3] This example is based on a similar problem examined in Paul E. Green and Donald S. Tull, *Research for Marketing Decisions*, 4th ed. © 1978, pp. 36, 385–392. Adapted by permission of Prentice-Hall, Inc., Englewood Cliffs, New Jersey. Green and Tull's treatment of the subject also includes the appropriate formulas for calculating the discriminant function coefficients for a two-group, two-variable discriminant analysis.

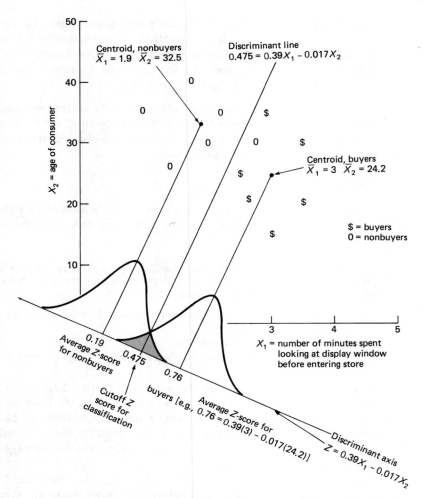

**Figure 16-5.** Discriminant analysis results for the observational study described in text. Note how Z-score combines both $X_1$ and $X_2$ into single measurement that falls along the discriminant axis.

bers of the two groups. The discriminant axis need not be parallel to a straight line through the centroids. (Remember that the discriminant axis is the direction along which between-group variation divided by within-group variation is maximized, and this is the only criterion for determining its direction.)

The *discriminant function*, which describes the Z-scores along the discriminant axis, is $Z = 0.39X_1 - 0.017X_2$. The average Z-score for buyers can be obtained by calculating $Z = 0.39(3.0) - 0.017(24.2)$, or 0.76; thus, on the discriminant axis, the average buyer is located at the $Z = 0.76$ position. In similar fashion, we can substitute the centroid values for the nonbuyer group into the discriminant function and obtain their average position, which is $Z = 0.19$. Note

---

**EXHIBIT 16-1**

**Classifying Potential Tenants**

From the limited perspective of a landlord, there are only two categories of people: (1) desirable tenants, and (2) undesirable tenants. To help landlords differentiate between the two, a number of agencies have sprung up which provide tenant screening services.

In addition to keeping records on eviction and credit files, one screening agency maintains computerized data reflecting newspaper coverage of drug incidents, murders, and other crimes in its area. Another lists any tenant who, for whatever reason, causes a financial loss for a landlord. In the latter case, a tenant may find herself listed even though she was in the right and the landlord was in the wrong.

Some have claimed to be innocent victims of misclassification. In one instance, a woman was listed because her name had been found in court eviction records. However, her attorney argued, these records were misleading because she was never actually evicted. In another case, a woman who liked playing bingo was identified as a "chronic excessive gambler" and listed accordingly.

*Source:* Based on Pam Belluck, "Tenants Cry Foul as Screening Companies Help Landlords Spot 'Problem' Applicants," *The Wall Street Journal*, December 27, 1985, p. 11.

---

how the discriminant function takes two different measurements and combines them into a single measurement, the $Z$ score.

The *discriminant line*, our "cutoff" point when classifying new individuals into one of the groups, is located halfway between the two centroids, and intersects the discriminant axis at $Z = 0.475$. If a potential customer of about 35 years of age ($X_2 = 35$), were to spend 4 minutes ($X_1 = 4$) looking at the display window, her $Z$ score would be $0.39(4) - 0.017(35)$, or $0.965$. Since $0.965$ exceeds the cutoff value of $0.475$, we would categorize this shopper into the "buyer" group, and presumably spend more attention on her during her visit. The equation for the discriminant line is $0.475 = 0.39X_1 - 0.017X_2$.

## Discriminant Analysis: Commentary

Discriminant analysis may also involve more than two groups, in which case it is known as *multiple discriminant analysis*. This is essentially an extension of the two-group approach, and involves the generation of more than one discriminant function. Because of its greater complexity, coverage of multiple groups in discriminant analysis is beyond the scope of this book.

Since discriminant analysis attempts to classify individuals or objects into groups, we can evaluate the success of a discriminant function by simply determining the proportion of individuals it is able to classify correctly. In this case, it is easiest to use the same individuals who were used in developing the function in the first place. For the data of Sam and Ollie's Shoes, Inc., the discriminant function correctly classifies 11 of the 12 persons observed. However, because of (1) small sample sizes, and (2) the "circular logic" of evaluating the function on the basis of the same data from which it was developed, it is preferable to judge the success of a discriminant function by using a separate sample of individuals. These can be a small proportion of the original observations (a "holdout" sample) or an entirely new set of individuals.

## FACTOR ANALYSIS

Multiple regression and discriminant analysis both assume that there is a dependent variable ($Y$), the value of which is a function of several independent variables ($X$'s). In this section and the next, we'll examine two approaches that treat all variables as "equals." The first of these techniques, *factor analysis*, is an increasingly popular tool of the practicing marketing researcher. Its two primary applications are (1) simplifying a set of data by reducing the number of variables, and (2) identifying the underlying structure or dimensionality of the data.

*Simplifying a set of data by reducing the number of variables.* In marketing research studies, we may end up with a large number of measurements, or variables for a set of respondents. This can lead to two difficulties: (1) the sheer number of variables may be a bit unwieldy for further analysis (e.g., a 100-variable multiple regression), and (2) some of the variables may be highly related to others, leading to reliability problems such as *multicollinearity*, discussed earlier in the chapter. Factor analysis can help reduce the number of variables to a level that is easier to manage, but that still contains most of the information found in the (much larger) original set. In survey research, it can be desirable to collect data by pretesting a questionnaire, then using factor analysis to "boil down" the questionnaire to those questions which are really measuring different things about the respondent. This saves money on survey copying and administration, shortens the questionnaire itself, and enhances our eventual response rate.

*Identifying the underlying structure, or dimensionality of the data.* While we may have 50 different variables, these may be measuring only five different basic characteristics of our sample. For example, in a housing study, such variables as number of rooms, lot size, number of baths, number of occupants, annual utility bill, and market value would tend to be identified by factor analysis as reflecting a single underlying dimension—in this case, the size of the home.

### Basic Principles of Factor Analysis

Typically starting with a matrix of the correlations between variables (e.g., Table 16-2), factor analysis attempts to generate "new" variables, each of which is a

**TABLE 16-2.** *The typical starting point for factor analysis is a matrix of the correlations between variables (X's). For this hypothetical matrix, the high correlation between variables 2 and 4 would lead to their being associated with (i.e., having a high factor loading with) the same underlying construct (factor).*

|       | $X_1$ | $X_2$ | $X_3$ | $X_4$ | $X_5$ |
|-------|-------|-------|-------|-------|-------|
| $X_1$ | 1.00  | 0.80  | 0.40  | 0.65  | 0.30  |
| $X_2$ |       | 1.00  | 0.70  | 0.90  | 0.15  |
| $X_3$ |       |       | 1.00  | 0.85  | 0.75  |
| $X_4$ |       |       |       | 1.00  | 0.50  |
| $X_5$ |       |       |       |       | 1.00  |

linear combination of the original variables. These new variables are called *factors*, and the coefficients in each linear combination are called *factor loadings*.

The *principal components* technique, probably the most popular approach to factor analysis, derives a set of factors that are totally uncorrelated—that is, their axes are perpendicular to each other. The first factor chosen is the one along which the data are most "spread out," and will account for the maximum possible variation in the data. The second factor, perpendicular to the first, is selected so that it will account for the greatest possible amount of the remaining variation in the data. Additional factors, each perpendicular to those that preceded, are selected until the amount of unexplained variation remaining is below an acceptable limit.

As an example of what a factor might look like, consider Figure 16-6, in which the first two factors are shown for a set of data in two dimensions. Note that the first factor, $F_1 = 0.95X_1 + 0.20X_2$, is along the direction of "greatest spread" of the data, and that the second factor is perpendicular to the first. In the original data, each respondent is represented by a position on $X_1$ and $X_2$. However, using the linear combination description for each factor, each individual may now be described in terms of his or her scores on factors 1 and 2. For example, a point originally described by ($X_1 = 4$ and $X_2 = 3$) can now be represented by [$F_1 = 0.95(4) + 0.20(3) = 4.4$ and $F_2 = 0.20(4) - 0.95(3) = -2.05$]. To better understand what has happened, just visualize the points staying in the same place, but the coordinate system axes being moved slightly.

When the original variables have been "standardized" (each expressed in terms of its standard deviation, and with mean corrected to zero), the factor loadings represent the correlation between each factor and the various original variables. For example, in Figure 16-6, the correlation between factor 1 and $X_1$ would be 0.95. This "standardization" is the reason why Figure 16-6 would have $X_1 = 0$ and $X_2 = 0$ as the origin of the two axes.

Once the set of factors has been obtained, and we have the correlations (factor loadings) between each factor and each original variable, we may find that it is relatively difficult to interpret the results (i.e., some variables may not be highly correlated with *any* of the factors). In this case, the coordinate system

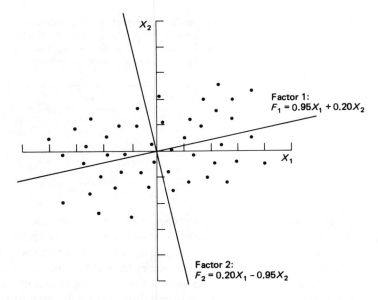

**Figure 16-6.**   As shown here, a *factor* is just a linear combination of the original variables. For these hypothetical data in two dimensions, factor 1 extends in the direction of greatest spread in the data, while the second factor is perpendicular (uncorrelated) with the first. (*Source:* Adapted from an example by H.W. Boyd, R. Westfall, and S.F. Stasch, *Marketing Research: Text and Cases*, 5th ed., Richard D. Irwin, Inc., Homewood, Ill., 1981, p. 521.)

represented by the factors can be "rotated" about its origin so that the correlations will tend to be either very high or very low. The goal is to come up with new factors, each of which has some variables highly correlated with it. Naturally, these new factors will also be perpendicular to each other.

## An Example

To further demonstrate how factor analysis works, let's consider the study that led to the information presented in Table 16-3. As part of their examination of cross-shoppers (consumers who shop different types of stores which carry the same merchandise), the researchers measured a sample of shoppers by means of the 23 statements shown in the table. Were they really measuring 23 different aspects of the sample or do the results suggest that the 23 measurements could be representative of a smaller number of more basic consumer characteristics? The answer would appear to be the latter possibility, as the 23 statements (variables) have been distilled by factor analysis into three major kinds of measurements, or factors:[4]

---

[4] Stanton G. Cort and Luis V. Dominguez, "Cross-Shopping and Retail Growth," *Journal of Marketing Research*, 14 (May 1977): 189, published by the American Marketing Association.

*Factor I.*   As shown in the table, each of the first 14 statements has a high loading, or correlation, with the first factor identified. Because of the common nature of these statements, the researchers identified this factor as representing a "fashion motivation and involvement" dimension.

*Factor II.*   The next five statements in the table have a high loading on the second factor identified, and the researchers have interpreted this factor as representing a "self-confidence and fashion opinion leadership" dimension.

*Factor III.*   The last four statements in the table are loaded on factor III, characterized by the authors as a "value motivation and opportunistic shopping" dimension.

Note that the factor loadings in Table 16-3 are such that each of the 23 statements tends to load heavily on one factor, and low on the other two. This is because the factors are the result of axes rotation designed for this purpose; as discussed earlier, such rotation makes it easier to interpret the meaning of the factors.

Table 16-3 includes a number of common factor analysis terms, some of which we have not yet considered. As with the factors themselves, these are among the typical output of a factor analysis application. They may be described as follows:

*Factor loadings:*   Discussed earlier, these are the correlations between the factors and the various original variables, and are shown in columns I, II, and III. For example statement 1, ("I like to be the person wearing the newest fashions at school or work") has a correlation of 0.80 with factor I, 0.21 with factor II, and 0.03 with factor III.

*Communalities:*   For each of the statements, the communality is the proportion of the statement's variability that is explained by the three factors shown. Sometimes identified as $h^2$, the communality is just the sum of the squared correlations for the statement and the three factors. For example, in the case of statement 1, the communality (0.69) is equal to $(0.80)^2 + (0.21)^2 + (0.03)^2$. As the table shows, the three factors are more successful in explaining the variability in statement 1 ($h^2 = 0.69$) than in explaining that of statement 2 ($h^2 = 0.62$). For 9 of the 23 statements, the three factors explain at least half of the variability in consumer responses to the statement.

*Eigenvalues:*   For each factor, the *eigenvalue* is the sum of the squared factor loadings for that factor. For example, for factor I, the eigenvalue is $(0.80)^2 + (0.77)^2 + \cdots + (-0.08)^2$, or 5.90. When we divide the eigenvalue by the number of statements, we obtain the proportion of the total variability that is explained by that factor. For factor I, we can calculate $5.90/23 = 0.257$ and determine that factor I explains 25.7% of the variance in the consumer responses to the 23 statements. As we proceed from factor

**TABLE 16-3.** *The result of applying the principal-components factor analysis technique to a series of 23 statements administered to a consumer sample. After factor rotation, each statement loads heavily on one of the factors and lightly on the other two. Factor analysis has helped to distill the original 23 statements down to three underlying dimensions, or factors. Terms in this table are common to most factor analysis solutions, and are described in text.*

| Statements | I | II | III | Communalities |
|---|---|---|---|---|
| "I like to be the person wearing the newest fashions at school or work." | 0.80 | 0.21 | 0.03 | 0.69 |
| "I like to be the person wearing the newest fashions at a party." | 0.77 | 0.13 | 0.08 | 0.62 |
| "Dressing smartly is an important part of my life." | 0.65 | 0.32 | 0.15 | 0.55 |
| "I spend a lot of time talking with my friends about fashions." | 0.64 | −0.21 | 0.22 | 0.50 |
| "I usually have one or two outfits that are the very newest styles." | 0.63 | 0.20 | 0.04 | 0.44 |
| "I often try new styles before my friends and neighbors do." | 0.62 | 0.30 | −0.04 | 0.48 |
| "I prefer to associate with people who buy and wear the very newest fashions." | 0.62 | −0.16 | 0.04 | 0.41 |
| "My friends and neighbors often come to me for advice on fashions." | 0.61 | 0.27 | 0.14 | 0.46 |
| "I often try the new hairdo styles when they change." | 0.57 | 0.08 | −0.04 | 0.33 |
| "I like to wear fashionable clothes around the house." | 0.57 | 0.09 | 0.08 | 0.34 |
| "I like to wear new fashions when shopping for food or household supplies." | 0.57 | 0.01 | 0.19 | 0.36 |
| "I read fashion magazines more regularly than most people do." | 0.55 | 0.04 | 0.07 | 0.31 |
| "I often buy fashions on impulse because a new style excites me." | 0.54 | 0.08 | −0.15 | 0.32 |
| "When I must choose between the two, I usually dress for fashion, not comfort." | 0.54 | 0.11 | −0.17 | 0.33 |
| "I think I have more self-confidence than most people." | 0.10 | 0.73 | 0.17 | 0.57 |
| "I like to be considered a leader." | 0.33 | 0.68 | 0.00 | 0.57 |
| "People come to me more often than I go to them for information." | 0.14 | 0.64 | 0.13 | 0.45 |
| "I think I have a lot of personal ability." | 0.20 | 0.58 | 0.08 | 0.38 |
| "I often seek my friends' advice on which fashions to buy." | 0.29 | −0.39 | 0.11 | 0.25 |

TABLE 16-3. (continued)

| Statements | Factors | | | Communalities |
| --- | --- | --- | --- | --- |
| | *I* | *II* | *III* | |
| "I usually watch fashion advertisements for announcements of sales." | 0.19 | −0.05 | 0.71 | 0.54 |
| "A person can save a lot of money on her own fashions by shopping for bargains." | −0.18 | 0.33 | 0.71 | 0.65 |
| "I shop a lot for fashion specials." | 0.32 | 0.23 | 0.67 | 0.60 |
| "I find myself checking the prices in fashion stores even for small ticket items." | −0.08 | 0.00 | 0.61 | 0.38 |
| Eigenvalues: | 5.90 | 2.53 | 2.10 | |
| Percent of variance explained: | 25.7% | 11.0% | 9.1% | |
| Cumulative percent of variance explained: | 25.7% | 36.7% | 45.8% | |

Source: Adapted from Stanton G. Cort and Luis V. Dominguez, "Cross-Shopping and Retail Growth," *Journal of Marketing Research*, 14 (May 1977): 189, published by the American Marketing Association.

I through factor III, we can observe that each factor helps explain part of the variability, and that the three factors combine to explain 45.8% of the variability in the consumer responses.

Factor analysis remains one of the more complex techniques available to the marketing researcher, this despite the fact that increased computer capacities and accessibility have made it relatively convenient to apply. The user is faced with a number of decisions that tend to provide the technique with an artistic as well as a mathematical dimension. For example, we must decide how many factors to extract from a given set of data, whether we will rotate the factors for better interpretability (and, if so, in what manner), and the form which our input data will take. In addition, identification of the resulting factors is a subjective process that may differ markedly from one researcher to the next. For readers with a strong interest in applying factor analysis to marketing data, it is suggested that they follow this rather introductory discussion by consulting a more specialized treatment of the subject.

## CLUSTER ANALYSIS

*Cluster analysis* is a multivariate technique that places either variables or objects into groups, or clusters, so that those within each group are more similar to each other than they are to members of other groups. The principal application of the technique is to cluster objects—for example, cities, consumers, product brands, and television programs. While there are many different computational algorithms for classifying objects into clusters, they all must begin with some measure of the similarities between the objects. In some cases, the similarities may simply consist of nominal data, such as whether or not the objects possess certain characteristics. With this in mind, individuals could be clustered on the basis of the kind of car they drive, the brand of TV set they own, or whether or not they like root beer.

Typically, clustering proceeds from a set of similarities data that are stronger than the nominal scale, and that reflect the objects' positions in what is essentially a multidimensional, interval-scale space. The basic configuration of objects is merely a ***starting point*** for cluster analysis.

### Clustering Techniques

After a measure of the similarities between the objects has been developed, there are a wide variety of clustering techniques that can be used for the actual selection of the clusters and the objects to be included in them. One family of approaches is described as ***hierarchical***, since it involves clustering at different levels of aggregation. In the first level of one such approach, each object is considered to be its own "cluster." At the next stage, the two closest objects are combined to form a new cluster, with this new cluster being described by its centroid. At each subsequent step, a point will join either another point or a cluster. This continues until the desired number of clusters have been formed. If the process were continued to its completion, every object would be included in just a single cluster—a solution that would be of little practical value.

An example of this approach is shown in Figure 16-7 and the steps may be explained as follows:

> ***Step 1.*** The shortest distance in the configuration is that between objects A and B, so they are joined to form a cluster.

> ***Step 2.*** The shortest distance in the configuration is now between objects E and F, so they are joined to form a cluster.

> ***Step 3.*** The shortest distance in the configuration is now between object C and the centroid of the AB cluster, so object C joins the AB cluster.

> ***Step 4.*** The shortest distance in the configuration is now between object D and the centroid of the ABC cluster, so object D joins the ABC cluster.

The hierarchical approach can be applied in the opposite direction (the "top-down" strategy), with the objects initially being members of just one or two very large clusters. During subsequent steps, objects are removed to form new, smaller clusters, until a satisfactory number of clusters have been formed. If this process were continued to its extreme, each object would end up being its own "cluster," the starting point for the hierarchical approach from the op-

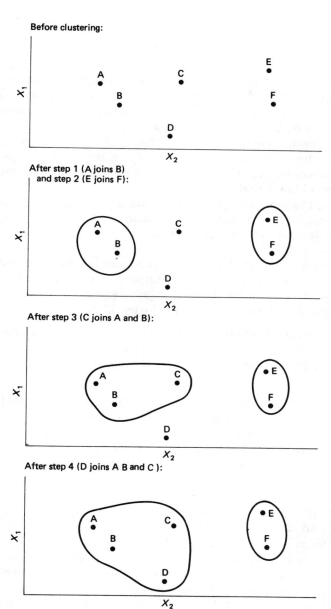

**Before clustering:**

**After step 1 (A joins B)
and step 2 (E joins F):**

**After step 3 (C joins A and B):**

**After step 4 (D joins A B and C ):**

**Figure 16-7.** An example of a hierarchical clustering approach. At the beginning, each object is its own "cluster." In each of the subsequent steps, a point will join either (1) another nearby point, or (2) the cluster whose centroid is nearest.

posite direction. Many other algorithms are also available for the clustering of objects.

## An Example

In a study of relationships between personality and product usage, Schaninger, Lessig, and Panton used a hierarchical approach in carrying out a cluster analysis of individuals who had been measured by 31 product-usage variables.[5] After examining solutions containing between 2 and 12 clusters, they found that the 3-cluster solution was the most meaningful for their data. Table 16-4 shows the mean personality and product usage scores for members of the three groups, along with the *F* ratio reflecting the significance of the difference among the group means for each individual variable.

As Table 16-4 shows, the three groups differed quite significantly on many of the measured variables. Based on their interpretation of the findings, the researchers summarized the three clusters of individuals:[6]

> *Group 1.* ". . . heavy consumers of fashion/socially oriented products and all types of alcohol. . . . Significantly less compliant and more ascendent and sociable than persons in clusters 2 and 3, as well as more responsible and vigorous and less detached than those in cluster 3."

> *Group 2.* ". . . low consumption of most types of alcohol and cigarettes and low readership of *Playboy* and *Penthouse*, higher scores on compliance, responsibility and vigor, and lower scores on ascendency and sociability than clusters 1 and 3."

> *Group 3.* ". . . exhibited heavy usage of all types of illegal drugs, alcohol, and other 'drug'-type products, lower scores on responsibility and vigor, and higher scores on detachment. They were more compliant and less ascendent than those in cluster 1 and tended (not significantly) to be less aggressive, emotionally stable, and cautious than those in clusters 1 and 2."

The subjects of the preceding analysis were male undergraduates at a large midwestern university, and the findings might not apply to the general population of the United States. However, the results demonstrate the ability of cluster analysis to categorize members of a group into clusters of similar individuals. This is perhaps the principal application of cluster analysis in marketing today, and the technique plays a key role in market segmentation: dividing an overall market into consumer groups that are different from each other, but

---

[5] Charles M. Schaninger, V. Parker Lessig, and Don B. Panton, "The Complementary Use of Multivariate Procedures to Investigate Nonlinear and Interactive Relationships between Personality and Product Usage," *Journal of Marketing Research*, 17 (February 1980): 119–24, published by the American Marketing Association.

[6] Ibid., pp. 121–22.

**TABLE 16-4.** *Average scores on personality and product-usage variables for members of the three groups identified by the cluster analysis study described in text. F-values and levels of significance reflect results of univariate analysis of variance for each of the variables.*

| | Group 1 (n = 38) | Group 2 (n = 79) | Group 3 (n = 25) | F |
|---|---|---|---|---|
| Personality measures | | | | |
| Compliant | 38.39 | 42.33 | 42.00 | 5.00[a] |
| Aggressive | 53.13 | 52.33 | 50.88 | 0.52 |
| Detached | 32.26 | 33.13 | 34.80 | 0.94 |
| Ascendency | 23.95 | 21.38 | 22.16 | 2.72[b] |
| Responsibility | 24.32 | 24.37 | 21.60 | 3.43[c] |
| Emotional stability | 25.29 | 24.73 | 23.64 | 0.53 |
| Sociability | 21.63 | 19.67 | 20.24 | 1.37 |
| Caution | 22.32 | 23.05 | 21.42 | 0.63 |
| Original thinking | 23.60 | 24.58 | 23.29 | 0.54 |
| Personal relations | 22.26 | 21.76 | 21.20 | 0.19 |
| Vigor | 25.05 | 25.61 | 22.92 | 1.87 |
| Product usage scores | | | | |
| Aspirin/headache | 2.87 | 2.64 | 3.04 | 1.49 |
| Mouthwash | 2.82 | 2.62 | 2.40 | 0.61 |
| Cologne | 3.42 | 3.18 | 2.76 | 1.74 |
| Hairspray | 0.24 | 0.14 | 0.16 | 0.87 |
| Shampoo | 4.58 | 4.34 | 4.64 | 3.23[c] |
| Hair dryer[d] | 0.34 | 0.30 | 0.44 | 0.78 |
| Stomach remedies | 2.13 | 2.01 | 2.28 | 0.61 |
| *Playboy* | 2.87 | 2.44 | 2.60 | 3.60[c] |
| *Penthouse* | 2.24 | 1.94 | 2.08 | 2.62[b] |
| Alcohol | 4.08 | 2.91 | 3.80 | 30.75[a] |
| Beer (frequency) | 3.71 | 2.59 | 3.40 | 15.74[a] |
| Beer (quantity) | 4.21 | 2.86 | 3.96 | 19.11[a] |
| Six-packs | 3.45 | 2.22 | 3.32 | 17.48[a] |
| Hard liquor (frequency) | 2.89 | 2.11 | 2.76 | 12.51[a] |
| Hard liquor (quantity) | 2.76 | 1.65 | 2.48 | 21.87[a] |
| Wine | 2.02 | 1.82 | 2.16 | 2.80[b] |
| Brush teeth | 3.66 | 3.57 | 3.56 | 0.16 |
| Fashion adoption | 3.26 | 2.76 | 2.40 | 8.29[a] |
| Complexion aids | 1.66 | 1.68 | 1.28 | 1.07 |
| Vitamins | 1.00 | 2.20 | 2.44 | 13.27[a] |
| Haircuts[d] | 3.55 | 3.78 | 3.88 | 3.50[c] |
| Cigarettes | 1.82 | 1.27 | 1.76 | 9.79[a] |
| Coffee | 2.37 | 2.05 | 2.04 | 0.88 |
| Gum | 2.61 | 2.34 | 2.40 | 0.60 |
| Aftershave | 3.39 | 2.64 | 1.92 | 7.64[a] |
| Milk | 4.34 | 5.15 | 4.80 | 3.17[c] |
| Marijuana/hashish | 2.08 | 2.08 | 5.58 | 54.84[a] |
| Previous marijuana/hashish | 2.79 | 2.54 | 6.50 | 45.32[a] |
| Hard drugs | 1.16 | 1.18 | 5.29 | 209.22[a] |
| Number hard drugs | 0.18 | 0.37 | 3.96 | 101.34[a] |
| Time since | 0.03 | 0.06 | 0.72 | 85.34[a] |

[a] $p < 0.01$. (Group means differ significantly at the 0.01 level.)

[b] $p < 0.10$. (Group means differ significantly at the 0.10 level.)

[c] $p < 0.05$. (Group means differ significantly at the 0.05 level.)

[d] Reverse coded.

*Source:* Reprinted from Charles M. Schaninger, V. Parker Lessig, and Don B. Panton, "The Complementary Use of Multivariate Procedures to Investigate Nonlinear and Interactive Relationships between Personality and Product Usage," *Journal of Marketing Research,* 17 (February 1980): 122, published by the American Marketing Association.

where the members of each group tend to be alike in one or more ways. In addition, cluster analysis is useful in many other marketing pursuits—for example, identifying similar cities for test marketing, grouping magazines and television programs, or positioning product brands into categories.

## OTHER MULTIVARIATE TECHNIQUES

### Multivariate Analysis of Variance

Where univariate analysis of variance tests whether the means of a number of groups are significantly different from one another, the *multivariate version is concerned with differences among centroids*. (Remember, a centroid is merely a point that represents the combination of two or more means, and is the multivariate counterpart to the mean.) The groups compared may be (1) clusters that have resulted from cluster analysis of a set of data, (2) demographic or other groups identified by previous measurements, or (3) treatment groups in an experiment.

While the calculation procedures are much more complex for multivariate analysis of variance, the basic idea is the same as for the univariate case. The hypotheses tested in the two approaches are:

#### Univariate analysis of variance

$H_0$: The groups came from the same population (or from populations having the same value for the univariate mean)

#### Multivariate analysis of variance

$H_0$: The groups came from the same population (or from populations having the same multivariate centroid)

As an example of the difference between the two techniques, consider the two parts of Figure 16-8. In part (a) of the figure, three groups have been measured on just one variable, while in part (b), the same three groups have been measured on the basis of two variables. Note that, in part (a), the variability *between* the groups is relatively large compared to that *within* the groups. This would tend to provide a large $F$ ratio and cause us to reject the possibility that the groups really came from the same population.

In part (b) of Figure 16-8, the variability between the groups is also rather large compared to that within the groups. This would tend to give us a large *multivariate F* ratio, and would also cause us to reject the possibility that the groups are from the same population.

Compared to the univariate approach, multivariate analysis of variance offers the advantage of allowing us to compare groups by *simultaneously* considering two or more measurements. This can be especially useful in experimental studies where we wish to measure more than one effect of the treatments

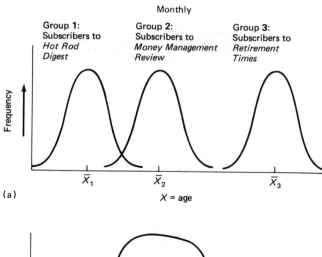

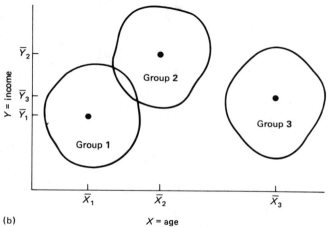

**Figure 16-8.** A contrast between the univariate (a) and multivariate (b) approaches to analysis of variance. While multivariate is more complex, both depend on comparing variability *between* groups to variability *within* groups. In the multivariate case, the centrality of each group is expressed by a centroid instead of a univariate mean.

administered to several groups. In addition, we retain the univariate capability of comparing the groups on just one variable at a time.

### Automatic Interaction Detector

*Automatic interaction detector* (AID) is a computerized procedure that sequentially splits an overall sample into smaller groups to better explain the scores of the sample members on a given dependent variable. At each step, the technique identifies the remaining independent variable that best separates high and low scores on the dependent variable.

The primary output of this form of analysis is the AID "tree," an example of which is shown in Figure 16-9. This diagram was the result of a study in which researchers examined the export marketing behavior of business firms

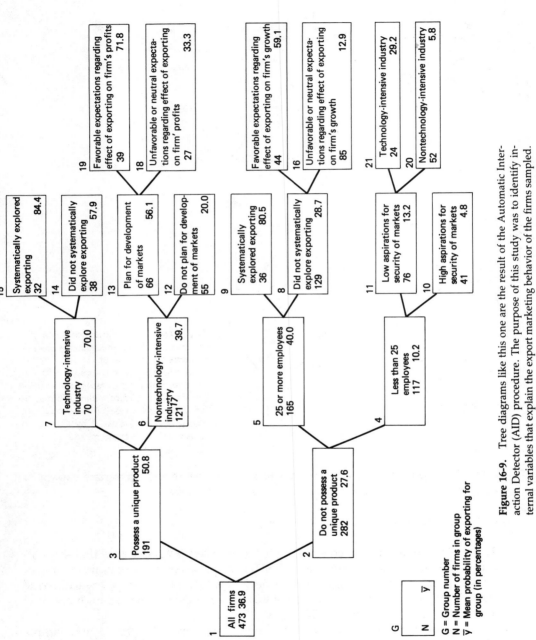

**Figure 16-9.** Tree diagrams like this one are the result of the Automatic Interaction Detector (AID) procedure. The purpose of this study was to identify internal variables that explain the export marketing behavior of the firms sampled. (*Source:* Reprinted from S. Tamer Cavusgil and John R. Nevin, "Internal Determinants of Export Marketing Behavior," *Journal of Marketing Research,* 18 (February 1981): 117, published by the American Marketing Association.)

G = Group number
N = Number of firms in group
$\overline{Y}$ = Mean probability of exporting for group (in percentages)

and the factors that appeared to have an effect on whether or not firms engaged in export marketing.[7] The first "split" in the AID procedure was according to the firm's possession of a "unique" product. Note that those possessing a unique product have a much higher exporting percentage than those which do not (50.8% versus 27.6% exporting).

Those who fall into the "possess a unique product" category are then split into two groups based on the predictor variable that best separates high and low exporting percentage. In this case, the distinction is according to the technology intensiveness of the firm's industry. Again, we can see that one group is much higher (70.0% versus 39.7% exporting) than another in terms of their export percentage.

The AID procedure continues to split each group into subgroups according to variables that best explain high and low measurements for the dependent variable (exporting percentage). The process stops when group size becomes too small or whenever making another split would not explain a sufficient amount of difference in the dependent variable.

While AID is quite useful in helping to explain the variation in a dependent variable, it does so at the expense of requiring a very large sample size. This is necessary in order to maintain satisfactory group sizes as successive partitions are formed from the original sample. However, it remains a popular research tool for identifying market segments and explaining marketing behavior on the basis of demographic and other predictor variables.

### Conjoint Analysis

Conjoint analysis begins with a rank order of product preferences, then proceeds to calculate utility values for each of the key features that describe the product type. The idea is to come up with a set of utilities that explain the order in which the products were ranked. For example, a racquetball racquet might be considered as having two primary features: price ($10, $30, or $50) and construction material (graphite, fiberglass, aluminum, or cast iron). This provides 3 × 4, or 12 different combinations of price and construction material. Note that a particular combination need not actually exist in the marketplace in order to present its set of features to the respondent.

Input to the conjoint analysis program would consist of a rank order of combinations preferred by a respondent—for example, a hypothetical respondent might provide the preferences shown in Table 16-5. Output consists of utility values for each level of the price and construction material variables. The procedure assumes that the overall preference (utility) of a particular racquet will be the sum of the utility values for the features it possesses.

The utility values in Figure 16-10 might be the result of a conjoint analysis

---

[7] S. Tamer Cavusgil and John R. Nevin, "Internal Determinants of Export Marketing Behavior: An Empirical Investigation," *Journal of Marketing Research*, 18 (February 1981): 114–19, published by the American Marketing Association.

**TABLE 16-5.** *Typical input for conjoint analysis consists of preference ordering of product feature combinations. This hypothetical ranking (1 = 1st choice, 2 = 2nd choice, etc.), of racquetball racquets involves 12 different combinations of price level and construction material.*

| | | Racquet construction | | | |
| --- | --- | --- | --- | --- | --- |
| | | *Graphite* | *Fiberglass* | *Aluminum* | *Cast iron* |
| *Racquet price* | $10 | 1 | 2 | 3 | 6 |
| | $30 | 4 | 7 | 8 | 11 |
| | $50 | 5 | 9 | 10 | 12 |

applied to the preferences revealed by our hypothetical racquet shopper. When the utility values of the component features are added, they tend to result in the same order of preferences he has indicated. For example, his first preference was the $10 graphite racquet (total utility = 0.90 for the $10 price plus 0.85 for graphite construction, or 1.75). His second choice was the $10 fiberglass racquet (total utility = 1.50), while his last choice was the expensive but durable $50 racquet of cast iron (total utility = 0.13).

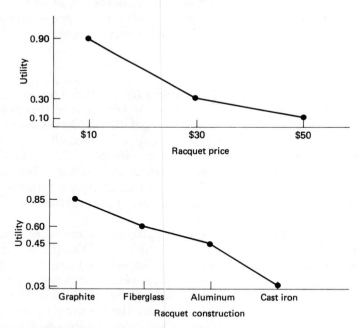

**Figure 16-10.** Conjoint analysis provides utility values like these for levels of various product features examined. These values, when added according to racquet price and construction, explain the racquet preferences shown in Table 16-5.

In this example, the rank order of utility totals is exactly the same as the respondent's preference order, a degree of success that is both rare and unnecessary in practice. The conjoint analysis procedure will typically derive underlying utility values that come as close as possible to the goal of reconstructing the rank order of preferences.

The intent of conjoint analysis is to use these utilities to describe the likely preference level for both existing and proposed products, with major emphasis currently on the latter application. Conjoint analysis has already been applied to many different products, ranging from shampoos and panty hose to cameras and car rental agencies.[8]

## ☐ SUMMARY

Multivariate techniques are those that involve more than two variables at the same time. One such technique, multidimensional scaling, was discussed in Chapter 7. Multivariate techniques are useful because many marketing situations and research questions require that more than just one or two variables be considered. Multivariate techniques may be classified according to the answers to three questions: (1) Are some of the variables dependent on others? (2) Is there more than one dependent variable? (3) What is the scale of measurement for the variables?

Multiple regression analysis is an extension of two-variable regression, and is typically used to (1) describe the nature of a linear relationship between one dependent variable and several independent variables, and (2) based on known values for the independent variables, to predict the value of the dependent variable. Multivariate correlation analysis determines the strength of the linear relationship between the dependent variable and the set of independent variables.

Discriminant analysis is a technique that, like multiple regression, has one dependent variable and a set of independent variables. However, in discriminant analysis, the dependent variable is always of the nominal scale and represents group membership. Discriminant analysis is used to classify objects into groups and to identify the descriptive variables that best determine group membership.

Factor analysis does not assume that some variables might be dependent on the values of others, and treats all variables as "equals." One important use of factor analysis is to simplify a set of data by reducing the number of variables to a level easier to manage, yet retaining most of the information found in the

---

[8] Paul E. Green and Donald S. Tull, *Research for Marketing Decisions*, 4th ed. © 1978, p. 491. Adapted by permission of Prentice-Hall, Inc., Englewood Cliffs, New Jersey.

original set. Another application is to identify the underlying structure, or dimensionality of the data. For example, while we may have 50 different variables, these may be measuring only five different basic characteristics of our sample.

Cluster analysis is a multivariate technique that places either variables or objects into groups, or clusters, so that those within each group are more similar to each other than they are to members of other groups. The technique can play an important role in market segmentation—dividing the overall market into consumer groups that are different from each other, but where the members of each group tend to be alike.

Multivariate analysis of variance is an extension of the univariate approach, but is concerned with comparing centroids (a centroid represents the combination of two or more means, and is the multivariate counterpart to the mean). The automatic interaction detector (AID) is a computerized procedure that sequentially splits an overall sample into smaller groups to better explain the scores of the sample members on a given dependent variable. At each step, the technique identifies the remaining independent variable that best separates high and low scores on the dependent variable.

Conjoint analysis begins with a rank order of product preferences, then calculates utility values for each of the key features that describe the product type. The result is a set of utilities that attempts to explain the order in which the products were ranked. A proposed combination of attributes can thus be evaluated even though no existing product may yet have that specific set of features.

□  **QUESTIONS FOR REVIEW**

1. The computer output below is the result of applying multivariate regression and correlation to the following variables for 1980–1984:

   International air travel, thousands of departures

   Flounder catch, millions of pounds of fish

   Energy research and development expenditure, millions of dollars

   Size of U.S. Postal Service, thousands of employees

   (*Data source: 1986 Statistical Abstract of the United States*, Bureau of the Census, U.S. Department of Commerce, pp. 237, 543, 579, 684.)

   a. Identify the dependent and independent variables along with the least-squares regression equation describing their linear relationship.
   b. What are the values of the regression coefficients? At the 0.10 level, determine if each one differs significantly from zero.
   c. What is the coefficient of multiple determination ($R^2$)? At the 0.10 level, does it differ significantly from zero?

REGRESSION ANALYSIS

HEADER DATA FOR: A:MULTREGX    LABEL: MISC. TIME SERIES
                                              DATA, 1980–1984.
NUMBER OF CASES: 5    NUMBER OF VARIABLES: 4

INT'L AIR DEPARTS. VS. FLOUNDER CATCH, ENERGY R&D, POSTAL
  WRKERS

| INDEX | NAME | MEAN | STD.DEV. |
|---|---|---|---|
| 1 | FLOUNDER | 224.0000 | 19.4294 |
| 2 | ENERGY | 3055.0000 | 488.1788 |
| 3 | POSTAL | 678.6000 | 13.8672 |
| DEP. VAR.: | DEPARTS | 19964.2000 | 958.7196 |

DEPENDENT VARIABLE: DEPARTS

| VAR. | REGRESSION COEFFICIENT | STD. ERROR | T(DF = 1) | PROB. | PARTIAL $r^2$ |
|---|---|---|---|---|---|
| FLOUNDER | − 16.1824 | 32.0074 | − .506 | .70200 | .2036 |
| ENERGY | − .0842 | 2.0362 | − .041 | .97368 | .0017 |
| POSTAL | 65.6770 | 51.7156 | 1.270 | .42464 | .6173 |
| CONSTANT | − 20722.0197 | | | | |

STD. ERROR OF EST. = 426.9407

R SQUARED = .9504
MULTIPLE R = .9749

ANALYSIS OF VARIANCE TABLE

| SOURCE | SUM OF SQUARES | D.F. | MEAN SQUARE | F RATIO | PROB. |
|---|---|---|---|---|---|
| REGRESSION | 3494294.4733 | 3 | 1164764.8244 | 6.390 | .2811 |
| RESIDUAL | 182278.3267 | 1 | 182278.3267 | | |
| TOTAL | 3676572.8000 | 4 | | | |

2. What is a dummy variable and how might such a variable be useful in multiple regression analysis?

3. Provide a real or hypothetical example in which discriminant analysis might be beneficial in the analysis of marketing data.

4. What descriptive variables do you think might be useful in separating joggers from non-joggers? Select any two of these variables and construct a hypothetical scatter diagram (use your imagination) in two-dimensional space. Include a discriminant line.

5. Explain what is meant by each of the following: discriminant function, centroid, misclassification.

6. Given the following graphical illlustration of a two-group discriminant analysis:

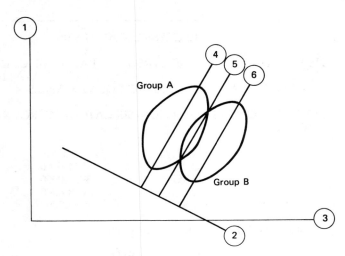

a. Which lines describe the two dimensions on which the group members have been measured?

b. Along which line is the between-group variability divided by within-group variability maximized?

c. Which line represents the discriminant axis?

d. Assuming that we wish to be able to classify consumers into the respective groups in such a way as to have a minimum number of "misclassifications," which line would best serve as the basis for classification?

e. Assuming that there is a very high cost associated with making the mistake of classifying a person into group B when he or she is, in fact, a member of group A, which line might we wish to use as the basis of classification?

7. When carrying out discriminant analysis in two dimensions, a discriminant line serves as the boundary when classifications are made. What form of geometric "divider" would exist in one-variable space? In three-variable space? In four-variable space?

8. After using data from 100 individuals to construct a discriminant function, a researcher tests the function by determining how many of these same 100 subjects are correctly classified. What weakness is present in this approach?

9. What is factor analysis and why is it useful in the analysis of marketing research data?

10. In factor analysis, what is the difference between a factor and a factor loading? What is meant by the eigenvalue associated with each factor?

11. What is cluster analysis and for what practical marketing applications is it useful?

12. An associate wishes to conduct a cluster analysis study of automobiles available in the U.S. market. What variables associated with the automobiles would you suggest that he or she measure?

13. What is the difference between the "top down" and the "bottom up" approaches to cluster analysis?

14. Suppose that a sporting-goods manufacturer has collected information on the fishing equipment expenditures of 1000 consumers. Members of this sample have also com-

pleted questionnaires measuring 20 different psychological variables and 15 different demographic variables. Discuss how each of the following could contribute to analysis of the data:
a. Cluster analysis.
b. Discriminant analysis.
c. Factor analysis.

15. Briefly explain how conjoint analysis is carried out and describe a hypothetical set of underlying curves for a product category of your choice.

## CASES FOR PART FOUR

### CASE 4-1

#### Mountain View Resort

Mountain View Resort, one of the more popular skiing areas in the western United States, has been attempting to find out what guests have liked and not liked during their visit. The medium is a short questionnaire left in each room the evening before guests are to check out. One of the questions asks "What did you least enjoy about your stay with us?" In a sampling of 50 questionnaires, the following responses were obtained:

1. "The prices in the lodge coffee shop are outrageous."
2. "Not enough ski lifts. We paid to ski, not stand in line."
3. "Too many different things to do and not enough time to do them."
4. "Staff was rude but still expected tips."
5. "Room service too slow."
6. "There wasn't really anything we didn't enjoy. It was a nice vacation."
7. "Need to control the noise after midnight. We hardly got to sleep because of the loud parties down the hall two nights in a row."
8. "Ski instructors are incompetent."
9. "Medical facilities should be improved. My husband broke his ankle and it took an hour and a half before he was seen by a doctor."
10. "Ski trails not well marked."
11. "Should have a better reservations system at the main restaurant. A lot of people who arrived after we did were seated before we were."
12. "The water in the swimming pool was too cold."
13. "Hiking trail goes past a cliff where someone could get hurt. You ought to put in a fence before some guy with a broken back sues and ends up owning this place."
14. "The day the intermediate slope was closed down, there didn't seem to be any danger of any avalanche. I think you were just trying to save a few bucks by shutting down the lift."
15. "Beds were like sleeping on a board."

16. "The whole experience was a nightmare from day one. We're never coming back."

17. "Every time the guy in the next room flushes the toilet, the water in the shower gets scalding hot. What idiot installed your plumbing anyway?"

18. "Desk clerk laughed when I said my name was Smith and made me show an ID."

19. "The drinking water tastes like rotten eggs."

20. "Some college kids down the hall set off the smoke alarm in the middle of the night."

21. "Not enough variety in the coffee shop menu."

22. "Our 8 A.M. wake-up call didn't happen until 9 A.M."

23. "The lift tickets cost too much. We paid a lot less at Vail."

24. "You need more sound insulation in the walls. Somebody in the next room snored all night and we had to play the radio to drown out the racket."

25. "The ski instructor put me on the advanced slope after only 10 minutes of lessons. I must have rolled a quarter mile before I hit that tree."

26. "Too much chlorine in the swimming pool."

27. "The so-called happy hour from 5 to 7 was like a funeral parlor."

28. "Hire more security people. Somebody stole my Sony Walkman while I was trying on a sweater in the Ski Shop."

29. "The travel agent was supposed to book us for Disney World. I don't know how we ended up here."

30. "Most of the people who come here seem to be snobs."

31. "I never did get to meet the girl in your magazine ad and that's the only reason I came here in the first place."

32. "The clock in our room was 3 minutes slow."

33. "The ski boots I rented were too small and hurt my feet."

34. "Nonsmoking area of the restaurant should be expanded. We went there to eat, not smell the cigar five tables away."

35. "TV in the room had a lousy picture."

36. "There weren't very many good-looking guys."

37. "The video game room shouldn't be next to the jazz bar. The teenagers made so much noise we could hardly hear the music."

38. "Not enough snow."

39. "Room service was terrible. We ended up using the same towels all weekend."

40. "The road to Mountain View needs resurfaced. We'll have to get our car's front end lined up when we get home."

41. "Shouldn't let people run snowmobiles in the same place where others are trying to cross-country ski."

42. "Most everything was OK. No complaints."
43. "Keep the faster skiers off the beginners' slope. I almost got killed out there."
44. "You said in your ad that you had experienced babysitters, but Friday night a 12-year-old showed up to babysit our kids."
45. "The gift shop ran out of postage stamps."
46. "Should have Nautilus equipment in the health spa."
47. "I don't know how to ski."
48. "It was awfully hard to find this place. You need a better map on your brochure."
49. "The waiter made us leave because we brought a six-pack into the restaurant."
50. "The shuttle bus to town should run more often than every two hours."

Given the preceding sample of responses: (a) set up a set of exhaustive and mutually exclusive categories, (b) code the responses into these categories and tabulate the results, then (c) provide management with advice regarding those characteristics of the resort that appear to be most in need of improvement or attention.

## CASE 4-2

### Evergreen University (B)

For the data set of Case 2-1, Evergreen University (A):

1. Construct a simple tabulation for each variable measured. For odometer readings, use intervals of your choice in converting the interval-scale data into nominal categories for determining frequencies.
2. Construct two body-style pie charts: one for imports, the other for domestic makes.
3. Construct a pictogram (using sketches of your choice) to display the frequencies with which the various body styles were observed.
4. Construct a two-way tabulation table for country of origin and transmission type, then use chi-square analysis to determine if these two variables are independent.
5. Construct a two-way tabulation table for country of origin and odometer reading. For the latter variable, use the same mileage intervals as in part 1. Use chi-square analysis to determine if these two variables are independent.

## CASE 4-3

### Shopping Area Survey

A survey was conducted comparing three major shopping areas in the community of Sharpsburg. The areas include a large, newer mall (Greenwood) in a suburban location along with an older facility (Royal) near the edge of town. The following questions were among those included, and results from 100 of the respondents are listed in the data set that follows. The coding summary below lists each question and associated data set columns, with corresponding response codes indicated in parentheses.

A. The frequency with which you shop at each shopping area (data set columns 1–3).

|  | 1. Greenwood Mall | 2. Downtown | 3. Royal Mall |
|---|---|---|---|
| 6 or more times/week | (1) | (1) | (1) |
| 4–5 times/week | (2) | (2) | (2) |
| 2–3 times/week | (3) | (3) | (3) |
| 2 times/week | (4) | (4) | (4) |
| 2–3 times/month | (5) | (5) | (5) |
| 0–1 time/month | (6) | (6) | (6) |

B. The approximate distance (in miles) from home to each shopping area (columns 4–6).

|  | 4. Greenwood Mall | 5. Downtown | 6. Royal Mall |
|---|---|---|---|
| 0–3 miles | (1) | (1) | (1) |
| 4–10 miles | (2) | (2) | (2) |
| 11–15 miles | (3) | (3) | (3) |
| Over 15 miles | (4) | (4) | (4) |

C. Approximately how much do you spend in each of the following shopping areas during a typical visit? *Check only one box under each shopping area* (columns 7–9).

|  | 7. Greenwood Mall | 8. Downtown | 9. Royal Mall |
|---|---|---|---|
| $200 or more | (1) | (1) | (1) |
| $150–$199 | (2) | (2) | (2) |
| $100–$149 | (3) | (3) | (3) |
| $50–$99 | (4) | (4) | (4) |
| $25–$49 | (5) | (5) | (5) |
| $15–$24 | (6) | (6) | (6) |
| $14 or less | (7) | (7) | (7) |

D. Please indicate your general attitude toward each of the shopping areas (columns 10–12).

| | 10. Greenwood Mall | 11. Downtown | 12. Royal Mall |
|---|---|---|---|
| Like very much | (1) | (1) | (1) |
| Like | (2) | (2) | (2) |
| Neutral | (3) | (3) | (3) |
| Dislike | (4) | (4) | (4) |
| Dislike very much | (5) | (5) | (5) |

E. Listed below are 25 statements. Evaluating each statement carefully, indicate which one shopping area best fits each description (columns 13–30).

| | Greenwood Mall | Downtown | Royal Mall | No Opinion |
|---|---|---|---|---|
| 13. Good delivery/service | (1) | (2) | (3) | (4) |
| 14. Easy to establish charge account | (1) | (2) | (3) | (4) |
| 15. Easy to return or exchange goods | (1) | (2) | (3) | (4) |
| 16. Easy to take the family along | (1) | (2) | (3) | (4) |
| 17. High quality of goods | (1) | (2) | (3) | (4) |
| 18. Low prices | (1) | (2) | (3) | (4) |
| 19. Good variety of sizes and styles | (1) | (2) | (3) | (4) |
| 20. Sales staff helpful and friendly | (1) | (2) | (3) | (4) |
| 21. Goods are attrractively displayed | (1) | (2) | (3) | (4) |
| 22. Convenient shopping hours | (1) | (2) | (3) | (4) |
| 23. Clean stores and surroundings | (1) | (2) | (3) | (4) |
| 24. Don't have to fight crowds | (1) | (2) | (3) | (4) |
| 25. A lot of bargain sales | (1) | (2) | (3) | (4) |
| 26. Good place for one-stop shopping | (1) | (2) | (3) | (4) |
| 27. The retailers know their products | (1) | (2) | (3) | (4) |
| 28. Ease of parking | (1) | (2) | (3) | (4) |
| 29. Comfortable place to shop | (1) | (2) | (3) | (4) |
| 30. Clean rest rooms and areas to relax | (1) | (2) | (3) | (4) |

F. Please rate each of the following in terms of its importance in your decision to choose a shopping area. Indicate "1" for "very important," "7" for "not important," and numbers from "2" through "6" for levels of importance that are in between (columns 31–48).

| | Very important | | | | | | Not important |
|---|---|---|---|---|---|---|---|
| 31. Good delivery/service | (1) | (2) | (3) | (4) | (5) | (6) | (7) |
| 32. Easy to establish charge account | (1) | (2) | (3) | (4) | (5) | (6) | (7) |
| 33. Easy to return or exchange goods | (1) | (2) | (3) | (4) | (5) | (6) | (7) |

| | Very important | | | | | | Not important |
|---|---|---|---|---|---|---|---|
| 34. Easy to take the family along | (1) | (2) | (3) | (4) | (5) | (6) | (7) |
| 35. High quality of goods | (1) | (2) | (3) | (4) | (5) | (6) | (7) |
| 36. Low prices | (1) | (2) | (3) | (4) | (5) | (6) | (7) |
| 37. Good variety of sizes and styles | (1) | (2) | (3) | (4) | (5) | (6) | (7) |
| 38. Sales staff helpful and friendly | (1) | (2) | (3) | (4) | (5) | (6) | (7) |
| 39. Goods are attractively displayed | (1) | (2) | (3) | (4) | (5) | (6) | (7) |
| 40. Convenient shopping hours | (1) | (2) | (3) | (4) | (5) | (6) | (7) |
| 41. Clean stores and surroundings | (1) | (2) | (3) | (4) | (5) | (6) | (7) |
| 42. Don't have to fight crowds | (1) | (2) | (3) | (4) | (5) | (6) | (7) |
| 43. A lot of bargain sales | (1) | (2) | (3) | (4) | (5) | (6) | (7) |
| 44. Good place for one-stop shopping | (1) | (2) | (3) | (4) | (5) | (6) | (7) |
| 45. The retailers know their products | (1) | (2) | (3) | (4) | (5) | (6) | (7) |
| 46. Ease of parking | (1) | (2) | (3) | (4) | (5) | (6) | (7) |
| 47. Comfortable place to shop | (1) | (2) | (3) | (4) | (5) | (6) | (7) |
| 48. Clean rest rooms and areas to relax | (1) | (2) | (3) | (4) | (5) | (6) | (7) |

G. To help us in interpreting the findings, please tell us a little about yourself. All information will be used only for summary purposes (columns 49–56).

**49.** Your sex: Male (1)    Female (2)

**50.** Number of years of school completed:       Less than 8 years (1)
8–12 years (2)
13–15 years (3)
16 or more years (4)

**51.** Marital status: Single (1)    Married (2)    Other (3)

**52.** Number of individuals in household:

1 (1)    2 (2)    3 (3)    4 (4)    5 (5)    6 or more (6)

**53.** Your occupation:

Housewife (1)                                    Business professional (2)

Salaried nonprofessional (3)                              Skilled worker (4)

Student (5)              Laborer (6)                              Other (7)

**54.** Your approximate yearly annual income:

Under $10,000 (1)        $30,000–$39,999 (5)

$10,000–$14,999 (2)        $40,000–$49,999 (6)

$15,000–$19,999 (3)        $50,000 or more (7)

$20,000–$29,999 (4)

**55.** Your age:

17–21 (1)        31–40 (3)        51–60 (5)

22–30 (2)        41–50 (4)        Over 60 (6)

**56.** How long have you lived in this area?

| | |
|---|---|
| 1–6 months (1) | 5–10 years (4) |
| 7–12 months (2) | 11–15 years (5) |
| 1–4 years (3) | over 15 years (6) |

*Note:* In the data set that follows, a coding of "." indicates the respondent did not answer the question.

1. Applying chi-square analysis to the results of Question C, test the hypothesis that the amount spent is independent of the area visited during a shopping trip.

2. Applying analysis of variance to the responses to Question D, compare the mean attitude scores toward the three shopping areas.

3. Based on the attributes described in Question E, evaluate the relative strengths and weaknesses of the three shopping areas.

4. On the average, based on Question F, which attributes of a shopping area seem to be most important and least important to the respondents in this sample?

5. Based on these analyses alone, what advice might be appropriate for presentation to decision makers associated with these shopping areas?

6. What other information could be valuable from these data and what kinds of techniques might be appropriate for their analysis?

| Respondent number | Responses for variables | | | | | |
|---|---|---|---|---|---|---|
| | *1–10* | *11–20* | *21–30* | *31–40* | *41–50* | *51–56* |
| 1 | 5551116772 | 2211111311 | 1112111111 | 5224112332 | 2212113223 | 145413 |
| 2 | 4661116771 | 2341141312 | 1313332111 | 6116111111 | 1222121123 | 155613 |
| 3 | 6561117771 | 3244334411 | 1412131111 | 4317113463 | 5312334413 | 155712 |
| 4 | 6461115774 | 2321412414 | 1112421111 | 6424112243 | 2313332223 | 165212 |
| 5 | 4631116763 | 3344111111 | 1114211111 | 1111111111 | 1411111123 | 145416 |
| 6 | 4361116772 | 34441.1211 | 1212411111 | 6627113243 | 3433232313 | 135411 |
| 7 | 5541117671 | 1321111311 | 1112311111 | 7754112332 | 3421342323 | 125413 |
| 8 | 5451116772 | 4241141312 | 1112312411 | 7547213562 | 4635473421 | 145512 |
| 9 | 4542115772 | 3313222314 | 4111331111 | 6111112141 | 1311172123 | 115413 |
| 10 | 3522314571 | 2241312311 | 1141131111 | 7111331211 | 1422352114 | 125243 |
| 11 | 6561116773 | 2411111311 | 1112214111 | 4414122265 | 3355232223 | 135712 |
| 12 | 5661117772 | 2321111111 | 1111131111 | 6117111141 | 1311151324 | 135123 |
| 13 | 6461117673 | 3322414312 | 2442344421 | 5337113354 | 4532372523 | 145111 |
| 14 | 5451117773 | 2344112311 | 1111334111 | 7437223342 | 2411274321 | 165713 |
| 15 | 6351116673 | 2322411324 | 1112122121 | 3412112434 | 2533262323 | 155113 |
| 16 | 5351117573 | 1342212322 | 1112224111 | 6115131142 | 2335232324 | 135223 |
| 17 | 4651116773 | 4344411414 | 1111211111 | 7717111141 | 3521211323 | 145213 |
| 18 | 4521115672 | 3222111331 | 1311331311 | 7717112462 | 5523222713 | 145513 |
| 19 | 5651115672 | 3444312113 | 1112332111 | 7527212552 | 3511423314 | 115326 |
| 20 | 6461117772 | 3444141112 | 1114444411 | 7777442675 | 4771473313 | 215113 |
| 21 | 6561117772 | 2244441314 | 1414314411 | 7767112475 | 5724577624 | 115523 |

| Respondent number | Responses for variables | | | | | |
|---|---|---|---|---|---|---|
| | 1–10 | 11–20 | 21–30 | 31–40 | 41–50 | 51–56 |
| 22 | 6451117772 | 2343331313 | 1311334114 | 3411111434 | 5521134523 | 155313 |
| 23 | 6561115761 | 2141111313 | 1313311111 | 6236212232 | 2322333423 | 165213 |
| 24 | 6563335571 | 2544411311 | 1111311111 | 7737121341 | 1441411123 | 315724 |
| 25 | 6561116672 | 2341112312 | 2211214111 | 7317111322 | 2331242323 | 145516 |
| 26 | 3562116772 | 3521111211 | 1113211111 | 6773777777 | 7274676723 | 165714 |
| 27 | 5452127772 | 3444114414 | 1114442141 | 4352434244 | 4635544714 | 215222 |
| 28 | 5651215772 | 3341411214 | 1114214111 | 7626222351 | 2312112614 | 125513 |
| 29 | 5551116771 | 3244111311 | 1112111111 | 7737211653 | 5522422523 | 135512 |
| 30 | 6431117674 | 1242212212 | 2112212121 | 5135277247 | 2532567213 | 115111 |
| 31 | 5461115762 | 3442111311 | 1111433211 | 6336112233 | 2312352423 | 115112 |
| 32 | 6551117772 | 2244111212 | 1113112133 | 5677776546 | 4454655413 | 145513 |
| 33 | 5661114772 | 3344111311 | 1113142111 | 7111113344 | 1442211313 | 125512 |
| 34 | 6661117772 | 1244412322 | 2424212124 | 7737112465 | 4423333513 | 165512 |
| 35 | 3651116672 | 2224111312 | 1112112111 | 1413212232 | 3522112213 | 145413 |
| 36 | 5321115762 | 2141121114 | 2112331131 | 6146113321 | 1111223513 | 155513 |
| 37 | 6451116773 | 1341422312 | 2144434141 | 4434112456 | 5533424423 | 145312 |
| 38 | 6561116772 | 2341111111 | 1113222114 | 6536113354 | 4432244513 | 135212 |
| 39 | 6441116772 | 2244412314 | 1433312131 | 7755112132 | 2421372223 | 155612 |
| 40 | 6341117771 | 3344141314 | 1111132114 | 7717111111 | 3313372223 | 135213 |
| 41 | 6551116773 | 3421111312 | 1113222111 | 7735111243 | 3424243523 | 145112 |
| 42 | 4561117772 | 2324441112 | 1211212111 | 6777711251 | 6612244523 | 165513 |
| 43 | 5451117672 | 1224212222 | 2212212111 | 7727112245 | 3224153313 | 135423 |
| 44 | 2641114751 | 3211111311 | 1111111111 | 1111111121 | 1741131123 | 233545 |
| 45 | 5.61113141 | 2221112322 | 2112312111 | 3325211342 | 4413473123 | 222734 |
| 46 | 3451117672 | 3321112311 | 2312131111 | 4423215343 | 1443112114 | 242634 |
| 47 | 3651115753 | 4541111414 | 1112114111 | 5317111421 | 1513135724 | 222425 |
| 48 | 6651116672 | 2244332314 | 2322434111 | 2211111441 | 1411213122 | 261246 |
| 49 | 3541115562 | 3442212322 | 2112312111 | 6337151231 | 1343412223 | 221565 |
| 50 | 6561117773 | 2242311312 | 1412342114 | 7121112352 | 7732231113 | 114116 |
| 51 | 4642225732 | 3214111314 | 1112314111 | 4444113442 | 4311312322 | 231433 |
| 52 | 5432124561 | 3341111311 | 1112311111 | 7754221122 | 6411422122 | 241323 |
| 53 | 5631117761 | 1344111314 | 1112334414 | 7737123754 | 3353744723 | 243334 |
| 54 | 6651227774 | 5144433333 | 4333334433 | 7652326665 | 4222662212 | 227266 |
| 55 | 4442226631 | 1111111311 | 1114311111 | 5511113573 | 3744422324 | 223223 |
| 56 | 6361117573 | 1342222222 | 2222222222 | 7752115756 | 5315654114 | 313425 |
| 57 | 4651115562 | 4241111321 | 2112134111 | 7521312462 | 3735733723 | 261546 |
| 58 | 5661116672 | 3342212322 | 1112312111 | 5216212142 | 1233213213 | 232544 |
| 59 | 5231116742 | 2241331312 | 2112232111 | 7731112321 | 2313223424 | 232434 |
| 60 | 3641116771 | 2211111321 | 1113121111 | 3221111121 | 1211111122 | 111264 |
| 61 | 5251116662 | 2344412444 | 4144432114 | 7774113575 | 5534324714 | 242436 |
| 62 | 3651116771 | 5244411414 | 4111114111 | 7121112213 | 1311111122 | 317165 |
| 63 | 5561115571 | 1324212424 | 2142414111 | 4512111221 | 3531332424 | 231526 |
| 64 | 5461112772 | 2344211312 | 1212332113 | 5525313342 | 6234434514 | 122423 |
| 65 | 6461114562 | 3411111312 | 1112212111 | 1114111231 | 1414111313 | 127226 |
| 66 | 4541117771 | 2121111111 | 1132134111 | 2422333232 | 3334433422 | 251122 |
| 67 | 6562124652 | 3341211311 | 1112311131 | 3327221222 | 2422222422 | 221323 |
| 68 | 6541114652 | 2211311312 | 1112332111 | 2223222232 | 2724222223 | 244434 |
| 69 | 2551117651 | 3311211312 | 1112331111 | 4123131242 | 2423222222 | 243323 |
| 70 | 5451115552 | 2211411311 | 1114332111 | 7766121325 | 2724242722 | 327216 |

| Respondent number | Responses for variables | | | | | |
|---|---|---|---|---|---|---|
| | *1–10* | *11–20* | *21–30* | *31–40* | *41–50* | *51–56* |
| 71 | 5151113742 | 3111211212 | 1114112111 | 5334112442 | 3714222323 | 242524 |
| 72 | 6661114562 | 2211211311 | 1112332111 | 7656112633 | 3732216622 | 117166 |
| 73 | 4651115762 | 4344111111 | 1113111111 | 3112113222 | 1332321122 | 241423 |
| 74 | 3361114472 | 1341424421 | 1444114141 | 1622122243 | 2435222223 | 247523 |
| 75 | 5561117772 | 3544411311 | 1111314114 | 7757112123 | 2521221312 | 112423 |
| 76 | 3641117752 | 3244411313 | 1413432111 | 7736112133 | 3323232613 | 134713 |
| 77 | 5561117772 | 2244442112 | 1112212111 | 7737114252 | 2412423714 | 112323 |
| 78 | 3541117772 | 3241112114 | 2112114411 | 1213313232 | 2123232413 | 11326. |
| 79 | 5551117672 | 1322112312 | 2112212121 | 1127112222 | 2222232213 | 112323 |
| 80 | 5361117773 | 1321212222 | 1232232332 | 5552113615 | 4327643213 | 242645 |
| 81 | 3561117771 | 2441111212 | 1113312111 | 7611131211 | 1737377714 | 262554 |
| 82 | 4451114552 | 2321111311 | 2112311111 | 5111111221 | 1546211224 | 112422 |
| 83 | 3461115572 | 1544112312 | 2122121114 | 7447121351 | 2223233523 | 155515 |
| 84 | 3361116372 | 2424242322 | 2122341112 | 7217111115 | 1317231723 | 113126 |
| 85 | 4561114673 | 3341111111 | 1113112111 | 6225112462 | 4313222224 | 112323 |
| 86 | 3141116473 | 2422112312 | 2122112131 | 2114132123 | 2253121124 | 122424 |
| 87 | 5521117773 | 2144434344 | 4411334331 | 1771435333 | 5531613514 | 222665 |
| 88 | 5351114462 | 3344412311 | 1114232211 | 4775712275 | 2542313714 | 115125 |
| 89 | 5531116772 | 22444.1113 | 431.334113 | 5323223244 | 3323333324 | 241523 |
| 90 | 3441117773 | 3344114414 | 1144114141 | 7737544311 | 1444314123 | 251734 |
| 91 | 5642126671 | 2123132211 | 1311231111 | 6311112341 | 1211111224 | 243424 |
| 92 | 5432114761 | 5244311313 | 1113131111 | 1121213342 | 4444423223 | 112113 |
| 93 | 5641117752 | 3133312313 | 2332333333 | 1112213242 | 3611233112 | 256236 |
| 94 | 4531117672 | 2444111311 | 1112314114 | 7313213463 | 4523745423 | 241433 |
| 95 | 1511114662 | 3423412321 | 1312334111 | 5361112754 | 7663457723 | 112616 |
| 96 | 5121115442 | 1221313311 | 2212212111 | 4213113343 | 3311321423 | 261535 |
| 97 | 2451117761 | 2241111311 | 1112131111 | 2213112131 | 1223221112 | 227166 |
| 98 | 4351117771 | 2444111311 | 1113231111 | 7536113362 | 3312431322 | 233434 |
| 99 | 3641116662 | 3231112114 | 2142114411 | 7714111142 | 2436222124 | 232536 |
| 100 | 6661214541 | 4341411413 | 1112314111 | 1552111261 | 6511134413 | 233635 |

(*Source:* Materials in this case have been provided courtesy of V.P. Taiani and Associates, Spring Church, Pa. Town and mall identities have been disguised.)

## CASE 4-4

## Softfab, Inc.

The Softfab Company, manufacturer of a well-known brand of fabric softener, has been considering their advertising agency's advice to enhance the product's image and sales by engaging in a comparative advertising campaign featuring the effectiveness of Softfab versus one or more of its major competitors. Softfab is currently the third-leading fabric softener on the market, and is better known for its relatively low price than for its effectiveness as a softening agent. The agency has already carried out consumer testing in which softness scores (rated on a scale of 0 to 10) have been obtained from independent samples of consumers evaluating the products. Two hundred consumers were divided into five groups, each of which judged the softness of just one product, yielding the following summary statistics:

| | Competitor A | Competitor B | Competitor C | Competitor D | Softfab |
|---|---|---|---|---|---|
| Mean softness score | 7.59 | 7.43 | 7.48 | 7.32 | 6.90 |
| Standard deviation (using $n - 1$) | 0.97 | 1.05 | 0.78 | 0.92 | 1.19 |
| Sample size | 40 | 40 | 40 | 40 | 40 |

1. Since Softfab did not score especially well compared to the other products, the company's ad agency is considering a campaign with the theme, "Independent laboratory testing proves that Softfab is fully comparable to other leading softeners, but at a price that saves you money." In backing up the claim, the agency's research personnel plan to use the softness scores and analysis of variance to statistically accept the null hypothesis that the population means could be equal for all five products. At the 0.05 level, could this conclusion be accepted? At the 0.01 level? Comment on the ethical considerations involved in reaching and publicizing such a conclusion.

2. Suppose that competitor A, after being shocked by the implications of the Softfab campaign, is allowed to examine the same data. In counterattacking with a comparative advertising campaign of their own, featuring their product versus Softfab, could they apply analysis of variance to the same data in order to statistically support a conclusion stating that brand A and Softfab are vastly different in terms of the softness they provide? If so, at what level of significance?

# 17

# MARKET ANALYSIS
# AND FORECASTING

=====

**Joel Hyatt Courts Middle-Class Legal Customers**

Shortly after the ban on the advertising of legal services was lifted in 1977, attorney Joel Hyatt left a New York law firm and opened an office in Cleveland as a first step in developing what was to become a national network catering to middle-class individuals previously underserved by attorneys. According to Wayne Willis, a partner in Hyatt Legal Services, Inc., both the poor and the rich had access to legal services, but the largest segment of our population—the middle class—either did not know how to go about choosing a lawyer or were afraid of the cost.

Analyzing the needs of the middle-class market segment, Hyatt identified five benefits that were important to this group:

- *Price.* Hyatt charges about 30% less than average.
- *Convenience.* Neighborhood centers combined with evening and Saturday hours.
- *Quality.* Along with experienced lawyers, Hyatt relies on internal training programs and expertise in specific areas, and uses checklists and flowcharts to deliver consistent quality among the branches.

---

*Source:* "Hyatt Targets Legal Market with Five Benefits," *Marketing News,* October 26, 1984, p. 6, published by the American Marketing Association.

**Figure 17-1.** The founder of Hyatt Legal Services, Joel Hyatt says, "I wanted to develop a mechanism whereby the large segment of our population who never had access to legal services would be able to obtain such access." (Courtesy of Hyatt Legal Services.)

- *Speed of service*. Computerized document production reduces the time required for legal paperwork.
- *Respect*. Lawyers' lack of respect for their clients is the leading cause of people's resistance to see a lawyer, a factor to which Hyatt is attentive.

Affiliation with H & R Block, Inc., the nation's largest income tax service, led to the Block Management Company and the combination of Block's administrative and marketing experience with Hyatt's legal expertise. From its Cleveland beginnings, Hyatt Legal Services has now expanded to over 200 offices across the nation, offering services ranging from will preparation to name changes, divorce, automobile accidents, and bankruptcy.

## INTRODUCTION

In preceding chapters we examined a variety of techniques that have proven useful to the practicing marketing researcher. In this one, we'll discuss several research topics that are also of key concern to the usual "customer" of marketing research: the marketing manager.

Analysis of one's market is a very important part of overall marketing strategy, and we will consider the topic in terms of two very essential ingredients: (1) market segmentation, and (2) estimating market potential. Unless you have the persuasive powers of Attila the Hun, your academic advisor will probably not allow you to substitute this chapter for a Marketing Management course. However, you should come away with a better understanding of these joint concerns of research and management, and why they are vital to the firm's marketing success.

In addition, we will examine the art and science of forecasting, long a concern of fortune tellers, weather persons, picnic planners, groundhogs, and marketing decision makers alike. Forecasting is an especially important function since many important corporate decisions—nonmarketing as well as marketing—depend heavily on our ability to gain insight into what the future holds.

Accordingly, our topics in this chapter will be presented in the following sections:

I. Market segmentation
II. Estimation of market potential
III. Forecasting

## MARKET SEGMENTATION

Consumers and products are in many ways like the customers of a computer dating service. Just as identifying "The Wabash Cannonball" as your favorite song is not a good way to obtain a date with a student of the opera, marketing an inexpensive, low-quality product is not likely to win the dollars of the prestige-conscious consumer. Fortunately, however, there are many members of the opposite sex who also enjoy country songs about trains, and many consumers who are perfectly content with a lower-quality product making no pretensions toward status.

Computer dating has its questionnaires and its matching processes to help arrange the meeting of compatible individuals. Marketing has a counterpart known as *market segmentation*—identifying groups of consumers who will tend to respond in a similar fashion when presented with a particular combination of our marketing inputs. As an example of how consumers might be categorized into segments, consider the different motives the spectators appear to have for attending the baseball game of Figure 17-2.

In following a segmentation strategy, a firm might decide to concentrate its efforts on a single market segment, such as Mercedes-Benz has done for many years in satisfying the needs of luxury-car customers. On the other hand, efforts may be taken to identify and satisfy a wide variety of segments, as General Motors has done with its wide selection of economy, family, and prestige models, ranging from Chevrolet to Oldsmobile and Cadillac.

### Bases for Market Segmentation

There are a great many variables that can be used in breaking up an overall market into meaningful segments. In general, they can be categorized as (1) geographic, (2) demographic, (3) psychographic, and (4) behavioristic.[1]

---

[1] Philip Kotler, *Marketing Management*: Analysis, Planning, and Control, 5th ed. (Englewood Cliffs, N.J.: Prentice-Hall Inc., 1984), p. 255, Copyright © 1984.

**Figure 17-2.** Different kinds of people may be attracted to different aspects of a product or marketing mix, a phenomenon that lies at the heart of the strategy known as market segmentation. Fans of the Arson City Flames may have a variety of reactions as the team ignites its late-inning rally.

### Geographic Segmentation

Geographic segmentation simply divides the market according to geographic location or geography-related characteristics, such as climate or population density. It can be applied on a variety of levels, ranging all the way from complete hemispheres to local neighborhoods.

Figure 17-3 shows two approaches to carving up the United States largely according to geographic area. Part (a) shows the nine regions used by the Bureau of the Census for data reporting and summarization.[2] In part (b), Management Horizon, Inc.'s segmentation strategy is shown. The latter approach considers geography along with a number of other characteristics, such as language, racial composition, energy resources, and metropolitan population. Since a lot of changes have taken place since the Bureau of the Census regions were identified

---

[2] *General Social and Economic Characteristics, United States Summary*, Bureau of the Census, U.S. Department of Commerce, 1980, p. 1–10a.

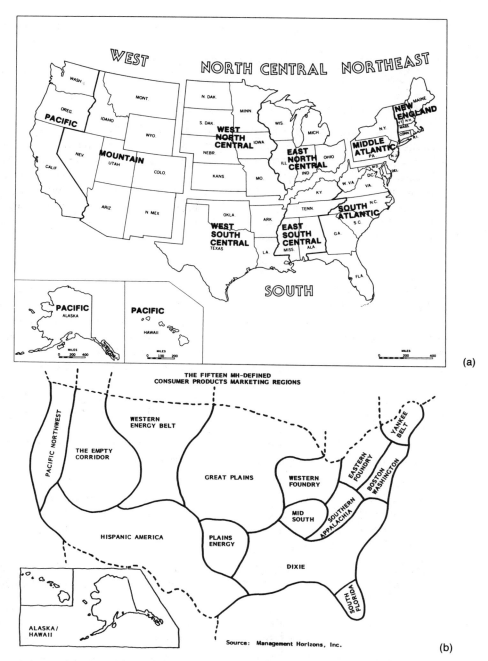

(a)

(b)

**Figure 17-3.** In existence for most of this century, the U.S. Bureau of the Census segmentation of the United States divides the nation into nine geographic regions (a). Management Horizons, Inc. has gone beyond this to include language, racial composition, metropolitan population, and other factors in segmenting the country into 15 "nations." (b). (*Sources:* (a) *General Social and Economic Characteristics, United States Summary,* Bureau of the Census, U.S. Department of Commerce, 1980, p. 1–10a; (b) Illustration courtesy of Management Horizons, Inc.)

in 1910, the "15 nations" categorization is said to be more relevant to making today's marketing decisions.[3]

### Demographic Segmentation

Age, sex, family size, income, occupation, and education are typical of the variables used in demographic segmentation, a very popular method of segmenting a market. These kinds of variables are especially useful because (1) they are relatively easy to measure, and (2) they are often related to consumer needs and purchasing behavior. In a demographic study of recreational vehicle buyers, it was found that first-time buyers are likely to be married, older, and more affluent than the overall U.S. population. Table 17-1 summarizes the demographic profile of these consumers.

### Psychographic Segmentation

Psychographic segmentation involves the individual's personality and general life-style. Just as one's approach to life is made up of many different characteristics, the bases for psychographic segmentation are equally diverse. As with the other types of segmentation, this one is frequently used in conjunction with those from the other three categories—that is, psychographic measures may be taken simultaneously with geographic, demographic and behavioristic descriptions.

As an example of this combined approach, consider a study in which men in the "married" demographic segment were further divided into subsegments on the basis of additional data, including life style analysis. Researchers discovered that, contrary to popular belief, many married men actually enjoy cooking. They describe five subsegments of married men:

*New breed husbands,* representing 32% of all married men, willingly share with their wives household chores such as cooking, cleaning, and grocery shopping. Usually under age 40, they are mostly white-collar workers and are well educated. Their wives work full-time and they probably have young children.

*Classics,* representing 25%, believe women shouldn't work unless it's an economic necessity. They'll share responsibilities, but insist on having the final word.

*Retired,* 16% of the total. Typically over age 40, they are less involved in decision making and remote from their families.

*Bachelor husband,* 15% of all married men, is usually under age 30 and a "bachelor at heart." He normally doesn't make decisions with his wife or ask for her advice and is less inclined to feel that the family comes first.

---

[3] Bernie Whalen, "Marketing Research Firm Segments U.S. into 15 Geodemographic Regions," *Marketing News,* May 13, 1983, sec. 2, p. 8, published by the American Marketing Association.

**TABLE 17-1.** *First-time buyers of recreational vehicles differ from the U.S. population on a variety of demographic variables.*

| First-Time Owners of RVs Compared to U. S. Population | | |
|---|---|---|
| | First-time RV owners | U. S. population |
| Home ownership | 92% | 65% |
| Married | 92% | 66% |
| Average age (years) | 49.1 | 31.3 |
| High school education or less | 53% | 63% |
| Some college education or more | 43% | 35% |
| Average income | $39.800 | $22,400 |

| Who Is the First-Time RV Buyer? | | | | | |
|---|---|---|---|---|---|
| | Total | Motor home | Travel trailer | Fold-down camper | Truck camper |
| Average age (years) | 49.1 | 53.7 | 49.7 | 41.5 | 45.3 |
| Married | 92% | 92% | 92% | 93% | 86% |
| Home ownership | 92% | 96% | 92% | 88% | 88% |
| Average income | $39,800 | $45,300 | $36,000 | $39,800 | $37,000 |
| High school or less | 53% | 44% | 60% | 52% | 56% |
| Some college or more | 43% | 52% | 36% | 47% | 36% |
| Employed full time | 55% | 45% | 56% | 71% | 57% |
| Retired | 25% | 35% | 24% | 10% | 18% |
| Avg. annual miles driven in RV | 5,900 | 9,100 | 4,300 | 2,800 | 5,800 |

Source: Recreation Vehicle Industry Association, "A Profile of the Typical RV Buyer," *Automotive News*, January 19, 1987, p. E2.

*Strugglers,* 12% of total, think of themselves as ship captains. They demand that their wives keep the house clean and want the final say. Strugglers are usually in lower-income brackets and are middle-aged.[4]

### Behavioristic Segmentation

This segmentation approach divides buyers into groups based on attitude, knowledge, usage, and similar variables related to the product and its attributes. Variants of this approach include segmentation according to product benefits, usage rate, and marketing-factor sensitivity.

*Benefit Segmentation.* An interesting variant of the behavioristic approach, benefit segmentation is concerned with the benefits that consumers seek when buying a product. In a study of bank customers, researchers identified two segments with very different motives for patronage—one group placing a high value on convenience, the other more concerned with the availability of banking

---

[4] "New Research Identifies Five Subsegments of Married Men," *Marketing News*, November 14, 1980, p. 7, published by the American Marketing Association.

---

**EXHIBIT 17-1**

**VALS Helps Tailor Ads to Bikers**

Developed by SRI International, the VALS approach to psychographic segmentation uses values and attitudes in dividing Americans into four major groups: Need-Driven, Outer Directed, Inner Directed, and Integrateds.[5]

In a study of motorcycle riders, Kenyon & Eckhardt had an advertising executive assume an undercover role at a biker hangout in California.[6] Results included a VALS-type psychographic segmentation describing the Outer-Directed segments (two-thirds of the market) as interested in touring and cruising bikes because of the success that these bikes imply. On the other hand, the Inner-Directed were more concerned with the riding experience and with getting the most out of life. In one of the ads resulting from the research, the (Outer-Directed) theme was "Introducing the Vulcan. If you don't look bad, we don't look good." In appealing to the Inner-Directeds, another ad proclaimed, "Introducing the Ninja 600R. You'll ride it out of your mind."

---

services.[7] Even MBA study can be viewed from the perspective of benefit segments. Based on a survey of MBA students, George Miaoulis and Michael D. Kalfus identified the segments shown in Table 17-2.

In another study involving benefit segmentation, six benefit segments were identified among potential vacation travelers to Canada. Figure 17-4 shows a perceptual map in which the segments are positioned, along with attitude vectors that help to explain the dimensionality of the configuration.

*Usage rate.* In segmentation by usage rate, individuals are categorized on the basis of the quantity of product that is typically consumed. For example, it has been found that a mere one-half of all beer drinkers account for nearly 90% of the beer consumed.[8] This pattern is typical for many products, and identification of the heavy user is a frequent goal of market segmentation studies.

*Marketing-factor sensitivity.* Segmentation on the basis of marketing-factor sensitivity assumes that some will respond differently than others when presented with one or more marketing stimuli. Some may be more receptive to price reductions, others to higher product quality or greater purchasing convenience. For example, some consumers are more responsive than others to special "deals," such as cents-off coupons, sales, and other promotional events.

---

[5] For an excellent discussion of these segments and the VALS approach, see James Atlas, "Beyond Demographics," *The Atlantic Monthly*, October, 1984, p. 49.

[6] Brad Edmondson, "Living with Kawasakis," *American Demographics*, October 1985, p. 18.

[7] W. Thomas Anderson, Eli P. Cox, and David G. Fulcher, "Bank Selection Decision and Market Segmentation," *Journal of Marketing*, January 1976, pp. 40–55, published by the American Marketing Association.

[8] Dik Warren Twedt, "How Important to Marketing Strategy Is the 'Heavy User'?" *Journal of Marketing*, January 1964, pp. 71–72, published by the American Marketing Association.

*TABLE 17-2. Ten benefit segments based on a study of MBA candidates.*

**10 MBA benefit segments**

BY GEORGE MIAOULIS and MICHAEL D. KALFUS

HERE ARE THE 10 BENEFIT SEGMENTS identified in a recent survey of candidates for the MBA degree.

1. QUALITY SEEKERS desire the highest quality education available in their communities. They are generally part-time students pursuing the MBA several years after their undergraduate education. They believe a first-rate education will benefit them throughout their business lives, ultimately leading to job advancement or career change. They seek an AACSB-accredited MBA program.

2. SPECIALTY SEEKERS desire a specialized education to become experts in their fields (insurance, health care, etc.). Concentrated, no-frills programs will fit their needs, and they will seek out institutions that offer them.

3. CAREER CHANGERS want different job positions or employers and believe the MBA degree will give them the opportunity for career advancement and mobility. They have worked for several years and typically perceive themselves to be in dead-end jobs, so the benefit they seek is career flexibility. They are part-time students who take one or two courses per term.

4. KNOWLEDGE SEEKERS want to learn and feel knowledge will lead to power. They believe a graduate MBA education will be an asset to any activity they undertake in their social, community, political, or corporate lives.

5. STATUS SEEKERS feel that graduate MBA coursework will lead to increased income and prestige. The MBA program which is conveniently located and inexpensive best fits their needs.

6. DEGREE SEEKERS believe the bachelor's degree is insufficient and that the MBA is essential to being "job-competitive" in today's business environment. They want programs which are "credible" and conveniently located. More than any other, this segment tends to have the highest proportion of full-time students. They are active, self-oriented, and independent.

7. PROFESSIONAL ADVANCERS strive to climb the corporate ladder. They want professional advancement, higher income, job flexibility, and upward mobility. They're serious, future-oriented, and want to build careers within their current corporate structures.

8. AVOIDERS seek the MBA programs which require them to invest the least effort. They feel all schools will give them essentially the same education. Their motivation is "other-directed" and they select low-cost, low-quality programs.

9. CONVENIENCE SEEKERS enroll in the MBA programs that are located near their homes or jobs and have simple registration procedures. They are interested in any school with these characteristics and low cost.

10. NONMATRICULATORS want to take MBA courses without completing formal application procedures. They are attracted to schools that allow them to begin the MBA program without GMAT or formal application. They want the opportunity to evaluate whether they really should participate in an MBA program. They are part-time students and typically take one course during their first year.

*Source:* From George Miaoulis and Michael D. Kalfus, "Benefit Segmentation Analysis Suggests Marketing Strategies for MBA Programs," *Marketing News,* August 5, 1983, sec. 1, p. 14, published by the American Marketing Association.

In one attempt to identify the segment most receptive to special deals, researchers found that car and home ownership "were strong predictors of deal proneness. Of the households that owned a car and home, 34.4% were deal prone. In contrast, only 20.5% of the households that did not own either a car or a home were deal prone."[9]

---

[9] Robert Blattberg, Thomas Buesing, Peter Peacock, and Subrata Sen, "Identifying the Deal Prone Segment," *Journal of Marketing Research,* August 1978, p. 377, published by the American Marketing Association.

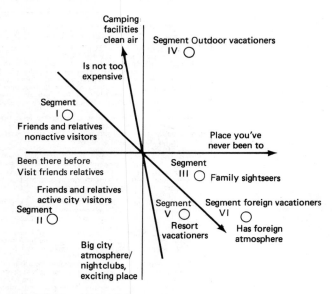

Segment I.   *Friends and relatives—nonactive visitors*
             Seek familiar surroundings in which to visit, but are not activity-
             oriented.

Segment II.  *Friends and relatives—active visitors*
             Similar to segment I, but are more likely to engage in sightseeing,
             shopping, entertainment, and cultural activities.

Segment III. *Family sightseers*
             Seek a new vacation place which would be an enrichening experience
             and a treat for the children.

Segment IV.  *Outdoor vacationers*
             Seek clean air, rest and quiet, and beautiful scenery. Many are campers
             and value availability of recreational facilities for themselves and
             their children.

Segment V.   *Resort vacationers*
             Prefer a popular place with a big-city atmosphere. Are most interested
             in water sports and good weather.

Segment VI.  *Foreign vacationers*
             Looking for a new place to vacation which has a foreign atmosphere and
             beautiful scenery. Money is of little concern, but much value is placed
             on good service and accommodations. Seek an exciting, enriching experience.

**Figure 17-4.**   A study of potential U.S. travelers to Canada led to the identifi-
cation of six benefit segments. In this mapping of their relative positions, the
vertical axis might be described as a "great outdoors" dimension, while the
horizontal axis appears to represent a "a new place to visit." (*Source:* Myron
Rusk, *Understanding the U.S. Vacationer: Summary of the Potential Vacation Trip
Market for Canada,* Marketing Research Office, Canadian Government, Ottawa,
Ontario; July 1974; in Shirley Young, Leland Ott, and Barbara Feigin, "Some
Practical Considerations in Market Segmentation," *Journal of Marketing Research,*
August 1978, pp. 405–12, published by the American Marketing Association.)

**TABLE 17-3.** *Markets can be segmented based on a variety of geographic, demographic, psychographic, and behavioral variables. Shown here are a number of popular bases for segmentation and their typical breakdowns.*

| Variable | Typical breakdowns |
|---|---|
| **Geographic** | |
| Region | Pacific, Mountain, West North Central, West South Central, East North Central, East South Central, South Atlantic, Middle Atlantic, New England |
| County size | A, B, C, D |
| City or SMSA size | Under 5,000; 5,000–20,000; 20,000–50,000; 50,000–100,000; 100,000–250,000; 250,000–500,000; 500,000–1,000,000; 1,000,000–4,000,000; 4,000,000 or over |
| Density | Urban, suburban, rural |
| Climate | Northern, southern |
| **Demographic** | |
| Age | Under 6, 6–11, 12–19, 20–34, 35–49, 50–64, 65+ |
| Sex | Male, female |
| Family size | 1–2, 3–4, 5+ |
| Family life cycle | Young, single; young, married, no children; young, married, youngest child under 6; young, married, youngest child 6 or over; older, married, with children; older, married, no children under 18; older, single; other |
| Income | Under $2,500; $2,500–$5,000; $5,000–$7,500; $7,500–$10,000; $10,000–$15,000; $15,000–$20,000; $20,000–$30,000; $30,000–$50,000; $50,000 and over |
| Occupation | Professional and technical; managers, officials, and proprietors; clerical, sales; craftsmen, foremen; operatives; farmers; retired; students; housewives; unemployed |
| Education | Grade school or less; some high school; high school graduate; some college; college graduate |
| Religion | Catholic, Protestant, Jewish, other |
| Race | White, black, Oriental |
| Nationality | American, British, French, German, Scandinavian, Italian, Latin American, Middle Eastern, Japanese |
| **Psychographic** | |
| Social class | Lower lowers, upper lowers, lower middles, upper middles, lower uppers, upper uppers |
| Lifestyle | Straights, swingers, longhairs |
| Personality | Compulsive, gregarious, authoritarian, ambitious |
| **Behavioral** | |
| Use occasion | Regular occasion, special occasion |
| Benefits sought | Quality, service, economy |
| User status | Nonuser, ex-user, potential user, first-time user, regular user |
| Usage rate | Light user, medium user, heavy user |
| Loyalty status | None, medium, strong, absolute |
| Readiness stage | Unaware, aware, informed, interested, desirous, intending to buy |
| Attitude toward product | Enthusiastic, positive, indifferent, negative, hostile |

*Source:* Philip Kotler, *Marketing Management: Analysis, Planning and Control*, 5th ed., © 1984, p. 256 Reprinted by permission of Prentice-Hall, Inc., Englewood Cliffs, New Jersey.

### Selecting a Basis for Segmentation

Table 17-3 summarizes the variables on which markets are often segmented; it includes those we've just discussed, plus a few more. In general, there are two major approaches for the identification of meaningful market segments: the a priori method and the clustering method.[10]

*A priori method.* In the a priori approach we decide in advance which variables are likely to prove useful, then conduct research to describe the members of these segments. In addition to measuring the proposed segmentation variables, we would also gather information concerning members' purchasing and product use habits and their media exposure patterns.

*Clustering method.* In the second method we use cluster analysis to find similar multivariate profiles based on many different variables. Naturally, some of the variables will include such relevant measures as purchasing, product use, and media viewing habits. In this approach, consumers are subjected to a large battery of measurements dealing with the potential variables, and cluster analysis is employed to determine which ones are actually meaningful as bases for segmentation.

## ESTIMATION OF MARKET POTENTIAL

In making decisions on the amount and the nature of our marketing efforts for a given product, it's helpful to have some idea regarding the potential which the market has to offer. As one observer points out:

> One of the most difficult aspects of allocating marketing effort between geographic markets, products, or components of a marketing mix is determining how much is to be gained from a given market, or from a particular product, or in response to one or more elements of the marketing mix. Without some knowledge of the demand response possible, the decision to allocate marketing effort and dollars must be made blindly and probably inefficiently.[11]

*Market potential* has been defined as "the limit approached by market demand as industry marketing effort goes to infinity, for a given environment."[12] This may be contrasted to the *market forecast*, which is the *expected* level of demand for the level of industry effort that is likely to be made. Hence, market potential will always be greater than the market forecast. These terms are graphically depicted in the diagram of Figure 17-5, which shows how the

---

[10] Further discussion of these two segmentation approaches may be found in R.E. Frank, W. Massy, and Y. Wind, *Market Segmentation* (Englewood Cliffs, N.J.: Prentice-Hall, Inc., 1977).

[11] Dan E. Schendel, "Estimating Market Potential: Established Products," in Robert Ferber (ed.), *Handbook of Marketing Research* (New York: McGraw-Hill Book Company, 1974), pp. 4.81–4.98. Used with permission.

[12] Kotler, *Marketing Management*, p. 230. The reader is also referred to Kotler for additional details regarding the market potential estimation approaches that follow.

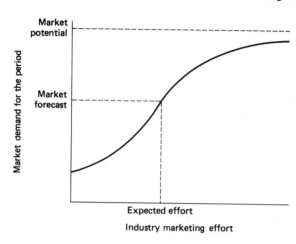

**Figure 17-5.** A graphical depiction of market potential, the "upper limit" for industry sales in a given economic and social environment. If the environment should change (e.g., via technological breakthroughs or legal constraints), this potential would move upward or downward for a given level of effort. Awareness of market potential helps us in allocating marketing resources and evaluating their effectiveness. (*Source:* Philip Kotler, *Marketing Management: Analysis, Planning and Control,* 5th ed., © 1984, p. 229. Adapted with permission of Prentice-Hall, Inc., Englewood Cliffs, N.J.)

growth in market demand slows as the upper limit (market potential) is approached.

Knowledge of market potential allows us to better allocate the dollars we spend on such marketing inputs as advertising, number of salespersons, or outlets. For example, if one geographic region has three times the market potential, it should tend to receive three times as much marketing effort. In addition, because market potential provides us with a standard for comparison, we are in a better position to set sales goals, evaluate and reward the performance of our sales force, and to generally assess the effectiveness of our marketing efforts.

There are a variety of methods used for the actual estimation of market potential. Since some are rather complex, we will limit our discussion here to (1) the chain ratio method, (2) the market buildup method, and (3) the weighted factor index method.

### Chain Ratio Method

Sometimes referred to as the "top-down" approach, the chain ratio method begins with the entire population of interest, then multiplies by a succession of factors to arrive at a smaller, more likely estimate of customers or sales. The factors used may be percentages, probabilities, or dollar amounts.

As a hypothetical example, let's assume that we've just developed a new watch for joggers, a formidable timepiece that employs a belt buckle with a mini-radar unit for measuring the jogger's speed. It uses the police-radar principle to compare the runner's speed with that of stationary objects along the course. In addition to measuring lap times, it allows the runner to monitor or maintain either instantaneous or average speeds. Naturally, such a product will be relatively expensive, so one of our multiplication factors will reflect income. The chain ratio approach to estimation for the potential for this product might look like this: Total population × percentage who jog × percentage with income over $60,000 × percentage who wear a watch while jogging × percentage who would consider purchase of the new watch × percentage who would be likely to actually buy one.

The numbers and percentages for this estimate would be based on census information, survey or secondary data on jogging habits and popularity, and survey data measuring the attractiveness of the new watch compared to current timing alternatives. If we were not the only company with the new watch, we could also include a factor reflecting the percentage of the market that we might expect to capture.

Table 17-4 shows the application of the chain ratio method in describing the potential undergraduate student market for women in the 25 to 45 age range

**TABLE 17-4.** *Using the chain ratio method to determine the market potential for women in the 25 to 45 age group who live near Northwestern University.*

|  | Total forecasted population 1980 |
|---|---|
| 1. *Base market (demographic)*<br>North Shore communities<br>(Evanston, Glencoe, Kenilworth, Wilmette, and Winnetka) | 138,000 |
| 2. *Population of census tracts with median 1970 income over $15,000 (demographic)* | 87,400 |
| 3. *Females 25 to 44 (demographic)* | 10,300 |
| 4. *% upper quartile on IQ*<br>Given the strong relationship between IQ and SES, probably close to 50% | 5,150 |
| 50% × 10,300 | |
| 5. *% females 25 to 44 in top quartile on SES, in top quartile of age cohort on academic aptitude, and who did not complete college within five years after high school graduation*<br>Probability of a female (top quartile on SES and academic aptitudes) graduating from a four-year college within five years after high school is 0.71. Thus probability of noncompletion is 0.29 | 1,493 |
| 0.29 × 5,150 | |
| 6. *% interested in attending college (stage of readiness)*<br>(Some will decide to continue working, doing volunteer work, etc.) | ? |
| 7. *% interested in attending Northwestern (loyalty status)* | ? |
| 8. *Further corrections must be made for:*<br>% able to arrange for household help, transportation, family agreement<br>% willing to cope with application process | |

*Source:* From Karen F. A. Fox, *Attracting a New Market to Northwestern's Undergraduate Programs: Older Women Living on the North Shore*, Northwestern University Program on Women, Evanston, Ill., 1979; in Philip Kotler and Karen F. A. Fox, *Strategic Marketing for Educational Institutions*, Prentice-Hall, Inc., Englewood Cliffs, N.J., 1985, p. 164.

who live near a midwestern university. At each stage, the preceding base number is multiplied by a percentage in order to arrive at the next base.

## Market Buildup Method

The market buildup method, sometimes called the "bottom-up" approach, requires that we divide the market into identifiable segments, then make separate estimates of potential sales to each. In the case of the radar-equipped jogging watch, we might select a two-way segmentation based on age and income, use the chain ratio method to estimate potential sales to each of these groups, then simply add up the segment potentials to arrive at an estimate of total potential sales for the product.

The market buildup method is especially useful in the industrial marketing setting, where *Census of Manufacturers* data can be used to estimate the market potential for each segment. These data are based on the Standard Industrial Classification (SIC) system and include such information as unit and dollar value of shipments according to product classification. For each product classification, the number of manufacturing establishments is provided, along with subclassifications according to location, number of employees, annual sales, and net worth.

One market buildup approach to the estimation of industrial market potential is simply to take a census of all actual and potential users of the product, asking them to estimate their requirements. However, since a census is not always practical, we can also estimate potential on the basis of (1) secondary data, or (2) survey results based on a sample of such customers.[13] Table 17-5 shows how the survey approach might be used to estimate the market potential for roller bearings in several selected industries. By using purchases per employee as an index, the results may be multiplied (extrapolated) to obtain an estimate for the entire United States. Similarly, we can estimate regional or local market potential by using the same index as a multiplier.

## Weighted Factor Index Method

Used primarily by marketers of consumer goods, the weighted factor index method measures the *relative* market potential of a region or territory—that is, the potential as a percentage of the total potential of all such regions or territories.

As an example of how this works, let's assume that the state in which you live has 5% of the total U.S. population. Using percent of population as a "factor," we would then predict that your state is a market for 5% of all ballpoint pens, 5% of all snowshoes, and 5% of all bathing suits. Naturally, just as a state is not likely to be equally attractive as a market for both bathing suits and snowshoes, a single factor is usually not sufficient for measuring the relative

---

[13] See William E. Cox, Jr., *Industrial Marketing Research* (New York: John Wiley & Sons, Inc., 1979), pp. 157–68, for a more detailed discussion of these approaches.

**TABLE 17-5.** *When a complete census of potential industrial users is impractical, survey results can be combined with the market buildup method to obtain estimates of market potential.*

| SIC code | Industry | (1) Product purchases[b] | (2) Number of production employees[c] | (3) Average purchases per employee[d] | (4) Total production employees in this industry[e] | (5) Estimated U.S. market potential[f] |
|---|---|---|---|---|---|---|
| | | | | **Market survey data[a]** | | |
| 3573 | Computers and related equipment | $201,627 | 8736 | $23.08 | 78,000 | $1,800,240 |
| 3585 | Refrigeration and heating equipment | 851,552 | 15,720 | 54.17 | 120,000 | 6,500,400 |
| 3721 | Aircraft industry | 292,692 | 20,020 | 14.62 | 130,000 | 1,900,600 |
| 3811 | Engineering and scientific instruments | 178,200 | 4950 | 36.00 | 25,000 | 900,000 |

[a] Based on personal interviews with known users of roller bearings.

[b] Product purchases from all suppliers in previous calendar year.

[c] Average employment during previous calendar year.

[d] Column 1 divided by column 2.

[e] Estimated from latest Bureau of the Census, U.S. Department of Commerce, *Annual Survey of Manufactures—General Statistics for Industry Groups and Industries.*

[f] Column 3 multiplied by column 4.

*Source:* Adapted from Francis E. Hummel, "Market Potentials in the Machine Tool Industry—A Case Study," *Journal of Marketing,* 19 (July 1954): 34—41; in William E. Cox, Jr., *Industrial Marketing Research,* John Wiley & Sons, Inc., New York, 1979, p. 162.

market potential of a state for a single product. (Note that there may be some exceptions to this general rule; for example, we might expect "number of births" to be an excellent factor in measuring the relative potential for diaper sales.)

Expanding to more than one factor, we end up with the relative market potential expressed as a weighted average of a number of factors that are considered relevant. The sum of the "weightings" typically is 1, and the individual weights may be arrived at either subjectively or through a quantitative approach—for example, multiple regression.

Such a multiple-factor index exists in the "Annual Survey of Buying Power" published by *Sales and Marketing Management* magazine. This index of relative market potential uses three factors—disposable income, retail sales, and population—and can be expressed as

$$B = 0.5I + 0.3R + 0.2P$$

## EXHIBIT 17-2
### Computer Mapping Replaces Pins on the Wall

Computer mapping, a relatively new technique in marketing research, uses secondary data to generate computerized maps describing market areas and providing insights on their market potential (see Figure 17-6). Geographic information within the database is obtained from such sources as the U.S. Postal Service, the Bureau of the Census, and the National Technical Information Service. Consumer data within an area may include population, income, occupation, age, auto registration, and other data, some of which are developed from custom surveys.

One of the capabilities of computer mapping is to match up census tracts with income data to plot a map in which localities are colored or shaded according to average income. Similarly, areas can be differentiated on the basis of age, occupation type, family size, or even Cadillac ownership. In the 1950s, the Cadillac Division of General Motors partially based new dealer site decisions on observational studies in which researchers simply drove through various neighborhoods and counted the number of Cadillacs they saw. Today, Cadillac uses an in-house mapping system with an auto registration database to produce color-coded maps showing areas of high Cadillac ownership as well as locales where competitive makes are especially popular.

American Express employs computer mapping to identify areas having high cardholder density and high incomes. The technique includes the ability to match these characteristics with restaurants honoring the American Express card and their geographic locations. Federal Express uses computer mapping to analyze trends in use of its overnight-delivery service. Mapping also allows computer companies to identify the areas with the greatest concentration of likely first-time buyers, households with children.

John P. Bowen, president of Geographic Systems, Inc., says that computer mapping is really just an extension of techniques that have been in use for years. Bowen points out that "most managers are very conscious of geography and its relationship to their businesses. They constantly think in geographic terms—sales territories, market areas. . . . Every sales manager's office has a map on the wall." According to Bowen, "In essence, what we did was take the map off the wall, take the pins out of the map, and give the person a computer to replace that whole technology that has been going on for generations."

With the combined availability of powerful microcomputers and extensive computer databases, computer mapping is more than ever within the capabilities of smaller firms. For example, Sammamish Data Systems, Inc. markets a desktop color-mapping software package for about $2000. Such "in-house" systems, besides allowing the firm to generate and experiment with computer-generated maps of its own, also provide a level of confidentiality that was impossible to guarantee when the company had to rely on services provided by commercial suppliers of computer mapping services.

*Source:* Based on Bernie Whalen, "'Cheap and Friendly' Software Lets 'Little Guys' Have In-House Mapping," *Marketing News*, March 16, 1984, p. 1, published by the American Marketing Association.

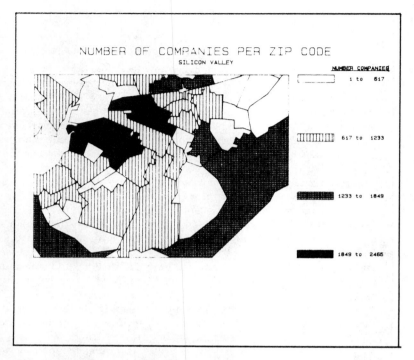

**Figure 17-6.** Computer mapping converts geographic and demographic information into a visual display describing the characteristics of areas and providing insights into their market potential. (Generated with Atlas Mapping Software from Strategic Locations Planning, Inc., San Jose, Calif.)

where

$B$ = percentage of total national buying power in a region

$I$ = percentage of national personal disposable income in the region

$R$ = percentage of national retail sales in the region

$P$ = percentage of national population located in the region

As an example, let's assume that you live in a state that happens to account for 10% of the nation's personal income, 12% of the nation's retail sales, and just 5% of the nation's population. The *Sales and Marketing Management* index of buying power for your state would be $0.5(10) + 0.3(12) + 0.2(5) = 9.6$.

According to *Sales and Marketing Management*, these weights are useful for products that are neither low-priced staples nor high-priced luxuries, so they might not be appropriate for all possible products. Thus, if you happen to be marketing generic chewing gum or crystal chandeliers, you may wish to (1) adjust these weights slightly, or (2) include additional factors (and their weights) that are better suited to your product.

## FORECASTING

For many, the word *forecasting* conjures up images of fat folks in smoke-filled rooms, or of computer specialists consulting their electronic seers through typewriterlike consoles. The truth is that forecasting is both of these, *and* many approaches that lie in between. Forecasting is both an art and a science, and its difficulty is best described by this quote: "Forecasting is like trying to drive a car blindfolded and following directions given by a person who is looking out the back window."[14]

In marketing, there are a wide variety of quantities that can be the object of a forecast, including such diverse variables as sales, market share, general business conditions, and technological developments. In addition, there are many different approaches that can be taken to the forecasting process. Since it isn't possible to cover all of these potential combinations here, we will concentrate primarily on *sales* as the object of our forecast, and we will discuss the topic of forecasting according to the structure shown in Figure 17-7. In general, forecasting can be divided into *formal* and *informal* approaches, with those of the formal variety being further classified according to *quantitative* and *qualitative*.[15] Because the informal forecast is typically a matter of judgment and intuition, two personal skills that are difficult to teach in a textbook, our discussion will emphasize the more structured, formal methods of forecasting.

### Quantitative Forecasting: Time-Series Based

In quantitative approaches based on time series, *past sales* and *time* are the key variables from which we try to make our predictions. While there are a wide variety of specific approaches, all involve using sales data from the past in order to estimate the level of sales in the future. Naturally, they differ considerably in terms of the way these past data are actually used.

In illustrating how some of these techniques work, we'll be considering the following yearly sales data from Uncle Dewey's Distillery, a hypothetical family-owned concern engaged in the production and marketing of beverages:

| Year | Uncle Dewey's sales (thousands of cases) |
|------|------------------------------------------|
| 1975 | 95 |
| 1976 | 130 |
| 1977 | 110 |
| 1978 | 120 |
| 1979 | 115 |
| 1980 | 140 |

---

[14] Anonymous, from Kotler, *Marketing Management*, p. 224.

[15] This structure is suggested by Spyros Makridakis and Steven C. Wheelwright, "Forecasting: Issues and Challenges for Marketing Management," *Journal of Marketing*, October 1977, pp. 24–38, published by the American Marketing Association.

| Year | Uncle Dewey's sales (thousands of cases) |
|------|------------------------------------------|
| 1981 | 145 |
| 1982 | 160 |
| 1983 | 180 |
| 1984 | 170 |
| 1985 | 155 |
| 1986 | 170 |
| 1987 | 200 |
| 1988 | 195 |

### Naive Methods

The *naive* forecast involves simply applying a crude rule of thumb to the data of the preceding year. For example, Uncle Dewey may forecast next year's sales as being the same as last year's sales—195,000 cases.[16] Alternatively, he may arbitrarily decide to apply a 1.05 growth factor, thus multiplying last year's sales by 1.05 and arriving at an estimate of 1.05 × 195,000, or 204,750 cases for the coming year. If he were dealing with monthly, instead of yearly, sales data, Uncle Dewey would base his prediction for next month on his sales for the preceding month, possibly considering seasonal (yearly) patterns of distilled beverage sales. For example, typically higher sales during the end-of-year holiday season might cause him to "bump" December's prediction up a bit more from the level observed in November.

While these approaches may not seem very impressive, this does not mean that they should be ignored. According to Makridakis and Wheelwright:

> An important application of such naive methods is to use their forecasting accuracy as a basis for comparing alternative approaches. It is not uncommon to find that one of these naive methods may provide adequate accuracy for certain situations. It may also be the case that more sophisticated methods (which are usually much more costly) do not give sufficient improvement in accuracy over these methods to justify their use.[17]

### Trend Extrapolation

The trend extrapolation method simply involves extrapolating past sales data into the future, and typically involves a graphical picture of past sales, as shown in Figure 17-8. This extrapolation can be done either visually (the "eyeball" approach) or mathematically (by fitting a linear or nonlinear regression equation to the data). Since Uncle Dewey's research analyst, Donald, is also his chief taste tester, he has asked Donald to forego the visual route in favor of a linear regression equation of the form $Y = a + bX$. The result, also shown in

---

[16] Makridakis and Wheelwright refer to this as the "naive I" method, with "naive II" having the same approach plus consideration of the seasonal patterns which tend to make some months higher or lower than others.

[17] Makridakis and Wheelwright, "Forecasting," p. 28.

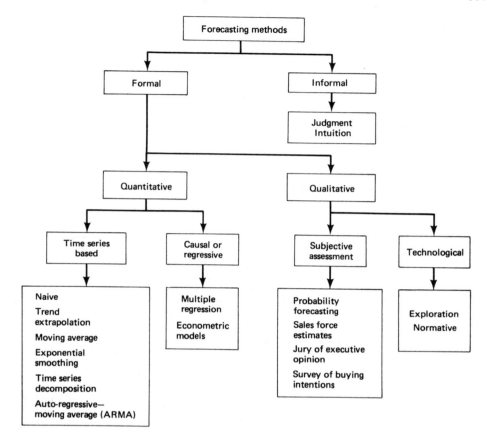

**Figure 17-7.** The major approaches to forecasting. Text concentrates on formal techniques, which can be categorized as quantitative and qualitative. (*Source:* Adapted from Spyros Makridakis and Steven C. Wheelwright, "Forecasting: Issues and Challenges for Marketing Management," *Journal of Marketing,* October 1977, pp. 24–38, published by the American Marketing Association.)

Figure 17-8, is $Y = 102.29 + 7.18X$, where $Y$ = sales (thousands of cases) and $X$ = number of years past 1975.

As Figure 17-8 indicates, a straight line is a very good "fit" to the past sales data (the coefficient of correlation is 0.928). Based on this method, 1989 sales would be predicted as $102.29 + 7.18(14)$, or 202,810 cases.

### Moving Average

With the moving average technique, we can take some of the "ups and downs" from the data, allowing us to more easily see bigger-picture trends and movement patterns. Each point in the moving average is actually the average of sales figures for several months or years. For example, if we converted Uncle

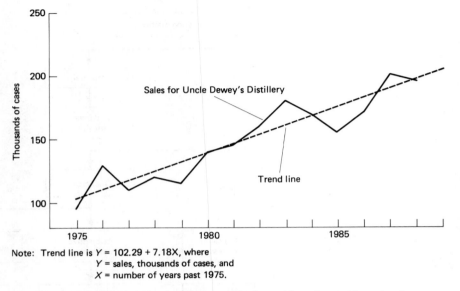

Note: Trend line is $Y = 102.29 + 7.18X$, where
$Y$ = sales, thousands of cases, and
$X$ = number of years past 1975.

**Figure 17-8.**   The trend extrapolation method provides a forecast by extending a regression equation fitted to past sales data.

Dewey's yearly sales data by means of a three-year moving average, the result would be as follows:

| Year | Uncle Dewey's sales (thousands of cases) | Three-year moving average |
|------|------------------------------------------|---------------------------|
| 1975 | 95  | —     |
| 1976 | 130 | 111.7 |
| 1977 | 110 | 120.0 |
| 1978 | 120 | 115.0 |
| 1979 | 115 | 125.0 |
| 1980 | 140 | 133.3 |
| 1981 | 145 | 148.3 |
| 1982 | 160 | 161.7 |
| 1983 | 180 | 170.0 |
| 1984 | 170 | 168.3 |
| 1985 | 155 | 165.0 |
| 1986 | 170 | 175.0 |
| 1987 | 200 | 188.3 |
| 1988 | 195 | —     |

In these calculations, the results of which are shown in Figure 17-9, each new data point is the average of three years. For example, for 1979, the moving average value is $(120 + 115 + 140)/3$, or 125.0. If we wished, we could use some other basis for these moving averages—for example, 5 years, 8 years, or 2 years. The more periods on which we base our moving average, the more of a "damping" effect we will have on the original sales data.

Since Uncle Dewey's sales growth curve is not very straight, a lot of variation can be removed through such damping. Notice that the moving average line of Figure 17-9 is a little smoother than the original data. The moving averages we've calculated here may be described as "centered" because each point represents the same number of years on both sides—the 1979 moving average value, for example, is a combination of the three years for which 1979 is in the center.

When we're dealing with monthly data, moving averages can be useful in helping us to identify and adjust for annual patterns in sales data. This ability is especially applicable for department stores and other retailers, who generally find that a disproportionally large percentage of their sales come during the final three months of the year. The key to this is to express sales on a monthly basis, then use a moving average that is based on 12-month periods. As the basis for your average proceeds over the years, each moving average will reflect one January, one February, . . . , one November, and one December.

### Exponential Smoothing

Like the moving average, the exponential smoothing approach allows us to "smooth" the data by reducing the amount of variation in it. It also allows us to give increased importance to the most recent sales figures. A typical approach to exponential smoothing is to express each year's forecast as a weighted combination of just two quantities: (1) the actual sales during the previous year, and (2) the forecast that was calculated for the previous year. A weighting value (referred to as the *smoothing constant*) determines how heavily the most recent

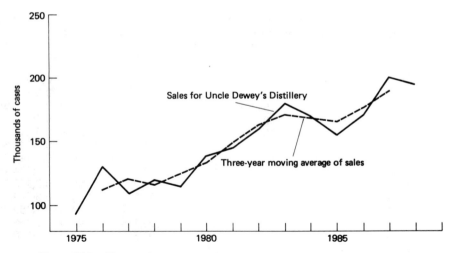

**Figure 17-9.** The moving average takes some of the "ups and downs" from the data and allows us to better see bigger-picture trends and patterns. Each point in the moving average is actually the average of sales for several months or years.

period contributes to the forecast. The formula for this approach is

sales forecast for next year

= $A$ [actual sales last year] + $(1 - A)$[sales level forecasted for last year]

The value of the smoothing constant, $A$, will be between 0 and 1, depending on how much importance is to be given to more recent values. The maximum value, $A = 1$, means that our forecast for each year will simply be "the same as last year."

Before applying exponential smoothing to Uncle Dewey's yearly sales, we must first decide on a value for our smoothing constant. In practice, this would be a relatively subjective decision, with different values tried until one is found that seems to provide satisfactory forecasts. The higher the value of the smoothing constant, the more quickly the curve will "adjust" to upward or downward changes in the chart of the actual sales data. For our example, we'll use $A = 0.7$.

The second decision, a more minor one, is to arbitrarily select a value for the (nonexisting) "first forecast." Since the formula demands a forecast value for each "previous year," it will not have a starting point unless we make up a value for what would have been forecasted for Uncle Dewey's first year, 1975. To make life a little easier, let's assume that sales of 95,000 cases had been forecast for 1975. This value will become of less and less importance, but we need it in order to get the process started.

Now that we've made these preliminary decisions, we can use exponential smoothing to help Uncle Dewey dampen his distillery's sales data. The results of our calculations will be as follows:

| Year | Uncle Dewey's sales (thousands of cases) | Sales forecasted for the year |
|------|------------------------------------------|-------------------------------|
| 1975 | 95  | 95 (arbitrarily selected) |
| 1976 | 130 | 95    = 0.7(95)  + 0.3(95) |
| 1977 | 110 | 119.5 = 0.7(130) + 0.3(95) |
| 1978 | 120 | 112.9 = 0.7(110) + 0.3(119.5) |
| 1979 | 115 | 117.9 = 0.7(120) + 0.3(112.9) |
| 1980 | 140 | 115.9 = 0.7(115) + 0.3(117.9) |
| 1981 | 145 | 132.8 = 0.7(140) + 0.3(115.9) |
| 1982 | 160 | 141.3 = 0.7(145) + 0.3(132.8) |
| 1983 | 180 | 154.4 = 0.7(160) + 0.3(141.3) |
| 1984 | 170 | 172.3 = 0.7(180) + 0.3(154.4) |
| 1985 | 155 | 170.7 = 0.7(170) + 0.3(172.3) |
| 1986 | 170 | 159.7 = 0.7(155) + 0.3(170.7) |
| 1987 | 200 | 166.9 = 0.7(170) + 0.3(159.7) |
| 1988 | 195 | 190.1 = 0.7(200) + 0.3(166.9) |
| 1989 |     | 193.5 = 0.7(195) + 0.3(190.1) |

Using exponential smoothing, with a smoothing constant of $A = 0.7$, our forecast for 1989 would be a weighted average of (a) 1988's actual sales, and (b) the forecast we had made for 1988. That is, we would forecast 0.7(195) +

0.3(190.1), or 193.5 thousand cases for 1989. Figure 17-10 compares these exponential smoothing forecasts with the actual sales enjoyed by Uncle Dewey over the years.

Uncle Dewey would probably not be in high spirits to observe that the smoothed curve tends to lag far behind actual sales, and that it does not do a very good job at "turning corners" when the sales curve suddenly changes direction. However, remember that the technique has only rearward vision, and that it is the simplest version of exponential smoothing models, which can involve a great deal more complexity.

### Time-Series Decomposition

As with the preceding methods, time-series decomposition is solely concerned with the variation of past sales data over time. However, in this approach, we attempt to break down the time series into four factors: three that also vary over time, and one that reflects random upward-downward movement. These factors are known as the trend, cyclical, seasonal, and random components of the time series.

**Trend.** The underlying tendency for sales to increase or decrease over the long run is known as the trend. This was our primary concern when we applied

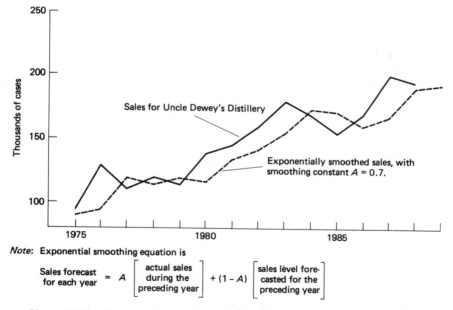

**Figure 17-10.**  Exponential smoothing provides a forecast for the coming period by using a weighted average of (1) sales in the last period, and (2) sales which had been forecasted for the last period. Higher values for the smoothing constant (*A*) cause more importance to be placed on more recent sales.

the linear regression equation to Uncle Dewey's sales over the years. This component is often the result of long-term increases in such variables as population, affluence, and technology. It is typically considered in terms of lengthy periods of time, and is most applicable to long-range forecasting.

*Cyclical variations.* Patterns that tend to repeat over a period of time greater than one year (i.e., more than one year elapses from peak to peak) are cyclical variations. The exact period of the cycle will generally not be very constant, thus making it one of the more troublesome components with which to deal. The general business cycle of economic activity affects the sales of many companies, but is not as predictable as some economists and government experts would like to believe.

*Seasonal variations.* Patterns that repeat on a yearly (or even shorter) basis are seasonal variations. We typically refer to the yearly period when considering this type of variation. For example, sales of weather-related products such as air conditioners, sleds, swimsuits, and fishing lures are highly seasonal. In addition, there are such non-weather-related phenomena as the annual back-to-school clothing frenzy, the purchase of Christmas gifts each December, and the ever-present George Washington's birthday sales.

Even shorter patterns may be caused by payday schedules at large plants, by the monthly receipt of welfare and Social Security payments, or by weekend spending for movies, travel, and other recreational activities.

*Random variations.* The unpatterned "noise" in the system due to random variations can include chance fluctuations as well as major events, such as strikes, oil embargoes, equipment breakdown, and either adverse or favorable publicity related to your product. This component can make it difficult to identify the other, more systematic factors that contribute to the overall movement of a time series of sales or other data.

Time-series decomposition models may assume that the relationship between sales and the contributing components is additive (i.e., sales = trend value + cyclical value + seasonal value + random value). Alternatively, the relationship may be viewed as multiplicative (i.e., sales = trend factor × cyclical factor × seasonal factor × random factor). These models can become rather complex in their attempts to uncover the underlying contributions of the four factors, and a more detailed discussion of them would stretch beyond the scope of this text.

### Autoregressive Moving Average

The autoregressive moving average (ARMA) method has been referred to as the most sophisticated of the single time-series approaches to forecasting. An ARMA model applies weights not only to past values of the main variable of interest (e.g., sales), but to past values of the forecast error as well. A popular model of this type is the *Box–Jenkins* technique, which statistically selects weighting values in order to minimize the forecasting error for any given time period.[18]

## Quantitative Forecasting: Causal or Regressive

In causal or regressive approaches to forecasting, sales are assumed to be more than just a function of time, with additional variables included in the model. Two techniques of this type are *multiple regression* and *econometric models*.

### Multiple Regression

Instead of simply expressing sales as a linear function of time (sales = $a$ + $b$ × time), multiple regression is used to express sales as a function of two or more variables. Typical independent variables used include (1) past values of sales, plus (2) current or past values of variables that are considered to have a causal effect on sales. Such causal variables might include advertising level, price, weather conditions, disposable income, or housing starts. The eventual set of independent variables used will depend on the product involved as well as on the importance of each variable in determining or accompanying sales.

### Econometric Models

Econometric methods typically involve complete *sets* of regression equations, and take into consideration that the independent variables themselves are often interrelated. For example, steel sales are partly a function of automobile sales and disposable income. However, disposable income and automobile sales are also related to each other. The resulting set of interrelated regression equations are solved simultaneously in order to provide a forecast of sales. As you can imagine, these methods can be both highly complex and very expensive.

## Qualitative Forecasting: Subjective Assessment

This qualitative family of forecasting techniques is based mainly on judgment, with various approaches differing primarily according to the types of individuals making the estimates and the ways in which their judgments are combined. We will consider four such methods: (1) probability forecasting, (2) sales force estimates, (3) jury of executive opinion, and (4) survey of buying intentions.

### Probability Forecasting

The probability approach involves generating (1) a set of the possible states of nature (i.e., possible sales levels), and (2) a set of probabilities associated with these states of nature. For example, Uncle Dewey could identify three different

---

[18] *Ibid.*, p. 29.

sales levels, and accompanying probabilities, for the coming year:

220,000 cases, probability = 0.3

200,000 cases, probability = 0.5

180,000 cases, probability = 0.2

Thus the expected sales level would be a weighted average of the three estimates, or 0.3(220,000) + 0.5(200,000) + 0.2(180,000), or 202,000 cases. Both the estimates and probabilities may be subjective, though quantitative forecasting techniques may be partially relied on to get Dewey "into the ballpark" of the range of possibilities.

### Sales Force Estimates

A method that is especially popular with marketers of industrial products is simply to sum up the estimates provided by individual salespersons in the field. In addition to estimating sales to a customer, the salesperson may be asked to provide an estimate of total customer requirements, sometimes involving such detail as identities and probable sales by key competitors. Naturally, such forecasts are heavily dependent on the salesperson's awareness of customers and their needs, and on his or her ability to make objective estimates. Because a salesperson's measure of success for the coming year may depend on his performance versus the estimate he has provided, such objectivity might be questionable. To help maintain objectivity, or to adjust for undue optimism or pessimism, interviews with the members of the sales force may prove useful.

### Jury of Executive Opinion

In this method, a set of company executives make their own estimates of expected sales for the forecast period, then the estimates are combined to form a single forecast. The "combining" process may involve: (1) an executive who resolves the differences and arrives at a single number, or (2) an open meeting in which the executives discuss, resolve, and adjust in order to arrive at a consensus.

Executives involved are likely to include representatives from marketing, finance, purchasing, production, and sales. The method is exceedingly simple, and allows input from a wide variety of presumably knowledgeable individuals, each with his or her own base of information and experience.

An extension of this method is known as the *Delphi* technique, which involves a "feedback" loop in which each expert is provided with a compilation of the forecasts made by all group members. Without communication with others, each individual is allowed to review this compilation and revise his or her own forecast accordingly. The general idea is to repeat this loop several times, encouraging participants to "converge" on either a single value or on a narrower range of values. The method helps to reduce the effects of group pressure and personality dominance that can occur in open discussions.

### Survey of Buying Intentions

As a forecasting approach, this method relies on survey techniques to measure the buying intentions or anticipated needs of our customers for the period ahead. For example, we may use mail, telephone, or personal interviews to find out if individuals intend to purchase a new car, refrigerator, or color television set during the coming year. Such approaches are useful in staying aware of the general conditions of the marketplace, but tend to suffer from respondent uncertainty or untruthfulness (i.e., response bias). It's one thing for a person to *say* that she will buy a new car next year, but quite another for her to actually reach into her bank account to make the purchase.

Intentions are not always reliable as an indicator of actual future behavior, especially for consumer products. This is why the more successful applications of this method have been in the industrial marketplace, where buyers are not only more identifiable but more knowledgeable, rational, and factual in anticipating and communicating their product needs.

### Qualitative Forecasting: Technological

Another category of qualitative forecasting is concerned with technological change, especially as it might affect (1) today's products, (2) current new-product plans, and (3) possible new products of the future. The *exploration* approach to technological forecasting involves using today's knowledge, along with the extrapolation of trends from the past, in an attempt to gain insight into the technological future. By contrast, the *normative* approach is based on future goals, then requires working backward to determine the technological developments that will be necessary in order to reach these goals.[19]

### Choice of a Forecasting Method

As you've seen, there are many different methods available for the forecasting of sales, and they range from the very simple to the highly complex. In selecting a technique from these methods, you should consider: (1) how much time you have to come up with the forecast, (2) the amount of accuracy you would like the forecast to have, (3) the kind of data you will need in order to make the forecast, and (4) the time horizon to which the forecast is to apply.

The last of these considerations, time horizon, is probably the most important, as it is closely related to the others—especially to the accuracy you can expect from each method. Table 17-6 summarizes the forecasting procedures

---

[19] *Ibid.*, p. 26.

*TABLE 17-6. In choosing a forecasting method, the time horizon for the forecast is a key consideration. This summary shows how extensively each method tends to be used for various horizons.*

| Forecasting technique | Time horizon and extensiveness of use[a] | | | |
|---|---|---|---|---|
| | *Less than one month* | *1–3 months* | *3 months to 2 years* | *2 years or more* |
| Quantitative | | | | |
| Naive | xxxx | xxxx | xx | |
| Trend extrapolation | | | xx | xxxx |
| Moving average | xxxx | xxxx | | |
| Exponential smoothing | xxxx | xxxx | | |
| Time-series decomposition | | xxxx | | |
| Autoregressive moving average (ARMA) | | xxxx | | |
| Multiple regression | xxxx | xxxx | xxxx | xx |
| Econometric models | x | xx | xxxx | |
| Qualitative | | | | |
| Probability forecasting | x | x | xxxx | x |
| Sales force estimates | | | xxxx | |
| Jury of executive opinion | | | xxxx | |
| Survey of buying intentions | | x | xxxx | |
| Technological | | | | |
| Exploration | | | x | xxxx |
| Normative | | | | xxxx |

[a] xxxx, extensive use; xx, medium use; x, limited use.

*Source:* Adapted from Spyros Makridakis and Steven C. Wheelwright, "Forecasting: Issues and Challenges for Marketing Management," *Journal of Marketing*, October 1977, pp. 24–38, published by the American Marketing Association.

we've covered, indicating the degree to which they are each used for time horizons ranging from very short (less than one month) to long (two years or more).

## ☐ SUMMARY

Market analysis, a key component of overall marketing strategy, is considered here in terms of (1) market segmentation, and (2) estimating market potential. Market segmentation helps us to identify and compare market opportunities, make finer adjustments in our marketing mix, and develop marketing plans with a clearer picture of how various segments are likely to respond. While there are a great many variables that can be used to segment an overall market, most can be categorized as geographic, demographic, psychographic, or behavioristic in nature.

Market potential provides us with an indicator of the relative strengths of various markets, allowing us to more efficiently allocate marketing resources to specific markets or segments. A variety of methods can be used for the estimation of market potential. Those discussed in the chapter include the chain ratio, market buildup, and weighted factor index methods.

Forecasting, a combination of art and science, may be used to predict the value of many different marketing variables, including sales, market share, general business conditions, and technological developments. Forecasting techniques may be categorized as either formal or informal, with the formal variety being further classified as either quantitative or qualitative.

Formal quantitative forecasting approaches may be time series based or causal-regressive. Among the former are the naive, trend extrapolation, moving average, exponential smoothing, time series decomposition, and autoregressive moving average methods. Causal or regressive methods in this category include multiple regression and econometric models.

Formal qualitative forecasting techniques often involve subjective assessment. Such approaches are probability forecasting, sales force estimates, jury of executive opinion, and the survey of buying intentions. Technological forecasting may be categorized as exploration or normative. The exploration approach involves using today's knowledge, along with the extrapolation of trends from the past, to gain insight into the technological future. The normative approach is based on future goals, then requires working backward to identify the technological developments that will be necessary in order to reach these goals.

## ☐ QUESTIONS FOR REVIEW

1. In what specific ways can a firm benefit by being aware of the different segments of its market?
2. Differentiate among geographic, demographic, psychographic, and behavioristic segmentation and provide two possible bases for each approach.
3. The text describes a psychographic study that identified five categories of married men. For each "type," list at least one magazine likely to be popular among members of that segment.
4. What specific benefit segments might be useful to an analyst studying:
   a. Athletic shoes?
   b. Wrist watches?
   c. Automobiles?
5. For each of the following, identify a market segmentation basis that might prove especially useful:
   a. Garden tractors.
   b. Motor oil.
   c. Clock radios.
   d. Racquetball racquets.
6. Briefly, what is the difference between the *a priori* and *clustering* approaches to market segmentation?
7. How might one apply the chain-ratio method in estimating the market potential for a spearmint-scented men's cologne?

8. Based on available secondary information, use the trend extrapolation technique to forecast the number of students enrolled in four-year colleges in 1995.

9. Suppose that a company's past yearly sales are 11, 12, and 16 for periods 1 through 3. The company's forecaster uses exponential smoothing with a smoothing constant of 0.4 and initial forecast (for period 1) = 11. Calculate the exponentially smoothed sales that would have been predicted for period 4.

10. Given the following sales data:

| | |
|---|---|
| 1975 | 200 units |
| 1976 | 160 |
| 1977 | 180 |
| 1978 | 190 |
| 1979 | 220 |
| 1980 | 250 |
| 1981 | 280 |
| 1982 | 240 |
| 1983 | 200 |
| 1984 | 180 |
| 1985 | 210 |
| 1986 | 230 |
| 1987 | 280 |
| 1988 | 300 |

   a. Fit a five-period centered moving average to the data.
   b. Fit an exponentially smoothed ($A = 0.6$) curve to the data.

11. Briefly, what is the difference between forecasting by (a) the time series approach and (b) the causal methods approach?

12. From a direction-of-causality standpoint, differentiate between the multiple regression and econometric-model approaches to forecasting.

13. For what types of products is the survey of buying intentions most likely to be useful? What is the primary weakness of this forecasting approach?

14. What is the difference between the exploration and normative approaches to technological forecasting?

15. Of the forecasting techniques discussed in the chapter:
   **a.** Which methods tend to be more popular for short-term (3 months or less) horizons?
   **b.** Which methods tend to be more popular for longer-term (2 years or more) horizons?

# 18

# PRESENTATION OF RESEARCH RESULTS

## Making It Perfectly Clear

Communication, a combination of oral, written, and visual stimuli, is the way researchers transmit findings to marketing management. It's desirable that this transmission be both clear and unlikely to be misunderstood. As David N. Dickson, executive vice-president of Carnation Company, puts it, "Management should expect marketing researchers to talk clearly and understandably about what is going on in the real world. More sophisticated (research) techniques can lead to a clearer understanding of the consumer, but they also can act as a mask to the clear thinking which leads to decisive action."[1]

Remarkably, a form of language has evolved which strangely enhances precision while detracting from the clarity that many readers seek—it has been described as Tech Speak.[2] Ironically, as shown in Figure 18-1, the use

---

[1] "Management Wants Researchers to 'Eschew Obfuscation,'" *Marketing News*, January 21, 1983, sec. 2, p. 12, published by the American Marketing Association.

[2] For an excellent discussion of this phenomenon, including a detailed examination of its applications and evolution, see Edward Tenner, "Cognitive Input Device in the Form of a Randomly Accessible Instantaneous-Read-Out Batch-Processed Pigment-Saturated Laminous-Cellulose Hard-Copy Output Matrix* (*Or magazine article in Tech Speak, which replaces the jargon of Indo-European herdsmen with a rigorous and logical language)," © *Discover Magazine*, May 1986, p. 58. Time, Inc.

**Figure 18-1.** As you're optically deriving cognitive input from this pulp-based instructional device, you may be receiving the thermal-transfer benefits of polyvinyl chloride, electromagnetically-actuated, shaft-mounted rotating airfoils designed to effect a negative epidermal temperature gradient through the propulsion of gaseous atmospheric media. While such precise descriptions may be technically accurate, they can get in the way of normal communication. The same holds true with the excessive use of statistical and research terminology in the discussion of marketing research results and how they were obtained. (Photo courtesy of Jim Wakefield.)

of very precise, technically-correct terms to describe even the simplest object or event can become an obstacle instead of an aid to the communication process.

## INTRODUCTION

In previous chapters we examined many strategies and techniques designed to help us in our pursuit of objective, meaningful marketing research. However, even the best of research efforts will be of little value unless the results can be summarized and communicated to marketing management in a form that is both understandable and useful.

In this chapter we will discuss two vital ingredients of this commmunication process: (1) the written research report, and (2) the oral presentation typically provided for those who occupy the executive suite. Along the way, we'll review some of the more popular devices for graphical and visual support, and how statistics can be used or misused.

We'll also take a look at how company politics can be used to your advantage in the presentation process, and provide some hints and tips that could prove useful when you happen to find yourself on the *receiving* end of a written or oral presentation of research findings. Accordingly, our discussion will be centered on the following topics:

I. Types of research reports
II. Report organization and writing
III. Graphical and visual aids
IV. Use and misuse of statistics
V. Oral presentations
VI. Political considerations
VII. On the receiving end . . .

## TYPES OF RESEARCH REPORTS

Depending on its intended audience, your research report may be either ***technical*** or ***popular*** in orientation. While both approaches describe the research study, its methodology, findings, conclusions, and recommendations, they can differ considerably in terms of detail, writing style, use of technical terms, and length of report. In general, the higher the executive status of the audience, the shorter the report will tend to be. Some audiences may be more impressed than others by technical jargon and stilted language—for them, the preceding sentence could be written: "There will be an inverse relationship betwen the verbal content of the written communication and the corporate status level of its readership."

### The Technical Report

The technical report is generally intended for other researchers, or for research managers, and will describe what you've done in considerable detail. The report should enable another researcher to critique your methodology, check your calculations and accuracy, and to follow everything you've done on a step-by-step basis.

In this report, you can feel free to use such terms as *degrees of freedom, nonresponse error, confidence interval, external validity,* and *test–retest reliability*. However, in the interests of your reader, you should provide a brief definition for any technical terms with which he or she might not be familiar.

As an "operational definition" of what a technical report tends to look like, consider the majority of articles that appear in the *Journal of Marketing Research*. While they usually do not include their raw data, authors of *JMR* articles tend to use a format and language style that is typical of the technical report.

### The Popular Report

The popular report is intended for a more general audience, one that isn't conversant with (or interested in) the details of research methods and terminology. This reader values the "big picture" and the "bottom line," and would quickly convey a complicated technical report to the circular file.The writing style and complexity will tend to resemble what we find in the business section of major newspapers or in periodicals such as *Business Week*.

Compared to the technical report, the presentation will be a bit more lively, with increased attention to headlines, flow diagrams, charts, tables, and occasional summaries for the purpose of stressing major points. In writing the popular report, try not to "talk down" to the audience—remember that your goal is to *inform* the reader, not to merely impress him or her with your own expertise.

As a professor, I feel that my students are not inferiors, but associates who just happen to have a little less knowledge than I in the areas I teach. As a marketing researcher, you should rely on the same philosophy when communicating your findings to others who may not share your own base of research expertise. Besides helping you in your communications, this philosophy should also be useful in improving your relations with influential members of management, advancing your career in the long run.

Admittedly, communicating research findings without talking down is like walking a tightrope, but don't forget that many nontechnical persons are easily "psyched out" or "turned off" by discussions that are in any way mathematical or statistical. Converting technical material into the English language isn't always easy, but it's definitely worth the effort.

Because different kinds of audiences may be interested in the results of the same marketing research study, it is sometimes necessary to write both a technical report and a popular report. Trying to write a single report that does both jobs is a difficult task, and such an effort could end up satisfying neither audience.

## *REPORT ORGANIZATION AND WRITING*

When you begin writing your research report, it's important that you organize your thoughts and materials into a structured format that provides an attractive "package" for the fruits of your labor. While no single format can satisfy the requirements of *all* reports, the components described here will tend to be useful in the majority of research reports. In reading our discussion of these components, you may decide that one or more of them may not be needed in communicating the results of your particular research study.

After deciding on the format components to be used, you should make an outline of the points you will discuss under each. In addition, there are some specific writing strategies that you may find helpful when you actually sit down and begin putting words on paper.

*TABLE 18-1. Typical format for a marketing research report*

| | |
|---|---|
| I. | Transmittal |
| II. | Title page |
| III. | Executive summary |
| IV. | Table of contents |
| V. | Introduction |
| VI. | Methodology |
| VII. | Findings |
| VIII. | Limitations |
| IX. | Conclusions and recommendations |
| X. | Appendices |
| XI. | Bibliography |

## Research Report Components

The following components, listed in Table 18-1, are presented here in the same order typically used for the actual report. Again, remember that these are merely a suggested format for your paper, and you may wish to eliminate or combine some of them as it best suits your purpose.

### Transmittal

The transmittal letter or memo is the "Here it is!" dimension of the report. An example is shown in Figure 18-2. The function of the transmittal is to introduce the report and say the kinds of things that you might say if you were to deliver it in person. It should be brief, to the point, and should include (1) a mention of the authorization for the report, (2) a "carbon copy" notation to indicate who is receiving copies of the transmittal and report, and (3) any specific comments you may have regarding the report or its findings. With regard to this last point, consider that the transmittal can also serve as a "preview" to pique the reader's interest.

### Title Page

The initial page of the report itself should include information such as (1) the title of the report, (2) the author(s) of the report, (3) for whom the report was prepared, and (4) the date on which the report was completed. While some of this may seem to duplicate the function of the transmittal, consider that the transmittal letter or memo will probably not accompany the report throughout its readership route, or make it to the company library or files where the report may be stored for future reference. Try to make the title brief, but descriptive of the study's intent. If you did a good job of thinking out the purpose of the study in the first place, you should have no trouble in arriving at a suitable title.

I.A. Wizarrd & Associates          1939 Yellow Brick Rd.      Oz, Calif. 99205

November 22, 1988

Ms. Greta Breckameer, President
Breckameer Cosmetics, Inc.
1313 Slowtraffic Lane
Frogswamp, Texas 76201

Dear Greta:

As authorized in our agreement dated October 15, we have carried out the requested brand-image study in the Miami, Florida market area.

Our study, described fully in the attached report, involved personal interviews with a representative sample of 900 females over age 15.

Overall, we found that Breckameer Cosmetics had a relatively low level of brand awareness among these women. Only 35% of those surveyed identified the Breckameer name with cosmetics.

In addition, of those who were aware of the Breckameer line, many tended to associate the name with high price and low product quality.

While these results may be somewhat disappointing, we feel that the information obtained will prove useful as you formulate your product and promotional plans for the coming year. Toward this end, we have made some specific recommendations which you may wish to consider as these plans are being made.

We appreciate this opportunity to be of service to you. Should you have further questions regarding this study or any related matter, please don't hesitate to contact us.

Sincerely,

*Dorothy*

Dorothy Tinman
Research Associate


dt:rmw

Enclosure

cc: F.D. Lyon
    S.A. Crow

**Figure 18-2.** The research report is usually accompanied by an explanatory letter or memo. This transmittal introduces the report and contains the kinds of comments you might have if you were to deliver it in person.

## Some examples:

"Student Attitudes toward the Availability of State-Owned Housing at Hower University"

"Star Power: The Effectiveness of Celebrity Endorsements"

"A Profile of Four-Wheel-Drive Owners in Boone County"

"Consumer Purchasing Patterns for Generic Grocery Products"

"Hard Contact Lenses: Is the Market Softening?"

The title should be descriptive, but "catchy" if possible. Again, remember that you're trying to inspire the reader's interest. Whatever you call your report, do not, do not, *do not* use "Research Report" as your title. While nobody minds if you saddle an unfortunate pet with the name "Dog," using "Research Report" for a title will immediately label you as someone who has one wheel stuck in the sand.

### Executive Summary

If your report is long, you should be realistic and assume that some key individuals may not have time to read it in its entirety. In addition, providing a summary of the report will help ensure that readers get the major points you are trying to make. The executive summary may range from a few paragraphs to one or two pages, depending on the length and detail of the report itself. When writing the summary, keep in mind that it could well be the most important section of the report, and keep it as short and nontechnical as possible. If you can't hold your breath while reading it, chances are it's too long.

### Table of Contents

The table of contents should follow the same format as the items listed in Table 18-1—at least for those components which you've decided are relevant to your particular report. For shorter reports (e.g., five pages), this step will not be necessary, especially if you have good headlines for the sections which the report contains. Each major section will be identified by a Roman numeral, with the appropriate page number following each section heading in the table.

### Introduction

Sometimes referred to as "Background" or "Background and Objectives," the introductory section should explain why the study was done in the first place—that is, what marketing problem or question led to its initiation. In some cases, the reader may not be familiar with the circumstances of the study, and a description of the company or product involved may be appropriate. In this section, you should also state very explicitly the objectives of the study.

### Methodology

In the preceding section you described what you were going to do, and why. In the "Methodology" section, you should indicate how you fulfilled these objectives. If your research involved a survey or other primary data collection, describe the methods by which the data were obtained, and the sample sizes involved. This is also a good place to provide at least a brief argument as to why you selected the approaches used (e.g., why you selected a mail questionnaire instead of using the personal interview or telephone survey techniques). However, you need not defend every aspect of your methodology—this could communicate to others that you're a bit uncertain about what you're doing. Support the main decisions, and readers will assume that you could also defend the rest (if asked).

This section is also appropriate for a discussion of the methods of analysis you employed, including the mention of statistical computer packages, if present. If you're writing a popular report, don't get too technical in this section, and don't hinder the readability by placing copies of the questionnaire, field-worker instructions, raw data, or calculations here. The appendix is a far better location for materials like this, since many readers will not be interested in such details.

### Findings

The "Findings" section is the "meat" of the report, and deserves your best efforts. A combination of text with relevant charts, tables, and diagrams will tend to work best, though this advice is sometimes easier said than done. Above all, you must be highly organized here, and must present your findings in a way that is clear, logical, and visually attractive.

Although it may be tempting to include *everything* you've learned, try to limit your presentation to those findings that are most relevant—others can be relegated to the appendix. A common problem, especially with student research papers, occurs when the author of a survey research report simply presents a series of response frequencies—one for each item on the questionnaire. This tends to communicate not only a lack of effort, but little creativity as well. Not all questions will lead to results that are either significant or interesting, and it's best to be discriminating in deciding which will make it into this section of your report.

While actual calculations (e.g., for chi-square analysis or analysis of variance techniques) are not welcome here, the tables that summarize the data can be quite effective in communicating your findings. In addition, confidence intervals or levels of significance can be expressed in either numerical (technical report) or verbal-plus-numerical (popular report) forms. While readers of the technical report will understand what a significance level means, those who receive a popular report may need a brief explanation. For example: "The difference between the attitudes of the two groups is highly significant. The probability is less than one out of one hundred that such a big difference could have occurred by chance. This indicates that the proposed ad copy change is highly effective in achieving its goals."

### Limitations

The "Limitations" section of the report presents a dilemma. On one hand, we are trying to impress the reader with our thoroughness and professionalism, to communicate our findings, and perhaps persuade him or her that certain

---

**EXHIBIT 18-1**

**Telling the Whole Story**

"Professional marketing researchers have an ethical obligation to report to their clients the major limitations and delimitations of their research. Hiding such information cheats the client and jeopardizes the integrity of the report and the researcher. . . . Revealing limitations and delimitations even may heighten the client's respect for the researcher's professionalism. In any case, the client's opportunity to make sound decisions based on the research results will be improved."

*Source:* John L. Beisel, "Identify Limitations, Delimitations in Marketing Research Reports," *Marketing News*, September 17, 1982, sec. 2, pp. 1, 24, published by the American Marketing Association.

---

courses of action might be advisable. On the other hand, no study is perfect, and there are many things that we might have done differently if we had only been given more time, money, or technical assistance. In addition, we might have experienced the kinds of problems that often arise in real-world efforts, research or otherwise—for example, due to illness, a field interviewer may have been replaced between the pre- and post-measurements of an experiment. This, in turn, may have led to the internal validity problem known as *instrumentation*.

Your choices in this situation fall somewhere between these two extremes:

1. *Totally omit the section.* This is the "ostrich" approach, and your employer or client is not being told the whole story regarding the study and its findings. Despite your best efforts, it may be possible that the city selected for an advertising experiment may not be fully representative of other cities across the United States. If the new ad campaign is used nationally, and fails, you may find yourself both embarrassed and unemployed because you issued your "limitations" section after the fact.

2. *Self-critique your report to death.* This choice will ensure that neither you nor your research findings get serious consideration from marketing management, and many will wonder why you even bothered to do the study at all.

Naturally, the proper course of action will be somewhere between these extremes, and will depend on your report and its readership. In an academic research report, it's better to gravitate toward alternative 2. In the context of a course, it's difficult to apply techniques while you're still learning about them, and it's not unusual for a student to have many after-the-fact concerns about his or her own study. In this case, lean towards a heavier self-critique, and your professor will probably appreciate both your honesty and the amount of insight you have obtained from the course. However, in a company or consultant setting, it's best to strike a balance in the "Limitations" section—just enough to show that you're not a wide-eyed idealist who doesn't understand the real world, but not enough to undermine the credibility of yourself and your findings.

### Conclusions and Recommendations

In the concluding section, briefly summarize your major findings and describe the implications these findings have for marketing decision making. While you may not have complete knowledge of all corporate factors involved in a marketing decision, this should not prevent you from suggesting courses of action that seem attractive on the basis of your study results. If you have carried out your study as a marketing consultant, your client is likely to *expect* such recommendations as part of your agreement (see Figure 18-3).

### Appendices

An appendix section is the place for those supportive materials that are too technical or cumbersome to place in the body of the report. Items such as raw data, statistical analysis, calculations, copies of the questionnaire, and interviewer instructions are best relegated to this location. With such placement, the interested reader will be able to find and evaluate them, while others will not have to stumble over them on the way through the report. If you have doubts as to whether something should be placed in the report or in an appendix, it probably belongs in the appendix.

### Bibliography

If portions of your report rely on secondary data, use a bibliography section to list the publications or sources that you've consulted. This part of the report can also be used for footnotes, since listing these in the text can also be a readability hurdle.

## Writing the Report

Writing style and ability are largely individual matters. However, in writing your report, there are a few general guidelines and strategies that you should keep in mind.

### Outlining

Before you hit the first typewriter key or keyboard button, it's best to spend a little time outlining each section of your report. Each major heading should be divided into subheadings, which in turn are subdivided as the need arises. The main idea is to end up with a cohesive, organized "skeleton" on which to hang the text and visuals that will follow.

### Level of Formality

When writing a formal report, it's best to avoid using the personal pronouns "I," "me," "we," "us," and "you."[3] Their use tends to make the report sound like a personal diary instead of a description of a serious research effort. With a little practice, you can avoid them. However, in the process, don't go to extremes and make your report into a stilted document that looks like it was written by an English butler. Here are some examples of how these words can be avoided:

1. "I stationed myself at the main entrance to the mall, then I used the systematic sampling method and interviewed every tenth person leaving the mall."
   *Better:* "Standing at the mall's main entrance, the author employed systematic sampling to interview every tenth person leaving the mall."
2. "Because of the complexity of the questions, I used personal interviews instead of mail questionnaires."
   *Better:* "Because of question complexity, personal interviews were used instead of mail questionnaires."
3. "Based on these findings, I believe you should delay product introduction until you're sure that legal uncertainties have been resolved."
   *Better:* "Based on these findings, it appears advisable to delay product introduction until legal uncertainties have been resolved."

### Selecting Your Words

When you actually sit down at the keyboard or legal pad, you'll be able to select from a wide variety of words that say the same thing—almost! Here's where a good *dictionary* or *thesaurus* can come in handy. Depending on the word you use in a specific instance, the meaning can change quite drastically in terms of emotional loading. The following examples illustrate how words can be used to portray favorable, neutral or unfavorable images of essentially the same object:[4]

| Positive | Neutral | Negative |
|----------|---------|----------|
| scholarly | well-educated | bookworm |
| meticulous | exact | nit-picker |
| fragrance | smell | odor |
| converse | talk | prattle |
| dignified | proud | arrogant |

---

[3] Robert E. Swindle, *The Business Communicator* (Englewood Cliffs, N.J.: Prentice-Hall, Inc., 1980), p. 357.

[4] Adapted from Paul R. Timm, *Managerial Communication* (Englewood Cliffs, N.J.: Prentice-Hall, Inc., 1980), p. 361.

## RECOMMENDATIONS

*Based upon results of an initial (1980) and follow-up (1981) telephone survey of public transit attitudes and awareness in Kalamazoo, Michigan.*

| **Target advertising featuring the benefits of riding the bus to:** | **Target advertising to nonriders, outlining the fare structure for riding the bus.** | **Target advertising to nonriders, emphasizing how close bus stops are to certain Kalamazoo area residents.** | **Target advertising to nonriders, emphasizing frequency of bus service, i. e., how often the bus comes by.** |
|---|---|---|---|
| * <u>males</u> for "work," "personal business," "school," & "when I don't have a car/when car is in garage" purposes . . <br><br> * <u>females</u> for "personal business," "shopping," & "visits or recreation" uses. (Radio spots could feature a male announcer for male-related purposes, & similarly, a female announcer for female-related uses.) | | | |
| *Reason: There was an increase in the number of <u>males</u> and <u>females</u> who used the bus for the purposes mentioned above.* | *Reason: A 12% increase among <u>nonriders</u> who did not know the cost for a ride on the bus.* | *Reason: 48% of <u>nonriders</u> in both surveys, who live 1 to 2 blocks from the nearest bus route, chose not to use the bus during the last year.* | *Reason: Approximately seven out 10 nonriders were initially unaware of the frequency of bus service, and remained so during follow-up interviewing.* |
| Question 6 (Pg. 36 of report) | Question 10 (Pg. 16 of report) | Question 12 (Pg. 24 of report) | Question 14 (Pg. 17 of report) |

| Recommendation | Reason | Question/Page |
| --- | --- | --- |
| **Service improvements (where feasible) in the areas of more convenient routes & more courteous drivers.** | *Reason: An increase among certain Kalamazoo area bus riders and nonriders who reported a need for the improvements mentioned above.* | Question 20 (Pg. 33–35 of report) |
| **\* Change negative attitudes that bus riding is inconvenient (via news stories for particularly good or unusual service).** **\* Point out comparative costs of auto use versus public transit.** | *Reason: More than nine out of 10 nonriders in both surveys reported "car" as their usual means of transportation.* | Question 34 (Pg. 25 of report) |
| **Target advertising to nonriders who own only one car.** **The message: "take the bus and save the family car for use by other members of the household."** | *Reason: Approximately one-third of nonriders in both surveys reported having only one automobile in their household.* | Question 35 (Pg. 26 of report) |
| **Continue using "other" media & "radio" advertising in addition to newspaper & television advertising.** | *Reason: Follow-up results for "other" media show a higher percentage of recall over initial survey results for heavy & other users, & for nonriders. Similar results were found for moderate users regarding recall of "radio" advertising.* | Conclusions (Pg. 51–54 of report) |

**Figure 18-3.** Since much research is carried out as an aid to decision-making, marketing management may expect the report to include recommendations based on the findings. A two-part format like this one can be used on a separate sheet to serve the dual purpose of summarizing the recommendations and briefly explaining how they have been reached. (*Source:* Nancy L. Frederick, "Two-Part Report Format Attracts Attention of Research Users," *Marketing News*, May 13, 1983, sec. 2, p. 18, published by the American Marketing Association.)

575

As these examples suggest, word selection can be very important to the meaning you convey to your audience. If you still have doubts, just pick up the nearest magazine and look at any ad placed by a major company. Now select any noun, verb, or adjective, and try to come up with a better word than the one they've used—chances are that you can't. This is what good writing is all about. While correct spelling and punctuation are obvious necessities, chances are that you can most easily improve the quality of your own writing by purchasing a good thesaurus, then using it.

### Using Jargon

Earlier it was stated that esoteric language and technical jargon tends to get in the way of real communication in a popular report. However, there may be times when a little jargon can be strategically inserted. Some people are just not impressed unless you give them a bit more than they really understand. In addition, others may actually *expect* it. For example, it has been my experience that government agencies tend to fall into the latter category, with plain English not being the language of the day.

While it is sometimes helpful to "flavor" your reports with a small pinch of jargon, determining the exact amount can be a highly subjective (and potentially dangerous) decision. For this reason, either avoid jargon altogether, or be very careful in attempting to use it for strategic purposes.

### The Fog Index

Since it can be difficult to objectively measure the readability of written reports, you may wish to use a device called *The Fox Index*. This index, developed by Robert Gunning, is based on the size of the words and the length of the sentences in a sample of written text. The index itself is intended to express the number of years of schooling a person requires in order to understand what he or she is reading. For a given sample of written text, the index can be calculated as follows:

1. Select a sample containing at least 100 words and ending in a complete sentence.
2. Count the number of words and the number of sentences, then calculate the average number of words per sentence.
3. Of the first 100 words in the sample, count how many have three or more syllables. Don't include (a) capitalized words, (b) words that make their third syllable by combining two words (e.g., "typewriter"), or (c) verbs that form the third syllable by adding *es* or *ed* (e.g., "completed").

**4.** Add the results you obtained from steps 2 and 3, then multiply by 0.4.[5]

Studies have shown that written material with a Fog Index greater than 10 or 11 tends to be very difficult to understand.[6] Naturally, this is only a rough measure of text readability, but it can be used to help ensure that your written work is appropriate for its intended audience.

## GRAPHICAL AND VISUAL AIDS

To keep the reader interested and help ensure his or her understanding of the points you're trying to make, tables, graphs, charts, and flow diagrams should be sprinkled liberally throughout the report. Just as some people open a magazine and merely look at the pictures (though they won't admit it), some of your readers may spend more time looking at the visuals than at the text. In order to accommodate these simple folk, and to help the visuals reinforce what most readers will find in the text, be sure to provide explanatory captions with each visual in the report.

In Chapter 12, we examined a number of popular visual approaches designed to bring a little "life" to our research findings. The techniques included graphs, bar charts, pictorial displays and sketches. When planning your report, you may wish to refer to this earlier discussion for some hints and tips on expressing your findings in an objective, visual fashion.

Unfortunately, not everyone is so objective in expressing information in graphical form, and it's possible to play some tricks on the unknowing reader. For example, consider the visuals in Figures 18-4 and 18-5. In Figure 18-4, the vertical scale of the graph has been given an extremely high end-point to make it look like Uncle Dewey's business is just about on the rocks. In Figure 18-5, a gap is created in the vertical scale to create the illusion that Family Theater's attendance has risen dramatically in the past few months.

In oral communications, which we'll examine very soon, visual aids are equally important and involve similar opportunities for either objectivity or distortion. The oral presentation allows the use of a wider range of devices, including chalkboards, posters, flip charts, overhead projectors, slides, movies, videotapes, tape recordings, and models. Of these devices, slides, flip charts and posters are the simplest to use, the best values for the money, and offer the added advantage of easy conversion to printed handouts that can be given to the audience after the presentation.[7]

---

[5] Adapted from P.D. Hemphill, *Business Communications with Writing Improvement Exercises* (Englewood Cliffs, N.J.: Prentice-Hall, Inc., 1976), pp. 246–47.

[6] Ibid., p. 247.

[7] Timm, *Managerial Communication*, p. 245.

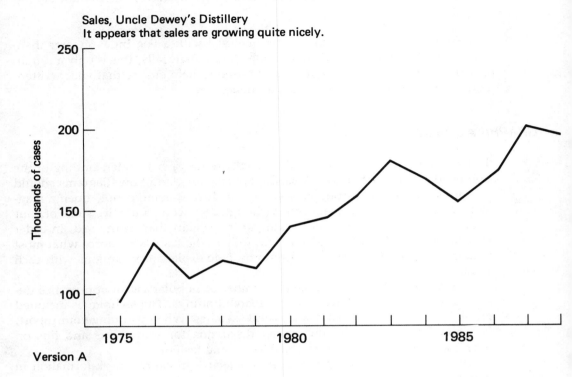

**Version A**

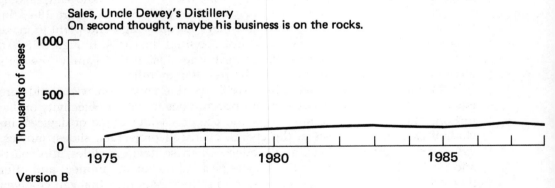

**Version B**

**Figure 18-4.**   By using a very high end-point for the vertical axis of a graph (version B), you can make a growing company look very stagnant. (For a more detailed discussion of this method of distorting visual presentations, see Ely Francis, *Using Charts to Improve Profits*, (Englewood Cliffs, N.J.: Prentice-Hall, Inc., 1962, pp. 42–43.)

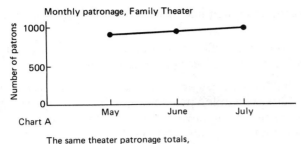

Monthly patronage, Family Theater

Chart A

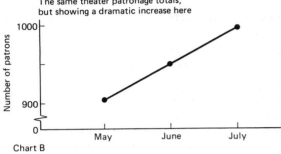

The same theater patronage totals,
but showing a dramatic increase here

Chart B

**Figure 18-5.** By inserting a convenient break in the vertical axis, the result is an exaggerated picture of Family Theater's patronage increase. (For a more detailed discussion of this method of distorting visual presentations, see Ely Francis, *Using Charts to Improve Profits*, (Englewood Cliffs, N.J.: Prentice-Hall, Inc., 1962, pp. 46–47.)

## USE AND MISUSE OF STATISTICS

Used properly, and in an ethical fashion, statistics can provide excellent support for both written and oral presentations. However, you should try to (1) avoid statistical terms with which your audience may not be familiar, and (2) simplify, or use plain, understandable language when introducing those that are absolutely necessary to your discussion. For example, in a popular report, you should use "average" instead of "mean," and "maximum error" instead of "confidence interval." Here are some other general guidelines that can be helpful, especially in oral presentations.[8]

1. Round off large numbers (e.g., 321,493 becomes 321,000 or 321,500.)

2. Interpret the numbers so they will be meaningful to the reader or listener. Percentages are helpful in this regard.

3. If possible, avoid the use of "probability," since this is a statistical term that could "psych out" some individuals. Instead of saying "a probability of 0.01," use "1 chance in 100."

4. When comparing figures, use the same basis—for example, don't compare percentages with fractions or means with medians.

In Chapter 12 we also discussed some of the common statistics used in describing research findings. These included measures of centrality (mean, median, and mode) and measures of dispersion (range, standard deviation, and variance). At that point, we also examined (1) how each is calculated, and (2)

---

[8] Adapted from Timm, *Managerial Communication*, p. 240.

how they could be misleading in certain instances. Here is a brief review of the key "offenders":

*Mean.* Representing the arithmetic average of the data, this quantity can be distorted by extreme values, either very high or very low.

*Median.* The value that has just as many points higher as lower, this could be described as the "50th percentile" position. It is likely to differ from the mean—for example, being much lower when we are expressing information like personal income and family expenditures.

*Mode.* This is the most frequently observed value, and likely to differ from both the mean and median.

*Range.* The difference between the highest and lowest values, this measure of dispersion is very strongly influenced by extremely high or low values.

Just as the thesaurus allows you to select words with positive or negative emotional loadings, a little knowledge of statistics allows you to present measures that distort research findings in one direction or another. As we saw in Chapter 12, results can differ quite considerably, depending on which one of the three measures of centrality we elect to use. The following are just a *few* of the other possibilities that exist for statistical distortion:

1. Using percentages that are based on a very small number of persons or objects.
2. Selecting a very demanding (e.g., 0.001) or a very "easy" (e.g., 0.20) significance level when deciding whether two variables are "significantly" related.
3. Using the same approach as (2) to drastically alter the "error term" of your (or someone else's) survey findings. If a survey has a maximum error of $\pm 3$ percentage points at the 90% confidence level, it will have a maximum error of $\pm 5.6$ percentage points at the more demanding 99.8% confidence level.

Again, we know that you're honest, objective, and will use statistics in a positive way. However, as this text has maintained throughout, we can never be so sure of the other person—and part of learning *how to* involves finding out how *not* to. The latter is especially important if you wish either (1) to be unethical, or (2) to protect yourself from those who are. The improper use of statistics can be a very persuasive weapon with which to wage war on the unknowing (but often trusting) research consumer.

## ORAL PRESENTATIONS

In addition to one or more written reports, it's possible that you will be called upon to brief key executives in an oral presentation of the research findings and implications. This is a difficult task, as it involves distilling (no relation to Uncle

**Figure 18-6.** The main idea of the oral presentation is to deliver research findings and implications in a concise, organized, and interesting fashion. You may have less than 30 minutes to describe what you've been working on for the past six months.

Dewey) a great deal of information into a concise, organized, and interesting presentation. The audience is likely to be very nontechnical, so you'll be severely challenged in your attempts to simplify and summarize. Like the poor soul in Figure 18-6, you may have less than 30 minutes to describe what you've been doing for the past six months—let's hope you do a better job than he did.

Above all, don't burden your audience with detail or complexity. When deciding on an outline of the presentation, be content to deal with relatively few major points (e.g., a half dozen, perhaps fewer). If you have trouble deciding which ones to discuss, pretend that you've just fallen from the top of the Sears Tower, and that you have to list your main points before you land. (If the

**TABLE 18-2.** *Your oral presentations will go much more smoothly if you keep these tips in mind.*

1. *Prepare yourself* by collecting primary and secondary data for your presentation.

2. *Get to know your audience* members and their interests before you make the presentation.

3. *Know your objectives.* Ask yourself: Why am I making the presentation? Develop a communicative strategy of how to combine the interest of your audience with your own goal. Practice the communication concept.

4. *Use notes.* Memorize the opening if you must.

5. *Just be yourself.* Nobody expects you to be Johnny Carson, Bob Hope, or Billy Graham.

6. *Start by outlining* the entire presentation in the form of four or five key topics on the screen or chalkboard. It helps your audience see where things fit together and where the presentation is going.

7. *Take time* to write clearly and draw carefully. Fight the tendency to draw quickly in the interest of saving time.

8. *Begin with your most dramatic* and convincing point or quickly build up to a climax so that you receive the full attention of the audience from the start.

9. *Swiftly move from the most important* to the least important points.

10. *Think of your presentation* as a service. Look at it from your audience members' viewpoints. Continuously ask yourself: How does the presentation help the audience? The organization? My own operation? What is in it for all? Establish mutual benefits. Think of the plus-plus relationship in transactional analysis.

11. *Keep it simple* and easy to understand. Use short sentences: subject, verb, object.

12. *Do not discuss too many points* and details; the main mission of your presentation may get lost.

13. *Be factual.* Your presentation's credibility will increase.

14. *Anticipate objections.* Recognize them if you cannot fight them. Stating an objection calmly takes the emotion out of it. You also show that you are aware of it.

15. *End with a positive note.* Summarize what the listeners might lose and what they will gain.

16. *Do you want a decision* right there? Then get the audience to act. Explain why immediate action is important.

17. *Remember, a presentation is not a sermon.* It is sharing ideas with your audience—ideas that may affect their jobs, their future.

18. *Don't talk down* to your audience. Use "we" instead of "I".

19. *Talk directly* to your audience. Don't lose personal contact by looking out of the window or at your shoes. Look people straight in the eyes.

20. *Use charts.* Don't overload them. Keep them simple. A chart should not say all there is to say. It can later be distributed.

21. *When you use charts,* talk to the audience, not to the chart.

22. *Look at your watch.* Finish your presentation on time.

*Source:* Reprinted from Hugh Kramer, "'Communication Concept' Would Offer Idea in Recipient's Terms," *Marketing News,* December 29, 1978, p. 4, published by the American Marketing Association.

audience consists of corporate vice-presidents, pretend that you've fallen from the fifth floor instead.)

As mentioned earlier, visual aids play an especially important role in the oral presentation, and there are a wide variety of devices from which to choose. In using them, don't rely on the same visual to make more than one point. If it takes more than 30 seconds for an audience to understand a visual, it's too "busy" and should be broken up into two or more different illustrations. Also, try to coordinate the visuals with the presentation in such a way that the audience will not be distracted from what you're saying. For example, if using a flip chart, don't turn to a new page until you're actually ready to discuss it—otherwise, people will be reading it instead of listening to you.

These tips, and more, are shown in Table 18-2. According to Hugh Kramer, who compiled this handy list, the points are based on the "communication concept," an interesting analogy to the marketing concept. Kramer explains that the concept "is a philosophy that strategically focuses the message on the receiver's needs and wants as the key to accomplishing communication goals."[9] By following these guidelines, you won't be guaranteed a superlative presentation, but your chances for success should be significantly greater.

## POLITICAL CONSIDERATIONS

In any research situation, there will be personalities and egos involved, and these can sometimes present more problems than nonresponse error, instrumentation validity, and all other research difficulties combined. As a researcher, you should not only be sensitive to the audience when you deliver the report, but also when you're in the process of conducting the research itself. This is not to say that you must arrive at conclusions that others would like to see, but that you should be aware of the potential difficulties when you don't.

In one of the better discussions available on company politics and research, Chester R. Wasson suggests a number of tips designed to help ensure that your research is taken seriously and put to constructive use:[10]

1. *Identify at an early stage the persons who might be affected.* Individuals who are likely to be affected by your report include top executives, "gatekeepers" in the line of communication to them, and may involve persons who are not directly within the marketing function of the firm. Wasson observes that, without the support of these individuals, "recommendations can be expected to be diluted on their way to the top and the presentation to lose force, or fail completely."[11]

2. *Test tentative findings conversationally.* By testing possible findings in advance, you can identify potential objections and resistance at an early stage of the study and be better prepared to deal with them when the results are actually obtained. According to Wasson, "Conducted systematically

---

[9] Hugh Kramer, "'Communication Concept' Would Offer Idea in Recipient's Terms," *Marketing News*, December 29, 1978, p. 4, published by the American Marketing Association.

[10] Chester R. Wasson, *Research Analysis for Marketing Decision* (New York: Appleton-Century-Crofts, 1965), pp. 227–32.

[11] Ibid., p. 228.

and well, this informal presentation process can sometimes clear the way so thoroughly that the final presentation is a mere formality."[12]

3. *Be cautious in recommending abrupt changes.* Some research findings may suggest that the firm move in a direction that is directly opposite its traditional approach to marketing. In this case, you should sympathize with the dismay of the decision maker and refer to the finding as a possibility that may require further research support before it is finally accepted. The recommendation will have a better chance in the long run if it is "sold" at a more gradual rate.

4. *In presenting results, think in the customer's terms and stress the benefits of the recommendations that will be most acceptable to him or her.* The research customer may not be receptive to *all* recommendations, so concentrate on those which are most likely to be accepted. This is also an "accentuate the positive" strategy. For example, instead of telling a decision maker that past practices have been inefficient, describe how operations might be made even *more* efficient.

5. *Understate potential benefits.* A strategy of understatement involves promising a little less than the results you believe will accrue from following your recommendations. Such understatement can help your credibility with the research customer and make him or her more confident in future recommendations you might provide. However, don't be *too* conservative in applying this strategy—otherwise, your recommendations may not seem promising enough for the firm to implement.

## ON THE RECEIVING END . . .

During most of this chapter, we've concentrated on strategies that are useful when you're writing reports or giving presentations to others. However, there will be times when you find yourself on the *receiving* end of the same kinds of communication. While these situations are simply opposite sides of the same coin, this section contains some advice that could prove helpful when *you* are the audience.

### Reading Reports

In general, critical reading of someone else's report involves subjecting it to the requirements posed earlier in this chapter. For example, you should ask questions such as: (1) Has the researcher explicitly stated the reasons for the study, then listed the objectives it was designed to satisfy? (2) Does the methodology seem appropriate for a study of this type? (3) Has the author described his or her methodology in sufficient detail for you to evaluate the procedures involved? If not, what is missing? The report may be covering up a fatal weakness. (4)

---

[12] Ibid., p. 229.

Has the author arrived at findings that are directly related to the objectives stated earlier? (5) Do the findings support the recommendations that have been made? How much is fact and how much seems to be opinion or speculation? (6) To what extent, if any, has the author described the limitations of the study and its findings? If a "Limitations" section is not present, there may be reason for suspicion and cause for a more in-depth examination of the methodology and conclusions.

### Listening to Presentations

Since you can think a lot faster than most people talk, this gives you a time advantage that can be used in your favor—provided that you put this time to proper use. Listen "between the lines" and try to pick up what the speaker is *really* saying. This requires sensitivity to nonverbal clues such as gestures, nervousness, facial expressions, and eye contact between speaker and audience. In addition, the time advantage gives you the opportunity to evaluate the content of the presentation as it is being made. You can also engage in periodic self-reviews of what has been said, and even speculate on the direction in which the presentation is headed.

## ☐ SUMMARY

Even the best research effort is of little value unless the results are summarized and communicated to marketing management in a form that is both understandable and useful. This chapter examines two vital ingredients of this communication process: (1) the written research report, and (2) the oral presentation that often accompanies the reporting of research findings.

Depending on the intended audience, a research report may be either technical or popular in orientation. The technical report is generally intended for other researchers, or for research managers, and will describe the study in considerable detail. This type of report will contain research terminology as necessary, and should enable another researcher to critique your methodology, check your calculations and accuracy, and to follow everything you've done on a step-by-step basis.

The popular report is intended for a more general audience, one that isn't conversant (or interested) in the details of research methods and terms. The writing style and level of complexity will be comparable to articles found in the business section of major newspapers or in periodicals such as *Business Week*. Compared to the technical report, the presentation will be more lively, with increased attention to headlines, flow diagrams, charts, tables, and occasional summaries for the purpose of stressing major points.

Because different audiences may be interested in the results of the same marketing research study, it is sometimes necessary to write both a technical report and a popular report. Trying to write a single report that serves both purposes is a difficult task, and such an effort could end up satisfying neither audience.

In writing the research report, it's important to organize your thoughts and materials into a structured format that provides an attractive "package" for your efforts. While no single format can satisfy the requirements of all reports, the following tend to be useful in a majority of research reports: transmittal, title page, executive summary, table of contents, introduction, methodology, findings, limitations, conclusions and recommendations, appendices, and bibliography.

While writing style and ability are largely individual matters, there are several general guidelines that should prove helpful: (1) Outline each section of the report before you actually begin writing. (2) When writing a formal report, avoid personal pronouns ("I," "me," "we," and "you"). (3) Because words vary significantly in their emotional loading, be careful to select the words that best convey your meaning. A thesaurus is invaluable for this purpose. (4) Try to avoid unnecessary use of jargon, but remember that some readers are just not impressed unless you sometimes give them just a bit more than they understand. (5) Use the Fog Index to measure the readability of your material.

To keep the reader interested and help ensure his or her understanding of the points you're trying to make, use tables, graphs, charts, and flow diagrams liberally throughout the report. Such visual reinforcement is especially important when making oral presentations. In using statistics to support your findings or recommendations, try to avoid statistical terms with which your audience may not be familiar. If the terms can't be totally avoided, provide a clear explanation of what they mean.

In any research situation, there will be personalities, egos, and possible political considerations with which to contend. As a researcher, you should not only be sensitive to the audience when you deliver the report, but also when you're in the process of conducting the research itself. While you need not arrive at conclusions that others would like to see, it helps to be aware of the potential difficulties when actual findings aren't the same as some may have wanted.

When on the receiving end of an oral or written research report, listen or read between the lines and subject the report to the same requirements you would follow if you were writing or presenting it yourself. In addition to considering what's being said, speculate on what is *not* being said, and on possible reasons why. Oral presentations offer the special advantage of providing nonverbal cues that may warn of possible weaknesses or deceptions in one or more phases of the study.

## ☐ QUESTIONS FOR REVIEW

1. Differentiate between the technical report and the popular report as applied to marketing research and the reporting of research findings and recommendations. Be sure to include all report dimensions (e.g., length, intended audience, organizational and writing strategies, etc.) that you feel are especially important to each approach.

2. Select an especially technical paragraph from a recent article in the *Journal of Marketing Research*, then rewrite the paragraph in language that might be more suitable for presentation in a popular report.

3. What practical functions are served by the letter of transmittal which accompanies the research report?

4. Re-phrase each of the following titles so that the communication will be on a more professional level.
   a. "A study of what students at Hower University like and don't like about their contact lenses."
   b. "A study to see if residents of Pine Oaks own different kinds of cars than the people who live in Dogwood City."
   c. "Age, income, education level, and some other demographic measurements describing households owning a Kenmore washer and dryer."

5. "In the *Methodology* section of your report, never leave anything open to question. Besides identifying each methodological approach taken, be sure to explain why this method was selected over each of the other alternatives available at the time of the decision." Comment.

6. Since few research studies can realistically claim perfection, a "Limitations" section is sometimes included in the report. What factors should be considered in (a) deciding on the possible inclusion of such a section, and (b) determining how extensively limitations are to be discussed?

7. Calculate the Fog Index of the following passage: "Due to unavoidable difficulties in occupying the preselected location for the disguised, structured observational study, it became advantageous to relocate to a position of greater distance from the checkout counter. This undoubtedly precipitated observational discrepancies and errors due to the impossibility of noting various of the fashion variables displayed by the subjects of the study."

8. Select any paragraph from this chapter, then use a thesaurus to help you rewrite it at the most complex level possible. Might there ever be any benefit from employing such language?

9. The pollster for presidential Candidate A has surveyed 1500 voters and found that 55% favor his candidate. The pollster for Candidate B quickly releases a public announcement that the survey should not be taken seriously because the maximum error with such a sample size is 10 percentage points, or twice the margin of preference supposedly enjoyed by Candidate A. Comment.

10. In presenting research findings to employers, clients and/or the general public, numerical statements are sometimes used which some would consider to be misleading. Provide two different examples, real or hypothetical, of statements which you feel fall into this category.

11. What advice might you provide to a research colleague who is faced with an upcoming meeting in which he or she must make an oral presentation of research findings to executives at the vice-presidential level?

12. What is the "communication concept," and how does it relate to the oral reporting of marketing research findings?

13. What are some of the political factors to be considered in planning, carrying out, and implementing the results of a marketing research study? How might each be approached for maximum success?

14. When reading a research report written by someone else, what strategies can you employ to help protect yourself from accepting findings which are either false or fraudulent?

15. "If, based on your test market, you feel that the company should introduce a new product, be conservative and underestimate by at least 20% the number of units you think are likely to be sold during the first year." Comment.

# 19

# SOCIAL AND ETHICAL ISSUES IN MARKETING RESEARCH

**Polls "Vital to Democracy," But Pollsters Concerned**

Public opinion surveys, a major activity within marketing research, have been described as essential to the American way of life. According to George H. Gallup, Jr., "Constant and accurate measurements of public opinion are vital to our democracy. . . . The modern poll can beam a bright and devastating light on the gap which too often exists between the will of the people and the translation of this will into law by legislation." In addition to noting their positive impact on government, Gallup credits surveys of public opinion with helping to guide companies in the generation and marketing of products that satisfy consumers and lead to "an improved quality of life."[1]

On the other hand, there is an undercurrent of concern about surveys, partially brought about by the manner in which the general public has sometimes been abused by unprofessional individuals and groups. As John P. Rupp, general counsel to the Council of American Survey Research Organizations, puts it, "Surveys that are too long or are conducted at inconvenient hours can stimulate legislative scrutiny. So can fundraising appeals that masquerade as survey research projects and telemarketing efforts involving high-pressure tactics. . . . During the past year alone, approximately 20 states con-

---

[1] "Public-Opinion Polls 'Vital to Democracy,'" *Marketing News*, August 1, 1986, p. 15, published by the American Marketing Association.

# The Marketing Research Process...
# Why It's Important to You

## Why do you ask for my opinion?

As marketing researchers it is our job to ask questions—to find out what *you* think of products, services, political leaders and contemporary issues. Manufacturers of products, providers of services and political figures all succeed only if they please you—the consumer, the public. Since only you know what you want and what you like, your opinion is important to them. They send us, marketing researchers, to obtain the answers to their questions—to get your opinions.

## But why should I answer—what's in it for me?

By answering the questions of marketing researchers, you are making your opinions on products, services, and issues known. This is your "voice"—a communication channel directly from you to those who can make the changes you want. And because these people care about pleasing you, it means they will incorporate your opinions, along with those of many others, into new products, new services, new procedures, all with one goal—to please you so they can keep your business or approval.

## Will someone try to sell me something?

Our interviewers just want your opinion. Their job is to ask questions, only. If a person represents himself or herself as someone taking a survey and then tries to sell you something, he or she is probably not a marketing researcher.

## How can I be sure it's a legitimate marketing research company asking for an interview?

If it is a face-to-face interview, you may ask to see identification. If it's a telephone interview you can ask the name of the interviewer's local company and check the telephone book for that company's listing. Some interviews are conducted by long distance telephone, however, and cannot be checked locally. If you are not convinced that it is a legitimate marketing research interview, you may wish to refuse to answer questions. In fact, you are never obligated to answer questions if it is inconvenient or you prefer not to.

## Why do you ask for my name, address and telephone number?

We need this information so a supervisor could, if necessary, call or write to confirm that the interview was done correctly. Only a small percentage of all interviews are checked like this, but in order to be sure that our information is correct and valid, we must ask for your name and address.

## Why do you ask personal questions about age, family, income or occupation?

Your background, family and education have a lot to do with your choices of products and services. We ask questions about these things to help us determine who is buying or selecting what, and why. Those who value your opinions then know whom to address in their advertising, their political campaigns, etc.

## Who are these interviewers who ask the questions?

They are employees of a marketing research company who have been trained to ask questions. They may also be young mothers, graduate students, retirees, career women—but all are part of the fast-growing marketing research industry.

## Why is it such a fast-growing industry and how big is it?

In today's economic environment, businesses cannot afford to make costly mistakes—to produce a product that will not sell or to change a product in a way that will not please the public. In order to avoid these costly mistakes, they go to marketing research to get answers. There are more than 600 research companies represented by members of the Marketing Research Association. Research companies are found in most large cities and towns and are usually owned by people who have lived in the community for many years. Many belong to the local Chamber of Commerce and are registered with the Better Business Bureau.

## How can I find out about opportunities in the marketing research field?

The Marketing Research Association has a pamphlet, "Employment and Career Opportunities in Marketing Research" which is available by writing to the address shown on the back of this brochure. Also check the yellow pages under "Marketing Research and Analysis" or "Public Opinion Research" for companies in your area. Then call and ask them about employment opportunities.

**Figure 19-1.** As part of the "Your Opinion Counts" program, informational materials like this are employed to help the public better understand the importance of marketing research and public opinion surveys. (*Source:* "Why Do You Ask? Why Should I Answer?" pp. 2–3. Courtesy of the Marketing Research Association, Chicago, Ill.)

sidered legislation that would have banned entirely various forms of unsolicited commercial telephone calls."[2]

In response to such concerns, the American Marketing Association has joined with several other professional organizations in a program called "Your Opinion Counts." According to the AMA, "YOC is an ongoing program to promote the importance and need for marketing research and opinion surveys in American society," and a major goal is to "combat growing consumer refusal rates for surveys."[3] In the process, educational messages like those in the brochure of Figure 19-1 play an important role.

## INTRODUCTION

As we examined the marketing research techniques and strategies of previous chapters, we carefully considered the potential for unethical behavior at every opportunity. If this were an accounting text, you'd already have sufficient training to be a pretty fair embezzler. However, remember the spirit in which this information was provided—that is, to develop your awareness for positive, defensive purposes, not to help you take unfair advantage of those not so familiar with research methods.

In this chapter, we're going to concentrate more specifically on the social and ethical dimensions of the marketing research function. We'll start by taking a look at how the scope of marketing has expanded to include some very professional efforts by those who happen to sell ideas, behavior patterns, and other "unconventional" products. Many of these products have strong social implications by themselves, and the involvement of marketing research in their success or failure is a matter deserving of your most serious consideration.

Next, we'll examine marketing research in the context of an old friend, the *marketing concept*: Is marketing research *really* just a management tool for finding out what the consumer wants? Following this, we'll see how marketing research can play an important (if controversial) role in key social settings, including those dealing with political and legal issues.

Finally, we'll return to a slightly more "micro" level, discussing the responsibilities and obligations generally considered to be "ethical practices" when researcher, client, and respondent join forces in a marketing research effort. Overall, our chapter discussion will be according to the following topics:

I. The widening scope of marketing

II. Research and the marketing concept

---

[2] "Self-Regulated Research: Guidelines May Thwart Future Governmental Action," *Marketing News*, January 2, 1987, p. 1, published by the American Marketing Association.

[3] "YOC to Fete Major Donors: Release Refusal-Rate Study," *Marketing News*, January 17, 1986, p. 4, published by the American Marketing Association.

### EXHIBIT 19-1
### *Research and Creativity*

According to a survey by *Advertising Age*, many creative directors believe marketing research tends to result in reduced diversity in advertising, leading to similar appeals like those of Figure 19-2. When different researchers use the same kinds of techniques in studying consumers, it is not unlikely for them to reach similar conclusions and recommendations. However, the issue is not quite so clear-cut. On the opposite side of the argument, advertising managers, creative people, and even company lawyers are said to share the blame whenever ads exhibit a sameness. According to Joel Peck, research director of Geer, Dubois, "Research is only a guidepost, not a substitute for creativity. Blaming research for mediocre advertising is like blaming reading tests for students' poor reading scores."

(*Source:* Merle Kingman, "Who's to Blame for Sameness in Ads? Not Us: Researchers," *Advertising Age*, February 2, 1981, p. 41. Copyright Crain Communications, Inc. Reprinted with permission.)

**Figure 19-2.**   Does the use of similar marketing research techniques lead to reduced creativity in advertising? While there is disagreement on the issue, similarities as striking as this one are rare. (*Source:* Merle Kingman, "Who's to Blame for Sameness in Ads? Not Us: Researchers," *Advertising Age*, February 2, 1981, p. 41. Copyright Crain Communications, Inc. Reprinted with permission.)

III. Social issues in marketing research

IV. Ethical issues in marketing research

V. Issues of the future

## THE WIDENING SCOPE OF MARKETING

In the hands of a carpenter, a hammer can be a positive force helping to build a school or hospital. When employed by a mugger, it can provide the "muggee" with a real Excedrin headache. Like the hammer, the marketing research function is a tool, one that is useful to any individual or organization desiring information about a market and how best to penetrate it. However, unlike the hammer, the marketing researcher is a human being with a conscience, and this conscience is likely to be severely tested more than ever as marketing is used by an increasingly wide variety of groups with an equally wide variety of objectives.

### Social Marketing

The object of our concern in this section is the activity that has been described as *social marketing*. It has been defined by Kotler and Zaltman as "the design, implementation, and control of programs calculated to influence the acceptability of social ideas and involving considerations of product planning, pricing, communications, distribution, and marketing research."[4] In other words, the marketing techniques are quite familiar, and marketing research plays a key role—however, the "product" is more likely to be an idea or belief instead of a can of taco sauce.

In their respective social marketing efforts, various organizations may attempt to persuade you to (1) quit smoking (see Figure 19-3), (2) stay on your high-blood-pressure medication, (3) join a car pool, (4) be a "Big Brother" to a fatherless child, (5) contribute to a charity or political party, or (6) fasten your seat belt when you drive. As described by Kotler, these groups range "from the Society for the Preservation and Encouragement of Barber Shop Quartet Singing in America to major foundations, colleges, hospitals, museums, charities, social agencies, and churches."[5]

While few would argue strenuously against barber shop quartets, other social products are significantly more controversial. For example, various interests may be simultaneously trying to persuade you to either accept or reject such ideas as (1) abortion, (2) gun control, (3) banning offshore oil drilling, (4)

---

[4] Philip Kotler and Gerald Zaltman, "Social Marketing: An Approach to Planned Social Change," *Journal of Marketing*, July 1971, pp. 3–12, published by the American Marketing Association.

[5] Philip Kotler, "Strategies for Introducing Marketing into Nonprofit Organizations," *Journal of Marketing*, January 1979, pp. 37–44, published by the American Marketing Association.

# SMOKING IS VERY SOPHISTICATED

**Figure 19-3.** Social marketing involves the application of proven marketing and marketing research techniques. However, the product is likely to be an idea, behavior, or political candidate instead of a breakfast cereal. (Courtesy of the American Cancer Society.)

socialized medicine, (5) birth-control clinics for teenagers, or (6) voluntary military service.

## Should the Best Marketer Win?

Ethics is a highly subjective matter, and what constitutes social marketing for one person may be regarded as "antisocial marketing" by another. For example, if you happen to belong to the National Rifle Association, you may regard the efforts of gun-control groups to be counter to the best interests of our society.

Like myself, you are probably not bothered by marketers' attempts to put Cheerios instead of Rice Krispies on your breakfast table, or to attract you to the wheel of a Hertz rental car instead of Avis. After all, isn't this what marketing is all about—good, healthy competition among those vying for our dollars? However, there is also a competition among those contending for our minds and our beliefs, and this is where the dilemma begins.

With many commercial products, the leading brand may not be physically different from its competitors. I once conducted a beer taste test in which only 60% of the participants could differentiate between Heineken and Iron City. Other, more formal studies have also shown that a bottle of beer tends to taste much better when your favorite label is on the bottle (even if your favorite beer isn't inside). According to the authors of one such study, "product distinctions or differences, in the minds of the participants, arose primarily through their receptiveness to the various firms' marketing efforts rather than through perceived physical product differences."[6]

Whether social or commercial, a good product can be the victim of marketing ineptness or inadequate funding. Likewise, marketing skills or resources can help a poor product enjoy more success than it really deserves in the marketplace. As suggested before, it's not a moral catastrophe when a candy bar or soft drink "wins" our dollars because of marketing excellence instead of physical merit. However, what about the *idea* or *belief* (e.g., abortion, gun control) that so often constitutes the social product? Does it deserve to capture our minds because its advocates are heavily funded or highly skilled in the techniques of marketing and marketing research—or should it have to depend on its ideological merits? Think about it.

Marketing scholars are just beginning to consider more seriously the ethical implications of social marketing in the battle for our minds. In their discussion of this subject, Laczniak, Lusch, and Murphy point out that "to pursue the path of increased marketing of social programs and ideas without anticipating possible ethical consequences would seem rather naive. Yet there has been little

---

[6] Ralph I. Allison and Kenneth P. Uhl, "Influence of Beer Brand Identification on Taste Perception," *Journal of Marketing Research*, August 1965, pp. 36–39, published by the American Marketing Association.

*TABLE 19-1.* *In this study of social marketing, respondents expressed varying degrees of concern over its ethical implications. Some felt that it could be a "thought-control" weapon wielded by well-funded or highly skilled marketers of social ideas.*

| Statement | Median responses[a] of: | | | |
|---|---|---|---|---|
| | *Professors of ethics (n = 71)* | *Economic Historians (n = 80)* | *Social Psychologists (n = 70)* | *Marketing Practitioners (n = 88)* |
| "The utilization of marketing techniques with respect to social issues or ideas will help communicate these causes in a more effective manner." | 3.8 | 3.8 | 4.0 | 4.5 |
| "The application of marketing techniques to diffuse social issues and ideas is not a beneficial development." | 3.4 | 3.0 | 2.5 | 2.0 |
| "The application of marketing techniques to diffuse social issues and ideas raises significant ethical questions." | 4.8 | 4.4 | 4.5 | 3.8 |
| "The application of marketing techniques to social issues and ideas is a step toward a society wherein the opinions held by the population can be manipulated." | 4.2 | 4.1 | 4.0 | 3.7 |
| "Marketers who assist others in diffusing social issues or ideas should be held strictly accountable for their actions." | 4.7 | 4.5 | 4.6 | 4.2 |
| "A professional certification board which would 'license' marketers (much like the American Bar Association certifies attorneys) should be formulated to control marketers working to diffuse social issues or ideas." | 2.9 | 1.6 | 3.3 | 2.0 |
| "Marketers working to diffuse social issues or ideas should be regulated by a new government review board." | 2.5 | 1.4 | 2.5 | 1.3 |

| | Median responses[a] of: | | | |
|---|---|---|---|---|
| **Statement** | *Professors of ethics (n = 71)* | *Economic Historians (n = 80)* | *Social Psychologists (n = 70)* | *Marketing Practitioners (n = 88)* |
| "When judging the application of marketing techniques to social programs or ideas in terms of their ethical appropriateness, one cannot separate the techniques from the ideas themselves." | 4.1 | 3.4 | 3.8 | 2.3 |

[a] Scores reported are median responses on the scale 1, strongly disagree; 2, moderately disagree; 3, neither agree nor disagree; 4, moderately agree; 5, strongly agree.

*Source:* Adapted from Gene R. Laczniak, Robert F. Lusch, and Patrick E. Murphy, "Social Marketing: Its Ethical Dimensions," *Journal of Marketing,* Spring 1979, pp. 29–36, published by the American Marketing Association.

discussion of the ethical dimensions of social marketing in the literature to date."[7]

In an effort to examine the possible social and ethical implications of social marketing, the authors sampled the expertise of four diverse groups: (1) professors of ethics, (2) economic historians, (3) social psychologists, and (4) marketing practitioners. As shown in Table 19-1, the groups tended to respond quite differently to each of the eight statements about social marketing, with the marketing practitioners generally having a more favorable viewpoint. Some of the survey participants were highly concerned about the implications of social marketing, and expressed their concern with grim warnings like these:

> Although ideas may be communicated more effectively with social marketing, those who have the dollars and power to use marketing techniques may communicate nonsocially-beneficial ideas.[8]
>
> Social marketing could ultimately operate as a form of thought control by the economically powerful.[9]

As you've gathered by now, I view the involvement of marketing research in social marketing as a highly significant social and ethical issue for the mar-

---

[7] Gene R. Laczniak, Robert F. Lusch, and Patrick E. Murphy, "Social Marketing: Its Ethical Dimensions," *Journal of Marketing,* Spring 1979, pp. 29–36, published by the American Marketing Association.

[8] Ibid., p. 31.

[9] Ibid., p. 32.

keting researcher. After we have explored some specific examples of such involvement in later sections of the chapter, I think that you will share this concern. There may be no easy answers to the social and ethical questions raised by the use of proven marketing and marketing research techniques in the battle for people's minds.

## RESEARCH AND THE MARKETING CONCEPT

At this stage of your marketing education, you have probably had numerous encounters with a philosophy called the *marketing concept*. Basically, this concept says, "Give the consumer what he or she wants." It implies that the consumer is the king or queen, and that the role of marketing research is to find out his or her wants so that we can come up with a set of marketing inputs that will satisfy them. This relationship is illustrated in Figure 19-4.

### Is the World Really This Simple?

Some highly regarded observers have pointed out that the marketing concept may be obsolete, that it is not as relevant as it was in the more simple and plentiful times of the 1950s. For example, Frederick Webster has suggested a "revised" marketing concept, "one which places public welfare ahead of consumer welfare as the ultimate criterion for socially responsible decision making in marketing."[10] In these days of resource depletion, technical complexity, environmental concern, and general societal needs, it might indeed make sense to place society first, and the individual consumer second in priority. However, the mechanisms to bring this about are not exactly in place and ready to operate—the result is more than a little uncertainty on the part of marketers and consumers alike. The individual consumer and the marketing concept are not easily abandoned—when was the last time you saw *society* reach into its pocket and buy a candy bar?

To further illustrate the dilemma, both consumers and manufacturers tend to prefer the convenience of throwaway beverage containers. Yet, such metal and plastic containers seem to be strewn throughout our landscape and along our highways. How can we solve this and similar problems? Webster has suggested that, without willingness on the part of both consumer and manufacturer, *legislation* may be necessary to help ensure the long-run quality of life, including a clean environment.[11] This is especially relevant to our later discussion of marketing research and social issues, since marketing research can play a key role in helping to formulate and evaluate the effectiveness of such legislation.

---

[10] Frederick E. Webster, Jr., *Social Aspects of Marketing* (Englewood Cliffs, N.J.: Prentice-Hall, Inc. 1974), p. 110.

[11] Ibid., p. 71.

**Figure 19-4.** According to the *marketing concept*, the consumer is king or queen, and marketing research is only a passive tool for finding out what products he or she wants. Is the world really this simple? Not quite.

### Is Marketing Research Just a Passive Tool?

In the diagram of Figure 19-4, marketing research was depicted as merely a passive measurement device to help us find out what the consumer wants. Is it possible that marketing research might also be used to identify the most promising strategies for persuading the consumer to desire what we'd *like* for him or her to want? The answer to this question is *yes*, and we'll examine this application of marketing research in the very next section. For now, it's sufficient that you just view both marketing research and the marketing concept in a slightly different light.

## SOCIAL ISSUES IN MARKETING RESEARCH

As suggested previously, marketing research can have significant impact on society in ways other than the simple measurement of what the consumer wants. Since this topic could easily become a book in itself, we'll limit our discussion to two especially relevant issues: marketing research in the political and legal arenas.

### Marketing Research in the World of Politics

Anyone who has ever observed a politician in action has seen a perfect example of applied marketing. According to Kotler, "Political campaigns have increasingly been compared to marketing campaigns in which the candidate puts himself in the voter market and uses modern marketing techniques, particularly marketing research and commercial advertising, to maximize voter 'purchases.' Candidates seeking to win elections cannot avoid marketing themselves. The only question is how to do it effectively."[12]

In every presidential election of recent years, each candidate has had a well-oiled campaign organization in which marketing research plays a key role. Voter attitudes and preferences are constantly monitored, and wise candidates are careful to check with their marketing advisors before making public announcements that might adversely affect their "positioning" in the voter's mind.[13]

The political candidate is but one example of those who engage in what Kotler refers to as "person marketing." Others include actors, singers, models, sports figures and entertainers of all sorts. However, unlike the political candidate, sports figures and entertainers are generally not entrusted with running the country. Therein lies the "social issue" dimension of marketing research as it relates to politics.

### *Marketing Research Helps Dump an Antidumping Proposition*

As a more specific example of the power that marketing research techniques can exert in a political situation, consider the case of the Los Angeles suburb of West Covina. Voters had been asked to approve a proposition that would ban the dumping of toxic wastes. Prior to the actual voting, business interests hired a political consulting firm, which proceeded to use demographic and attitude information to segment the voters. Each segment then received an appeal that was designed just for them. For example, conservatives received a

---

[12] Philip Kotler, *Marketing for Nonprofit Organizations* (Englewood Cliffs, N.J.: Prentice-Hall, Inc., 1975), p. 366.

[13] For an excellent, more detailed discussion of the political benefits of marketing research, see "Reagan's $2 Million Marketing Research Budget Paid Off," *Marketing News*, March 5, 1982, p. 12, published by the American Marketing Association.

mailing indicating that Jane Fonda and activist husband Tom Hayden supported the proposal. In the end, the measure failed to pass, this despite an initial survey showing that 60% of all registered voters favored the ban, with only 24% opposed, and the rest undecided.[14]

## Marketing Research in the Legal Environment

The use of marketing research techniques in the legal arena has grown by leaps and bounds in recent years. In this section, we will discuss the role of marketing research in (1) the regulatory process, (2) legislation, and (3) judicial proceedings.

### The Regulatory Process

Government agencies, in their efforts to formulate, monitor, and enforce regulations, often rely on information provided by marketing research. For example, the Federal Trade Commission, in deciding whether an advertisement is deceptive, is likely to employ attitude research to find out what meaning the ad has conveyed to the viewer or listener. Likewise, if a corrective advertising program is required, the same techniques can be used to determine at what point the program has succeeded in cancelling the initial, deceptive message.[15]

The same techniques can also be used by companies on the other side of an FTC inquiry. After it had been alleged that the "Safety Champion" brand name was misleading, the Firestone Tire and Rubber Company conducted a consumer survey to refute the allegation of deception. In the survey, only 1.4% of the participants identified the tire named "Safety Champion" as having unique characteristics that made it safer than other tires.[16]

Sometimes the research is conducted by neither regulatory agency nor manufacturer, but by an interest group. In 1981, the National Highway Traffic Safety Administration considered lowering the 5-mph bumper protection standard required for new cars. On the eve of the NHTSA hearing on the possible change, the Insurance Institute for Highway Safety released the results of a research study they had commissioned. Based on a survey of 1013 owners of 1979–1982 cars (the models having 5-mph bumper protection), the IIHS reported that 83% were satisfied with current bumper protection, 70% were aware that their bumpers offered protection at 5 mph, and 92% felt that it was a good feature.[17]

---

[14] See Robert J. Wagman, "New Tools of Political Trade," *The Wagman File*, Newspaper Enterprise Association; in *The Indiana Gazette*, December 11, 1981, p. 2.

[15] "FTC Now Conducts Attitude Research before Entering Costly Legal Battles," *Marketing News*, May 16, 1980, p. 1, published by the American Marketing Association.

[16] Dorothy Cohen, "The FTC's Advertising Substantiation Program," *Journal of Marketing*, Winter 1980, pp. 26–35, published by the American Marketing Association.

[17] "Survey on 5-mph Bumpers Reports Owner Satisfaction," *Automotive News*, November 30, 1981, p. 52.

### Legislation

By measuring and reporting public sentiment, marketing research plays an important role in the legislative process at all levels of government. (Ironically, it was probably such public sentiment that prompted consideration of the West Covina proposition to ban the dumping of toxic wastes, discussed earlier.) State and national legislators routinely survey their constituents to find out how they feel about key issues, including present and pending legislation. Others, including companies, business associations, and special-interest groups, also conduct such surveys.

Using the results from 2300 personal interviews, Warner Communications determined that nearly $3 billion worth of prerecorded music and other audio entertainment was being taped at home each year. According to Warner, such taping harms members of the recording industry: "Clearly these infringements of copyrights deprive artists, musicians, publishers, songwriters, producers, and recording companies of fair and reasonable royalties."[18] Warner, in announcing the results of its survey, said that it had joined a coalition of recording interests in support of then-pending bills in both houses of Congress that would levy royalty fees on blank recording tapes and other home audio equipment.

As you might expect, when different organizations or groups conduct legislation-related research, they often come up with conflicting results. In 1972, Oregon enacted a bill requiring a refundable deposit for all beverages sold in bottles or cans. Subsequently, a number of studies were carried out to measure the impact of what was known as the "Oregon Bottle Bill." A review of the results of these studies reported that:[19]

> A study by a major container manufacturer found that returnable bottles produced 4.5 times as much energy waste as nonreturnable bottles. A study by two Oregon State professors revealed the opposite: that nonreturnable bottles would waste 3.9 times as much energy as the returnable type.
>
> A study by an environmentalist group found that beverage-related litter was reduced by 88% in the year following enactment of the bill. A firm hired by the state found that litter was reduced by just 66%.
>
> The study by the professors revealed that the bill increased employment by 365 workers, while the state-hired firm found that the bill decreased employment by about 170 people.

### Judicial Proceedings

In recent years, courts at both state and federal levels have increasingly tended to admit consumer surveys as courtroom evidence.[20] The problem of

---

[18] "Home Taping Hurts Music Industry," *The Indiana Gazette*, March 27, 1982, p. 7.

[19] Michael D. Geurts and Gloria E. Wheeler, "Converging Conflicting Research Findings: The Oregon Bottle Bill Case," *Journal of Marketing Research*, November 1980, pp. 552–57, published by the American Marketing Association.

[20] Fred W. Morgan, "The Admissibility of Consumer Surveys as Legal Evidence in Courts," *Journal of Marketing*, Fall 1979, pp. 33–40, published by the American Marketing Association.

**TABLE 19-2.** *Marketing research is increasingly finding its way into the courtroom. When developing and presenting survey results for one of the parties in a judicial proceeding, these guidelines should prove useful.*

1. Be convinced and prepared to argue that the survey relates strongly to the issue in question and is superior to alternative forms of evidence.
2. Remember that interested persons (judge and jury) with little background in survey research methods will be trying to understand the results.
3. Eliminate methodological flaws which could appear to affect results.
4. If possible, utilize surveys conducted prior to litigation.
5. Be prepared for an all-out adversary evaluation of the survey.
6. Be prepared to offer a concise interpretation of the survey findings.

*Source:* Fred W. Morgan, "The Admissibility of Consumer Surveys as Legal Evidence in Courts," *Journal of Marketing*, Fall 1979, p. 35, published by the American Marketing Association.

trademark infringement has been especially amenable to survey inputs. In deciding whether one brand has infringed on the trademark of another, it can be valuable for courts to learn how the typical consumer perceives each of the brands involved—for example, to what extent does the consumer believe that both were produced by the same company?[21]

In any judicial dispute, there will be two sides to the issue involved, and either party (or both) may commission a marketing research study to support its case. For example, suppose that an applicant for a bicycle dealer franchise were to be turned down because her location is said to be too close to one of the company's existing franchises. The unhappy applicant may conduct a study of consumer shopping patterns in the geographic area involved. Naturally, she would hope to find that her proposed franchise isn't likely to attract a significant number of consumers from the market served by the existing dealer.

Because of the relative newness of marketing research in the courtroom, the researcher is likely to find himself in an unfamiliar and potentially uncomfortable setting. Attorneys, expert witnesses, and possible research results from the other litigating party will subject his or her findings and methodology to the most severe scrutiny. Should you find yourself in a situation where you have been asked to provide survey research support and testimony for one of the parties in a legal dispute, the guidelines shown in Table 19-2 should prove helpful.

## ETHICAL ISSUES IN MARKETING RESEARCH

Accompanying the growing concern with marketing research in the political and legal settings, there remains the more traditional issue of ethics within the research process itself. In examining this topic, a Washington, D.C., research firm

---

[21] George Miaoulis and Nancy D'Amato, "Consumer Confusion and Trademark Infringement," *Journal of Marketing*, April 1978, pp. 48–55, published by the American Marketing Association.

asked over 500 marketing researchers how they, their companies, and competing companies might respond when faced with a variety of settings involving research ethics. Their findings, which may be a little shocking, are summarized in Figure 19-5.

## A Code of Ethics

In order to establish guidelines as to what constitutes ethical behavior in their fields, many professional organizations have drawn up codes of ethics for their practicing members. The Marketing Research Association, Inc. is no exception, and has developed such a code for those engaged in marketing research ac-

| Research Strategies | % Affirmative Responses* | | |
|---|---|---|---|
| | A | B | C |
| 1. Researcher poses as graduate student working on a thesis. Researcher tells source that dorm phones are very busy, so researcher will call back rather than have phone calls returned. This way, researcher's real identity is protected. | 39.6 | 42.6 | 75.6 |
| 2. Researcher calls the vice president while he is at lunch, hoping to find the secretary who may have some information but is less likely to be suspicious about researcher's motives. | 60.6 | 68.7 | 81.7 |
| 3. Researcher calls competitor's suppliers and distributors, pretending to do a study of the entire industry. Researcher poses as a representative of a private research firm and works at home during the project so that the company's identity is protected. | 46.1 | 54.6 | 81.0 |
| 4. The competitor's representative is coming to a local college to recruit employees. Researcher poses as a student job-seeker to learn recruiting practices and other general information about competitor. | 30.1 | 35.4 | 62.0 |
| 5. The researcher is asked to verify rumors that the competitor is planning to open a new plant in a small southern town. The researcher poses as an agent from a manufacturer looking for a site similar to the one that the competitor supposedly would need. Researcher uses this cover to become friendly with local representatives of the Chamber of Commerce, newspapers, realtors, etc. | 42.4 | 49.1 | 75.5 |
| 6. Researcher corners a competitor employee at a national conference, such as (one held by the) American Marketing Association, and offers to buy drinks at the hotel bar. Several drinks later, the researcher asks the hard questions. | 70.6 | 67.1 | 86.8 |
| 7. Researcher finds an individual who works for the competitor to serve as an informant to researcher's company. | 39.1 | 39.1 | 73.8 |

*KEY  A=Researcher's own company would use this technique.
B=Researcher would use this technique.
C=Researcher believes other companies use this technique.

**Figure 19-5.** When asked how they would react in a variety of hypothetical situations, researchers in this study tended to attribute less ethical behavior to their competitors than to themselves. (*Source:* Bernie Whalen, "Report Rise in Use of 'J.R.' Research Tactics," *Marketing News,* May 25, 1984, sec. 1, p. 31, published by the American Marketing Association.)

---

*EXHIBIT 19-2*

*The Code of Professional Ethics
and Practices of the
MARKETING RESEARCH ASSOCIATION, INC.
is subscribed to as follows:*

1. To maintain high standards of competence and integrity in marketing and survey research.

2. To exercise all reasonable care and to observe the best standards of objectivity and accuracy in the development, collection, processing and reporting of marketing and survey research information.

3. To protect the anonymity of respondents and hold all information concerning an individual respondent privileged, such that this information is used only within the context of the particular study.

4. To thoroughly instruct and supervise all persons for whose work I am responsible in accordance with study specifications and general research techniques.

5. To observe the rights of ownership of all materials received from and/or developed for clients, and to keep in confidence all research techniques, data and other information considered confidential by their owners.

6. To make available to clients such details on the research methods and techniques of an assignment as may be reasonably required for proper interpretation of the data, providing this reporting does not violate the confidence of respondents or clients.

7. To promote the trust of the public for marketing and survey research activities and to avoid any procedure which misrepresents the activities of a respondent, the rewards of cooperation or the uses of the data.

8. To refrain from referring to membership in this organization as proof of competence, since the organization does not so certify any person or organization.

9. To encourage the observance of the principles of this code among all people engaged in marketing and survey research.

(*Source:* Reprinted courtesy of the Marketing Research Association, Inc., Chicago, IL.)

---

tivities. This has been reprinted in Exhibit 19-2 and deserves your serious attention.

Naturally, neither this nor any other code can include all possible ethical dilemmas that may arise. Some settings may come up that are relatively unique. For example, the following problematic circumstances are among those listed by one observer of the ethics-in-research issue.[22]

---

[22] Richard Crosby, "Uniform Ethical Code Is Impractical Due to Shifting Marketing Research Circumstances," *Marketing News*, September 18, 1981, p. 16, published by the American Marketing Association. Crosby presents an excellent discussion of these and other situations in examining the difficulties of a uniform ethical code for all research activities.

1. Should we use questions developed for one client in putting together a questionnaire to be used for another client?
2. Without getting the permission of one client, should we insert a simple question for another client in the first client's questionnaire?
3. Should we price identical studies differently for different clients?
4. Should we accept a research assignment even if we know that it can't be finished on time?

When you find yourself in a situation that appears to be ethically compromising, try to view it from the point of view of the other party involved: How would you feel if you were in *their* shoes? As a practical matter, if you have a lot of trouble deciding whether a particular course of action is ethical, chances are it's not.

### The Research Triad

As shown in Figure 19-6, there are three parties directly involved in the marketing research process: (1) the manager or client, (2) the researcher, and (3) the subject or respondent. Most responsibilities for ethical behavior fall upon the user and the researcher, since the primary duty of the respondent is simply to be honest in his or her behaviors and responses. We can't expect too much on the part of participants—after all, getting involved in a research study probably wasn't their idea in the first place. Figure 19-6 also shows two other parties: competitors and society at large. While they are not directly involved, their interests are often affected by marketing research activities and findings.

#### *Responsibilities of the Manager or Client*

The manager or client should be honest with both the researcher and those to whom the research findings are to be disseminated. For the latter group, such honesty is especially important when research is done for the purpose of promoting a product or supporting a legal or political viewpoint. For example, suppose that an objective researcher has conducted a product comparison test in which 97% of the respondents had no preference, 2% favored brand A, and 1% favored brand B. Based on such results, it would be a bit unethical for the marketer of brand A to claim that "of those expressing a preference, our brand was favored by a 2-to-1 margin."

The responsible manager or client will not encourage a researcher to be anything but objective in his or her search for factual results. Being realistic, you should realize that managers or clients will often have a strong vested interest in the eventual findings of your study. Nevertheless, any overt attempts to nudge you from the straight and narrow path of objectivity must be strongly resisted.

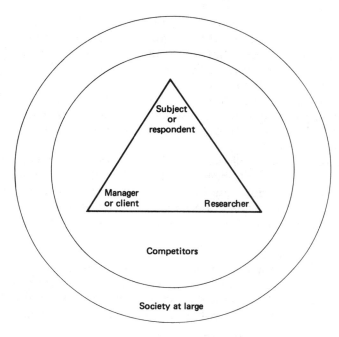

**Figure 19-6.** This research "triad" shows the three parties directly involved in marketing research. While competitors and society at large may not be directly involved in research, their interests are often affected by marketing research and its findings.

### Responsibilities of the Researcher

The researcher's responsibilities tend to be more comprehensive than those of the manager or client. This is to be expected, since he or she must deal with both of the other members of the triad, the manager or client with just one.

***Responsibilities to the manager or client.*** As a researcher, your primary responsibilities here are honesty, integrity, and confidentiality. For example, if you know that the desired work can be accomplished with less money than the client has to spend, it's not ethical to inflate your proposal to better match the funds available—and besides, such integrity will help in avoiding problems if cost overruns are incurred during a future project.

***Responsibilities to yourself and your profession.*** Conflicts might arise between your short-term and long-term career success. By prostituting your research skills to arrive at predetermined "results," it's possible that you might be well rewarded in the short run. However, the tainted reputation you develop as a researcher will result in reduced credibility and diminished success over the long haul.

***Responsibilities to the subject or respondent.*** If the Humane Society specialized in people instead of animals, the research subject or respondent might well be the object of their enthusiastic efforts. When we collect telephone survey data from a respondent, we obviously benefit by obtaining valuable information.

However, what immediate benefits does the respondent get after being yanked from the bathtub or dinner table, or from his or her favorite television program? Some may argue that the respondent feels a little more important because someone is interested in what he does or thinks. Others could claim that, without survey techniques, his favorite television show might not even be on the air—how would we or the sponsors know that it *is* the favorite? While these arguments have merit, the fact remains that survey respondents are often abused, with too many researchers feeling that a mere "Thank you" is sufficient reward for a half hour of an individual's time.

Perhaps the most blatant abuse of respondents is the despicable practice of using the "We're doing a survey" line to begin a sales pitch to the consumer. While someone may indeed have a slight amount of interest in the "data" obtained, the primary goal is sales by means of deception. Encyclopedias, home improvements, magazines, and other products have often been involved in such schemes.

Potential respondents may have had previous experiences with such impostors, making it difficult for established, professional research firms to gain access for legitimate research purposes. These suspicions are sometimes reduced by "paving the way" with public announcements such as that shown in Figure 19-7. In this way, the potential respondent will know that he or she is really

---

TRENDEX HOLDS AREA PHONE INTERVIEWS

Some 150 Indiana area residents are scheduled to be interviewed by telephone soon through a quarterly buyership survey conducted by the Trendex Market Research Co. The survey is one phase of a number of similar surveys taken at various locations throughout the United States.

Trendex, Inc. has been in the survey business for over 25 years and is one of the top market research companies in the country and is a member of the American Marketing Association and the American Association of Public Opinion Research. The studies are of a consumer or market research nature and there is absolutely no selling involved.

The company's national buyership study is conducted four times each year. It is the second largest survey conducted in the United States—the largest being the United States Census. The survey is conducted entirely by telephone and the numbers are selected at random.

The purpose of the survey is to determine the number of various products acquired within a specific time period and to gather information regarding the circumstances of the acquisition and use of products in the home.

All interviewing is conducted according to standards set by Trendex, Inc. and all information gathered is strictly confidential.

---

**Figure 19-7.**  Newspaper announcements like this one can help smooth the way for legitimate survey research. Respondents are assured that the true purpose is really an interview, not a sales pitch for aluminum siding, magazine subscriptions, or a rebuilt furnace. (*Source: The Indiana Evening Gazette,* April 3, 1982, p. 17.)

---

### EXHIBIT 19-3

### Relentless Robot Rousts Resting Respondents

One of the newer and more controversial technologies of marketing is the availability of automated dialing that can enable researchers to record brief question responses or salespersons to deliver a prerecorded sales message. In one instance, a health club used a programmed "phone robot" to call prospective members automatically and deliver a sales pitch. Unfortunately, a human supervisor forgot to turn the machine off at the assigned time, 8 P.M. As a result, both the health club and many local residents received a rude awakening. True to its advertised virtues as "a business associate that doesn't take breaks, follows instructions, and won't quit," the persistent device conscientiously continued its efforts until 8 A.M. the next morning. The telemarketing firm from whom the machine had been contracted spent nearly an entire day calling and apologizing to the individuals contacted.

(*Source:* "Phone Robot Angers Prospects," *Marketing News,* November 25, 1983, sec. 1, p. 4, published by the American Marketing Association.)

---

taking part in a research project instead of being asked to buy aluminum siding, magazine subscriptions, or a rebuilt furnace.

As a consumer self-defense note, consider these two strategies the next time *you* get hit with a "pseudo-survey": (1) Provide a few choice words and hang up or close the door as soon as you realize that a sales pitch is on the way, or (2) if you've *really* been inconvenienced, or you're just in a mischievous mood, provide just enough encouragement to allow the pitch to continue to the point where the sale is about to be "closed," then express some second thoughts and turn it down. If you enjoy observing human behavior, you owe it to yourself to try this at least once. Aside from letting the Doberman loose, the worst thing you can do to these impostors is to waste *their* time by being an impostor yourself.

Another key issue regarding the respondent is that research studies can be considered an invasion of his or her privacy. The 1974 Privacy Act applies to government agencies and their research suppliers, and provides for the protection of this privacy.[23] The act stresses that respondents have:

**The right to choose.** This includes the right to be informed that they do not have to participate in a study. Believe it or not, some respondents are apt to think that they are required to answer survey questions, especially if the study is government-sponsored. However, such mandatory participation is only required in the national census conducted every ten years.

---

[23] See Cynthia J. Frey and Thomas Kinnear, "Legal Constraints and Marketing Research: Review and Call to Action," *Journal of Marketing Research,* August 1979, pp. 295–302, for an excellent discussion of the Privacy Act and other legal constraints that have implications for the marketing research profession.

*The right to safety.*   This includes the respondent's anonymity as well as freedom from physical or psychological harm. (Imagine, for example, the possibility that a hypochondriac might suddenly "notice" an entirely new set of symptoms after taking part in a survey measuring his awareness of early-warning signals for various ailments.)

*The right to be informed.*   This includes knowing who is sponsoring the study, why it is being undertaken, and how he or she might be affected by the results. Individuals must also be told of their right to examine and correct the information they have provided.

As you can imagine, such disclosure requirements can make it very difficult, if not impossible, to conduct some types of valuable research. For example, observational studies, projective techniques, experiments, and other approaches often depend on less-than-full disclosure in order to achieve their effectiveness. Abuses by survey impostors and unethical researchers, along with the normal (but minimal) inconvenience which accompanies legitimate research, may combine to make the ethical researcher's job a great deal more difficult in the future.

*Responsibilities to competitors.*   While an "all's fair in love, war, and business" philosophy may seem appropriate in research activities involving competitors, there are some practices that clearly go beyond ethical limits. For example, one might engage a competitor's janitor to pilfer correspondence and product information from the nightly trash collection. In general, such tools of espionage are not considered to be within the bounds of ethical behavior.

*Responsibilities to society at large.*   Issues involving responsibilities toward the general public are woven throughout much of the previous discussion of

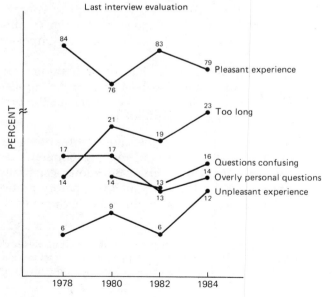

**Figure 19-8.**   While most respondents find their interview experience to be "pleasant," this series of studies found adverse trends to exist regarding personal questions and interview duration. (*Source:* "Survey Participation Is Leaving a Sour Taste with Respondents, According to Image Study," *Marketing News,* February 15, 1985, p. 1, published by the American Marketing Association.)

this chapter. One of the primary ways in which we can satisfy our obligations to society is to appreciate that members of the public are the "raw materials" on which present and future research depends. Without their good will and cooperation, our task would be considerably more difficult. As shown in Figure 19-8, most interview respondents find their involvement to be a pleasant experience. However, as suggested by the adverse trends for "too long" and "unpleasant experience," problems still exist that are deserving of our professional attention.

As researchers, we can probably best serve the public by being honest and objective in the research we conduct, and by helping to ensure the same objectivity when results are disseminated to members of society. As suggested during our discussions involving social marketing and marketing research in the political and legal settings, marketing research is a powerful tool that can easily be turned into a weapon.

## ISSUES OF THE FUTURE

If the social and ethical dimensions of marketing research seem a bit murky now, consider that these issues are likely to become even more difficult in the years ahead. Many of the issues we've discussed are practically in their infancy.

From the social perspective, social marketers are likely to continue their increasing trend toward using marketing and marketing research techniques to sell their ideas, behaviors, and political candidates. Marketing research will probably be highly influential in encouraging people to do such positive things as donating blood, better attending to their personal health, buckling up their seat belts, and getting out to vote. It will also be influential in helping them decide *for whom to vote*, and some observers of society will abhor such research involvements as representing thought control.

From a legal standpoint, governmental concern with respondent rights and privacy will increasingly affect marketing research activities. This applies especially to types of research that utilize the telephone or mail media, or that rely on the respondent's having less than full information about the purposes of the study. We can also expect increased use of marketing research in the formulation and enforcement of governmental agency regulations, in legislation at all levels of government, and by litigants involved in judicial proceedings.

As has been discussed in much of the text, marketing research techniques can be either professionally used or unethically abused. The advent of new technologies, such as electronic databases, computerized interviewing, voice stress and brain wave analysis, and automated dialing may further complicate the already delicate interface between marketing research and our society. There are probably only two things concerning marketing research about which we can be certain: (1) it is a constantly developing behavioral science that is rapidly evolving newer and better techniques for a broader range of applications, and (2) these changes, along with their social and ethical implications, will increasingly be the subject of scrutiny by government and social observers alike.

☐ **SUMMARY**

The scope of marketing has expanded to include some very professional efforts by those who happen to sell ideas, behavior patterns, and other "unconventional" products. Many of these products have strong social implications by themselves, and the involvement of marketing research in their success or failure is a matter deserving of serious consideration.

Social marketing, the marketing of ideas, has been applied to car-pooling, charitable contributions, and seat-belt usage as well as to antismoking and political campaigns. While some objects of social marketing are unarguably beneficial to society, others are the subject of controversy. What constitutes social marketing for one person may be regarded as distinctly "antisocial" by another.

Whether social or commercial, a good product can be the victim of marketing ineptness or inadequate funding. Likewise, marketing skill or resources can help a poor product enjoy more success than it really deserves in the marketplace. The key question: Does an idea or belief deserve to capture our minds because its advocates are heavily funded or highly skilled in the techniques of marketing and marketing research—or should it have to depend on its ideological merits? Some feel that social marketing might eventually function as a form of "thought control" practiced by those of economic means. The marketing concept implies that the consumer is king or queen, and that the role of marketing research is to find out his or her wants so that we can come up with a set of marketing inputs that will satisfy them. In the chapter, it is argued that the world really isn't this simple, and that marketing research is more than just a passive tool for information collection.

Marketing research can have significant impact on society in ways other than the simple measurement of what the consumer wants. In recent years, every major presidential candidate has had a well-oiled campaign organization in which marketing research plays a key role. Voter attitudes and preference are constantly monitored, and wise candidates are careful to check with their marketing advisors before making public statements that might adversely affect their "positioning" in the voter's mind. Marketing research is also increasingly applied during the legislative process, in formulating and evaluating legislation, and in judicial proceedings.

Accompanying the growing concern with marketing research in the political and legal settings, there remains the more traditional issue of ethics within the research process itself. In order to establish guidelines as to what constitutes ethical behavior, associations within the profession have developed codes of ethics for those engaged in marketing research activities. However, since some settings are always unique, it is difficult to construct (let alone have all practitioners obey) a universal code of research ethics.

Most responsibilities for ethical behavior fall upon the researcher and the research user, since the primary duty of the respondent is simply to be honest in his or her behaviors or responses. Competitors and society at large are also indirectly involved, because their interests can be affected by marketing research activities and findings.

In the future, social marketers are likely to continue their increasing trend toward using marketing and marketing research techniques to sell their ideas, behaviors, and political candidates. The advent of new technologies will also serve to complicate matters. While some new techniques may help compensate for legal constraints on research activities, others may create still further ethical problems. One thing is certain about the social and ethical future of marketing research: Its continuing evolution will increasingly be the subject of scrutiny by government and social observers alike.

## ☐ QUESTIONS FOR REVIEW

1. What is *social marketing* and how is it related to marketing research ethics in today's world?

2. Provide three examples of organizations or interests that some feel are engaged in "antisocial" social marketing—that is, the ideas or beliefs may be viewed by some as detrimental to our societal welfare.

3. Can a marketing researcher using his or her expertise to advance the acceptability of a socially-undesirable behavior be likened to a scientist applying his or her knowledge to invent a more effective nerve gas? If your response is "yes," what do you feel is the answer to this dilemma faced by the conscientious marketing researcher? If your answer is "no," how might the marketing researcher in such a situation answer his or her critics?

4. How would each of these observers tend to view marketing research and the role that it plays in our modern society? Which of these positions, if either, do you feel is the more correct?
   a. "The consumer is king."
   b. "Today's marketing techniques have transformed the consumer into a puppet."

5. Provide a real or hypothetical situation in which a marketing researcher finds himself/herself in a state of conflict between (a) his/her professional, ethical, and personal responsibilities, and (b) his/her role as an employee of a large commercial organization. How do you think the individual *should* resolve the conflict? How do you think the individual *would* end up resolving the conflict?

6. In what ways might marketing research prove to be a useful tool for those aspiring to national political office?

7. How might marketing research prove valuable to both sides of a judicial dispute in which a well-known celebrity is bringing suit against a company for employing someone who he thinks resembles him in one of their ads?

8. How might marketing research be employed by a candy manufacturer who claims that a competitor has infringed on its trademark by introducing a new product that is very likely to be confused with the company's own brand?

9. Drivers for a city transit authority are striking for higher wages. City government claims the increases are unreasonable and beyond what riders can bear. How might

both sides employ marketing research to increase their likelihood of winning the dispute?

10. What are some of the difficulties in (a) drawing up, and (b) having practitioners universally adhere to a marketing research code of ethics?

11. A client wishes to hire your research firm to conduct a study, but has hinted that the likelihood of future contracts between your firms will be greatly enhanced if the desired results are obtained in the proposed investigation. How should you respond?

12. What steps can legitimate marketing researchers take to help minimize the adverse effect which unethical marketers have on the public's receptivity to honest research studies?

13. Provide two examples, real or hypothetical, in which marketing research is used as a weapon rather than as a tool designed to improve a firm's marketing efficiency.

14. Select a newspaper or magazine article in which a "research study" is mentioned. Critique the article in terms of (a) study details and methodology, if provided, and (b) whether the study sponsor had a strong interest in the outcome of the study. Based on your knowledge of marketing research, suggest at least three strategies the sponsor could have used to ensure the desired results.

15. What are the key responsibilities which a marketing researcher has toward:
   a. Client or employer?
   b. Respondents?
   c. The marketing research profession?

# CASES FOR PART FIVE

## CASE 5-1

### Baxter Nail Company

The Baxter Nail Company is examining possible approaches to making sales forecasts with a one-year horizon. Among the alternatives being examined are exponential smoothing and trend extrapolation. Baxter's researchers are evaluating these techniques based on how well they would have forecast the sales levels for years 1981 through 1988. Sales from 1975 through 1988 were as follows:

| Year | Sales (millions of dollars) |
|------|-----------------------------|
| 1975 | 31 |
| 1976 | 23 |
| 1977 | 27 |
| 1978 | 30 |
| 1979 | 35 |
| 1980 | 33 |
| 1981 | 38 |

| Year | Sales (millions of dollars) |
|---|---|
| 1982 | 49 |
| 1983 | 56 |
| 1984 | 67 |
| 1985 | 65 |
| 1986 | 52 |
| 1987 | 55 |
| 1988 | 46 |

1. Beginning with an initial forecast of $31 million sales for 1975, use a smoothing constant of $A = 0.5$ to fit an exponentially smoothed sales curve to the data.
2. Beginning with an initial forecast of $31 million sales for 1975, use a smoothing constant of $A = 0.7$ to fit an exponentially smoothed sales curve to the data.
3. Based on past sales data that would have been available for each forecast, use either regression analysis or a visually fitted trend line to predict sales for years 1981 through 1988 (e.g., sales for 1981 would be predicted on the basis of either regression analysis or visual trend extension using years 1975 through 1980).
4. Compare the accuracy of the sales forecasts for 1981–1988 generated in parts 1, 2, and 3. As a basis for comparison, use the mean absolute deviation between the actual and forecasted sales values. [The mean absolute deviation for each method is just the average "error" (regardless of the direction of the error) for each forecasting approach.]
5. Evaluate the applicability of exponential smoothing and trend extrapolation to the sales data provided. What other approaches might be used either to replace or to supplement those involved here?

## CASE 5-2

### Car Safety Comparisons

In the October 3, 1986 edition of *The Wall Street Journal*, General Motors placed a full-page ad on p. 22, explaining that of the 10 best 1983–1985 passenger cars in terms of overall injury claim experience as determined by the Highway Loss Data Institute, 7 of them were GM models, including the top two. Upon examining the top-10 list, one finds that 9 of the 10 are either station wagons or four-door sedans.

In the August 26, 1985 edition of *Automotive News*, an article on page 56 pointed out that small Japanese-made cars fared relatively poorly in injury and vehicle damage losses for 1982–1984 models sold in the U.S. These data were also prepared by the Highway Loss Data Institute.

Question:

There can be little doubt that when larger cars collide with smaller cars, people in the smaller cars will tend to suffer greater injuries. However, could the findings in the two paragraphs above be due partially to the types of individuals who may tend to buy various types of cars and the manner in which they operate them? Evaluate this possibility, including arguments to support your position.

## CASE 5-3

### Tapetrex International

Tapetrex International, a manufacturer of high-quality audio and video blank tape cassettes for the home consumer market, is concerned about the legal controversy regarding the use of such cassettes to reproduce the copyrighted work of recording artists and movie studios. Tapetrex is especially alarmed at the possibility that they and other companies might have to pay a per-cassette royalty compensation fee that would be divided up among the owners of such copyrights.

The company's position has been that its customers do not build up large tape libraries for selling or swapping, but merely use the tapes in the home in order to expand their range of entertainment choices. In particular, the company claims that televised movies and other special programs are merely recorded for viewing at a more convenient time, then the tape erased as other movies or programs are likewise recorded for viewing at the customer's greater convenience.

To fortify their position that customers are not infringing on copyright restrictions or intentions, Tapetrex has conducted a mail questionnaire survey to determine the product usage patterns of over 3000 consumers of their audio and video tape cassettes. In the cover letter accompanying the questionnaire, the purpose of the study is described and respondents are reminded that unauthorized use or sale of copyrighted materials may be illegal. In addition, the respondent is reminded that future regulations could cause substantial increases in the low prices he now enjoys for the company's fine products.

According to the survey results, 85% of the respondents have never sold or swapped tapes, and 90% of blank videotape buyers say they record movies only for viewing at a more convenient time. Over 98% of the respondents say they would oppose the idea of imposing a royalty compensation fee that would raise the prices of the blank cassettes they buy. In response to a special inquiry on the questionnaire, 93% of the respondents provided their signature and gave permission for their name to be used "when national legislators are contacted with the results of this survey."

1. From an ethical standpoint, is this an appropriate application of marketing research techniques? If you say "no," what about the argument that in-

terests on the other side of the issue have every opportunity to employ marketing research methods to help them sell *their* side of the controversy?

2. From a practical standpoint, how might you have reacted if you were the researcher placed in charge of this attempt to bolster the company's position by means of survey research?

## CASE 5-4

### The $14.80 Questionnaire

The author received an eight-question survey card from a firm with a very official-sounding (as in *government*) name. Along with the brief questionnaire on TV viewing habits was a notification that each respondent would receive one of 20 computer preselected prizes. One of the more attractive prize possibilities was a 7-day vacation for two in Acapulco, Mexico. Another was prize number 12, a lifetime supply of film, providing free color film of any size or exposure for each roll developed. This gift was described as including up to 40% off on the cost of developing. A set of instructions accompanied the questionnaire. One item instructed the respondent to include a check or money order to the amount of $14.80 "to cover the cost of shipping, handling, postage, printing and administration of this testing procedure." As this was being written, the author called the number listed on the survey instruction sheet and found it to be disconnected.

As a future marketing person, comment on this survey and its implications for the marketing research profession.

# APPENDIX
# Statistical Tables

**TABLE I.** *Random numbers.*

|    | 1 | 2 | 3 | 4 | 5 | 6 | 7 | 8 | 9 | 10 |    |
|----|-------|-------|-------|-------|-------|-------|-------|-------|-------|-------|----|
| 1  | 48461 | 14952 | 72619 | 73689 | 52059 | 37086 | 60050 | 86192 | 67049 | 64739 | 1  |
| 2  | 76534 | 38149 | 49692 | 31366 | 52093 | 15422 | 20498 | 33901 | 10319 | 43397 | 2  |
| 3  | 70437 | 25861 | 38504 | 14752 | 23757 | 59660 | 67844 | 78815 | 23758 | 86814 | 3  |
| 4  | 59584 | 03370 | 42806 | 11393 | 71722 | 93804 | 09095 | 07856 | 55589 | 46020 | 4  |
| 5  | 04285 | 58554 | 16085 | 51555 | 27501 | 73883 | 33427 | 33343 | 45507 | 50063 | 5  |
| 6  | 77340 | 10412 | 69189 | 85171 | 29082 | 44785 | 83638 | 02583 | 96483 | 76553 | 6  |
| 7  | 59183 | 62687 | 91778 | 80354 | 23512 | 97219 | 65921 | 02035 | 59847 | 91403 | 7  |
| 8  | 91800 | 04281 | 39979 | 03927 | 82564 | 28777 | 59049 | 97532 | 54540 | 79472 | 8  |
| 9  | 12066 | 24817 | 81099 | 48940 | 69554 | 55925 | 48379 | 12866 | 51232 | 21580 | 9  |
| 10 | 69907 | 91751 | 53512 | 23748 | 65906 | 91385 | 84983 | 27915 | 48491 | 91068 | 10 |
| 11 | 80467 | 04873 | 54053 | 25955 | 48518 | 13815 | 37707 | 68687 | 15570 | 08890 | 11 |
| 12 | 78057 | 67835 | 28302 | 45048 | 56761 | 97725 | 58438 | 91528 | 24645 | 18544 | 12 |
| 13 | 05648 | 39387 | 78191 | 88415 | 60269 | 94880 | 58812 | 42931 | 71898 | 61534 | 13 |
| 14 | 22304 | 39246 | 01350 | 99451 | 61862 | 78688 | 30339 | 60222 | 74052 | 25740 | 14 |
| 15 | 61346 | 50269 | 67005 | 40442 | 33100 | 16742 | 61640 | 21046 | 31909 | 72641 | 15 |
| 16 | 66793 | 37696 | 27965 | 30459 | 91011 | 51426 | 31006 | 77468 | 61029 | 57108 | 16 |
| 17 | 86411 | 48809 | 36698 | 42453 | 83061 | 43769 | 39948 | 87031 | 30767 | 13953 | 17 |
| 18 | 62098 | 12825 | 81744 | 28882 | 27369 | 88183 | 65846 | 92545 | 09065 | 22655 | 18 |
| 19 | 68775 | 06261 | 54265 | 16203 | 23340 | 84750 | 16317 | 88686 | 86842 | 00879 | 19 |
| 20 | 52679 | 19595 | 13687 | 74872 | 89181 | 01939 | 18447 | 10787 | 76246 | 80072 | 20 |
| 21 | 84096 | 87152 | 20719 | 25215 | 04349 | 54434 | 72344 | 93008 | 83282 | 31670 | 21 |
| 22 | 63964 | 55937 | 21417 | 49944 | 38356 | 98404 | 14850 | 17994 | 17161 | 98981 | 22 |
| 23 | 31191 | 75131 | 72386 | 11689 | 95727 | 05414 | 88727 | 45583 | 22568 | 77700 | 23 |
| 24 | 30545 | 68523 | 29850 | 67833 | 05622 | 89975 | 79042 | 27142 | 99257 | 32349 | 24 |
| 25 | 52573 | 91001 | 52315 | 26430 | 54175 | 30122 | 31796 | 98842 | 37600 | 26025 | 25 |
| 26 | 16586 | 81842 | 01076 | 99414 | 31574 | 94719 | 34656 | 80018 | 86988 | 79234 | 26 |
| 27 | 81841 | 88481 | 61191 | 25013 | 30272 | 23388 | 22463 | 65774 | 10029 | 58376 | 27 |
| 28 | 43563 | 66829 | 72838 | 08074 | 57080 | 15446 | 11034 | 98143 | 74989 | 26885 | 28 |
| 29 | 19945 | 84193 | 57581 | 77252 | 85604 | 45412 | 43556 | 27518 | 90572 | 00563 | 29 |
| 30 | 79374 | 23796 | 16919 | 99691 | 80276 | 32818 | 62953 | 78831 | 54395 | 30705 | 30 |
| 31 | 48503 | 26615 | 43980 | 09810 | 38289 | 66679 | 73799 | 48418 | 12647 | 40044 | 31 |
| 32 | 32049 | 65541 | 37937 | 41105 | 70106 | 89706 | 40829 | 40789 | 59547 | 00783 | 32 |
| 33 | 18547 | 71562 | 95493 | 34112 | 76895 | 46766 | 96395 | 31718 | 48302 | 45893 | 33 |
| 34 | 03180 | 96742 | 61486 | 43305 | 34183 | 99605 | 67803 | 13491 | 09243 | 29557 | 34 |
| 35 | 94822 | 24738 | 67749 | 83748 | 59799 | 25210 | 31093 | 62925 | 72061 | 69991 | 35 |
| 36 | 34330 | 60599 | 85828 | 19152 | 68499 | 27977 | 35611 | 96240 | 62747 | 89529 | 36 |
| 37 | 43770 | 81537 | 59527 | 95674 | 76692 | 86420 | 69930 | 10020 | 72881 | 12532 | 37 |
| 38 | 56908 | 77192 | 50623 | 41215 | 14311 | 42834 | 80651 | 93750 | 59957 | 31211 | 38 |
| 39 | 32787 | 07189 | 80539 | 75927 | 75475 | 73965 | 11796 | 72140 | 48944 | 74156 | 39 |
| 40 | 52441 | 78392 | 11733 | 57703 | 29133 | 71164 | 55355 | 31006 | 25526 | 55790 | 40 |
| 41 | 22377 | 54723 | 18227 | 28449 | 04570 | 18882 | 00023 | 67101 | 06895 | 08915 | 41 |
| 42 | 18376 | 73460 | 88841 | 39602 | 34049 | 20589 | 05701 | 08249 | 74213 | 25220 | 42 |
| 43 | 53201 | 28610 | 87957 | 21497 | 64729 | 64983 | 71551 | 99016 | 87903 | 63875 | 43 |
| 44 | 34919 | 78901 | 59710 | 27396 | 02593 | 05665 | 11964 | 44134 | 00273 | 76358 | 44 |
| 45 | 33617 | 92159 | 21971 | 16901 | 57383 | 34262 | 41744 | 60891 | 57624 | 06962 | 45 |
| 46 | 70010 | 40964 | 98780 | 72418 | 52571 | 18415 | 64362 | 90636 | 38034 | 04909 | 46 |
| 47 | 19282 | 68447 | 35665 | 31530 | 59832 | 49181 | 21914 | 65742 | 89815 | 39231 | 47 |
| 48 | 91429 | 73328 | 13266 | 54898 | 68795 | 40948 | 80808 | 63887 | 89939 | 47938 | 48 |
| 49 | 97637 | 78393 | 33021 | 05867 | 86520 | 45363 | 43066 | 00988 | 64040 | 09803 | 49 |
| 50 | 95150 | 07625 | 05255 | 83254 | 93943 | 52325 | 93230 | 62668 | 79529 | 65964 | 50 |

*Source:* From F. James Rohlf and Robert R. Sokal, *Statistical Tables*, 2nd ed., W. H. Freeman and Company, Publishers, San Francisco. Copyright © 1981.

**TABLE II.** *The standard normal distribution.*

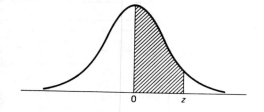

| z | .00 | .01 | .02 | .03 | .04 | .05 | .06 | .07 | .08 | .09 |
|---|---|---|---|---|---|---|---|---|---|---|
| 0.0 | .0000 | .0040 | .0080 | .0120 | .0160 | .0199 | .0239 | .0279 | .0319 | .0359 |
| 0.1 | .0398 | .0438 | .0478 | .0517 | .0557 | .0596 | .0636 | .0675 | .0714 | .0753 |
| 0.2 | .0793 | .0832 | .0871 | .0910 | .0948 | .0987 | .1026 | .1064 | .1103 | .1141 |
| 0.3 | .1179 | .1217 | .1255 | .1293 | .1331 | .1368 | .1406 | .1443 | .1480 | .1517 |
| 0.4 | .1554 | .1591 | .1628 | .1664 | .1700 | .1736 | .1772 | .1808 | .1844 | .1879 |
| 0.5 | .1915 | .1950 | .1985 | .2019 | .2054 | .2088 | .2123 | .2157 | .2190 | .2224 |
| 0.6 | .2257 | .2291 | .2324 | .2357 | .2389 | .2422 | .2454 | .2486 | .2517 | .2549 |
| 0.7 | .2580 | .2611 | .2642 | .2673 | .2704 | .2734 | .2764 | .2794 | .2823 | .2852 |
| 0.8 | .2881 | .2910 | .2939 | .2967 | .2995 | .3023 | .3051 | .3078 | .3106 | .3133 |
| 0.9 | .3159 | .3186 | .3212 | .3238 | .3264 | .3289 | .3315 | .3340 | .3365 | .3389 |
| 1.0 | .3413 | .3438 | .3461 | .3485 | .3508 | .3531 | .3554 | .3577 | .3599 | .3621 |
| 1.1 | .3643 | .3665 | .3686 | .3708 | .3729 | .3749 | .3770 | .3790 | .3810 | .3830 |
| 1.2 | .3849 | .3869 | .3888 | .3907 | .3925 | .3944 | .3962 | .3980 | .3997 | .4015 |
| 1.3 | .4032 | .4049 | .4066 | .4082 | .4099 | .4115 | .4131 | .4147 | .4162 | .4177 |
| 1.4 | .4102 | .4207 | .4222 | .4236 | .4251 | .4265 | .4279 | .4292 | .4306 | .4319 |
| 1.5 | .4332 | .4345 | .4357 | .4370 | .4382 | .4394 | .4406 | .4418 | .4429 | .4441 |
| 1.6 | .4452 | .4463 | .4474 | .4484 | .4495 | .4505 | .4515 | .4525 | .4535 | .4545 |
| 1.7 | .4554 | .4564 | .4573 | .4582 | .4591 | .4599 | .4608 | .4616 | .4625 | .4633 |
| 1.8 | .4641 | .4649 | .4656 | .4664 | .4671 | .4678 | .4686 | .4693 | .4699 | .4706 |
| 1.9 | .4713 | .4719 | .4726 | .4732 | .4738 | .4744 | .4750 | .4756 | .4761 | .4767 |
| 2.0 | .4772 | .4778 | .4783 | .4788 | .4793 | .4798 | .4803 | .4808 | .4812 | .4817 |
| 2.1 | .4821 | .4826 | .4830 | .4834 | .4838 | .4842 | .4846 | .4850 | .4854 | .4857 |
| 2.2 | .4861 | .4864 | .4868 | .4871 | .4875 | .4878 | .4881 | .4884 | .4887 | .4890 |
| 2.3 | .4893 | .4896 | .4898 | .4901 | .4904 | .4906 | .4909 | .4911 | .4913 | .4916 |
| 2.4 | .4918 | .4920 | .4922 | .4925 | .4927 | .4929 | .4931 | .4932 | .4934 | .4936 |
| 2.5 | .4938 | .4940 | .4941 | .4943 | .4945 | .4946 | .4948 | .4949 | .4951 | .4952 |
| 2.6 | .4953 | .4955 | .4956 | .4957 | .4959 | .4960 | .4961 | .4962 | .4963 | .4946 |
| 2.7 | .4965 | .4966 | .4967 | .4968 | .4969 | .4970 | .4971 | .4972 | .4973 | .4974 |
| 2.8 | .4974 | .4975 | .4976 | .4977 | .4977 | .4978 | .4979 | .4979 | .4980 | .4981 |
| 2.9 | .4981 | .4982 | .4982 | .4983 | .4984 | .4984 | .4985 | .4985 | .4986 | .4986 |
| 3.0 | .4987 | .4987 | .4987 | .4988 | .4988 | .4989 | .4989 | .4989 | .4990 | .4990 |

*Source:* John E. Freund, *Statistics: A First Course,* 3/E, © 1981, pp. 422–423. Reprinted by permission of Prentice-Hall, Inc., Englewood Cliffs, New Jersey.

**TABLE III.** *The t distribution.*

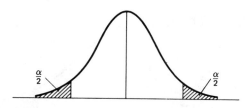

| Two-tail area ($\alpha$) | | .20 | .10 | .05 | .02 | .01 |
|---|---|---|---|---|---|---|
| d.f. | 1 | 3.078 | 6.314 | 12.706 | 31.821 | 63.657 |
| | 2 | 1.886 | 2.920 | 4.303 | 6.965 | 9.925 |
| | 3 | 1.638 | 2.353 | 3.182 | 4.541 | 5.841 |
| | 4 | 1.533 | 2.132 | 2.776 | 3.747 | 4.604 |
| | 5 | 1.476 | 2.015 | 2.571 | 3.365 | 4.032 |
| | 6 | 1.440 | 1.943 | 2.447 | 3.143 | 3.707 |
| | 7 | 1.415 | 1.895 | 2.365 | 2.998 | 3.499 |
| | 8 | 1.397 | 1.860 | 2.306 | 2.896 | 3.355 |
| | 9 | 1.383 | 1.833 | 2.262 | 2.821 | 3.250 |
| | 10 | 1.372 | 1.812 | 2.228 | 2.764 | 3.169 |
| | 11 | 1.363 | 1.796 | 2.201 | 2.718 | 3.106 |
| | 12 | 1.356 | 1.782 | 2.179 | 2.681 | 3.055 |
| | 13 | 1.350 | 1.771 | 2.160 | 2.650 | 3.012 |
| | 14 | 1.345 | 1.761 | 2.145 | 2.624 | 2.977 |
| | 15 | 1.341 | 1.753 | 2.131 | 2.602 | 2.947 |
| | 16 | 1.337 | 1.746 | 2.120 | 2.583 | 2.921 |
| | 17 | 1.333 | 1.740 | 2.110 | 2.567 | 2.898 |
| | 18 | 1.330 | 1.734 | 2.101 | 2.552 | 2.878 |
| | 19 | 1.328 | 1.729 | 2.093 | 2.539 | 2.861 |
| | 20 | 1.325 | 1.725 | 2.086 | 2.528 | 2.845 |
| | 21 | 1.323 | 1.721 | 2.080 | 2.518 | 2.831 |
| | 22 | 1.321 | 1.717 | 2.074 | 2.508 | 2.819 |
| | 23 | 1.319 | 1.714 | 2.069 | 2.500 | 2.807 |
| | 24 | 1.318 | 1.711 | 2.064 | 2.492 | 2.797 |
| | 25 | 1.316 | 1.708 | 2.060 | 2.485 | 2.787 |
| | 26 | 1.315 | 1.706 | 2.056 | 2.479 | 2.779 |
| | 27 | 1.314 | 1.703 | 2.052 | 2.473 | 2.771 |
| | 28 | 1.313 | 1.701 | 2.048 | 2.467 | 2.763 |
| | 29 | 1.311 | 1.699 | 2.045 | 2.462 | 2.756 |
| | 30 | 1.310 | 1.697 | 2.042 | 2.457 | 2.750 |
| | 40 | 1.303 | 1.684 | 2.021 | 2.423 | 2.704 |
| | 60 | 1.296 | 1.671 | 2.000 | 2.390 | 2.660 |
| | 120 | 1.289 | 1.658 | 1.980 | 2.358 | 2.617 |
| | $\alpha$ | 1.282 | 1.645 | 1.960 | 2.326 | 2.576 |

*Source:* Paul Hoel, *Elementary Statistics*, 3rd ed. John Wiley & Sons, Inc., New York, 1971.

**TABLE IV.** *The $\chi^2$ distribution.*

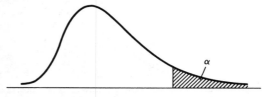

| d.f. \ α | .10 | .05 | .025 | .010 | .005 |
|---|---|---|---|---|---|
| 1 | 2.71 | 3.84 | 5.02 | 6.63 | 7.88 |
| 2 | 4.61 | 5.99 | 7.38 | 9.21 | 10.6 |
| 3 | 6.25 | 7.81 | 9.35 | 11.3 | 12.8 |
| 4 | 7.78 | 9.49 | 11.1 | 13.3 | 14.9 |
| 5 | 9.24 | 11.1 | 12.8 | 15.1 | 16.7 |
| 6 | 10.6 | 12.6 | 14.4 | 16.8 | 18.5 |
| 7 | 12.0 | 14.1 | 16.0 | 18.5 | 20.3 |
| 8 | 13.4 | 15.5 | 17.5 | 20.1 | 22.0 |
| 9 | 14.7 | 16.9 | 19.0 | 21.7 | 23.6 |
| 10 | 16.0 | 18.3 | 20.5 | 23.2 | 25.2 |
| 11 | 17.3 | 19.7 | 21.9 | 24.7 | 26.8 |
| 12 | 18.5 | 21.0 | 23.3 | 26.2 | 28.3 |
| 13 | 19.8 | 22.4 | 24.7 | 27.7 | 29.8 |
| 14 | 21.1 | 23.7 | 26.1 | 29.1 | 31.3 |
| 15 | 22.3 | 25.0 | 27.5 | 30.6 | 32.8 |
| 16 | 23.5 | 26.3 | 28.8 | 32.0 | 34.3 |
| 17 | 24.8 | 27.6 | 30.2 | 33.4 | 35.7 |
| 18 | 26.0 | 28.9 | 31.5 | 34.8 | 37.2 |
| 19 | 27.2 | 30.1 | 32.9 | 36.2 | 38.6 |
| 20 | 28.4 | 31.4 | 34.2 | 37.6 | 40.0 |
| 21 | 29.6 | 32.7 | 35.5 | 38.9 | 41.4 |
| 22 | 30.8 | 33.9 | 36.8 | 40.3 | 42.8 |
| 23 | 32.0 | 35.2 | 38.1 | 41.6 | 44.2 |
| 24 | 33.2 | 36.4 | 39.4 | 43.0 | 45.6 |
| 25 | 34.4 | 37.7 | 40.6 | 44.3 | 46.9 |
| 26 | 35.6 | 38.9 | 41.9 | 45.6 | 48.3 |
| 27 | 36.7 | 40.1 | 43.2 | 47.0 | 49.6 |
| 28 | 37.9 | 41.3 | 44.5 | 48.3 | 51.0 |
| 29 | 39.1 | 42.6 | 45.7 | 49.6 | 52.3 |
| 30 | 40.3 | 43.8 | 47.0 | 50.9 | 53.7 |

*Source:* Adapted with permission from *Standard Mathematical Tables*, 26th ed., William H. Beyer (ed.), CRC Press, Inc., Boca Raton, Fla., 1983.

**TABLE V.** *The F Distribution.*

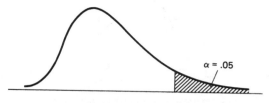

$\alpha = .05$

$V_1$ = **Degrees of Freedom Between Groups**

| | 1 | 2 | 3 | 4 | 5 | 6 | 7 | 8 | 9 | 10 | 12 | 15 |
|---|---|---|---|---|---|---|---|---|---|---|---|---|
| 1 | 161.4 | 199.5 | 215.7 | 224.6 | 230.2 | 234.0 | 236.8 | 238.9 | 240.5 | 241.9 | 243.9 | 245.9 |
| 2 | 18.51 | 19.00 | 19.16 | 19.25 | 19.30 | 19.33 | 19.35 | 19.37 | 19.38 | 19.40 | 19.41 | 19.43 |
| 3 | 10.13 | 9.55 | 9.28 | 9.12 | 9.01 | 8.94 | 8.89 | 8.85 | 8.81 | 8.79 | 8.74 | 8.70 |
| 4 | 7.71 | 6.94 | 6.59 | 6.39 | 6.26 | 6.16 | 6.09 | 6.04 | 6.00 | 5.96 | 5.91 | 5.86 |
| 5 | 6.61 | 5.79 | 5.41 | 5.19 | 5.05 | 4.95 | 4.88 | 4.82 | 4.77 | 4.74 | 4.68 | 4.62 |
| 6 | 5.99 | 5.14 | 4.76 | 4.53 | 4.39 | 4.28 | 4.21 | 4.15 | 4.10 | 4.06 | 4.00 | 3.94 |
| 7 | 5.59 | 4.74 | 4.35 | 4.12 | 3.97 | 3.87 | 3.79 | 3.73 | 3.68 | 3.64 | 3.57 | 3.51 |
| 8 | 5.32 | 4.46 | 4.07 | 3.84 | 3.69 | 3.58 | 3.50 | 3.44 | 3.39 | 3.35 | 3.28 | 3.22 |
| 9 | 5.12 | 4.26 | 3.86 | 3.63 | 3.48 | 3.37 | 3.29 | 3.23 | 3.18 | 3.14 | 3.07 | 3.01 |
| 10 | 4.96 | 4.10 | 3.71 | 3.48 | 3.33 | 3.22 | 3.14 | 3.07 | 3.02 | 2.98 | 2.91 | 2.85 |
| 11 | 4.84 | 3.98 | 3.59 | 3.36 | 3.20 | 3.09 | 3.01 | 2.95 | 2.90 | 2.85 | 2.79 | 2.72 |
| 12 | 4.75 | 3.89 | 3.49 | 3.26 | 3.11 | 3.00 | 2.91 | 2.85 | 2.80 | 2.75 | 2.69 | 2.62 |
| 13 | 4.67 | 3.81 | 3.41 | 3.18 | 3.03 | 2.92 | 2.83 | 2.77 | 2.71 | 2.67 | 2.60 | 2.53 |
| 14 | 4.60 | 3.74 | 3.34 | 3.11 | 2.96 | 2.85 | 2.76 | 2.70 | 2.65 | 2.60 | 2.53 | 2.46 |
| 15 | 4.54 | 3.68 | 3.29 | 3.06 | 2.90 | 2.79 | 2.71 | 2.64 | 2.59 | 2.54 | 2.48 | 2.40 |
| 16 | 4.49 | 3.63 | 3.24 | 3.01 | 2.85 | 2.74 | 2.66 | 2.59 | 2.54 | 2.49 | 2.42 | 2.35 |
| 17 | 4.45 | 3.59 | 3.20 | 2.96 | 2.81 | 2.70 | 2.61 | 2.55 | 2.49 | 2.45 | 2.38 | 2.31 |
| 18 | 4.41 | 3.55 | 3.16 | 2.93 | 2.77 | 2.66 | 2.58 | 2.51 | 2.46 | 2.41 | 2.34 | 2.27 |
| 19 | 4.38 | 3.52 | 3.13 | 2.90 | 2.74 | 2.63 | 2.54 | 2.48 | 2.42 | 2.38 | 2.31 | 2.23 |
| 20 | 4.35 | 3.49 | 3.10 | 2.87 | 2.71 | 2.60 | 2.51 | 2.45 | 2.39 | 2.35 | 2.28 | 2.20 |
| 21 | 4.32 | 3.47 | 3.07 | 2.84 | 2.68 | 2.57 | 2.49 | 2.42 | 2.37 | 2.32 | 2.25 | 2.18 |
| 22 | 4.30 | 3.44 | 3.05 | 2.82 | 2.66 | 2.55 | 2.46 | 2.40 | 2.34 | 2.30 | 2.23 | 2.15 |
| 23 | 4.28 | 3.42 | 3.03 | 2.80 | 2.64 | 2.53 | 2.44 | 2.37 | 2.32 | 2.27 | 2.20 | 2.13 |
| 24 | 4.26 | 3.40 | 3.01 | 2.78 | 2.62 | 2.51 | 2.42 | 2.36 | 2.30 | 2.25 | 2.18 | 2.11 |
| 25 | 4.24 | 3.39 | 2.99 | 2.76 | 2.60 | 2.49 | 2.40 | 2.34 | 2.28 | 2.24 | 2.16 | 2.09 |
| 26 | 4.23 | 3.37 | 2.98 | 2.74 | 2.59 | 2.47 | 2.39 | 2.32 | 2.27 | 2.22 | 2.15 | 2.07 |
| 27 | 4.21 | 3.35 | 2.96 | 2.73 | 2.57 | 2.46 | 2.37 | 2.31 | 2.25 | 2.20 | 2.13 | 2.06 |
| 28 | 4.20 | 3.34 | 2.95 | 2.71 | 2.56 | 2.45 | 2.36 | 2.29 | 2.24 | 2.19 | 2.12 | 2.04 |
| 29 | 4.18 | 3.33 | 2.93 | 2.70 | 2.55 | 2.43 | 2.35 | 2.28 | 2.22 | 2.18 | 2.10 | 2.03 |
| 30 | 4.17 | 3.32 | 2.92 | 2.69 | 2.53 | 2.42 | 2.33 | 2.27 | 2.21 | 2.16 | 2.09 | 2.01 |
| 40 | 4.08 | 3.23 | 2.84 | 2.61 | 2.45 | 2.34 | 2.25 | 2.18 | 2.12 | 2.08 | 2.00 | 1.92 |
| 60 | 4.00 | 3.15 | 2.76 | 2.53 | 2.37 | 2.25 | 2.17 | 2.10 | 2.04 | 1.99 | 1.92 | 1.84 |
| 120 | 3.92 | 3.07 | 2.68 | 2.45 | 2.29 | 2.17 | 2.09 | 2.02 | 1.96 | 1.91 | 1.83 | 1.75 |
| ∞ | 3.84 | 3.00 | 2.60 | 2.37 | 2.21 | 2.10 | 2.01 | 1.94 | 1.88 | 1.83 | 1.75 | 1.67 |

$V_2$ = **Degrees of Freedom Within Groups**

**TABLE V.** *The F distribution (continued).*

$$\alpha = .01$$

## $V_1$ = Degrees of Freedom Between Groups

| | 1 | 2 | 3 | 4 | 5 | 6 | 7 | 8 | 9 | 10 | 12 | 15 |
|---|---|---|---|---|---|---|---|---|---|---|---|---|
| 1 | 4052 | 4999.5 | 5403 | 5625 | 5764 | 5859 | 5928 | 5982 | 6022 | 6056 | 6106 | 6157 |
| 2 | 98.50 | 99.00 | 99.17 | 99.25 | 99.30 | 99.33 | 99.36 | 99.37 | 99.39 | 99.40 | 99.42 | 99.43 |
| 3 | 34.12 | 30.82 | 29.46 | 28.71 | 28.24 | 27.91 | 27.67 | 27.49 | 27.35 | 27.23 | 27.05 | 26.87 |
| 4 | 21.20 | 18.00 | 16.69 | 15.98 | 15.52 | 15.21 | 14.98 | 14.80 | 14.66 | 14.55 | 14.37 | 14.20 |
| 5 | 16.26 | 13.27 | 12.06 | 11.39 | 10.97 | 10.67 | 10.46 | 10.29 | 10.16 | 10.05 | 9.89 | 9.72 |
| 6 | 13.75 | 10.92 | 9.78 | 9.15 | 8.75 | 8.47 | 8.26 | 8.10 | 7.98 | 7.87 | 7.72 | 7.56 |
| 7 | 12.25 | 9.55 | 8.45 | 7.85 | 7.46 | 7.19 | 6.99 | 6.84 | 6.72 | 6.62 | 6.47 | 6.31 |
| 8 | 11.26 | 8.65 | 7.59 | 7.01 | 6.63 | 6.37 | 6.18 | 6.03 | 5.91 | 5.81 | 5.67 | 5.52 |
| 9 | 10.56 | 8.02 | 6.99 | 6.42 | 6.06 | 5.80 | 5.61 | 5.47 | 5.35 | 5.26 | 5.11 | 4.96 |
| 10 | 10.04 | 7.56 | 6.55 | 5.99 | 5.64 | 5.39 | 5.20 | 5.06 | 4.94 | 4.85 | 4.71 | 4.56 |
| 11 | 9.65 | 7.21 | 6.22 | 5.67 | 5.32 | 5.07 | 4.89 | 4.74 | 4.63 | 4.54 | 4.40 | 4.25 |
| 12 | 9.33 | 6.93 | 5.95 | 5.41 | 5.06 | 4.82 | 4.64 | 4.50 | 4.39 | 4.30 | 4.16 | 4.01 |
| 13 | 9.07 | 6.70 | 5.74 | 5.21 | 4.86 | 4.62 | 4.44 | 4.30 | 4.19 | 4.10 | 3.96 | 3.82 |
| 14 | 8.86 | 6.51 | 5.56 | 5.04 | 4.69 | 4.46 | 4.28 | 4.14 | 4.03 | 3.94 | 3.80 | 3.66 |
| 15 | 8.68 | 6.36 | 5.42 | 4.89 | 4.56 | 4.32 | 4.14 | 4.00 | 3.89 | 3.80 | 3.67 | 3.52 |
| 16 | 8.53 | 6.23 | 5.29 | 4.77 | 4.44 | 4.20 | 4.03 | 3.89 | 3.78 | 3.69 | 3.55 | 3.41 |
| 17 | 8.40 | 6.11 | 5.18 | 4.67 | 4.34 | 4.10 | 3.93 | 3.79 | 3.68 | 3.59 | 3.46 | 3.31 |
| 18 | 8.29 | 6.01 | 5.09 | 4.58 | 4.25 | 4.01 | 3.84 | 3.71 | 3.60 | 3.51 | 3.37 | 3.23 |
| 19 | 8.18 | 5.93 | 5.01 | 4.50 | 4.17 | 3.94 | 3.77 | 3.63 | 3.52 | 3.43 | 3.30 | 3.15 |
| 20 | 8.10 | 5.85 | 4.94 | 4.43 | 4.10 | 3.87 | 3.70 | 3.56 | 3.46 | 3.37 | 3.23 | 3.09 |
| 21 | 8.02 | 5.78 | 4.87 | 4.37 | 4.04 | 3.81 | 3.64 | 3.51 | 3.40 | 3.31 | 3.17 | 3.03 |
| 22 | 7.95 | 5.72 | 4.82 | 4.31 | 3.99 | 3.76 | 3.59 | 3.45 | 3.35 | 3.26 | 3.12 | 2.98 |
| 23 | 7.88 | 5.66 | 4.76 | 4.26 | 3.94 | 3.71 | 3.54 | 3.41 | 3.30 | 3.21 | 3.07 | 2.93 |
| 24 | 7.82 | 5.61 | 4.72 | 4.22 | 3.90 | 3.67 | 3.50 | 3.36 | 3.26 | 3.17 | 3.03 | 2.89 |
| 25 | 7.77 | 5.57 | 4.68 | 4.18 | 3.85 | 3.63 | 3.46 | 3.32 | 3.22 | 3.13 | 2.99 | 2.85 |
| 26 | 7.72 | 5.53 | 4.64 | 4.14 | 3.82 | 3.59 | 3.42 | 3.29 | 3.18 | 3.09 | 2.96 | 2.81 |
| 27 | 7.68 | 5.49 | 4.60 | 4.11 | 3.78 | 3.56 | 3.39 | 3.26 | 3.15 | 3.06 | 2.93 | 2.78 |
| 28 | 7.64 | 5.45 | 4.57 | 4.07 | 3.75 | 3.53 | 3.36 | 3.23 | 3.12 | 3.03 | 2.90 | 2.75 |
| 29 | 7.60 | 5.42 | 4.54 | 4.04 | 3.73 | 3.50 | 3.33 | 3.20 | 3.09 | 3.00 | 2.87 | 2.73 |
| 30 | 7.56 | 5.39 | 4.51 | 4.02 | 3.70 | 3.47 | 3.30 | 3.17 | 3.07 | 2.98 | 2.84 | 2.70 |
| 40 | 7.31 | 5.18 | 4.31 | 3.83 | 3.51 | 3.29 | 3.12 | 2.99 | 2.89 | 2.80 | 2.66 | 2.52 |
| 60 | 7.08 | 4.98 | 4.13 | 3.65 | 3.34 | 3.12 | 2.95 | 2.82 | 2.72 | 2.63 | 2.50 | 2.35 |
| 120 | 6.85 | 4.79 | 3.95 | 3.48 | 3.17 | 2.96 | 2.79 | 2.66 | 2.56 | 2.47 | 2.34 | 2.19 |
| ∞ | 6.63 | 4.61 | 3.78 | 3.32 | 3.02 | 2.80 | 2.64 | 2.51 | 2.41 | 2.32 | 2.18 | 2.04 |

$V_2$ = Degrees of Freedom Within Groups

*Source:* Adapted with permission from *Standard Mathematical Tables*, 26th ed., William H. Beyer (ed.), CRC Press, Inc., Boca Raton, Fla., 1983.

# FIRM AND ORGANIZATION INDEX

# NAME INDEX

# SUBJECT INDEX